Why are many EMDEs less resilient to external shocks now than during the global recession of 2009? How can the disappointing path of output growth in these economies during the last decade be explained? and What can policy makers do looking forward? With strong analysis of the evidence, this book answers these three fundamental questions thoroughly and systematically; and it is done in a splendidly clear way. The book is a must-read for researchers, policy makers, and practitioners around the globe seeking to understand the complex challenges facing EMDEs to achieve sustained economic growth in a highly uncertain international environment.

Liliana Rojas-Suarez

Senior Fellow and Director of the Latin America Initiative
Center for Global Development

Just as the 2008 global financial crisis caught the world by surprise, the aftermath of the crisis has proved to be both puzzling and disappointing. This book meticulously documents the anemic recovery, especially among emerging market and developing economies. It also conveys a clear message: with fewer buffers than they had in 2008, these economies are particularly vulnerable to the next global downturn. Central bank governors and finance ministers—and the citizens to whom they are accountable—should read this book.

Shantayanan Devarajan

Professor of the Practice, Science in Foreign Service
Georgetown University

The world has witnessed weakening global growth momentum with significant downside risks. This book provides succinct discussions of economic and financial developments that emerging market and developing economies have experienced since the 2009 global recession. It also suggests useful policies for these economies in an uncertain and risky global environment.

Jong-Wha Lee

Professor of Economics
Korea University

A Decade after the Global Recession

A Decade after the Global Recession

Lessons and Challenges for Emerging and Developing Economies

M. Ayhan Kose and Franziska Ohnsorge
Editors

1818 H Street NW, Washington, DC 20433
Telephone: 202-473-1000; Internet: www.worldbank.org

1 2 3 4 23 22 21 20

ISBN (paper): 978-1-4648-1527-0
ISBN (electronic): 978-1-4648-1528-7
DOI: 10.1596/978-1-4648-1527-0

Library of Congress Control Number: 2020914242

Summary of Contents

Contents

Boxes

Figures

Tables

Foreword

This year marks the 10-year anniversary of the 2009 global recession. Many emerging market and developing economies (EMDEs) weathered the global recession relatively well, in part thanks to large, prompt, and global policy support. A short-lived rebound in activity has been followed, however, by a decade of protracted weakness in the global economy. EMDEs have also experienced repeated growth disappointments during this period amid bouts of financial market stress, weak trade, and slowing poverty reduction.

This book takes stock of the past decade and asks whether EMDEs are ready to face the next global downturn. To this end, it assesses the macroeconomic and financial developments over this period and draws lessons for EMDEs that should help policy makers as they prepare their countries for the next possible global downturn.

The book offers three main conclusions.

First, perhaps for the first time, many EMDEs were able to implement large-scale countercyclical fiscal and monetary policy during the last global recession. They were in a position to stimulate activity because they could draw on sizable policy buffers accumulated during the prerecession period of strong growth: government debt had fallen, current account and fiscal deficits narrowed, and inflation had moderated. Those EMDEs with more resilient economies and with more forceful stimulus experienced milder growth slowdowns during the 2009 global recession.

Second, looking ahead, the good news is that policy makers are now equipped with stronger policy frameworks than in earlier global downturns. Rule-based approaches to policy setting are more common among EMDEs, with many adopting fiscal rules and inflation-targeting regimes to implement counter-cyclical policy. Such frameworks served these economies well during the global recession. EMDEs that have adopted—and credibly implemented—these policy frameworks will likely be in a better position to weather the next downturn and establish the foundations for robust and sustainable growth.

Third, on the flip side, there is some not so good news. The book cautions EMDE policy makers that their economies are now less well prepared to face a global downturn than before the 2009 global recession. Vulnerabilities to external shocks have grown, including through higher debt and weaker fiscal positions, accompanied by diminished long-term growth prospects, undermining the effectiveness of a possible response to the next downturn. Those EMDEs that rely on commodity exports also face a world where demand growth for their commodities will likely be weaker than before the global recession. International trade more generally, the foundation of many of the success stories among EMDEs, is under threat from a changing geopolitical and multilateral landscape. The past decade was also a lost opportunity to undertake the types of business and governance reforms that bring about strong and sustained long-term growth.

The World Bank Group's response to the global recession was unprecedented in both financing volume and country coverage and prioritized the areas of finance, infrastructure, fiscal management, and social protection. The Bank introduced new crisis response facilities to improve its assistance to EMDEs. It completed two global campaigns to boost its capital adequacy in part to be better prepared for future crises. It improved its monitoring functions of global macroeconomic developments to more effectively flag risks. In addition, the internal work practices of the Bank were reformed with a more coordinated institutional strategy on financing and advisory activities.

History repeats itself. And it is not kind to those who forget its lessons. The question is not whether the next global downturn will take place. It is rather when it will take place. Irrespective of its timing, though, the big lesson of the past decade for EMDEs is clear: because they are less well prepared to face a downturn today than before the 2009 episode, they urgently need to undertake cyclical and structural policy measures to be able to effectively confront the next downturn when it happens.

Ceyla Pazarbasioglu
Former Vice President
Equitable Growth, Finance and Institutions
World Bank Group

Acknowledgments

This book is the culmination of major efforts by many more people than those whose names appear on the cover. The eight chapters were prepared by Carlos Arteta, Sergiy Kasyanenko, Wee Chian Koh, Franz Ulrich Ruch, Naotaka Sugawara, Marco E. Terrones, Lei Sandy Ye, and Shu Yu. Sinem Kilic Celik, Jongrim Ha, Csilla Lakatos, and Temel Taskin contributed pieces that zoomed in on particularly timely issues for emerging market and developing economies. The production of the book was coordinated by Franz Ulrich Ruch.

The end result would not have been possible without comprehensive comments from Eduardo Borensztein, Stijn Claessens, Kevin Clinton, Graham Hacche, Ugo Panizza, Zia Qureshi, Sunil Sharma, and Christopher Towe. We also thank World Bank Group colleagues Rabah Arezki, Ciro Avitabile, Dilek Aykut, Kevin Barnes, Priya Basu, Merli Baroudi, Zeljko Bogetic, Cesar Calderon, Mena Cammett, Gianfilippo Carboni, Michael Carson, Pierre Laurent Chatain, Jeff Chelsky, Derek Chen, Tristan Cooper, Souleymane Coulibaly, Eugeniu Croitor, Francesca de Nicola, Franz Drees-Gross, Persephone Economou, Alison Evans, Luisa Felino, Erik Feyen, Lisa Finneran, Roberta Gatti, Rangeet Ghosh, Delfin Sia Go, David Gould, Margaret Grosh, Stephane Hallegatte, Camilla Holmemo, Bingjie Hu, Ergys Islamaj, Charlotte Nan Jiang, Henry Kerali, Patrick Kirby, Aurelien Kruse, Praveen Kumar, Jean Pierre Lacombe, Eric Le Borgne, Daniel Lederman, Andy Mason, Aaditya Mattoo, Alvaro Morales, Bexi Mota, Lili Motthagi, Cedric Mousset, Peter Nagle, Moritz Nebe, Nadia Novak, Martin Raiser, Martin Rama, Sheila Redzepi, Julio Revilla, Claudia Ruiz, Frederico Gil Sander, Jigyasa Sharma, Saurabh Shome, Jovana Stojanovic, Ashley Taylor, Mark Thomas, Hans Timmer, Charles Undeland, Dana Vorisek, Jessica Wade, Christina Wood, Hassan Zaman, Albert Zeufack, and Johannes Zutt for their constructive comments. We also owe a great debt of gratitude to Shihui Liu, Shijie Shi, and in particular Jinxin Wu for their excellent research assistance.

We are grateful to our colleagues who worked on the production of the book. Adriana Maximiliano and Quinn Sutton assembled the print publication. Graeme Littler provided editorial and website support. Maria Hazel Macadangdang produced the index. Mark Felsenthal and Alejandra Viveros managed media relations and dissemination.

The production of this book was managed by the Prospects Group under the general guidance of Ceyla Pazarbasioglu, Former Vice President for Equitable Growth, Finance and Institutions of the World Bank Group.

Finally, we thank the participants in the panel discussion "New Challenges for Emerging and Developing Economies," moderated by Ceyla Pazarbasioglu at the 2019 Annual Meetings of the World Bank Group and International Monetary

Fund. The panel discussion previewed the main findings of this book and provided insights on the experience of emerging market and developing economies since the 2009 global recession. The policy messages here benefited from insightful interventions by the panelists, including Reza Baqir (Governor, State Bank of Pakistan), Patrick Njoroge (Governor, Central Bank of Kenya), Eswar Prasad (Nandlal P. Tolani Senior Professor of Trade Policy and Professor of Economics, Cornell University), and Liliana Rojas-Suarez (Senior Fellow and Director of the Latin America Initiative, Center for Global Development).

About the Authors

Carlos Arteta, Prospects Group, World Bank

Sinem Kilic Celik, Prospects Group, World Bank

Jongrim Ha, Prospects Group, World Bank

Sergiy Kasyanenko, Prospects Group, World Bank

Wee Chian Koh, Prospects Group, World Bank

M. Ayhan Kose, Prospects Group, World Bank; Brookings Institution; Centre for Economic Policy Research; and Centre for Applied Macroeconomic Analysis

Csilla Lakatos, Prospects Group, World Bank

Franziska Ohnsorge, Prospects Group, World Bank; and Centre for Applied Macroeconomic Analysis

Franz Ulrich Ruch, Prospects Group, World Bank

Naotaka Sugawara, Prospects Group, World Bank

Temel Taskin, Prospects Group, World Bank

Marco E. Terrones, Department of Economics and Finance, Universidad del Pacifico, Peru

Lei Sandy Ye, Prospects Group, World Bank

Shu Yu, Prospects Group, World Bank

Abbreviations

ARA	Assessing Reserve Adequacy
ASEAN	Association of Southeast Asian Nations
BIS	Bank for International Settlements
CCTs	conditional cash transfer schemes
CDOs	collateralized debt obligations
CDS	credit default swaps
CEPR	Centre for Economic Policy Research
CFMs	capital flow management measures
CPI	consumer price index
CRS	U.S. Congressional Research Service
CRW	crisis response window
DDO	deferred drawdown option
DeMPA	Debt Management Performance Assessment
DPL	development policy lending
DRS	Debtor Reporting System
EAP	East Asia and Pacific
ECA	Europe and Central Asia
ECB	European Central Bank
EM7	seven largest emerging market and developing economies (Brazil, China, India, Indonesia, Mexico, Russian Federation, and Turkey)
	exchange rate mechanism
EMBI	J.P. Morgan Emerging Market Bond Index
EMDEs	emerging market and developing economies
ERM	European Union
EU	fragility, conflict, and violence
FCV	foreign direct investment
FDI	U.S. Federal Reserve
Fed	Financial Stability Board
FSB	Financial Stability Oversight Council
FSOC	Group of Twenty (Argentina, Australia, Brazil, Canada, China, France,
G20	Germany, India, Indonesia, Italy, Japan, Republic of Korea, Mexico, Russian Federation, Saudi Arabia, South Africa, Turkey, United Kingdom, United States, and European Union)
GCRP	Global Crisis Risk Platform
GDP	gross domestic product
GEP	*Global Economic Prospects*
GFSN	Global Financial Safety Net
GMR	*Global Monitoring Report*
G-SIB	global systemically important bank
GTFP	Global Trade Finance Program
GTLP	Global Trade Liquidity Program
HICs	high-income countries
HIPCs	heavily indebted poor countries
IBRD	International Bank for Reconstruction and Development

IDA	International Development Association
IEA	International Energy Agency
IEG	Independent Evaluation Group
IEO	Independent Evaluation Office
IFC	International Finance Corporation
IFI	international financial institution
IIF	Institute of International Finance
IILS	International Institute for Labour Studies
ILO	International Labour Organization
IMF	International Monetary Fund
LAC	Latin American and the Caribbean
LICs	low-income countries
LMICs	lower-middle-income countries
MCPP	Managed Co-Lending Portfolio Program
MDGs	Millennium Development Goals
MDRI	Multilateral Debt Relief Initiative
MFD	Maximizing Finance for Development Approach
MIGA	Multilateral Investment Guarantee Agency
MNA	Middle East and North Africa
MSCI	Morgan Stanley Capital International
NAFTA	North American Free Trade Agreement
NBER	National Bureau of Economic Research
NIRP	negative interest rate policy
ODA	official development assistance
OECD	Organisation for Economic Co-operation and Development
OPEC	Organization of the Petroleum Exporting Countries
PRIO	Peace Research Institute Oslo
PSW	Private Sector Window
RFAs	regional financing arrangements
SALL	Sustainable Annual Lending Level
SAR	South Asia
SMEs	small and medium-sized enterprises
SSA	Sub-Saharan Africa
TFP	total factor productivity
UMICs	upper-middle-income countries
UNCTAD	United Nations Conference on Trade and Development
VAT	value added tax
WEO	*World Economic Outlook*
WGI	Worldwide Governance Indicators
WTO	World Trade Organization

PART I

Context

The real question is what will happen when the turmoil moves to debt markets. Many countries have built up substantial reserves, and are now issuing far more debt in domestic currency. Of course, the option of inflating away debt is hardly a panacea. Unfortunately, there is surely more drama to come over the next few years.

Kenneth Rogoff (2014)

Professor of Public Policy and Economics
Harvard University

CHAPTER 1

A Decade after the Global Recession: Lessons and Challenges

Although emerging market and developing economies (EMDEs) weathered the global recession a decade ago relatively well, they now appear less well placed to cope with the substantial downside risks facing the global economy. In many EMDEs, the room for monetary and fiscal policies to respond to shocks has eroded, underlying growth potential has slowed, and the momentum for improving policy frameworks, institutions, and business climates seems to have slackened. The experience of the 2009 global recession highlights once again the critical role of policy room in shielding economic activity during adverse shocks. The subsequent decade of anemic growth underlines the need for sound policy frameworks, institutions, and business environments to promote sustained growth. With the global growth outlook weakening and vulnerabilities rising, the policy priority for EMDEs is now to improve resilience to shocks and to lift long-term growth prospects.

Introduction

A decade ago, the global economy was reeling under the impact of the deepest global recession in the post-World War II period. In 2009, emerging market and developing economies (EMDEs) weathered the global recession relatively well. However, following a short-lived initial rebound in activity in 2010, the global economy, and especially EMDEs, has suffered a decade of weak growth despite unprecedented monetary policy accommodation and several rounds of fiscal stimulus in major economies (figure 1.1).

There has been a concern that the global economy may again experience a downturn in the near future. The baseline forecast for global growth in 2019 is likely to be softer than previously projected, partly reflecting recent data showing broad-based weakness in industrial activity and world trade. Although global growth is expected to stabilize in 2020, this assumes that global financing conditions will remain benign, encouraging a modest recovery of EMDE capital inflows. It also assumes no further escalation in trade tensions between major economies and stability in commodity prices. But the growth momentum is fragile and the risks are tilted to the downside.

Are EMDEs ready to face a global downturn, if it materializes? To answer this question, this study examines developments of the past decade, draws lessons for EMDEs, and discusses policy options. It is the first comprehensive analysis on the topic with a truly EMDE focus.

The study carries three main messages.

First, perhaps for the first time, many EMDEs were able to implement large-scale countercyclical fiscal and monetary policy during the global recession. They were in a

Note: This chapter was prepared by M. Ayhan Kose and Franziska Ohnsorge.

FIGURE 1.1 A decade since the 2009 global recession

A decade ago, a financial crisis that originated in the Unites States was followed by a global recession with an exceptionally severe output contraction in advanced economies. Capital flows to EMDEs and global trade sharply decelerated, and commodity prices fell. A coordinated international policy stimulus led to a rebound of activity in 2010. Growth since then, however, has been subpar, especially in EMDEs.

A. Growth

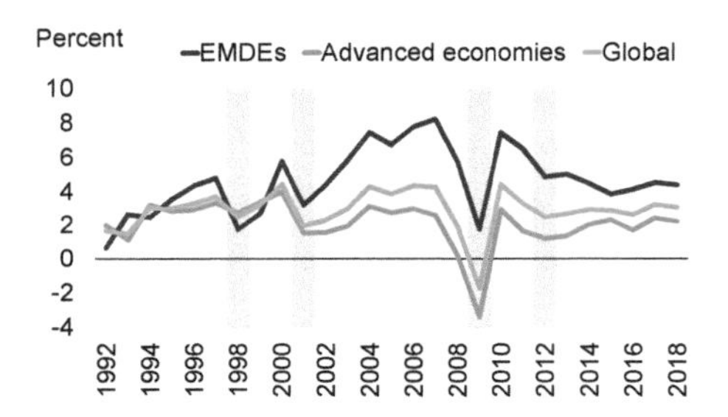

B. EMDE growth around global recessions

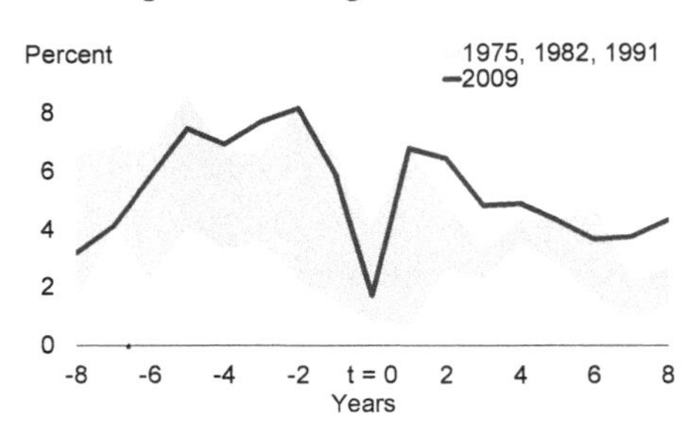

C. Advanced-economy growth around global recessions

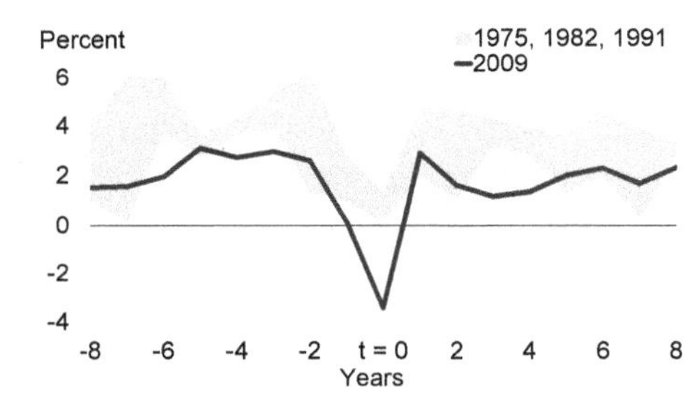

D. Private capital inflows to EMDEs around recessions

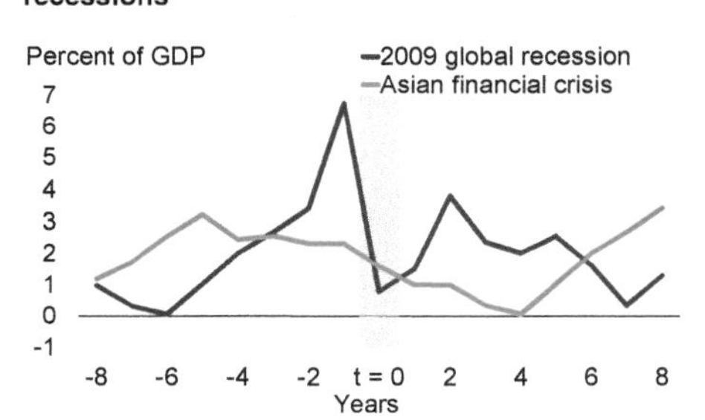

E. Global export and investment growth

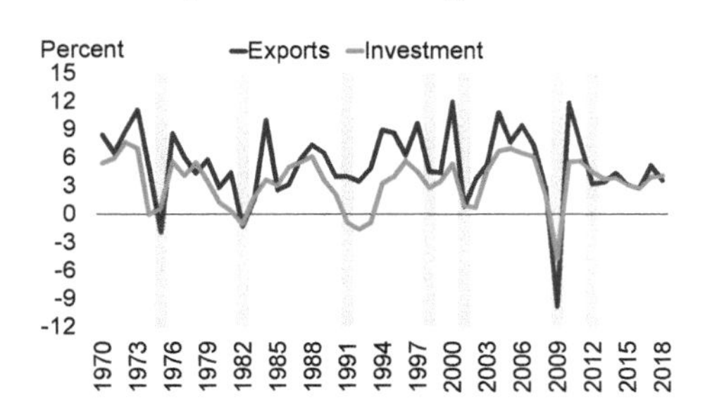

F. Commodity prices

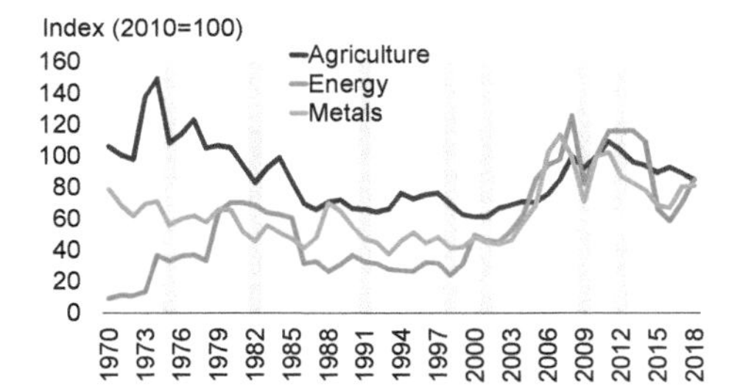

Sources: Chinn and Ito (2006); Haver Analytics; World Bank.

Note: EMDEs = emerging market and developing economies.

A. Shaded bars indicate global recessions and slowdowns.

B. C. Shaded areas are the range of GDP growth in previous global recessions as defined by Kose and Terrones (2015).

D. t = 0 indicates 2009 for "2009 global recession" and 1998 for "Asian financial crisis."

F. Prices measured in real terms (2010 U.S. dollars).

position to stimulate activity because they could draw on sizable policy buffers accumulated during the prerecession period of strong growth: government debt had fallen, current account and fiscal deficits narrowed, and inflation had moderated. Those EMDEs with more resilient economies and with more forceful stimulus experienced milder growth slowdowns during the global recession.

Second, on a more cautionary note, this study warns that, were a sharp global downturn to happen now, the average EMDE would be less prepared to address it than before the 2009 recession. EMDEs generally are more vulnerable to external shocks, in part because of mounting debt, weakening demand for commodity exports, and slower underlying domestic growth. Trade disputes among major economies are chipping away at an important engine of EMDE growth. At the same time, weaker fiscal positions would make it more difficult for EMDEs to support activity with expansionary fiscal policy.

Third, there are a few reasons for optimism. Since the 1997-98 Asian crisis and the 2001 U.S. recession—the two global downturns that preceded the 2009 global recession—policy frameworks in EMDEs have become more resilient. For example, the number of EMDEs with inflation-targeting monetary policy regimes and the number with fiscal rules have risen considerably since 1997. Although their effectiveness varied, these rules-based policy frameworks facilitated effective countercyclical responses by these economies during the global recession of 2009, and could be a source of strength in the face of future shocks.

These three messages underscore the need for EMDE policy makers to draw on the principal lessons of the 2009 global recession—the importance of strengthening their economies' ability to avoid or minimize the effects of adverse shocks and of having in place the policy room to act when such shocks inevitably occur. This means rebuilding fiscal space, raising foreign reserves where they are insufficient, and, in some economies, further strengthening policy frameworks. It also means putting in place financial sector policies that enable EMDEs to adapt to changing international financial conditions and mitigate systemic risks. Such policies would aim to strengthen home-host financial supervisory coordination and empower prudential authorities to act. Perhaps most important, it also means putting in place the structural policies needed to help offset the projected decline in potential growth over the next decade, focusing particularly on improving human capital, closing infrastructure gaps, and improving governance and institutions. These policies are also critical in reducing poverty and promoting shared prosperity.

This study builds on these themes by extending the literature on lessons from the global recession in several dimensions. First, whereas the previous literature focused on the experience of advanced economies, this study explores in depth the experience of a large group of EMDEs.[1] Second, whereas previous work focused either on macroeconomic

[1] Several studies focus exclusively or predominantly on advanced economies, including IMF (2018a, 2018b), OECD (2018), and Liang, McConnell, and Swagel (2018).

developments and policies (IMF 2018a), financial sector issues (IMF 2018b; World Bank 2019a), or structural reforms (OECD 2018), this study presents a unified review of these critical aspects from the perspective of EMDEs. Third, whereas the literature has covered specific aspects of financial market developments in EMDEs since the global recession (IMF 2015; World Bank 2018a), this is the first study to comprehensively document these changes.

This introductory chapter first briefly describes the main features of global recessions and recoveries to put the 2009 episode into a historical context. It then discusses macroeconomic and financial market developments in EMDEs before, during, and after the 2009 global recession. The subsequent two sections present lessons and challenges faced by EMDEs today and policy options to meet these challenges, including World Bank Group policies that can support such efforts. The last section provides a synopsis of the remaining chapters of this book.

Global recessions: Infrequent, but always costly

Since 1950, the global economy has experienced a global recession—defined as a contraction in global real per capita gross domestic product (GDP)—in almost every decade (1975, 1982, 1991, and 2009; figure 1.2). These four episodes were characterized by highly synchronized downturns in global trade, industrial production, capital flows, employment, and energy consumption (chapter 2). They were triggered by different types of shocks and each exhibited unique features, but they were all accompanied by financial crises.[2]

The global recession of 1975 followed the shock to global oil prices triggered by the Arab oil embargo in October 1973. Although the embargo ended in March 1974, the supply shock associated with the sharp rise in oil prices quickly translated into a substantial increase in inflation and a significant decline in growth in many countries (Ha, Ivanova et al. 2019). Monetary and fiscal policy easing, especially by advanced economies, helped spur a rebound of growth in 1976, but also ushered in an era of stagflation with disappointing growth but high and unstable inflation.

The global recession in 1982 was triggered by several developments, including a second oil price shock, a tightening of monetary policies in advanced economies, and the Latin American debt crisis. Oil prices rose sharply in 1979, partly owing to disruptions caused by the Iranian revolution, and this increase helped push inflation to new highs in several advanced economies. In response, monetary policies were tightened significantly, especially in the United States, causing sharp declines in activity and significant increases in unemployment rates in many advanced economies in 1982-83. The increase in global interest rates and a collapse of commodity prices in the early 1980s made it difficult for several Latin American countries to service their debts, resulting in debt crises in the region. Even though advanced economies were able to recover quickly, the debt crisis

[2] The events surrounding these episodes are discussed in detail in Knoop (2004), Reinhart and Rogoff (2009), and Kose and Terrones (2015). Barsky and Kilian (2004) and Hamilton (2011) present surveys of the history of oil shocks and the subsequent economic downturns.

FIGURE 1.2 Global recessions: Costly and synchronous

Since 1950, the world economy has experienced a global recession—defined as a contraction in global real per capita GDP—in almost every decade (in 1975, 1982, 1991, and 2009). The proportion of countries in recession rose sharply during these episodes. In addition to these four global recessions, the global economy experienced global downturns in 1958, 1998, 2001, and 2012.

A. World per capita output

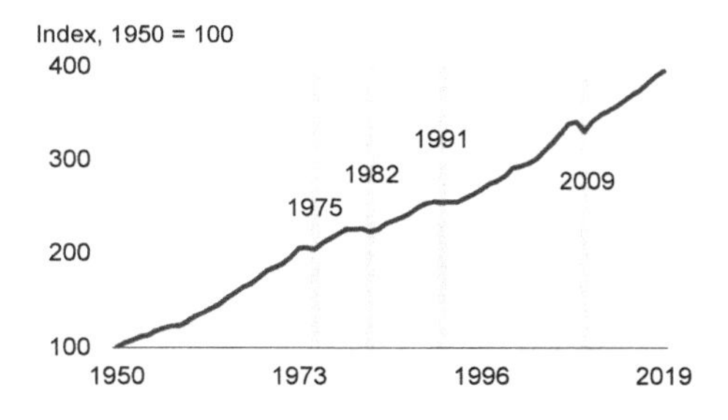

B. World per capita growth

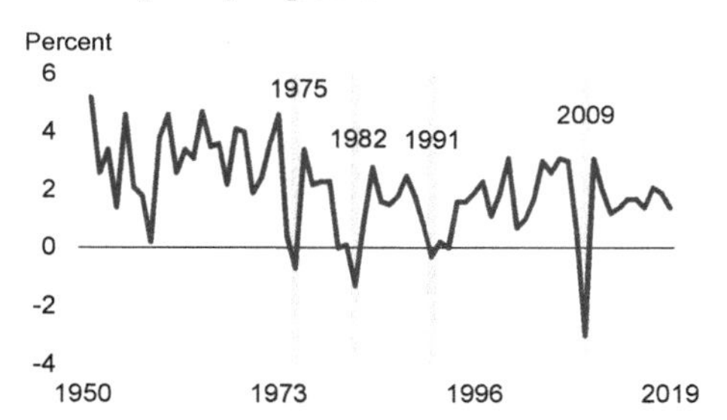

C. World per capita output during global recessions and downturns

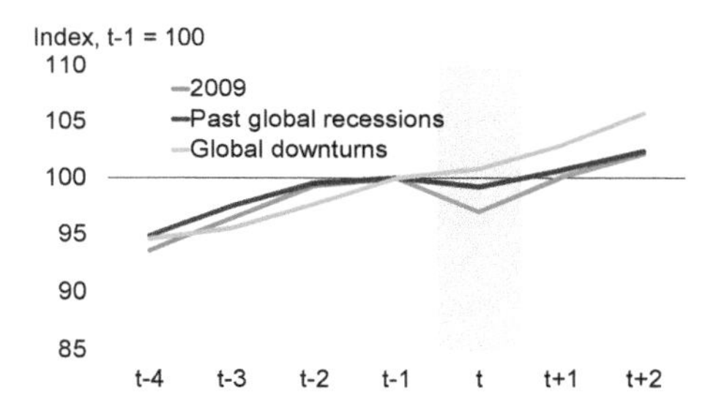

D. World industrial production during global recessions and downturns

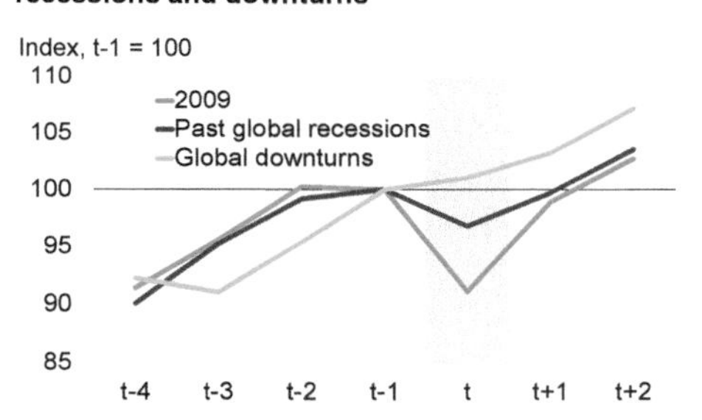

E. World per capita growth during global recessions and downturns

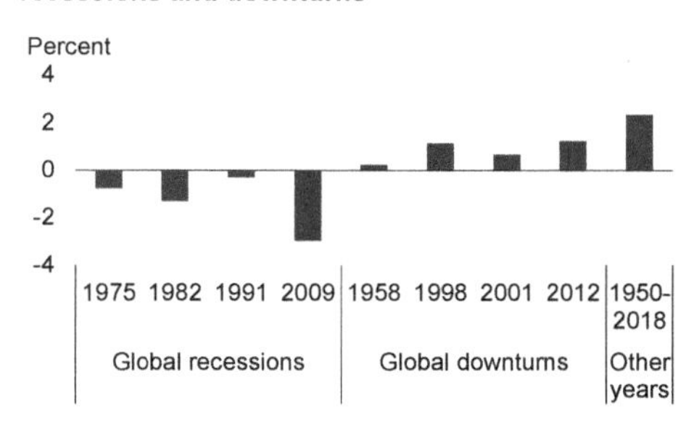

F. Synchronization of recessions

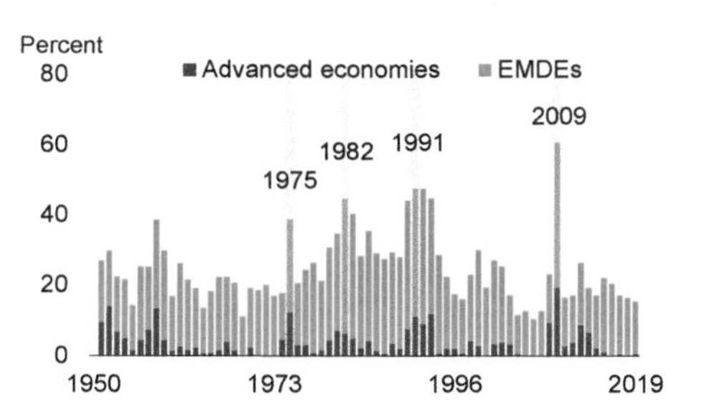

Source: World Bank.

Note: Aggregated using GDP at 2010 prices and market exchange rates. EMDEs = emerging market and developing economies.

A. Shaded bars indicate global recessions.

C.D. Time t denotes the year of global recessions and slowdowns (shaded in gray). The line for past global recessions is an average of 1975, 1982, and 1991 global recessions, whereas the one for global downturns is an average of global downturns of 1958, 1998, 2001, and 2012.

E. Each bar shows world per capita output growth for the relevant years of global recessions and downturns, as well as average growth during nonrecession/nondownturn years.

F. Recession is defined as a contraction in per capita GDP (unweighted). Global recession years are 1975, 1982, 1991, and 2009.

contributed to long-lasting growth slowdowns in many EMDEs in Latin America and the Caribbean (LAC) and in Sub-Saharan Africa (SSA).

The 1991 global recession resulted from the confluence of a wide range of shocks. The Gulf War was associated with heightened geopolitical uncertainty and a sharp increase in oil prices, which adversely affected global activity. In Central and Eastern Europe and the former USSR, the transition to a market economy was accompanied by high inflation and output contractions. In the United States, widespread weakness of lending institutions from the mid-1980s weighed on the housing market, especially during the credit crunch of 1990-91. Scandinavian countries had severe banking crises in the early 1990s, following the liberalization of financial sectors and rapid expansion in credit markets in the 1980s. In the European Union (EU), problems with the European Monetary System's exchange rate mechanism in 1992 were accompanied by sharp declines in activity in many member countries. In Japan, the bursting of an asset price bubble resulted in a recession and a prolonged period of low growth and near-zero inflation. The broad-based financial distress in multiple large economies meant that the recovery from the 1991 recession was subdued.

The 2009 global recession followed the worst financial crisis since the Great Depression. As discussed in detail later, the crisis followed a period of loosening regulation and supervision of financial markets and institutions, asset price and credit booms in a number of countries, and the rapid expansion of high-risk lending, particularly in U.S. mortgage markets. Although the epicenter of the crisis was the U.S. mortgage market, it quickly spread to other financial market segments and countries, becoming global in its reach. Banking crises in many European countries erupted in 2008 and culminated in a sovereign debt crisis in the euro area in 2011-12. The high degree of financial interconnectedness contributed to the transmission of the crisis to other advanced economies and some EMDEs. The aftermath featured prolonged asset price busts and credit crunches, a collapse in global trade, and synchronized recessions.

EMDEs, with the exception of those heavily exposed to the euro area debt crisis, weathered the 2009 global recession relatively well. With policy room that had been built since the Asian crisis—such as low debt, deficits, and inflation as well as high international reserves—many EMDEs were able to undertake countercyclical policy measures and used flexible exchange rates as shock absorbers. EMDEs also benefitted from exceptional policy stimulus in advanced economies. The extraordinary policy stimulus, provided especially by advanced economies but also many EMDEs, laid the foundation for a strong global rebound in 2010. Despite this recovery, the crisis had long-lasting and damaging effects on global growth, which has remained lackluster during the subsequent decade.

Global downturns. In addition to the four global recessions, the global economy experienced low growth in 1958, 1998, 2001, and 2012. World output per capita grew at slightly less than 1 percent during these four years, the lowest growth rates the global economy registered during the past seven decades, except during global recessions and the years before and after them.

Each of these downturns falls short of qualifying as a global recession because world real GDP per capita did not contract. For example, in 1958, global growth was weak because of slow growth or outright recessions in some major advanced economies. In 1997-98, economic activity in many EMDEs, particularly those in Asia, slowed sharply, but growth in advanced economies held up. In 2001, conversely, many advanced economies had mild slowdowns or recessions, but growth in major EMDEs, such as China and India, remained robust. In 2012, the global downturn was mainly driven by the euro area debt crisis.

Moreover, during the years of global downturns, the behavior of other global indicators was mixed, implying that these episodes did not display the features of a global recession. For example, the main activity indicators did not suggest a broad-based weakness in the global economy in 1998. In 2001, although industrial production fell and the rate of global unemployment picked up slightly, both global trade flows and oil consumption increased. Equity prices declined substantially in 2001, and prices of commodities fell significantly in both episodes. During the global downturn of 2012, some activity indicators did not show much weakness, but global capital flows slowed, equity prices collapsed, and inflation declined.

National recessions in many economies. Global recessions are highly synchronized events internationally, with many economies sliding simultaneously into recession. Remarkably, the proportion of economies in recession during successive global recessions has increased over time: it was close to 40 percent in the 1975 episode and about 61 percent in the 2009 global recession. The proportion of countries in recession typically starts rising ahead of the recession year. The 2006-07 period stands out for the historically low number of countries in recession, but it was followed by a sharp reversal of fortune. In 2009, almost all advanced economies and roughly half of EMDEs were in recession. The degree of synchronicity in the last global recession was the highest in the past 70 years, possibly reflecting the depth of the global financial crisis and stronger international trade and financial linkages compared to prior decades.

The U.S. economy during global recessions and downturns. Although the four global recessions between 1975 and 2009 coincided with recessions in the United States, not every U.S. recession was associated with a global recession. The United States experienced six additional recessions during 1950-2019, including recessions in 1958 and 2001 that coincided with global downturns; but its economy grew strongly during the 1998 global downturn and, to a lesser extent, during the 2012 global downturn.

Before the recession: A seemingly golden era

During 2001-07, the world economy appeared to be enjoying a golden era of growth. During this period, average output growth reached its highest pace since the early 1970s. Not only was growth buoyant, but inflation appeared to have been tamed in what was termed "the Great Moderation" (figure 1.3). EMDEs were expanding rapidly as global supply chains and financial institutions expanded around the world.

A confluence of favorable circumstances fueled global trade and commodity demand. Advanced economies enjoyed a cyclical upturn after the global downturn of 2001, with

FIGURE 1.3 Global output, inflation, and poverty

The global recession of 2009 featured an exceptionally severe output contraction in advanced economies and a collapse of capital market valuations notwithstanding widespread monetary policy accommodation. The recovery has been anemic. The decline in global poverty continued, albeit at a somewhat slower pace, because poverty was concentrated in regions less affected by the global recession.

A. Growth

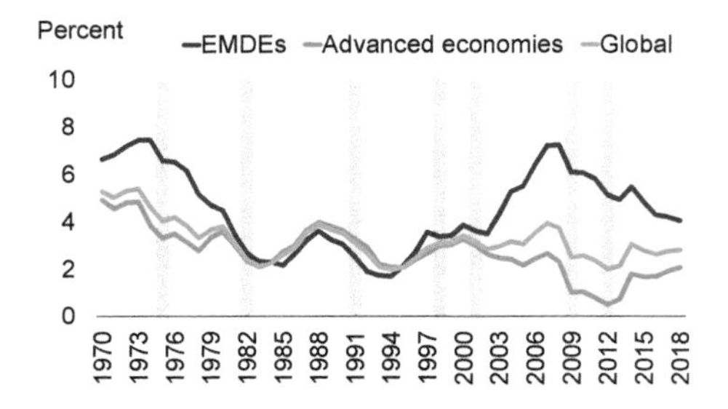

B. EMDE growth

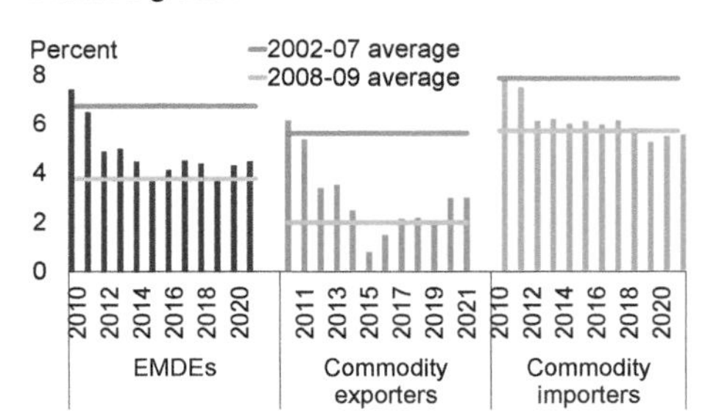

C. Monetary policy rates

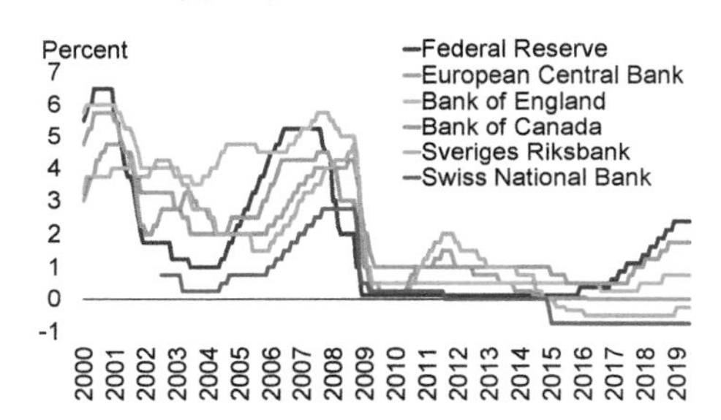

D. Equity markets

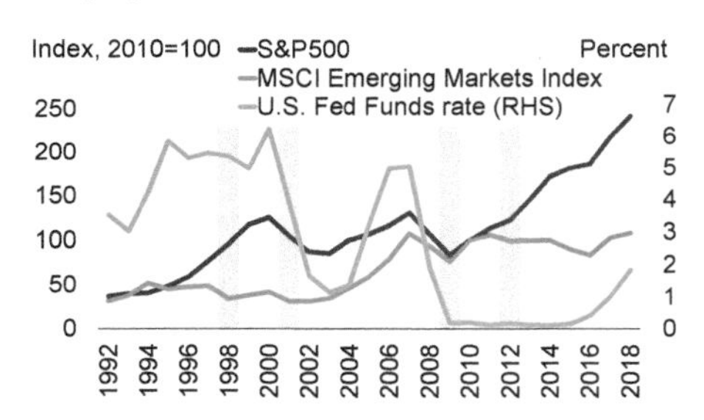

E. Inflation

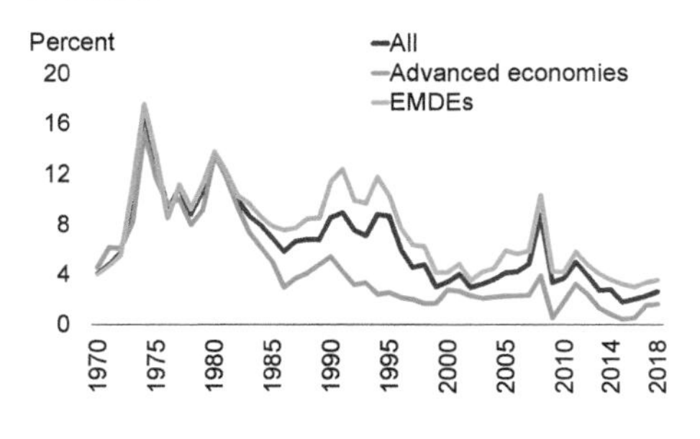

F. Poverty

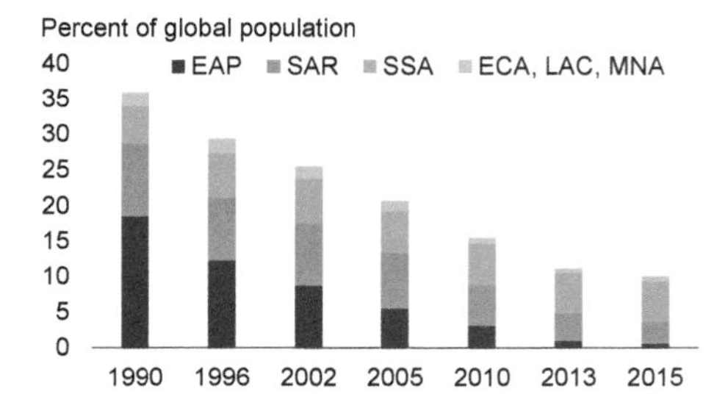

Sources: Haver Analytics; International Monetary Fund; PovCalNet; U.S. Federal Reserve Economic Data; World Bank.

Note: EAP = East Asia and Pacific; ECA = Europe and Central Asia; EMDEs = emerging market and developing economies; LAC = Latin America and the Caribbean; MNA = Middle East and North Africa; MSCI = Morgan Stanly Capital International (emerging markets index); SAR = South Asia; SSA = Sub-Saharan Africa.

A. Five-year rolling averages.

A.B. GDP-weighted averages at 2010 prices and exchange rates.

D. Shaded bars indicate global recessions and slowdowns.

E. Median year-on-year consumer price inflation for 29 advanced economies and 126 EMDEs.

F. Poverty defined as number of people living on $1.90 per day or less, as in World Bank (2018d).

output growth strengthening from 1.5 percent in 2001 to 2.6 percent in 2007. China was also growing rapidly as it integrated into global trade networks and supply chains, with its output almost doubling from the time of its World Trade Organization (WTO) accession in 2001 until 2007 (chapter 3).

Prolonged accommodative monetary policy in major advanced economies and rapidly growing savings in some large EMDEs helped maintain low global real interest rates and encouraged capital flows to EMDEs. Partly as a result of search for yield, gross capital inflows to EMDEs excluding foreign direct investment (FDI) swelled nearly sevenfold (from 1 percent of GDP in 2001 to 6.5 percent of GDP in 2007). FDI flows to these economies also expanded rapidly, almost doubling relative to GDP during the same period; and remittance flows to these economies rose by one-and-a-half times.

This benign external environment supported EMDE financial markets and domestic demand. EMDE equity market valuations, as measured by the Morgan Stanley Capital International (MSCI) index, more than quadrupled during 2002-07; EMDE bond spreads, as captured by J.P. Morgan's Emerging Market Bond Index (EMBI), and sovereign credit default swap (CDS) spreads in major EMDEs decreased by more than half between January 2005 and June 2007. Benign financing conditions supported strong investment growth, and private consumption was supported by strong employment and income growth. Except in Europe and Central Asia (ECA), EMDE banks were the main source of domestic private sector credit and were mostly funded by local deposits, thus limiting external funding risks (chapter 4). In ECA, however, EU accession was accompanied by credit booms in several economies that were funded by large EU-headquartered banks.

Rapid EMDE growth helped reduce global poverty. The number of low-income countries (LICs) declined to 49 in 2007, from 64 in 2001. Between 1990 and 2008, extreme poverty halved to 18 percent of the global population. China's rapid expansion accounted for about three-fifths of this decline, and the remainder mostly reflected progress in Brazil, India, Indonesia, and Pakistan. Rapid EMDE growth reduced between-country inequality, halving the global Gini index—an indicator of income inequality—between the 1990s and 2005-07. In most EMDEs, within-country inequality also declined, albeit only marginally.

Robust economic growth allowed EMDEs to improve their fiscal and external positions and strengthen their macroeconomic and financial sector policy frameworks (chapters 3-5; figure 1.4). On average, fiscal balances improved from a deficit of 0.8 percent of GDP in 2002 (after some deterioration during the 2001 global slowdown) to a surplus of 2.4 percent of GDP in 2007. Government debt declined steeply from 76 percent of GDP to 45 percent of GDP. Subdued inflation allowed central banks to maintain low policy rates, narrowing deficits improved fiscal positions, and rising international reserves strengthened external buffers. EMDE current account deficits narrowed from 3.5 percent of GDP in 2001 to 1.2 percent GDP in 2007. About 70 percent of EMDEs increased their international reserves by more than 10 percentage points of external debt, whereas 25 percent of EMDEs increased them by more than 50 percentage points.

FIGURE 1.4 Fiscal and external positions

The prerecession global expansion helped EMDEs improve their fiscal and external positions. Since 2007, fiscal and current account deficits have widened, debt has risen, and international reserves have declined.

A. Fiscal balances

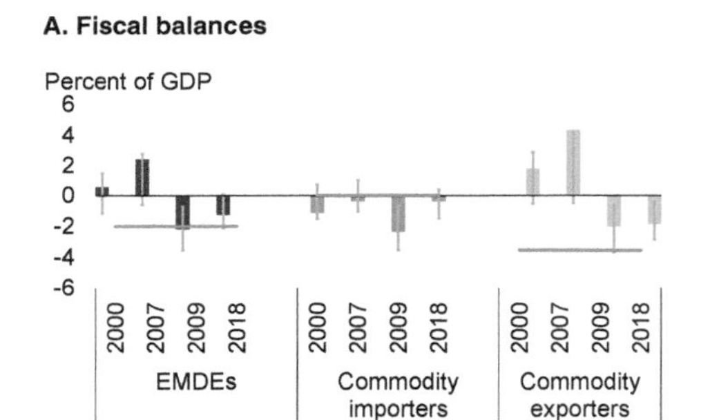

B. Government debt

Percent of GDP
100
80
60
40
20
0
2000
2007
2009
2018
EMDEs
Commodity importers
Commodity exporters

C. Current account balances

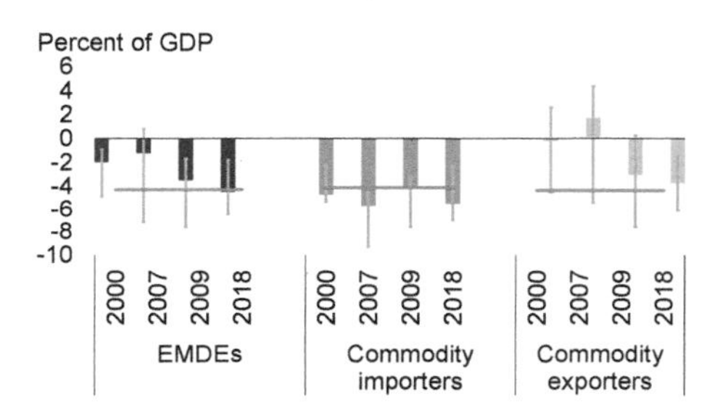

D. International reserves in months of imports

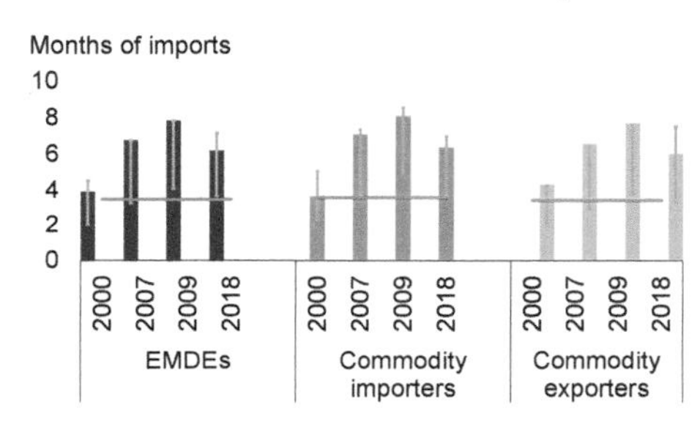

Sources: International Monetary Fund; Kose, Kurlat et al. (2017); World Bank.

Note: Blue bars denote unweighted averages for emerging market and developing economies (EMDEs). Orange whiskers denote intertercile ranges. Green lines denote 1980-99 averages.

Thanks to reforms in response to previous financial crises, many EMDEs entered the 2009 global recession with improved financial oversight frameworks.

During the recession: A highly synchronized contraction

The demise of this seemingly golden era of growth was swift, as rapid financial system growth during 2001-07 sowed the seeds for the global financial crisis and subsequent global recession. In the second half of 2007 and early 2008, with numerous defaults in the subprime mortgage market, the U.S. financial system teetered under increasing stress; and the failure of Lehman Brothers in September 2008 unleashed a full-blown crisis. A run on key funding markets exposed the fragility of other financial institutions, including major banks, investment dealers, and insurance companies that were involved in subprime mortgage lending or dependent on short-term wholesale funding.

FIGURE 1.5 Activity and monetary policy during the global recession

EMDEs weathered the 2009 global recession better than advanced economies did, despite a steep drop in global trade and investment growth. This resilience in part reflected the effects of exceptionally accommodative monetary policy in both advanced economies and EMDEs.

A. Global export and investment growth

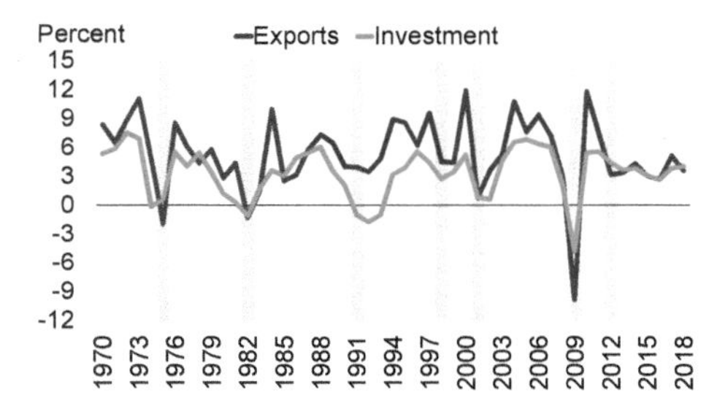

B. EMDE export and investment growth

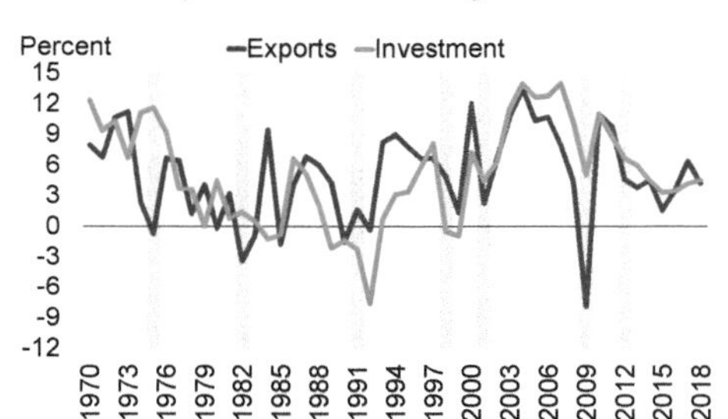

C. Central bank balance sheets

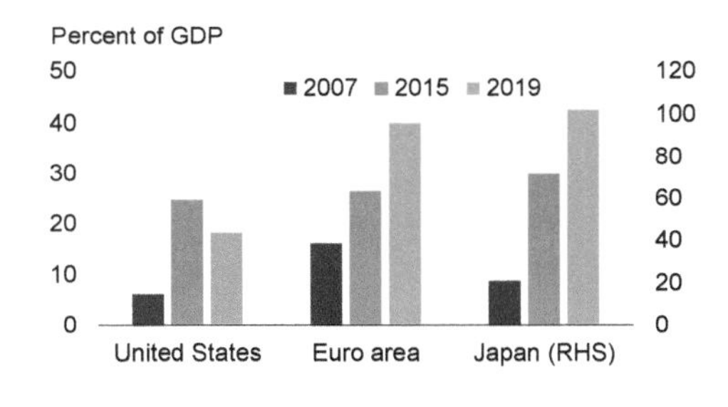

D. EMDE policy interest rates compared with previous banking crises

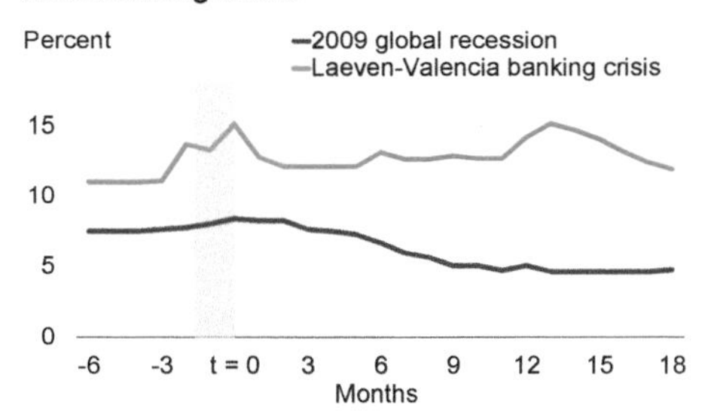

Source: World Bank.

A.B. Shaded areas are the range of GDP growth in previous global recessions and downturns as defined by Kose and Terrones (2015).

C. Assets of the U.S. Federal Reserve, the European Central Bank (euro area) and the Bank of Japan (Japan) in percent of GDP, for end-2007, end-2015, and July 2019.

D. Median policy rates. The country sample of banking crisis episodes consists of Argentina, Bulgaria, Colombia, Croatia, the Czech Republic, Hungary, Malaysia, Philippines, the Russian Federation, and Vietnam. The starting dates (t = 0) are defined by Laeven and Valencia (2018). The country sample in the global recession consists of 26 emerging market and developing economies (EMDEs).

The financial crisis was followed by a severe recession in the United States, during which output contracted by more than in any other U.S. recession since the Great Depression. Contagion quickly spread the crisis and recession to other advanced economies where consumer durables and investment spending plunged. Growth in advanced economies reversed from 2.6 percent in 2007 to -3.4 percent in 2009, leading to a global recession. Global per capita GDP contracted by 2.9 percent in 2009—more than in any previous global recession since the end of World War II.

Global trade plummeted, with global exports dropping 9.9 percent in 2009, compared to a 7.3 percent expansion in 2007 (figure 1.5). Countries dependent on manufacturing exports in sectors with high income elasticities of demand, especially electronics and motor vehicles, suffered large export contractions. Commodity prices, particularly for energy and industrial metals commodities, declined sharply.

In a broad-based flight to safety, portfolio investment and foreign lending flows to EMDEs reversed sharply in 2008, rocking EMDE financial markets. Between June 2007 and December 2008, the EMBI bond spread widened by nearly 600 basis points, the MSCI equity market index halved, and average CDS spreads in major EMDEs increased by 375 basis points (figure 1.3). At the peak of the global recession, from September 2008 to March 2009, currencies in EMDEs with some of the most liquid financial markets (Indonesia, Mexico, Poland) weakened by more than 20 percent against the U.S. dollar.[3]

Despite these developments, EMDE output growth remained positive, although it did slow sharply, from 8.2 percent in 2007 to 5.9 percent in 2008 and 1.7 percent in 2009 (chapter 3). Although steep, this slowdown was somewhat milder than during some previous global recessions (figure 1.1). Three-fifths of EMDEs avoided output contractions entirely.

EMDEs weathered the global recession relatively well thanks to large, prompt, and global policy support. Coordinated by the Group of Twenty (G20), the largest advanced economies and EMDEs implemented unprecedented monetary and fiscal stimulus in 2009 and 2010.[4] EMDE governments employed fiscal packages that included infrastructure investment, tax cuts, and social protection programs. EMDE central banks lowered policy interest rates, having tamed inflation before the crisis; and some EMDEs used their foreign reserves, accumulated before the crisis, to stabilize their currencies. On average in EMDEs, private sector credit relative to GDP declined only moderately and was considerably more stable than in their past episodes of financial distress (chapter 4). The incidence of sudden stops in capital inflows tipping countries into financial distress was about half of that before 2008, and centered in economies where precrisis credit booms had been funded by large capital inflows and where banks had a narrow deposit base, such as some economies in ECA (Feyen et al. 2014).

Although EMDEs as a whole weathered the global recession well, the effects varied across regions (chapter 3). Most EMDEs in ECA suffered severe output contractions, particularly those EMDEs that were highly dependent on cross-border financing. Countries that were heavily reliant on commodity sectors for export receipts and fiscal revenues, such as those in LAC and the Middle East and North Africa (MNA), also fared relatively badly. EMDEs elsewhere withstood the crisis better, because they were less exposed to the financial turmoil and recession in advanced economies, and because they pursued countercyclical policies.

The experience of the seven largest EMDEs, the EM7 (Brazil, China, India, Indonesia, Mexico, the Russian Federation, and Turkey), was heterogeneous (figure 1.6). The differences reflected, in part, the extent of each country's trade links to other crisis-hit

---

[3] The ECA region was the hardest hit. Exchange rates depreciated against the U.S. dollar by more than 30 percent in Belarus, Georgia, Serbia, and the Russian Federation and by more than 50 percent in Ukraine.

[4] The G20, founded in 1999, includes Argentina, Australia, Brazil, Canada, China, France, Germany, India, Indonesia, Italy, Japan, the Republic of Korea, Mexico, the Russian Federation, Saudi Arabia, South Africa, Turkey, the United Kingdom, the United States, and the EU.

FIGURE 1.6 EMDE growth

A synchronous and persistent slowdown has been underway in EMDEs since the postrecession rebound of 2010, notwithstanding a modest recovery in 2017-18. The growth slowdown during 2007-09 was particularly pronounced in EMDEs that were more open to trade and finance, had higher vulnerabilities and policy imbalances (external debt, credit growth, fiscal deficits, and inflation), and implemented less policy support (monetary easing, fiscal stimulus, and reserve drawdown).

A. Growth by region

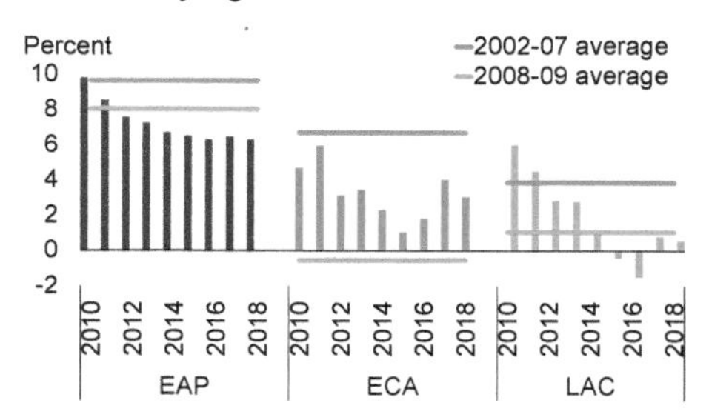

B. Growth by region (continued)

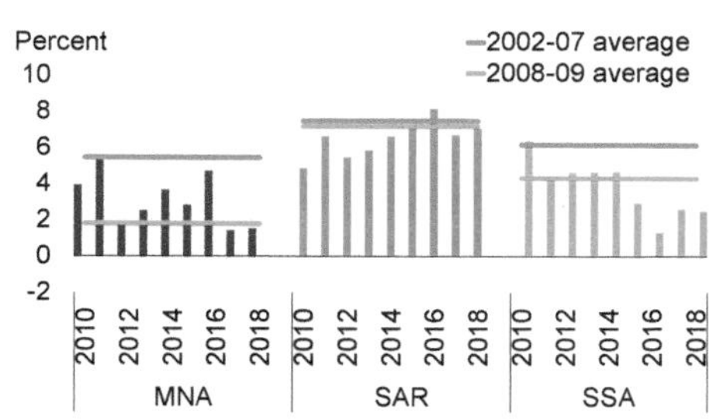

C. Growth in selected commodity importers

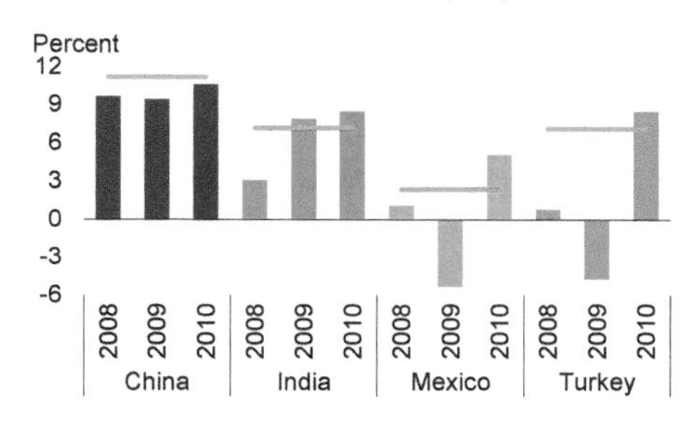

D. Growth in selected commodity exporters

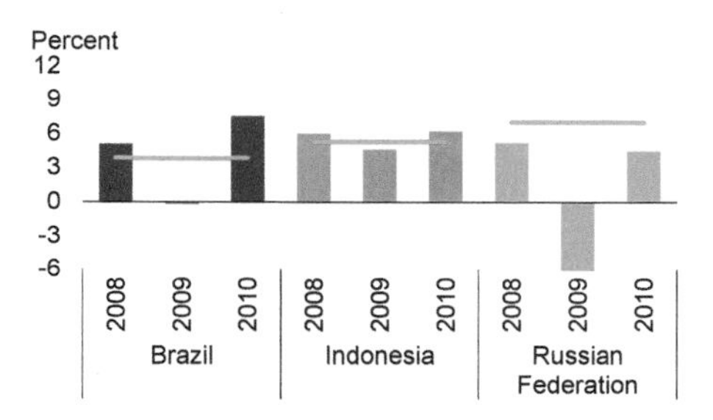

E. EMDE growth slowdowns in 2007-09, by precrisis structural indicators

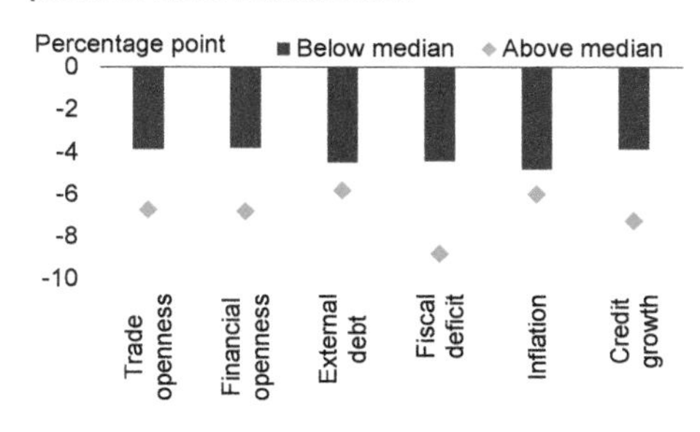

F. EMDE growth slowdowns in 2007-09, by policy intervention

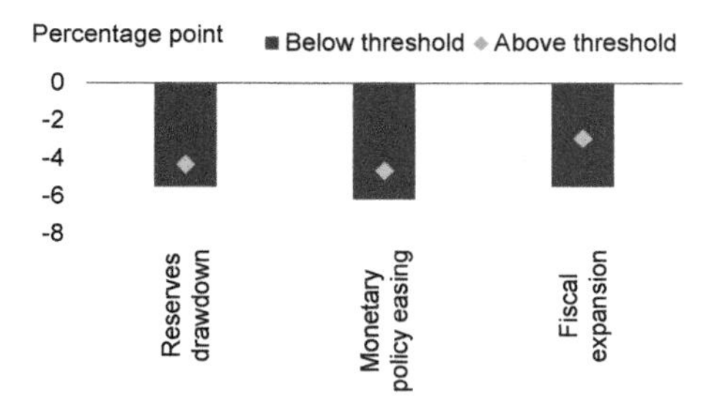

Source: World Bank.

Note: EAP = East Asia and Pacific; ECA = Europe and Central Asia; EMDEs = emerging market and developing economies; LAC = Latin America and the Caribbean; MNA = Middle East and North Africa; SAR = South Asia; SSA = Sub-Saharan Africa.

C.D. Blue bars denote 2002-07 averages.

E.F. Growth slowdown is the GDP growth differential between 2007 (precrisis) and 2009. Depending on data availability for each indicator, the number of EMDEs ranges from 80 to 154.

E. Trade openness is proxied by trade (exports and imports) in percent of GDP and financial openness is based on the Chinn-Ito index. External debt and fiscal deficit are in percent of GDP. Inflation is the annual change in the consumer price index. Credit growth is the annual change in domestic credit to the private sector.

F. The threshold for reserves drawdown is 10 percent of the reserve-to-debt ratio. Monetary easing refers to the lowering of interest rates, with a 0.5-percentage-point threshold. Fiscal expansion refers to growth in real government consumption expenditure, with a 10-percentage-point threshold.

countries, their precrisis vulnerabilities, and the speed, size, and effectiveness of policy stimulus (chapter 3). China and India, for example, were successful in mitigating the adverse impact of the global recession by putting in place large fiscal and monetary stimulus and using their sizeable international reserves (India) or capital controls (China) to stabilize currency markets. More broadly, EMDEs with stronger fiscal and external positions, lower inflation, sound financial sectors, better institutions, or lesser dependence on external demand and foreign finance fared better, as did those that used countercyclical policies decisively to support activity (see also Balakrishnan et al. 2011; Berkmen et al. 2012; Blanchard et al. 2010; Cetorelli and Goldberg 2011; Fratzscher 2012). Together with the globally coordinated expansionary policies, these characteristics helped limit the magnitude of economic and financial disruptions in many EMDEs.

During the global recession, the World Bank Group nearly doubled its annual financing commitments and provided support to large numbers of crisis-affected countries (box 1.1; chapter 8). Its extensive and rapid response made effective use of traditional financing instruments alongside new crisis-specific facilities. Drawing on this experience, the World Bank Group has since enhanced its surveillance of the global economy, rebuilt its capital, and refined its financing and operating model.

After the recession: The lackluster recovery

The sizable, prompt, and global monetary and fiscal stimulus in the largest advanced economies and major EMDEs initially supported a strong rebound in global trade, commodity prices, and capital markets. Capital flows returned to EMDEs although flows other than FDI initially remained below precrisis peaks. Stock markets rallied, and sovereign bond spreads retreated: by end-2010, the MSCI and EMBI spreads had already nearly returned to precrisis (mid-2007) levels.

This rebound, however, proved short-lived. The following decade has been marked by protracted weakness in the global economy. Since 2011, global trade growth has averaged 4.1 percent, well below precrisis rates (7.3 percent, 2002-07). Trade weakness has reflected a combination of factors, including weak demand growth in advanced economies, shifts in the composition of global demand, the maturation of global supply chains, and trade tensions between major economies (World Bank 2015a).

In 2011, commodity prices—at first metals and agricultural prices and, later, oil prices—began to decline sharply from their peaks, reaching a trough in early 2016 and then recovering only moderately. The decline reflected both slowing demand growth, including in China, and ample supply after a period of rapid global investment in the resource sectors (World Bank 2015b, 2016a, 2016b). The Organization of the Petroleum Exporting Countries (OPEC) initially tried to stabilize oil prices in the face of surging U.S. shale oil production, but abandoned this strategy in mid-2014. Oil prices then plunged to a trough in 2016, causing widespread disruption to oil-exporting countries (Baffes et al. 2015). At end-2018, energy prices were still 32 percent below their 2011 highs, industrial metals prices 20 percent below, and agricultural commodity prices 29 percent below. The decline in commodity prices—compounded by policy

BOX 1.1 World Bank Group response to the global recession

The World Bank Group's response to the global financial crisis and the subsequent global recession was unprecedented in scale. The World Bank Group has since strengthened its balance sheet, financing instruments, and analytical tools so that it is well positioned to provide the support that member countries may need during the next global downturn.

The global financial crisis and the subsequent global recession sharply slowed growth and exacerbated poverty in World Bank Group client countries. This situation led the World Bank Group to provide new levels of financing support and advisory services to its members.

The World Bank Group's response to the global financial crisis was unprecedented in financing volume and broadly distributed across countries (chapter 8). Within two years, financing commitments nearly doubled and loans were extended to more than 100 countries, with the largest regional increases in Latin America and the Caribbean and Europe and Central Asia (figure B1.1.1). In addition to its traditional financing instruments, the World Bank Group adopted several new facilities to support crisis-impaired activities such as trade finance and infrastructure investment. The World Bank Group's crisis response relied heavily

FIGURE B1.1.1 World Bank Group financing during the global recession

The World Bank Group's lending rose significantly in response to the global financial crisis and subsequent global recession.

A. Financing commitments

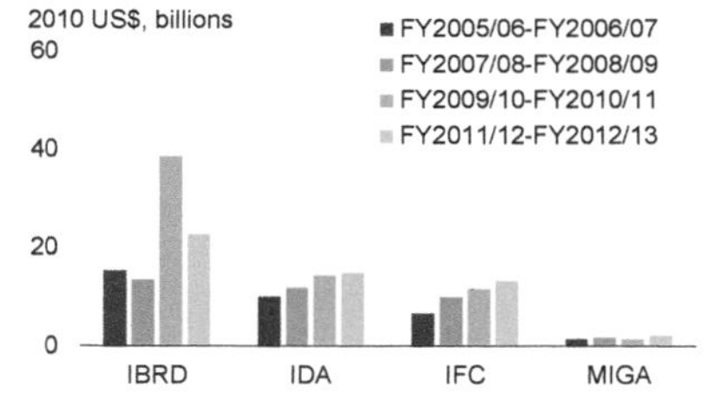

B. Lending commitments, by region

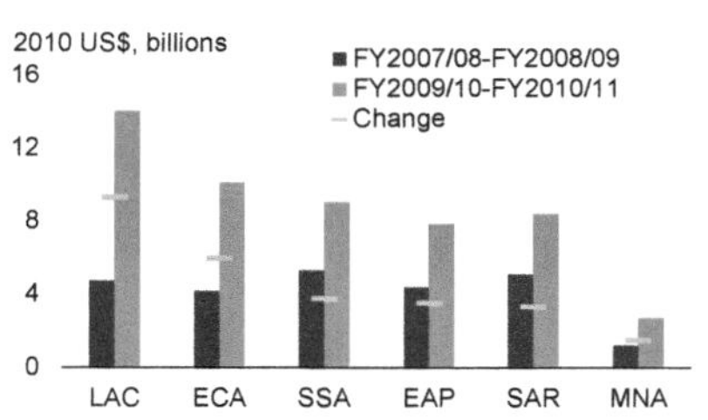

Source: World Bank.

Note: EAP = East Asia and Pacific; ECA = Europe and Central Asia; LAC = Latin America and the Caribbean; MNA = Middle East and North Africa; SAR = South Asia; SSA = Sub-Saharan Africa; IBRD = International Bank for Reconstruction and Development; IDA = International Development Association; IFC = International Finance Corporation; MIGA = Multilateral Investment Guarantee Agency.

A. Annual averages over the periods denoted. Data for IBRD/IDA refer to commitments. Data for IFC refer to investment commitments from own accounts. Data for MIGA refer to guarantee issuances.

B. Each column shows annual averages over fiscal years denoted for the IBRD and IDA.

Note: This box was prepared by Lei Sandy Ye.

BOX 1.1 World Bank Group response to the global recession *(continued)*

on development policy lending and prioritized the areas of finance, fiscal management, infrastructure, and social protection.

In its recent work, the World Bank Group has drawn on its experience during the global recession. It has improved its monitoring of global macroeconomic and financial developments, allowing it to more effectively flag risks in the world economy. It has completed two global campaigns to improve its capital adequacy, partly to be better prepared for future crises. It has refined its operating model by introducing new crisis response facilities and implementing a more coordinated Bank-wide strategy in its lending and advisory activities, helping to enhance its ability to respond quickly and flexibly should a future crisis arise. Although there may be room for further improvements (chapter 8), the World Bank Group's current policy toolkit contains a comprehensive set of instruments to help countries reduce risk, mitigate the consequences of crises, and build longer-term growth and shared prosperity.

tightening as resource revenues collapsed and reserves declined—dampened growth in the two-thirds of EMDEs that rely heavily on commodity exports (World Bank 2018b).

Capital flows to EMDEs have been volatile since the global recession, with repeated spikes in borrowing cost since mid-2013. Following the postrecession rebound, global capital flows have declined with episodes of sharp outflows in 2013, 2015, and 2018.[5] During these episodes, on average, the EMBI spread rose by about 50 basis points, the MSCI stock price index declined by 7.7 percent, capital inflows to EMDEs slowed sharply, and EMDE currencies depreciated against the U.S. dollar (figure 1.7). Whereas portfolio and other investment flows to EMDEs underwent bouts of reversals, FDI flows and remittances to EMDEs have remained more stable.

EMDE growth has slowed since 2010 to a trough of 4.1 percent in 2016 before a modest recovery took hold (chapter 4). The growth slowdown during 2011-16 was synchronous (affecting more than three-fifths of EMDEs) and protracted, with the steepest slowdowns in LAC and the mildest in South Asia (SAR). In LICs, growth slowed from 6.9 percent in 2012 to a trough of 4.8 percent in 2016. Amid this broad-based growth weakness, EMDEs have struggled to fully unwind fiscal and monetary stimulus (World Bank 2015a, 2017a, 2019a).

Most components of EMDE demand growth slowed concurrently. Investment and export growth suffered especially sharp declines, to less than half their rates before the

[5] These episodes were especially pronounced in the third quarter of 2013, third quarter of 2015, and second quarter of 2018.

FIGURE 1.7 EMDE financial markets during periods of financial stress

Since the global recession, there have been several bouts of financial market stress in EMDEs.

A. Exchange rates

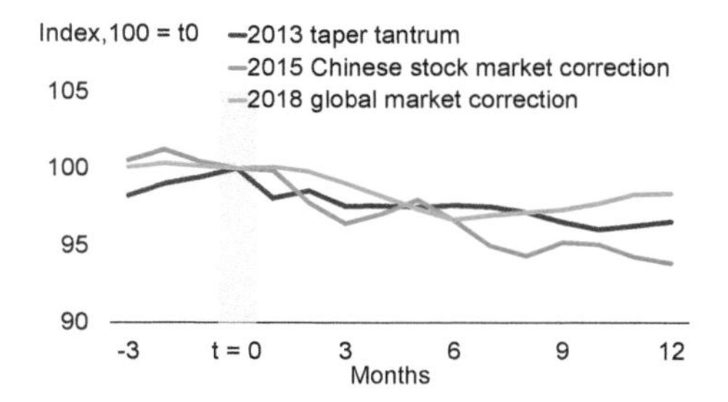

B. Financial market volatility

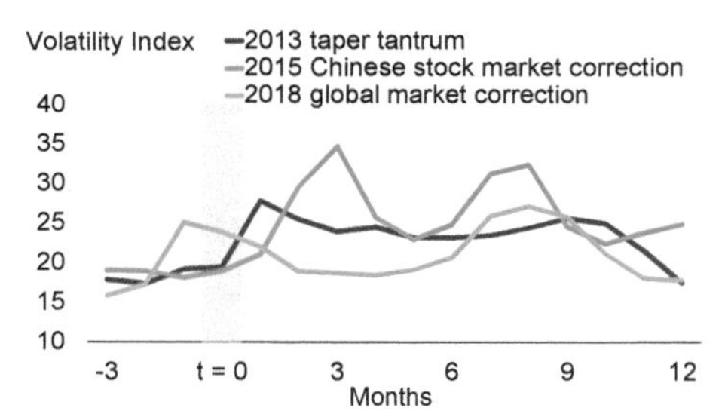

C. EMBI spreads

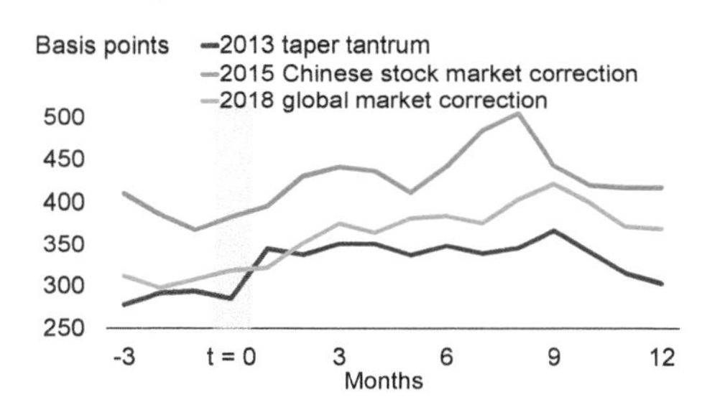

D. MSCI stock index

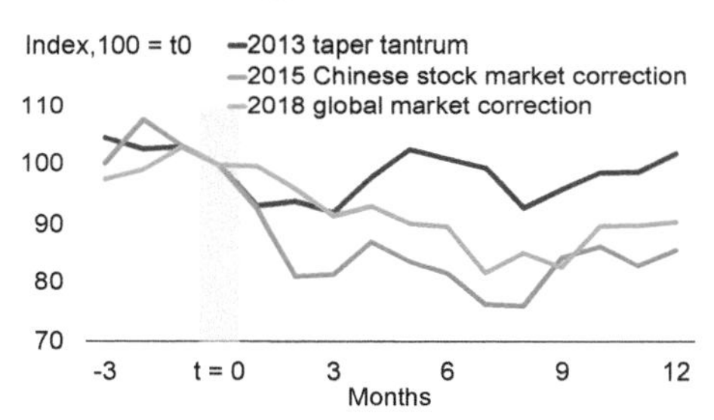

Sources: Haver Analytics; World Bank.

Note: t = 0 indicates May 2013, June 2015, and March 2018. The taper tantrum refers to a period of market turbulence related to changes in the Federal Reserve's quantitative easing program. EMDEs = emerging market and developing economies.

A. J.P. Morgan's nominal broad effective exchange rate for emerging markets.

B. Chicago Board Options Exchange emerging market exchange traded funds volatility index.

C. EMBI is J.P. Morgan's emerging market bond spread index.

D. MSCI is Morgan Stanley's emerging market stock market index.

global recession (World Bank 2017b, 2019a). In 2017, EMDEs saw a mild cyclical recovery, led by growth in exports and investment as global manufacturing and trade picked up, but EMDE growth has since slowed again. Much of the postcrisis slowdown appears to have been structural in nature. Potential output growth in EMDEs slowed from an estimated 5.9 percent a year in 2003-07 to 4.8 percent a year in 2013-17, reflecting the effects of weak investment on capital stocks, demographic trends turning from tailwinds to headwinds, and slower productivity growth (chapter 7).

This slowing in growth has meant a reversal of rapid precrisis convergence with per capita incomes in advanced economies. In 2019, per capita income gaps with advanced economies are expected to widen in about one-third of EMDEs—and more in LAC, MNA, and SSA. That said, in SSA especially, there is wide heterogeneity. In the largest three economies (Angola, Nigeria, South Africa), per capita income growth has been negative since 2015-16. Some metal exporters and countries affected by fragility, conflict, and violence have also had weak per capita growth. In contrast, some non-resource-intensive economies have had robust per capita income growth. Weak EMDE growth has also slowed the pace of decline in between-country inequality. Although the within-country Gini index of income inequality declined in 79 percent of EMDEs between 2005-07 and 2015-17, this change often left behind those living on incomes in the bottom 40 percent of the distribution. Since about 2009 (the first year for which data are available), the average income of households in the bottom 40 percent of the income distribution has fallen relative to the economy-wide average income in almost one-half of EMDEs with available data.

A weak global economy has coincided with country-specific challenges in some large EMDEs. In China, with the unwinding of policy stimulus, efforts were also made to guide the economy away from investment- and export-driven growth toward more balanced growth. The resulting slowdown in China, from growth of 11.3 percent on average during 2002-07 to 6.3 percent in 2018, has weighed on growth in its trading partners and in commodity exporters (Huidrom, Kose, Matsuoka, and Ohnsorge 2019; World Bank 2016a). In some other major EMDEs, episodes of policy uncertainty, social tensions, geopolitical events, and civil wars caused sharp losses in confidence (chapter 3).

EMDE financial systems have continued to evolve. Since the global recession, new regulatory frameworks across the world have, on net, strengthened the global banking system (chapter 4); however, they have also encouraged a retrenchment by crisis-hit global banks from several EMDE regions—ECA and, to a lesser extent, LAC and SSA—where lending by international banks was an important source of finance (figure 1.8). The exit of foreign banks has allowed a rapidly expanding footprint of EMDE-headquartered banks in some EMDE regions, particularly in SSA. It has also been associated with increased reliance by EMDEs on other types of international capital inflows, including sales of local currency-denominated bonds to foreign portfolio investors.

The global recession initially boosted structural reform efforts in EMDEs, but this momentum was short-lived and confined to a few areas. Since the global recession, there have been reforms to strengthen business climates (which, however, lost momentum after 2010), as well as reforms to improve access to finance, strengthen financial supervision, reduce trade cost, and lower energy subsidies (which were mostly sustained). In contrast, governance has deteriorated to 1990s levels, and EMDEs have become less open to international capital flows.

A clouded horizon: Prospects and risks

After a decade of lackluster growth following the global recession, EMDEs are confronted by formidable short- and long-term challenges. Global growth in 2019 is now expected to be slower than previously projected, reflecting broad-based weakness in industrial activity and world trade (figure 1.9). Global growth is forecast to stabilize in 2020, with slowing expansions in some major economies countered by a modest cyclical recovery in other EMDEs.

FIGURE 1.8 Financial market developments

For EMDEs, the financial landscape has shifted since the 2009 global recession. As EU- and U.S.-headquartered banks retreated from EMDEs, EMDE-headquartered banks and regional banks expanded. Amid record-low interest rates in advanced economies, many EMDEs have accessed international capital markets with sizable bond issues.

A. Net capital inflows to EMDEs and exchange rate volatility

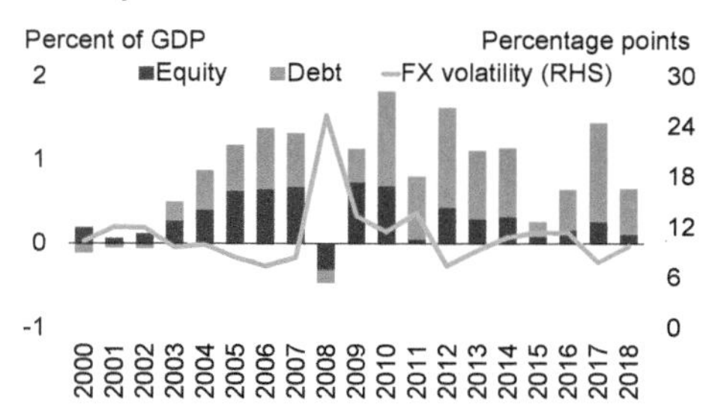

B. Change in bank credit to the private sector during financial crises

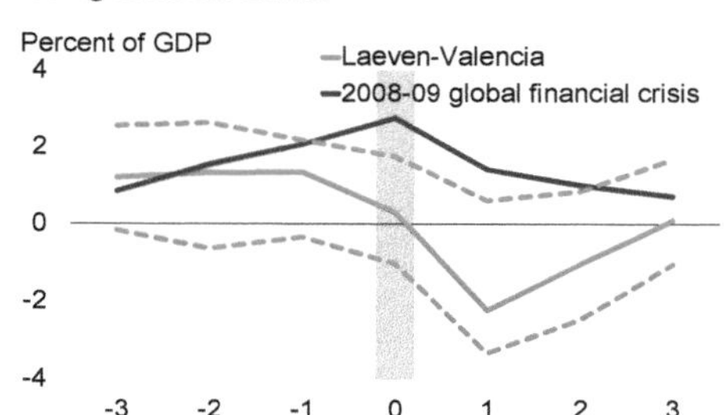

C. Foreign bank share of banking system assets

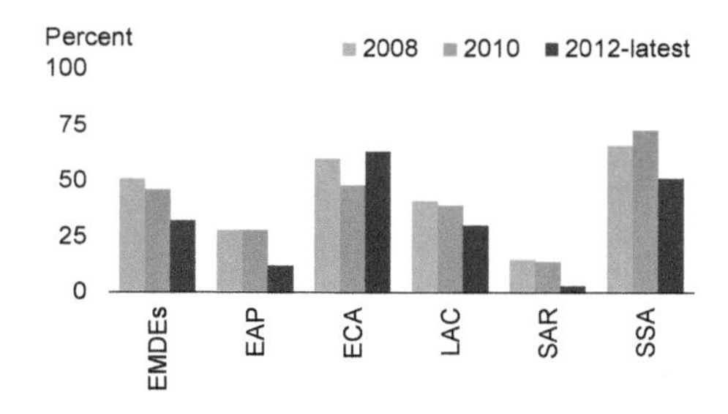

D. Panregional banks in EMDEs

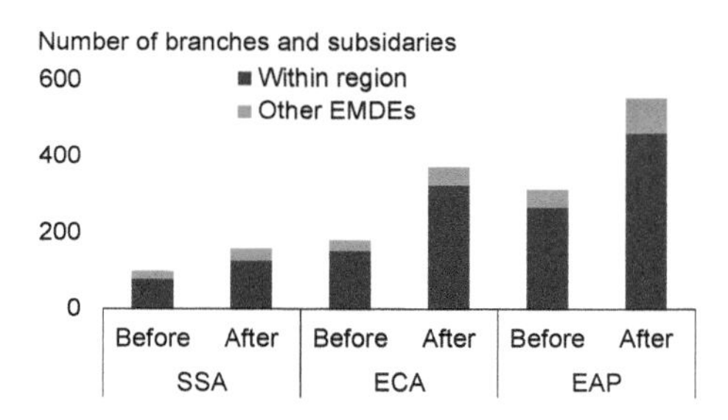

E. Global assets of 10 largest G-SIBs, by bank domicile

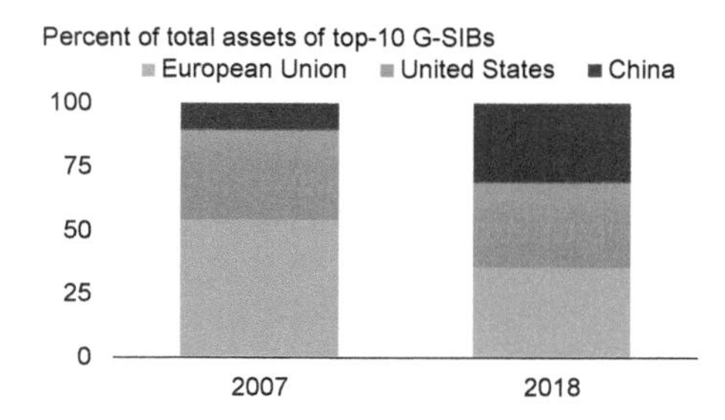

F. Share of EMDEs in a financial crisis following a sudden stop in capital flows

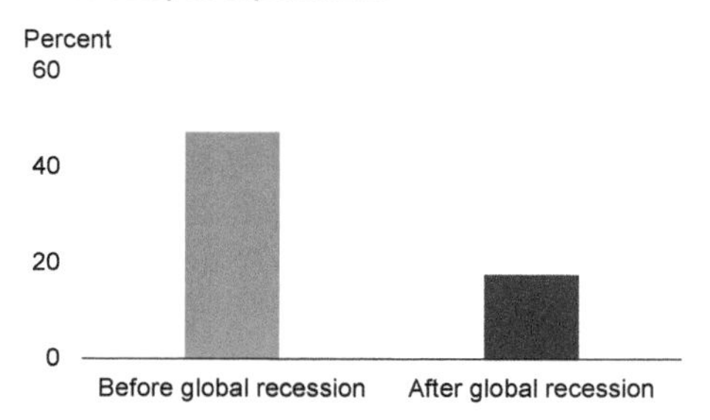

Sources: Bank for International Settlements; Bloomberg; Eichengreen and Gupta (2016); International Monetary Fund; Institute of International Finance; Laeven and Valencia (2018); World Bank (2018a).

A. FX volatility is the J.P. Morgan VXY Global Index, a turnover-weighted index of the implied volatility of three-month at-the-money options on 23 USD currency pairs.

B. t = 0 indicates the year when crisis started. 2009 recession and global recessions show averages across all emerging market and developing economies (EMDEs). Global recession years are 1975, 1982 and 1991. Financial crises denote averages across EMDEs that went through a systemic banking crisis at t = 0 (103 episodes from 1980-2014 as identified by Laeven and Valencia 2018).

D. Based on annual bank statements. "Before" indicates before global recession (2008 or 2009, depending on data availability); "After" indicates 2018 or latest data available.

E. Based on the Financial Stability Board's list of global systemically important banks (G-SIBs). European Union includes Deutsche Bank, BNP Paribas, Barclays and HSBC Holdings; United States includes Bank of America, J.P. Morgan Chase, Goldman Sachs Group and Citigroup; China includes Industrial and Commercial Bank of China and Bank of China.

F. Data include 36 sudden stops in EMDEs during 1993-2014 (Eichengreen and Gupta 2016). Each bar indicates the share of EMDEs that went through a financial crisis (as identified in Laeven and Valencia 2018) within two years of a sudden stop.

FIGURE 1.9 EMDE growth prospects

Following a further deceleration in 2019, GDP growth in EMDEs is expected to recover in 2020-21, as headwinds are assumed to dissipate in key economies. A slowdown in potential growth among EMDEs, however, will mean that the pace of convergence toward per capita incomes in advanced economies is expected to remain slow.

A. GDP growth

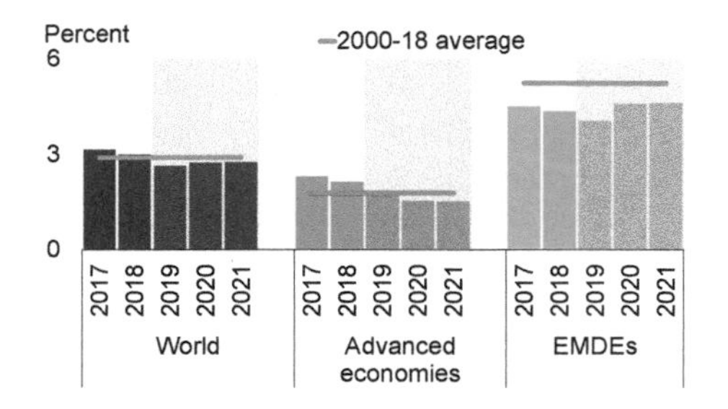

B. Per capita growth differential between EMDEs and advanced economies

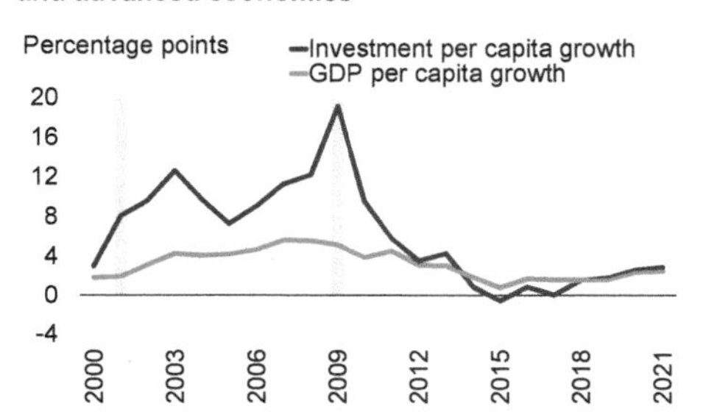

Sources: Consensus Economics; Haver Analytics; World Bank.
Note: EMDEs = emerging market and developing economies.
A. Average growth rates are calculated using constant 2010 U.S. dollar GDP weights. Shaded areas indicate forecasts.
B. Weights based on real GDP and Investment in 2010 U.S. dollars. Investment refers to public and private real gross fixed capital formation. Sample consists of 50 EMDEs. Shaded areas indicate global recessions and slowdowns.

This baseline assumes that the effects of earlier financial pressure and policy uncertainties that have weighed on some large EMDEs will begin to dissipate, and that global financing conditions will remain benign, encouraging a modest recovery of EMDE capital inflows. It also assumes no further escalation in trade tensions between major economies and broad stability in commodity prices. Uncertainty, however, is wide around this global growth outlook, with risks to baseline forecasts heavily tilted to the downside. Although the probability of a full-fledged global recession remains very low, it could increase materially for several reasons.

Trade tensions and other adverse policy shocks. Rising policy uncertainty in major economies has already weakened confidence and investment spending (figure 1.10). An intensification of such uncertainties, including through a further sharp escalation in trade tensions between China and the United States or a disorderly exit of the United Kingdom from the EU, could have significant consequences for trade and investment.

Trade relations between the United States and several of its major trading partners, most notably China, remain fragile. A further increase in U.S. tariffs, and a subsequent retaliation by China, would result in substantial economic losses for exporters and would increase costs for many other sectors, although there could be some short-run benefits from trade diversion for some countries (Freund et al. 2018). Higher tariffs on U.S. imports of automobiles and parts could disrupt global value chains, which are tightly integrated. Perhaps most worrisome is the danger that these tensions could spill over and undermine the broader commitment to free trade, with potentially even more damaging effects. For example, estimates suggest that a global escalation of tariffs up to limits

FIGURE 1.10 Risks to EMDE growth prospects and vulnerabilities

Risks to the growth outlook for EMDEs are rising and mainly to the downside. They include heightened global policy uncertainty amid trade disputes and slowing growth in major economies. Since the 2009 global recession, EMDE vulnerabilities to adverse events, including those due to high debt, have risen.

A. World policy uncertainty

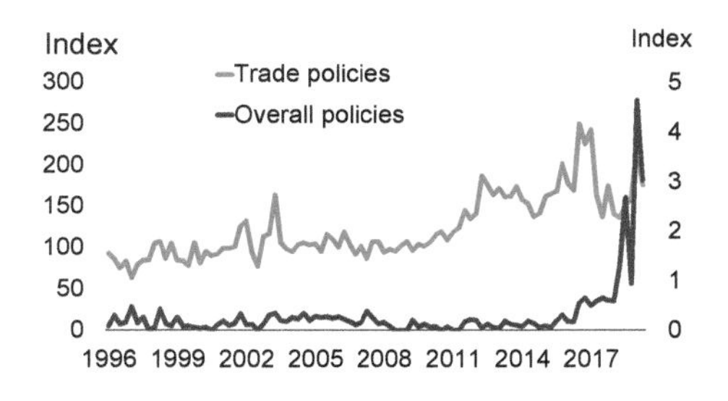

B. Growth spillovers from major economies

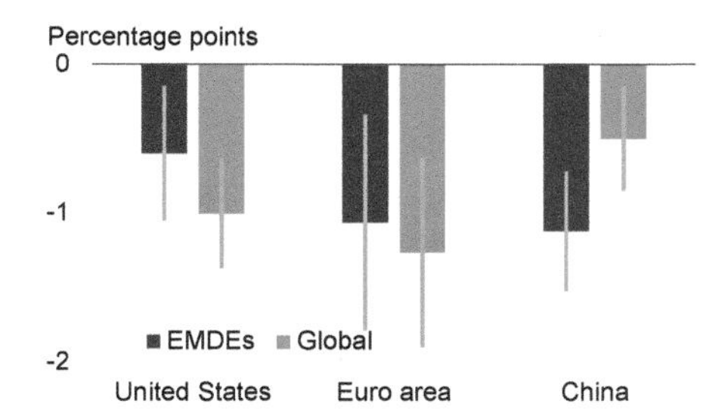

C. Gross government debt in EMDEs

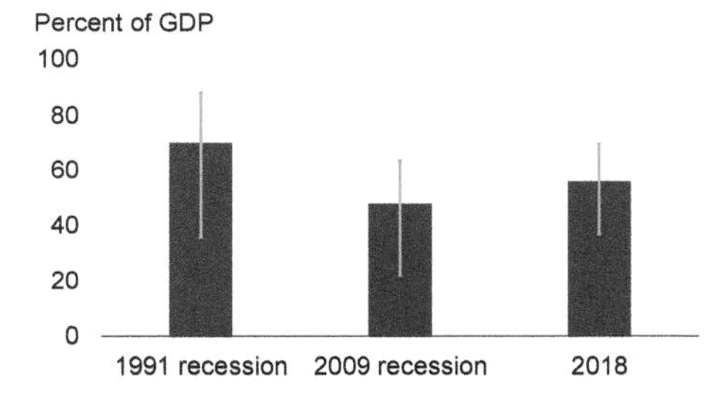

D. Nonfinancial private debt in EMDEs

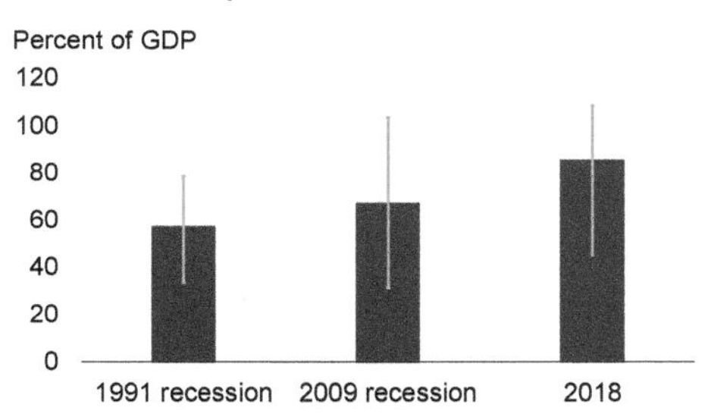

Sources: Ahir, Bloom, and Furceri (2018); International Monetary Fund; Huidrom, Kose, Matsuoka, and Ohnsorge (2019); World Bank.
A. News-based index by Ahir, Bloom, and Furceri (2019) for 143 countries.
B. Median cumulative impulse response of emerging market and developing economy (EMDE) and global GDP growth after one year to a 1-percentage-point decline in U.S., euro area and Chinese GDP growth. Based on vector autoregression of world GDP (excluding the source country of spillovers), output growth in the source country of the shock, the U.S. 10-year sovereign bond yield plus J.P. Morgan's Emerging Market Bond Index (EMBI), output in EMDEs excluding China, and oil price as an exogenous variable (in the case of China's spillover, the order of growth is third). The "global" sample includes 22 advanced economies (Canada, 19 euro area countries, Japan, and the United Kingdom) and 19 EMDEs for 1998Q1-2016Q2.
C. Blue bars show median government debt (in percent of GDP) for EMDEs two years before recession/crisis. Whiskers show interquartile range. Data available for 98 EMDEs with data available for 1989.
D. Private sector debt is proxied by private sector credit in percent of GDP. Blue bars show median private sector debt (in percent of GDP) for EMDEs two years before recession/crisis. Whiskers show interquartile range. Based on 10 EMDEs with data available for 1989.

allowed under the General Agreement on Tariffs and Trade (GATT) could shave 9 percent from global trade flows—similar to the drop observed during the 2009 global recession (Kutlina-Dimitrova and Lakatos 2017).

A disorderly Brexit from the EU could severely affect the United Kingdom and, to a lesser extent, European trading partners if it results in trade diversion or large disrupttions and delays at border crossings. An abrupt interruption in financial relationships and cross-border financial flows could also trigger financial instability.

Renewed financial stress. A prolonged period of low global interest rates and prospects for its continuation have encouraged a search for yield among investors that may contribute to growing vulnerabilities. Renewed financial market stress could have increasingly pronounced and widespread effects in view of rising indebtedness. Such episodes could be triggered or amplified by several factors.

- *Corporate debt and complex instruments.* An increase in corporate default rates could lead to a rapid deterioration in financial market sentiment, a repricing of risks, and a spike in bond spreads for more vulnerable borrowers (FSB 2019a). This result is especially likely in light of the increased use of riskier, less transparent debt instruments such as leveraged loans, which have now risen above their precrisis highs, and collateralized loan obligations (CLOs) in advanced economies. A broad-based loss of investment-grade status would place both corporate and sovereign borrowers under stress, especially in view of the low interest coverage afforded by corporate earnings in several sectors and large volumes of bond refinancing scheduled in coming years (BIS 2019).

- *Currency movements.* Large currency depreciations in EMDEs could be triggered by unexpected tightening of U.S. monetary policy, sharp commodity price declines, concerns about debt sustainability, or domestic policy uncertainties. Renewed financial stress in large EMDEs could be contagious if accompanied by heightened investor risk aversion and shifts in portfolio allocations.

- *Sovereign bank nexus.* Government guarantees to the financial system, either explicit or implicit, coupled with large bank holdings of government debt, can create self-reinforcing feedback effects. As a result of increased bank holdings of government debt, this sovereign bank nexus has become more pronounced in EMDEs since the 2009 global recession, as well as in some advanced economies, especially in the euro area (Feyen and Zuccardi 2019).

Geopolitical risks and conflict. The number of armed conflicts has risen significantly, to 51 during 2015-17 compared to 35 in 2000-14. The potential for further conflict is elevated by increased polarization of public opinion in some countries, increased income inequality, and heightened economic and political disputes between countries.

- *Conflict.* Renewed conflict could disrupt regional and global economic activity, as well as financial and commodity markets in the short term, while setting back potential growth and increasing refugee flows over the medium term. Conflict near important shipping bottlenecks could lead to disruptions in global trade and spikes in commodity prices.

- *Terrorist attacks and cybersecurity.* Terrorist attacks could hinder confidence, travel, and tourism, and could increase risk aversion and transaction and insurance costs (World Bank 2016a). Cyber attacks could disrupt political processes and economic activity, especially if they affect critical information and communications infrastructure.

- *Climate events.* Growth in a number of countries would also be set back by severe weather events, which have been increasing in frequency, severity, and cost (IPCC

2018). The interplay of climate change with basic needs insecurity (related to food, water, and land), natural resource destruction, and population displacement creates fertile ground for conflict. Refugee flows from affected countries could put strain on neighboring areas and trigger a further shift toward protectionist and populist policies.

Risks of abrupt slowdown in major economies. Recessions often follow rapid increases in debt and elevated asset price valuations (Claessens, Kose, and Terrones 2012). Such buildups tend to unwind suddenly, often during or shortly after the end of a period of monetary policy tightening (Sims and Tao 2006). In the United States, three of the last four periods of monetary tightening were followed by a recession within a year and a half, with the most severe contractions following unsustainable housing market booms (Mian and Sufi 2009).

The recent rise in U.S. private debt is less pronounced than that observed before previous recessions, mostly because of deleveraging by households and banks since 2009. U.S. corporate debt has risen significantly, however, increasing the likelihood that corporate bond defaults could amplify the next downturn (FSOC 2018). In the euro area, the risk of a sharper-than-expected slowdown has risen amid growth disappointments since mid-2018, decelerating global trade, and elevated policy uncertainty. Renewed financial stress in vulnerable economies would lead to slower investment, higher unemployment, and new concerns about banking sector health.

Risks to China's growth outlook are also tilted to the downside. Although fiscal and monetary policy stimulus could offset the adverse effect of trade tensions with the United States, it would delay efforts to contain credit growth and the buildup of balance sheet vulnerabilities of nonfinancial corporations, local governments, and financial institutions (World Bank 2018b). The materialization of these risks could have significant adverse repercussions on activity. Although the authorities hold policy levers to mitigate such repercussions in the near term, continued fiscal and monetary stimulus could become ineffective over time while adding further leverage to private and public sectors. Providing stimulus through state-owned enterprises may eventually undermine economy-wide productivity growth. In other EMDEs, private debt levels and growth rates have been well above those during previous credit booms—two-thirds of which ended in growth slowdowns and more than one-third in financial crisis (Acharya et al. 2015).

Combination of risks leading to global downturn. The pervasiveness of vulnerabilities increases the danger of a broad-based downturn in major economies that could trigger a global downturn. The United States, the euro area, and China together account for nearly 50 percent of global GDP and are the primary sources of spillovers to EMDEs other than China via trade, financial, commodity, and confidence channels (Huidrom, Kose, Matsuoka, Ohnsorge 2019; Kose, Lakatos et al. 2017; World Bank 2016a). After one year, a 1-percentage-point growth shock in these economies could curtail global growth by 1.7 percentage points and EMDE growth (excluding China) by 1.4 percentage points.

FIGURE 1.11 Long-term growth prospects

Long-term growth prospects have slowed substantially from precrisis rates. Potential growth is expected to decline in the next decade.

A. Consensus long-term growth forecasts

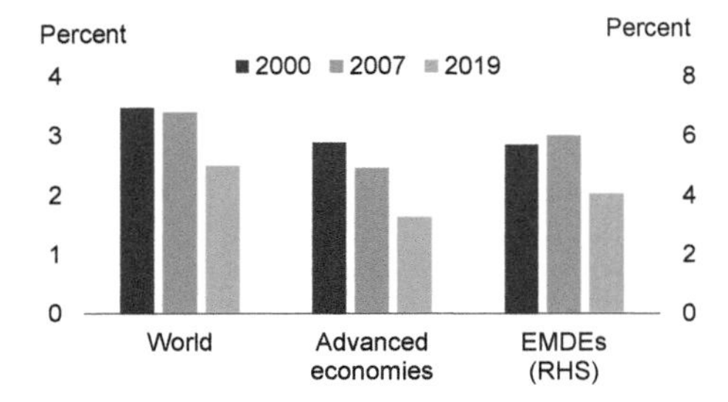

B. Potential growth

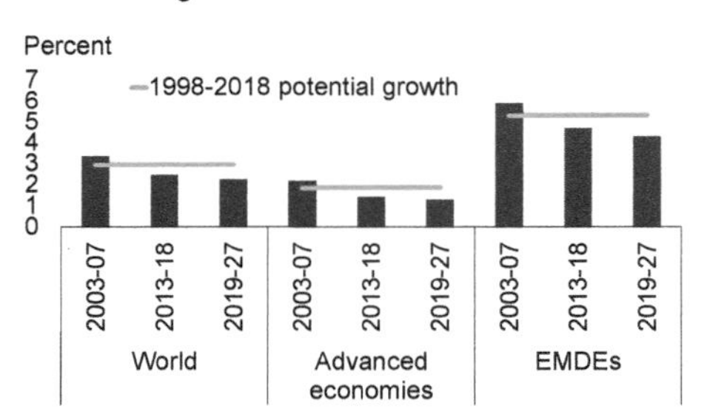

Sources: Consensus Economics; Haver Analytics; Penn World Table; United Nations Population Prospects; World Bank.

A. Bars show long-term (10 years ahead) average annual growth forecasts surveyed in respective years. Sample comprises 38 countries—20 advanced economies and 18 emerging market and developing economies (EMDEs)—for which consensus forecasts are consistently available during 1998-2018. Aggregate growth rates calculated using constant 2010 U.S. dollar GDP weights.

B. Period average of annual GDP-weighted averages. Estimates based on production function approach. World sample comprises 50 EMDEs and 30 advanced economies.

Long-term challenges. EMDEs face a further weakening of potential growth over the next decade (figure 1.11). Their potential growth is expected to be about 1.6 percentage points weaker than before the global recession, at 4.3 percent on average in 2019-27 (World Bank 2018b). Productivity growth has declined as the growth of productivity-enhancing investment has slowed, gains in factor reallocation (including the migration of labor from agriculture to manufacturing and services) have faded, and growth in global value chains has moderated. Slower investment growth has tempered capital accumulation. Demographic trends have also turned less favorable to growth since the share of working-age populations in EMDEs peaked around 2010. Many of these factors will weigh on potential growth over the next decade. Commodity exporters face the additional challenge of prospects for weaker commodity demand growth over the next decade (Baffes et al. 2018).

Poverty reduction goals at risk. The rate of poverty reduction has slowed since the 2009 global recession (World Bank 2018c). Poverty declined by 1.25 percentage points per year between 2011 and 2013, but by only 0.6 percentage points per year between 2013 and 2015. Forecasts for these trends to 2018 suggest a further slowdown to 0.5 percentage points per year. Over the longer term, weaker long-term growth prospects put at risk the achievement of the target of lowering the global extreme poverty rate to 3 percent of the population by 2030. Even if the growth rates of 2005-15 are maintained, the world will not be able to reach the 3 percent global poverty rate target set for 2030 (figure 1.12).[6] This target will not be met because more than half of the global poor now

[6] For more detailed discussions, see Dollar, Kleineberg, and Kraay (2013); Dollar and Kraay (2002); Foster and Székely (2008); Ravallion and Chen (2003); Santos, Dabus, and Delbianco (2019); and World Bank (2018c).

FIGURE 1.12 Poverty

At current growth projections, the goal of reducing extreme poverty to 3 percent of the global population by 2030 is unlikely to be met.

A. Projections of global extreme poverty

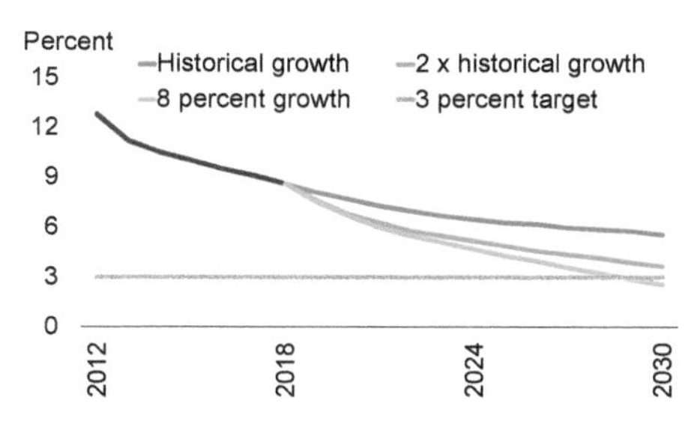

B. Distribution of poverty

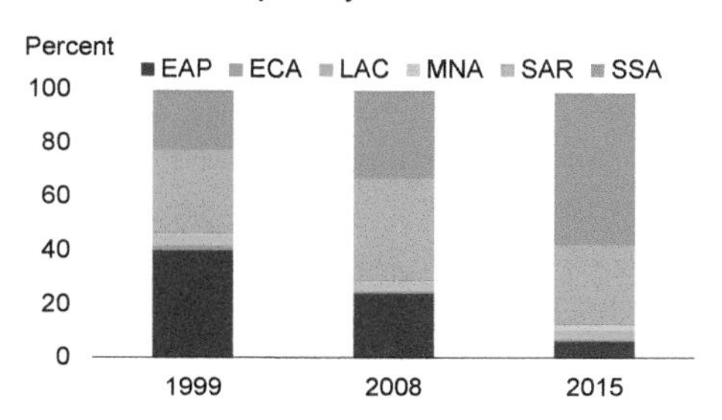

Source: World Bank's PovcalNet.

Note: EAP = East Asia and Pacific; ECA = Europe and Central Asia; LAC = Latin America and the Caribbean; MNA = Middle East and North Africa; SAR = South Asia; SSA = Sub-Saharan Africa.

A. Data based on global real per capita growth. "8 percent growth" assumes 8 percent growth in per capita incomes of the poorest 40 percent of households and 4.7 percent growth in per capita incomes for all other households, such that per capita income growth averages 6 percent in all countries in every year until 2030 .

B. Regional aggregation based on 2011 purchasing power parity (PPP) and $1.90 per day poverty line.

reside in SSA, where per capita growth is feeble. If current trends continue, the share of global poor living in SSA will likely increase to 87 percent by 2030.[7]

Lessons and policy challenges

Lessons

The 2009 global recession and the long shadow it has cast over the subsequent decade offer important lessons for EMDE policy makers today.

In a recession, early policy action is critical. The sizable, prompt, and coordinated policy stimulus that was implemented at the height of the global financial crisis in 2008 could not prevent the subsequent global recession, but it did help dampen its severity (chapter 3). EMDEs benefitted from their own policy stimulus as well as that of major advanced economies. They were able to engage in such stimulus because they had accumulated policy room before the crisis.

Policy room is needed to respond to adverse shocks. The global recession has shown, once again, not only the importance of taking action to prevent crises and their repercussions but also the importance of creating and preserving policy room to enable

[7] To reach the 2030 goal of global poverty rate of 3 percent, GDP per capita in SSA would need to grow by 6 percent per year, with the bottom 40 percent of the population achieving 8 percent growth, that is, there would have to be a reduction in income inequality. The last three years, 2017-19, have seen no per capita growth in SSA. In fact, only a small and declining proportion of EMDEs have achieved such growth in any year since 2009 (World Bank 2019a).

countries to act when their economies are hit by crises and other shocks. Low inflation allowed central banks to implement monetary stimulus, ample foreign currency reserves allowed them to dampen exchange rate volatility, and sound fiscal positions (narrow deficits and low debt) permitted them to support activity with fiscal stimulus. The global recession also underscored the challenges of unwinding stimulus in an anemic postcrisis environment (chapter 3).

Sound policy frameworks help create policy room. The prevalence of flexible exchange rate arrangements and inflation targets served EMDEs well during the global recession by helping create policy room before the recession (chapter 5). In the runup to the global recession, exchange rate flexibility had helped discourage the buildup of large foreign currency exposures that might have exacerbated stress during the recession. During the global financial crisis and subsequent global recession, exchange rate flexibility acted as a shock absorber. The shift to inflation-targeting regimes had helped several EMDEs lower inflation in the runup to the global recession, and fiscal rules had supported the elimination of fiscal deficits in the global expansion leading up to the 2009 recession (Ha, Kose et al. 2019).

Countercyclical policies are no substitute for vigorous reforms in support of long-term growth. Despite the initial rebound from the global recession of 2009, the subsequent decade has been one of tepid growth punctuated by bouts of financial market stress and a commodity price collapse. This experience has illustrated the limitations of macroeconomic stimulus in supporting demand beyond the short term and underscores the need for reforms that can help durably improve long-term growth (chapter 7). The momentum of structural reforms in EMDEs increased in some areas in the immediate aftermath of the crisis, but was not maintained. The quality of governance in EMDEs even relapsed to 1990s levels.

Economic diversification supports resilience. Economies that were particularly reliant on the production of consumer durables (during the global recession), the euro area banking system (shortly after the global recession), or exports of commodities (in the long shadow of the global recession) suffered sharp or chronic declines when adverse shocks hit (chapter 3). They provide examples of how lack of diversification tends to make economies more vulnerable to shocks. Successful diversification of economies requires investment in human capital, technology, and institutions, as well as sound regulation that can, over time, become the source of rapid productivity growth.

Sound financial systems strengthen resilience. During the global recession and subsequent euro area crisis, the most severe credit crunches occurred in economies where credit booms had been funded by large capital flows and where banks had a narrow deposit base, such as in parts of ECA (chapter 4). In some of these economies, deep recessions increased nonperforming loans and eroded bank capital to an extent that they substantially amplified the negative shocks, and necessitated extensive government support of the financial system. The more resilient economies were the ones that had strong financial regulatory and supervisory regimes that encouraged robust bank capitalization, the reliance on stable funding sources, and effective risk management systems.

Robust resolution frameworks help the recovery. Since the global recession, nonperforming loans have risen in several countries. Until resolved, nonperforming loans erode bank balance sheet health and weigh on lending (chapter 7). Stronger corporate bankruptcy and bank resolution regimes can help resolve nonperforming loans and return financial system balance sheets to health.

Macroprudential measures and capital flow management policies can lower volatility. The global recession has shifted the debate in the economics profession to a wider recognition of the roles of macroprudential policies and capital flow management measures in preventing and containing crises. Aimed at limiting the buildup of systematic risks, macroprudential policies can prevent the emergence of vulnerabilities that amplify the impact of recessions (chapters 5 and 6). Capital flow management measures can reduce the volatility of capital flows during times of economic stress, provided they are accompanied by sound macroeconomic policies (chapter 7).

Policy challenges

Differences between 2009 and 2019. EMDEs would now be hard pressed to replicate the successful policy response of a decade ago, for several reasons.

- *Limited fiscal policy space.* During the 2009 global recession, the G20 recognized that the "global crisis require[d] global solutions." These solutions included robust, rapid, and coordinated macroeconomic policy stimulus (G20 2009). The fiscal response in G20 countries, measured as the cumulative change in the primary fiscal balance from 2009 to 2011, averaged 6.6 percent of GDP. This was two-and-a-half times larger than the average response to 45 other banking crises since 1990 (Laeven and Valencia 2018). The simultaneous fiscal expansion helped speed the recovery from crisis as the positive impact of fiscal stimulus in one country spilled over to its neighbors (Blagrave et al. 2017). Today, G20 economies have higher average public debt levels than before the 2009 global recession. In EMDEs, average government debt as a share of GDP has risen by 10 percentage points, to 54 percent of GDP in 2018. These higher debt levels reduce policy makers' ability to respond with deficit spending, because there is less room for additional borrowing and stimulus tends to be less effective under weak fiscal positions (Huidrom, Kose, Lim, and Ohnsorge 2019). Although, for now, global borrowing costs remain low, past experience suggests that they can rise steeply during financial market stress and heavily restrict EMDE governments' room to maneuver (World Bank 2019b).

- *Limited monetary policy space.* During the 2009 global recession, monetary policy in G20 countries also responded aggressively. Policy rates were lowered by 360 basis points, on average, between September 2007 and December 2009. The U.S. Federal Reserve lowered rates by over 500 basis points in less than two years and reached the effective zero lower-bound by December 2008. To respond to U.S. dollar funding shortages, bilateral swap lines were established between the U.S. Federal Reserve and 14 other central banks, including EMDE institutions, as well as among central banks in Europe. With policy rates effectively at zero in most advanced economies, and negative in some, policy makers turned to unconventional policies, including quantitative easing and forward guidance, to further stimulate activity. Today, in advanced economies, low policy rates leave little room for further conventional monetary accommodation. The initial provision of unconventional monetary policy stimulus that was effective following the 2009 global recession may be subject to diminishing returns. Although many EMDEs still have monetary policy room, amid low inflation and with policy rates well above zero, they may be compelled to tighten policy regardless of output weakness if financial market stress materializes.

- *Weaker commitment to multilateralism.* During the global recession, the G20 made a commitment to strengthen multilateral cooperation. The group took a stand "to fight against protectionism"—by not raising existing or implementing new barriers to trade or investment—and "committed to further trade liberalization" (G20 2009). These commitments were generally upheld with little increase in protectionism in the years immediately following the crisis (Kee, Neagu, and Nicita 2013). More recently, however, commitments to multilateralism and trade liberalization have weakened, with an increasing number of new trade restrictions. New import-restrictive measures were imposed on 3.5 percent of G20 imports between May and mid-October 2018—a sixfold increase compared to the previous six-month period and the largest increase on record (WTO 2018). Further restrictions and tariffs were imposed subsequently.

More encouraging have been financial sector reforms and the expansion of country-specific, regional, and multilateral funding mechanisms included in the global financial safety net. These have increased the resilience of the global financial system (ECB 2018). Generally, banks in advanced economies are now better capitalized and less leveraged than in 2008-09 (IMF 2018b). The size of the global financial safety net tripled between 2007 and 2016 including through the creation of regional financing arrangements and the expansion of International Monetary Fund resources and international reserve holdings (IMF 2017). There are also now an estimated 160 bilateral swap lines between central banks around the world (Bahaj and Reis 2018). The People's Bank of China alone maintains over 100 active swap lines with more than 40 countries, including many EMDEs, and the Chiang Mai Initiative establishes swap lines between countries belonging to the Association of Southeast Asian Nations (Bahaj and Reis 2018).

Countercyclical policy in a constrained environment. A successful response to a future global downturn would require an effective and coordinated macroeconomic policy response alongside a strong commitment to preserve an open, fair, and rules-based global trading system. For advanced economies, such a response would include the operation of automatic fiscal stabilizers and—where fiscal room permits—increased discretionary spending in productive areas or well-targeted tax cuts, as well as clear and credible monetary policy actions and guidance that bolster market confidence. Although large potential capital flows may limit monetary policy room in some EMDEs, monetary policy makers in other EMDEs may have room to implement conventional policy stimulus or, where this approach is insufficient, shift to unconventional policies (Cavallino and Sandri 2018; Gopinath 2017; Rey 2015). Policy makers should ensure that fiscal stimulus is timely (to promptly mitigate demand shortfalls), temporary (to be reversed as the economy recovers), and well-targeted (at households and firms with the most severe liquidity constraints) to ensure that benefits outweigh the possible negative effects of increased debt.

Macroprudential policy tools, which have expanded in use and number in the last decade, can provide a buffer in the event that systemic risks materialize (IMF, FSB, and BIS 2016). Countercyclical capital buffers could help absorb asset deterioration when crisis hits. Limits on banks' foreign exchange positions and reserve requirements on foreign funding could help EMDEs avoid currency mismatches, and lower loan-to-value ratios could help limit the build-up of leverage in balance sheets. New challenges posed by financial technology may need to be navigated carefully, and in some EMDEs, the capacity of regulators and supervisors needs to be built to adjust to rapidly evolving financial market developments (World Bank 2019a).

Promoting domestic growth and resilience. Heightened downside risks to global growth highlight the need for policy makers to reinforce domestic policy room against possible negative shocks, and to shore up domestic growth prospects. In EMDEs, policy makers need to use the opportunity provided by still-benign financing conditions to rebuild fiscal and monetary policy room to confront future shocks, while safeguarding or expanding growth-enhancing investment. Amid adverse debt dynamics and narrowing fiscal space, policy makers need to strengthen domestic revenue mobilization, prioritize growth-enhancing spending, and improve debt management and transparency. Increased public sector efficiency (including reining in poorly targeted subsidies to households or state-owned enterprises) and measures to foster private sector investments will also be key to meet large infrastructure needs and achieve critical development goals.

In countries where progress has flagged, steps are needed to reinvigorate sustainable growth (figure 1.13; chapter 8). A key area of focus should be to improve policy and regulatory environments in ways that support stronger potential growth and social cohesion. This approach includes efforts to draw groups that are only marginally attached to the labor market into formal employment, to encourage skills development and entrepreneurial activity, and to expand private investment (G20 2018). Greater financial inclusion of groups lacking access to finance could also help increase productivity.

Measures to strengthen financial resilience are needed to address rising financial vulnerabilities. They can include initiatives to improve credit quality, insurance regulation, loan restructuring mechanisms, adequately enforced bankruptcy laws, recognition of nonperforming loans, cross-border bank resolution, buffers in bank and nonbank institutions, and the introduction of centralized clearing for derivatives transactions (IMF 2018b).

Policy priorities. Policy priorities are necessarily country-specific. That said, they exhibit some general patterns. For example, countries facing weak demand but having ample fiscal or monetary space may want to activate macroeconomic stimulus policies. Countries with precarious fiscal sustainability may want to prioritize strengthening fiscal positions in a manner that is the least damaging to output. Doing so would likely require a focus on spending efficiency and domestic revenue mobilization. Countries with high foreign exchange exposures may want to prioritize macro- and microprudential measures. Countries with large informal sectors may want to prioritize

FIGURE 1.13 Structural policies in EMDEs

A significant number of reforms was introduced in the immediate aftermath of the 2009 global recession. Since then, however, business regulatory reform momentum has slowed whereas there have been several spurts of financial regulatory reform and, most recently, trade reforms.

A. EMDEs with fiscal rules or inflation targeting

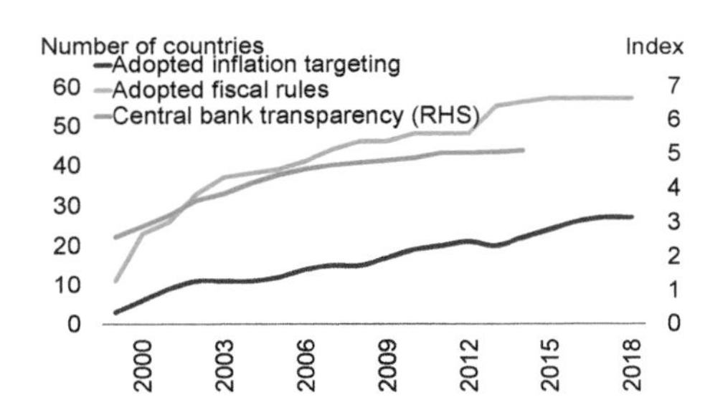

B. EMDE GDP governed by fiscal rules, inflation targeting, or flexible exchange rates

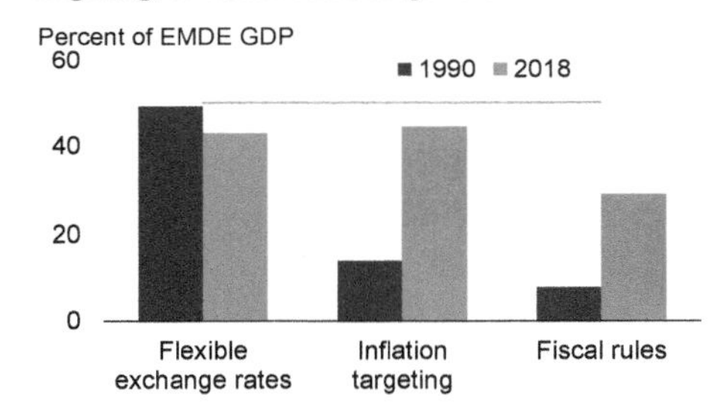

C. Macroprudential policy in EMDEs

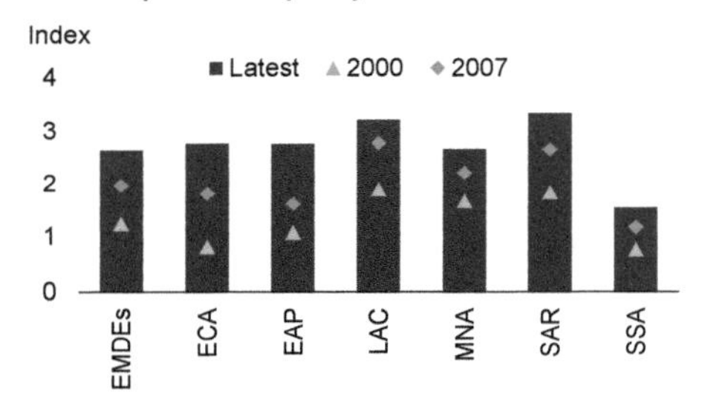

D. Business regulatory environment

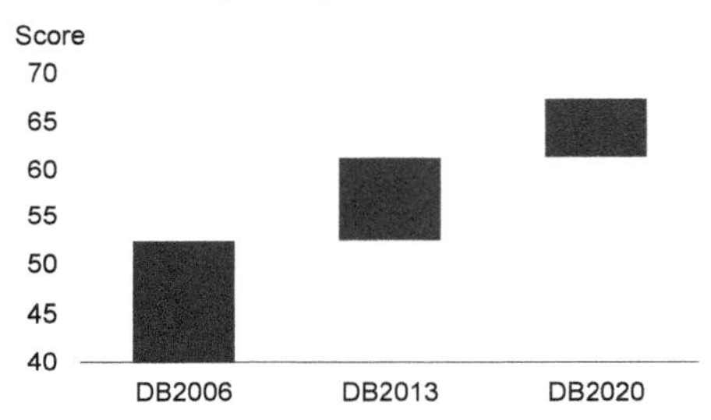

E. Financial regulatory environment

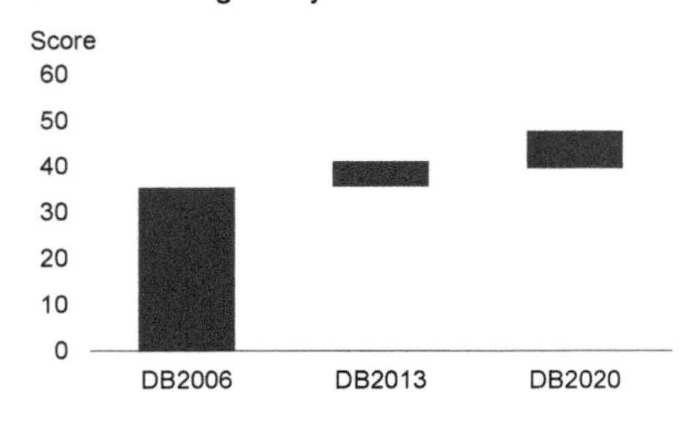

F. Trade environment

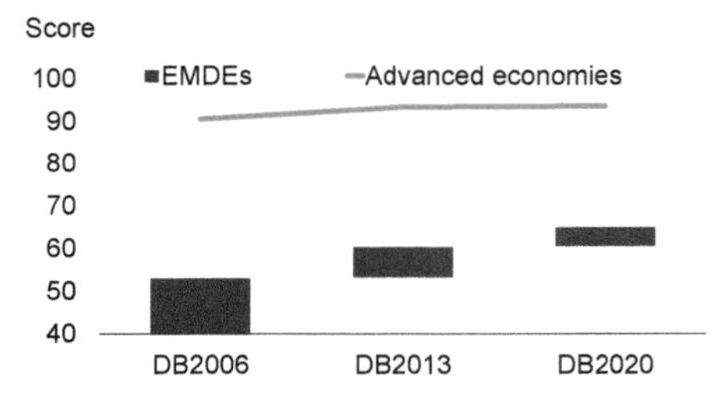

Sources: Cerutti, Claessens, and Laeven (2017); Dincer and Eichengreen (2014); Ha, Kose, and Ohnsorge (2019); International Monetary Fund; Kose, Kurlat et al. (2017); World Bank.

A.B. An economy is considered to be implementing a fiscal rule if it has one or more fiscal rules on expenditure, revenue, budget balance or debt. Inflation targeting as classified in the International Monetary Fund's Annual Report of Exchange Arrangements and Exchange Restrictions.

B. Flexible exchange rate regimes are defined as "floating" or "freely floating" exchange rate regimes. GDP aggregation at 2010 prices and exchange rates. Gray line indicates 50 percent.

C. Sample includes 123 emerging market and developing economies (EMDEs). Unweighted average of the Macroprudential Policy Index of Cerutti, Claessens, and Laeven (2017). The Macroprudential Policy Index measures the number of tools used by authorities and is based on a simple sum of up to 12 including, but not limited to, the countercyclical capital buffer and loan-to-value ratios.

D.E.F. An economy's score is measured on a scale from 0 to 100, where 0 represents the lowest performance and 100 the frontier, which is constructed from the best performances across all economies and across time. "DB" before the year indicates the related *Doing Business* publication.

F. Scores are unweighted averages of 31 advanced economies and 129 EMDEs. The trading across borders indicator is spliced backward where methodological changes affected the level.

investing in education, expanding access to finance and markets, and streamlining (and effectively enforcing) business and tax regulations (World Bank 2019c). Countries with flagging potential growth as a result of demographic trends may want to prioritize reforms to benefit systems as well as strengthen education and health systems; those with slowing potential growth as a result of weak investment or productivity may want to focus on removing policy uncertainty and strengthening business and regulatory environments. Countries under severe political pressures may be forced to postpone much-needed reforms and instead focus on narrower agendas.

Multilateral initiatives. Multilateral fora would again have an important role to play in the event of another sharp global downturn. Improving and expanding the global financial safety net would help boost confidence and bolster financial resilience (IMF 2017). Well-coordinated support from international financial institutions could help governments stimulate activity and protect vulnerable populations. Collaboration between various financial authorities could help EMDEs mitigate contagion from international financial stress. Extended foreign exchange swap lines could help ease

funding, and help prevent bank failures (Goldberg, Kennedy, and Miu 2010). Creditors to EMDEs can intensify efforts to improve the reporting and transparency of debt, especially to nontraditional creditors.

The global community also needs to focus on new threats to sustainable and inclusive growth and financial stability. International cooperation is needed to address the fast pace of financial technology development, cybersecurity risks, and the role of credit institutions outside the ambit of prudential authorities (FSB 2019b). Transformative technologies could bring higher productivity as well as new economic opportunities that raise employment and incomes; however, the transition will likely create challenges. To harness technology for broad-based faster growth and productivity, policies need to support people who face disruptions from new technologies, including job losses, and address related distributional issues (G20 2018).

Synopsis

The remainder of this chapter presents summaries of the remaining chapters. After discussing the motivation of the chapter, each summary explains the main questions, contributions to the literature, and analytical findings.

Chapter 2: What Happens during Global Recessions?

Global recession has been a recurring topic of debate over the past decade, reflecting the breadth and severity of the 2007-09 global financial crisis, the halting nature of the recovery, and the more recent fears that the global economy was on the edge of another downturn. A better understanding of global recessions requires an appreciation of the growing importance of EMDEs and of cross-border trade and financial linkages. The increasing role of EMDEs means that it is no longer sufficient to monitor cyclical fluctuations in advanced economies to understand the global business cycle. It implies that the need for a better understanding of the global business cycle requires going beyond the usual set of advanced economies to a much broader group that also includes EMDEs.

Against this background, chapter 2 examines the main features of global recessions and the ensuing recoveries and expansions. Specifically, it addresses the following questions:

- What happens during global recessions and recoveries?
- How do global recessions and recoveries vary across different groups of countries, particularly advanced economies, EMDEs, and LICs?
- What happens during global expansions, and how does the current global expansion compare with previous ones?

Chapter 2 begins by documenting turning points of the global business cycle, in line with Kose and Terrones (2015). These turning points are identified by means of two methods widely used in the analysis of national business cycles: a statistical method and a judgmental method. The former defines a global recession as taking place when there is a decline in annual global real GDP per capita. The judgmental method considers whether there is strong evidence for a broad-based decline in multiple key indicators of global economic activity in any given year. Chapter 2 focuses on six main global activity indicators: real GDP per capita, industrial production, trade, capital flows, oil consumption, and employment. These two methods together provide an intuitively appealing characterization of the turning points of the global business cycle and translate into a concrete definition of a global recession.

Specifically, a global recession is defined as a contraction in global real GDP per capita accompanied by a broad decline in various other measures of global activity. The definition of a global recovery also closely follows the standard definition used in the context of national business cycles. The recovery phase is the period after the trough and is defined here as the one- or three-year period following the trough of the cycle. The recovery is thus the earlier part of the expansion phase, which refers to the whole period between two recessions.

The chapter presents the following findings.

First, in the 70 years since 1950, the world economy has experienced four global recessions: in 1975, 1982, 1991, and 2009. In each of these episodes, there was a contraction in annual real per capita global GDP and broad-based weakness in other key indicators of global economic activity. These episodes were highly synchronized, involving severe economic and financial disruptions in many countries around the world. The 2009 global recession was by far the deepest and most synchronized episode among the four.

Second, global recoveries usually involved a broad-based rebound in macroeconomic and financial activity. Among the four episodes, the recovery from the 1975 recession saw the highest growth during the recovery. Thanks to large, prompt, and globally coordinated policy support, the recovery following the 2009 recession was the second strongest among the four global recessions.

Third, average per capita growth declined more in advanced economies than in EMDEs during global recessions. As the epicenter of the financial crisis, advanced economies also felt the brunt of the 2009 global recession. In contrast, EMDE output growth remained positive during the recession. The East Asia and Pacific (EAP) and SAR regions even continued expanding during global recessions; however, the other four EMDE regions, particularly those with more reliance on exports of industrial commodities, experienced per capita output declines. LICs were able to continue growing during the 2009 global recession whereas their per capita growth had plummeted in the previous episodes.

Fourth, although the post-2009 global expansion was the weakest of the four in advanced economies, EMDEs delivered a stronger recovery post-2009 than after any of the three previous global recessions. The duration of the global expansions varied from 6 to 17 years. The latest global expansion registered average per capita growth comparable with that of previous episodes.

Fifth, monetary and fiscal policies often became expansionary going into global recessions, and they typically supported the ensuing global recoveries. Following the 2009 global recession, monetary policy remained highly accommodative for most of the 2010s, with advanced economy central banks introducing a wide range of unconventional measures to ease credit. After the initial implementation of large, coordinated, fiscal stimulus programs during 2008-09, however, advanced economies withdrew fiscal support, out of concerns for the growth of public debt, and government expenditures fell after 2010. By contrast, EMDEs have generally employed expansionary fiscal and monetary policies during the current expansion, while adjusting the settings of their monetary policy instruments in response to cyclical conditions.

Chapter 2 builds on an extensive literature on global business cycles in four dimensions. First, it covers a longer time span of annual series (1950-2018) and a larger set of economies (181). Second, the chapter is the first study that presents an analysis of the phases of the global business cycle with quarterly output series of 105 countries over the period 1960Q1-2019Q2. Third, it expands on the set of macroeconomic and financial variables that Kose and Terrones (2015) analyzed to present a broader perspective on the evolution of the global business cycle. Fourth, it presents a detailed analysis of global expansions and puts the current global expansion in context by comparing it with previous such episodes.

Chapter 3. Macroeconomic Developments

Chapter 3 documents macroeconomic developments in EMDEs before, during, and after the global recession of 2009. It shows that, overall, EMDEs weathered the global recession relatively well. EMDEs with stronger precrisis fundamentals—such as adequate foreign exchange reserves, sound fiscal positions, and low inflation—suffered milder growth slowdowns, in part because of their greater capacity to engage in monetary and fiscal stimulus. LICs were also resilient, because foreign aid and inflows of remittances remained relatively stable. In contrast, EMDEs that were heavily dependent on short-term capital flows—such as portfolio investment and cross-border bank lending—fared less well, especially those in ECA. A key lesson for EMDEs is the need to strengthen macroeconomic frameworks and create policy space to prepare for future global downturns.

Specifically, chapter 3 addresses the following questions:

- How strong were the economic fundamentals in EMDEs before the global recession?
- How did EMDEs fare during the recession and in its aftermath?
- What explains the sluggish postrecession recovery in EMDEs?

Chapter 3 documents the following trends.

First, before the 2009 global recession, EMDEs benefitted from broad-based and rapid growth, supported by strong domestic demand and a benign external environment. On the eve of the global financial crisis, EMDEs accounted for almost one-third of global output and global exports, up from about one-quarter in 2001. EMDEs became a key source of global savings during the precrisis period. In EMDEs, gross saving as a share of GDP rose by 10 percentage points between 2001 and 2007, and benign financing conditions encouraged strong investment growth. EMDEs accumulated sizeable current account surpluses, reduced fiscal deficits, lowered debt, and built foreign exchange reserves.

Second, EMDEs weathered the global recession relatively well, particularly those with strong fundamentals that allowed the use of expansionary macroeconomic policies and those that were less exposed to global trade and finance. EMDEs that had built central bank credibility, established low inflation, and secured sound fiscal positions had space to engage in monetary and fiscal stimulus and thus fared better during the crisis, as did those that had accumulated ample foreign exchange reserves that could be used to stabilize exchange rates. EMDEs that were heavily reliant on more volatile financing sources (such as portfolio investment and cross-border bank lending), especially those in ECA, suffered steeper recessions.

Third, postcrisis growth in EMDEs has been disappointing. Although still well above growth in advanced economies, EMDE growth slowed steadily after the global recession, from a peak of 6.5 percent in 2011 to a trough of 3.8 percent in 2015, continuing at a moderate 4.3 percent a year during 2017-18. This slowdown had both cyclical and structural origins. It reflected weaker growth in advanced economies; the phasing out of policy stimulus in several large EMDEs and advanced economies; a slowdown in potential growth in many EMDEs, including China; China's shift toward a more balanced growth model; a sharp decline in commodity prices in 2012; bouts of financial stress in major EMDEs; and episodes of policy uncertainty that dampened confidence and weighed on investment.

Fourth, although growth is expected to stabilize somewhat, it will likely remain subdued in the near future—and subject to downside risks—and slow further over the longer term (World Bank 2019b). Population dynamics in EMDEs reached a turning point in 2010 when the share of the working-age population stabilized after several decades of rapid increases. Productivity growth is expected to remain lackluster as diminishing growth prospects weigh on investment, contributing to a potential growth slowdown of about 1.6 percentage points from precrisis rates, to an annual average of 4.3 percent in 2019-27 (World Bank 2018b).

Fifth, ample policy room, sound institutions, and international policy coordination helped mitigate the adverse effects of the 2009 global recession. The window of opportunity for rebuilding resilience before the next downturn materializes may be narrowing, which in turn highlights the urgent need to rebuild policy space to enhance the resilience of those EMDEs with eroded policy room.

Chapter 3 makes several contributions to a growing literature, drawing lessons from the global financial crisis and the 2009 global recession. First, the chapter expands on earlier studies of the global recession by introducing an EMDE focus and extending the horizon of the discussion. Previous studies examined the initial impact of the global financial crisis on EMDEs but did not reach far into the postcrisis period (Berkmen et al. 2012; Blanchard, Faruqee, and Das 2010; World Bank 2009). Other studies focused on the cross-border transmission of the crisis among advanced economies (Arestis and Karakitsos 2013; Blinder 2013; Imbs 2010; Mishkin 2011). A third set of studies examined the impact of the financial crisis on the real economy in advanced economies (Ball 2014; Bernanke 2018; Gertler and Gilchrist 2018; Perri and Quadrini 2018) or the lasting nature of the macroeconomic effects of the financial crisis (Chen, Mrkaic, and Nabar 2019; IMF 2018a). Second, the chapter delves deeper into developments in specific EMDE regions and the largest emerging markets. Third, it draws lessons from the global recession that are relevant for today's policy challenges.

Chapter 4. Financial Market Developments

Across EMDEs, robust economic growth before the 2009 global recession was accompanied by rapid financial deepening. In the runup to the global recession, EMDE banks were the main source of domestic private sector credit and were mostly funded by local deposits. This situation softened the impact of the global liquidity tightening in 2008-09. After the global recession, however, several EMDEs went through credit booms fueled by supportive macroeconomic policies, large capital inflows, and accommodative global financial conditions. These booms have left a legacy of elevated private debt. EMDE financial markets became more interconnected as capital flows increased and cross-border lending between EMDEs expanded.

Against this backdrop, chapter 4 considers the following questions:

- How were EMDE financial markets affected by the global recession?
- How have financial markets in EMDEs evolved since the global recession?

- What implications do these changes have for financial stability and policies in EMDEs?

Chapter 4 documents the following findings.

First, during the global recession private sector deleveraging in EMDEs was milder than in previous episodes of financial distress. In 2009-10, nonfinancial private sector debt in EMDEs was broadly flat as a percent of GDP, compared to large decreases after past crises. The most severe credit crunches occurred in economies where precrisis credit booms had been funded by large capital flows and where banks had a narrow deposit base, such as some economies in ECA (Feyen et al. 2014).

Second, credit growth and capital flows resumed in many EMDEs following a brief pause after the global recession as benign international financial conditions encouraged nonfinancial corporations and governments in EMDEs to access international capital markets (Feyen et al. 2015). Several EMDEs experienced credit booms during 2011-16. Although these booms have largely subsided, they have left a legacy of high private sector debt that makes nonfinancial corporations more vulnerable to financing shocks (World Bank 2018c). By end-2018, total debt in EMDEs had surged to 169 percent of GDP on average from 98 percent of GDP at end-2007. Private sector debt nearly doubled over the decade to end-2018, to 118 percent of GDP on average.

In several EMDEs, increased borrowing in international capital markets has raised foreign currency-denominated debt. On average, foreign-currency-denominated corporate debt as a share of GDP rose by 7 percentage points between 2007 and 2018, exposing EMDE corporate sectors and banks to risks from large currency devaluations.

Third, tighter regulations and a retrenchment by crisis-hit global banks have significantly curtailed foreign bank credit in several EMDE regions—ECA, LAC, and SSA—where lending by international banks was an important source of finance for the government and the private sector (IMF 2016; World Bank 2018d). The retrenchment of global banks has opened space for the rapid expansion of EMDE-headquartered banks in some regions, such as SSA.

Finally, financial intermediation in EMDEs with systemically important financial sectors is now larger and more complex, opaque, and internationally interconnected than at the onset of the crisis. This outcome raises new regulatory challenges. For example, the nonbank financial sector in several large economies (especially China) is less heavily regulated than banks and is playing a growing role in supplying credit to corporate borrowers (Ehlers, Kong, and Zhu 2018).

Chapter 4 expands a limited literature on postrecession financial market developments in EMDEs in several directions. First, it documents the extent to which the global financial crisis and subsequent global recession affected financial systems in EMDEs across a much larger sample of economies and in broader dimensions than in earlier exercises. Previous studies have focused on financial systems in advanced economies and associated global financial regulation. Other studies have focused on developments in EMDE banking systems, with limited integration of the discussion into the broader context of global capital markets. Chapter 4 brings these different strands together into an overall assessment of EMDE financial systems over the past decade.

Chapter 5: Macroeconomic and Financial Sector Policies

Unprecedented monetary policy accommodation in advanced economies and a large, coordinated fiscal stimulus by G20 countries helped to support a solid rebound in global output in 2010. This experience highlights the benefits of well-timed, appropriately calibrated stabilization policies and illustrates how international cooperation and coordination can enhance the effectiveness of policies to cope with global downturns and restore financial stability. Against this backdrop, chapter 5 examines the following questions:

- What macroeconomic and financial sector policies characterized the environment before the global recession?
- How have macroeconomic and financial sector policies evolved since the global recession?

Chapter 5 reports the following findings.

First, during the global recession, unprecedented coordinated monetary stimulus in advanced economies and fiscal stimulus in G20 countries supported a rapid recovery in global growth. Three-fifths of EMDEs with floating exchange rates had lowered their policy interest rates by the first quarter of 2009. EMDEs also made use of other monetary policy stimulus measures such as reducing reserve requirements; accepting a broader range of collateral as lender of last resort; injecting liquidity into, and recapitalizing, domestic banks; and channeling government-supported lending through development banks. G20 countries introduced fiscal packages equivalent to 1.4 percent of global GDP. China had the largest stimulus package at 12.7 percent of GDP.

Second, since the global recession, monetary policy has remained accommodative and fiscal stimulus has not been fully unwound in many EMDEs. By 2018, fiscal balances had returned to 2007 levels in only one-quarter of EMDEs and real interest rates had returned to 2007 levels in only one-half of them. Most of the EMDEs that have unwound their crisis-related fiscal stimulus are commodity importers. Many commodity-exporting EMDEs implemented procyclical policy tightening in response to the steep commodity price decline of 2011-16. Rising external, corporate, household, and government debt stocks, combined with wider fiscal and current account deficits, have increased EMDEs' vulnerabilities to shocks.

Third, since the global recession, all advanced economies and about 70 percent of EMDEs have strengthened their macroprudential policy frameworks and the resilience of their financial systems. Several new instruments have been developed under the Basel III framework to reduce systemic risk. Relative to advanced economies, EMDEs have made greater use of macroprudential tools such as foreign exchange and liquidity policies (for instance, limits on foreign currency loans and foreign exchange countercyclical reserve requirements) to mitigate their exposure to volatile capital inflows.

Fourth, the legitimacy of capital controls as a tool to promote financial stability in appropriate circumstances has gained greater acceptance. During the global recession, many EMDEs strengthened existing capital controls while others introduced new ones. Measures such as reserve requirements on foreign investment, taxes on currency outflows, taxes on interest and capital gains earned by nonresidents, minimum term requirements for holdings of central bank securities, and limits on foreign currency positions have been used often by EMDEs over the past decade.

Fifth, the global recession offers important lessons for policy priorities. Fiscal and monetary policies can provide effective stabilization tools if they are implemented swiftly and are coordinated in response to global shocks. However, policy stimulus can have unintended consequences in sowing the seeds of vulnerability to the next crisis if the stimulus is not unwound in a timely manner and if financial sector supervision and regulation are inadequate. Hence, policy makers need to balance short-term gains and long-term sustainability risks of proactive macroeconomic policies and ensure coherence between their macroeconomic and financial sector policies.

Chapter 5 constitutes the first extensive stocktaking of the evolution of macroeconomic policies used by EMDEs before, during, and after the global recession. Previous studies focused on subsets of policies, such as monetary policies or fiscal policies (Cukierman 2013; de Haan et al. 2018; Ramey 2019), policies during or shortly after the global recession (Akerlof et al. 2014; Blanchard et al. 2016; Taylor 2014), or macrofinancial linkages that propagated the financial crisis (Blanchard, Faruqee, and Das 2010; Claessens and Kose 2018). Most of these existing studies do not distill policy lessons specifically for EMDEs. Chapter 5 also provides a detailed overview of financial sector policies in EMDEs whereas the previous literature on such policies focuses on advanced economies (IMF 2018b). Third, the chapter distills lessons from the global recession that are relevant to EMDE policy makers today.

Chapter 6: Prospects, Risks, and Vulnerabilities

EMDE growth has repeatedly disappointed since the global recession. EMDEs continue to face multiple downside risks to the current subdued growth outlook. If these risks materialize, their impact on EMDEs depends on the magnitude of spillovers and domestic vulnerabilities. Since the 2009 global recession, external, corporate sector, and sovereign vulnerabilities have risen in most EMDEs, leaving them less prepared for future shocks. Over the longer run, EMDEs also face weakening potential growth, reflecting decelerations in capital accumulation and productivity growth, as well as demographic headwinds.

Against this background chapter 6 addresses the following questions:

- What are EMDEs' growth prospects?

- What are the main global and regional risks to growth faced by EMDEs?

- How have external and domestic vulnerabilities evolved over the past decade, and how do they compare to developments following previous crises?

Chapter 6 presents the following findings.

First, EMDE growth has generally disappointed in the past decade, with repeated and significant forecast downgrades—and 2019 is no different. Income gaps with advanced economies are expected to widen again in 2019 in one-third of EMDEs, especially in LAC, MNA, and SSA. The prospects for progress of today's LICs, which are increasingly clustered in SSA, to middle-income levels are dimmer than before the global recession, in part because of a rising number of countries affected by fragility, conflict, and violence; the prospect of weaker demand for primary commodities; and higher vulnerability to extreme weather, especially in agriculture-dependent economies (World Bank 2019b). Sustained robust per capita income growth, however, is needed for EMDEs to meaningfully reduce poverty, improve shared prosperity, and converge to income levels in advanced economies.

Second, near-term risks to EMDEs' growth outlook are tilted to the downside. At the global level, EMDEs face risks related to trade tensions between the United States and other major economies, especially China; broader threats to the international trade system; the risk of a disorderly exit of the United Kingdom from the EU; and the possibility of financial market disruptions. Some EMDEs also face risks related to security, geopolitical tensions, and severe weather events. Even in the case of risks outside EMDEs' control, effective monitoring and a thorough understanding of their likely effects can help develop appropriate policy responses to dampen their eventual impact.

Third, long-term growth prospects for EMDEs are weakening, as fundamental drivers lose momentum. In the mid-2000s, potential growth in EMDEs was 5.9 percent a year. It slowed to 4.7 percent a year in 2013-18 and, on current trends, is expected to decelerate further over the next decade. This slowdown reflected a marked slowdown in capital accumulation and productivity growth amid pronounced investment weakness, as well as demographic headwinds. Weakening growth prospects do not bode well for poverty reduction in EMDEs; in fact, evidence is that the pace of poverty reduction has already started to slow.

Fourth, EMDEs' vulnerabilities to adverse events have risen since the 2009 global recession. Today's average EMDE has higher government and private debt, wider fiscal deficits, and only slightly smaller current account deficits than the average EMDE before past financial crises. These vulnerabilities may be partly mitigated by greater exchange rate flexibility and more robust monetary, prudential, and fiscal policy frameworks compared to previous crises as well as financial sector reforms and the expansion of country-specific, regional, and multilateral financial safety nets since the global recession.

Chapter 6 contributes to the existing literature in several dimensions. First, the chapter updates earlier World Bank Group work on short- and long-term growth prospects, with granular regional and group perspectives (IMF 2019; World Bank 2018b). Second, it provides a comprehensive overview of vulnerabilities for the largest sample of EMDEs yet. Existing studies, such as Chitu and Quint (2018), Dahlhaus and Lam (2018), IMF (2019), and Rojas-Suarez (2015), for example, limit their analysis to a few, mainly large, EMDEs. In addition, this chapter is the first study that compares specific domestic and external vulnerabilities across a comprehensive list of nearly 300 previous EMDE crises since 1980, building on the work of Laeven and Valencia (2018).

Chapter 7: Policy Challenges

Unprecedented and coordinated policy stimulus supported a rebound from the global recession in 2010. Since then, amid anemic postcrisis growth, most EMDEs have not been able to fully unwind the policy stimulus put in place in response to the crisis. External, fiscal, and corporate vulnerabilities have increased since 2007. Several EMDEs are highly indebted, have elevated levels of foreign currency-denominated debt, or rely on portfolio or bank flows to finance large current account deficits. In addition, structural factors have eroded potential growth since the global recession.

Against this backdrop, chapter 7 addresses the following questions:

- What macroeconomic policies should be implemented to build resilience?
- What financial sector policies should be employed to maintain financial stability?
- How have structural reforms evolved, and what policies are needed to boost growth?

Chapter 7 reports the following findings.

First, it documents the extent to which current macroeconomic policies undermine EMDEs' resilience to shocks. Over 60 percent of EMDEs have primary fiscal deficits that are too large to stabilize or reduce their debt levels based on current macroeconomic and financial conditions. In several EMDEs, international reserves are currently inadequate.

Second, chapter 7 points to several policy implications. EMDEs with unsustainable fiscal positions should prioritize rebuilding policy space by raising revenues and improving spending efficiency while maintaining growth-enhancing expenditure. Measures to enhance tax revenues include broadening the tax base, improving tax collection systems, reducing loopholes, and empowering tax administrators with greater technical skills. To improve spending efficiency, policy makers can enhance the institutions and mechanisms used to determine investment projects and procurement, and to monitor spending, including on government administration and social services. Separately, EMDEs with inadequate international reserves could focus on rebuilding them and restraining foreign currency borrowing.

Third, to improve longer-term resilience, EMDEs need to strengthen fiscal and monetary policy frameworks by adopting transparent and rules-based approaches. Fiscal rules, if effectively implemented, can help countries maintain sustainable finances and accumulate resources when the economy is doing well. Better fiscal frameworks also assist monetary policy by restraining procyclical fiscal policy. A transparent and independent central bank will be better placed to maintain price stability, thereby helping to create a macroeconomic environment that is conducive to strong growth.

Fourth, proactive financial sector supervision and regulation can mitigate risks, especially in countries with financial markets that are developing rapidly and becoming more integrated globally. In EMDEs without a prudential authority or institutions with prudential powers, creating or empowering these institutions is a priority. In EMDEs with the appropriate institutions, flexible and well-targeted tools are needed to manage balance sheet mismatches, foreign currency risk, and asset price misalignment with fundamentals. In EMDEs facing destabilizing capital flows, capital flow management measures—in conjunction with sound macroeconomic policies, exchange rate policy, and sufficient levels of financial and institutional development—can reduce the risk of financial instability (IMF 2012). In regions where EMDE-headquartered banks have gained prominence, efforts to strengthen home-host supervisor coordination may pay dividends during the next episode of financial stress.

Fifth, although EMDEs were able to make some progress in improving their business climates in the three years prior and during the global recession, in many areas momentum was not maintained. Governance in EMDEs has failed to improve since the 1990s, and some EMDEs have taken steps to reduce openness to international capital flows. Reform priorities include building institutions that support economic growth and resilience; enhancing productivity and encouraging investment; building human capital; investing in growth-enhancing public infrastructure; helping to address, as well as adapting to, climate change; improving governance; strengthening competition; and reducing regulatory burdens.

Chapter 7 adds to the existing literature in several ways. First, the chapter assesses both the progress and impact of structural reforms in EMDEs since the global recession. Most studies focus either on quantifying the impact of a subset of these reforms on output (Bailiu and Hajzler 2016; Égert 2018) or on the evolution of specific aspects of structural reforms (World Bank 2019d, 2019e). Second, compared to existing studies that focus on individual structural reforms, chapter 7 brings together the policy priorities most relevant at the current juncture, alongside a review of the related literature analyzing the likely impact of their implementation, with a focus on possible complementarities and tradeoffs.

Chapter 8: The Role of the World Bank Group

The global financial crisis and the subsequent global recession not only adversely affected global growth and poverty but also demonstrated the limitations and challenges of unilateral responses by national governments. The global recession required rapid and targeted responses by international financial institutions—in particular, it led the World Bank Group to provide unprecedented financing support and advisory services to its member countries.

Specifically, chapter 8 examines the following questions:

- How did the World Bank Group respond during the global recession?
- What is the assessment of the World Bank Group's response?
- How have the World Bank Group's strategy and operating model changed since the global recession?
- What policies can the World Bank Group offer to reduce vulnerabilities and build resilience ahead of future crises?

Chapter 8 documents the following findings.

World Bank Group's financing during the global recession was unprecedented in volume. Financing commitments of the World Bank Group nearly doubled in real terms (in 2010 U.S. dollars), from an annual average of $37 billion during the fiscal years 2007/08 and 2008/09 to an annual average of $66 billion during the fiscal years 2009/10 and 2010/11. This World Bank Group financing was larger than during earlier crises, with lending commitments made to more than 100 economies. The World Bank Group's disbursements during the crisis were also larger than those of any other major international financial institution.

The forms of World Bank Group financing were diverse across its multiple entities. Lending by the International Bank for Reconstruction and Development (IBRD) nearly tripled, and that of the International Development Association (IDA) rose by about 20 percent. The support of the International Finance Corporation (IFC) and Multilateral Investment Guarantee Agency (MIGA) did not surge, but the former provided investments and the latter provided financial guarantees targeted at sectors and regions that were especially hard-hit by the global recession.

Lending during the global recession increased the most for LAC and ECA, the two regions most affected by the crisis. About one-fifth of World Bank (IBRD and IDA) lending was provided to LICs, equivalent to about 1 percent of their GDP. Upper-middle-income countries (UMICs) and lower-middle-income countries (LMICs) each received about 40 percent of World Bank crisis commitments, but these represented much smaller shares of recipient GDP than was the case for LICs.

As in previous global crises, the World Bank Group prioritized its lending in the areas of social protection, infrastructure investment, fiscal management, and financial sector development. Although investment lending served as the primary lending tool during the global recession, the World Bank Group provided development policy lending more heavily than during noncrisis periods because of its faster pace of deployment. It also adopted crisis-specific facilities in targeted areas, such as trade finance and infrastructure investment, where the World Bank Group has long-standing expertise.

The World Bank Group has built upon its experience during the global recession in its subsequent work. It has improved its monitoring and surveillance of global macroeconomic and financial developments, allowing it to more effectively flag risks in the world economy. It has completed two global campaigns to improve its capital adequacy, partly to make it better prepared for future crises. It has refined its operating model by introducing new crisis response facilities and implementing a more coordinated Bank-wide strategy in its financing and advisory activities, helping to enhance its ability to respond quickly and flexibly should a future crisis arise. The World Bank Group has an extensive set of both traditional and new support instruments to help members reduce the risk and impact of crises and to build longer-term resilience against future crises. These instruments constitute an important strategic capability that better enables it to advance its twin goals of poverty reduction and shared prosperity, including by mitigating the reversals that occur during economic downturns.

Chapter 8 links the World Bank Group's response to the global recession with the evolution of its policy toolkit in the subsequent decade. Although an exhaustive analysis of the World Bank Group's role during the global recession is beyond its scope, chapter 8 adds to a set of studies that have examined the World Bank Group's response to the global recession. Most prominently, the World Bank Group's Independent Evaluation Group (IEG) conducted two comprehensive studies that examined the World Bank Group's response. The first described the overall response of the World Bank Group, presented an early evaluation of its effectiveness, and drew initial lessons (IEG 2011). The second analysis, a year later, examined the effectiveness of the World Bank Group's crisis response in the areas of social protection, financial sector policies, and fiscal management (IEG 2012). These and other studies have documented that the World Bank Group largely retained its lending models and focus areas through the crisis and the subsequent global recession (Guven 2012; Hall 2015; IEG 2012).

Chapter 8 contributes to these works in three ways. First, it analyzes the World Bank Group's crisis response under the lens of the subsequent decade, a longer time span than the existing work. Second, it analyzes how the global recession affected World Bank Group operations. It documents that, while the World Bank Group demonstrated a consistent overall policy position that prioritized its traditional areas of expertise, such as social protection, it has also in the last decade made refinements to its strategy and operating model that were motivated by its experience responding to the global recession. Third, the chapter shows that, partly drawing on the lessons from the global recession response, the World Bank Group current crisis-response strategy in financing and advisory functions combines crisis risk and impact mitigation with longer-term efforts to build structural resilience.

References

Acharya, V., S. Cecchetti, J. Gregorio, Ş. Kalemli-Özcan, P. Lane, and U. Panizza. 2015. "Corporate Debt in Emerging Economies: A Threat to Financial Stability?" Brookings Institution Report, Washington, DC.

Ahir, H., N. Bloom, and D. Furceri. 2018. "The World Uncertainty Index." https//www.policyuncertainty.com/media/WUI_mimeo_10_29.pdf.

Akerlof, G., O. Blanchard, D. Romer, and J. Stiglitz. 2014. *What Have We Learned?: Macroeconomic Policy after the Crisis*. Cambridge, MA: MIT Press.

Arestis, P., and E. Krakitosos. 2013. *Financial Stability in the Aftermath of the 'Great Recession.'* London: Palgrave Macmillan.

Baffes, J., A. Kabundi, P. Nagle, and F. Ohnsorge. 2018. "The Role of Major Emerging Markets in Global Commodity Demand." Policy Research Working Paper 8495, World Bank, Washington, DC.

Baffes, J., M. A. Kose, F. Ohnsorge, and M. Stocker. 2015. "The Great Plunge in Oil Prices: Causes, Consequences and Policy Responses." Policy Research Note 1, World Bank, Washington, DC.

Bahaj, S., and R. Reis. 2018. "Central Bank Swap Lines." Staff Working Paper 741, Bank of England, London.

Bailliu, J., and C. Hajzler. 2016. "Structural Reforms and Economic Growth in Emerging-Market Economies." *Bank of Canada Review* 2016 (Autumn): 47-60.

Balakrishnan, R., S. Danninger, S. Elekdag, and I. Tytell. 2011. "The Transmission of Financial Stress from Advanced to Emerging Economies." *Emerging Markets Finance and Trade* 47 (sup2): 40-68.

Ball, L. 2014. "Long-Term Damage from the Great Recession in OECD Countries." NBER Working Paper 20185, National Bureau of Economic Research, Cambridge, MA.

Barsky, R. B., and L. Kilian. 2004. "Oil and the Macroeconomy since the 1970s." *Journal of Economic Perspectives* 18 (4): 115-34.

Berkmen, S. P., G. Gelos, R. Rennhack, and J. P. Walsh. 2012. "The Global Financial Crisis: Explaining Cross-Country Differences in the Output Impact." *Journal of International Money and Finance* 31 (1): 42-59.

Bernanke, B. S. 2018. "The Real Effects of Disrupted Credit: Evidence from the Global Financial Crisis." *Brookings Papers on Economic Activity Conference Drafts,* September 13-14, 2018, Brookings Institution, Washington, DC.

BIS (Bank for International Settlements). 2019. *BIS Quarterly Review.* March. Basel: Bank for International Settlements.

Blagrave, P., G. Ho, K. Koloskova, and E. Vesperoni. 2017. "Fiscal Spillovers: The Importance of Macroeconomic and Policy Conditions in Transmission." *Spillover Notes* 17/02, International Monetary Fund, Washington, DC.

Blanchard, O. J., H. Faruqee, and M. Das. 2010. "The Initial Impact of the Crisis on Emerging Market Countries." *Brookings Papers on Economic Activity* (Spring): 263-323.

Blanchard, O., R. Rajan, K. Rogoff, and L. Summers. 2016. *Progress and Confusion: The State of Macroeconomic Policy.* Cambridge, MA: MIT Press.

Blinder, A. 2013. *After the Music Stopped: The Financial Crisis, the Response, and the Work Ahead.* London: The Penguin Press.

Cavallino, P., and D. Sandri. 2018. "The Expansionary Lower Bound: Contractionary Monetary Easing and the Trilemma." IMF Working Paper 18/236, International Monetary Fund, Washington, DC.

Cerutti, E., S. Claessens, and L. Laeven. 2017. "The Use and Effectiveness of Macroprudential Policies: New Evidence." *Journal of Financial Stability* 28 (February): 203-24.

Cetorelli, N., and L. S. Goldberg. 2011. "Global Banks and International Shock Transmission: Evidence from the Crisis." *IMF Economic Review* 59 (1): 41-76.

Chen, W., M. Mrkaic, and M. Nabar. 2019. "The Global Economic Recovery 10 Years After the 2008 Financial Crisis." Working Paper 19/83, International Monetary Fund, Washington, DC.

Chinn, M. D., and H. Ito. 2006. "What Matters for Financial Development? Capital Controls, Institutions, and Interactions." *Journal of Development Economics* 81 (1): 163-92.

Chitu, L., and D. Quint. 2018. "Emerging Market Vulnerabilities - A Comparison with Previous Crises." ECB Economic Bulletin 8/2018, European Central Bank, Frankfort.

Claessens, S., and M. A. Kose. 2018. "Frontiers of Macrofinancial Linkages." BIS Papers 95, Bank for International Settlements, Basel.

Claessens, S., M. A. Kose, and M. Terrones. 2012. "How Do Business and Financial Cycles Interact?" *Journal of International Economics* 87 (1): 178-90.

Cukierman, A. 2013. "Monetary Policy and Institutions before, during, and after the Global Financial Crisis." *Journal of Financial Stability* 9 (3): 373-84.

Dahlhaus, T., and A. Lam. 2018. "Assessing Vulnerabilities in Emerging-Market Economies." Discussion Paper 2018-13, Bank of Canada, Ottawa.

de Haan, J., C. Bodea, R. Hicks, and S. Eijffinger. 2018. "Central Bank Independence Before, During, and After the Crisis." *Comparative Economic Studies* 60 (2): 183-202.

Dincer, N. N., and B. Eichengreen. 2014. "Central Bank Transparency and Independence: Updates and New Measures." *International Journal of Central Banking* 10 (1): 189-259.

Dollar, D., T. Kleineberg, and A. Kraay. 2013. "Growth Still Is Good for the Poor." Policy Research Working Paper 6568, World Bank, Washington DC.

Dollar, D. and A. Kraay. 2002. "Growth Is Good for the Poor." *Journal of Economic Growth* 7 (3): 195-225.

ECB (European Central Bank). 2018. "Strengthening the Global Financial Safety Net." Occasional Paper 207, ECB, Frankfurt am Main.

Égert, B. 2018. "The Quantification of Structural Reforms: Extending the Framework to Emerging Market Economies." CESifo Working Paper 6921, Center for Economic Studies and Ifo Institute, Munich.

Ehlers, T., S. Kong, and F. Zhu. 2018. "Mapping Shadow Banking in China: Structure and Dynamics." BIS Working Paper 701, Bank for International Settlements, Basel.

Eichengreen, B., and P. Gupta. 2016. "Managing Sudden Stops." Policy Research Working Paper 7639, World Bank, Washington, DC.

Feyen, E., and I. Zuccardi. 2019. "The Sovereign-Bank Nexus in EMDEs: What Is It, Is It Rising, and What Are the Policy Implications?" Policy Research Working Paper 8950, World Bank, Washington, DC.

Feyen E., S. Ghosh, K. Kibuuka, and S. Farazi. 2015. "Global Liquidity and External Bond Issuance in Emerging Markets and Developing Economies." Policy Research Working Paper

7363, World Bank, Washington, DC.

Feyen, E., R. Letelier, I. Love, S. Maimbo, and R. Rocha. 2014. "The Impact of Funding Models and Foreign Bank Ownership on Bank Credit Growth: Is Central and Eastern Europe Different?" Policy Research Working Paper 6783, World Bank, Washington, DC.

Foster, J. E., and M. Székely. 2008. "Is Economic Growth Good for the Poor? Tracking Low Incomes Using General Means." *International Economic Review* 49 (4): 1143-72.

Fratzscher, M. 2012. "Capital Flows, Push versus Pull Factors and the Global Financial Crisis." *Journal of International Economics* 88 (2): 341-56.

Freund, C., M. J. Ferrantino, M. Maliszewska, and M. Ruta. 2018. "Impacts on Global Trade and Income of Current Trade Disputes." MTI Practice Notes, Number 2, World Bank, Washington, DC.

FSB (Financial Services Board). 2019a. *Global Monitoring Report on Non-Bank Financial Intermediation 2018.* Basel: Switzerland.

FSB (Financial Services Board). 2019b. "Cyber Security: Finding Responses to Global Threats." Remarks by Dietrich Domanski, Secretary General, Financial Stability Board, at G7 conference "Cybersecurity: Coordinating Efforts to Protect the Financial Sector in the Global Economy," May 10, Paris.

FSOC (Financial Stability Oversight Council). 2018. *Annual Report 2018.* Washington, DC: Financial Stability Oversight Council.

G20 (Group of Twenty). 2009. "Leaders' Statement: The Pittsburgh Summit." Pittsburgh, PA.

G20 (Group of Twenty). 2018. "G20 Leaders' Declaration: Building Consensus for Fair and Sustainable Development." Buenos Aires, Argentina.

Gertler, M., and S. Gilchrist. 2018. "What Happened: Financial Factors in the Great Recession." *Journal of Economic Perspectives* 32 (3): 3-30.

Goldberg, L. S., C. Kennedy, and J. Miu. 2010. "Central Bank Dollar Swap Lines and Overseas Dollar Funding Costs." Federal Reserve Bank of New York Staff Reports, New York.

Gopinath, G. 2017. "Rethinking Macroeconomic Policy: International Economy Issues." Paper presented at conference "Rethinking Macroeconomic Policy," Peterson Institute for International Economics, October 12-13, Washington, DC.

Guven, A. B. 2012. "The IMF, the World Bank and the Global Economic Crisis: Exploring Paradigm Continuity." *Development and Change* 43 (4): 869-98.

Ha, J., M. A. Kose, and F. Ohnsorge, eds. 2019. *Inflation in Emerging and Developing Economies: Evolution, Drivers, and Policies.* Washington, DC: World Bank.

Ha, J., A. Ivanova, F. Ohnsorge, and D. F. Unsal. 2019. "Inflation: Concepts, Evolution, and Correlates." Policy Research Working Paper 8738, World Bank, Washington, DC.

Ha, J., M. A. Kose, H. Matsuoka, and D. Vorisek. 2019. "Inflation Expectations: Review and Evidence." In *Inflation in Emerging and Developing Economies: Evolution, Drivers and Policies* edited by J. Ha, M. A. Kose and F. Ohnsorge. Washington, DC: World Bank.

Hall, A. 2015. "More of the Same: The World Bank's Social Policy Response to Global Economic Crisis." *Global Social Policy* 15 (1): 88-90.

Hamilton, J. D. 2011. "Historical Oil Shocks." NBER Working Paper 16790, National Bureau of Economic Research, Cambridge, MA.

Huidrom, R., M. A. Kose, H. Matsuoka, and F. Ohnsorge. 2019. "How Important are Spillovers from Major Emerging Markets?" *International Finance* 2019: 1-17

Huidrom, R., M. A. Kose, J. J. Lim, and F. Ohnsorge. 2019. "Why Do Fiscal Multipliers Depend on Fiscal Positions?" *Journal of Monetary Economics*. Advance online publication. https://doi.org/10.1016/j.jmoneco.2019.03.004.

IEG (Independent Evaluation Group). 2011. *The World Bank Group's Response to the Global Economic Crisis: Phase 1*. Washington, DC: World Bank.

IEG (Independent Evaluation Group). 2012. *The World Bank Group's Response to the Global Economic Crisis: Phase 2*. Washington, DC: World Bank.

Imbs, J. 2010. "The First Global Recession in Decades." *IMF Economic Review* 58 (2): 327-54.

IMF (International Monetary Fund). 2012. "The Liberalization and Management of Capital Flows—An Institutional View." IMF Policy Paper, International Monetary Fund, Washington, DC.

IMF (International Monetary Fund). 2015. *Pan-African Banks—Opportunities and Challenges for Cross-Border Oversight*. Washington, DC: International Monetary Fund.

IMF (International Monetary Fund). 2016. *Financial Integration in Latin America*. Washington, DC: International Monetary Fund.

IMF (International Monetary Fund). 2017. *Adequacy of the Global Financial Safety Net—Considerations for Fund Toolkit Reform*. Washington, DC: International Monetary Fund.

IMF (International Monetary Fund). 2018a. *World Economic Outlook: Challenges to Steady Growth*. October. Washington, DC: International Monetary Fund.

IMF (International Monetary Fund). 2018b. *Global Financial Stability Report: A Decade after the Global Financial Crisis: Are We Safer?* October. Washington, DC: International Monetary Fund.

IMF (International Monetary Fund). 2019. *World Economic Outlook: Growth Slowdown, Precarious Recovery*. April. Washington, DC: International Monetary Fund.

IMF, FSB, and BIS (International Monetary Fund, Financial Stability Board, and Bank for International Settlements). 2016. "Elements of Effective Macroprudential Policies: Lessons from International Experience." Joint publication.

IPCC (Intergovernmental Panel on Climate Change). 2018. *Global Warming of 1.5°C*. Geneva: Intergovernmental Panel on Climate Change.

Kee, H. L., C. Neagu, and A. Nicita. 2013. "Is Protectionism on the Rise? Assessing National Trade Policies during the Crisis of 2008." *Review of Economics and Statistics*, 95 (1): 342-46.

Knoop, T. A. 2004. *Recessions and Depressions: Understanding Business Cycles*. Westport, CT: Praeger.

Kose, M. A., and M. Terrones. 2015. *Collapse and Revival*. Washington, DC: International Monetary Fund.

Kose, M. A., S. Kurlat, F. Ohnsorge, and N. Sugawara. 2017. "A Cross-Country Database of Fiscal Space." Policy Research Working Paper 8157, World Bank, Washington, DC.

Kose, M. A., C. Lakatos, F. Ohnsorge, and M. Stocker. 2017. "The Global Role of the U.S. Economy: Linkages, Policies and Spillovers." Policy Research Working Paper 7962, World Bank, Washington, DC.

Kutlina-Dimitrova, Z., and C. Lakatos. 2017. "The Global Costs of Protectionism." Policy Research Working Paper 8277, World Bank, Washington, DC.

Laeven, L., and F. Valencia. 2018. "Systemic Banking Crises Revisited." IMF Working Paper 18/206, International Monetary Fund, Washington, DC.

Liang, N., M. M. McConnell, and P. Swagel. 2018. "Responding to the Global Financial Crisis: What We Did and Why We Did It: Evidence on Outcomes." Preliminary Discussion Draft, Brookings Institution.

Mian, A., and A. Sufi. 2009. "The Consequences of Mortgage Credit Expansion: Evidence from the U.S. Mortgage Default Crisis." *The Quarterly Journal of Economics* 124 (4): 1449-96.

Mishkin, F. 2011. "Over the Cliff: From the Subprime to the Global Financial Crisis." *Journal of Economic Perspectives* 25 (1): 49-70.

OECD (Organisation for Economic Co-operation and Development). 2018. "OECD on the Crisis and After: 10 Years, 10 Stories." *OECD Observer* website, http://oecdobserver.org/news/fullstory.php/aid/6067/OECD_on_the_crisis_and_after:_10_years_10_stories.html.

Perri, F., and V. Quadrini. 2018. "International Recessions." *American Economic Review* 108 (4-5): 935-84.

Ramey, V. 2019. "Ten Years After the Crisis: What Have We Learned from the Renaissance in Fiscal Research?" *Journal of Economic Perspectives* 33 (2): 89-114.

Ravallion, M., and S. Chen. 2003. "Measuring Pro-Poor Growth." *Economics Letters* 78(1): 93-9.

Reinhart, C. M., and K. S. Rogoff. 2009. *This Time is Different: Eight Centuries of Financial Folly.* Princeton, NJ: Princeton University Press.

Rey, H. 2015. "Dilemma Not Trilemma: The Global Financial Cycle and Monetary Policy Independence." NBER Working Paper 21162, National Bureau of Economic Research, Cambridge, MA.

Rogoff, K. 2014. "How Fragile are Emerging Markets?" The Guardian, February 6, 2014. Available at https://www.theguardian.com/business/2014/feb/06/emerging-markets-how-fragile-kenneth-rogoff.

Rojas-Suarez, L. 2015. "Emerging Market Macroeconomic Resilience to External Shocks: Today Versus Pre-Global Crisis." Center for Global Development, Washington, DC.

Santos, M. E., C. Dabus, and F. Delbianco. 2019. "Growth and Poverty Revisited from a Multidimensional Perspective." *The Journal of Development Studies* 55 (2): 260-77.

Sims, C., and Z. Tao. 2006. "Does Monetary Policy Generate Recessions?" *Macroeconomic Dynamics* 10 (2): 231-72.

Taylor, J. 2014. "The Role of Policy in the Great Recession and the Weak Recovery." *American Economic Review* 104 (5): 61-6.

World Bank. 2009. *Global Monitoring Report: A Development Emergency.* Washington, DC: World Bank.

World Bank. 2015a. *Global Economic Prospects: Having Fiscal Space and Using It.* January. Washington, DC: World Bank.

World Bank. 2015b. *Global Economic Prospects: Global Economy in Transition.* June. Washington, DC: World Bank.

World Bank. 2016a. *Global Economic Prospects: Spillovers amid Weak Growth.* January. Washington, DC: World Bank.

World Bank. 2016b. *Commodity Markets Outlook: Weak Growth in Emerging Market Economies.* April. Washington, DC: World Bank.

World Bank. 2017a. *Global Economic Prospects: A Fragile Recovery.* June. Washington, DC: World Bank.

World Bank. 2017b. *Global Economic Prospects: Weak Investment in Uncertain Times.* January. Washington, DC: World Bank.

World Bank. 2018a. *Global Financial Development Report: Bankers without Borders.* Washington, DC: World Bank.

World Bank. 2018b. *Global Economic Prospects: Broad-Based Upturn, but for How Long?* January. Washington, DC: World Bank.

World Bank. 2018c. *Poverty and Shared Prosperity Report: Piecing Together the Poverty Puzzle* Washington, DC: World Bank.

World Bank. 2018d. *Global Economic Prospects: The Turning of the Tide?* June. Washington, DC: World Bank.

World Bank. 2019a. *Global Financial Development Report: Bank Regulation and Supervision a Decade after the Global Financial Crisis.* Washington, DC: World Bank.

World Bank. 2019b. *Global Economic Prospects: Heightened Tensions, Subdued Investment.* June. Washington, DC: World Bank.

World Bank. 2019c. *Global Economic Prospects: Darkening Skies.* January. Washington, DC: World Bank.

World Bank. 2019d. *Mainstreaming Disruptive Technologies at the World Bank Group.* Washington, DC: World Bank.

World Bank. 2019e. *Harvesting Prosperity: Technological Progress and Productivity Growth in Agriculture.* Washington, DC: World Bank.

WTO (World Trade Organization). 2018. *Report on G20 Trade Measures: Mid-May 2018 to Mid-October 2018.* November. Geneva: World Trade Organization.

The effects of the global financial crisis were deep, powerful, and lasting. Some are being felt to this very day.

Patrick Njoroge (2018)
Governor
Central Bank of Kenya

CHAPTER 2

What Happens during Global Recessions?

The world economy has experienced four global recessions over the past seven decades: in 1975, 1982, 1991, and 2009. During each of these episodes, annual real per capita global output contracted, and this contraction was accompanied by weakening of other key indicators of global economic activity. The global recessions were highly synchronized internationally, with severe economic and financial disruptions in many countries around the world. The 2009 global recession, set off by the global financial crisis, was by far the deepest and most synchronized of the four recessions. As the epicenter of the crisis, advanced economies felt the brunt of the recession. The subsequent expansion has been the weakest since World War II in advanced economies as many of them have struggled to overcome the legacies of the crisis. In contrast, most emerging market and developing economies weathered the 2009 global recession relatively well and delivered a stronger recovery than after previous global recessions.

Introduction

"Global recession" has been a recurrent topic of debate over the past decade, reflecting the breadth and severity of the 2007-09 global financial crisis, the halting nature of the recovery, and, recently, fears that the global economy was on the edge of another downturn. In 2009, the interest was understandably focused on the severity of the global recession and its devastating consequences. Attention shifted to the signs of a flourishing global recovery in 2010-11, but hopes that this recovery would be sustained were soon curtailed by the possibility of another global recession due to the euro area debt crisis. Financial pressures in the euro area eased in late 2012, but in 2015-16 fears of a global recession reemerged partly because of financial market turbulence in China. Since mid-2018, concerns about a global recession have returned as the world economy experienced a synchronized slowdown largely driven by extraordinary weakness in trade and manufacturing amid elevated trade tensions and heightened policy uncertainties.

Despite the interest in global recessions, the term does not have a widely accepted definition. It is difficult to map the most practical definition of national recessions—at least two consecutive quarters of decline in national output—to a global context, not only because reliable quarterly data for global output are unavailable without a significant lag but also because the global economy rarely registers a contraction: 2009 was the only year since World War II to register a decline in annual global output.

A better understanding of global recessions requires an appreciation of the growing importance of emerging market and developing economies (EMDEs) and of cross-border trade and financial linkages. First, the increasing role of EMDEs means that it is

Note: This chapter was prepared by M. Ayhan Kose, Naotaka Sugawara, and Marco E. Terrones.

FIGURE 2.1 Contributions of country groups to world output and growth

Contributions of EMDEs to world output and output growth have increased over the past seven decades.

A. World output

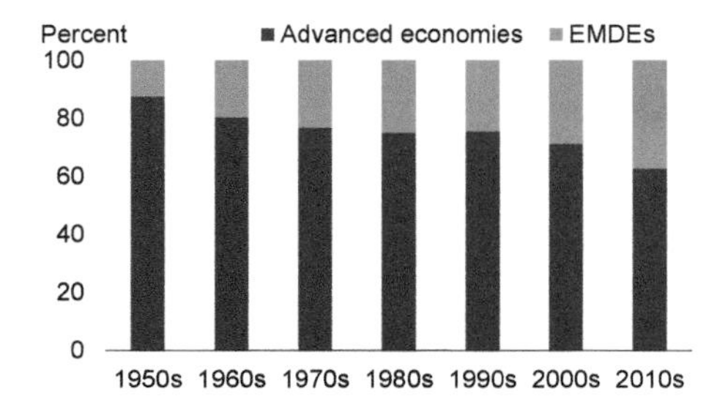

B. World output growth

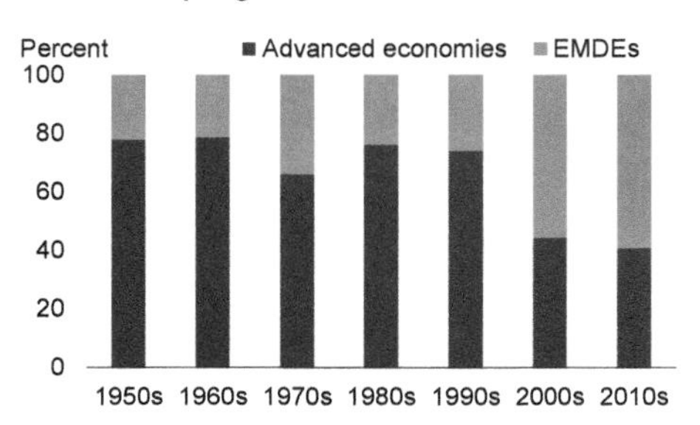

Sources: Feenstra, Inklaar, and Timmer (2015); Kose and Terrones (2015); World Bank.
Note: EMDEs = emerging market and developing economies.
A. Bars show the average distribution of world output among country groups in the decade indicated (computed using market exchange rates). The 2010s period refers to 2010-19, which includes a forecast for 2019.
B. Bars correspond to the average of each country group's contribution to growth in world output in the decade indicated.

no longer sufficient to monitor cyclical fluctuations in advanced economies, the United States in particular, to understand the global business cycle. Advanced economies on average accounted for about 80 percent of global output and 75 percent of global growth over the period 1950-90 (figure 2.1). By the 2010s, however, the average share of advanced economies in world output had declined to about 60 percent and their contribution to world output growth had fallen to about 40 percent. As a result, business cycles in advanced economies have become a much less reliable proxy indicator for the global business cycle. The smaller contribution from advanced economies implies that a better understanding of the global business cycle requires going beyond the usual set of advanced economies to a much broader group that also includes EMDEs.

Second, cross-border trade and financial linkages have become stronger over the past seven decades. In the 1950s, global trade openness—measured by the sum of exports and imports of goods and services in percent of global gross domestic product (GDP)—was on average less than 20 percent (figure 2.2). By the 2010s, it had increased to more than 55 percent. Global financial openness, defined as the sum of foreign assets and liabilities in percent of GDP, also increased, from about 50 percent in the 1970s to almost 400 percent in the latest decade. These stronger linkages have increased the feedback, in both directions, between business cycles in advanced economies and those in EMDEs. They also ultimately raise the odds of more pronounced, and more synchronous, movements in the global business cycle.

Against this background, this chapter examines the main features of global recessions and the ensuing recoveries and expansions. Specifically, it addresses the following questions:

- What happens during global recessions and recoveries?

FIGURE 2.2 World trade and financial integration

Cross-border trade and financial linkages have become stronger over the past seven decades.

A. Trade openness

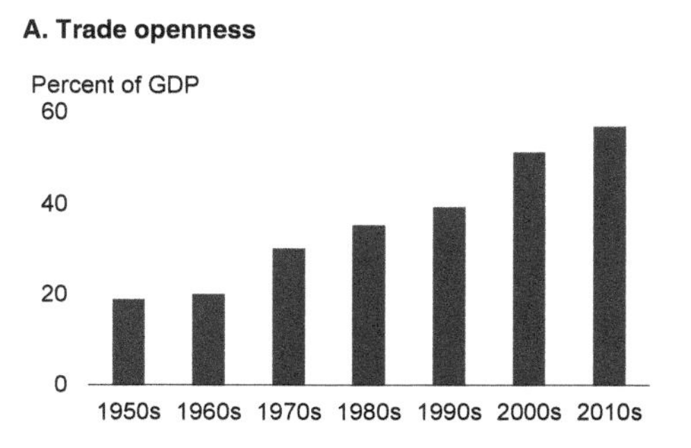

B. Financial openness

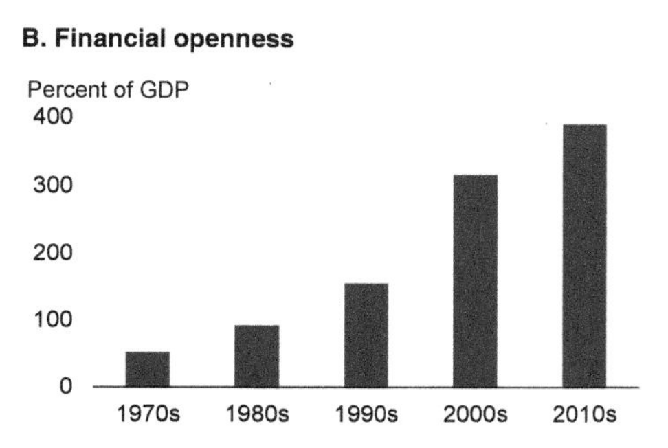

Sources: Feenstra, Inklaar, and Timmer (2015); International Monetary Fund; Lane and Milesi-Ferretti (2018); World Bank.
Note: Trade openness is the ratio of world exports and imports to world GDP. Financial openness is the sum of foreign assets and liabilities in percent of GDP across all countries. Each bar corresponds to the average in the decade indicated. The 2010s period refers to 2010-19, with estimates for 2019 based on data for the first two quarters.

- How do global recessions and recoveries vary across different groups of countries, particularly advanced economies, EMDEs, and low-income countries (LICs)?
- What happens during global expansions, and how does the current global expansion compare with previous ones?

Contributions. The chapter builds on an extensive literature on various aspects of global and national business cycles.[1] A branch of this research documents the growing importance of global business cycles in explaining national cycles. A second branch focuses on the roles played by trade and financial linkages in the cross-border transmission of business cycles. A third branch studies the turning points of the global business cycle and its phases.

Our study is closely related to Kose and Terrones (2015; KT going forward), who present the first detailed account of global recessions. KT mostly focus on global recessions and recoveries using annual data for 163 countries over 1960-2012. They present a detailed review of the relevant literature, analyze how financial crises lead to recessions, and examine the interactions between global and national cycles. Their work builds on Rogoff, Robinson, and Bayoumi (2002), who briefly examine whether the 2001 worldwide downturn was a global recession. That study focuses on movements in

[1] Most of the earlier studies in the literature focused on the dependence of EMDEs on advanced economies (for example, Chui et al. 2002; Currie and Vines 1988). For studies on the growing importance of the global business cycle, see Kose, Otrok, and Whiteman (2003, 2008) and Mumtaz, Simonelli, and Surico (2011). For transmission of cross-border business cycles, see Diebold and Yilmaz (2015); di Giovanni and Levchenko (2010); di Giovanni, Levchenko, and Mejean (2018); and Kose and Yi (2006). For the turning points of the global business cycle, see Camacho, Martinez-Martin (2015); Kose and Terrones (2015); and Martínez-García, Grossman, and Mack (2015). For forecasting global growth, see Cuba-Borda, Mechanick, and Raffo (2018); Ferrara and Marcilli (2019); Golinelli and Parigi (2014); and Rossiter (2010). Zarnowitz (1992) reviews earlier research program on business cycle fluctuations across countries.

per capita GDP growth to identify episodes that could be labeled as global recessions. It emphasizes the importance of statistical and judgmental approaches to identify the turning points of the global business cycle.

This chapter extends the literature in four dimensions. First, it covers a longer time span of annual series (1950-2018) and a larger set of economies (181). Second, the chapter is the first study that presents an analysis of the phases of the global business cycle with quarterly output series of 105 countries from 1960Q1 to 2019Q2. Third, it expands on the set of macroeconomic and financial variables that KT analyzed to present a broader perspective on the evolution of the global business cycle. Specifically, it analyzes the behavior of confidence, uncertainty, and measures of global financial conditions that have recently attracted increasing attention in research and policy circles. Fourth, it presents a detailed analysis of global expansions and puts the current global expansion in context by comparing it with previous such episodes.

Approach. This study, like KT, employs global real GDP per capita to track movements in the global business cycle. This variable is a primary indicator of global well-being that takes into account variations in population growth rates over time and across countries.

Turning points of the global business cycle are identified by means of two methods widely used in the analysis of national business cycles: a statistical method and a judgmental method. The former defines a global recession as taking place when there is a decline in annual global real GDP per capita. The judgmental method, similar to the method used for the United States by the Business Cycle Dating Committee of the National Bureau of Economic Research (NBER), considers whether there is strong evidence for a broad-based decline in multiple key indicators of global economic activity in a given year. This chapter focuses on six main global activity indicators: real GDP per capita, industrial production, trade, capital flows, oil consumption, and employment. These two methods together provide an intuitively appealing characterization of the turning points of the global business cycle and translate into a concrete definition of a global recession.

For the purposes of this study, and following KT, a global recession is defined as a contraction in global real GDP per capita accompanied by a broad decline in various other measures of global activity. The definition of a global recovery also closely follows the standard definition used in the context of national business cycles. The recovery phase is the period after the trough and defined here as the one- or three-year period following the trough of the cycle. The recovery is thus the earlier part of the expansion phase, which refers to the whole period between two recessions.

Main findings. In the seventy years since 1950, the world economy has experienced four global recessions: in 1975, 1982, 1991, and 2009. In each of these episodes, there was a contraction in annual real per capita global GDP and broad-based weakness in other key indicators of global economic activity. These episodes were highly synchronized internationally, involving severe economic and financial disruptions in many countries around the world. The 2009 global recession was by far the deepest and most synchronized episode among the four.

- *Global recoveries.* A global recovery usually involves a broad-based rebound in macroeconomic and financial activity. Among the four episodes, the strongest recovery occurred after the 1975 recession. Thanks to large, prompt, and globally coordinated policy support, the recovery following the 2009 recession was the second-strongest.

- *Impact across country groups and regions.* The impact of global recessions varied across different groups of countries. Average per capita growth declined more in advanced economies than in EMDEs during global recessions. LICs on average suffered larger declines in per capita growth than did the average EMDE. The East Asia and Pacific (EAP) and South Asia (SAR) regions even continued expanding during global recessions. The other four EMDE regions, particularly those with more reliance on exports of industrial commodities, experienced per capita output declines.

- *Relatively good performance of EMDEs during the latest global recession.* As the epicenter of the financial crisis, advanced economies felt the brunt of the 2009 global recession. In contrast, EMDE output growth remained positive during the recession, and EMDEs delivered a stronger recovery after 2009 than after any of the three previous episodes. LICs were able to continue growing during the most recent global recession whereas their per capita growth had plummeted in the previous episodes.

- *Global expansions.* The duration of the global expansions varied, with a minimum of six years (following the 1975 recession) and a maximum of 17 years (following the 1991 recession). The latest global expansion registered average per capita growth comparable with that of previous episodes. The post-2009 expansion was the weakest of the four in advanced economies, because many of them struggled to overcome the legacies of the global financial crisis. Among EMDEs, the recovery of per capita output growth has been exceptionally robust, despite a gradual slowdown after 2012.

- *Policies.* Monetary and fiscal policies often became expansionary going into global recessions, and they have typically supported the ensuing global recoveries. Following the 2009 global recession, monetary policy remained highly accommodative for most of the 2010s, with advanced economy central banks introducing a wide range of unconventional measures to ease credit. After the initial implementation of large, coordinated, fiscal stimulus programs during 2008-09, however, advanced economies withdrew fiscal support, out of concerns for the growth of public debt, and government expenditures fell after 2010. By contrast, EMDEs have generally employed expansionary fiscal and monetary policies during the current expansion, while adjusting the settings of their monetary policy instruments in response to cyclical conditions.

The remainder of this chapter is organized as follows. The following section introduces the database and methodology. It is followed by a discussion of the identification of the turning points of the global business cycle and a summary of the main events associated with each global recession. The next section documents the main features of global recessions, recoveries and expansions. The last section concludes with a discussion of results and future research directions.

Identification of turning points of the global business cycle

Database. Multiple data sources are employed to construct world GDP growth at annual and quarterly frequencies over a long period. The annual GDP series covers 181 economies—36 advanced economies and 145 EMDEs—over the period 1950-2018, though the country sample size varies by year. The quarterly series covers 105 economies over the period 1960Q1-2019Q2.[2] In addition to data on GDP growth, a wide range of measures of global economic and financial activity are employed. Indicators of economic activity include trade, industrial production, unemployment, and oil consumption. Financial variables include capital flows, credit, equity and house prices, inflation, short-term nominal and real interest rates, and an index of broad financial conditions. In light of their roles in determining activity, some additional series, such as indicators of uncertainty and confidence, are also examined. Annex 2B presents the list of countries, and annex 2C includes a summary of all variables in the database with their definitions, coverage, and sources.

Measure of the global business cycle. The main measure of the global business cycle is the growth rate of world real GDP per capita.[3] Real GDP per capita is considered as a primary measure of average economic well-being because it takes into account differences in population growth. The difference between per capita GDP growth rates in advanced economies and EMDEs is generally smaller than the difference between their aggregate GDP growth rates.[4]

The growth rate of world real GDP is a weighted average of national real GDP growth rates. Two types of weights are employed: market exchange rate weights and purchasing power parity (PPP) weights. The baseline results refer to market exchange rate weights, which are calculated as national GDP measured in domestic currencies, converted into U.S. dollar terms using market exchange rates, as a share of world GDP in U.S. dollar terms. Global trade and transactions in financial markets are conducted at market exchange rates, and the baseline specification uses this weighting scheme.

PPP exchange rates are calculated as the rates at which the currency of one country would have to be converted into the currency of another to equalize the values of a

[2] In addition to historical growth data, annual growth forecasts for 2019-20 are included in the database. Forecasts are taken from the World Bank's Global Economic Prospects report, which covers 181 economies. The quarterly data collected begin in 1950Q1, but data availability is quite limited during the 1950s, so data before 1960 were excluded.

[3] Hamilton (2019) develops a monthly indicator of global activity, based in the industrial production for countries in the Organisation for Economic Co-operation and Development (OECD) plus Brazil, China, India, Indonesia, the Russian Federation, and South Africa.

[4] Over the period 1950-2018, average GDP growth rate was 3.3 percent for advanced economies and 4.7 percent for EMDEs. Population growth in EMDEs (1.8 percent) was also higher than in advanced economies (0.8 percent) over 1950-2018. Per capita output growth was then, on average, 2.4 percent in advanced economies and 2.8 percent in EMDEs.

common and broadly defined basket of goods and services. PPP exchange rates differ from market exchange rates particularly because goods and services that are not traded internationally tend to be cheaper in lower-income countries than in higher-income countries. As a result, the value of output in lower-income countries tends to be relatively greater using PPP than using market exchange rates (Callen 2007). Thus, PPP weights, which are calculated as national GDP valued at PPP as a share of world GDP, tend to be higher for lower-income countries than do market exchange rate weights. As growth in lower-income countries tends to be greater than that in higher-income countries, global GDP growth is often higher with PPP weights than with market weights.[5]

For measuring living standards and aggregating welfare, PPP weights are more appropriate because they capture the amount of consumption affordable to households for comparable consumption baskets. Whereas PPP weights capture the fact that some goods are cheaper in lower-income countries, market rates capture how much an economy could "buy" in global markets. Hence, weights based on market exchange rates are used here to provide the baseline measure of economic size (Cooper 2014; Frankel 2014).

Methodology. Two approaches are employed to identify the turning points of the global business cycle: a statistical method and a judgmental method. The methods are complementary but employ different information sets. Both follow the "classical" definition of a business cycle (Burns and Mitchell 1946), under which business cycle expansions are marked by increases in many measures of economic activity, and contractions by broad declines in activity. Both are widely used in the context of national business cycles and often arrive at similar turning points.

The statistical dating method used here was introduced by Harding and Pagan (2002).[6] The method is convenient because the turning points identified are robust to the inclusion of newly available data. The method makes it possible to identify global recessions, defined as taking place when the annual growth rate of per capita global real GDP is negative. Per capita real GDP growth alone, however, may not be sufficient as an indicator of the cyclical evolution of economic activity. For this reason, the Business Cycle Dating Committees of the U.S. NBER and the Europe-based Centre for Economic Policy Research (CEPR) employ broad sets of economic indicators and apply a "judgmental method" to identify the turning points of national or regional cycles.

---

[5] For example, the average annual growth rate of world GDP over the period 1950-2018 was 3.7 percent or 4.0 percent, using market weights and PPP weights, respectively. Average annual global GDP growth over the past 20 years was 2.9 percent with market weights and 3.7 percent with PPP weights. In per capita terms, average annual GDP growth was 1.7 percent with market weights and 2.5 percent with PPP weights.

[6] It extends the algorithm developed by Bry and Boschan (1971), to identify the turning points in the log of per capita GDP (refer to Kose, Sugawara, and Terrones 2020 for details). This dating algorithm is widely used to identify the turning points of business and financial cycles (Claessens, Kose, and Terrones 2009, 2011, and 2012; Grjebine, Szczerbowicz, and Tripier 2018; Harding and Pagan 2016; Herman, Igan, and Solé 2017; Meller and Metiu 2017; Pagan and Sossounov 2003). Other methodologies consider how a variable fluctuates around its trend, but the estimation of trend is sensitive to sample period.

The judgmental method involves analyzing a broad set of macroeconomic indicators and reaching a judgment on whether the evidence points to expansion or recession. The NBER uses this method to determine the dates of cyclical turning points, expansions, and recessions in the U.S. economy; and the CEPR does so for the euro area. The NBER examines, for example, movements in real GDP, industrial production, retail sales, employment, and disposable income; it states that "[the] Committee does not have a fixed definition of economic activity" (NBER 2020). Because different indicators can exhibit conflicting signals about the direction of activity, the judgmental method may not be straightforward to apply in real time. The CEPR's task may be considered even more complex than that of the NBER because it has to determine cyclical conditions in the multicountry context of the euro area.

The judgmental method is applied at the global level through analysis of a selected set of indicators of global activity—movements in real GDP per capita, industrial production, trade, capital flows, oil consumption, and unemployment. Some of the variables used by the NBER and CEPR are not available for a large enough number of countries over a sufficiently long period. The measures employed here, however, capture the essentials of the information supplied by the country-specific variables used by these institutions. Moreover, they provide a reasonably comprehensive perspective on the evolution of the global business cycle. In addition to the standard activity measures, such as GDP, industrial production, and unemployment, other variables capture the changes in global commerce and finance (trade and capital flows) and global energy consumption (oil consumption).

Using these two methods, a global recession is defined as an annual contraction in world real per capita GDP accompanied by a broad decline in various other measures of global economic activity. A global recession begins just after the world economy reaches a peak of activity and ends when it reaches its trough. The recovery is defined as the early part of the expansion phase.[7] The recovery phase is often considered to be the first year following the trough of the business cycle; however, to obtain a broader understanding, developments in the first three years following a global recession are also examined. The global expansion phase is the period between the end of one recession and the beginning of the next one.

Global recessions and recoveries: Dates and events

Turning points of the global business cycle

Global recessions. The baseline statistical method identifies four declines (troughs) in annual real global per capita GDP, using market exchange rate weights, since 1950—in

[7] In the context of national cycles, a number of studies examine the dynamics of recoveries (see Balke and Wynne 1995; Bec, Bouabdallah, and Ferrara 2015; Eckstein and Sinai 1986; Graetz and Michaels 2017; Mussa 2009; Stock and Watson 2012). Some studies focus on business cycles of subnational entities, such as U.S. states (Francis, Jackson, and Owyang 2018; Owyang, Piger, and Wall 2005). Hausmann, Rodríguez, and Wagner (2006) define the recovery as the time it takes for output to rebound from its trough to its peak level before the recession, whereas Cerra, Panizza, and Saxena (2013) assume that the recovery is the year of positive growth immediately after a sequence of years with negative growth. Others associate the recovery with growth achieved after a certain time period, such as four or six quarters, following the trough (Calderón and Fuentes 2014; Sichel 1994).

FIGURE 2.3 Evolution of world output and world output per capita

World per capita output declined during the four global recessions.

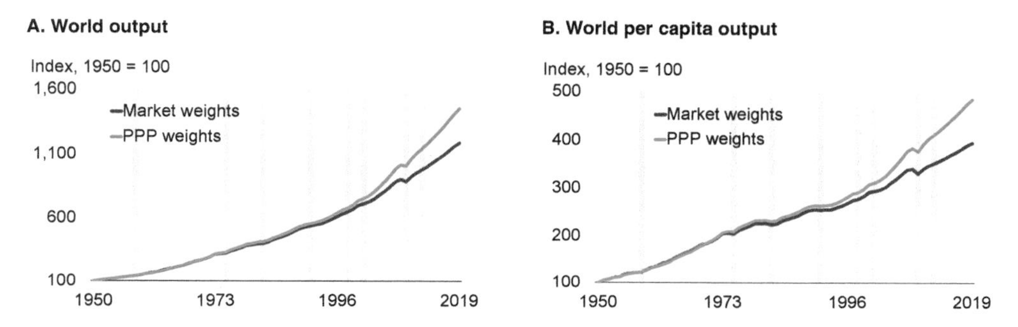

Sources: Feenstra, Inklaar, and Timmer (2015); Kose and Terrones (2015); World Bank.
Note: Shaded areas indicate global recessions in 1975, 1982, 1991, and 2009, and global downturns in 1958, 1998, 2001, and 2012. PPP = purchasing power parity.

1975, 1982, 1991, and 2009 (figure 2.3). The use of PPP weights rather than market exchange rate weights does not affect the dates of the troughs. With market exchange rate weights, which are tilted toward advanced economies, global per capita GDP growth is lower especially during global recessions when many advanced economies experience synchronized contractions in activity (figure 2.4). With both sets of weights, the dates of peaks in the global business cycle are found to be 1974, 1981, 1990, and 2008, with the annual data showing each global recession lasting just one year.[8]

Some employ the definition of global recession that relies on a simple threshold (The Economist 2001, 2008). The findings here suggest that it is misleading to employ a simple growth threshold (such as below 2.5 percent annual growth in global GDP) to identify global recessions. For example, if one assumes that a global recession takes place whenever world real GDP growth with market (PPP) weights is less than 2.5 percent, there are 16 (11) global recessions over the period 1950-2018 (figure 2.4). If per capita growth rates with market (PPP) weights are used and the threshold is 1 percent, then 14 (11) global recessions are identified over the same period. The annual growth of world real GDP needs to fall below 1.1 percent to register a contraction in per capita GDP given the population growth in 2018, but, of course, population growth is time variant with substantial changes from one decade to another.[9]

The judgmental method is applied at the global level by looking at movements in several indicators of global activity—real GDP per capita, industrial production, trade, capital flows, oil consumption, and employment. This method also results in the same four

[8] This finding echoes the results from the literature on national recessions. For example, Claessens, Kose, and Terrones (2012) report that the average duration of roughly 250 recessions in advanced economies and EMDEs since 1960 is about one year.

[9] Global population growth has slowed by 0.7 percentage point since the 1950s to 1.2 percent a year over 2010-18.

FIGURE 2.4 Growth of world output

Each recession saw a contraction in per capita world output, but the 2009 recession was the only one with a decline in world output.

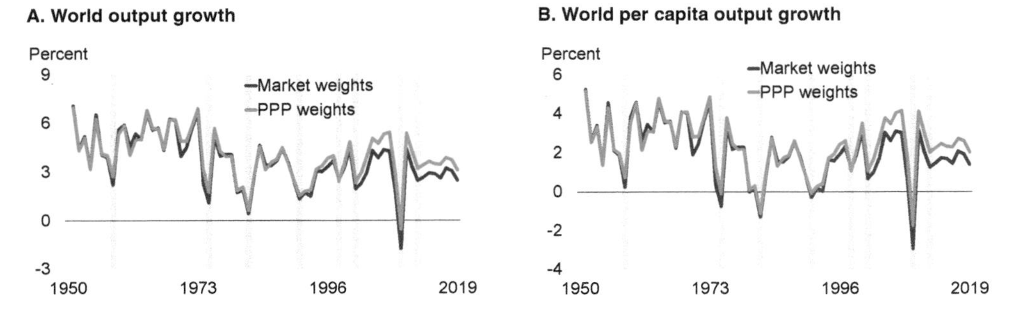

Sources: Feenstra, Inklaar, and Timmer (2015); Kose and Terrones (2015); World Bank.
Note: Shaded areas indicate global recessions in 1975, 1982, 1991, and 2009, and global downturns in 1958, 1998, 2001, and 2012. PPP = purchasing power parity.

dates as the years of global recessions: most of these indicators point to an obvious contraction in global economic activity in these years, after a peak in the preceding year. The behavior of the indicators during the global recessions is discussed below.

The turning points of the global business cycle identified using the quarterly data are consistent with those from the annual data series. The statistical approach identifies four global recessions in the quarterly series since 1960, including 1974Q1-1975Q1, 1981Q4-1982Q3, 1990Q4-1991Q1, and 2008Q3-2009Q1 (figure 2.5; table 2A.1). With the quarterly data, the average duration of global recessions was slightly less than one year. In addition to these four recession episodes, global per capita output contracted in 1970Q4 (-0.7 percent), 1980Q2 (-4.8 percent), 1981Q2 (-0.3 percent), 1998Q1 (-0.3 percent), and 2001Q3 (-0.6 percent).[10] These contractions lasted for only a quarter without translating into global recessions. Some of these short-lived global contractions, however, were associated with recessions in major economies that took place ahead of global recessions (1982) or coincided with global downturns (1998 and 2001).[11]

[10] Global quarterly per capita growth is measured as the difference between quarter-on-quarter annualized growth of seasonally adjusted real GDP, aggregated with market weights, and annual population growth (annex 2C). For details about the database, see Kose, Sugawara, and Terrones (2020).

[11] The United States experienced a recession in 1969Q4-1970Q4 with per capita GDP contracting by more than 5 percent in 1970Q4. This recession coincided with one in Japan (where per capita growth dropped to negative 2.7 percent). Per capita output in the Unites States contracted by about 9 percent in 1980Q2, whereas a number of advanced economies also experienced contractions, including Japan (with a contraction in per capita output of about 4 percent) and the United Kingdom (with a decline of about 8 percent). Over 1960-2019, world per capita output growth was close to but above zero in several quarters because of contractions in some major economies, for example in 1960Q4 (contraction in the United States with expansions in other major economies), 1963Q1 (contractions in France, Germany, and the Netherlands), 1987Q1 (Germany), and 1989Q2 (Japan).

FIGURE 2.5 Growth of world output, quarterly

The dates of global recessions based on the quarterly per capita GDP series are consistent with those identified with the annual series.

A. World output growth

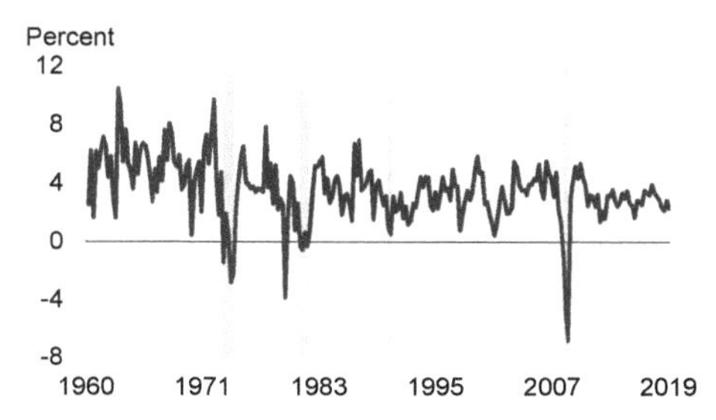

B. World per capita output growth

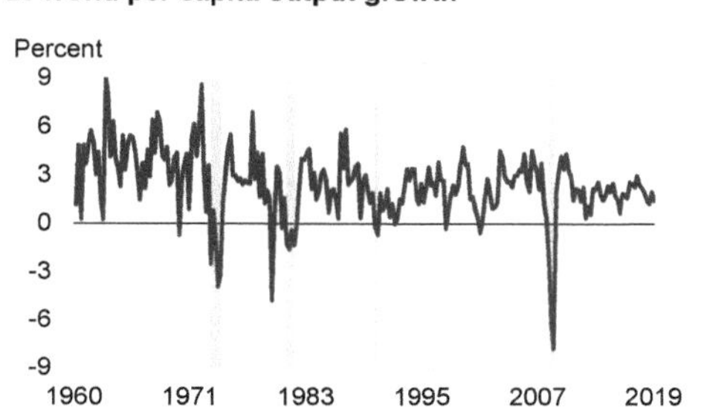

Sources: Feenstra, Inklaar, and Timmer (2015); Haver Analytics; Organisation for Economic Co-operation and Development; World Bank.

Note: Shaded areas show global recessions, which are identified using per capita output data and the algorithm in Harding and Pagan (2002). Last observation is 2019Q2. Refer to annex 2C for details.

Global downturns. In addition to the four global recessions, the global economy experienced low growth in 1958, 1998, 2001, and 2012: in these four years, the global economy registered its lowest growth rates of the past seven decades, except for the years of global recession and the two years before and after each of them.[12] World output per capita grew by slightly less than 1 percent a year, on average, over these four downturns (table 2A.2). These downturns fall short of qualifying as global recessions because world real GDP per capita did not contract and there was no broad-based weakness in multiple indicators of global activity.

In 1958, global growth was weak because of low growth or outright recessions in several major economies, including the United States and some European economies (Federal Reserve Board 1958; United Nations 1959).[13] In the United States, monetary policy was tightened to control inflation (Eckstein and Sinai 1986; Romer and Romer 2012). In some European countries, also, domestic demand weakened as policy measures to contain inflationary pressures were implemented. Growth in other parts of the world, however, remained resilient.

In 1997-98, economic activity in many EMDEs, particularly those in Asia, weakened sharply. In fact, the global economy experienced a contraction in per capita GDP in 1998Q1 as the East Asian financial crisis took a heavy toll on emerging market

[12] The statistical method identifies the local minimum in each episode. There were years in which global growth was lower than in the years of global downturns, but those years were always within two years before or after these recession and downturn episodes (for example, 1980).

[13] In 1958, per capita GDP contracted in the United States (by 2.4 percent), Canada (by 1 percent), and several European countries (for example, Belgium, by 1.2 percent; the Netherlands, by 2.4 percent; Switzerland, by 3.5 percent; and the United Kingdom, by 0.1 percent). Per capita growth was strong in other parts of the world, including Australia (4.6 percent), Germany (3.7 percent), Italy (4.1 percent), and Japan (5.3 percent).

economies in the region. The world economy did not experience a recession in 1998, however, because growth in advanced economies held up.

In 2001, many advanced economies experienced mild slowdowns or recessions: global per capita output declined in 2001Q3, when per capita growth turned negative in a number of advanced economies, including the United States (-2.7 percent, annualized) and Japan (-4.2 percent, annualized). Growth in some major EMDEs, such as China and India, remained robust, helping the global economy escape a recession.

The 2012 global downturn was mainly driven by the euro area debt crisis.[14] Although world per capita output did not contract in any of the quarters of 2012, growth was very low (0.4 percent in 2012Q2). The global economy was supported by growth in the United States and some major EMDEs.

During these four global downturns, the behavior of other global indicators was mixed, again implying that these episodes do not qualify as global recessions. For example, industrial production, trade, and consumption did not suggest a broad-based weakness in the global economy in 1998. In 2001, although industrial production fell and the rate of global unemployment picked up slightly—and although equity prices and business confidence declined sharply and policy uncertainty increased significantly following the 9/11 terrorist attacks—both global trade flows and oil consumption continued increasing. During the 2012 global downturn, some activity indicators did not show much weakness, but capital flows slowed, equity prices collapsed, and inflation declined.

The U.S. economy during global recessions and downturns. Although the four global recessions coincided with recessions in the United States, not every U.S. recession was associated with a global recession. In fact, the United States experienced six additional recessions during 1950-2019, including recessions in 1958 and 2001 that coincided with global downturns. But its economy grew strongly during the 1998 global downturn and, to a lesser extent, during the 2012 global downturn.[15]

Events surrounding the global recessions

The four global recessions identified above were all characterized by severe economic and financial disruptions in many countries around the world. But each recession had its own unique features.[16] In particular, the shocks that contributed to the global recessions

[14] Some euro area countries experienced financial crisis (Greece in 2012 and Cyprus in 2011-13), and some others went through periods of fiscal distress (Ireland and Portugal) (Laeven and Valencia 2018; Medas et al. 2018). A number of other euro area countries also registered relatively low economic growth during this period. The euro area recorded its lowest output growth (-0.9 percent) since 2009. Indeed, CEPR identifies the period 2011Q3 to 2013Q1 as a recession in the area.

[15] Average per capita GDP growth in the United States during the global recessions and global downturns identified previously was -2.1 percent and 0.6 percent a year, respectively. Whereas U.S. per capita output contracted in the 1958 global downturn (by 2.4 percent) and was virtually stable in 2001, it expanded in 1998 and 2012 (by 3.2 percent in the former case and 1.4 percent in the latter).

[16] The events surrounding these episodes are discussed in detail by Allen (2009), Knoop (2004), Kose and Terrones (2015), and Reinhart and Rogoff (2009). Baffes et al. (2015), Barsky and Kilian (2004), and Hamilton (2013) present surveys of the history of oil shocks and the associated economic downturns.

were different. The 1975 global recession was driven mainly by a global supply shock—the oil price shock of 1973-74. The 1982 episode followed a series of shocks, including the oil price shock of 1979; the subsequent rise in global inflation; monetary policy responses to that increase in inflation, especially the marked monetary tightening by the U.S. Federal Reserve; and the Latin American debt crisis.

Similarities also exist, however, across the global recessions, including in their origins. A number of countries experienced financial crises during the four global recessions.[17] In the 1991 global recession, a wide range of national shocks were transmitted across borders, including financial disruptions and exchange rate crises in some advanced economies, especially in Europe, and a major shift in political and economic systems in many Eastern European countries. The 2009 episode originated mainly from problems in the U.S. financial sector that started to become evident in 2007. These problems rapidly propagated to other advanced economies and some EMDEs through trade and financial linkages.

The global recession of 1975 followed the shock to world oil prices from the Arab oil embargo initiated in October 1973. Although the embargo ended in March 1974, the supply shock and associated sharp rise in oil prices triggered a substantial increase in inflation and a significant weakening of growth in a number of countries. Monetary and fiscal policy easing, especially by some major advanced economies, helped spur a rebound of growth in 1976. Five of the Group of Seven (G7) countries—Canada, France, Italy, the United Kingdom, and the United States—however, experienced persistent and high inflation, and the 1975 global recession was the beginning of a half-decade of stagflation, with low output growth and high inflation (Knoop 2004).[18]

The global recession of 1982 was triggered by several developments, including the second oil shock of 1979, a tightening of monetary policies in the United States and other advanced economies, and the Latin American debt crisis. Oil prices rose sharply in 1979, partly owing to disruptions caused by the Iranian revolution, and helped push inflation to new highs in several advanced economies. Partly in response, monetary policies were tightened significantly in several major advanced economies, including Germany, Italy, Japan, the United Kingdom, and the United States, causing sharp declines in activity and significant increases in unemployment rates in many cases in 1982-83. The increase in global interest rates and a collapse in commodity prices that stemmed from the weakening of global growth made it difficult for many Latin American countries to service their debts, resulting in debt crises in the region. Advanced economies were generally able to begin their recoveries relatively quickly, although unemployment in some cases remained relatively high. But the debt crisis

[17] Financial crises—including banking, currency, and sovereign debt crises—took place in 15, 62, 67, and 38 economies during the 1975, 1982, 1991, and 2009 global recessions, including the two years before and after the recession years (see Laeven and Valencia 2018). Most of the financial crises in the 1975 global recession were currency crises in EMDEs, whereas Chile and Spain experienced systemic banking crises.

[18] The other two G7 economies are Germany and Japan. By 1980, immediately after the second oil shock, inflation had risen to levels higher than those seen after the first oil shock in all G7 countries except Japan and the United Kingdom, while inflation in Germany remained relatively moderate.

contributed to long-lasting growth slowdowns in many EMDEs, especially in Latin America and the Caribbean (LAC) and Sub-Saharan Africa (SSA).

The 1991 global recession also resulted from the confluence of a wide range of factors (Perry and Schultze 1993). The 1990-91 Gulf War was associated with heightened geopolitical uncertainty and another sharp increase in oil prices. In the United States, widespread weakness of lending institutions, evident since the mid-1980s, weighed on the housing market, especially during the credit crunch of 1990-91 (Bernanke and Lown 1991; Hall 1993). Scandinavian countries had severe banking crises in the early 1990s, following the liberalization of financial sectors and rapid expansion in credit markets in the 1980s. In Europe, problems with the European Monetary System's exchange rate mechanism (ERM) in 1992 were accompanied by sharp declines in activity in many member countries. In Japan, the bursting of an asset price bubble resulted in a recession and a prolonged period of low growth and near-zero inflation. In Central and Eastern Europe and the former USSR, the transition to market economies was accompanied by high inflation and output contractions.

The 2009 global recession followed the worst financial crisis since the Great Depression. The crisis started in mid-2007 in major advanced economies, and followed a period of loosening regulation and supervision of financial markets and institutions, asset price and credit booms in a number of countries, and the rapid expansion of high-risk lending, particularly in U.S. mortgage markets. The collapse of Lehman Brothers, in September 2008, triggered a full-blown financial and macroeconomic crisis. Although the initial trigger for the crisis was the U.S. mortgage markets, the high degree of interconnectedness between U.S. and other financial markets caused the crisis to spread to other advanced economies and some EMDEs. Banking crises erupted in many European countries in 2008, causing financial crises in the euro area in 2011-13. These events caused sharp asset price declines and severe credit crunches, a collapse in global trade, and highly synchronized recessions in a record number of countries around the world. As discussed in the next section, however, with the exception of some of those in the Europe and Central Asia (ECA) region, EMDEs weathered the 2009 global recession relatively well.

Synchronization of national recessions

Global recessions are highly synchronized events internationally. The fraction of countries in recession increased during the four global recessions (figure 2.6). The GDP-weighted fraction of countries in recession was about 50 percent in the first three global recessions, but rose to slightly more than 80 percent in the latest episode. The unweighted fraction of countries in recession reached local peaks during the global recession years. For example, it was about 60 percent during the 2009 episode.[19] In all

[19] Imbs (2010), using monthly industrial production data, concludes that the degree of cross-country business cycle correlation during the latest recession was the highest over the past three decades. Other research also indicates that shocks originating in credit markets have been influential in driving global activity during global recessions, including the 2009 episode (Bacchetta and van Wincoop 2016; Eickmeier and Ng 2015; Helbling et al. 2011; Perri and Quadrini 2018).

FIGURE 2.6 International synchronization of recessions

Global recessions are highly synchronized events, with many countries experiencing contractions in national per capita GDP.

A. Countries in recession, weighted

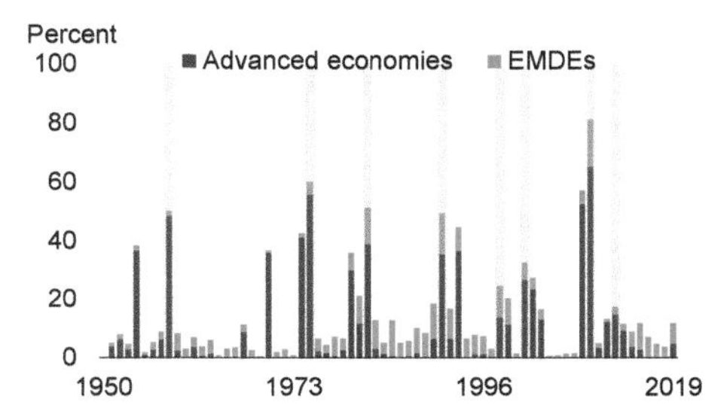

B. Countries in recession, unweighted

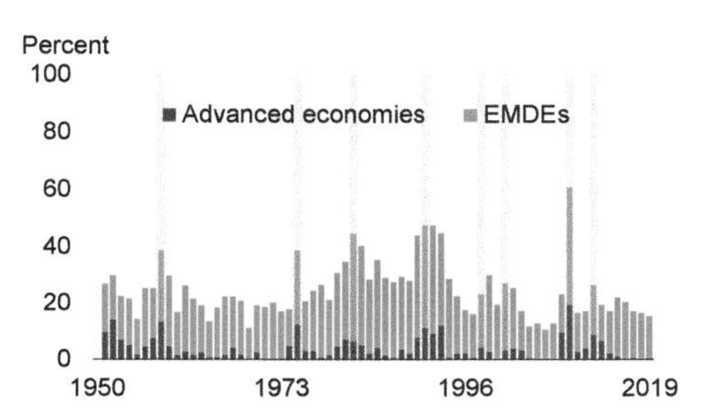

Sources: Feenstra, Inklaar, and Timmer (2015); Kose and Terrones (2015); World Bank.
Note: Shaded areas indicate global recessions in 1975, 1982, 1991, and 2009, and global downturns in 1958, 1998, 2001, and 2012. Recessions are defined as a contraction in per capita GDP. EMDEs = emerging market and developing economies.
A. Weighted by GDP at 2010 prices and market exchange rates.

four global recessions, the fraction of countries in recession started picking up ahead of the recession year.

The number of countries in recession was often relatively low two to three years before each global recession. The 2006-07 period stands out for the historically low number of countries in recession, but this was followed by a sharp reversal of fortune. In 2009, almost all advanced economies (35 out of 36) and roughly half of EMDEs were in recession. The degree of international synchronicity in the last global recession was the highest in the past 70 years, possibly reflecting the unusual depth of the global financial crisis and much stronger international trade and financial linkages than in earlier episodes.

Main features of global recessions, recoveries, and expansions

Global recessions

The behavior of the main macroeconomic and financial variables displays a number of regularities during the four global recessions. The 2009 global recession, which saw by far the largest declines in many indicators of activity, otherwise followed a pattern broadly similar to the previous episodes. The impact of these episodes often varied across different groups of countries and regions.

Sharp contraction in real activity. In the four global recessions, per capita global output (market exchange rate weighted) declined on average by 1.3 percent, which is 3.5 percentage points below the average annual growth rate of 2.2 percent during the 1950-

2018 expansion years (table 2A.3). With PPP weights, the decline in per capita output during global recessions was, on average, 0.8 percent, whereas growth during expansion years was 2.5 percent.

Among the four global recessions, the 2009 episode was by far the deepest. It involved the only annual contraction in real global GDP since 1950.[20] The least severe episode in terms of per capita output growth was the 1991 recession. Average annual growth of output over the four global recession episodes was 0.3 percent, about 3.6 percentage points lower than average world growth during expansion years (3.9 percent).

World per capita output, industrial production, trade, and oil consumption often started to slow down two years before the global recessions (figure 2.7.A). Moreover, investment, industrial production, and trade typically declined much more than output during the global recessions. Although private consumption generally held up relatively well, its growth was much weaker than in nonrecession years. Oil consumption declined in every global recession except the 1991 episode.[21]

Depressed financial markets and business confidence. Asset prices and credit on average began decelerating about two years ahead of each global recession (figure 2.7.B). The average annual rate of credit growth during the global recessions was about two-fifths of the annual average observed in nonrecession years, and both house and equity prices fell, with the decline in the former on average three times larger than in the latter. Financial conditions often tightened before the global recessions but then quickly loosened as monetary policy became accommodative. Inflation typically fell during global recessions, which gave further license for central banks to reduce interest rates (figure 2.7.C).

The behavior of real interest rates varied widely across the episodes. For example, real rates declined in the 1991 and 2009 episodes, but went up during the 1975 and 1982 recessions. Business confidence fell in all global recession episodes. Economic policy uncertainty increased during the two episodes—1991 and 2009—for which data are available (Baker and Bloom 2013; Caldara et al. 2019).

Differences across country groups. The impact of global recessions has varied across different groups of countries and regions (table 2A.4). In advanced economies, average per capita growth fell to -1.1 percent during the global recession years, from 2.7 percent during nonrecession years. In EMDEs, the decline was to 0.2 percent from 3 percent (LICs on average suffered larger declines in per capita growth than did other EMDEs). Thus, the drop in growth was 1 percentage point greater for advanced economies than for EMDEs. In addition, both trade and industrial production registered much larger contractions in advanced economies than in EMDEs.

---

[20] On the basis of the quarterly data, average annual per capita output growth in the four global recessions was -2.4 percent (table 2A.1). The deepest recession is again seen to be that of 2009 and the least severe that of 1991: average annual growth rates in the four recessions were -1.9 percent (1974Q1-1975Q1), -1.2 percent (1981Q4-1982Q3), -0.5 percent (1990Q4-1991Q1), and -5.4 percent (2008Q3-2009Q1). Per capita growth was negative in each quarter of the four recessions, except in 1974Q2 when growth picked up to 0.8 percent for one quarter only.

[21] Oil consumption declined in only 9 years of the past 70. These episodes coincided with the global recessions or were within two years before or after them.

FIGURE 2.7.A Economic activity during global recessions

Global recessions have been associated with broad-based declines in multiple measures of economic activity.

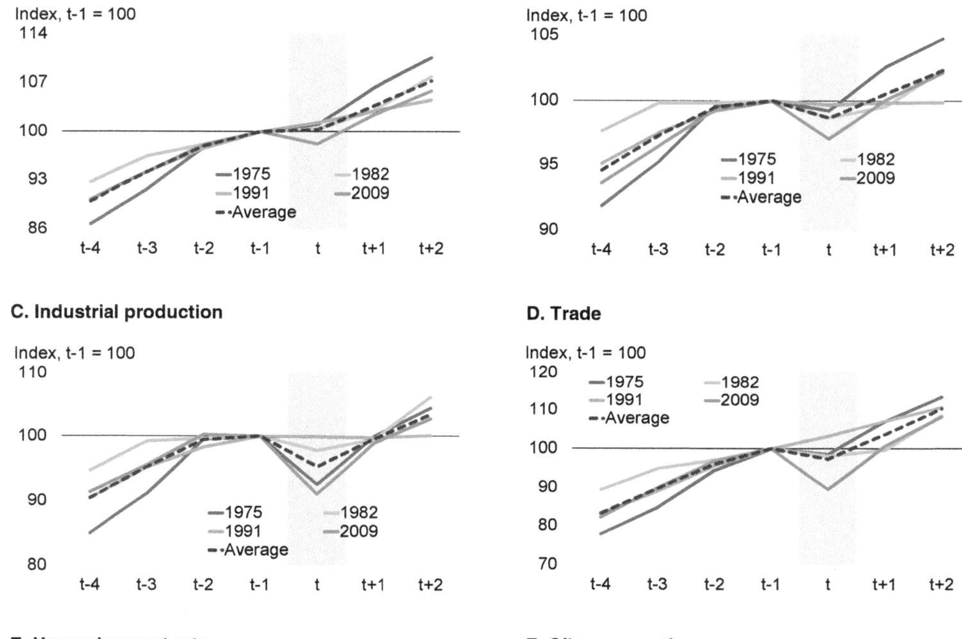

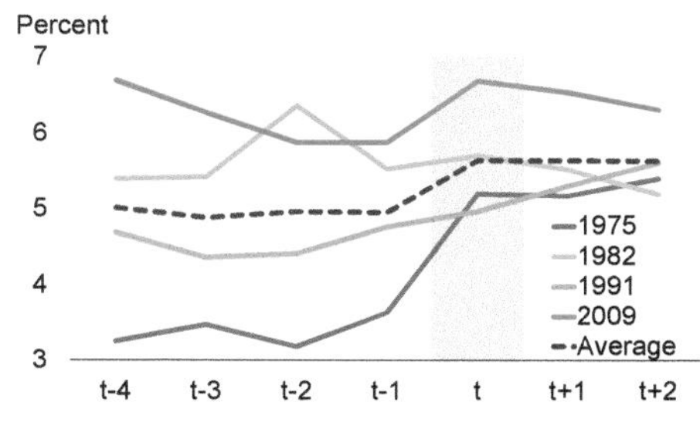

F. Oil consumption

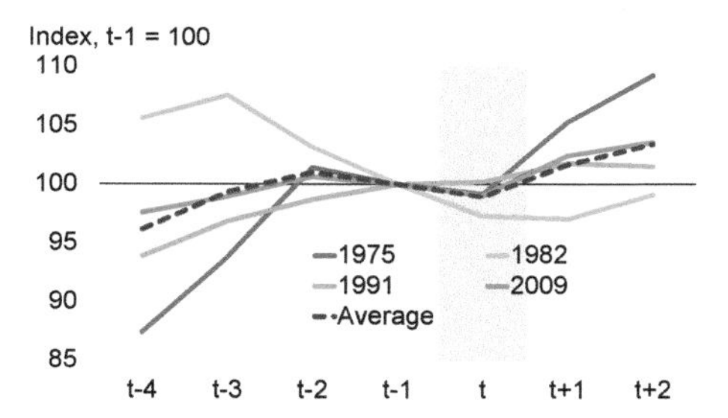

Sources: British Petroleum; Feenstra, Inklaar, and Timmer (2015); Haver Analytics; International Monetary Fund; Kose and Terrones (2015); Organisation for Economic Co-operation and Development; World Bank.

Note: Year "t" denotes the year of the respective global recessions (shaded in gray). Average refers to an average of four global recessions with available data. Output, output per capita, industrial production, trade, and oil consumption are index numbers equal to 100 one year before year "t" (that is, t-1 = 100). Aggregates for output, output per capita, and industrial production are market-weighted. Refer to annex 2C for details.

Some EMDE regions have been able to weather global recessions better than others. For example, the EAP and SAR regions continued expanding during the past four global recessions whereas the other four regions all on average experienced declines in per capita output (though aggregate output continued growing, on average, in LAC and SSA). One explanation for this outcome is that, whereas EAP and SAR mostly comprise relatively fast-growing commodity importers (including the large economies of China in

FIGURE 2.7.B Financial markets during global recessions

Substantial declines in financial markets have been a common feature of global recessions. As activity slowed, inflation often fell.

A. Capital flows

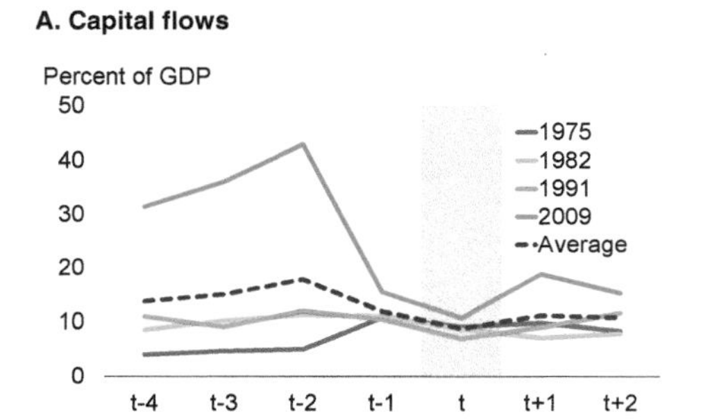

B. Credit

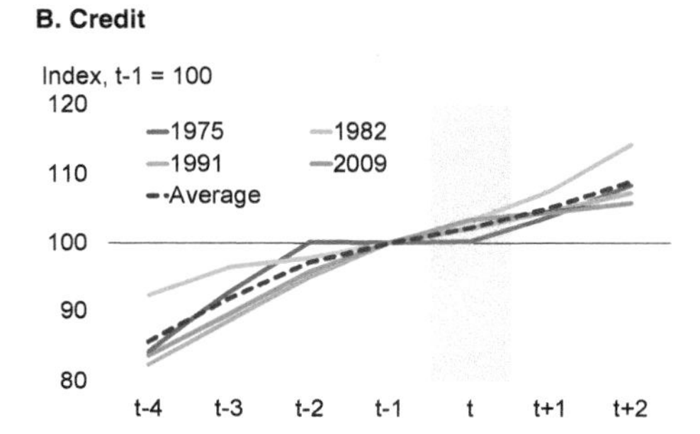

C. Equity prices

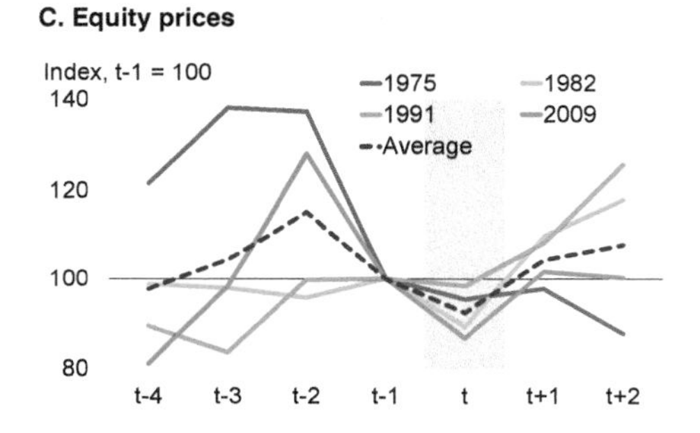

D. House prices

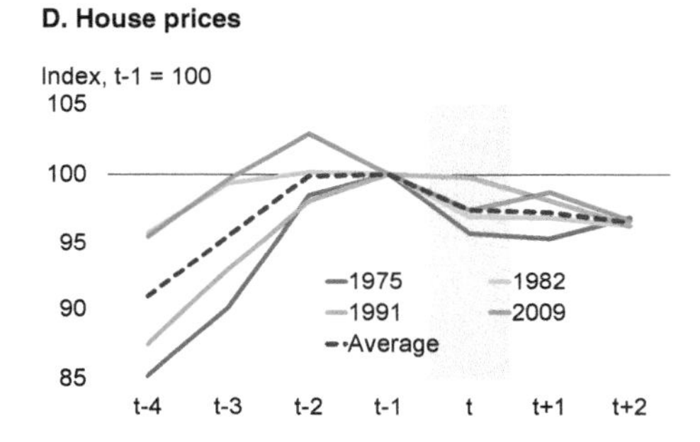

E. Financial conditions

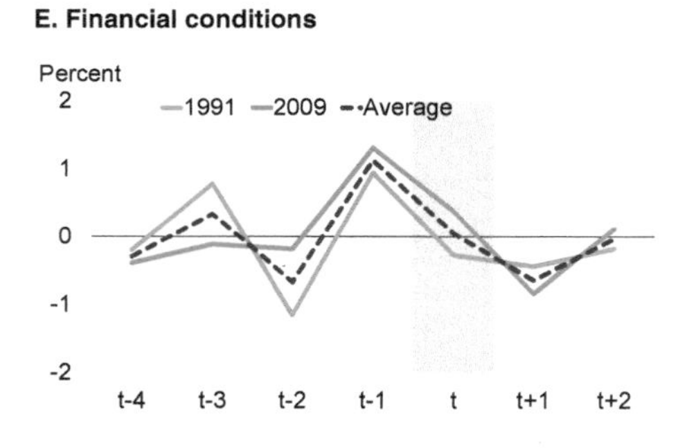

F. Inflation

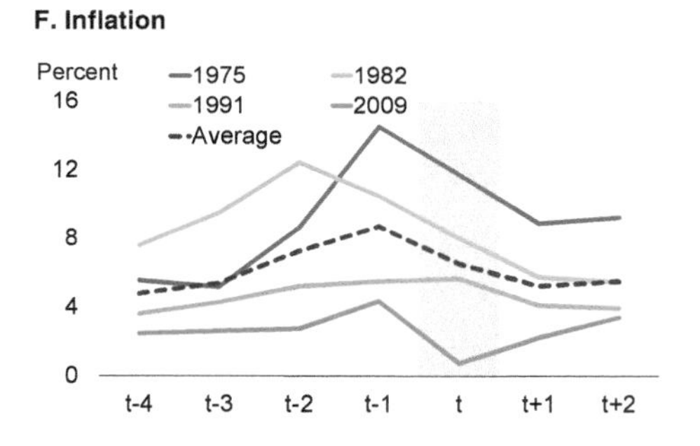

Sources: Bank for International Settlements; Bloomberg; Haver Analytics; International Monetary Fund; Kose and Terrones (2015); Organisation for Economic Co-operation and Development; World Bank.

Note: Year "t" denotes the year of the respective global recessions (shaded in gray). Average refers to an average of four global recessions with available data. Equity prices, house prices, financial conditions, and inflation are weighted by GDP in U.S. dollars. Credit, equity prices, and house prices are index numbers equal to 100 one year before year "t" (that is, t-1 = 100). Refer to annex 2C for details.

EAP and India in SAR), the other four regions consist more of commodity exporters that have been severely affected by the collapses in demand for commodities associated with global recessions.

The 2009 recession. The unusually sharp declines in a wide range of economic indicators, especially growth in both aggregate and per capita global output, highlight

FIGURE 2.7.C Interest rates, confidence, and uncertainty during global recessions

Nominal interest rates fell in the year of each global recession as monetary policy turned expansionary. Confidence plummeted and policy uncertainty rose during global recessions.

A. Nominal interest rate

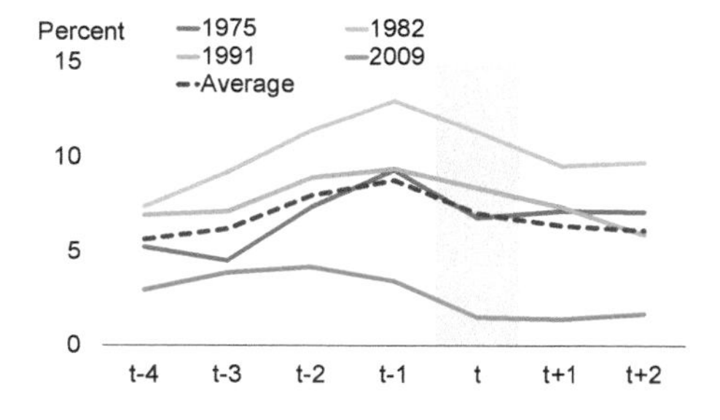

B. Real interest rate

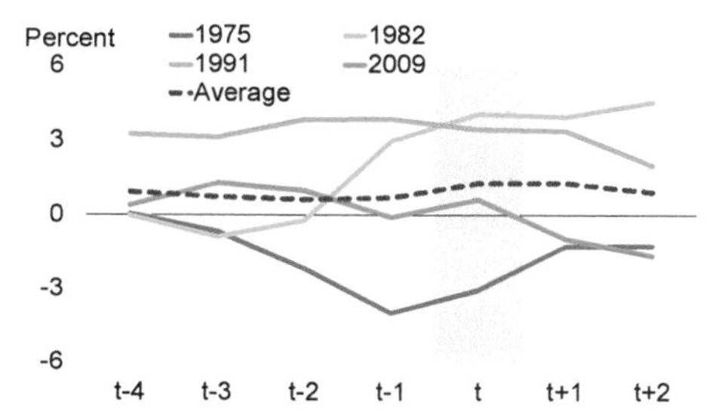

C. Business confidence

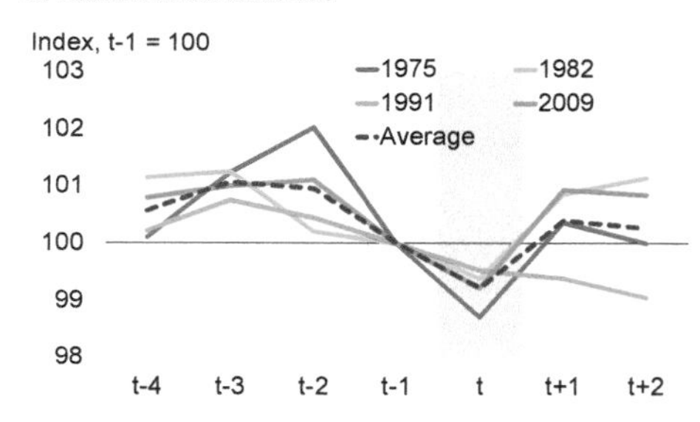

D. Policy uncertainty

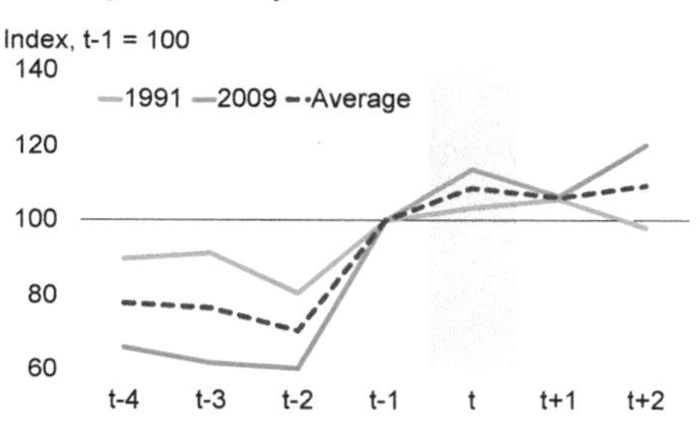

Sources: Bank for International Settlements; Davis (2016); European Commission; Haver Analytics; International Monetary Fund; Kose and Terrones (2015); Organisation for Economic Co-operation and Development; country sources; World Bank.

Note: Year "t" denotes the year of the respective global recessions (shaded in gray). Average refers to an average of four global recessions with available data. Variables are weighted by GDP in U.S. dollars at market exchange rates. Business confidence and policy uncertainty are index numbers equal to 100 one year before year "t" (that is, t-1 = 100). Refer to annex 2C for details.

the severity of the 2009 global recession. The global impact was amplified by the growing importance of international linkages through trade and financial flows. Although the globalization of national manufacturing chains was a major force driving the growth of world trade in the two decades before the global recession, it appears to have been instrumental in driving the sharp contraction of cross-border trade during 2009.[22] The 2009 episode also saw the largest increase in the index of global policy uncertainty, and the second-sharpest decline in business confidence (the largest decline took place during the 1975 global recession).

---

[22] The contraction in international trade also appears to have been driven partly by other factors, including a sharp fall in trade credit, the increased role of durable consumer goods (with relatively high income elasticity of demand) in trade, accumulated inventories by importing firms, and the strong cross-border spillovers associated with demand shocks. The collapse of trade (relative to output) during the 2009 global recession is much larger than that predicted by standard business cycle models. For potential explanations, see Alessandria, Kaboski, and Midrigan (2010); Amiti and Weinstein (2011); Bems, Johnson, and Yi (2010); Chor and Manova (2012); Freund (2009); and Levchenko, Lewis, and Tesar (2010).

Global capital flows registered their sharpest fall during the 2009 global recession. After overshadowing the growth of global trade flows over the previous two decades, global capital flows had reached unprecedented levels in 2007. But they rapidly dried up in the last quarter of 2008, as the global financial crisis spread from advanced economies to EMDEs. Variations among countries in the decline of capital flows appear to have been related to the degrees of trade and financial openness, the nature of financial linkages (for example, reliance on bank flows), and domestic macroeconomic conditions.[23]

As the epicenter of the financial crisis, advanced economies felt its brunt the most (figure 2.7.D; table 2A.4). Almost all of them experienced much larger declines in output than in the previous global recessions, and on average their per capita output growth declined to -4.0 percent in 2009, more than 6 percentage points below their average growth rate during nonrecession years. Contractions in trade, industrial production, and employment were also much sharper in these economies than in EMDEs.

In contrast, EMDE output growth remained positive, although it did slow sharply, from 8.2 percent in 2007 to 5.7 percent in 2008 and 1.8 percent in 2009 (chapter 3). EMDEs delivered their strongest recovery following the 2009 episode, as discussed in the following section (Kose, Otrok, and Prasad 2012). LICs were also able to continue growing during the 2009 global recession whereas their growth fell to negative rates in per capita terms in the previous episodes.

In the 2009 episode, there were some stark differences across EMDE regions (figure 2.7.D; table 2A.5). ECA took the largest hit partly because the withdrawal of Western European banks caused a severe credit crunch, and the region's per capita output declined by more than 5 percent in 2009. Per capita output in LAC and the Middle East and North Africa (MNA) also contracted as commodity prices and exports collapsed. In EAP and SAR, expansions continued, partly reflecting heavy use of monetary and fiscal stimulus in the largest economies to support activity (World Bank 2009, 2010a, 2010b). Unlike in previous global recessions, when SSA experienced declines in per capita output, the region was able to avoid recession in 2009 partly because it had limited exposure to global financial markets but stronger linkages, especially through trade, with the large emerging market economies of EAP, which continued growing (Fosu 2013).

Global recoveries

A global recovery typically involves broad-based rebounds in multiple measures of economic activity and financial markets. The strength of recoveries differs across countries and country groups. For instance, evidence suggests that the recovery in countries with fixed exchange rate regimes is weaker than that in countries with more flexible regimes (Terrones 2019). Following the 2009 global recession, advanced economies experienced the weakest recovery among the four episodes whereas EMDEs enjoyed their strongest.

---

[23] For discussion of movements in capital flows, see Claessens (2017); Koepke (2019); Lane and Milesi-Ferretti (2018); and Milesi-Ferretti and Tille (2011).

FIGURE 2.7.D Economic activity during global recessions, by country group

The impact of global recessions has differed between advanced economies and EMDEs. Output and trade have tended to decline more in advanced economies than in EMDEs.

A. Output per capita, advanced economies

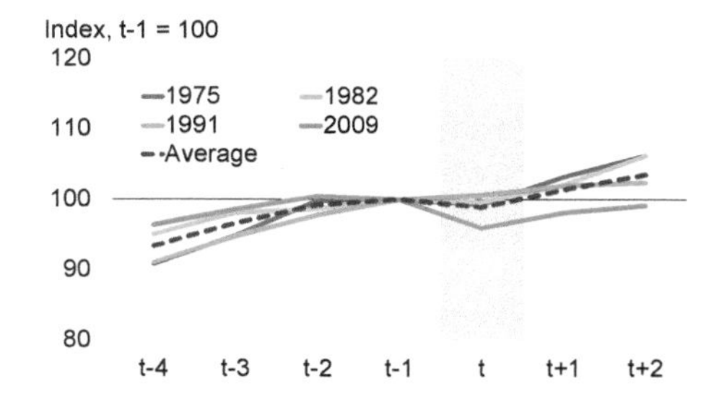

B. Output per capita, EMDEs

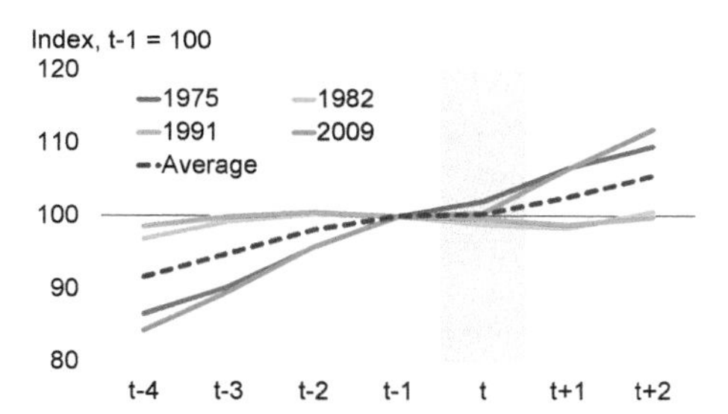

C. Trade, advanced economies

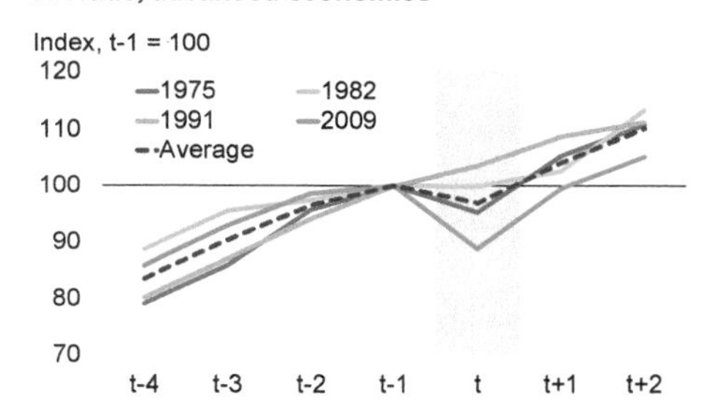

D. Trade, EMDEs

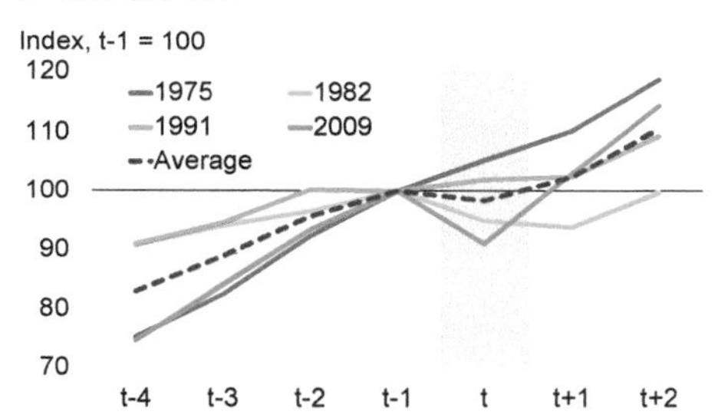

E. Credit, advanced economies

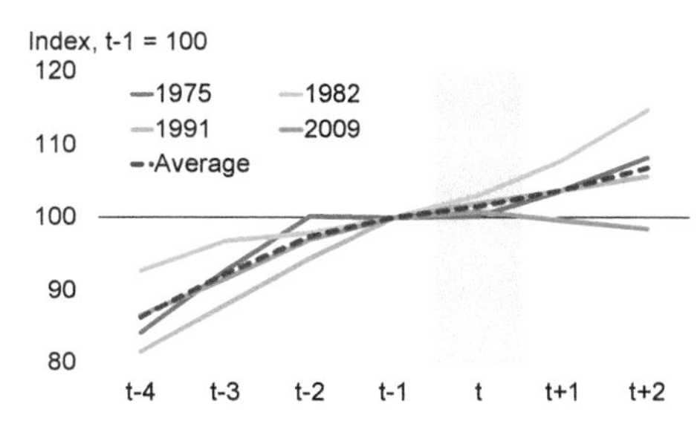

F. Credit, EMDEs

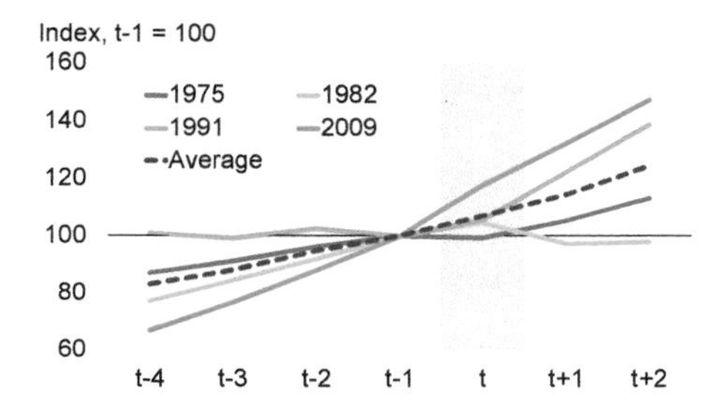

Sources: Bank for International Settlements; Feenstra, Inklaar, and Timmer (2015); Haver Analytics; International Monetary Fund; Kose and Terrones (2015); World Bank.

Note: Year "t" denotes the year of the respective global recessions (shaded in gray). Average refers to an average of four global recessions with available data. Variables are index numbers equal to 100 one year before year "t" (that is, t-1 = 100). Aggregates for output per capita are market-weighted. Refer to annex 2C for details. EMDEs = emerging market and developing economies.

Broad rebound in activity. Most indicators of global activity started expanding in the first year of each recovery (figure 2.8.A). The average growth rate of global output in the first year (or the first three years) of recoveries was close to the average growth rate in a typical year of the full sample period (table 2A.6). The growth rates of consumption, investment, and international trade picked up in the first year of each recovery while oil

FIGURE 2.8.A Economic activity during global recoveries

Global recoveries have typically involved a broad-based rebound in economic activity.

A. Output

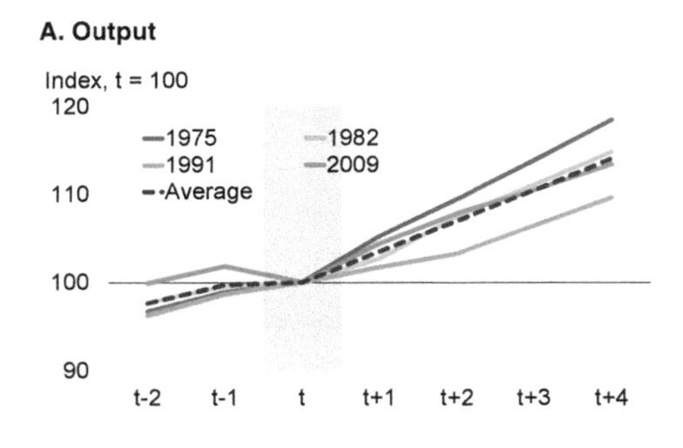

B. Output per capita

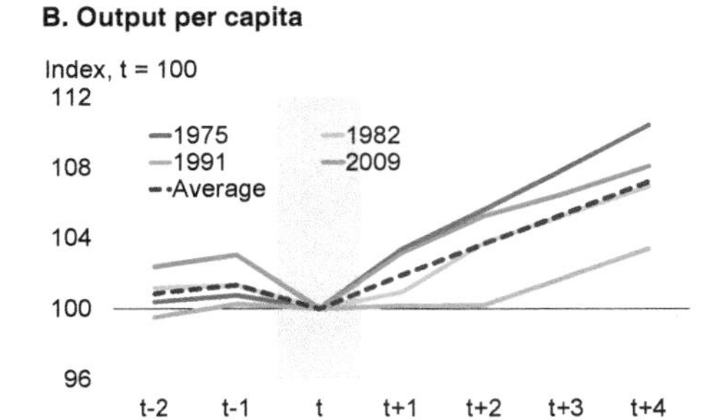

C. Industrial production

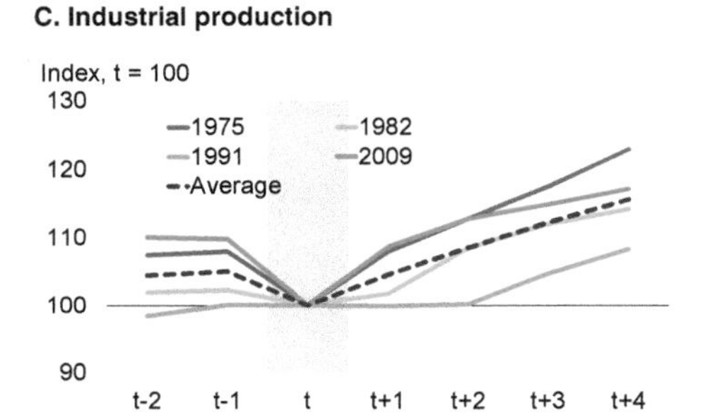

D. Trade

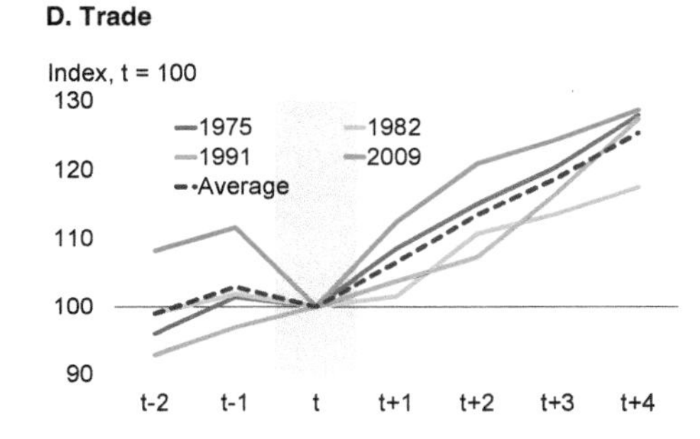

E. Unemployment rate

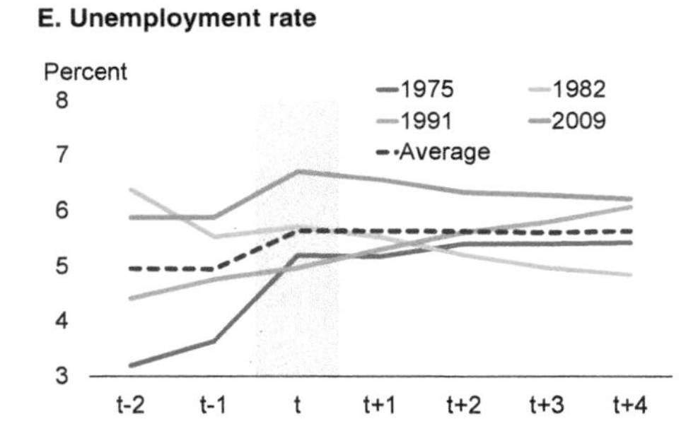

F. Oil consumption

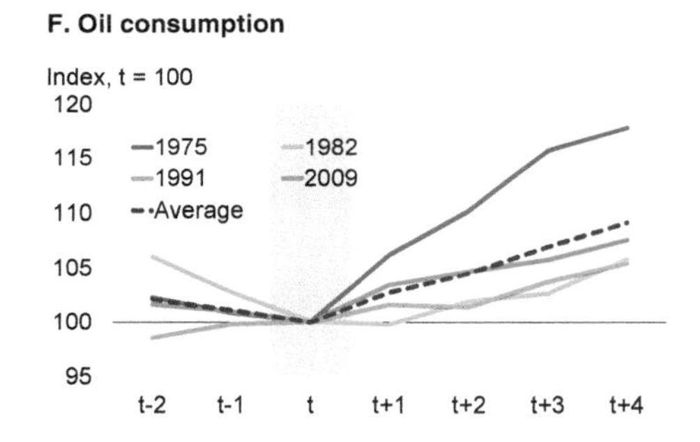

Sources: British Petroleum; Feenstra, Inklaar, and Timmer (2015); Haver Analytics; International Monetary Fund; Kose and Terrones (2015); Organisation for Economic Co-operation and Development; World Bank.

Note: Year "t" denotes the year of the respective global recessions (shaded in gray). Average refers to the average of the four global recessions identified. Output, output per capita, industrial production, trade, and oil consumption are index numbers equal to 100 in recession years. Aggregates for output, output per capita, and industrial production are market-weighted. Refer to annex 2C for details.

consumption tended to increase. The global recovery from the 1975 recession was the strongest in terms of average output growth in the first three years of the recovery, as well as in terms of growth in the first year. The recovery after the 1991 global recession was the weakest.

Recoveries in financial markets. Global financial markets have tended to rally as recoveries have strengthened over time (figure 2.8.B). In the recoveries from both the

FIGURE 2.8.B Financial markets during global recoveries

Global financial markets have tended to rally as recoveries have strengthened over time.

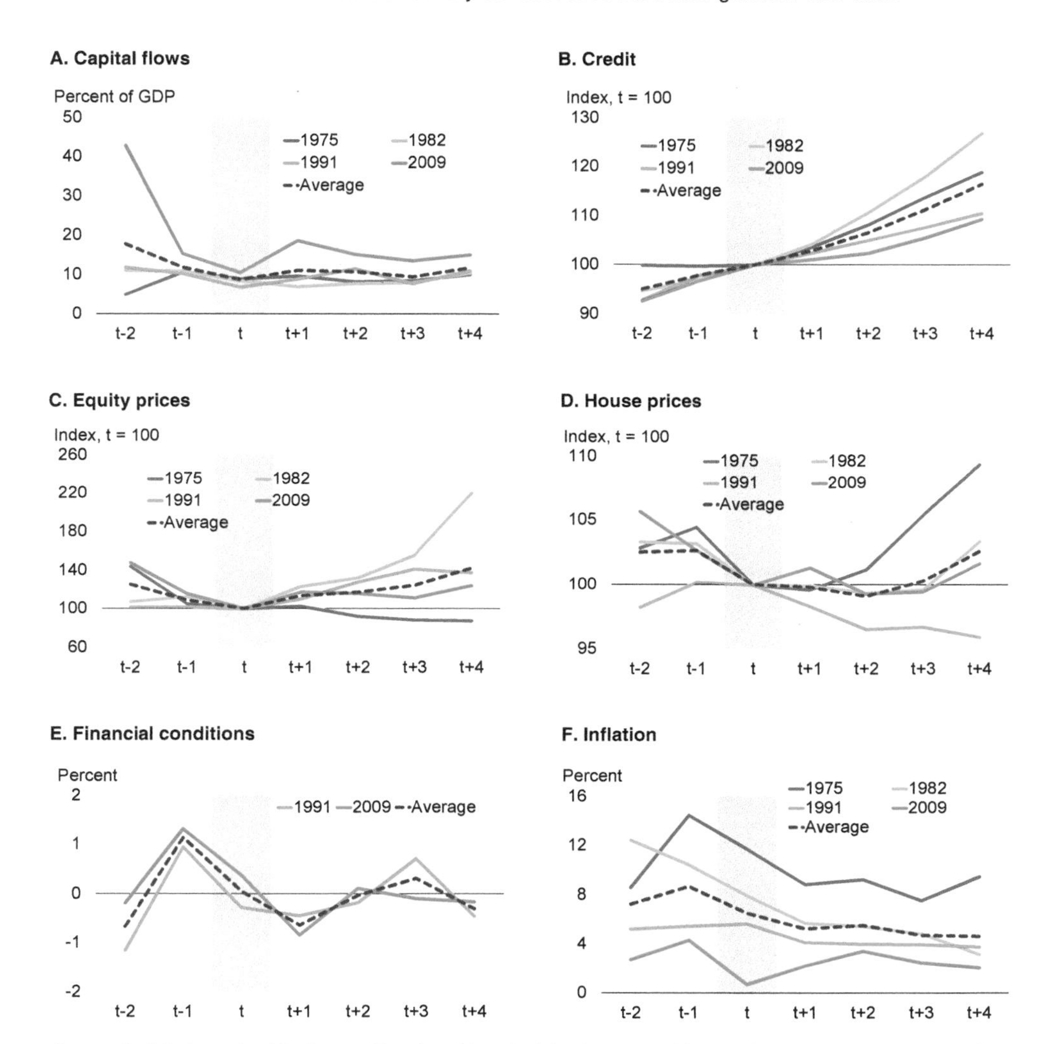

Sources: Bank for International Settlements; Bloomberg; Haver Analytics; International Monetary Fund; Kose and Terrones (2015); Organisation for Economic Co-operation and Development; World Bank.

Note: Year "t" denotes the year of the respective global recessions (shaded in gray). Average refers to an average of four global recessions with available data. Equity prices, house prices, financial conditions, and inflation are weighted by GDP in U.S. dollars. Credit, equity prices, and house prices are index numbers equal to 100 in recession years. Refer to annex 2C for details.

1991 and 2009 recessions, for which these estimates are available, broad financial conditions loosened further in the first year of the recovery but then gradually tightened. Although global equity prices on average have picked up quickly in the first year of recoveries, house prices have tended to remain depressed for two to three years. Credit growth has also generally taken longer to attain the rates observed during nonrecession periods. Housing markets were depressed mostly during the recoveries following the three most recent global recessions. Equity markets remained weak during the recovery

FIGURE 2.8.C Interest rates, confidence, and uncertainty during global recoveries

Nominal interest rates have usually declined during recoveries. Business confidence has often improved as policy uncertainty has faded.

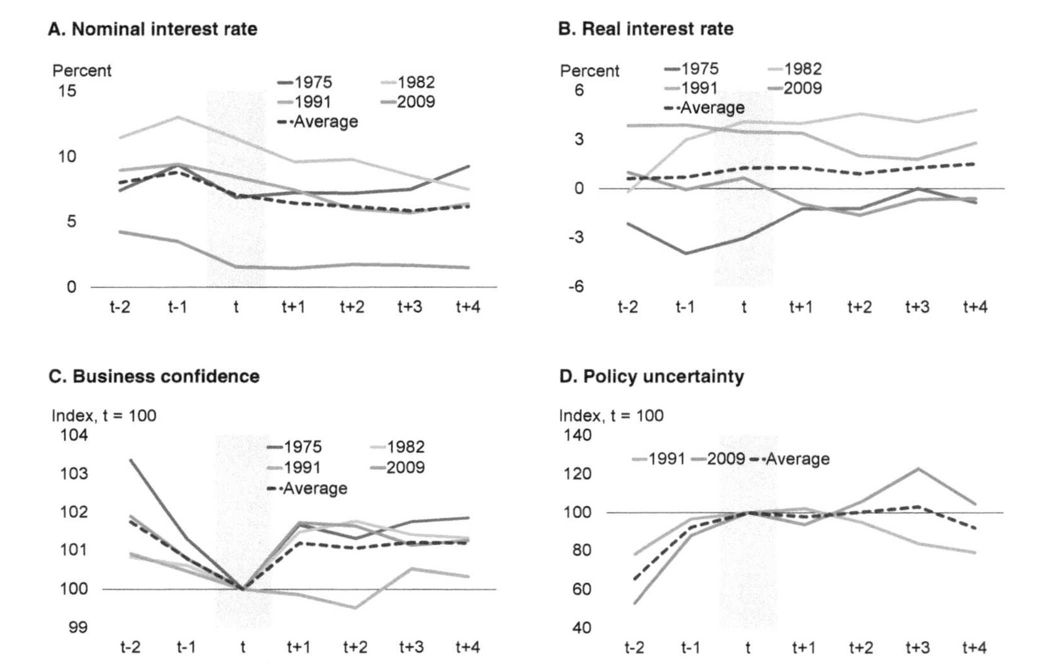

Sources: Bank for International Settlements; Davis (2016); European Commission; Haver Analytics; International Monetary Fund; Kose and Terrones (2015); Organisation for Economic Co-operation and Development; country sources; World Bank.

Note: Year "t" denotes the year of the respective global recessions (shaded in gray). Average refers to an average of four global recessions with available data. Variables are weighted by GDP in U.S. dollars. Business confidence and policy uncertainty are index numbers equal to 100 in recession years. Refer to annex 2C for details.

from the 1975 recession, partly reflecting the stagflation in several major advanced economies.

The 2009 episode, which saw the lowest rate of inflation during a recession, was followed in 2010 by a further dip of inflation to near zero. It thereafter rose quite modestly, to stabilize at a rate in the low single digits. Because of the depressed inflation after 2009, accommodative monetary policies kept nominal interest rates low, and real interest rates remained somewhat below zero (figure 2.8.C). Nominal rates declined during and after previous recessions too, but there was a less consistent pattern to real rates. For example, although real interest rates remained negative after the 1975 and 2009 episodes, they went up following the recession of 1982. Business confidence quickly recovered to the prerecession levels except after the 1991 recession because of the financial turbulence in Europe.

Differences across country groups. The four global recoveries featured many commonalities, but they also displayed important differences across country groups and

FIGURE 2.8.D Economic activity during global recoveries, by country group

Recoveries have differed between advanced economies and EMDEs. In advanced economies, the recovery from the most recent recession (over the first three years) was the weakest in the past 70 years in terms of output and output per capita. In contrast, EMDEs, as a group, enjoyed their strongest recovery of the past 70 years following the 2009 global recession.

A. Output per capita, advanced economies

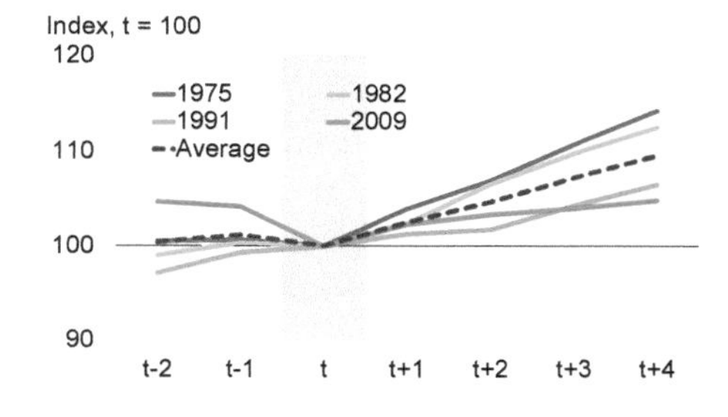

B. Output per capita, EMDEs

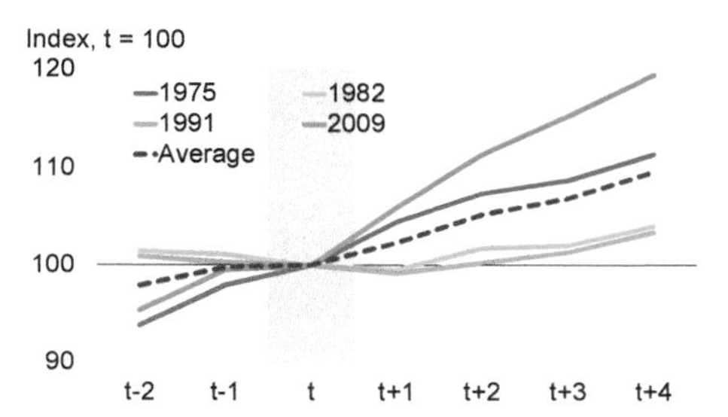

C. Trade, advanced economies

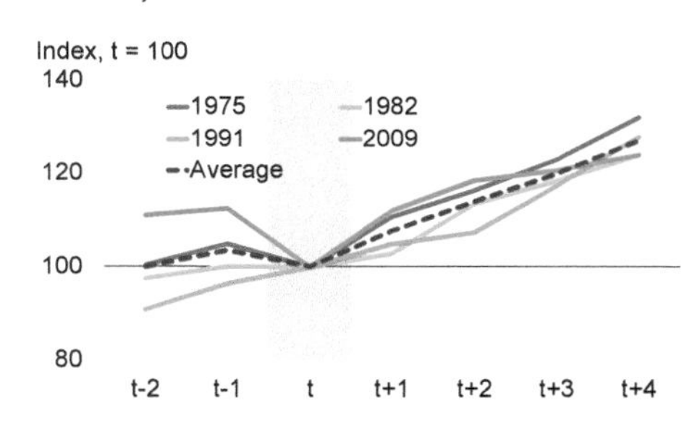

D. Trade, EMDEs

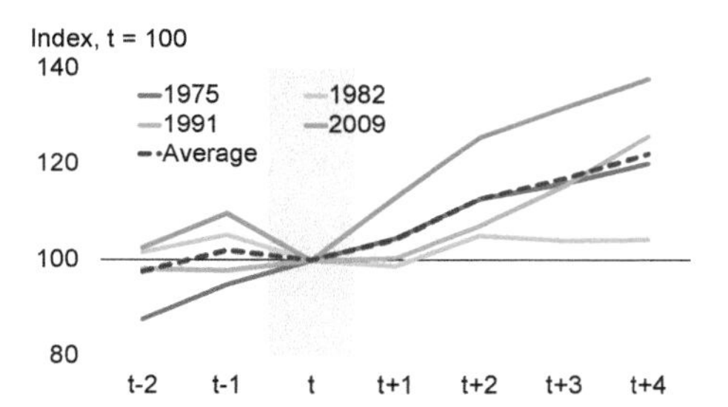

E. Credit, advanced economies

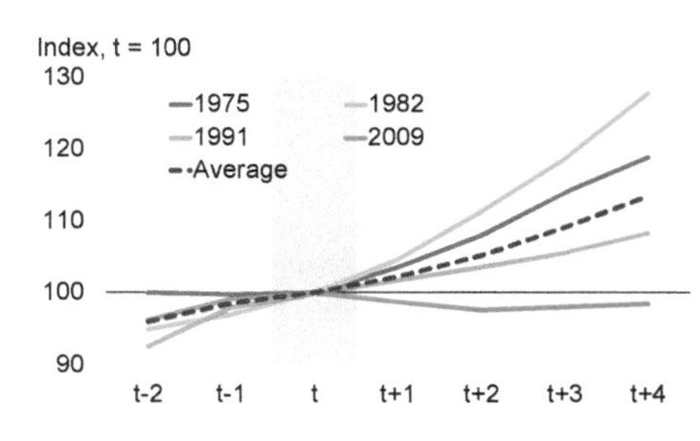

F. Credit, EMDEs

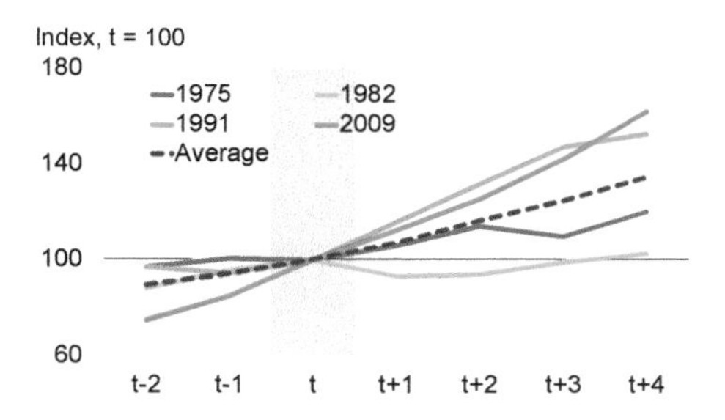

Sources: Bank for International Settlements; Feenstra, Inklaar, and Timmer (2015); Haver Analytics; International Monetary Fund; Kose and Terrones (2015); World Bank.

Note: Year "t" denotes the year of the respective global recessions (shaded in gray). Average refers to an average of the four global recessions identified. Variables are index numbers equal to 100 in recession years. Aggregates for output per capita are market-weighted. Refer to annex 2C for details. EMDEs = emerging market and developing economies.

EMDE regions (figure 2.8.D; table 2A.7). First, advanced economies on average delivered better per capita GDP growth outcomes (in the first three years) during the first three recoveries than did EMDEs. They also experienced faster trade growth during these episodes. Second, per capita GDP growth in LICs was much weaker than in the broader group of EMDEs, as well as advanced economies, during the global recoveries. Third, whereas EAP and SAR experienced robust recoveries, other regions suffered significant contractions during some recovery episodes mostly because of region-specific factors (table 2A.8). For example, LAC and SSA saw slumps in per capita output during the 1983-85 recovery because of the debt crises engulfing these regions, and ECA experienced a serious recession during the 1992-94 global recovery driven by challenges of transition.

Recovery following the 2009 recession. The trajectory of per capita global output in the most recent recovery was slightly weaker than that of the period following the 1975 global recession (figure 2.8.A). After the latest recession, there were stronger rebounds in industrial production and trade in the first three years than in the previous three recoveries. The pattern of global unemployment during the latest global recovery follows that of the previous episodes, but the average rate of unemployment remained elevated in 2010-12.

Financial markets experienced a subdued recovery after 2009 (figures 2.8.B and 2.8.C). Credit registered its weakest growth among the four episodes while both housing and equity markets struggled in the first three years. The latest recovery was characterized by the lowest inflation and nominal interest rates. Capital flows, however, picked up quite strongly in the first year of the recovery, and then stabilized at a lower level than the average over the 2003-07 period.

The global recovery from the 2009 recession was significantly different from the previous three episodes, particularly in its uneven nature and especially in the differences in performance between advanced economies and EMDEs (figure 2.8.D; table 2A.7). Advanced economies were the engines of previous global recoveries, but EMDEs accounted for the lion's share of global growth after the 2009 global recession: the average contribution of advanced economies to global growth during the previous three global recoveries (that is, over 1976-78, 1983-85, and 1992-94) was 75 percent, but that average dropped to 35 percent in 2010-12.

For advanced economies, the most recent recovery, in 2010-12, was the weakest in terms of both output and output per capita. This reflects in part the legacies of the global financial crisis, particularly the deterioration in credit and housing markets as well as in labor markets. The balance sheets of households and financial sectors were severely damaged, resulting in a sharp contraction of investment, especially in construction. Some countries in the euro area, including Cyprus and Greece, also struggled to finance their public debt and experienced severe sovereign debt crises in 2011-13. Compared to the previous episodes, growth rates of consumption and investment were much weaker in advanced economies. Reflecting anemic income growth in these economies, unemployment declined only slowly during the recovery, especially in the euro area.

In contrast, EMDEs, as a group, enjoyed their strongest recovery following the 2009 global recession. Despite an unfavorable external environment, both industrial production and trade rebounded strongly, supported by a sharp increase in credit growth (table 2A.7). EMDEs weathered the global recession relatively well thanks to the large, prompt, and globally coordinated policy support, as discussed below. The strong performance of EMDEs during the early years of the recovery also reflects previous structural improvements such as more well-regulated financial systems and stronger macroeconomic policy frameworks that allowed them to pursue more credible and effective countercyclical policies (Kose and Prasad 2010).

Although this period saw a relatively robust recovery for EMDEs generally, its strength differed among the regions, with growth stronger in EAP, SAR, and LAC than in ECA and MNA. For example, the ECA region suffered a financial shock qualitatively similar to that in many advanced economies, and its growth was slower than the other regions in the first year of the recovery.[24] Among the four global recoveries examined, the most recent was the first in which LICs were able to deliver positive per capita GDP growth, partly because of a sharp increase in their exports.

Policy responses during recessions and recoveries. In response to the prospect of large output and employment losses in the wake of the financial turbulence of 2008, a number of advanced economies and EMDEs employed wide-ranging expansionary fiscal policy measures during 2008–09. These coordinated measures were instrumental in supporting global demand at the height of the global financial crisis and in limiting the decline in activity. As public debt and financing requirements rose significantly, however, market pressures and—perhaps more important—political constraints led advanced economies to withdraw fiscal support in 2010.[25]

The change in fiscal policy stance led to an unprecedented outcome, with advanced economies taking quite different paths for government expenditures than in past recoveries, when policy was expansionary for longer, with continued increases in real primary government expenditures (figure 2.9). In contrast, in EMDEs, the recovery was accompanied by expansionary fiscal policy (Kose et. al 2017). EMDE governments employed fiscal packages that included infrastructure investment, tax cuts, and social protection programs.

Monetary policies in advanced economies remained exceptionally accommodative during the latest recovery—more so than in earlier episodes (Arteta et al. 2015; Ha, Kose, and Ohnsorge 2019). Monetary policy played a key role in restoring financial sector health, limiting the economic downturn, and supporting the recovery. During the early stages of the global financial crisis, central banks in the major advanced economies sharply reduced interest rates, expanded their liquidity facilities, and started large-scale purchases of longer-term assets. The combination of near-zero policy interest rates and

[24] The incidence of sudden stops in capital inflows tipping countries into financial distress was about half of that before 2008, and centered in economies where precrisis credit booms were funded by large capital inflows and where banks had narrow deposit bases, such as some economies in ECA (Feyen et al. 2014). Data from Forbes and Warnock (2012) show that more than 80 percent of countries in the sample experienced sudden stops in 2009, whereas the share was about 46 percent, on average, in 1982 and 1991. In addition, many sudden stops episodes were observed during the global downturns of 1998 and 2001. Eichengreen and Gupta (2016) also document the high incidence of sudden stops during the 2009 global recession.

[25] In advanced economies, government expenditures have increased gradually since 2015 as public investment picked up in major economies. A number of countries have implemented tax reforms to stimulate activity over the past decade (IMF 2019; OECD 2019).

FIGURE 2.9 Fiscal and monetary policies during global recessions and recoveries

Unusually, fiscal and monetary policies followed different trajectories in advanced economies after the 2009 recession. Whereas monetary policies have remained highly accommodative during the recovery, fiscal policies were expansionary during the recession but have not supported activity during the recovery. In EMDEs, both fiscal and monetary policies have remained accommodative during the recovery.

A. World, government expenditure

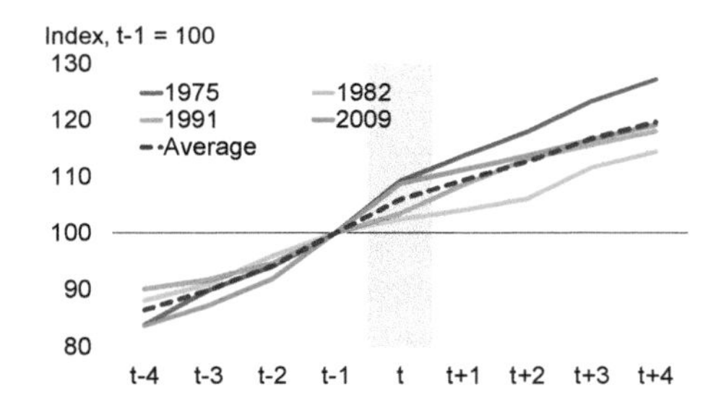

B. World, policy interest rate

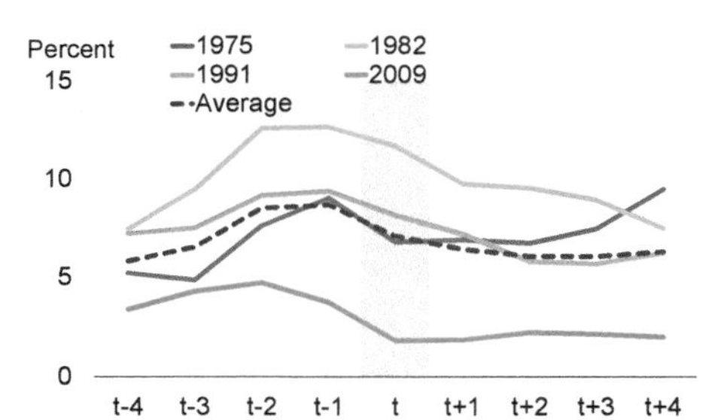

C. Advanced economies, government expenditure

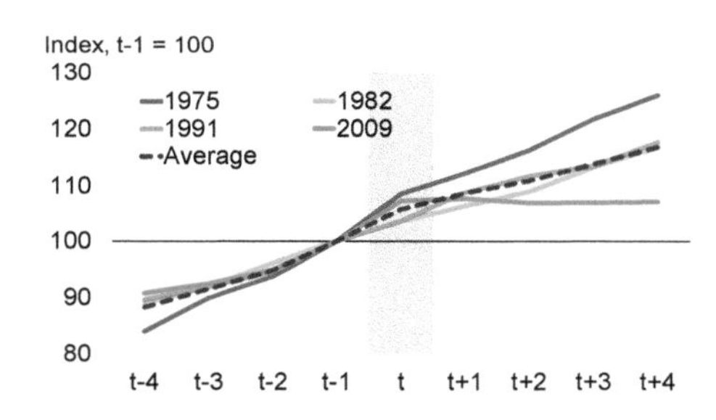

D. Advanced economies, policy interest rate

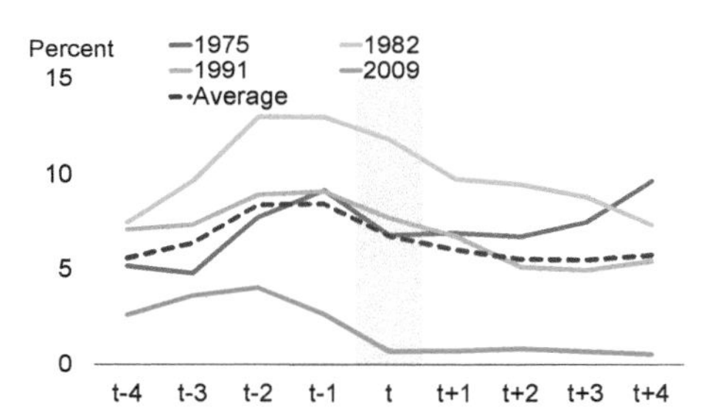

E. EMDEs, government expenditure

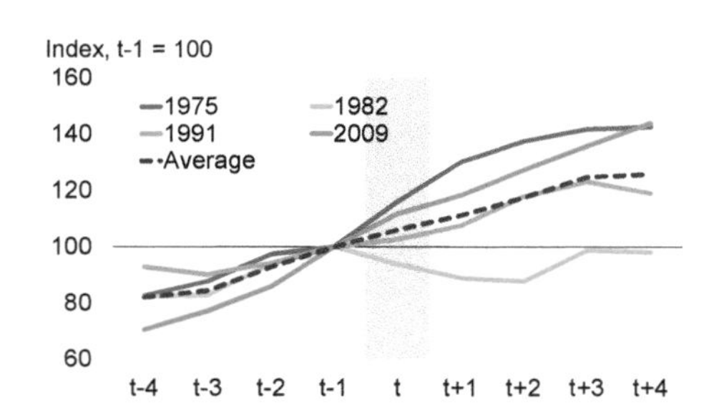

F. EMDEs, policy interest rate

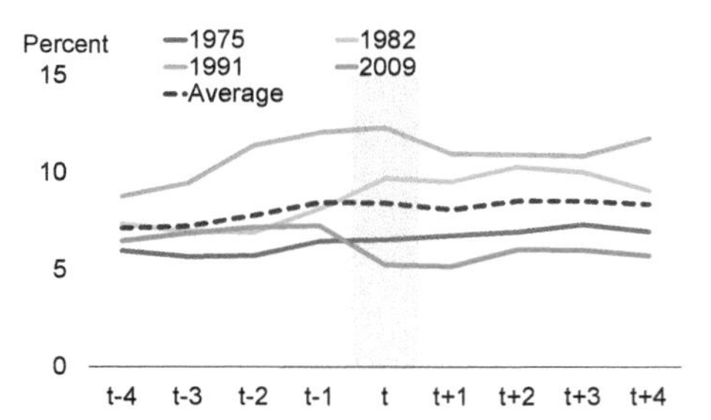

Sources: Bank for International Settlements; Haver Analytics; International Monetary Fund; Kose and Terrones (2015); Mauro et al. (2015); Organisation for Economic Co-operation and Development; World Bank.

Note: Year "t" denotes the year of the respective global recessions (shaded in gray). Average refers to an average of four global recessions with available data. Government expenditure is an index number equal to 100 one year before year "t" (that is, t-1 = 100). Aggregates are market-weighted. Refer to annex 2C for details. EMDEs = emerging market and developing economies.

the record expansion of central bank balance sheets was unprecedented. Policy rates remained at, or close to, the zero lower bound, and below zero in some cases; and central bank balance sheets were expanded further. In addition, central banks began or intensified the use of forward guidance about the direction of monetary policy to help manage expectations and lower longer-term interest rates. EMDE central banks too lowered policy interest rates, which was made easier by their success in taming inflation before the crisis; and some EMDEs intervened in foreign exchange markets to support their currencies, having accumulated ample foreign reserves before the crisis (chapter 3).

Global expansions

The global expansion phase refers to the period between two global recessions. The world economy has experienced four expansions since the 1975 recession: 1976–81, 1983–90, 1992–2008, and the current expansion, which started in 2010.

Different durations. Global expansions since 1975 have varied in duration, between 6 years (following the 1975 recession) and 17 years (following the 1991 recession). The longest global expansion, 1992–2008, coincided with the information technology revolution, the integration of China and many other emerging market economies into the global economy, a sharp increase in commodity prices, and rapid growth in international trade and financial flows. Although this benign period of macroeconomic stability acquired the label of "The Great Moderation," it did witness global downturns in 1998 and 2001, during which the world economy came close to outright recession. The latest global expansion, which turned 10 years old in 2019, has seen a global downturn episode in 2012, but also the longest U.S. expansion in history.

Changes in amplitude over time. The world economy on average registered 3.3 percent annual output growth in the four global expansions (figure 2.10.A; table 2A.9). The strongest expansion was the one that followed the 1982 recession. Reflecting the support of accommodative policies, recoveries in confidence, pent-up demand, and ample spare capacity, the growth of activity in the first year after each global recession has tended to be faster than average growth over the expansion phase.

The post-2009 global expansion. The current global expansion has registered average annual per capita GDP growth similar to that of previous episodes. It is distinguished, however, by the lowest average growth in industrial production of all four expansions (when their initial years are excluded). The current expansion has also seen the weakest growth in global trade. Since 2011, average annual global trade growth has been 3.9 percent, well below the 5.7 percent average of previous global expansions. This weakening of trade growth has reflected a combination of factors, including weak demand growth in advanced economies, shifts in the composition of global demand, the maturation of global supply chains, and increased trade tensions between major economies, particularly involving the United States.

The current expansion has also seen the lowest growth in capital flows. Sluggish investment growth has been reflected in a decline in global capital flows since 2011. Capital flows to EMDEs have been sluggish, with repeated spikes in borrowing costs

FIGURE 2.10.A Economic activity and financial markets during global expansions

Per capita output growth in the current expansion has been little different from previous ones.

A. Output per capita

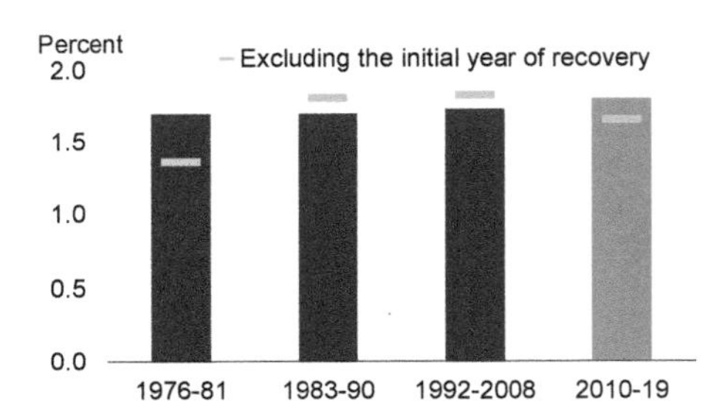

B. Trade

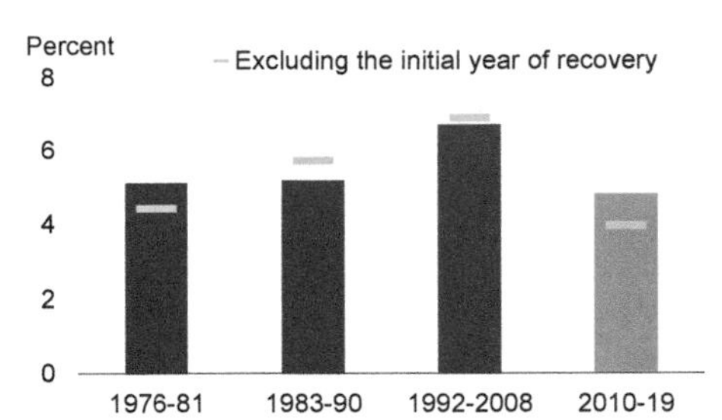

C. Unemployment rate

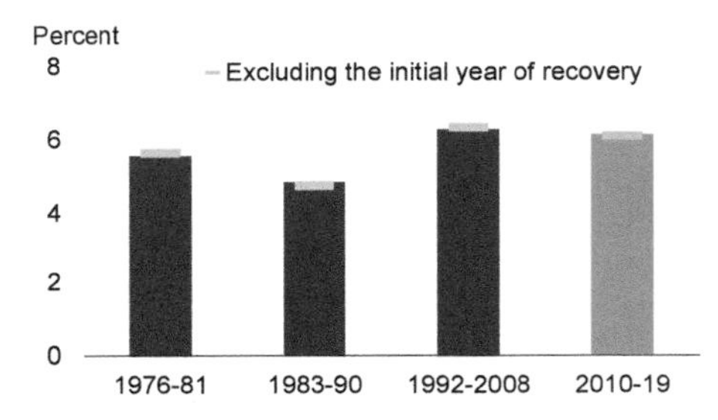

D. Credit

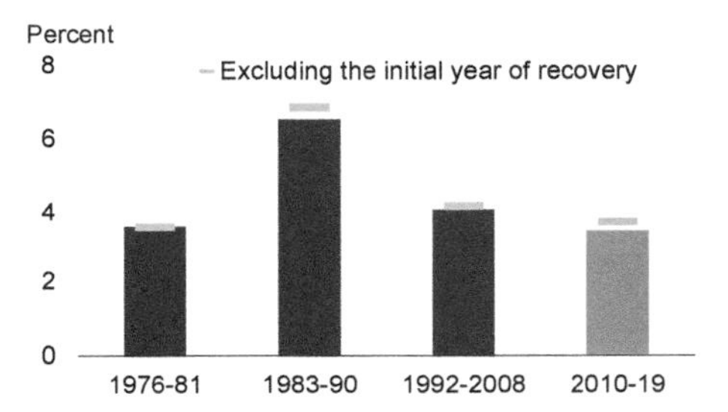

E. Equity prices

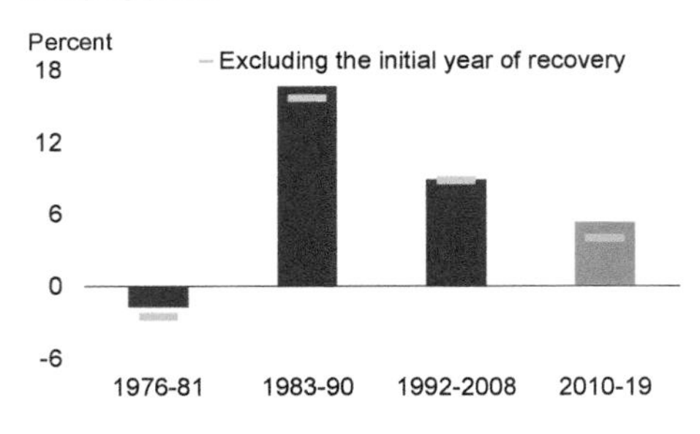

F. House prices

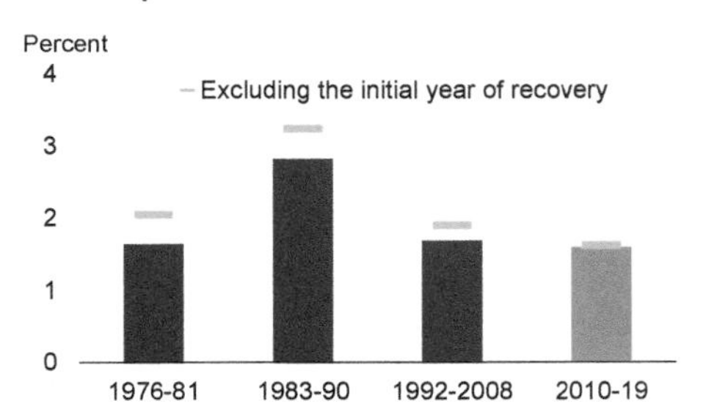

Sources: Bank for International Settlements; Feenstra, Inklaar, and Timmer (2015); Haver Analytics; International Monetary Fund; Kose and Terrones (2015); Organisation for Economic Co-operation and Development; World Bank.

Note: Each bar represents average growth during the periods of global expansions. Aggregates for output per capita, equity prices, and house prices are market-weighted.

since mid-2013. Following an initial rebound after the recession, global capital flows have declined (chapter 3).

Weak expansion in advanced economies. The expansions in advanced economies following the 1991 and 2009 global recessions were the weakest of the four episodes. Despite the marked difference in the severity of these two recessions, their underlying

FIGURE 2.10.B Global expansions, by country group

Of the four expansions examined, the current expansion has been the weakest in advanced economies but the strongest in EMDEs.

A. Output per capita, advanced economies

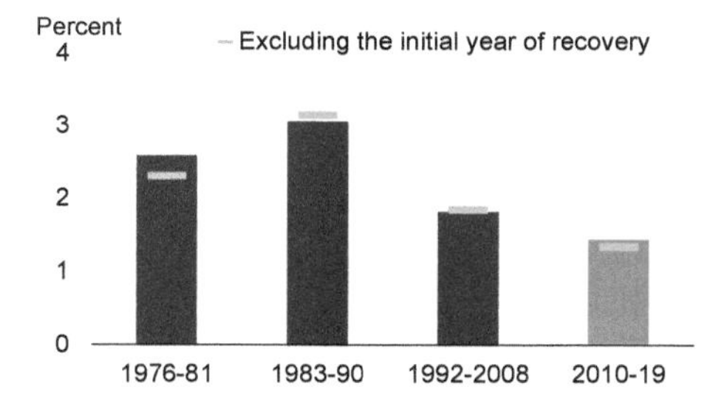

B. Output per capita, EMDEs

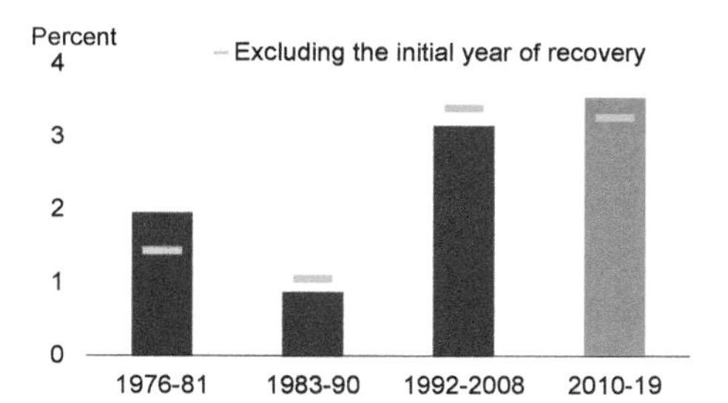

C. Trade, advanced economies

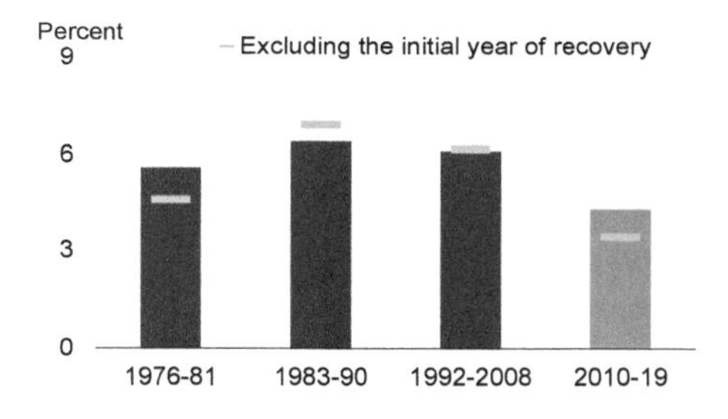

D. Trade, EMDEs

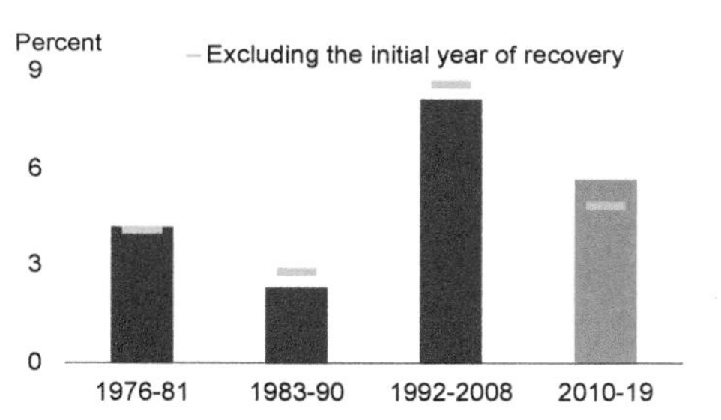

E. Credit, advanced economies

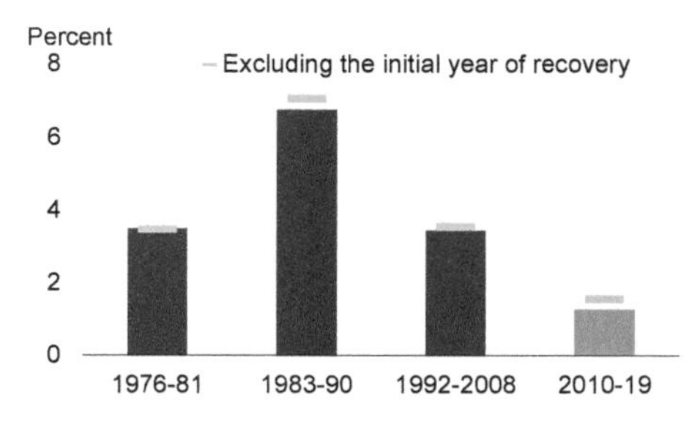

F. Credit, EMDEs

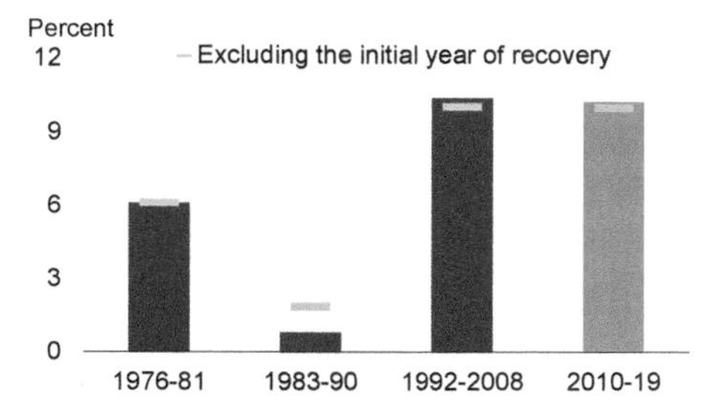

Sources: Bank for International Settlements; Feenstra, Inklaar, and Timmer (2015); Haver Analytics; International Monetary Fund; Kose and Terrones (2015); World Bank.

Note: Each bar represents average growth during the periods of global expansions. Aggregates for output per capita are market-weighted. EMDEs = emerging market and developing economies.

causes and the evolution of activity during the following expansions share remarkable similarities for advanced economies (figure 2.10.B; table 2A.10). Both recessions were associated with disruptions in credit and housing markets in the major advanced economies. In particular, the global expansion following the 1991 recession was adversely affected by the ripple effects of collapses in credit and asset markets in Japan and the United States. Similarly, the deep 2009 global recession was associated with substantial problems in credit and housing markets in the United States and a number of other advanced economies, including France, Denmark, Iceland, Ireland, Spain, the United Kingdom, and the Baltic countries.

The expansions following the 1991 and 2009 global recessions were also both slowed by particular challenges in Europe. Both the latest expansion and the one following the 1991 global recession were hampered by problems in the European Monetary System—the ERM crisis in 1992 and crises in the euro area in 2011-13. Downturns in many European countries in the wake of the ERM crisis involved significant increases in interest rates in several countries and took a severe toll on confidence. The euro area debt crisis in 2012-13 also weakened growth in several of its members. Growth in the area has remained generally sluggish throughout the expansion, with the highest annual output growth of 2.4 percent in 2017, leaving unemployment still high in a number of countries.

Reversal of fortunes for EMDEs. The latest global expansion was the strongest one for EMDEs in terms of per capita output growth. After enjoying the strongest recovery immediately following the 2009 global recession, EMDEs have since experienced a protracted slowdown following the drop in commodity prices in 2012 (figure 2.10.B; tables 2A.10 and 2A.11). EMDE GDP growth slowed from 7.4 percent in 2010 to a trough of 3.8 percent in 2015 (Didier et. al 2015). The growth slowdown during 2011-15 was synchronous (affecting more than three-fifths of EMDEs) and protracted, with the steepest slowdowns in LAC and the mildest in SAR. In LICs, GDP growth slowed from 6.9 percent in 2012 to a trough of 4.9 percent in 2016. In 2017, many EMDEs saw a mild cyclical recovery, led by growth in exports and investment as global manufacturing and trade picked up, but EMDE growth has since weakened again.

Weakening global economic growth has coincided with country-specific challenges in some large EMDEs. In China, for example, with the unwinding of policy stimulus, efforts have also been also made to guide the economy away from investment- and export-driven growth toward more balanced growth that relies more on consumer spending. The resultant slowdown in China, from growth of 8.9 percent on average during the previous global expansions to 6.6 percent in 2018, has weighed on growth in its trading partners and in commodity exporters (Huidrom et al. 2019; World Bank 2016). In some other major EMDEs, episodes of policy uncertainty, social tensions, geopolitical events, and civil wars have caused sharp losses in confidence (chapter 3).

Repeated short-term growth disappointments. The latest global recovery has also seen repeated downgrades in short-term global growth forecasts (figure 2.11). Over 2010-19, on average, current-year growth projections in consensus forecasts have been downgraded from a year earlier in about 55 percent of economies. Downgrades affected growth forecasts for both advanced economies (54 percent of economies) and EMDEs (57 percent of economies), but with forecasts for EMDEs revised down by a wider margin. For EMDEs, since 2009, growth has been revised down by an average of 0.3 percentage point for the current year forecast, relative to the one made a year earlier.

FIGURE 2.11 Global growth forecasts

There have been multiple downgrades in short-term global growth forecasts since the 2009 global recession. Long-term, 10-year-ahead, global growth forecasts have also been downgraded repeatedly.

A. Current-year growth forecast revisions

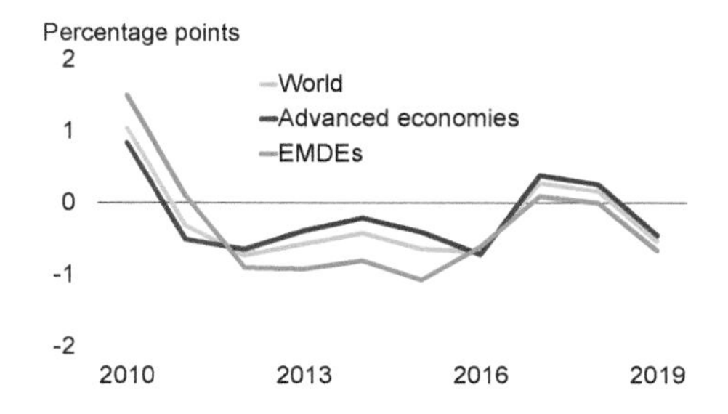

B. Long-term growth forecasts

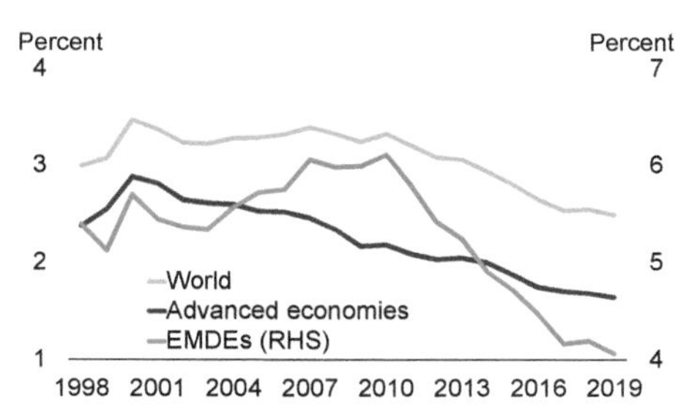

Sources: Consensus Economics; World Bank.

A. Differences in growth forecasts for current years as of September of the year and those made a year ago, in percentage points. The latest forecast survey in 2019 is September. Sample includes 85 economies, consisting of 33 advanced economies and 52 emerging market and developing economies (EMDEs), weighted by GDP in U.S. dollars.

B. The horizontal axis refers to the year of consensus forecast surveys. Annual averages of results from multiple surveys conducted in each year are presented. Forecasts in 2019 are based on surveys in January, April, and July. Sample includes 38 economies, consisting of 20 advanced economies and 18 EMDEs, weighted by GDP in U.S. dollars.

Diminishing long-term growth projections. The 2009 global recession marked a turning point in long-term (10-year-ahead) global growth projections. Long-term forecasts for global GDP growth increased from 3.0 percent in 1998 to 3.3 percent in 2008. Since then, they have steadily declined, to 2.5 percent in 2019. Growth forecasts for advanced economies began to be downgraded after the 1991 global recession. After a brief period of upgrades in the late 1990s, they resumed their gradual decline in the early 2000s. In contrast, EMDEs enjoyed improving growth prospects up to the 2009 global recession. Since then, long-term forecasts have materially deteriorated for both groups of economies.

Before the 2009 global recession, growth prospects were supported by a rapid expansion of investment, trade, and financial flows. During the most recent global expansion, however, cyclical factors, such as the anemic recovery in advanced economies, a sharp collapse in commodity prices, and weak investment growth, have been compounded by structural weaknesses, including slower productivity growth, and a slowdown in the growth of working-age populations.

These structural factors have been eroding global potential growth—the growth rate that the global economy would sustain at full capacity utilization and full employment. In 2013-17, global potential growth is estimated to have been roughly 1 percentage point a year lower than a decade earlier, as a result of weaker productivity growth, sluggish expansion of investment, and a broadening slowdown in working-age population growth. Annual potential growth estimates for advanced economies were reduced to 1.4 percent on average in 2013-17, from 2.2 percent a decade earlier. Potential output growth in EMDEs is also estimated to have slowed, from 5.9 percent a year in the mid-

2000s to 4.8 percent a year in 2013-17, reflecting the effects of weak investment, adverse demographic trends, and slower productivity growth.

In light of the protracted weakness of economic growth, together with chronically low inflation (persistently below target in most cases), and despite unprecedented monetary policy accommodation maintained over several years and historically low long-term interest rates, some observers have argued that advanced economies have been facing "secular stagnation," owing to structural weakness in aggregate demand (Rachel and Summers 2019; Summers 2015; Teulings and Baldwin 2014).[26] Many factors may have contributed to such demand weakness, including increased saving originating partly from demographic factors, and reduced investment spending stemming partly from the reduced costs of capital goods, which have increasingly embodied information technology. Financial crises may also have contributed through higher risk aversion, increased costs of financial intermediation, and increased debt overhangs. Recent research concludes that, in light of the Japanese experience after its banking crisis in the early 1990s, some major euro area economies might suffer a long period of stagnation because of structural headwinds associated with demographic trends and persistent weakness in productivity growth (Hoshi and Kashyap 2015).

Conclusion

The year 2019 is the 10th anniversary of the last global recession. Yet 2019 also marks an intensifying speculation about whether another such episode is looming. Over the past year, global growth forecasts have been repeatedly downgraded as a highly synchronized slowdown has enveloped both advanced economies and EMDEs. Trade tensions between major economies have led to unprecedented policy uncertainty and taken a heavy toll on global industrial production and trade.

In light of the resurgence of interest on the topic, this chapter analyzes the main features of global recessions and the ensuing global recoveries and expansions.

What happens during global recessions and recoveries? Both statistical and judgmental methods identify four global recessions since 1950: in 1975, 1982, 1991, and 2009. During these four years, there was a contraction in annual real per capita global GDP and broad-based weakness in the main indicators of global activity. Quarterly data yield similar recession dates, and confirm that the duration of a typical global recession is about one year—which is also the average duration of national recessions. Global recessions are highly synchronized events, with severe economic and financial disruptions occurring simultaneously in many countries around the world. Although the four global recessions coincided with recessions in the United States, not every U.S. recession coincided with a global recession: in fact, the United States experienced six additional recessions during 1950-2019.

[26] Hansen (1939) argues that the Great Depression could lead to a prolonged period of stagnation and high unemployment because of the decline in the birth rate and excessive savings that constrain aggregate demand. For a theoretical formulation of secular stagnation, see Eggertsson, Mehrotra, and Robbins 2019. Hamilton et al. (2016) argue that the secular stagnation hypothesis confuses a delayed recovery with chronically weak aggregate demand. Others consider the case for secular stagnation to be weak (Rogoff 2013; Taylor 2014).

The world economy suffered a sizable contraction in per capita output during the four global recessions since 1950: the average decline in per capita output (market exchange rate weighted) was about 1.3 percent, 3.5 percentage points lower than the average annual growth rate (2.2 percent) in the years of expansion during 1950-2018. Financial conditions tended to tighten, business confidence declined, and policy uncertainty increased during the global recessions. The 2009 global recession was by far the deepest and most internationally synchronized among the four: it saw the only outright annual contraction in global output and the largest declines in global trade, capital flows, and industrial production.

In addition to the four global recessions, the global economy experienced relatively slow growth in 1958, 1998, 2001, and 2012. During these episodes, which we refer to as "global downturns," the global economy registered its lowest growth rates of the past seven decades, except for the years of and around the four global recessions. These episodes fall short of qualifying as recessions, however, because world real GDP per capita did not contract and because several activity indicators remained robust.

Global recoveries have generally been characterized by a broad-based rebound in economic activity and normalization of financial conditions. The average growth rate of global output in the first year (or over the first three years) of recoveries has been close to the longer-term average. Financial conditions often remained loose in the first year of the recovery but then gradually tightened. Among the four episodes, the recovery from the 1975 recession saw the steepest acceleration in growth in its first year. Thanks to large, prompt, and globally coordinated policy support, the recovery following the 2009 recession was the second-strongest.

How do global recessions and recoveries vary across different groups of countries? First, per capita output growth declined more in advanced economies than in EMDEs during global recessions, with some EMDE regions consistently faring better than others. The EAP and SAR regions continued expanding in each of the past four global recessions whereas the other four regions all experienced declines in average per capita output. Second, LICs on average suffered larger declines in growth than did the broader group of EMDEs. Third, in all four global recessions, both trade and industrial production registered much larger contractions in advanced economies than in EMDEs.

The magnitude of the 2009 global recession varied across the country groups. As the epicenter of the financial crisis, advanced economies felt the initial brunt of the recession but also suffered the weakest recovery in terms of output and output per capita compared with previous episodes. In contrast, EMDE output growth remained positive during the 2009 recession, and EMDEs' subsequent recovery was the strongest of the four global recessions examined. LICs also were able to continue growing during the 2009 global recession, whereas their growth plummeted in the previous episodes.

What happens during global expansions, and how does the current global expansion compare with previous ones? The duration of global expansions has varied from six years (following the 1975 recession) to 17 years (following the 1991 recession). The latest global expansion turned 10 years old in 2019. It includes a global downturn in 2012 but also the longest U.S. expansion in history. The latest expansion has registered average per capita growth comparable with previous episodes, but it has also seen the weakest growth in global trade and capital flows.

The current expansion has been the weakest in advanced economies because many of them have struggled to overcome the legacies of the global financial crisis and structural weaknesses in demand. In contrast, it has been the strongest one for EMDEs in terms of per capita output growth. EMDEs have, however, also experienced a slowdown in growth during the expansion as a result of both external and domestic factors.

Monetary and fiscal policies often become expansionary leading into global recessions, and typically continue supporting the ensuing global recoveries. In advanced economies, monetary policies remained highly accommodative for almost the whole post-2009 decade, with central banks introducing a wide range of unconventional measures to ease credit conditions. After the implementation of large, coordinated, fiscal stimulus programs during 2008-09, however, fiscal support was withdrawn shortly into the recovery. By contrast, EMDEs have generally employed expansionary fiscal and monetary policies during most of the expansion, apart from some adjustments of monetary policy in response to cyclical conditions and financial stability concerns.

Short- and long-term global growth forecasts have both been repeatedly downgraded during the latest global expansion. During 2010-19, on average, current-year global growth forecasts have been downgraded from a year earlier in about 55 percent of countries. The long-term forecasts for global GDP growth have also steadily declined, from 3.3 percent in 2008 to 2.5 percent in 2019. These downgrades reflect not just persistently mediocre growth outturns in many countries but also protracted weakness in the fundamental drivers of growth, including productivity and investment.

Despite significant progress in our understanding of the global business cycle and its phases since the 2009 global recession, there remain a number of research avenues to explore. First, there is clear need to better understand the sources of the subdued growth performance that has been the hallmark of the current global expansion. Second, future work needs to focus on the cross-border spillovers and their interactions with domestic real and financial cycles. Third, global spillovers from national macrofinancial linkages require further scrutiny in light of the strong connections among financial entities in different countries.

ANNEX 2A Main features of recessions, recoveries, and expansions

TABLE 2A.1 Main features of recessions and expansions (with quarterly series)

	Duration (quarters)	Amplitude (percent)	Average (percent)
Recessions			
1974Q1-1975Q1	5	-9.3	-1.9
1981Q4-1982Q3	4	-4.5	-1.2
1990Q4-1991Q1	2	-0.9	-0.5
2008Q3-2009Q1	3	-15.3	-5.4
Average	*3.5*	*-7.5*	*-2.2*
Quarters with negative growth			
1970Q4		-0.7	-0.7
1980Q2	1	-4.8	-4.8
1981Q2	1	-0.3	-0.3
1998Q1	1	-0.3	-0.3
2001Q3	1	-0.6	-0.6
Expansions			
1975Q2-1981Q3	26		2.5
1982Q4-1990Q3	32		2.7
1991Q2-2008Q2	69		2.2
2009Q2-2019Q2	41		2.1
Average	*42*		*2.4*

Sources: Feenstra, Inklaar, and Timmer (2015); Haver Analytics; Organisation for Economic Co-operation and Development; World Bank.

Note: The table shows the periods identified as recessions and expansions, using the algorithm in Harding and Pagan (2002), or those with negative per capita growth. Amplitude and average are based on per capita global GDP growth. "Amplitude" is measured as a percent change in per capita output during each period (that is, a cumulative change over the denoted period). "Average" refers to average annualized growth during each period.

TABLE 2A.2 Output growth during global downturns

	Global downturns					Global	Non-	All years
	1958	1998	2001	2012	Average	recessions	recessions	
World								
Output	2.2	2.5	1.9	2.5	2.3	0.3	3.9	3.7
Output per capita	0.2	1.1	0.7	1.2	0.8	-1.3	2.2	2.0
Output (PPP)	2.7	2.4	2.3	3.2	2.7	0.8	4.2	4.0
Output per capita (PPP)	0.7	1.0	1.1	2.0	1.2	-0.8	2.5	2.3
Advanced economies								
Output	1.6	2.7	1.5	1.2	1.8	-0.4	3.5	3.3
Output per capita	0.4	2.1	0.9	0.6	1.0	-1.1	2.7	2.4
Output (PPP)	1.5	2.7	1.5	1.2	1.7	-0.4	3.5	3.3
Output per capita (PPP)	0.3	2.1	0.9	0.6	1.0	-1.1	2.7	2.5
EMDEs								
Output	6.2	1.8	3.2	4.9	4.0	2.1	4.9	4.7
Output per capita	3.8	0.3	1.8	3.5	2.4	0.2	3.0	2.8
Output (PPP)	6.4	1.9	3.4	5.0	4.2	2.4	4.9	4.8
Output per capita (PPP)	4.0	0.4	2.0	3.6	2.5	0.5	3.0	2.9

Sources: Feenstra, Inklaar, and Timmer (2015); Kose and Terrones (2015); World Bank.

Note: All variables show percent changes. "Global recessions" refers to average growth rates during the four global recessions (1975, 1982, 1991, and 2009). "Nonrecessions" refers to averages during 1950-2018 excluding years of global recessions. "All years" refers to averages of all years. EMDEs = emerging market and developing economies; PPP = purchasing power parity.

TABLE 2A.3 Main features of global recessions

	Global recessions					Non-recessions	Global downturns	All years
	1975	1982	1991	2009	Average			
Activity								
Output	1.1	0.4	1.3	-1.8	0.3	3.9	2.3	3.7
Output per capita	-0.7	-1.3	-0.3	-3.0	-1.3	2.2	0.8	2.0
Industrial production	-7.4	-2.2	-0.1	-8.9	-4.6	4.0	0.3	3.5
Trade	-1.4	-1.8	3.2	-10.4	-2.6	6.3	2.2	5.8
Unemployment rate	1.6	0.2	0.2	0.8	0.7	0.0	0.2	0.1
Oil consumption	-0.8	-2.7	0.2	-1.0	-1.1	2.6	0.9	2.3
Investment	0.7	-1.1	-1.0	-5.0	-1.6	4.7	2.0	4.4
Consumption	2.6	1.6	1.9	-0.1	1.5	3.7	2.7	3.6
Output (PPP)	1.8	0.6	1.5	-0.6	0.8	4.2	2.7	4.0
Output per capita (PPP)	-0.1	-1.1	-0.1	-1.7	-0.8	2.5	1.2	2.3
Financial markets								
Capital flows	-1.6	-2.3	-3.2	-4.8	-3.0	0.5	-3.8	0.2
Credit	0.2	3.2	2.2	3.4	2.2	5.5	3.8	5.3
Equity prices	-4.8	-10.9	-1.7	-13.5	-7.7	6.2	-2.9	5.3
House prices	-4.3	-3.1	-0.2	-2.6	-2.6	2.2	1.5	1.8
Financial conditions	...	...	-0.3	0.4	0.0	0.0	0.1	0.0
Inflation	-2.8	-2.5	0.2	-3.6	-2.2	0.2	-0.2	0.0
Interest rates, confidence, and uncertainty								
Nominal interest rate	-2.5	-1.6	-1.0	-1.9	-1.8	0.1	-0.4	0.0
Real interest rate	0.9	1.1	-0.4	0.7	0.6	-0.1	0.1	0.0
Business confidence	-1.3	-0.6	-0.5	-0.8	-0.8	0.1	-0.7	0.0
Policy uncertainty	...	...	3.5	13.9	8.7	3.3	31.5	3.6
Policies								
Government expenditure	9.2	2.3	3.4	8.8	5.9	4.7	4.8	4.8
Policy rate	-2.3	-1.0	-1.2	-1.9	-1.6	0.1	-0.6	0.0

Sources: Bank for International Settlements; Bloomberg; British Petroleum; Davis (2016); European Commission; Feenstra, Inklaar, and Timmer (2015); Haver Analytics; International Monetary Fund; Kose and Terrones (2015); Mauro et al. (2015); Organisation for Economic Co-operation and Development; U.S. Energy Information Administration; country sources; World Bank.

Note: All variables show percent changes, except in capital flows, unemployment rate, inflation, nominal and real interest rates, and policy rate, in which percentage-point changes of these variables are reported. "Nonrecessions" refers to averages during 1950-2018 excluding years of global recessions. "All years" refers to averages of all years. "Global downturns" refers to averages during the four global downturns (1958, 1998, 2001, and 2012). "..." indicates that data are either unavailable or not reported because country samples to compute data for aggregated groups are too small to be representative. PPP = purchasing power parity.

TABLE 2A.4 Main features of global recessions, by country group

	Global recessions					Non-recessions	Global downturns	All years
	1975	1982	1991	2009	Average			
Advanced economies								
Output	0.2	0.3	1.3	-3.4	-0.4	3.5	1.8	3.3
Output per capita	-0.7	-0.3	0.6	-4.0	-1.1	2.7	1.0	2.4
Industrial production	-7.8	-2.5	-0.2	-12.4	-5.7	3.6	-0.3	3.0
Trade	-4.7	-0.1	3.7	-11.1	-3.1	6.4	1.7	5.9
Unemployment rate	1.5	1.3	0.6	2.2	1.4	-0.1	0.0	0.0
Output (PPP)	0.2	0.3	1.3	-3.3	-0.4	3.5	1.7	3.3
Output per capita (PPP)	-0.7	-0.4	0.6	-4.0	-1.1	2.7	1.0	2.5
Credit	0.2	3.1	2.0	0.9	1.6	4.9	3.0	4.7
Government expenditure	8.6	3.5	3.6	7.3	5.7	4.1	3.5	4.2
Policy rate	-2.4	-1.2	-1.4	-2.0	-1.7	0.1	-0.7	0.0
EMDEs								
Output	4.2	0.9	1.5	1.8	2.1	4.9	4.0	4.7
Output per capita	2.0	-1.2	-0.4	0.4	0.2	3.0	2.4	2.8
Industrial production	...	...	0.4	-0.2	0.1	5.4	3.1	5.0
Trade	5.3	-5.1	2.0	-9.0	-1.7	6.1	3.8	5.6
Unemployment rate	...	-0.4	0.1	0.4	0.0	-0.1	0.2	-0.1
Output (PPP)	4.2	1.1	1.9	2.3	2.4	4.9	4.2	4.8
Output per capita (PPP)	2.1	-0.9	0.0	0.9	0.5	3.0	2.5	2.9
Credit	-0.7	4.5	5.7	17.7	6.8	8.0	9.8	7.9
Government expenditure	16.0	-6.2	2.6	11.7	6.0	5.8	6.5	5.8
Policy rate	0.1	1.5	0.2	-2.0	0.0	0.0	0.4	0.0
LICs								
Output	0.1	1.0	-0.5	5.9	1.6	3.9	3.6	3.8
Output per capita	-2.3	-1.6	-3.3	3.0	-1.1	1.3	0.9	1.1
Trade	3.6	-5.6	-1.4	4.6	0.3	6.4	7.5	6.0
Output (PPP)	0.5	0.9	-0.2	5.0	1.6	4.0	3.6	3.9
Output per capita (PPP)	-1.9	-1.7	-3.1	2.1	-1.2	1.4	1.0	1.2

Sources: Bank for International Settlements; Feenstra, Inklaar, and Timmer (2015); Haver Analytics; International Monetary Fund; Kose and Terrones (2015); Mauro et al. (2015); Organisation for Economic Co-operation and Development; World Bank.

Note: All variables show percent changes, except in unemployment rate and policy rate, in which percentage-point changes of these variables are reported. "Nonrecessions" refers to averages during 1950-2018 excluding years of global recessions. "All years" refers to averages of all years. "Global downturns" refers to averages during the four global downturns (1958, 1998, 2001, and 2012). "..." indicates that data are either unavailable or not reported since country samples to compute data for aggregated groups are too small to be representative. EMDEs = emerging market and developing economies; LICs = low-income countries; PPP = purchasing power parity.

TABLE 2A.5 Main features of global recessions, by region

	Global recessions					Non-recessions	Global downturns	All years
	1975	1982	1991	2009	Average			
East Asia and Pacific								
Output	6.6	6.3	8.3	7.5	7.2	7.0	6.7	7.0
Output per capita	4.4	4.6	6.7	6.7	5.6	5.4	5.4	5.4
Industrial production	...	...	11.1	8.0	9.5	10.0	6.3	9.9
Trade	0.2	-2.1	16.6	-6.4	2.1	9.0	4.0	8.6
Output (PPP)	6.4	6.0	8.2	7.3	7.0	6.9	6.2	6.9
Output per capita (PPP)	4.3	4.3	6.6	6.5	5.4	5.3	5.0	5.3
Europe and Central Asia								
Output	6.2	3.0	-5.8	-5.1	-0.4	3.5	1.5	3.2
Output per capita	5.3	2.1	-6.2	-5.4	-1.0	2.9	1.3	2.6
Industrial production	...	...	...	-8.7	-8.7	3.8	1.3	3.3
Trade	8.5	-1.5	-17.1	-14.3	-6.1	5.8	3.0	5.0
Output (PPP)	6.2	3.1	-5.9	-5.4	-0.5	3.4	1.4	3.2
Output per capita (PPP)	5.2	2.2	-6.3	-5.6	-1.1	2.8	1.3	2.6
Latin America and the Caribbean								
Output	3.8	-0.6	3.3	-1.8	1.2	4.1	2.6	3.9
Output per capita	1.4	-2.8	1.4	-2.9	-0.7	2.0	0.8	1.8
Industrial production	...	...	0.3	-6.5	-3.1	2.1	0.4	1.7
Trade	-1.7	-10.4	11.2	-10.9	-3.0	6.1	2.5	5.5
Output (PPP)	3.7	-0.8	3.6	-2.0	1.2	4.0	2.6	3.8
Output per capita (PPP)	1.3	-2.9	1.7	-3.1	-0.8	1.9	0.8	1.8
Middle East and North Africa								
Output	-1.3	-6.4	6.9	0.5	-0.1	5.3	5.0	5.0
Output per capita	-4.0	-9.5	4.4	-1.6	-2.7	2.7	2.8	2.4
Industrial production	...	...	...	...	...	...	...	...
Trade	5.0	-7.3	13.4	-7.0	1.0	5.4	7.5	5.2
Output (PPP)	-0.5	-5.1	7.2	0.4	0.5	5.2	4.7	4.9
Output per capita (PPP)	-3.2	-8.2	4.7	-1.6	-2.1	2.7	2.6	2.4
South Asia								
Output	7.5	3.8	2.3	4.8	4.6	5.0	5.3	5.0
Output per capita	5.0	1.3	0.1	3.3	2.4	3.0	3.5	3.0
Industrial production	...	...	...	...	...	...	...	...
Trade	6.7	5.3	7.4	-6.5	3.2	6.9	4.8	6.7
Output (PPP)	7.6	3.9	2.3	4.7	4.6	5.1	5.3	5.0
Output per capita (PPP)	5.1	1.4	0.1	3.2	2.5	3.0	3.4	3.0
Sub-Saharan Africa								
Output	0.3	0.3	0.2	3.2	1.0	4.0	3.7	3.8
Output per capita	-2.3	-2.6	-2.6	0.4	-1.8	1.2	1.0	1.1
Industrial production	...	...	...	...	...	...	...	...
Trade	6.4	-10.3	4.5	-9.9	-2.3	4.7	2.7	4.3
Output (PPP)	0.3	0.4	0.3	3.6	1.1	4.0	3.8	3.9
Output per capita (PPP)	-2.4	-2.5	-2.6	0.8	-1.6	1.3	1.1	1.1

Sources: Feenstra, Inklaar, and Timmer (2015); Haver Analytics; Kose and Terrones (2015); Organisation for Economic Co-operation and Development; World Bank.

Note: All variables show percent changes. "Nonrecessions" refers to averages during 1950-2018 excluding years of global recessions. "All years" refers to averages of all years. "Global downturns" refers to averages during the four global downturns (1958, 1998, 2001, and 2012). "..." indicates that data are either unavailable or not reported because country samples to compute data for aggregated groups are too small to be representative. PPP = purchasing power parity.

TABLE 2A.6 **Main features of global recoveries**

	Global recoveries (initial year)					Global recoveries (first three years)					All years
	1976	1983	1992	2010	Average	1976-78	1983-85	1992-94	2010-12	Average	
Activity											
Output	5.2	2.7	1.7	4.4	3.5	4.4	3.6	2.1	3.4	3.4	3.7
Output per capita	3.4	0.9	0.2	3.1	1.9	2.6	1.7	0.6	2.1	1.8	2.0
Industrial production	7.9	1.7	-0.1	8.6	4.5	5.5	3.9	1.6	4.8	3.9	3.5
Trade	8.5	1.5	3.8	12.4	6.6	6.4	4.4	5.4	7.6	6.0	5.8
Unemployment rate	0.0	-0.2	0.3	-0.1	0.0	0.1	-0.2	0.3	-0.1	0.0	0.1
Oil consumption	6.2	-0.2	1.6	3.4	2.8	5.0	0.9	1.3	1.9	2.2	2.3
Investment	5.6	1.8	-1.8	5.3	2.7	5.0	2.8	0.3	5.0	3.3	4.4
Consumption	4.7	3.3	2.7	3.0	3.4	4.3	3.5	2.7	2.7	3.3	3.6
Output (PPP)	5.6	2.8	1.8	5.3	3.9	4.6	3.5	2.3	4.2	3.7	4.0
Output per capita (PPP)	3.8	1.0	0.3	4.1	2.3	2.8	1.7	0.8	3.0	2.1	2.3
Financial markets											
Capital flows	0.5	-1.5	2.0	8.1	2.3	-0.2	-0.1	0.3	1.0	0.2	0.2
Credit	3.7	4.3	2.4	1.1	2.9	4.4	5.7	2.5	1.8	3.6	5.3
Equity prices	2.6	23.2	10.2	17.3	13.3	-3.9	16.2	12.4	4.1	7.2	5.3
House prices	-0.4	-0.1	-1.7	1.3	-0.2	1.8	-0.1	-1.1	-0.2	0.1	1.8
Financial conditions	...	...	-0.4	-0.8	-0.6	...	...	0.0	-0.3	-0.1	0.0
Inflation	-2.8	-2.3	-1.5	1.5	-1.3	-1.4	-1.0	-0.6	0.6	-0.6	0.0
Interest rates, confidence, and uncertainty											
Nominal interest rate	0.4	-1.8	-1.0	-0.1	-0.6	0.2	-0.9	-0.9	0.0	-0.4	0.0
Real interest rate	1.8	-0.1	-0.1	-1.6	0.0	1.0	0.0	-0.5	-0.4	0.0	0.0
Business confidence	1.7	1.5	-0.1	1.7	1.2	0.6	0.5	0.2	0.4	0.4	0.0
Policy uncertainty	...	...	2.1	-6.5	-2.2	...	...	-5.6	7.5	1.0	3.6
Policies											
Government expenditure	4.1	1.7	5.0	2.3	3.3	4.1	2.9	3.8	2.3	3.3	4.8
Policy rate	0.1	-1.9	-1.0	0.0	-0.7	0.2	-0.9	-0.8	0.1	-0.3	0.0

Sources: Bank for International Settlements; Bloomberg; British Petroleum; Davis (2016); European Commission; Feenstra, Inklaar, and Timmer (2015); Haver Analytics; International Monetary Fund; Kose and Terrones (2015); Mauro et al. (2015); Organisation for Economic Co-operation and Development; U.S. Energy Information Administration; country sources; World Bank.

Note: All variables show percent changes, except in capital flows, unemployment rate, inflation, nominal and real interest rates, and policy rate, in which percentage-point changes of these variables are reported. "All years" refers to averages of all years. "..." indicates that data are either unavailable or not reported because country samples to compute data for aggregated groups are too small to be representative. PPP = purchasing power parity.

TABLE 2A.7 Main features of global recoveries, by country group

	Global recoveries (initial year)					Global recoveries (first three years)					All years
	1976	1983	1992	2010	Average	1976-78	1983-85	1992-94	2010-12	Average	
Advanced economies											
Output	4.8	3.1	2.0	2.9	3.2	4.2	3.8	2.1	1.9	3.0	3.3
Output per capita	3.9	2.4	1.3	2.3	2.5	3.5	3.2	1.4	1.3	2.3	2.4
Industrial production	7.8	2.3	-0.3	7.6	4.3	5.5	3.9	1.3	3.4	3.5	3.0
Trade	10.7	2.8	5.0	12.0	7.6	7.2	5.8	5.5	6.5	6.3	5.9
Unemployment rate	0.0	0.3	0.6	0.3	0.3	0.0	-0.1	0.3	0.0	0.1	0.0
Output (PPP)	4.9	3.2	2.1	3.0	3.3	4.3	3.9	2.2	2.0	3.1	3.3
Output per capita (PPP)	4.1	2.5	1.4	2.4	2.6	3.6	3.2	1.5	1.4	2.4	2.5
Credit	3.6	4.7	1.7	-1.2	2.2	4.5	5.9	1.8	-0.6	2.9	4.7
Government expenditure	3.4	2.8	5.1	0.4	2.9	3.9	3.1	3.1	-0.1	2.5	4.2
Policy rate	0.1	-2.0	-1.0	0.0	-0.7	0.2	-1.0	-0.9	0.0	-0.4	0.0
EMDEs											
Output	6.7	1.6	0.9	7.4	4.2	5.0	2.8	2.1	6.3	4.0	4.7
Output per capita	4.5	-0.5	-0.8	6.0	2.3	2.9	0.7	0.5	4.9	2.2	2.8
Industrial production	...	...	1.4	11.0	6.2	...	...	3.6	7.9	5.7	5.0
Trade	4.6	-1.2	0.5	13.2	4.3	5.1	1.4	5.0	9.8	5.3	5.6
Unemployment rate	...	-0.5	0.3	-0.3	-0.2	...	-0.3	0.3	-0.2	-0.1	-0.1
Output (PPP)	6.7	2.2	1.4	7.5	4.5	5.0	2.9	2.4	6.3	4.2	4.8
Output per capita (PPP)	4.6	0.2	-0.3	6.1	2.6	2.9	0.9	0.7	4.9	2.3	2.9
Credit	6.0	-6.8	15.8	12.4	6.9	3.3	-0.2	13.8	12.4	7.3	7.9
Government expenditure	12.1	-5.2	4.8	6.0	4.4	7.0	2.0	6.3	6.7	5.5	5.8
Policy rate	0.2	-0.1	-1.3	-0.1	-0.3	0.3	0.1	-0.5	0.2	0.0	0.0
LICs											
Output	0.9	1.3	-1.7	6.9	1.9	0.7	2.0	-0.4	6.4	2.2	3.8
Output per capita	-1.5	-1.4	-4.5	4.0	-0.8	-1.7	-0.8	-3.3	3.5	-0.6	1.1
Trade	-2.3	0.9	-6.3	15.1	1.8	4.7	7.9	-0.8	13.8	6.4	6.0
Output (PPP)	1.3	1.4	-1.3	7.2	2.1	1.0	2.1	0.0	6.3	2.3	3.9
Output per capita (PPP)	-1.1	-1.4	-4.1	4.2	-0.6	-1.4	-0.7	-2.9	3.3	-0.4	1.2

Sources: Bank for International Settlements; Feenstra, Inklaar, and Timmer (2015); Haver Analytics; International Monetary Fund; Kose and Terrones (2015); Mauro et al. (2015); Organisation for Economic Co-operation and Development; World Bank.

Note: All variables show percent changes, except in unemployment rate and policy rate, in which percentage-point changes of these variables are reported. "All years" refers to averages of all years. "..." indicates that data are either unavailable or not reported because country samples to compute data for aggregated groups are too small to be representative. EMDEs = emerging market and developing economies; LICs = low-income countries; PPP = purchasing power parity.

TABLE 2A.8 Main features of global recoveries, by region

	Global recoveries (initial year)					Global recoveries (first three years)					All years
	1976	1983	1992	2010	Average	1976-78	1983-85	1992-94	2010-12	Average	
East Asia and Pacific											
Output	3.4	7.5	10.9	9.8	7.9	6.7	8.3	11.0	8.6	8.6	7.0
Output per capita	1.4	5.8	9.5	8.9	6.4	4.8	6.5	9.6	7.8	7.2	5.4
Industrial production	...	...	10.4	14.5	12.5	...	...	13.0	11.6	12.3	9.9
Trade	2.6	7.7	16.0	18.1	11.1	8.6	9.3	17.8	12.3	12.0	8.6
Output (PPP)	3.9	7.1	10.5	9.6	7.8	6.8	7.8	10.6	8.4	8.4	6.9
Output per capita (PPP)	1.9	5.4	9.0	8.8	6.3	4.9	6.0	9.2	7.6	6.9	5.3
Europe and Central Asia											
Output	6.1	4.3	-9.4	4.6	1.4	4.9	2.7	-7.3	4.6	1.2	3.2
Output per capita	5.2	3.4	-9.8	4.2	0.8	4.0	1.9	-7.6	4.1	0.6	2.6
Industrial production	...	...	-1.7	9.5	3.9	...	...	-0.7	7.6	3.5	3.3
Trade	5.9	0.9	-22.4	11.9	-0.9	6.8	5.3	-7.1	8.4	3.3	5.0
Output (PPP)	6.1	4.3	-9.8	4.5	1.3	4.9	2.7	-7.8	4.4	1.1	3.2
Output per capita (PPP)	5.2	3.4	-10.1	4.2	0.7	4.0	1.9	-8.1	4.1	0.5	2.6
Latin America and the Caribbean											
Output	6.0	-2.5	2.5	6.7	3.2	4.8	1.8	4.0	4.6	3.8	3.9
Output per capita	3.5	-4.6	0.7	5.5	1.3	2.4	-0.4	2.2	3.5	1.9	1.8
Industrial production	...	...	0.6	7.9	4.2	...	...	4.2	3.2	3.7	1.7
Trade	1.9	-5.3	12.1	17.6	6.6	5.1	1.6	10.5	9.8	6.8	5.5
Output (PPP)	5.4	-2.4	2.9	6.7	3.1	4.6	1.6	4.2	4.7	3.8	3.8
Output per capita (PPP)	3.0	-4.5	1.0	5.5	1.2	2.2	-0.6	2.3	3.5	1.9	1.8

TABLE 2A.8 Main features of global recoveries, by region (*continued*)

	Global recoveries (initial year)					Global recoveries (first three years)					All years
	1976	1983	1992	2010	Average	1976-78	1983-85	1992-94	2010-12	Average	
Middle East and North Africa											
Output	15.7	-1.5	5.8	4.8	6.2	6.1	-0.4	3.2	4.5	3.3	5.0
Output per capita	12.5	-4.8	3.5	2.6	3.4	3.1	-3.7	1.1	2.2	0.7	2.4
Industrial production	...	...	...	...	...	...	...	...	...	...	...
Trade	6.2	-3.9	6.6	1.3	2.6	2.4	-7.0	2.3	4.8	0.6	5.2
Output (PPP)	15.6	-0.5	5.3	4.1	6.1	5.9	0.1	2.9	3.5	3.1	4.9
Output per capita (PPP)	12.4	-3.8	3.0	2.0	3.4	2.9	-3.2	0.7	1.3	0.5	2.4
South Asia											
Output	2.3	6.7	5.3	9.6	6.0	4.9	5.4	5.3	7.3	5.7	5.0
Output per capita	-0.1	4.1	3.1	8.0	3.8	2.5	2.9	3.1	5.8	3.6	3.0
Industrial production	...	...	...	...	...	...	...	...	...	...	...
Trade	8.0	9.0	14.6	14.6	11.6	9.3	4.4	12.7	13.7	10.0	6.7
Output (PPP)	2.3	6.7	5.3	9.6	6.0	5.0	5.5	5.3	7.2	5.7	5.0
Output per capita (PPP)	-0.1	4.2	3.1	8.0	3.8	2.5	3.0	3.1	5.8	3.6	3.0
Sub-Saharan Africa											
Output	4.9	-1.5	-0.8	6.5	2.3	2.3	1.2	0.3	5.2	2.3	3.8
Output per capita	2.1	-4.3	-3.5	3.7	-0.5	-0.4	-1.7	-2.5	2.4	-0.6	1.1
Industrial production	...	...	...	...	...	...	...	...	...	...	...
Trade	-1.0	-7.2	-3.8	7.4	-1.2	4.1	-0.9	3.5	6.3	3.2	4.3
Output (PPP)	5.1	-1.5	-0.6	6.8	2.5	2.5	1.2	0.3	5.3	2.3	3.9
Output per capita (PPP)	2.3	-4.3	-3.4	4.0	-0.3	-0.2	-1.7	-2.5	2.5	-0.5	1.1

Sources: Feenstra, Inklaar, and Timmer (2015); Haver Analytics; Kose and Terrones (2015); Organisation for Economic Co-operation and Development; World Bank.

Note: All variables show percent changes. "All years" refers to averages of all years. "..." indicates that data are either unavailable or not reported because country samples to compute data for aggregated groups are too small to be representative. PPP = purchasing power parity.

TABLE 2A.9 Main features of global expansions

	Global expansions					Global expansions (excluding initial years)					All years
	1976-81	1983-90	1992-2008	2010-19	Average	1977-81	1984-90	1993-2008	2011-19	Average	
Activity											
Output	3.5	3.5	3.1	3.0	3.3	3.1	3.6	3.2	2.8	3.2	3.7
Output per capita	1.7	1.7	1.7	1.8	1.7	1.4	1.8	1.8	1.6	1.7	2.0
Industrial production	3.7	3.5	2.8	2.9	3.2	2.8	3.7	3.0	2.3	3.0	3.5
Trade	5.1	5.2	6.7	4.7	5.4	4.4	5.7	6.9	3.9	5.2	5.8
Unemployment rate	0.1	-0.1	0.1	-0.1	0.0	0.1	-0.1	0.0	-0.1	0.0	0.1
Oil consumption	1.6	1.8	1.5	1.7	1.7	0.7	2.1	1.5	1.5	1.4	2.3
Investment	3.4	3.8	3.4	3.8	3.6	2.9	4.1	3.8	3.7	3.6	4.4
Consumption	3.4	3.4	3.1	2.7	3.2	3.1	3.5	3.1	2.7	3.1	3.6
Output (PPP)	3.6	3.5	3.6	3.7	3.6	3.2	3.6	3.7	3.5	3.5	4.0
Output per capita (PPP)	1.8	1.7	2.2	2.5	2.1	1.4	1.8	2.4	2.4	2.0	2.3
Financial markets											
Capital flows	0.3	0.2	0.5	0.2	0.3	0.2	0.5	0.4	-0.8	0.1	0.2
Credit	3.6	6.5	4.1	3.8	4.5	3.6	6.8	4.2	4.1	4.7	5.3
Equity prices	-1.7	16.6	8.9	5.3	7.3	-2.5	15.7	8.8	3.9	6.5	5.3
House prices	1.6	2.8	1.7	1.6	1.9	2.0	3.2	1.9	1.6	2.2	1.8
Financial conditions	...	0.2	0.0	-0.1	0.0	...	0.2	0.0	0.0	0.1	0.0
Inflation	-0.2	-0.3	-0.1	0.1	-0.1	0.3	0.0	0.0	0.0	0.1	0.0
Interest rates, confidence, and uncertainty											
Nominal interest rate	1.0	-0.2	-0.3	0.1	0.1	1.2	0.0	-0.2	0.1	0.2	0.0
Real interest rate	1.0	0.0	-0.2	-0.1	0.2	0.9	0.0	-0.2	0.1	0.2	0.0
Business confidence	0.1	0.2	0.0	0.1	0.1	-0.2	0.0	0.0	0.0	-0.1	0.0
Policy uncertainty	...	0.0	2.8	5.7	2.8	...	0.0	2.9	7.0	3.3	3.6
Policies											
Government expenditure	4.2	3.0	4.1	2.8	3.5	4.3	3.2	4.0	2.9	3.6	4.8
Policy rate	1.0	-0.3	-0.3	0.1	0.1	1.2	-0.1	-0.2	0.1	0.2	0.0

Sources: Feenstra, Inklaar, and Timmer (2015); Haver Analytics; Kose and Terrones (2015); Organisation for Economic Co-operation and Development; World Bank.

Note: All variables show percent changes, except in capital flows, unemployment rate, inflation, nominal and real interest rates, and policy rate, in which percentage-point changes of these variables are reported. "All years" refers to averages of all years. "..." indicates that data are either unavailable or not reported because country samples to compute data for aggregated groups are too small to be representative. PPP = purchasing power parity.

TABLE 2A.10 Main features of global expansions, by country group

	Global expansions					Global expansions (excluding initial years)					All years
	1976-81	1983-90	1992-2008	2010-19	Average	1977-81	1984-90	1993-2008	2011-19	Average	
Advanced economies											
Output	3.3	3.7	2.5	1.9	2.9	3.0	3.8	2.5	1.8	2.8	3.3
Output per capita	2.6	3.1	1.8	1.4	2.2	2.3	3.2	1.8	1.4	2.2	2.4
Industrial production	3.5	3.5	2.0	1.9	2.7	2.7	3.7	2.1	1.2	2.4	3.0
Trade	5.6	6.4	6.1	4.3	5.6	4.6	6.9	6.2	3.4	5.3	5.9
Unemployment rate	0.2	-0.2	0.0	-0.3	-0.1	0.3	-0.3	-0.1	-0.4	-0.1	0.0
Output (PPP)	3.4	3.8	2.6	2.0	2.9	3.1	3.8	2.6	1.9	2.8	3.3
Output per capita (PPP)	2.6	3.1	1.9	1.5	2.3	2.3	3.2	2.0	1.4	2.2	2.5
Credit	3.5	6.8	3.4	1.2	3.7	3.5	7.1	3.5	1.5	3.9	4.7
Government expenditure	3.9	3.3	2.9	1.1	2.8	4.1	3.3	2.8	1.2	2.8	4.2
Policy rate	1.0	-0.3	-0.3	0.0	0.1	1.2	-0.1	-0.3	0.0	0.2	0.0
EMDEs											
Output	4.0	3.0	4.7	4.9	4.1	3.5	3.2	4.9	4.6	4.0	4.7
Output per capita	2.0	0.9	3.2	3.5	2.4	1.4	1.1	3.4	3.3	2.3	2.8
Industrial production	...	...	5.6	5.1	5.3	...	...	5.8	4.5	5.1	5.0
Trade	4.2	2.3	8.1	5.6	5.0	4.1	2.8	8.6	4.8	5.1	5.6
Unemployment rate	-3.5	0.0	0.1	0.0	-0.9	-3.5	0.0	0.1	0.0	-0.9	-0.1
Output (PPP)	4.0	3.2	4.8	5.2	4.3	3.4	3.3	5.1	4.9	4.2	4.8
Output per capita (PPP)	1.9	1.1	3.3	3.8	2.5	1.4	1.2	3.6	3.6	2.4	2.9
Credit	6.1	0.8	10.4	10.7	7.0	6.1	1.9	10.1	10.5	7.1	7.9
Government expenditure	6.9	1.4	7.1	5.7	5.3	5.8	2.4	7.2	5.7	5.3	5.8
Policy rate	0.3	0.3	-0.3	0.0	0.1	0.3	0.4	-0.2	0.0	0.1	0.0
LICs											
Output	1.3	2.5	4.0	5.9	3.4	1.4	2.6	4.3	5.8	3.5	3.8
Output per capita	-1.1	-0.4	1.1	3.0	0.6	-1.1	-0.3	1.5	2.8	0.7	1.1
Trade	1.7	4.5	7.4	8.8	5.6	2.5	5.0	8.2	8.2	6.0	6.0
Output (PPP)	1.6	2.6	4.2	6.1	3.6	1.6	2.8	4.5	6.0	3.7	3.9
Output per capita (PPP)	-0.9	-0.3	1.3	3.1	0.8	-0.8	-0.1	1.6	3.0	0.9	1.2

Sources: Bank for International Settlements; Feenstra, Inklaar, and Timmer (2015); Haver Analytics; International Monetary Fund; Kose and Terrones (2015); Mauro et al. (2015); Organisation for Economic Co-operation and Development; World Bank.

Note: All variables show percent changes, except in unemployment rate and policy rate, in which percentage-point changes of these variables are reported. "All years" refers to averages of all years. "..." indicates that data are either unavailable or not reported because country samples to compute data for aggregated groups are too small to be representative. EMDEs = emerging market and developing economies; LICs = low-income countries; PPP = purchasing power parity.

TABLE 2A.11 Main features of global expansions, by region

	Global expansions					Global expansions (excluding initial years)					All years
	1976-81	1983-90	1992-2008	2010-19	Average	1977-81	1984-90	1993-2008	2011-19	Average	
East Asia and Pacific											
Output	6.8	8.0	8.7	7.1	7.6	7.5	8.0	8.5	6.8	7.7	7.0
Output per capita	5.0	6.0	7.6	6.4	6.2	5.7	6.1	7.5	6.1	6.3	5.4
Industrial production	...	12.7	10.4	8.0	10.4	...	12.7	10.4	7.3	10.1	9.9
Trade	10.2	10.1	12.5	7.2	10.0	11.7	10.4	12.2	6.0	10.1	8.6
Output (PPP)	6.8	7.7	8.3	7.0	7.5	7.4	7.8	8.2	6.7	7.6	6.9
Output per capita (PPP)	5.0	5.8	7.3	6.3	6.1	5.7	5.8	7.2	6.0	6.2	5.3
Europe and Central Asia											
Output	2.8	1.9	2.2	3.2	2.5	2.1	1.6	2.9	3.0	2.4	3.2
Output per capita	1.9	1.1	2.1	2.7	1.9	1.2	0.8	2.8	2.5	1.8	2.6
Industrial production	...	...	3.5	4.2	3.9	...	...	3.9	3.6	3.7	3.3
Trade	4.5	1.0	6.2	4.9	4.2	4.3	1.0	8.0	4.2	4.3	5.0
Output (PPP)	2.8	1.9	2.1	3.0	2.4	2.1	1.5	2.8	2.9	2.3	3.2
Output per capita (PPP)	1.9	1.1	2.0	2.6	1.9	1.2	0.7	2.7	2.4	1.8	2.6
Latin America and the Caribbean											
Output	4.9	2.0	3.2	2.2	3.1	4.7	2.6	3.3	1.7	3.1	3.9
Output per capita	2.5	-0.1	1.7	1.1	1.3	2.3	0.6	1.8	0.6	1.3	1.8
Industrial production	...	...	3.0	0.5	1.7	...	...	3.1	-0.3	1.4	1.7
Trade	7.5	4.6	7.2	4.7	6.0	8.6	6.1	6.9	3.3	6.2	5.5
Output (PPP)	4.8	1.9	3.2	2.4	3.1	4.7	2.5	3.3	1.9	3.1	3.8
Output per capita (PPP)	2.4	-0.2	1.7	1.2	1.3	2.3	0.4	1.8	0.8	1.3	1.8

TABLE 2A.11 Main features of global expansions, by region (*continued*)

	Global expansions					Global expansions (excluding initial years)					All years
	1976-81	1983-90	1992-2008	2010-19	Average	1977-81	1984-90	1993-2008	2011-19	Average	
Middle East and North Africa											
Output	4.5	1.8	4.1	3.0	3.3	2.3	2.3	4.0	2.8	2.8	5.0
Output per capita	1.4	-1.3	2.1	0.9	0.8	-0.8	-0.8	2.1	0.7	0.3	2.4
Industrial production	...	...	...	...	...	...	...	...	...	...	...
Trade	0.7	0.0	5.4	3.2	2.3	-0.4	0.6	5.3	3.4	2.2	5.2
Output (PPP)	4.1	2.0	4.0	2.6	3.2	1.8	2.3	3.9	2.5	2.6	4.9
Output per capita (PPP)	1.0	-1.1	2.1	0.7	0.7	-1.3	-0.7	2.0	0.5	0.1	2.4
South Asia											
Output	4.1	5.6	6.1	6.9	5.7	4.5	5.4	6.2	6.7	5.7	5.0
Output per capita	1.6	3.1	4.2	5.6	3.6	2.0	3.0	4.2	5.3	3.6	3.0
Industrial production	...	...	...	...	...	...	...	...	...	...	...
Trade	7.2	5.1	13.0	7.0	8.1	7.0	4.5	12.9	6.2	7.7	6.7
Output (PPP)	4.1	5.6	6.1	6.9	5.7	4.5	5.4	6.2	6.7	5.7	5.0
Output per capita (PPP)	1.7	3.2	4.2	5.6	3.7	2.0	3.0	4.3	5.4	3.7	3.0
Sub-Saharan Africa											
Output	2.5	2.2	4.0	3.7	3.1	2.0	2.7	4.3	3.4	3.1	3.8
Output per capita	-0.2	-0.7	1.3	0.9	0.3	-0.7	-0.2	1.6	0.6	0.3	1.1
Industrial production	...	...	...	...	...	...	...	...	...	...	...
Trade	3.9	1.0	7.2	3.6	3.9	4.9	2.2	7.9	3.1	4.5	4.3
Output (PPP)	2.5	2.3	4.1	3.9	3.2	2.0	2.9	4.4	3.6	3.2	3.9
Output per capita (PPP)	-0.3	-0.6	1.4	1.1	0.4	-0.8	-0.1	1.7	0.8	0.4	1.1

Sources: Feenstra, Inklaar, and Timmer (2015); Haver Analytics; Kose and Terrones (2015); Organisation for Economic Co-operation and Development; World Bank.

Note: All variables show percent changes. "All years" refers to averages of all years. "..." indicates that data are either unavailable or not reported because country samples to compute data for aggregated groups are too small to be representative. PPP = purchasing power parity.

ANNEX 2B List of economies in the database

Advanced economies (36)			
Australia	France	Korea, Rep.	Singapore
Austria	Germany	Latvia	Slovak Republic
Belgium	Greece	Lithuania	Slovenia
Canada	Hong Kong SAR, China	Luxembourg	Spain
Cyprus	Iceland	Malta	Sweden
Czech Republic	Ireland	Netherlands	Switzerland
Denmark	Israel	New Zealand	Taiwan, China
Estonia	Italy	Norway	United Kingdom
Finland	Japan	Portugal	United States
Emerging market and developing economies (145)			
East Asia and Pacific (22)			
Cambodia	Malaysia	Papua New Guinea	Tonga
China	Marshall Islands	Philippines	Tuvalu
Fiji	Micronesia, Fed. Sts.	Samoa	Vanuatu
Indonesia	Mongolia	Solomon Islands	Vietnam
Kiribati	Myanmar	Thailand	
Lao PDR	Palau	Timor-Leste	
Europe and Central Asia (24)			
Albania	Croatia	Moldova	Serbia
Armenia	Georgia	Montenegro	*Tajikistan*
Azerbaijan	Hungary	North Macedonia	Turkey
Belarus	Kazakhstan	Poland	Turkmenistan
Bosnia and Herzegovina	Kosovo	Romania	Ukraine
Bulgaria	Kyrgyz Republic	Russian Federation	Uzbekistan
Latin America and the Caribbean (31)			
Antigua and Barbuda	Colombia	Guyana	Peru
Argentina	Costa Rica	*Haiti*	St. Kitts and Nevis
Bahamas, The	Dominica	Honduras	St. Lucia
Barbados	Dominican Republic	Jamaica	St. Vincent and the Grenadines
Belize	Ecuador	Mexico	Suriname
Bolivia	El Salvador	Nicaragua	Trinidad and Tobago
Brazil	Grenada	Panama	Uruguay
Chile	Guatemala	Paraguay	

Emerging market and developing economies (145) - *continued*			
Middle East and North Africa (16)			
Algeria	Iran, Islamic Rep.	Lebanon	Saudi Arabia
Bahrain	Iraq	Morocco	Tunisia
Djibouti	Jordan	Oman	United Arab Emirates
Egypt, Arab Rep.	Kuwait	Qatar	West Bank and Gaza
South Asia (8)			
Afghanistan	Bhutan	Maldives	Pakistan
Bangladesh	India	*Nepal*	Sri Lanka
Sub-Saharan Africa (44)			
Angola	Côte d'Ivoire	Lesotho	*Rwanda*
Benin	Equatorial Guinea	*Liberia*	Senegal
Botswana	*Eritrea*	*Madagascar*	Seychelles
Burkina Faso	Eswatini	*Malawi*	*Sierra Leone*
Burundi	*Ethiopia*	*Mali*	South Africa
Cabo Verde	Gabon	Mauritania	Sudan
Cameroon	*Gambia, The*	Mauritius	*Tanzania*
Chad	Ghana	*Mozambique*	*Togo*
Comoros	*Guinea*	Namibia	*Uganda*
Congo, Dem. Rep.	*Guinea-Bissau*	*Niger*	Zambia
Congo, Rep.	Kenya	Nigeria	Zimbabwe

Source: World Bank.

Note: The number of countries is in parentheses next to the country group name. Those in italics are low-income countries (based on the World Bank classification for FY2020).

ANNEX 2C Definitions and sources of variables

Variable	Definition	Source
Activity		
Output	GDP in constant 2010 U.S. dollars (market weighted), taken from the World Bank. Before 1960, the series is extended using data from the Penn World Tables 9.1 (PWT 9.1). Sample includes 181 economies, including 36 advanced economies and 145 EMDEs. For PPP-weighted series, GDP is in constant 2010 international dollars.	Feenstra, Inklaar, and Timmer (2015); World Bank
Output per capita	GDP per capita, in constant 2010 U.S. dollars (market weighted), taken from the World Bank. Before 1960, both GDP and population series are extended using data from PWT 9.1. Sample includes 181 economies. For PPP-weighted series, GDP per capita is in constant 2010 international dollars.	Feenstra, Inklaar, and Timmer (2015); World Bank
Industrial production	Industrial production index (if not available, manufacturing production index is used). Data are obtained at a quarterly frequency and used as annual averages of year-on-year growth rates. For aggregated groups, market-weighted output is used as a weight. The main source of the series is the World Bank and, for economies and quarters without data, the series is extended using growth rates of data from the OECD and Haver Analytics.	Haver Analytics, OECD, World Bank
Trade	Exports plus imports of goods and services, in constant 2010 U.S. dollars, taken from the World Bank. Before 1960, the series of exports and imports are extended using data from PWT 9.1. Trade for aggregated groups is the sum of exports and imports of individual economies.	Feenstra, Inklaar, and Timmer (2015); World Bank
Unemployment rate	Unemployment, in percent of labor force, taken from the International Monetary Fund. Data for aggregated groups are computed as the sum of those unemployed in individual economies divided by the sum of labor force.	International Monetary Fund
Oil consumption	Oil consumption, in thousand barrels per day. Oil consumption in advanced economies and EMDEs is computed as the sum of consumption in individual economies. If there are differences between the world total and the sum of advanced economies and EMDEs, the residuals are added to the EMDE aggregate. The number of world oil consumption for 2019 is based on data over the first nine months of the year.	British Petroleum, U.S. Energy Information Administration

ANNEX 2C Definitions and sources of variables (*continued*)

Variable	Definition	Source
Financial market		
Capital flows	Total capital flows, defined as the sum of absolute values of outflows (net acquisition of financial asset, including direct, portfolio, and other assets) and inflows (net incurrence of liabilities, including direct, portfolio, and other liabilities), in current U.S. dollars, taken from the International Monetary Fund Balance of Payments Statistics (sixth edition). The figures for 2019 show data over the first two quarters of the year. For the historical series, the statistics based on the fifth edition are also used. The series is shown as a percent of GDP, which is taken from the World Bank and PWT 9.1.	Feenstra, Inklaar, and Timmer (2015); International Monetary Fund; World Bank
Credit	Nominal credit provided by banks and other financial corporations, deflated by the consumer price index (CPI). Data are at a quarterly frequency and shown as annual averages of year-on-year growth of real credit. Nominal credit series is taken from the International Monetary Fund's International Financial Statistics (IFS), titled claims on private sector (by depository or financial corporations), and the Bank for International Settlements. CPI is taken from the Bank for International Settlements, Haver Analytics, and the International Monetary Fund. Credit for aggregated groups is computed as follows. First, real credit (in local currency) is converted to constant 2010 U.S. dollars, and then U.S.-dollar real credit in individual economies is aggregated into respective groups.	Bank for International Settlements, Haver Analytics, International Monetary Fund
Equity prices	Share price index, deflated by CPI. Data are at a quarterly frequency and used as annual averages of year-on-year growth of real equity prices. Data are from the International Monetary Fund (IFS) and Haver Analytics and available as period averages and end-of-period values. The one with longer data availability is used as the main series. Growth in aggregated groups is computed with market-weighted output as a weight. CPI is taken from the Bank for International Settlements, Haver Analytics, and the International Monetary Fund.	Bank for International Settlements, Haver Analytics, International Monetary Fund, World Bank
House prices	House (or property) prices, deflated by CPI. Data are at a quarterly frequency and used as annual averages of year-on-year growth of real house prices. Data are from the Bank for International Settlements, Haver Analytics, and OECD. Growth in aggregated groups is computed with market-weighted output as a weight. CPI is taken from the Bank for International Settlements, Haver Analytics, and the International Monetary Fund.	Bank for International Settlements, Haver Analytics, International Monetary Fund, OECD, World Bank

ANNEX 2C Definitions and sources of variables *(continued)*

Variable	Definition	Source
Financial conditions	An index of financial conditions, computed as a weighted average of short-term and long-term interest rates, trade-weighted dollar, an index of credit spreads, and the ratio of equity prices to the 10-year average of earnings per share, as explained in Hatzius and Stehn (2018). Higher index numbers reflect tighter financial conditions. Data are at a monthly frequency and used as annual averages of year-on-year growth of the index. Growth in aggregated groups is computed with market-weighted output as a weight.	Bloomberg, Goldman Sachs, World Bank
Inflation	Change in CPI in percent. Data are at a quarterly frequency and used as annual averages of year-on-year percent changes of CPI. The series is taken from the Bank for International Settlements, Haver Analytics, and the International Monetary Fund. Inflation in aggregated groups is computed with market-weighted output as a weight. In order to eliminate an effect of countries with a history of high inflation, countries whose average inflation over the entire sample period (based on quarterly data) is above the top 20th percentile, are excluded.	Bank for International Settlements, Haver Analytics, International Monetary Fund, World Bank
Interest rates, confidence, and uncertainty		
Short-term interest rate (nominal and real)	Treasury bill rates or money market rates, with the maturity of three months or less. In countries where 3-month rates are unavailable, shorter maturity rates (including overnight rates) are used. Data are at a quarterly frequency and used as annual averages. The real short-term interest rate is the difference between nominal rate and inflation in the following quarter (as a proxy of expected inflation). Data are taken from different sources, and the data series with the longest time coverage is used as the main series. Then, the main series is spliced with those from other data sources. Data for aggregated groups are computed with market-weighted output as a weight.	Bank for International Settlements, Haver Analytics, International Monetary Fund, OECD, World Bank
Business confidence	Business confidence index, originally taken from the European Commission, OECD, and country sources (including statistical offices, central banks, academic institutions, and think tanks). The series is obtained as quarterly data and used as annual averages. Data from different sources are first standardized and converted to an index equal to 100 in 2015-18. Confidence for aggregated groups is computed with market-weighted output as a weight.	European Commission, OECD, country sources, World Bank
Policy uncertainty	Economic policy uncertainty index, which is based on the frequency of articles in domestic newspapers mentioning economic policy uncertainty. Country-level indexes are at a monthly frequency and used as annual averages. Data are first converted to a 6-month moving average and then an index equal to 100 in 2015-18. Aggregated policy uncertainty is computed with market -weighted output as a weight, based on 20 economies with available data.	Davis (2016); World Bank

ANNEX 2C Definitions and sources of variables (*continued*)

Variable	Definition	Source
Policies		
Government expenditure	Government primary expenditure (that is, government total expenditure excluding interest expense) in local currency, deflated by GDP deflator. The expenditure series is first taken from the International Monetary Fund and then extended with data in Mauro et al. (2015). GDP deflator is taken from the International Monetary Fund, PWT 9.1, and the World Bank. Real government expenditure growth in aggregated groups is computed with market-weighted output as a weight.	International Monetary Fund; Mauro et al. (2015); World Bank
Policy interest rate	Nominal central bank policy rates. Data are at a quarterly frequency and used as annual averages. Data are taken from different sources, and the data series with the longest time coverage is used as the main series. Then, the main series is spliced with those from other data sources. Data for aggregated groups are computed with market-weighted output as a weight.	Bank for International Settlements; Haver Analytics; International Monetary Fund; OECD; World Bank
Quarterly series		
Output (per capita) growth	Quarterly real GDP is taken from Haver Analytics and OECD. Quarter-on-quarter annualized growth rates of seasonally adjusted real GDP are computed. If the original data are not seasonally adjusted, the U.S. Census X-13 program is used to perform seasonal adjustment first. Quarterly growth for aggregated groups is computed with market-weighted annual output as a weight—the same weights are applied to four quarters in given years. In computing per capita growth, population data are used on an annual basis and taken from the World Bank and PWT, and therefore, the same population growth numbers are used in four quarters in given years. As a result, output per capita growth is calculated as the difference between aggregated annualized quarterly GDP growth and annual population growth. When computing growth rates over two quarters with different samples, economies are restricted to the common samples between these two quarters and with GDP and population. Sample includes 105 economies, though the sample size varies by quarter, over 1960:1-2019:2. Data for the 1950s are excluded because of the limited data availability.	Feenstra, Inklaar, and Timmer (2015); Haver Analytics; OECD; World Bank

Source: World Bank.

Note: Country-group aggregates are not computed, if the sample size is limited—specifically, data need to be available for at least 10 economies in all variables except in financial conditions, short-term interest rates, business confidence, and policy uncertainty (at least 4 economies, because of more limited data availability in the original series). The sample coverage mentioned in the table is the maximum number of countries and the sample size varies by year or quarter. Output from other data sources is also used for comparison purposes: the International Monetary Fund World Economic Outlook (October 2019) has annual data available since 1980 and the United Nations National Accounts Main Aggregates Database has annual data starting in 1970. OECD = Organisation for Economic Co-operation and Development.

References

Alessandria, G., J. P. Kaboski, and V. Midrigan. 2010. "The Great Trade Collapse of 2008-09: An Inventory Adjustment?" *IMF Economic Review* 58 (2): 254-94.

Allen, R. E. 2009. *Financial Crises and Recession in the Global Economy*. Third Edition. Northampton: Edward Elgar.

Amiti, M., and D. E. Weinstein. 2011. "Exports and Financial Shocks." *Quarterly Journal of Economics* 126 (4): 1841-77.

Arteta, C., M. A. Kose, F. Ohnsorge, and M. Stocker. 2015. "The Coming U.S. Interest Rate Tightening Cycle: Smooth Sailing or Stormy Waters?" Policy Research Note 15/02, World Bank, Washington, DC.

Bacchetta, P., and E. van Wincoop. 2016. "The Great Recession: A Self-Fulfilling Global Panic." *American Economic Journal: Macroeconomics* 8 (4): 177-94.

Baffes, J., M. A. Kose, F. Ohnsorge, and M. Stocker. 2015. "The Great Plunge in Oil Prices: Causes, Consequences, and Policy Responses." Policy Research Note 15/01, World Bank, Washington, DC.

Baker, S. R., and N. Bloom. 2013. "Does Uncertainty Reduce Growth? Using Disasters as Natural Experiments." NBER Working Paper 19475, National Bureau of Economic Research, Cambridge.

Balke, N. S., and M. A. Wynne. 1995. "Recessions and Recoveries in Real Business Cycle Models." *Economic Inquiry* 33 (4): 640-63.

Barsky, R. B., and L. Kilian. 2004. "Oil and the Macroeconomy since the 1970s." *Journal of Economic Perspectives* 18 (4): 115-34.

Bec, F., O. Bouabdallah, and L. Ferrara. 2015. "Comparing the Shape of Recoveries: France, the UK and the US." *Economic Modelling* 44: 327-34.

Bems, R., R. C. Johnson, and K.-M. Yi. 2010. "Demand Spillovers and the Collapse of Trade in the Global Recession." *IMF Economic Review* 58 (2): 295-26.

Bernanke, B. S., and C. S. Lown. 1991. "The Credit Crunch." *Brookings Papers on Economic Activity* 1991 (2): 205-47.

Bry, G., and C. Boschan. 1971. *Cyclical Analysis of Time Series: Selected Procedures and Computer Programs*. New York: National Bureau of Economic Research.

Burns, A. F., and W. C. Mitchell. 1946. *Measuring Business Cycles*. New York: National Bureau of Economic Research.

Caldara, D., M. Iacoviello, P. Molligo, A. Prestipino, and A. Raffo. 2019. "Does Trade Policy Uncertainty Affect Global Economic Activity?" FEDS Notes, September 4, Board of Governors of the Federal Reserve System, Washington, DC.

Calderón, C., and J. R. Fuentes. 2014. "Have Business Cycles Changed over the Last Two Decades? An Empirical Investigation." *Journal of Development Economics* 109: 98-123.

Callen, T. 2007. "PPP versus the Market: Which Weight Matters?" *Finance & Development* 44 (1): 50-51.

Camacho, M., and J. Martinez-Martin. 2015. "Monitoring the World Business Cycle." *Economic Modelling* 51: 617-25.

Cerra, V., U. Panizza, and S. C. Saxena. 2013. "International Evidence on Recovery from Recessions." *Contemporary Economic Policy* 31 (2): 424-39.

Chor, D., and K. Manova. 2012. "Off the Cliff and Back? Credit Conditions and International Trade during the Global Financial Crisis." *Journal of International Economics* 87 (1): 117-33.

Chui, M., P. Levine, S. M. Murshed, and J. Pearlman. 2002. "North-South Models of Growth and Trade." *Journal of Economic Surveys* 16 (2): 123-65.

Claessens, S. 2017. "Global Banking: Recent Developments and Insights from Research." *Review of Finance* 21 (4): 1513-55.

Claessens, S., M. A. Kose, and M. E. Terrones. 2009. "What Happens during Recessions, Crunches, and Busts?" *Economic Policy* 24 (60): 653-700.

Claessens, S., M. A. Kose, and M. E. Terrones. 2011. "Financial Cycles: What? How? When?" In *NBER International Seminar on Macroeconomics 2010*, edited by R. Clarida and F. Giavazzi, 303-43. Chicago: University of Chicago Press.

Claessens, S., M. A. Kose, and M. E. Terrones. 2012. "How Do Business and Financial Cycles Interact?" *Journal of International Economics* 87 (1): 178-90.

Cooper, R. N. 2014. "Will China's Economy Surpass the United States' in 2014?" Caixin Online, June 5. https://scholar.harvard.edu/files/cooper/files/century5.14chinagdp.pdf.

Cuba-Borda, P., A. Mechanick, and A. Raffo. 2018. "Monitoring the World Economy: A Global Conditions Index." IFDP Notes, June, Board of Governors of the Federal Reserve System, Washington, DC.

Currie, D., and D. Vines, eds. 1988. *Macroeconomic Interactions between North and South*. New York: Cambridge University Press.

Davis, S. J. 2016. "An Index of Global Economic Policy Uncertainty." NBER Working Paper 22740, National Bureau of Economic Research, Cambridge, MA.

Didier, T., M. A. Kose, F. Ohnsorge, and L. S. Ye. 2015. "Slowdown in Emerging Markets: Rough Patch or Prolonged Weakness?" Policy Research Note 15/04, World Bank, Washington, DC.

Diebold, F. X., and K. Yilmaz. 2015. *Financial and Macroeconomic Connectedness: A Network Approach to Measurement and Monitoring*. New York: Oxford University Press.

di Giovanni, J., and A. A. Levchenko. 2010. "Putting the Parts Together: Trade, Vertical Linkages, and Business Cycle Comovement." *American Economic Journal: Macroeconomics* 2 (2): 95-104.

di Giovanni, J., A. A. Levchenko, and I. Mejean. 2018. "The Micro Origins of International Business-Cycle Comovement." *American Economic Review* 108 (1): 82-108.

Eckstein, O., and A. Sinai. 1986. "The Mechanisms of the Business Cycle in the Postwar Era." In *The American Business Cycle: Continuity and Change*, edited by R. J. Gordon, 39-122. Chicago: University of Chicago Press.

Economist, The. 2001. "Going Downhill." *The Economist*, September 27, 2001. https://www.economist.com/finance-and-economics/2001/09/27/going-downhill.

Economist, The. 2008. "The Global Slumpometer." *The Economist*, November 6, 2008. https://www.economist.com/finance-and-economics/2008/11/06/the-global-slumpometer.

Eggertsson, G. B., N. R. Mehrotra, and J. A. Robbins. 2019. "A Model of Secular Stagnation: Theory and Quantitative Evaluation." *American Economic Journal: Macroeconomics* 11 (1): 1-48.

Eichengreen, B., and P. Gupta. 2016. "Managing Sudden Stops." In *Monetary Policy and Global Spillovers: Mechanisms, Effects and Policy Measures*, edited by E. G. Mendoza, E. Pastén, and D. Saravia, 9-47. Santiago: Central Bank of Chile.

Eickmeier, S., and T. Ng. 2015. "How Do US Credit Supply Shocks Propagate Internationally? A GVAR Approach." *European Economic Review* 74: 128-45.

Federal Reserve Board. 1958. "Federal Reserve Bulletin." October, Board of Governors of the Federal Reserve System, Washington, DC.

Feenstra, R. C., R. Inklaar, and M. P. Timmer. 2015. "The Next Generation of the Penn World Table." *American Economic Review* 105 (10): 3150-82.

Ferrara, L., and C. Marsilli. 2019. "Nowcasting Global Economic Growth: A Factor-Augmented Mixed-Frequency Approach." *World Economy* 42 (3): 846-75.

Feyen, E., R. Letelier, I. Love, S. M. Maimbo, and R. Rocha. 2014. "The Impact of Funding Models and Foreign Bank Ownership on Bank Credit Growth." Policy Research Working Paper 6783, World Bank, Washington, DC.

Forbes, K. J., and F. E. Warnock. 2012. "Capital Flow Waves: Surges, Stops, Flight, and Retrenchment." *Journal of International Economics* 88 (2): 235-51.

Fosu, A. K. 2013. "Impact of the Global Financial and Economic Crisis on Development: Whither Africa?" *Journal of International Development* 25 (8): 1085-104.

Francis, N., L. E. Jackson, and M. T. Owyang. 2018. "Countercyclical Policy and the Speed of Recovery after Recessions." *Journal of Money, Credit and Banking* 50 (4): 675-704.

Frankel, J. 2014. "China Is Not Yet Number One." VoxEU.org, May 9, 2014.

Freund, C. 2009. "The Trade Response to Global Downturns: Historical Evidence." Policy Research Working Paper 5015, World Bank, Washington, DC.

Golinelli, R., and G. Parigi. 2014. "Tracking World Trade and GDP in Real Time." *International Journal of Forecasting* 30 (4): 847-62.

Graetz, G., and G. Michaels. 2017. "Is Modern Technology Responsible for Jobless Recoveries?" *American Economic Review* 107 (5): 168-73.

Grjebine, T., U. Szczerbowicz, and F. Tripier. 2018. "Corporate Debt Structure and Economic Recoveries." *European Economic Review* 101: 77-100.

Ha, J., M. A. Kose, and F. Ohnsorge, eds. 2019. *Inflation in Emerging and Developing Economies: Evolution, Drivers, and Policies.* Washington, DC: World Bank.

Hall, R. E. 1993. "Macro Theory and the Recession of 1990-1991." *American Economic Review* 83 (2): 275-79.

Hamilton, J. D. 2013. "Historical Oil Shocks." In *Routledge Handbook of Major Events in Economic History*, edited by R. E. Parker and R. Whaples, 239-65. London: Routledge.

Hamilton, J. D. 2019. "Measuring Global Economic Activity." *Journal of Applied Econometrics*, September 8, 2019. https://doi.org/10.1002/jae.2740.

Hamilton, J. D., E. S. Harris, J. Hatzius, and K. D. West. 2016. "The Equilibrium Real Funds Rate: Past, Present, and Future." *IMF Economic Review* 64 (4): 660-707.

Hansen, A. H. 1939. "Economic Progress and Declining Population Growth." *American Economic Review* 29 (1): 1-15.

Harding, D., and A. Pagan. 2002. "Dissecting the Cycle: A Methodological Investigation." *Journal of Monetary Economics* 49 (2): 365-81.

Harding, D., and A. Pagan. 2016. *The Econometric Analysis of Recurrent Events in Macroeconomics and Finance*. Princeton, NJ: Princeton University Press.

Hatzius, J., and S. J. Stehn. 2018. "The Case for a Financial Conditions Index." Global Economic Paper, July 16, Goldman Sachs, New York.

Hausmann, R., F. Rodriguez, and R. Wagner. 2006. "Growth Collapses." CID Working Paper 136, Center for International Development, Harvard University, Cambridge, MA.

Helbling, T., R. Huidrom, M. A. Kose, and C. Otrok. 2011. "Do Credit Shocks Matter? A Global Perspective." *European Economic Review* 55 (3): 340-53.

Herman, A., D. Igan, and J. Solé. 2017. "The Macroeconomic Relevance of Bank and Nonbank Credit: An Exploration of U.S. Data." *Journal of Financial Stability* 32: 124-41.

Hoshi, T., and A. K. Kashyap. 2015. "Will the U.S. and Europe Avoid a Lost Decade? Lessons from Japan's Postcrisis Experience." *IMF Economic Review* 63 (1): 110-63.

Huidrom, R., M. A. Kose, H. Matsuoka, and F. L. Ohnsorge. 2019. "How Important Are Spillovers from Major Emerging Markets?" *International Finance* 2019: 1-17.

Imbs, J. 2010. "The First Global Recession in Decades." *IMF Economic Review* 58 (2): 327-54.

IMF (International Monetary Fund). 2019. *Fiscal Monitor: Curbing Corruption*. April. Washington, DC: International Monetary Fund.

Knoop, T. A. 2004. *Recessions and Depressions: Understanding Business Cycles*. Westport, CT: Praeger.

Koepke, R. 2019. "What Drives Capital Flows to Emerging Markets? A Survey of the Empirical Literature." *Journal of Economic Surveys* 33 (2): 516-40.

Kose, M. A., S. Kurlat, F. Ohnsorge, and N. Sugawara. 2017. "A Cross-Country Database of Fiscal Space." Policy Research Working Paper 8157, World Bank, Washington, DC.

Kose, M. A., C. Otrok, and E. Prasad. 2012. "Global Business Cycles: Convergence or Decoupling?" *International Economic Review* 53 (2): 511-38.

Kose, M. A., C. Otrok, and C. H. Whiteman. 2003. "International Business Cycles: World, Region, and Country-Specific Factors." *American Economic Review* 93 (4): 1216-39.

Kose, M. A., C. Otrok, and C. H. Whiteman. 2008. "Understanding the Evolution of World Business Cycles." *Journal of International Economics* 75 (1): 110-30.

Kose, M. A., and E. S. Prasad. 2010. *Emerging Markets: Resilience and Growth amid Global Turmoil*. Washington, DC: Brookings Institution Press.

Kose, M. A., N. Sugawara, and M. E. Terrones. 2020. "Global Recessions." Policy Research Working Paper 9172, World Bank, Washington, DC.

Kose, M. A., and M. E. Terrones. 2015. *Collapse and Revival: Understanding Global Recessions and Recoveries*. Washington, DC: International Monetary Fund.

Kose, M. A., and K.-M. Yi. 2006. "Can the Standard International Business Cycle Model Explain the Relation between Trade and Comovement?" *Journal of International Economics* 68 (2): 267-95.

Laeven, L., and F. Valencia. 2018. "Systemic Banking Crises Revisited." IMF Working Paper 18/206, International Monetary Fund, Washington, DC.

Lane, P. R., and G. M. Milesi-Ferretti. 2018. "The External Wealth of Nations Revisited: International Financial Integration in the Aftermath of the Global Financial Crisis." *IMF Economic Review* 66 (1): 189-222.

Levchenko, A. A., L. T. Lewis, and L. L. Tesar. 2010. "The Collapse of International Trade during the 2008-09 Crisis: In Search of the Smoking Gun." *IMF Economic Review* 58 (2): 214-53.

Martínez-García, E., V. Grossman, and A. Mack. 2015. "A Contribution to the Chronology of Turning Points in Global Economic Activity (1980-2012)." *Journal of Macroeconomics* 46: 170-85.

Mauro, P., R. Romeu, A. Binder, and A. Zaman. 2015. "A Modern History of Fiscal Prudence and Profligacy." *Journal of Monetary Economics* 76: 55-70.

Medas, P., T. Poghosyan, Y. Xu, J. Farah-Yacoub, and K. Gerling. 2018. "Fiscal Crises." *Journal of International Money and Finance* 88: 191-207.

Meller, B., and N. Metiu. 2017. "The Synchronization of Credit Cycles." *Journal of Banking and Finance* 82: 98-111.

Milesi-Ferretti, G.-M., and C. Tille. 2011. "The Great Retrenchment: International Capital Flows during the Global Financial Crisis." *Economic Policy* 26 (66): 285-342.

Mumtaz, H., S. Simonelli, and P. Surico. 2011. "International Comovements, Business Cycle and Inflation: A Historical Perspective." *Review of Economic Dynamics* 14 (1): 176-98.

Mussa. M. 2009. "World Recession and Recovery: A V or an L?" Paper presented at the fifteenth semiannual meeting on Global Economic Prospects, Peterson Institute of International Economics, April 7, Washington, DC.

NBER (National Bureau of Economic Research). 2020. *The NBER's Business Cycle Dating Committee.* http://www.nber.org/cycles/recession.html.

Njoroge, P. 2018. "Keynote Address at the 7th Kenya Bankers Association Annual Banking Conference." September. Nairobi. https://www.centralbank.go.ke/uploads/speeches/843020292_Governor's%20Remarks%20-%207th%20Annual%20Banking%20Research%20Conference.pdf.

OECD (Organisation for Economic Co-operation and Development). 2019. *Tax Policy Reforms 2019: OECD and Selected Partner Economies.* Paris: OECD Publishing.

Owyang, M. T., J. Piger, and H. J. Wall. 2005. "Business Cycle Phases in U.S. States." *Review of Economics and Statistics* 87 (4): 604-16.

Pagan, A., and K. A. Sossounov. 2003. "A Simple Framework for Analysing Bull and Bear Markets." *Journal of Applied Econometrics* 18 (1): 23-46.

Perri, F., and V. Quadrini. 2018. "International Recessions." *American Economic Review* 108 (4-5): 935-84.

Perry, G., and C. L. Schultze. 1993. "Was This Recession Different? Are They All Different?" *Brookings Papers on Economic Activity* 1993 (1): 145-211.

Rachel, Ł., and L. H. Summers. 2019. "On Falling Neutral Real Rates, Fiscal Policy, and the Risk of Secular Stagnation." BPEA conference draft, Brookings Institution, March 7-8, Washington, DC.

Reinhart, C. M., and K. S. Rogoff. 2009. *This Time Is Different: Eight Centuries of Financial Folly.* Princeton, NJ: Princeton University Press.

Rogoff, K. 2013. "What's the Problem with Advanced Economies?" *Project Syndicate,* December 4, 2013. https://www.project-syndicate.org/commentary/kenneth-rogoff-asks-whether-we-need-to-know-what-s-ailing-the-advanced-economies-in-order-to-boost-growth?barrier=accesspaylog.

Rogoff, K., D. Robinson, and T. Bayoumi. 2002. "Was It a Global Recession?" Box in *World Economic Outlook: Recessions and Recoveries,* by the International Monetary Fund, April, International Monetary Fund, Washington, DC.

Romer, C. D., and D. H. Romer. 2012. "A Rehabilitation of Monetary Policy in the 1950's." *American Economic Review* 92 (2): 121-27.

Rossiter, J. 2010. "Nowcasting the Global Economy." Bank of Canada Discussion Paper 2010-12, Bank of Canada, Ottawa.

Sichel, D. E. 1994. "Inventories and the Three Phases of the Business Cycle." *Journal of Business & Economic Statistics* 12 (3): 269-77.

Stock, J. H., and M. W. Watson. 2012. "Disentangling the Channels of the 2007-09 Recession." *Brookings Papers on Economic Activity* 2012 (Spring): 81-135.

Summers, L. H. 2015. "Have We Entered an Age of Secular Stagnation? IMF Fourteenth Annual Research Conference in Honor of Stanley Fischer, Washington, DC." *IMF Economic Review* 63 (1): 277-80.

Taylor, J. B. 2014. "The Economic Hokum of 'Secular Stagnation.'" *Wall Street Journal,* January 1, 2014. https://www.wsj.com/articles/the-economic-hokum-of-8216secular-stagnation8217-1388613709.

Terrones, M. E. 2019. "Do Fixers Perform Worse than Non-fixers during Global Recessions and Recoveries?" MPRA Paper 98608, University Library of Munich, Munich.

Teulings, C., and R. Baldwin, eds. 2014. *Secular Stagnation: Facts, Causes and Cures.* London: CEPR Press.

United Nations. 1959. *World Economic Survey 1958.* New York: United Nations.

World Bank. 2009. *East Asia and Pacific Economic Update: Transforming the Rebound into Recovery.* November. Washington, DC: World Bank.

World Bank. 2010a. *Middle East and North Africa Economic Update: Recovering from the Crisis.* April. Washington, DC: World Bank.

World Bank. 2010b. *South Asia Economic Update: Moving Up, Looking East.* June. Washington, DC: World Bank.

World Bank. 2016. *Global Economic Prospects: Spillovers amid Weak Growth.* January. Washington, DC: World Bank.

Zarnowitz, V. 1992. *Business Cycles: Theory, History, Indicators, and Forecasting.* Chicago: University of Chicago Press.

PART II

In the Rearview Mirror

Policymakers' swift, forceful, and determined response [following the Great Financial Crisis] played an instrumental role in navigating economies through very challenging times and averting much worse outcomes.

Agustín Carstens (2019)
General Manager
Bank for International Settlements

CHAPTER 3
Macroeconomic Developments

Emerging market and developing economies (EMDEs) weathered the 2009 global recession relatively well, but the impact of the recession varied across economies. EMDEs with stronger precrisis fundamentals—such as large foreign exchange reserves, sound fiscal positions, and low inflation—suffered milder growth slowdowns, in part because of their greater capacity to engage in monetary and fiscal stimulus. Low-income countries were also resilient, because foreign aid and inflows of remittances remained relatively stable. In contrast, EMDEs that were heavily dependent on short-term capital flows—such as portfolio investment and cross-border bank lending—fared less well, especially those in Europe and Central Asia. A key lesson for EMDEs is the need to strengthen macroeconomic frameworks and create policy space to prepare for future global downturns.

Introduction

Just over a decade ago, the world economy experienced the most severe recession of the post-World War II period. In 2009, global output contracted by 1.8 percent, global trade collapsed by 9.9 percent, and investment declined by 9.0 percent, after robust expansions in output, trade, and investment in 2007 (of 4.3 percent, 7.3 percent, and 5.0 percent, respectively). The recession in advanced economies was particularly pronounced, with activity declining by 3.4 percent in 2009. Despite unprecedented stimulus, the postcrisis recovery in advanced economies was anemic.

Although the crisis originated in the United States, the subsequent collapse in global trade and capital flows affected emerging market and developing economies (EMDEs) as well. That said, EMDEs on the whole managed the global recession relatively well, especially those that were less dependent on external trade and finance, and those with strong precrisis fundamentals. Overall, EMDE output grew at a lower rate (at 1.6 percent) in 2009 but did not contract. This resilience partly reflected precrisis policies that reduced the vulnerabilities of EMDEs to external shocks and allowed the use of countercyclical policy stimulus during the crisis. The postcrisis decade, however, was marked by slowing or weak EMDE growth amid a series of financial and commodity price shocks and weakening fundamental drivers of growth.

Because advanced economies were more adversely affected by the financial crisis, the role of EMDEs increased in the global economy. By 2018, the share of EMDEs in the global economy had increased to 39 percent of global gross domestic product (GDP), from 31 percent in 2007, at 2010 market exchange rates. EMDEs' share of global trade also increased, to 36 percent during 2011-18 from 30 percent during 2002-07. In 2018, the seven largest EMDEs (EM7) alone accounted for 20 percent of global trade, compared

Note: This chapter was prepared by Wee Chian Koh and Shu Yu.

to 15 percent in 2007.[1] EMDEs continued to be the largest source of commodity demand growth (Baffes et al. 2018). During 2008-16, the EM7 accounted for almost all of the increase in global consumption of metals and energy and a sizeable share of the increase in consumption of grains (corn, rice, wheat; Baffes et al. 2018).

Given the growing role of EMDEs in the world economy, major economic disruptions are more likely to be felt by developing countries today than during the global recession. This risk coincides with a subdued outlook for EMDEs amid weak investment, rising debt and heightened policy uncertainty. A valuable lesson from the global recession is the importance of strong economic fundamentals, prudent financial systems, and sufficient policy room for governments and central banks to act when their economies are hit by shocks. Many EMDEs, however, have not yet rebuilt the policy buffers that were deployed successfully during the 2009 global recession. In order to enhance their resilience to shocks and lift long-term growth prospects amid subdued global growth, EMDEs urgently need to restore policy space.

Against this backdrop, this chapter reviews macroeconomic developments in EMDEs before, during, and after the 2009 global recession by addressing the following questions:

- How strong were economic fundamentals in EMDEs before the global recession?
- How did EMDEs fare during the global recession and in its aftermath?
- What explains the sluggish postrecession recovery in EMDEs?

Contributions to the literature. Chapter 3 makes several contributions to a growing literature drawing lessons from the global financial crisis and the 2009 global recession. First, the chapter expands on earlier studies of the global recession by introducing an EMDE focus and extending the horizon of the discussion. Previous studies examined the initial impact of the global financial crisis on EMDEs but did not reach far into the postcrisis period (Berkmen et al. 2012; Blanchard, Faruqee, and Das 2010; World Bank 2009a). Some studies focused on the international transmission of the crisis with an advanced-economy focus (Arestis and Karakitsos 2013; Blinder 2013; Imbs 2010; Mishkin 2011). Other studies examined the transmission from the financial crisis to the real economy in advanced economies (Ball 2014; Bernanke 2018; Gertler and Gilchrist 2018; Perri and Quadrini 2018) and the lasting nature of the macroeconomic effects of the financial crisis (Chen, Mrkaic, and Nabar 2019; IMF 2018). Second, the chapter delves deeper into developments in specific EMDE regions and the largest emerging markets (boxes 3.1 and 3.2). Third, it draws lessons from the experience of the global recession that are relevant for today's policy challenges.

Main findings. This chapter reports the following findings. First, before the 2009 global recession, EMDEs benefitted from broad-based and rapid growth, supported by strong domestic demand and a benign external environment. On the eve of the global financial

[1] The EM7 are Brazil, China, India, Indonesia, Mexico, the Russian Federation, and Turkey.

crisis, EMDEs accounted for almost one-third of global output and global exports, up from about one-quarter in 2001. EMDEs became a key source of global saving during the precrisis period. Gross saving in EMDEs rose by 10 percentage points of GDP between 2001 and 2007, while benign financing conditions encouraged strong investment growth. During this period, EMDEs accumulated sizeable current account surpluses, reduced fiscal deficits, lowered debt, and built foreign exchange reserves.

Second, EMDEs weathered the global recession relatively well, particularly those with strong fundamentals that allowed the use of countercyclical (expansionary) policy tools and those that were less exposed to global trade and finance. EMDEs that had built central bank credibility, established low inflation, and secured sound fiscal positions had space to engage in monetary and fiscal stimulus and thus fared better during the crisis, as did those that had accumulated ample foreign reserves that could be used to stabilize exchange rates. EMDEs that were heavily reliant on more volatile financing sources (such as portfolio investment and cross-border bank lending), especially those in Europe and Central Asia, suffered steeper recessions.

Third, although well above growth in advanced economies, EMDE growth slowed steadily after the global recession, from a peak of 6.5 percent in 2011 to a trough of 3.8 percent in 2015, continuing at a moderate 4.3 percent a year during 2017-18. This slowdown had both cyclical and structural origins. It reflected weaker growth in advanced economies; the phasing out of policy stimulus in several large EMDEs and advanced economies; a slowdown in potential growth in many EMDEs, including China; China's shift toward a more balanced growth model; a sharp decline in commodity prices in 2012; bouts of financial stress in major EMDEs; and episodes of policy uncertainty that dampened confidence and weighed on investment.

Fourth, over the next two years, growth is expected to stabilize somewhat but to remain subdued. EMDE growth is expected to average 4.4 percent a year in 2019-21 compared to the precrisis average of 6.7 percent a year in 2002-07 (World Bank 2019a). This short -term outlook is subject to considerable risks, predominantly on the downside, including the possibility of escalating trade tensions and elevated financial market stress. A further slowdown is expected over the longer term. Population dynamics in many EMDEs reached a turning point in 2010 when the share of the working-age population stabilized after several decades of rapid increase. Productivity growth is expected to remain lackluster as diminishing growth prospects weigh on investment. Developments in the drivers of potential growth will contribute to an expected slowdown of about 1.6 percentage points from precrisis rates, to an annual average of 4.3 percent in 2019-27 (World Bank 2018a, 2019b).

Finally, solid policy buffers, sound institutions, and international policy coordination helped mitigate the impact of the 2009 global recession. The window of opportunity for rebuilding resilience before the next shock materializes may be narrowing, which in turn highlights the urgent need to rebuild policy space to enhance the resilience of those EMDEs with eroded policy buffers.

The rest of the chapter is organized as follows. First, the chapter describes the period of strong growth in EMDEs before the global recession. Subsequently, it shows how

EMDEs fared during the global recession, followed by a discussion of the challenging postrecession decade. Finally, the chapter concludes with a summary and policy lessons.

Before the global recession: Strong growth

During 2002-07, in a benign external environment, EMDEs witnessed broad-based and rapid growth, averaging 6.7 percent a year—more than twice as fast as during the preceding two decades (figure 3.1). EMDEs' growth in this period is surpassed only by their growth spurt in the early to mid-1970s (7.2 percent a year, on average). Rapid, export-driven growth amid a commodity price boom allowed many EMDEs to accumulate sizable current account surpluses, reduce fiscal deficits, and build foreign exchange reserves (World Bank 2018c).

Benign external environment. A cyclical upturn in advanced economies, where output growth strengthened from 1.5 percent in 2001 to 2.6 percent in 2007, coincided with the integration of China into global trade networks after its World Trade Organization (WTO) accession in 2001, a wave of new or recently agreed free trade agreements, and the rapid expansion of global value chains. These developments fueled global trade and commodity demand and exploration (Khan et al. 2016). Global trade volumes grew by 6.7 percent a year in 2002-07, in part reflecting a rebound from tepid growth following the Asian financial crisis of 1997-98 (World Bank 2015a). EMDE exports grew from 27 percent of EMDE output in 2001 to 34 percent in 2007.[2] Rapid growth in China contributed to a doubling of energy and metals prices and a 1.7-fold increase in agricultural commodity prices. This increase buoyed activities in commodity exporters, which account for almost two-thirds of EMDEs.

In addition to their growing importance in global trade, EMDEs also became a key source of global savings during this period. Gross savings in EMDEs rose by 10 percentage points of GDP between 2001 and 2007 (figure 3.1). In particular, China's saving rate reached 51 percent of GDP in 2007, outpacing domestic investment and contributing to the widening of its current account surplus to 9.9 percent of GDP in 2007 from 1.3 percent in 2001. By contrast, in Europe and Central Asia (ECA), gross investment exceeded gross saving by a wide margin as economies transformed from centrally planned to market economies, resulting in large current account deficits (box 3.2).

Prolonged accommodative monetary policy in major advanced economies and rapidly growing savings in some major EMDEs helped maintain low global real interest rates and encouraged capital flows to EMDEs (Bernanke 2005; Hall 2017; Lin 2008).[3] Partly in search of yield, gross capital inflows to EMDEs (excluding foreign direct investment

[2] All EMDE regions except Europe and Central Asia increased their share of exports in GDP during 2001-07. The East Asia and Pacific and Middle East and North Africa regions had the largest increases.

[3] After the "dot-com" crash, the U.S. federal funds rate was cut repeatedly, from 6.5 percent in December 2000 to 1.0 percent in June 2003, and then maintained at this low level until May 2004. The European Central Bank also reduced its primary interest rate from 3.75 percent in October 2000 to 1.0 percent in June 2003-November 2005.

FIGURE 3.1 Global developments, 1991-2018

EMDEs grew rapidly in 2002-07, the period immediately before the global recession and after China joined the World Trade Organization, which helped fuel global trade and commodity demand. EMDEs became a key source of global saving. Capital inflows to EMDEs surged, partly owing to low interest rates in advanced economies.

A. Output growth

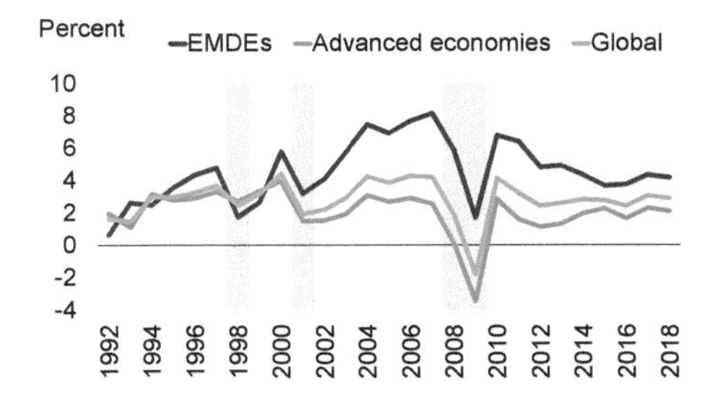

B. Saving

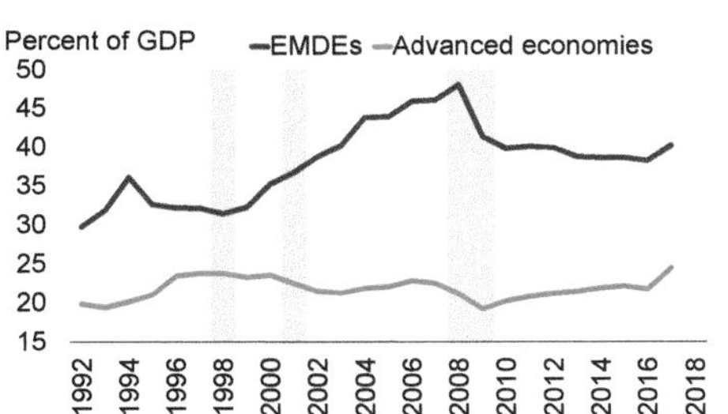

C. EMDE capital inflows

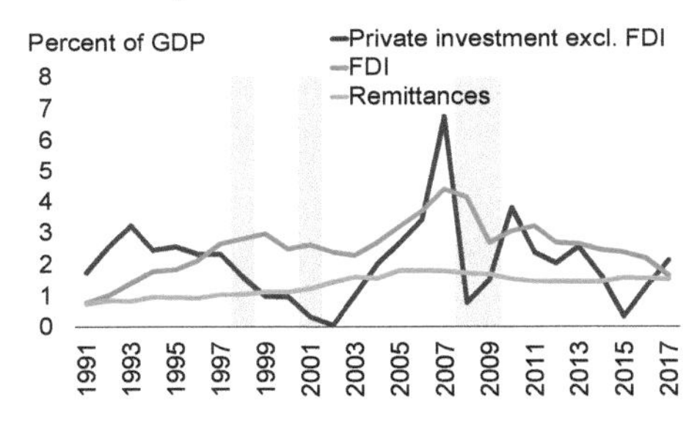

D. Financial markets

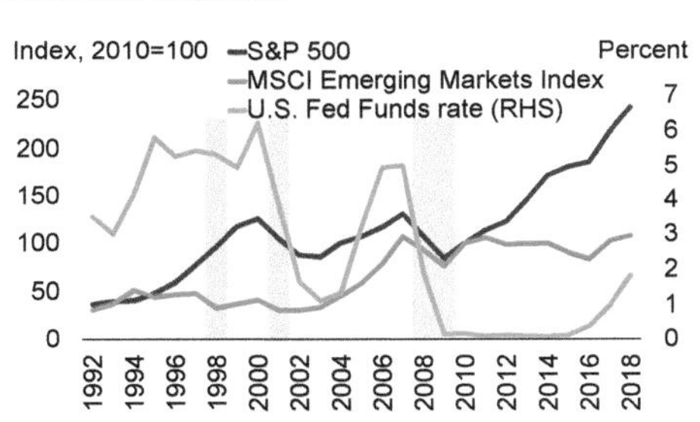

Sources: Araujo et al. (2015); Haver Analytics; International Monetary Fund; U.S. Federal Reserve Economic Data; World Bank.
Note: Shaded bars indicate global recessions and slowdowns. EMDEs = emerging market and developing economies; FDI = foreign direct investment; MSCI = Morgan Stanley Capital International.
C. Private investment flows comprise portfolio investment, other investment, and financial derivatives.

[FDI]) swelled to 6.5 percent of EMDE GDP in 2007, from less than 1 percent in 2001. FDI in EMDEs also rose, from 2.5 percent to 4.3 percent of GDP between 2001 and 2007; and remittances from EMDE nationals working in foreign countries increased from 1.3 to 1.8 percent of EMDE output during the same period.

Rapid reserve accumulation. International reserve holdings in EMDEs averaged 20 percent of GDP in 2007. This reserve accumulation reflected precautionary demand against balance-of-payment shocks and, by some estimates, support for competitiveness.[4] The reserve buildup was most pronounced in East Asia and Pacific (EAP) and Latin America and the Caribbean (LAC), largely accounted for by China and Brazil. The

[4] The precautionary motive was more important following the emerging market crises of the 1990s and the Asian financial crisis of 1997-98, but undervaluation of exchange rates that supported export-led growth was more important in the 2000s (Aizenman and Lee 2007; Dooley, Folkerts-Landau, and Garber 2003; Ghosh, Ostry, and Tsangarides 2012).

BOX 3.1 EM7 performance during the global recession

This box presents a summary of macroeconomic developments and policy measures in the seven largest emerging market economies (EM7) during the global financial crisis and recession. Some EM7 countries weathered the crisis considerably better than others, in part by implementing a swift and large policy stimulus made possible by greater policy space accumulated before the crisis. Closer trade links to relatively resilient economies also helped EM7 countries weather the crisis. Those that fared less well generally had deeper trade and financial links with economies that experienced steep recessions and had less effective policy responses.

Introduction

Emerging market and developing economies (EMDEs) as a whole weathered the 2009 global recession well, although their economic growth slowed significantly.[a] On average, growth in the seven largest EMDEs (EM7)—Brazil, China, India, Indonesia, Mexico, the Russian Federation, and Turkey—slowed by 3.9 percentage points, from 4.6 percent in 2008 to 0.7 percent in 2009. This slowdown caused considerable spillovers to EMDEs more broadly. On average, a 1-percentage-point slowdown in EM7 growth is associated with a 0.8-percentage-point decline in overall EMDE growth in the subsequent year (Huidrom et al. 2019).

Some EM7 countries, however, fared much better than others during the global recession (figure B3.1.1). The heterogeneity in the experiences of the EM7 also affected their respective trading and financial partners. China's resilience supported growth around the world, whereas a severe recession in Russia exacerbated the effects of the global financial crisis and recession on its regional trading partners. On average, for every 1-percentage-point growth pickup in China, growth in other EMDEs was higher by 0.6 percentage point in the following year (World Bank 2016c). Developments in Russia also had sizable growth spillovers in the Europe and Central Asia (ECA) region, and those in Brazil affected some of its neighbors; but developments in the other EM7 economies had limited spillovers.

Against this backdrop, this box describes developments during the global financial crisis and recession in each of the EM7. Those that did better had above-average fiscal stimulus implemented swiftly (China, India) or were close trading partners of China (Brazil, Indonesia). Those that fared less well were close trading partners of the United States (Mexico) or the European Union (Russia, Turkey), or experienced sharp capital flow reversals (Russia, Turkey), or were heavily dependent on the oil sector for fiscal and export revenues, which suffered from a plunge in oil prices (Mexico, Russia).

Note: This box was prepared by Wee Chian Koh.

a. The seven economies account for more than one-quarter of global output (at market exchange rates) and more than half of global output growth during 2010-15 (Huidrom et al. 2019).

BOX 3.1 EM7 performance during the global recession *(continued)*

FIGURE B3.1.1 EM7 macroeconomic developments

East Asian countries weathered the crisis well despite steep contractions in exports. The Russian Federation and Turkey suffered large output and investment contractions, partly owing to sharp capital flow reversals. As a result of China's resilience and strong recovery, Brazil and Indonesia, with their close trade links to China, were also more resilient. Mexico, Russia, and Turkey, which had deeper ties with the United States or the European Union, fared less well.

A. Output growth in commodity importers

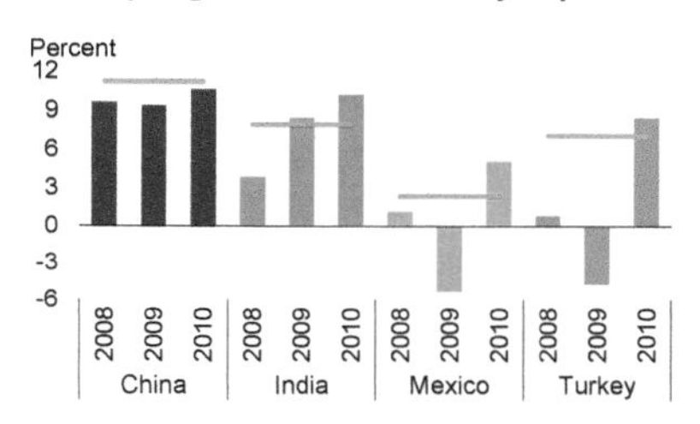

B. Output growth in commodity exporters

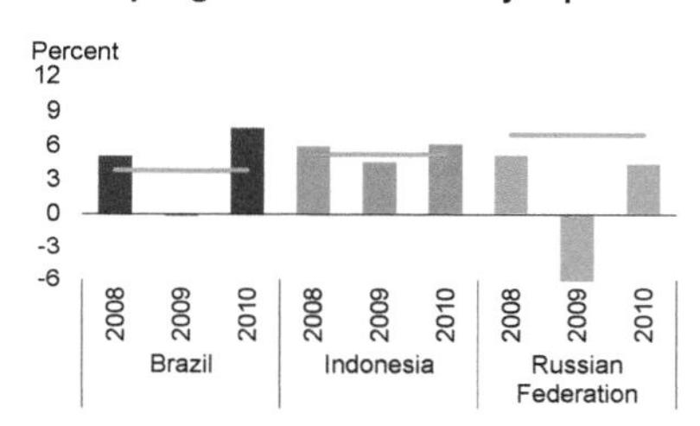

C. Investment growth in commodity importers

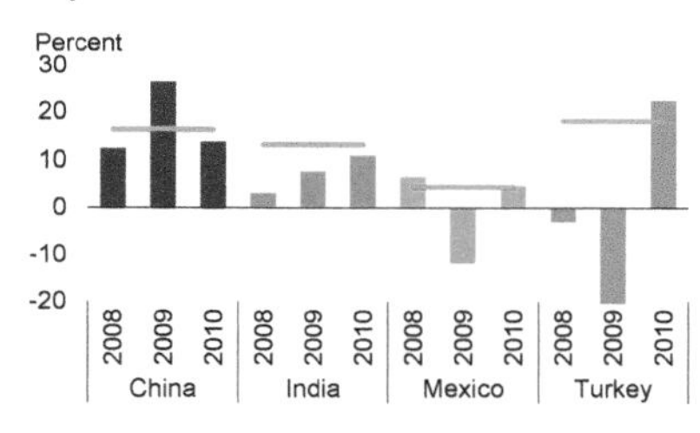

D. Investment growth in commodity exporters

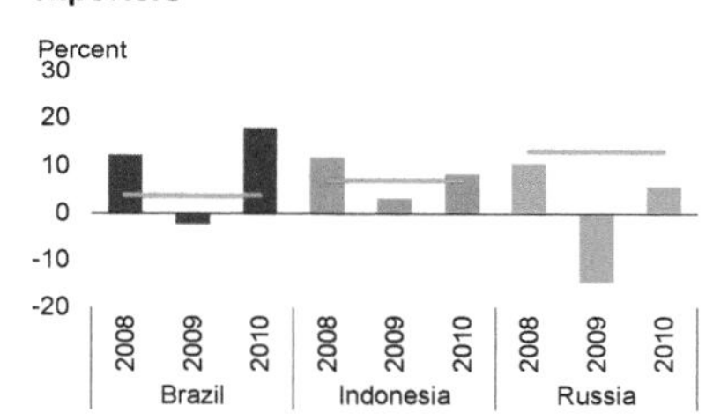

E. Export growth in commodity importers

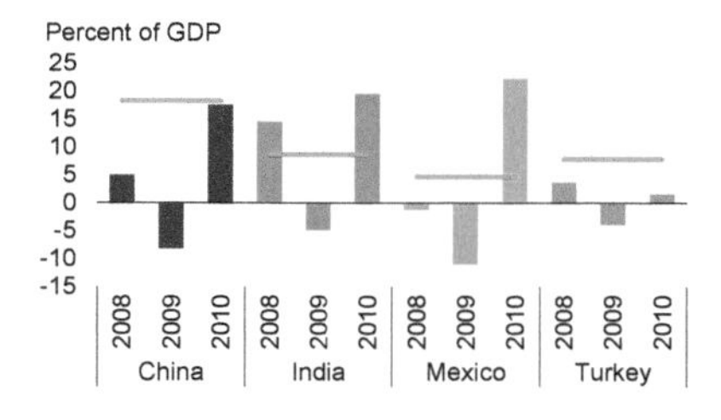

F. Export growth in commodity exporters

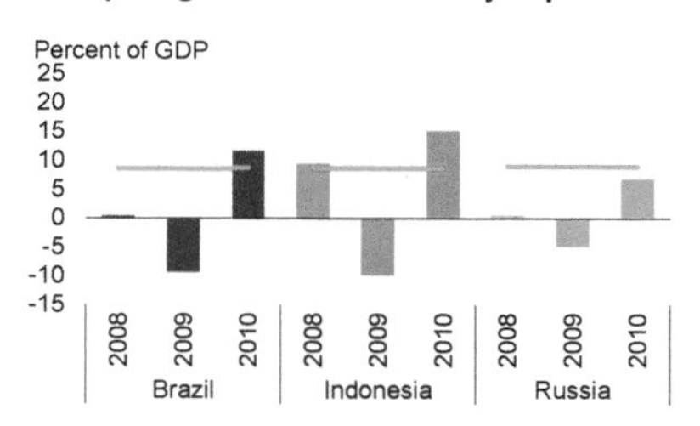

Source: World Bank.

Note: The EM7 are the seven largest emerging market economies.

A-D. Blue horizontal lines are 2002-07 averages.

BOX 3.1 EM7 performance during the global recession *(continued)*

Commodity-importing EM7: China, India, Mexico, and Turkey

In those commodity-importing EM7 economies that were less exposed to global financial stress (China, India) and global trade (India), growth continued, but at reduced rates, during the 2008-09 global financial crisis and recession. In contrast, those that were highly open to global financial markets (Mexico, Turkey) and heavily reliant on trade with the United States, the epicenter of the crisis (Mexico), or with the European Union (EU), which also experienced deep downturns (Turkey), suffered severe output contractions notwithstanding large monetary and fiscal stimulus (figure B3.1.2).

China. Growth slowed from an average of 11.3 percent a year during 2002-07 to 9.5 percent a year in 2008-09 before recovering to 10.6 percent in 2010. This robust growth performance reflected large-scale policy stimulus to mitigate severe export weakness as well as China's limited exposure to the global financial market turmoil.

After joining the World Trade Organization (WTO) in late 2001, China's exports grew from 21 percent of gross domestic product (GDP) in 2001 to 36 percent of GDP in 2007. This export-led growth was accompanied by large foreign direct investment (FDI) inflows (90 percent to the manufacturing sector), which grew from 3.5 percent to 4.4 percent of GDP over the same period. By 2007, China had become the world's second-largest exporter of merchandise goods and the largest FDI recipient among EMDEs. During the crisis, China's export-oriented industries, especially capital and technology-intensive industries, suffered a severe contraction. Export growth collapsed from 18.4 percent per year, on average, in 2002-07 to -8.1 percent in 2009. In contrast to its export-oriented industries, China's financial system was largely insulated from global financial stress by strict capital flow restrictions (Yang and Huizenga 2010). China faced currency appreciation pressures instead, and the central bank engaged in foreign exchange intervention to maintain the exchange rate at competitive levels; the renminbi appreciated by 6 percent in effective terms during September 2008-March 2009.

China's policy response to the global recession was swift and large (IMF 2010a). The government announced a fiscal stimulus package for 2009-10 that amounted to 12.7 percent of GDP. The three largest components of the package focused on development of public transport infrastructure, reconstruction after the earthquake in the Sichuan Province, and construction of public housing in urban areas. The authorities also raised tax rebates, reduced export insurance premium rates, and established an export financing guarantee system to promote exports. Monetary policy was eased, beginning in September 2008: by the end of the year, the People's Bank of China's benchmark interest rate had been reduced from 7.5 percent to 5.3 percent. The required reserve ratios of banks in China were also

BOX 3.1 EM7 performance during the global recession *(continued)*

FIGURE B3.1.2 Debt, deficits, and policy measures in EM7

All EM7 countries loosened monetary policy to stimulate aggregate demand during the global recession. China and India also took swift and large fiscal stimulus measures.

A. Government debt in commodity importers

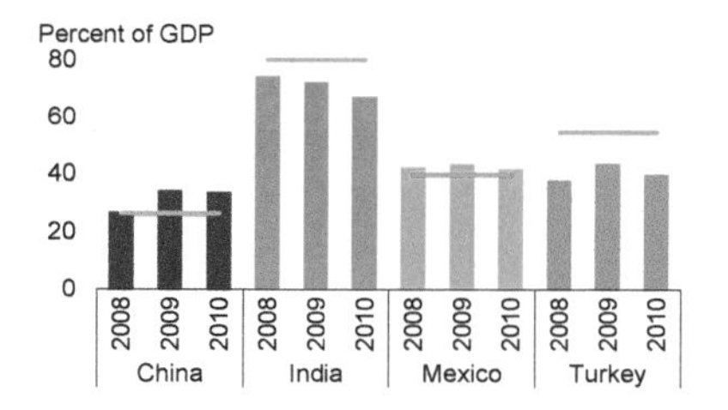

B. Government debt in commodity exporters

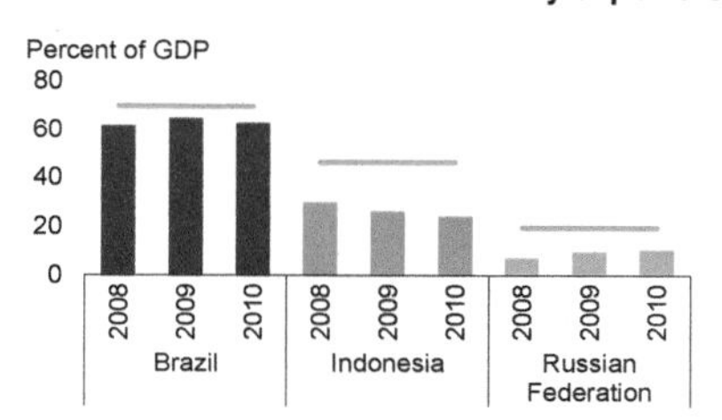

C. Fiscal balance in commodity importers

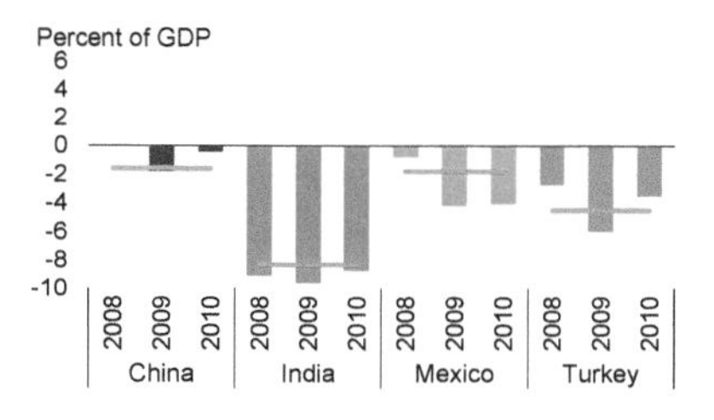

D. Fiscal balance in commodity exporters

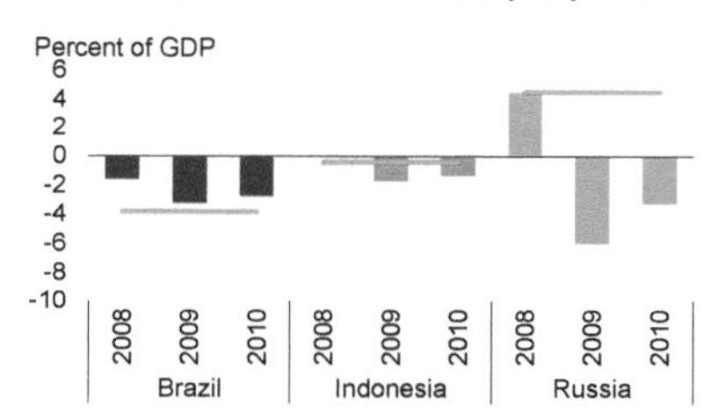

E. Policy interest rates and fiscal stimulus in commodity importers

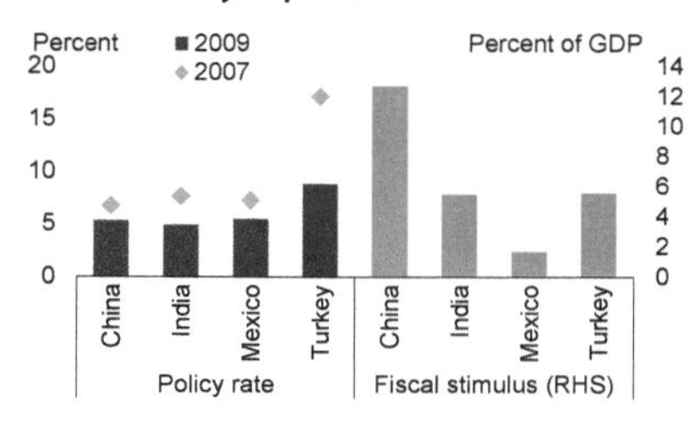

F. Policy interest rates and fiscal stimulus in commodity exporters

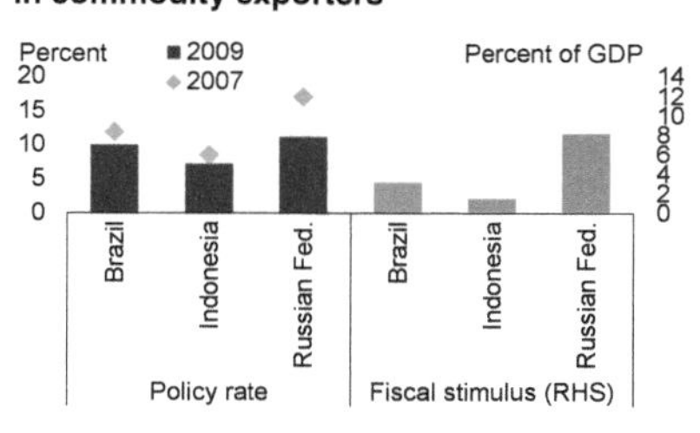

Sources: Bank for International Settlements; International Monetary Fund; World Bank.
Note: The EM7 are the seven largest emerging market economies. Russian Fed. = Russian Federation.
A-D. Blue horizontal lines are 2002-07 averages.

lowered to encourage banks to expand lending in support of the fiscal stimulus package.

Although fiscal and monetary stimulus helped China weather the global recession, in the postrecession period China has been confronted with large debt buildups. Stimulus during the recession, combined with two additional rounds of stimulus

BOX 3.1 EM7 performance during the global recession *(continued)*

spending in 2015-16 and 2018-19, have virtually doubled government debt in China as a proportion of GDP, from 26 percent on average during 2002-07 to 50 percent in 2018, and more than tripled the fiscal deficit-to-GDP ratio from 1.5 percent to 4.8 percent over the same period. Meanwhile, corporate debt rose from 108 percent of GDP in 2006 to 158 percent of GDP in 2017, before dropping slightly to 152 percent of GDP in 2018.

India. The economy managed the recession well, despite a sharp contraction in exports. Growth slowed from 7.2 percent a year on average in 2002-07 to 3.1 percent in 2008, but rebounded to 7.9 percent in 2009 and 8.5 percent in 2010. The rebound was supported by resilient FDI and remittance inflows, and swift policy stimulus (figure B3.1.3).

At the time the global financial crisis erupted, India had become significantly more integrated into the global economy than a decade earlier, with the ratio of exports to GDP having doubled to 21 percent in the decade to 2007 and the ratio of gross capital flows to GDP having doubled to 8 percent in the same period. During the global recession, export growth collapsed from 18.4 percent a year on average in 2002-07 to -4.8 percent in 2009. Capital inflows (excluding FDI) fell from 7.8 percent of GDP in 2007 to 4.1 percent of GDP on average in 2008-09. The decline in non-FDI capital inflows was accompanied by a mild currency depreciation (3 percent) in effective terms during September 2008-March 2009. FDI inflows continued to increase, however, and remittance inflows continued to grow strongly through the recession.

The authorities responded with large fiscal stimulus, monetary policy loosening, and large-scale foreign exchange market intervention (IMF 2009a). In February 2008, right before the financial crisis, the government had already planned a fiscal stimulus of 3.5 percent of GDP. In the three months starting in December 2008, the government announced three additional fiscal stimulus packages amounting to 2 percent of GDP for 2009-10 that included government-guaranteed funds for infrastructure, tax cuts, salary hikes for public servants, and credit to small and medium enterprises and exporters (Kumar and Vashisht 2009). The Reserve Bank of India lowered the cash reserve ratio from 9 percent in October 2008 to 5 percent in March 2009, the policy repo rate from 9 percent in September 2008 to 4.75 percent in June 2009, and the reverse repo rate from 6 percent to 3.25 percent over the same period. The Indian rupee depreciated in a controlled manner as the central bank intervened in foreign exchange markets by drawing down 13 percent of reserves between September 2008 and March 2009.

After the 2009 global recession, fiscal and monetary stimulus by the central government were only partially unwound, and in 2016 policy loosening resumed. Nevertheless, in 2018, the fiscal deficit fell back below precrisis levels, to 6.7 percent of GDP, compared with an average deficit of 8.2 percent of GDP during

BOX 3.1 EM7 performance during the global recession *(continued)*

FIGURE B3.1.3 Credit and capital inflows to EM7

EM7 central banks provided liquidity to support their domestic banking sectors. Capital inflows to EM7 increased with the exceptions of the Russian Federation and Turkey.

A. Increase in private sector credit provided by banks in commodity importers

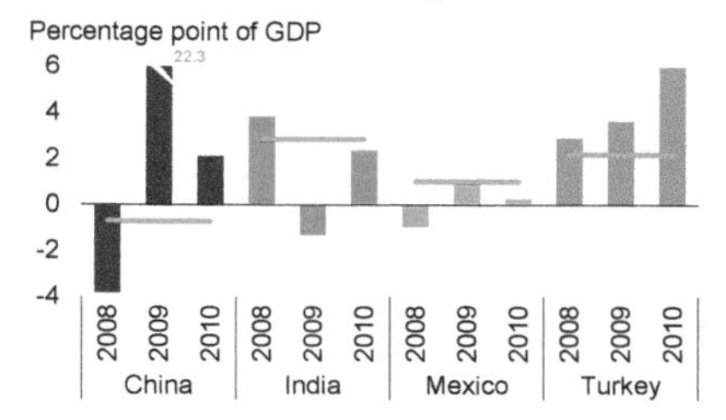

B. Increase in private sector credit provided by banks in commodity exporters

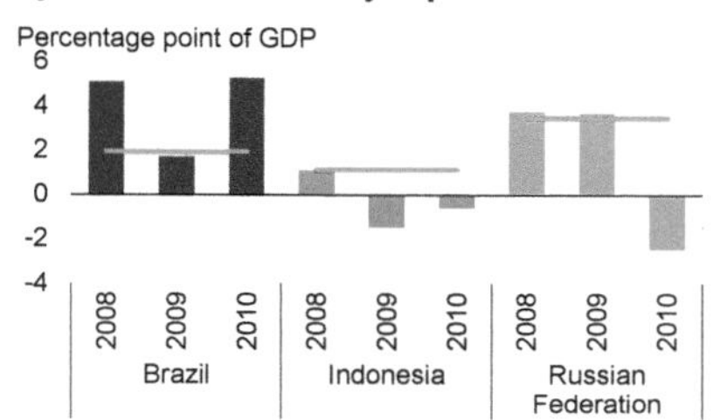

C. Capital inflows to commodity importers

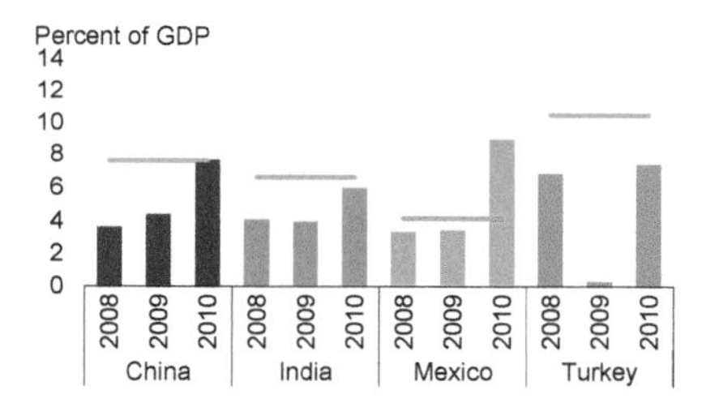

D. Capital inflows to commodity exporters

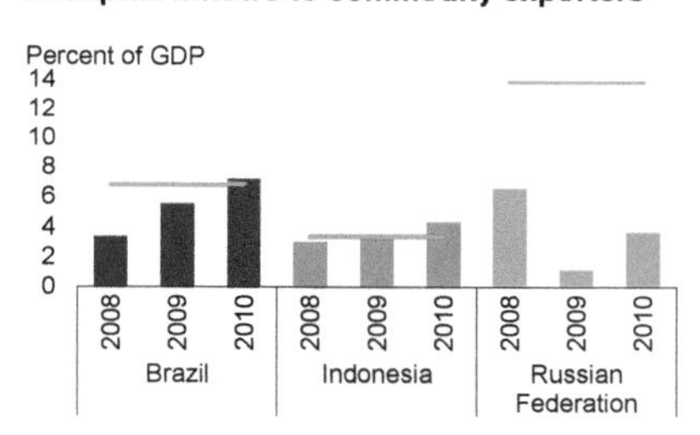

Sources: Araujo et al. (2015); International Monetary Fund; World Bank.

Note: The EM7 are the seven largest emerging market economies.

A.B. Percentage point of GDP change over previous year. Blue horizontal lines are 2002-07 averages. Bank credit to the private sector in China surged 22 percentage points of GDP in 2009.

C.D. Capital inflows comprise direct investment, portfolio investment, other investment, and derivatives. Blue horizontal lines are 2006-07 averages.

2002-07. Government debt also declined, from 80 percent of GDP on average during 2002-07 to 70 percent of GDP in 2018.

Mexico was the hardest-hit country in Latin America, in part because it was the most exposed to the U.S. economy, the epicenter of the financial crisis. It suffered its worst recession in six decades. Output contracted by 5.3 percent in 2009 after growing 2.4 percent a year in 2002-07; however, the economy rebounded sharply, with 5.1 percent growth in 2010, following the implementation of monetary and fiscal stimulus measures and large liquidity injections into foreign exchange and credit markets.

The crisis hit Mexico hard and fast. Exports fell by 1.0 percent in 2008 and 10.9 percent in 2009 as demand from the United States, which accounted for four-fifths of Mexican exports, collapsed. Declining prices and production in the oil

BOX 3.1 EM7 performance during the global recession *(continued)*

sector, the largest source of government revenue, exacerbated fiscal and balance-of-payments pressures. Capital inflows declined from 6.0 percent of GDP in 2007 to 3.4 percent of GDP in 2008 and 3.5 percent of GDP in 2009, but remittances held up well, falling by only 0.3 percentage point of GDP to 2.3 percent in 2008. As investors rebalanced their portfolios away from EMDEs, Mexico experienced a run on the peso, which caused a steep depreciation of 25 percent in effective terms between September 2008 and March 2009. The depreciation caused severe U.S. dollar liquidity shortages for large corporations that had engaged in complex derivative operations.

The Bank of Mexico intervened swiftly to restore orderly functioning of financial markets. It carried out U.S. dollar auctions, paid interest on U.S. dollar deposits at the central bank to disincentivize the liquidation of positions, and made use of a swap arrangement with the U.S. Federal Reserve. Between September 2008 and March 2009, the central bank drew down 14 percent of its foreign reserves. It also expanded the range of eligible assets that could be used as collateral to support funding for domestic banks. In the first half of 2008, the policy focus was to contain inflation and mitigate the impact of higher food prices (IMF 2009b). The central bank raised the policy rate by 0.75 percentage point over the summer months but subsequently loosened its policy stance, lowering its policy rate from 8.25 percent in December 2008 to 4.50 percent in August 2009. The government also increased credit lines with the World Bank, International Monetary Fund, and Inter-American Development Bank. Notwithstanding sharply lower government revenues from the oil sector, in 2009 the government implemented a fiscal stimulus package amounting to 1.7 percent of GDP, which expanded infrastructure spending, energy subsidies, and social safety nets (Celasun et al. 2015).

After the global recession, the fiscal stimulus was only partially unwound, leaving a fiscal deficit of 2.3 percent of GDP in 2018, down from 4.1 percent in 2009 but higher than the average of 1.7 percent in the precrisis years 2002-07. By end-2018, government debt had increased by about 14 percentage points of GDP from the precrisis average of 40 percent of GDP.

Turkey suffered a severe output contraction during the 2009 global recession. Growth faltered from 7.1 percent a year on average in 2002-07 to 0.8 percent in 2008 and -4.7 percent in 2009. It rebounded strongly to 8.5 percent in 2010, reflecting the resilience of the Turkish banking system as well as aggressive policy stimulus.

Capital-intensive goods—motor vehicles, electrical machinery, ferrous metals, petroleum products, and industrial machinery—have constituted the bulk of Turkey's exports (70 percent in 2008). As demand for durable goods from the European Union (Turkey's largest export market) collapsed during the recession,

BOX 3.1 EM7 performance during the global recession *(continued)*

export growth declined from an average of 8 percent a year in 2002-07 to 3.8 percent in 2008 and -3.7 percent in 2009. Capital inflows plunged virtually to zero (0.3 percent of GDP in 2009) from 9.2 percent of GDP in 2007. The Turkish lira depreciated by 19 percent in effective terms between September 2008 and March 2009.

Turkey's banking system remained resilient because it had limited exposure to cross-border financing, wholesale funding, and foreign currency-denominated liabilities (IMF 2010b). As shares of total liabilities in 2008, funding from customer deposits was stable at 62 percent whereas foreign currency liabilities had declined to 35 percent from 45 percent in 2003. Turkish banks also had solid profitability and low levels of nonperforming loans, which had decreased from 11.5 percent of total loans outstanding in 2003 to 3.7 percent in 2008.

The Central Bank of Turkey took various measures to ensure the orderly functioning of foreign exchange and credit markets. It used foreign reserves to support the foreign exchange liquidity needs of the banking system, acted as an intermediary in the foreign exchange deposit market, and doubled the export rediscount credit limit to facilitate lending to various industries. Between September 2008 and March 2009, the central bank drew down 13 percent of its foreign reserves. The central bank cut the policy rate from 16.75 percent in October 2008 to 6.50 percent in December 2009 and also lowered reserve requirement ratios. Turkey's fiscal balance had greatly improved in the years before the crisis, which allowed the government to implement a sizable fiscal stimulus package for 2009-10 equivalent to 5.6 percent of GDP, including increased infrastructure spending, reductions in social security contributions, salary hikes for public servants, and temporary tax cuts (Rawdanowicz 2010).

Since 2009, Turkey has been struggling to curb its rising spending and maintained negative real policy interest rates. This situation has resulted in double-digit inflation and rapid credit growth since 2017. The fiscal deficit decreased from 5.9 percent of GDP in 2009 to 3.6 percent in 2018. Government debt has declined from 44 percent of GDP to 29 percent over the same period.

Commodity-exporting EM7: Brazil, Indonesia, and Russia

The EM7 commodity exporters that were close trading partners of China—Brazil and Indonesia—benefitted from China's resilience through the 2009 global recession. Brazil and Indonesia also entered the recession with ample policy room and so were able to provide decisive policy stimulus, whereas Russia's policy response was delayed, constrained by high inflation and a rapidly deteriorating fiscal position.

Brazil. Output contracted marginally, by 0.1 percent, in 2009, following robust growth of 3.9 percent in 2002-07—a contraction much less severe than in the

BOX 3.1 EM7 performance during the global recession (*continued*)

1980s debt crisis. Growth rebounded swiftly to 7.5 percent in 2010. This resilience reflected strong recovery of demand from China (Brazil's largest export destination) as well as the use of foreign exchange intervention and monetary and fiscal stimulus.

As a large commodity exporter with highly open and internationally integrated financial markets, Brazil is vulnerable to external shocks. Export growth collapsed from an average of 8.8 percent a year in 2002-07 to 0.4 percent in 2008 and -9.2 percent in 2009. Capital inflows also dropped sharply, from 8.9 percent of GDP in 2007 to 3.4 percent of GDP in 2008 and rebounded slightly to 5.6 percent of GDP in 2009. The decline in commodity prices and drop in capital inflows led to a depreciation of the Brazilian real by 15 percent between September 2008 and March 2009. Although this depreciation was moderate compared to previous crises, it magnified the effects of corporate sector exposure to foreign currency debt. Brazil also faced a severe U.S. dollar liquidity squeeze.

Unlike in previous crises, Brazil entered the 2009 global recession with ample policy space. It had accumulated large foreign reserves (75 percent of external debt in 2007) and narrowed the fiscal deficit to 1.8 percent of GDP in 2007. The Central Bank of Brazil drew on its reserves to intervene heavily in foreign exchange markets to stabilize the exchange rate and to facilitate export financing and corporate debt rollover. It sold U.S. dollars in the spot market and in repo auctions, introduced foreign exchange loan auctions for banks to support trade finance, and offered foreign exchange swaps to Brazilian companies to roll over foreign currency debt. Between September 2008 and February 2009, the Central Bank drew down 9 percent of its foreign reserves. In October 2008, it established a currency swap arrangement with the U.S. Federal Reserve. The Central Bank reduced the policy interest rate from 13.75 percent in December 2008 to 8.75 percent in August 2009, and also lowered reserve requirements. Fiscal stimulus in 2009 amounted to 3.2 percent of GDP. This stimulus was partly channeled through the Brazilian Development Bank—which doubled its balance sheet between 2007 and 2009—to ease credit conditions. The stimulus package also included support for social programs, expansion of unemployment insurance, and provision of low-cost housing (Celasun et al. 2015).

Failure to unwind fiscal stimulus after its effective use in 2010 resulted in an erosion of policy space, contributing to the recession in 2015-16 and increasing the buildup of debt. The fiscal deficit has deteriorated markedly since the recession, widening from 3.2 percent of GDP in 2009 to 10.2 percent in 2015, before a limited improvement to 6.8 percent in 2018. Government debt has also been on the rise, increasing from 65 percent of GDP in 2009 to 88 percent in 2018.

BOX 3.1 EM7 performance during the global recession *(continued)*

Indonesia emerged from the global recession largely unscathed. Output grew by 6.0 percent in 2008—above its 2002-07 annual average of 5.3 percent—and merely slowed to 4.6 percent in 2009 before rebounding to 6.2 percent in 2010. This resilience reflected strong precrisis economic fundamentals as well as timely policy stimulus and the rapid rebound in China, Indonesia's largest export destination.

After the 1997-98 Asian financial crisis, Indonesia had vastly improved its macroeconomic framework. By 2007, it had a current account surplus and large foreign reserves, and it had trimmed external debt considerably, reduced financial sector vulnerabilities, and adopted a flexible exchange rate regime. Exports fell sharply, by 9.7 percent, in 2009, but capital inflows in 2008-09, at 3.3 percent of GDP, moderated only slightly compared to 2007, when they stood at 4.0 percent of GDP.

The central bank took proactive measures to address liquidity concerns during 2008-09. It lowered the overnight repurchase rate by 2.5 percentage points, lengthened the tenor of foreign exchange swaps from seven days to one month, and reduced the minimum reserve requirements for both rupiah and foreign exchange deposits. It lowered the policy interest rate from 9.5 percent in November 2008 to 6.5 percent in September 2009, in contrast to the hike in rates needed to defend the rupiah during the Asian crisis. The government also executed spending measures in a timely way (IMF 2009c). In contrast to fiscal consolidation during the Asian crisis, the Indonesian government had fiscal space that allowed it to undertake stimulus in 2009 amounting to 1.5 percent of GDP, including both tax cuts and social safety net expansion (Doraisami 2011).

Since the 2009 global recession, Indonesia has been struggling to unwind the fiscal stimulus undertaken during the crisis. Government debt has increased, though only slightly, from 26 percent of GDP in 2009 to 29 percent in 2018.

Russia. As a result of the dual shocks of declining oil prices and capital flow reversals, Russia was hardest hit by the global recession and its repercussions among the EM7 countries. Output growth collapsed from 7.0 percent a year, on average, in 2002-07 to -7.8 percent in 2009—a steeper contraction than occurred in the country's 1998 crisis. Growth rebounded to 4.5 percent in 2010, significantly below its prerecession rate. Russia's subdued recovery reflected its undiversified economy and high dependence on oil, weak banking system, poor governance and low business confidence, and limited effectiveness of policy stimulus.

Russia is a major oil producer, accounting for 12 percent of global oil production in 2007. Oil exports fell by 5 percent in 2009, as demand weakened and oil prices declined. Capital inflows dried up quickly, declining from 16.6 percent of GDP in

BOX 3.1 EM7 performance during the global recession *(continued)*

2007 to 6.6 percent of GDP in 2008 and 1.2 percent of GDP in 2009. This drop in capital inflows, combined with the weak domestic banking system, resulted in a credit crunch for Russian corporations. The Russian ruble depreciated by 19 percent in effective terms between September 2008 and March 2009, despite heavy central bank intervention in foreign exchange markets.

The initial policy response was aimed at avoiding a disorderly currency depreciation and maintaining financial sector stability (IMF 2009d). The Central Bank of Russia resisted sharp depreciations of the ruble by drawing down one-third of its foreign reserves between September 2008 and March 2009, but eventually allowed more flexible adjustments to take place. It also delayed monetary policy easing until inflation and capital outflows had somewhat stabilized, reducing the policy rate from 13.00 percent in March 2009 to 7.75 percent in June 2010. The fiscal policy response was constrained by a rapidly deteriorating fiscal position resulting from the drop in oil revenues and by rising inflation as a result of the depreciation. The initial fiscal stimulus was modest, at 1.8 percent of GDP, and consisted of the mobilization of funds for state-owned banks to extend credit to corporations in the natural resources sector and metal industries to repay external debt. In 2009, the government announced a larger stimulus package amounting to 6.4 percent of GDP, which prioritized tax cuts and transfer payments to affected households and sectors, but had limited effects in stimulating the economy (Ponomarenko and Vlasov 2010). The fiscal balance deteriorated from a surplus of 6.2 percent of GDP in 2007 to a deficit of 5.2 percent of GDP in 2009.

After 2009, Russia successfully unwound its large fiscal stimulus, with the fiscal balance restored to a surplus of 2.8 percent of GDP in 2018. Government debt rose from 10 percent of GDP in 2009 to 14 percent in 2018, but it remains comparatively small.

sterilized interventions of EMDEs in foreign exchange markets prompted accusations of protectionism (Dadush and Stancil 2011; Portes 2010).

Robust domestic demand growth. Low global borrowing costs, combined with accommodative monetary policy, supported EMDE financial markets and domestic demand (figure 3.1). Benefitting from a broad-based global decline in inflation, almost half of EMDEs had interest rates that were negative in real terms in at least one year during 2002-07.[5] EMDE equity market valuations, as reflected by the Morgan Stanley

[5] Based on data for 135 EMDEs.

Capital International (MSCI) index, more than quadrupled during 2002-07; EMDE bond spreads, as captured by the J.P. Morgan Emerging Market Bond Index (EMBI), and sovereign credit default swap (CDS) spreads in major EMDEs more than halved between January 2005 and June 2007. Benign financing conditions encouraged strong investment growth (12 percent a year, on average, during 2002-07) in EMDEs. More than one-quarter of EMDEs witnessed an investment surge in at least one year during 2002-07.[6] Most of these investment surges were fueled by credit booms (Ohnsorge and Yu 2016). Meanwhile, private consumption growth remained robust (6.3 percent a year, on average, during 2002-07) as household incomes grew and employment opportunities expanded.

Faster-than-expected decline in global poverty. In September 2000, the international community adopted the Millennium Development Goals. Among them was the goal to halve the share of the global population living on less than $1.25 a day between 1990 and 2015. As a result of rapid EMDE growth, the goal was achieved five years earlier than targeted, in 2010. China's rapid expansion accounted for about three-fifths of this decline in global poverty, and the remainder mostly reflected progress in Brazil, India, Indonesia, and Pakistan (World Bank 2016b). The number of low-income countries (LICs) declined to 49 in 2007 from 64 in 2001. Rapid LIC growth (4.6 percent a year, on average, during 2001-07), supported by several factors—such as the commodity price boom, debt relief, receding armed conflicts, and trade integration—facilitated their transition to middle-income status (World Bank 2019a).

During the global recession: Resilience

The global recession affected EMDEs through trade and financial channels. In many EMDEs, trade collapsed. The plunge in commodity prices weighed on growth in commodity-exporting countries, and reversals of financial flows, especially portfolio investment and cross-border bank lending, led to severe credit crunches. That said, EMDEs weathered the recession better than advanced economies did. First, EMDEs' linkages with the financial institutions and markets at the center of the crisis in advanced economies were limited. Second, services trade and flows of FDI, remittances, and foreign aid were resilient. Third, swift policy actions were taken to stabilize financial systems and stimulate aggregate demand.

Global financial crisis and global recession. Triggered by defaults in the U.S. subprime mortgage market, the U.S. financial system came under increasingly severe stress in the second half of 2007 and early 2008, culminating in a collapse in housing prices in late 2008 (figure 3.2). The bankruptcy of Lehman Brothers in September 2008 triggered a run on key funding markets. This situation exposed the fragility of banks that were dependent on short-term wholesale funding, which had been essential to the rapid growth of securitization, and also reflected inadequate regulatory oversight (Duffie 2019).

---

[6] Based on data for 132 EMDEs. An investment surge is defined as an episode during which the real gross fixed investment-to-GDP ratio is at least one standard deviation above the Hodrick-Prescott-filtered trend (Ohnsorge and Yu 2017; World Bank 2016a).

FIGURE 3.2 Developments around global recessions and downturns

Advanced economies were hit hard by the global financial crisis, which was triggered by problems in the subprime mortgage market in the United States. The recession in advanced economies spilled over to emerging market and developing economies through trade and financial linkages.

A. House prices

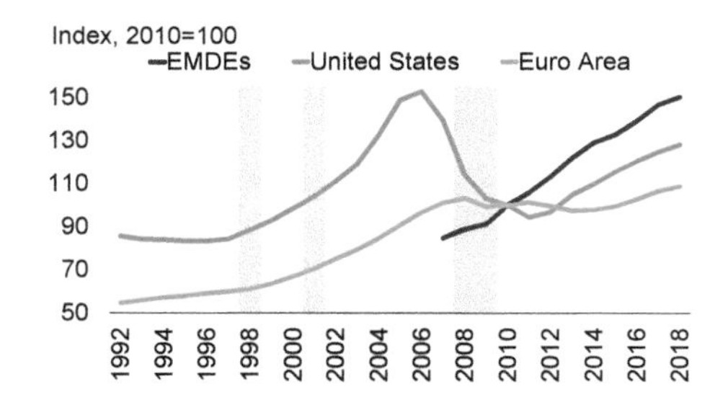

B. Advanced economies growth around global recessions

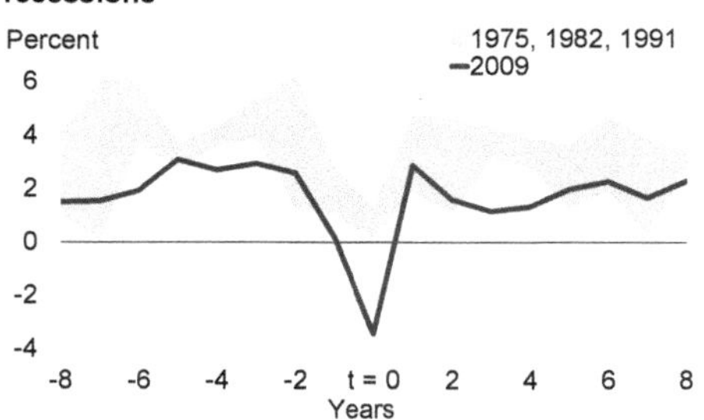

C. Global trade and investment growth

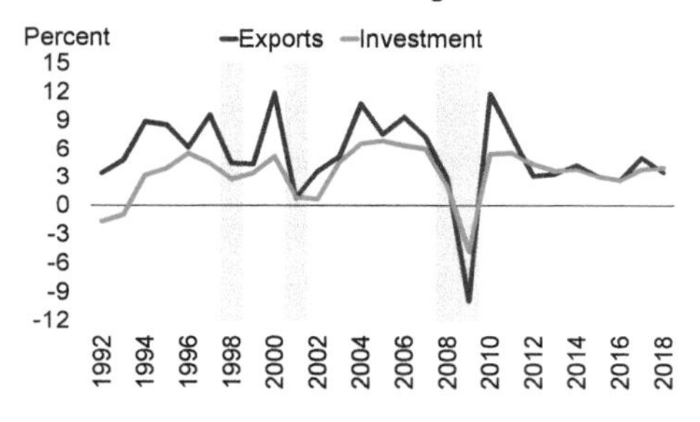

D. Global commodity prices

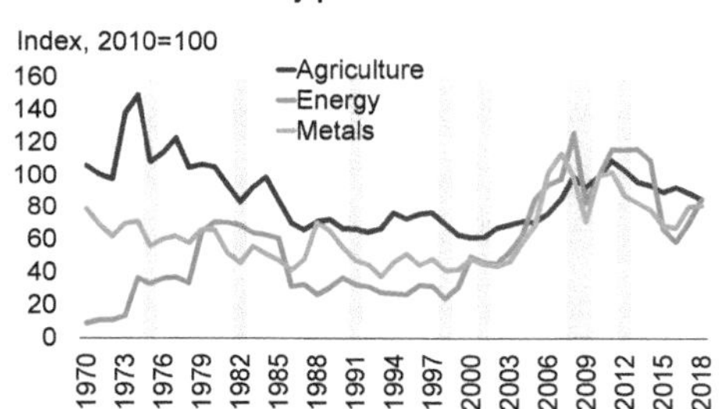

Sources: International Monetary Fund; World Bank.
Note: EMDEs = emerging market and developing economies.
A.C.D. Shaded areas indicate global recessions and slowdowns.
B. Shaded areas are the range of output growth in previous global recessions as defined by Kose and Terrones (2015).

Amid heightened concerns about the solvency of the financial system, credit markets froze as liquidity dried up in interbank funding markets; some banks experienced deposit runs. A severe U.S. recession ensued, during which U.S. output contracted by 4.0 percent between 2008Q3 and 2009Q2—more than in any other U.S. recession in the post-World War II period. Growth in advanced economies dropped from 2.6 percent in 2007 to -3.4 percent in 2009, resulting in a global recession. Global per capita GDP contracted by 2.9 percent in 2009—more than in any previous global recession since the end of World War II (Bolt et al. 2018).

EMDEs generally proved remarkably resilient, however, in part because some of them had limited vulnerabilities to global shocks and effectively used the policy room accumulated before the global recession for countercyclical policies. Among the EM7, growth remained robust during the global recession in China and India, supporting activity in their trading partners Brazil and Indonesia, but output contracted sharply in Mexico, the Russian Federation, and Turkey (box 3.1).

BOX 3.2 Regional developments during the global recession

This box documents how the six regions of emerging markets and developing economies (EMDEs) fared during the global financial crisis and recession. Although EMDEs as a whole weathered the global recession well, the effects varied across regions (figure B3.2.1). Most countries in Europe and Central Asia (ECA) suffered severe output contractions, particularly those that were highly dependent on cross-border financing. Countries that were heavily reliant on commodity export receipts for fiscal revenues also fared relatively badly, such as countries in Latin America and the Caribbean (LAC) and in Middle East and North Africa (MNA). Elsewhere, EMDEs withstood the crisis better because they were less exposed to the financial turmoil and recession in advanced economies, and also because they pursued countercyclical policies.

East Asia and Pacific (EAP) continued to expand throughout the recession, although at reduced rates (7.7 percent in 2009 compared to 12.2 percent in 2007). This growth contrasts sharply with EAP's experience a decade earlier during the Asian financial crisis, partly thanks to lessons learned for macroeconomic policy management (Rhee and Posen 2013). In particular, this resilience reflected the heavy use of stabilization policies to support activity in the region's large economies, which had been made possible by the policy room accumulated before the more recent crisis, and also limited exposure to risks in international financial markets.

Although growth in China and Indonesia slowed in 2009, it was still relatively high, at 9.4 percent and 4.6 percent, respectively, and near precrisis rates. Growth in both countries had remained high thanks to robust consumption and investment growth, supported by fiscal and monetary loosening. In countries dependent on capital- and technology-intensive exports, such as Malaysia and Thailand, output contracted by 1.5 percent and 0.7 percent, respectively, as global demand for consumer durables collapsed (Goldstein and Xie 2009). Compared to similar export-oriented countries in ECA (Turkey) and LAC (Mexico), these output declines were mild because the financial systems in these countries were less integrated into U.S. and euro area financial systems and so avoided financial distress. In Myanmar and Vietnam, growth remained robust in 2009, at 10.6 percent and 5.4 percent, respectively, because their principal exports (clothing, garments, and textiles) characterized by labor-intensive production and income-inelastic demand, declined only moderately.

ECA took the largest hit, with regional output contracting by 5.2 percent in 2009, following a 7.3 percent expansion in 2007. The withdrawal of Western European banks had a notable effect, causing a severe credit crunch (Tong and Wei 2009; World Bank 2011). Developments in ECA during the 2009 global recession resembled some of the features of EAP economies after the Asian

Note: This box was prepared by Wee Chian Koh.

BOX 3.2 Regional developments during the global recession *(continued)*

FIGURE B3.2.1 Growth in EMDE regions

Europe and Central Asia experienced the largest growth setback during the recession, partly owing to a sharp withdrawal of cross-border bank financing. Latin America and the Caribbean also experienced a decline in regional output as exports collapsed amid the plunge in commodity prices. East Asia and Pacific and South Asia fared much better thanks to swift policy stimulus implemented in the largest economies in these regions. In Middle East and North Africa and Sub-Saharan Africa, relatively weak trade and financial linkages with economies in deep recessions limited the impact of the crisis on growth.

A. East Asia and Pacific

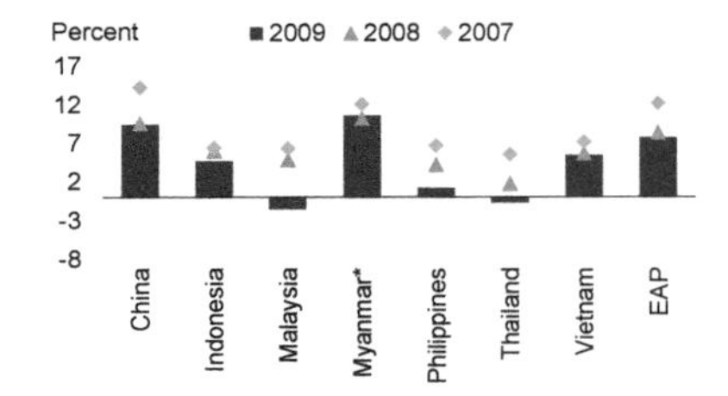

B. Europe and Central Asia

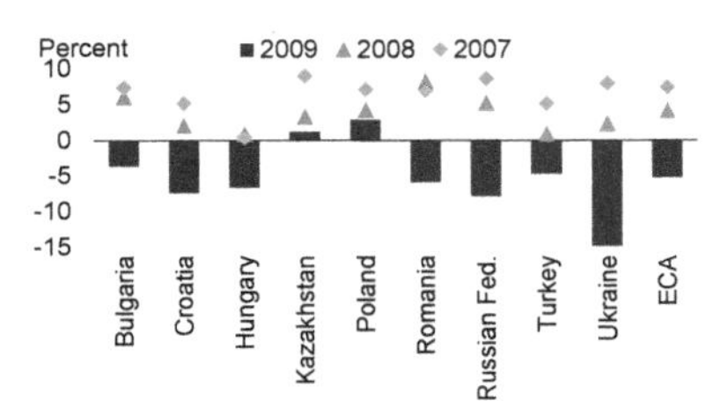

C. Latin America and the Caribbean

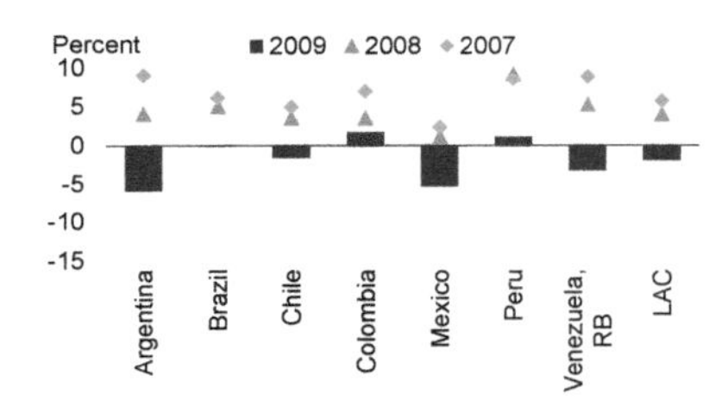

D. Middle East and North Africa

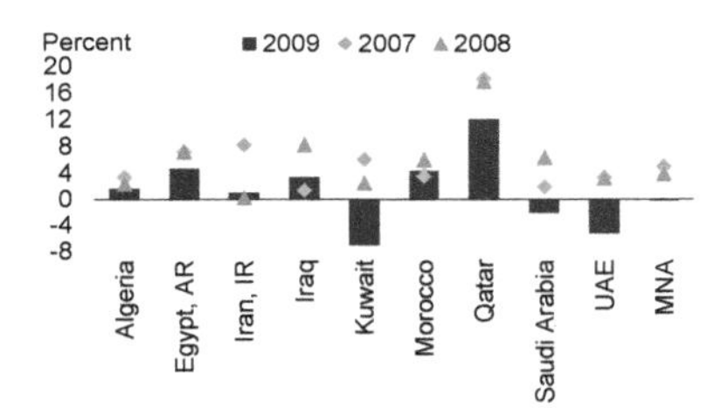

E. South Asia

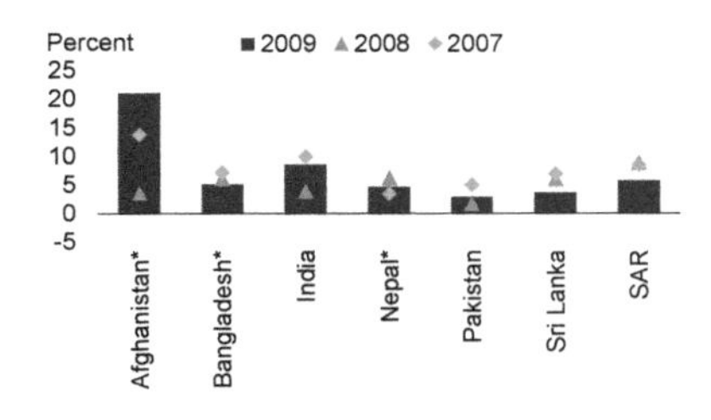

F. Sub-Saharan Africa

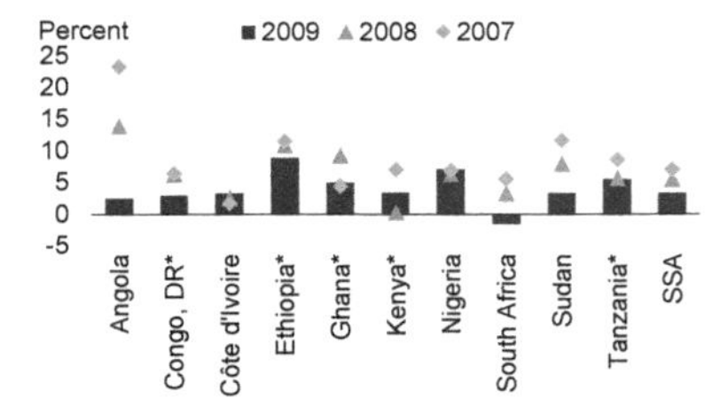

Source: World Bank.

Note: * denotes classification as a low-income country in 2009. Congo, DR = Democratic Republic of Congo; EAP = East Asia and Pacific; ECA = Europe and Central Asia; Egypt, AR = Arab Republic of Egypt; Iran, IR = Islamic Republic of Iran; LAC = Latin America and the Caribbean; MNA = Middle East and North Africa; Russian Fed. = Russian Federation; SAR = South Asia; SSA = Sub-Saharan Africa; UAE = United Arab Emirates.

BOX 3.2 Regional developments during the global recession *(continued)*

financial crisis in 1998 (World Bank 2018b). Countries in ECA had relied much more heavily on loans from foreign banks (especially Western European banks) than other EMDE regions had (Balakrishnan et al. 2009). Contractions were particularly severe in Bulgaria, Croatia, Romania, and Ukraine, with growth rates falling by more than 10 percentage points between 2007 and 2009. Ukraine, which registered the largest growth decline of 14.8 percent in 2009, experienced a collapse in exports (by 22 percent) and sharp capital flow reversals; in particular, cross-border claims on Ukraine fell by 8.7 percentage points of gross domestic product (GDP). Meanwhile, Bulgaria, Croatia, and Romania were exposed to large currency and maturity mismatches (Ranciere, Tornell, and Vamvakidis 2010).

Hungary, which had a strong export orientation, particularly in car manufacturing, with a concentration of exports to the euro area, experienced an output contraction of 6.6 percent in 2009 owing to a collapse in exports (ECB 2010). In the Russian Federation, output contracted by 7.8 percent in 2009 as a result of deep recessions in trading partners and exacerbated by a temporary plunge in oil prices. Kazakhstan continued to grow, but at a much reduced pace because of lower oil revenues. Alone in the European Union, Poland avoided a contraction, in part because of fiscal stimulus (largely infrastructure spending) that had been approved before the global financial crisis.

LAC, a region heavily dependent on commodity exports, saw its regional output contract by 1.9 percent in 2009 after a solid expansion of 5.7 percent in 2007, largely because of adverse terms of trade shocks. GDP declined by 5.9 percent in Argentina and by 3.2 percent in Republica Bolivariana de Venezuela amid collapses in commodity exports. Similarly, in Chile, Colombia, and Peru, growth slowed or turned negative owing to falls in commodity exports. These countries fared better than Argentina and República Bolivariana de Venezuela, thanks to better macroeconomic policies, including independent monetary policies delivering low inflation and flexible exchange rate regimes (De Gregorio 2014). Mexico's economy contracted by 5.3 percent in 2009 as manufacturing exports to the United States, which accounted for four-fifths of its total exports, plunged. Brazil averted a contraction largely owing to supportive policy measures, including large-scale foreign exchange interventions that were made possible by exceptionally large reserves accumulated during 2001-07 (equivalent to 60 percentage points of total external debt; Ocampo 2009).

MNA experienced only a small regional output contraction, of 0.2 percent, in 2009, compared to a robust expansion of 4.8 percent in 2007. This small contraction, however, masks a wide difference between oil exporters and importers. Growth in oil-exporting countries slowed markedly as declines in

BOX 3.2 Regional developments during the global recession *(continued)*

global oil consumption and prices were only partially offset by large fiscal stimulus. The steepest growth declines in 2009 were registered in Kuwait (-7.1 percent), the United Arab Emirates (-5.2 percent), and Saudi Arabia (-2.1 percent) despite expansionary fiscal policies. In contrast, oil-importing countries continued to grow moderately in 2009 (for example, the Arab Republic of Egypt by 4.7 percent, and Morocco by 4.2 percent), reflecting limited international financial and trade integration of this part of the region (World Bank 2016a).

South Asia was relatively sheltered from the adverse effects of the global recession because the region had less integrated trade and financial linkages with countries that suffered steep recessions. Regional growth merely slowed to 5.7 percent in 2009 from 8.4 percent in 2007. India's growth remained robust at 8.5 percent in 2009, reflecting resilient financial inflows (FDI and remittances) as well as large policy stimulus. In Bangladesh, Pakistan, and Sri Lanka, growth declined only moderately owing partly to high intraregional trade and the composition of exports, which consists mainly of goods like cotton, textiles, and apparels characterized by labor-intensive production and income-inelastic demand. Remittance inflows to these countries also remained resilient during the crisis, as did official development assistance (ODA).

Sub-Saharan Africa (SSA), home to 29 of the 40 low-income countries in 2009, continued to grow, although more slowly than before the global recession (5.4 percent growth in 2008 and 3.3 percent in 2009, compared to 6.9 percent in 2007). The recession came on top of food and energy price spikes through mid-2008, putting severe pressure on food- and oil-importing countries (Laborde, Lakatos, and Martin 2019). The subsequent plunge in commodity prices led to a growth slowdown in most commodity-exporting countries (World Bank 2015d). Nonetheless, the region displayed strong resilience, in part due to its low level of international financial integration (Louis, Léonce, and Taoufik 2009). Only eight out of the 48 countries in SSA registered an output decline in 2009 (and only four in 2008). Trade was one of the key channels through which the crisis affected the region. In Botswana, the Democratic Republic of Congo, Nigeria, and South Africa, exports fell by more than 15 percent in 2009. In other countries, such as Lesotho, Liberia, São Tomé and Príncipe, and Sierra Leone, declines in ODA or remittance inflows contributed to slower growth. Countries that had the capacity to implement fiscal stimulus packages, such as Gabon, Kenya, Nigeria, and Tanzania, escaped the crisis relatively unscathed (Osakwe 2010). The fiscal injections were mostly used to finance infrastructure and other public investments.

Global trade collapse. The contraction in global output was accompanied by a collapse in global trade, with export growth dropping from 7.3 percent in 2007 to -9.9 percent in 2009 (figure 3.2). The countries that showed the most pronounced export contractions were those most heavily reliant on manufacturing exports of goods with high income elasticities of demand, especially in the electronics and motor vehicle sectors, because spending on consumer durables plunged in advanced economies (Goldstein and Xie 2009). The trade collapse was also particularly pronounced in those countries that relied heavily on arm's length trade rather than intrafirm trade (Lakatos and Ohnsorge 2017). Thus, EMDEs in EAP (Indonesia, Malaysia, Thailand), ECA (Hungary, Ukraine), and Mexico that exported capital- and technology-intensive products experienced double-digit export collapses (box 3.2).

In contrast, export declines were more modest (below 5 percent) in South Asia (SAR; for example, Bangladesh and India), because these EMDEs relied more on exports of nondurable consumer goods with lower income elasticities of demand. The global trade collapse was compounded by shrinking trade finance. In LAC, for instance, in the first quarter of 2009, banks renewed just 50-60 percent of the previous year's trade credit lines (BIS 2009). Amid this trade collapse, EMDE manufacturing sectors shed large numbers of jobs (Banerji et al. 2014). Services exports of EMDEs were considerably more resilient than goods exports, although a decline in tourism dampened activity in EMDEs such as those in the Caribbean islands and some Sub-Saharan African (SSA) countries (Mauritius, Seychelles) where tourism is important.

Commodity price collapse. The global recession was accompanied by a short-lived collapse in commodity prices, particularly for energy and industrial metals. Commodity exporters, especially those that lack economic diversification, faced sharp drops in export revenues and deteriorations in their external and fiscal positions. In major oil-exporting countries such as Saudi Arabia, Nigeria, Russia, and República Bolivariana de Venezuela, the value of exports declined by more than one-third in 2009. Saudi Arabia's current account surplus narrowed by 20 percentage points of GDP; Russia's fiscal position flipped from a surplus of 5.6 percent of GDP in 2008 to a deficit of 5.2 percent of GDP in 2009. In part as a result of the commodity price collapse, headline inflation in EMDEs fell abruptly, averaging 4 percent in 2009 compared to 10 percent in the previous year.

Financial market turmoil and sudden stops. Portfolio investment and foreign lending flows to EMDEs fell steeply in 2008, reflecting a broad-based flight to safety in response to U.S. financial stress (Tong and Wei 2009; figure 3.3). In the fourth quarter of 2008, cross-border lending to EMDEs from banks declined by more than 60 percent of the cumulative inflows during the preceding three quarters (BIS 2009).[7] Between June 2007 and December 2008, the EMBI bond spread rose nearly 600 basis points, the MSCI equity market index halved, and average CDS spreads in major EMDEs increased by

[7] Cross-border bank lending to EMDEs had been dominated by Western European banks whereas portfolio investments were primarily from investors in North America. In European EMDEs, loans from foreign banks accounted for more than 50 percent of GDP, compared to an average of 20 percent of GDP in other EMDE regions (Balakrishnan et al. 2009).

FIGURE 3.3 Financial developments in EMDEs

Capital flows to EMDEs dropped sharply during 2008-09 and 1997-98, with portfolio and other investment flows being particularly volatile. Equity prices in EMDEs plunged. However, domestic bank credit remained resilient.

A. Private capital inflows

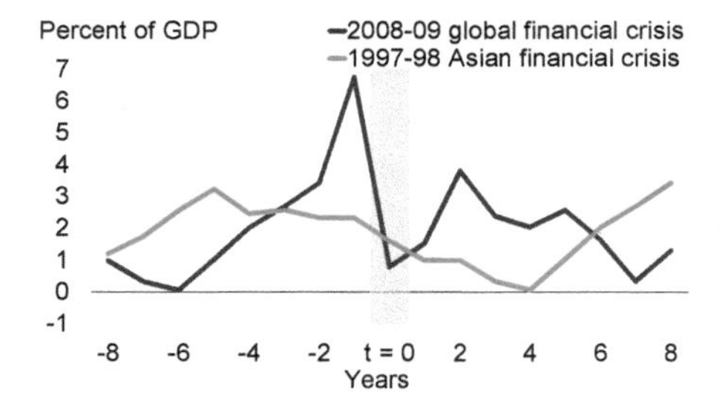

B. Equity markets

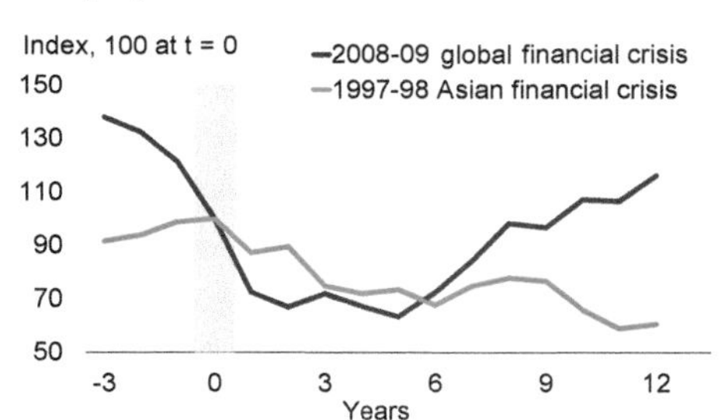

C. Domestic bank credit to the private sector

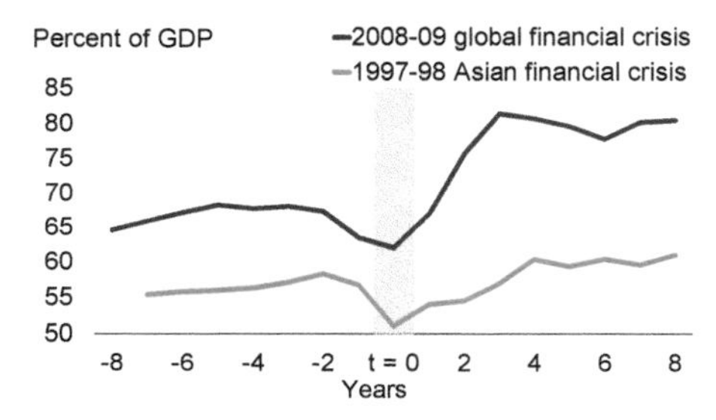

D. FDI inflows

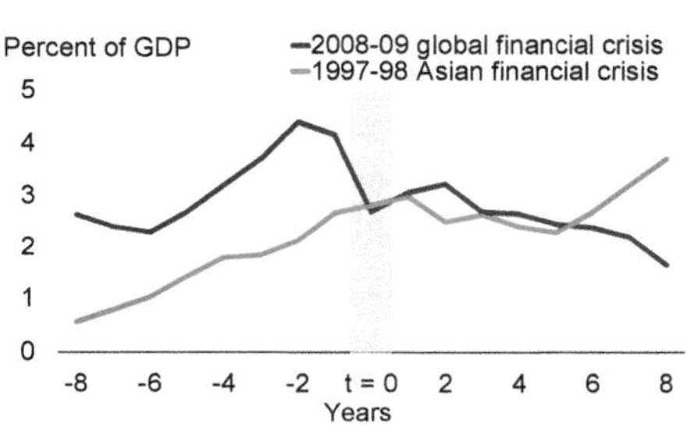

Sources: Araujo et al. (2015); Bank for International Settlements; Haver Analytics; International Monetary Fund; World Bank.
Note: EMDEs = emerging market and developing economies; FDI = foreign direct investment.
A. Private capital flows include portfolio investment, other investment, and financial derivatives. t = 0 in the crisis episodes are 1998 and 2008.
B. t = 0 in the crisis episodes are July 1997 and September 2008.
C.D. t = 0 in the crisis episodes are 1998 and 2009.

375 basis points. Particularly affected by rising financing costs and reduced external finance were countries with large current account deficits, especially in ECA, where the sudden decline in capital flows led to sharp exchange rate depreciations. During September 2008-March 2009, the currencies of several of these EMDEs (Hungary, Mexico, Poland, Ukraine) depreciated by more than 20 percent in effective terms.

Severe liquidity and solvency pressures, exacerbated by currency and maturity mismatches, also afflicted financial systems in EMDEs, particularly those dependent on cross-border credit from European banks and short-term borrowing in foreign currencies, such as Bulgaria, Croatia, and Romania (Binici and Yörükoğlu 2011; Ranciere, Tornell, and Vamvakidis 2010).[8] In EMDEs with more robust external

[8] By contrast, EAP and LAC had limited currency and maturity mismatches (Goldstein and Xie 2009). Taking lessons from previous crises, they also accumulated large foreign reserves to insure against worsening external financing conditions.

positions, such as Brazil, Malaysia, and South Africa, capital flow declines significantly affected the corporate sector: corporations that had borrowed heavily in international debt and credit markets faced difficulties in rolling over their debt.

Resilient domestic bank credit. Despite sharp declines in cross-border bank lending, EMDE domestic bank credit to the private sector continued to grow, albeit at reduced rates. At the peak of the crisis—between the fourth quarter of 2008 and the first quarter of 2009—year-on-year credit growth still averaged 6.7 percent. Domestic bank credit rose swiftly thereafter, reaching 80 percent of GDP by the end of 2009, higher than the precrisis average of 64 percent of GDP in 2002-07 (figure 3.3). Domestic credit growth in EMDEs was supported by monetary policy accommodation as well as by generally resilient EMDE banking systems that entered the crisis with solid profitability, high regulatory capital ratios (exceeding the 8 percent Basel I threshold), and low non-performing loan ratios.

Moderation in longer-term capital flows. FDI inflows into EMDEs, in relation to GDP, declined moderately in 2008 but remained higher than during the Asian financial crisis. FDI fell more sharply in 2009 and, after a brief rebound, continued to decelerate during the past decade (figure 3.3). Remittance inflows to EMDEs fell less than other financial inflows, but the decline dampened activity in the EMDEs most reliant on remittances.[9] Although stable in most EMDEs, official development assistance (ODA) flows to a few ODA-dependent countries (Liberia, São Tomé and Príncipe, Sierra Leone) dropped by more than 9 percentage points of GDP as some donors allocated fewer resources to aid (Allen and Giovannetti 2011).

Expected crisis impact on EMDEs: De-coupling. At the onset of the crisis, some analysts and commentators expected EMDEs to be largely spared its adverse effects (Akin and Kose 2007; IMF 2007). Many EMDEs entered the crisis with ample foreign exchange reserves, moderate debt and deficits, room for countercyclical policies, improved banking systems, and growing intraregional trade. With business cycles already less synchronized between advanced economies and EMDEs, despite rapid trade and financial integration, there seemed to be a prospect of "de-coupling" of EMDEs from advanced economy stress (Imbs 2010; Kose and Prasad 2010). Although the financial market stress and recession in advanced economies did spill over to EMDEs through trade and financial linkages, and to LICs through reduced remittances and aid, EMDEs were surprisingly resilient during the global recession.

Impact on EMDEs: Relatively moderate growth slowdown. EMDE output growth slowed from 8.2 percent in 2007 to 5.9 percent in 2008 and 1.7 percent in 2009 (figure 3.4). Although steep, this slowdown was somewhat milder than during some previous

[9] For example, in LAC, a sharp domestic currency depreciation dampened the impact of slowing dollar-denominated remittances (Ocampo 2009). The countries that experienced marked declines in remittances in 2007-09 were Bosnia and Herzegovina, El Salvador, Jamaica, Lesotho, Liberia, the Marshall Islands, and the Republic of Yemen. Remittances account for between 10 and 25 percent of GDP in these economies.

FIGURE 3.4 EMDE growth during the global recession

EMDEs weathered the global recession relatively well. Countries with stronger precrisis macroeconomic fundamentals and those with more aggressive countercyclical policies experienced milder slowdowns.

A. EMDE growth around global recessions

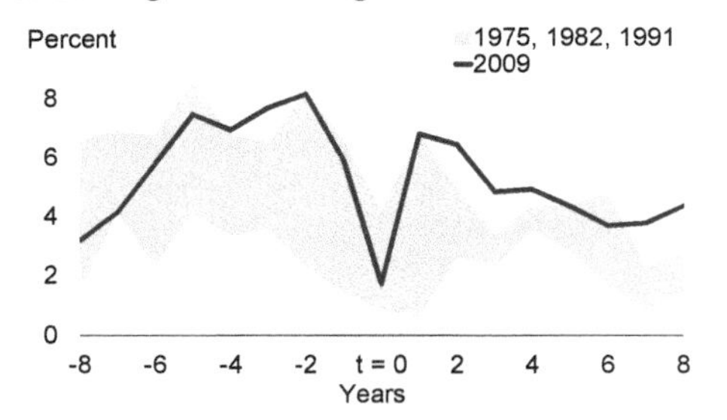

B. EMDE trade and investment growth

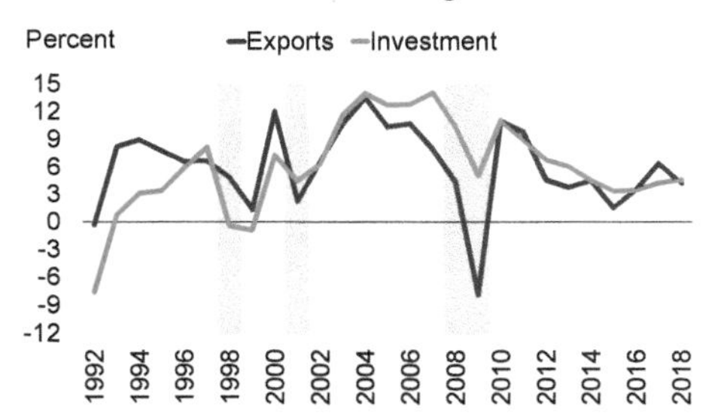

C. EMDE growth slowdowns in 2007-09, by precrisis structural indicators

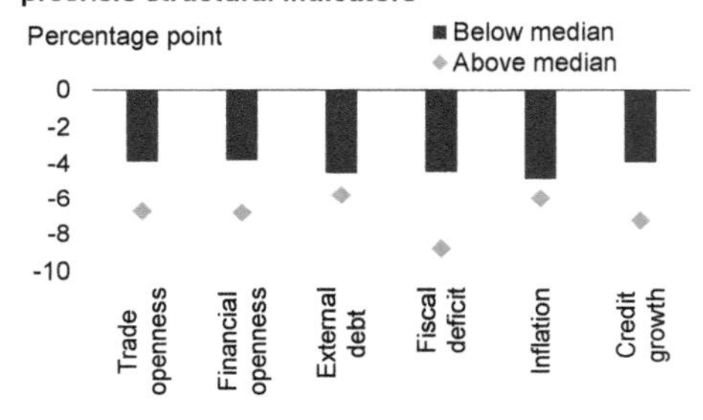

D. EMDE growth slowdowns in 2007-09, by policy intervention

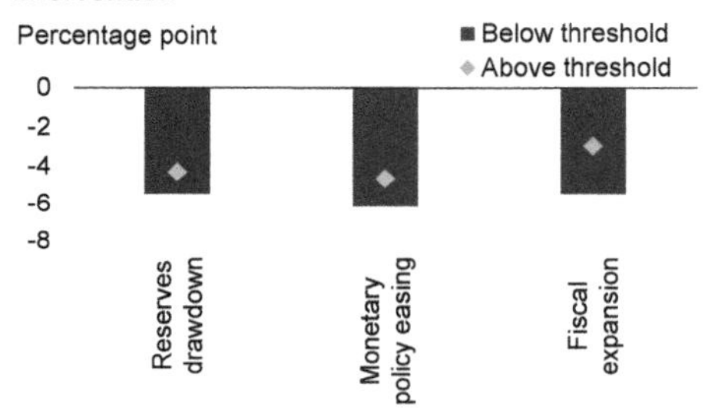

Sources: Chinn and Ito (2006); Haver Analytics; World Bank.

Note: EMDEs = emerging market and developing economies.

A. Shaded areas are the range of output growth in previous global recessions (that is, t = 0 for year 1975, 1982, and 1991) as defined by Kose and Terrones (2015). t = 0 shown in the blue line is for year 2009.

B. Shaded bars indicate global recessions and slowdowns.

C. Growth slowdown is the GDP growth differential between 2007 (precrisis) and 2009. Trade openness is proxied by trade as a share of GDP, and financial openness is based on the Chinn-Ito index. External debt and fiscal deficit are in percent of GDP. Inflation is the annual change in the consumer price index. Credit growth is the annual change in domestic credit to the private sector.

D. Growth slowdown is the GDP growth differential between 2007 (precrisis) and 2009. The threshold for reserves drawdown is 30 percentage points of the reserve-to-debt ratio. Monetary easing refers to the lowering of interest rates, with a 0.5-percentage-point threshold. Fiscal expansion refers to growth in real government consumption expenditure, with a 10-percentage-point threshold.

C.D. Depending on data availability for each indicator, the number of EMDEs ranges from 80 to 154.

global recessions, with three-fifths of EMDEs avoiding output contractions.[10] Exports shrank by 7.9 percent in 2009, in a sharp reversal from their robust 10 percent average annual growth in 2002-07, and investment growth slowed. Broadly speaking, countries with stronger fiscal positions, lower inflation, more sound financial sectors, or less dependence on external demand and foreign finance, fared better, as did those that used countercyclical policies decisively to support activity.

[10] For instance, during the Asian financial crisis, growth in the EAP region fell from 7.1 percent to 1.7 percent in 1997-98 whereas, in the global financial crisis, growth slowed from 8.4 percent to 7.7 percent in 2008-09. Similarly, in the Latin America debt crisis, LAC growth fell from 6.3 percent to 0 percent in 198081 whereas, in the global financial crisis, growth decreased from 4.1 percent to -0.1 percent in 2008-09.

The impact of the crisis varied across EMDE regions (box 3.2). ECA took the largest hit because the withdrawal of Western European banks caused a severe credit crunch. Output in LAC also contracted as commodity exports collapsed, accompanied by a plunge in commodity prices. Elsewhere, expansions continued although at reduced rates. In EAP, MNA, and SAR, this expansion reflected the heavy use of monetary and fiscal stimulus in large economies to support activity (World Bank 2009b, 2010a, 2010b). SSA had limited exposure to risks in international financial markets.

Resilience of LICs. LICs continued to grow during the crisis, although more slowly (4.9 percent in 2008 and 5.3 percent in 2009, compared to 6.0 percent in 2007), because domestic demand was supported by public investment in part financed by robust FDI and remittances and broadly stable foreign aid (World Bank 2019a). FDI inflows to LICs averaged 3.3 percent of GDP during 2008-09 compared to 2.5 percent of GDP during the precrisis period (2002-07). Remittances into LICs averaged 5.9 percent of GDP during 2008-09, an increase of 1.3 percentage points over the precrisis average. ODA to LICs declined marginally to 9.2 percent of GDP from 10.3 percent of GDP over the same period. Exports were also less adversely affected. In the median LIC, exports rose by 2.2 percent in 2009, compared to -6.1 percent in other EMDEs.

Slowing poverty reduction during the global recession. The pace of poverty reduction slowed or poverty increased in some EMDEs with steep recessions (Habib et al. 2010).[11] In ECA, following a large growth setback during the global recession, the proportion of people living in extreme poverty declined, on average, by only 0.2 percentage point a year in 2008-10, compared to the average decline of 0.7 percentage point a year in 2005-08.[12] In LAC, where output also contracted during the global recession, the average improvement in the proportion of people living in extreme poverty slowed to 0.4 percentage point a year in 2008-10 from 1.0 percentage point a year in 2005-08. More broadly for EMDEs, because of strong growth in EAP and SAR during the global recession, poverty declined by 1.2 percentage points a year in 2008-10. Previous studies show that the impact of economic crisis varies across income groups, often resulting in rising income inequality (Habib et al. 2010; Ravallion 2009). In regions such as MNA and SSA, the average Gini coefficient, a commonly used measure of inequality, increased during the global recession.

After the global recession: Protracted weakness

An easing in global fiscal and monetary policy promoted a rapid growth rebound in 2010. The following year, however, was the start of a decade of protracted weakness in the global economy. Global trade growth slowed sharply from prerecession rates, and

[11] It was initially estimated that the global financial crisis would add 64 million people to the population living under $2 a day (Ravallion and Chen 2009). For advanced economies, there is evidence of adverse impacts of the 2009 global recession on poverty and health (Bitler, Hoynes, Kuka 2017; Schwandt and von Wachter 2019; Seeman et al. 2018).

[12] People living in extreme poverty are those living on less than $1.90 a day at 2011 purchasing power parity. Data are obtained from https://databank.worldbank.org/source/poverty-and-equity-database.

commodity prices fell. The euro area plunged into a debt crisis in 2010-11. In 2013, as financial markets began to anticipate the reduction of large-scale asset purchases by the U.S. Federal Reserve, financing conditions tightened for EMDEs. This sluggish and volatile external backdrop coincided with country-specific challenges in some major EMDEs. Meanwhile, the weakness of investment that accompanied the global downturn and less favorable demographic trends continued eroding potential growth (that is, the growth rate an economy can sustain at full employment and capacity utilization).

Sharp, stimulus-driven initial rebound. In 2010, supported by stimulus in the largest advanced economies and EMDEs, global trade rebounded, commodity prices rallied, and financial conditions eased with many interest rates reaching historic lows. Capital flows returned to EMDEs but remained below peaks reached before the global recession. Stock markets rallied, and sovereign bond spreads retreated: by end-2010, the MSCI and EMBI spreads had already nearly returned to their prerecession levels (mid-2007).

Growth in EMDEs rebounded swiftly to 6.8 percent in 2010, from 1.7 percent in 2009. Even in the worst-affected regions (ECA, LAC), output rose above prerecession peaks in 2010. This rebound was sharper than after previous global recessions and EMDE crises. For instance, it had taken Indonesia about five years to reach its precrisis output levels following the 1997-98 Asian financial crisis. It had taken Mexican output about six years to recover to its precrisis level following the debt crises in Latin America in the 1980s. The initial 2010 rebound was followed by protracted weakness in the global economy.

Weak global trade growth. Since 2011, global trade growth has slowed to 4.1 percent a year on average, well below the prerecession average of 7.6 percent a year during 2002-07. This weakness appears to reflect five main factors: weak demand growth in advanced economies, a shifting composition of global demand, weakness in arm's-length trade, the maturation of global supply chains, and slowing momentum in trade liberalization and increased trade tension (World Bank 2015a).

- *Anemic demand growth in advanced economies.* Advanced economies account for about 60 percent of global import demand and are the destinations for about half of EMDE exports. Import growth in advanced economies averaged 3.6 percent a year in 2011-18 compared with 6.0 percent a year in 2002-07. A series of adverse events set back growth in the United States, the euro area, and Japan during 2011-18 (Didier et al. 2015; Lin and Volker 2012; Stocker et al. 2018).[13]

- *Changing composition of global demand.* The composition of global demand shifted toward less trade-intensive sectors (Obstfeld 2015). In advanced economies, growth in investment—which tends to be more trade-intensive than other components of

[13] The events included the euro area debt crisis of 2010-12, which raised questions about the area's viability; the 2014-16 oil price collapse that disrupted the rapidly growing U.S. shale oil sector; and concerns about the effectiveness of the expansionary strategy known as "Abenomics" in Japan.

demand—remained below long-term averages during 2011-16 (World Bank 2015b). In China, the rebalancing of the economy from exports, investment, and manufacturing toward consumption and services also reduced import demand growth from 18.5 percent a year in 2002-07 to 7.8 percent a year in 2011-18. Demographic change (population aging) has also contributed to the shift in demand toward services (health care, recreation, so on).

- *Postcrisis weakness in arm's-length trade.* Arm's-length trade—trade between unaffiliated firms—accounts disproportionately for the overall postrecession trade slowdown (Lakatos and Ohnsorge 2017). This is partly because arm's-length trade depends more heavily on EMDEs than intrafirm trade does, where output growth has slowed sharply from elevated prerecession rates, and on sectors with rapid prerecession growth that boosted arm's-length trade prerecession but that have languished postrecession. Compounding such compositional effects, arm's-length trade is also more sensitive to changes in demand and real exchange rates.

- *Maturing supply chains.* The pace of expansion of global supply chains, which strongly supported trade growth prerecession, has slowed. In particular, Chinese imports of parts and components have declined from their peak of 60 percent of merchandise exports in the mid-1990s to 35 percent of merchandise exports in 2012, reflecting the progressive substitution of domestic inputs for foreign ones (Constantinescu, Mattoo, and Ruta 2016; Kee and Tang 2016).

- *Slowing momentum in trade liberalization, and increased trade tensions.* The pace of easing impediments to trade has slowed since the global recession. Nontariff barriers have increased, and several countries have put trade restrictions in place (UNCTAD 2010; WTO 2018). Since 2017, increased trade tensions between the United States and several other countries, particularly China, have also weighed on global trade growth (World Bank 2019a).

Steep commodity price slide. The 2002-07 global expansion had been accompanied by surging demand for primary commodities, particularly metals, in part because of rapid demand growth in China (World Bank 2015b; Baffes et al. 2018). Between 2000 and 2010, China accounted for 89 percent of the increase in global demand for industrial metals, 54 percent of the increase in global energy demand, and 17 percent of the increase in global demand for food. The resulting prerecession surge in commodity prices encouraged commodity exploration and discovery, leading to rapid expansion in mining capacity and unconventional energy extraction, especially for shale and offshore oil and gas (World Bank 2015b, 2015c; Khan et al. 2016).

Metal prices reached a peak in early 2011 and then began to decline sharply, reaching a trough in early 2016. A moderate recovery followed. The decline reflected both slowing demand growth, including in China, and increased supply after a period of rapid global resource investment. Although Organization of Petroleum Exporting Countries (OPEC) policy initially supported stable oil prices despite surging U.S. oil production, a shift in OPEC policy in mid-2014 triggered an oil price plunge during 2014-16 that caused widespread disruption to oil-exporting countries.[14] At end-2018, energy prices were 32 percent below their 2001Q1 levels, industrial metals prices 37 percent below, and agricultural commodity prices 35 percent below. The broad-based decline in commodity prices weighed heavily on growth in the almost two-thirds of EMDEs that are commodity exporters.[15]

Intermittent spikes in EMDE borrowing costs. The postrecession period was marked by considerable volatility in capital flows to EMDEs and, from mid-2013, occasional spikes in borrowing costs. Following the rebound, global capital flows declined, with sharp outflows in 2013Q3, 2015Q3, and 2018Q2 related to episodes of heightened uncertainty in financial markets.[16] During these episodes, on average, the EMBI spread rose by about 50 basis points, the MSCI declined by 7.7 percent, capital inflows to EMDEs slowed sharply, and EMDE currencies depreciated (figure 3.5). From end-2015, after the U.S. Federal Reserve had started to tighten monetary conditions, the EMBI spread fell as U.S. long-term bond yields rose, before a partial reversal in early 2018 amid deteriorating growth prospects and heightened global uncertainty. From their trough of 0.3 percent of GDP in 2015, capital flows to EMDEs recovered to 2.1 percent of GDP in 2017 but slowed again in 2018.

Whereas portfolio and other short-term investment flows to EMDEs underwent bouts of reversals, FDI flows and remittances remained more stable (De et al. 2019; Eichengreen, Gupta, and Masetti 2017; Ratha, Mohapatra, and Silwal 2011; World Bank 2015a). FDI inflows declined only moderately to 2.2 percent of GDP in 2011-18 from 3.1 percent of GDP in 2002-07.[17] Remittance flows to EMDEs averaged 1.6 percent of GDP in 2018, broadly in line with the 2011-18 average (1.5 percent of GDP) and the prerecession average (1.7 percent of GDP, 2002-07).

Protracted EMDE growth weakness. Whereas growth in advanced economies recovered steadily from a trough in 2012, EMDE growth slowed continuously from 2010 to a trough of 3.7 percent in 2016 (which coincided with the trough in commodity prices) before a modest recovery took hold (figure 3.6). The growth differential between

[14] The oil price plunge had both supply- and demand-related origins: increased efficiency in U.S. shale oil production, weak global demand, U.S. dollar appreciation, less-than-expected supply disruptions from geopolitical uncertainty, and OPEC's policy change to target market share instead of oil prices (Baffes et al. 2015). A detailed analysis of sources and implications of the oil price collapse is available in Baffes et al. (2015) and World Bank (2015a, 2018a, 2018c).

[15] In particular, Brazil (iron ore, soybeans), Chile (copper ore, refined copper), Guinea (aluminum ore), the Philippines (nickel ore), Qatar (liquefied natural gas), Saudi Arabia (crude oil), and Thailand (rice) account for more than one-fifth of global exports of these commodities.

[16] In May 2013, the Chairman of the U.S. Federal Reserve Board, in testimony to U.S. Congress, noted that a robust U.S. economy might warrant a tapering of asset purchases; this policy change led to the "taper tantrum" (Arteta et al. 2015). In June 2015, a period of turbulence began in the Chinese stock market: by mid-July the Shanghai Stock Exchange had lost one-third of its value, and in August it dropped by more than 20 percent in a week, triggering widespread concerns about financial stability and growth in China. In March 2018, investor sentiment shifted to expectations of rising inflation and tightening monetary policy in the U.S., and this was followed by sharp capital outflows from EMDEs.

[17] The decline in part reflected lower rates of return as well as slowing expansion of global value chains (UNCTAD 2018).

FIGURE 3.5 EMDE financial markets since the global recession

Bouts of policy uncertainty since the global recession have triggered volatility in EMDE financial markets and borrowing costs.

A. EMBI bond spread around key events

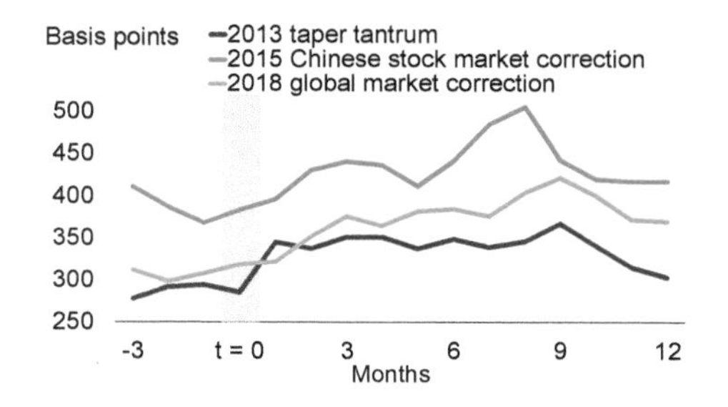

B. MSCI stock index around key events

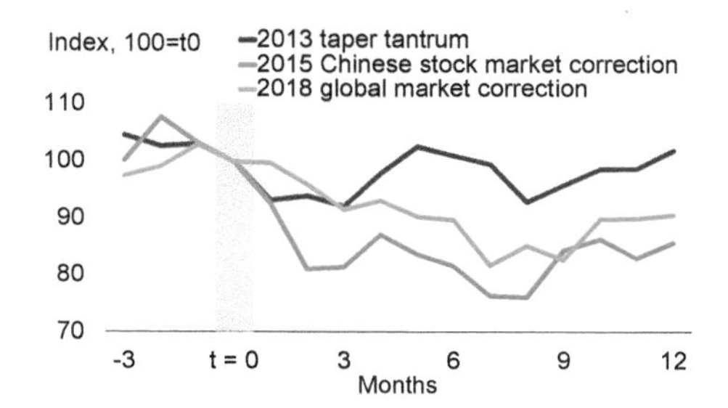

C. EMDE net portfolio flows and nominal exchange rate

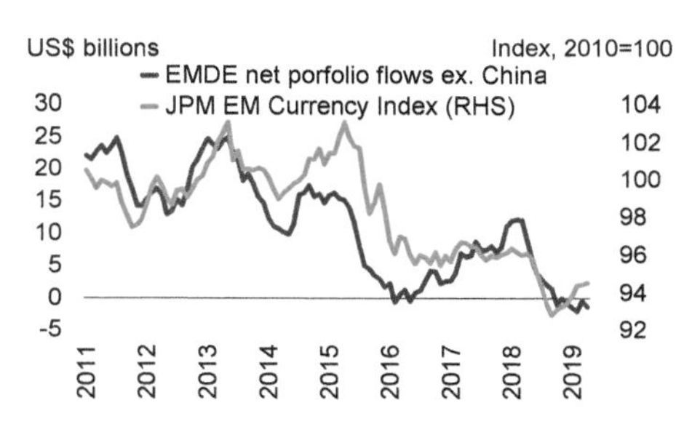

D. EMDE bond spreads and global uncertainty

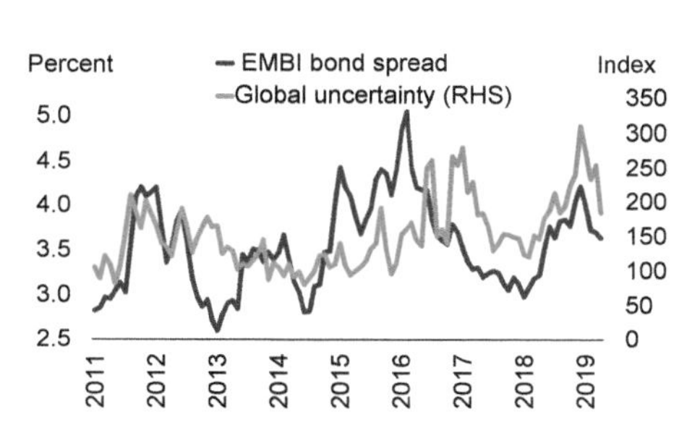

Sources: Araujo et al. (2015); Davis (2016); Haver Analytics; Institute of International Finance; International Monetary Fund; J.P. Morgan; World Bank.

Note: EMDEs = emerging market and developing economies.

A.B. t = 0 for the 3 events are May 2013, June 2015, and March 2018. MSCI = Morgan Stanley Capital International.

C. Net portfolio flows are 12-month moving averages. The nominal exchange rate is based on the J.P. Morgan Emerging Market Currency Index (labeled JPM EM Currency Index).

D. EMDE bond spread is based on the J.P. Morgan's Emerging Market Bond Index Plus (EMBI+). Global uncertainty is based on the Global Economic Policy Uncertainty Index developed by Davis (2016), where 100 = mean of 2007 (or first year).

C.D. Last observation is April 2019.

EMDEs and advanced economies has since narrowed to about 2 percentage points, the smallest since the early 2000s. The growth slowdown during 2011-16 was synchronous (affecting more than three-fifths of EMDEs) and protracted, with the steepest slowdowns in LAC and the mildest in SAR (Didier et al. 2015). In the 20 largest EMDEs, growth in 2016 was, on average, 3.1 percentage points lower than in 2011. In LICs, growth slowed from 6.3 percent in 2012 to a trough of 3.2 percent in 2016.

Most components of EMDE demand slowed concurrently (Kose et al. 2017). Investment and export growth suffered especially sharp declines, falling to less than half their prerecession rates. Gross fixed investment growth averaged 5.2 percent a year in 2011-18 compared to 11.9 percent a year in 2002-07. Export growth declined to 4.8

FIGURE 3.6 EMDE growth since the global recession

A synchronous and persistent slowdown has been underway in EMDEs since the postcrisis rebound of 2010, notwithstanding a modest recovery in 2017-18. As a result, the growth differential between EMDEs and advanced economies has narrowed.

A. Growth in EMDE commodity exporters and importers

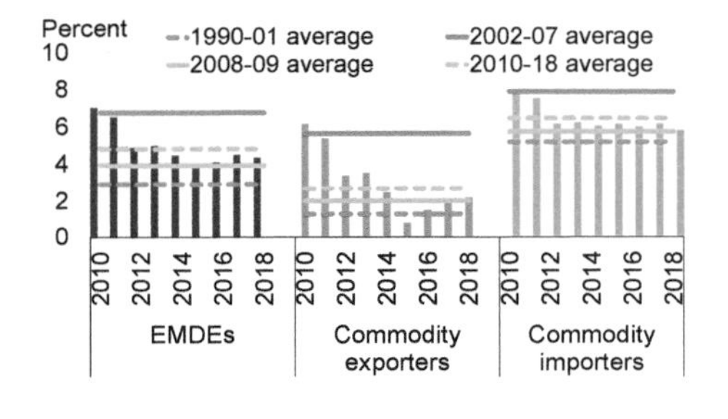

B. Growth by region

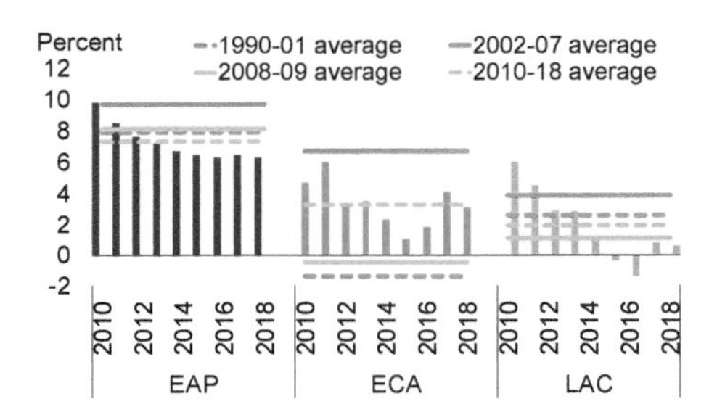

C. Growth by region (continued)

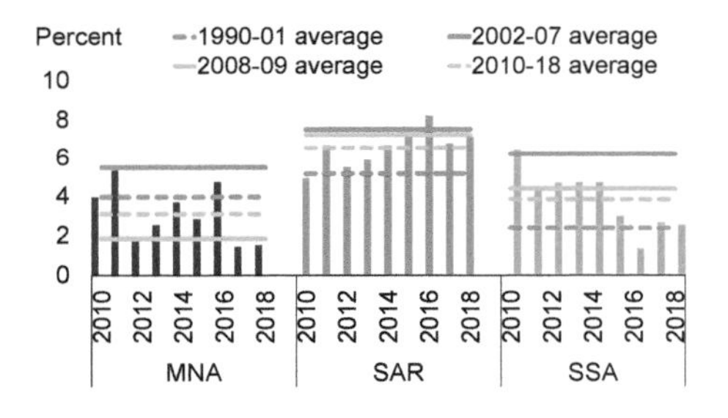

D. Growth differential with advanced economies

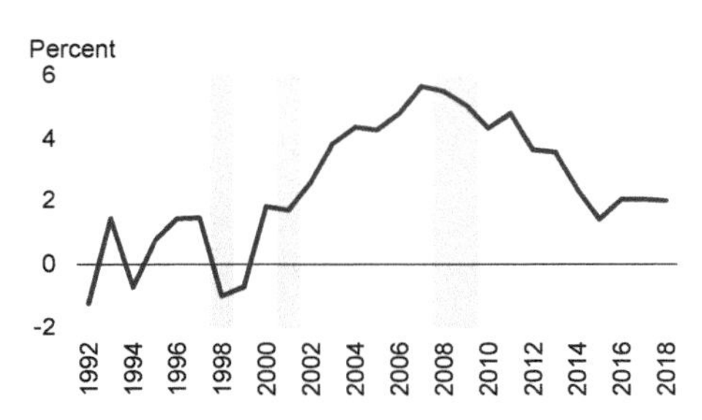

Source: World Bank.
Note: EAP = East Asia and Pacific; ECA = Europe and Central Asia; EMDEs = emerging market and developing economies; LAC = Latin America and the Caribbean; MNA = Middle East and North Africa; SAR = South Asia; SSA = Sub-Saharan Africa.
D. EMDE growth minus advanced economy's growth. Shaded bars indicate global recessions and slowdowns.

percent from 10.0 percent between the same periods. The weakness of investment growth reflected subdued global trade growth, low commodity prices, moderating FDI inflows, considerable policy uncertainty in major economies, and tightening financial conditions (Kose et al. 2017; Vashakmadze et al. 2017; World Bank 2017). This investment weakness has contributed to an EMDE total factor productivity growth slowdown from 2.5 percent a year on average in 2003-07 to 1.7 percent in 2018, with particularly pronounced declines in ECA, LAC, and MNA.

Weak global economic growth coincided with country-specific challenges in some large EMDEs. Episodes of political uncertainty, social tensions (especially in MNA), geopolitical events, civil wars, and unorthodox policy decisions triggered bouts of sharply weaker confidence (World Bank 2016c, 2017, 2018a). In China, recession-related policy stimulus was unwound intermittently, and policies guided the economy away from investment-driven growth toward more balanced growth. The growth slowdown in China, from 11.3 percent a year on average during 2002-07 to 6.3 percent in 2018, has hindered growth in its trading partners and in commodity exporters (Huidrom et al. 2019; World Bank 2016c).

The erosion of policy buffers employed during the global recession made it difficult to stem the growth slowdown through countercyclical policies. The large drop in commodity prices in 2014-16 further dampened growth in EMDE commodity exporters, with growth 2.8 percentage points lower than in 2011-13, on average (figure 3.6). It was exacerbated by procyclical policy tightening. As government revenues from the resources sector fell sharply and fiscal positions deteriorated, several EMDEs (Angola, Ecuador, Nigeria, Saudi Arabia) undertook fiscal consolidation despite weak growth. Adverse terms of trade movements also led to sharp currency depreciations (Angola, Azerbaijan, Colombia, Russia), prompting central banks to raise policy rates, intervene in foreign exchange markets, or allow greater exchange rate flexibility. In commodity-importing EMDEs, the growth benefits from rising real incomes due to falling prices of oil and other commodities did not materialize; instead, growth slowed by 0.6 percentage points between 2011-13 and 2014-16. Nonetheless, inflation subsided, and fiscal and current account balances improved in several countries (India, Poland, Romania, Thailand; World Bank 2015c).[18]

Recent growth trends and short-term outlook. Many EMDEs saw a mild cyclical recovery in 2017, led by growth in exports and investment as global manufacturing and trade picked up. Energy and metal prices rebounded from their lows in early 2016, but have been volatile since the second half of 2018 amid bouts of intensifying trade and geopolitical tensions. Growth in global trade is projected to weaken in 2019 to the slowest pace since the global recession, from 5.5 percent in 2017. EMDE growth is forecast to remain weak at 4.4 percent on average in 2019-21, from 4.5 percent in 2017 (World Bank 2019a).

The subdued short-term growth outlook is, in addition, subject to heightened downside risks. A further escalation in trade tensions could trigger a sharper-than-expected slowdown in global trade and activity and could threaten the stability of the rules-based multilateral trading system. Sharper-than-expected slowdowns in the United States, the euro area, and China—which together account for more than half of global GDP—could generate adverse spillovers for EMDEs through trade, financial, commodity, and confidence channels. A rise in borrowing cost could trigger financial stress in EMDEs with elevated debt or large financing requirements.

EMDE long-term growth prospects remain clouded by the confluence of demographic headwinds, rising debt levels, volatile financing conditions, limited policy space, elevated policy uncertainty and trade tensions, slowing capital accumulation and productivity

---

[18] EMDE commodity importers' current account balances improved from an average deficit of 0.3 percent of GDP in 2011-13 to an average surplus of 0.8 percent of GDP in 2014-16. By contrast, in EMDE commodity exporters, the average current account balance deteriorated from 2.3 to -1.1 percent of GDP over the same period.

growth, and lackluster reform progress that weakens potential growth.[19] Moreover, the prospects for progression of today's LICs to middle-income levels are dim compared to those in the precrisis period because of a larger prevalence of countries affected by fragility, conflict, and violence; geographical disadvantages in external trade; weaker commodity demand as China shifts toward less resource-intensive sectors; and higher vulnerability to extreme weather that threatens livelihoods in agriculture-dependent economies (World Bank 2019a).

Conclusion

Strong domestic demand and a benign external environment supported broad-based and rapid growth in EMDEs before the global recession. During 2002-07, EMDEs grew by 6.7 percent per year—twice as fast as during the previous two decades and surpassed only by their growth spurt during the early to mid-1970s. As a result, the share of EMDEs in global GDP increased to 31 percent in 2007 from 26 percent in 2001. In turn, favorable economic conditions allowed EMDEs to accumulate sizeable current account surpluses and foreign exchange reserves and to reduce fiscal deficits and government debt.

Triggered by defaults in the U.S. subprime mortgage market, the U.S. financial system came under severe stress in the second half of 2007 and early 2008. Heightened concerns about the solvency of the financial system, the shortage of liquidity in interbank funding markets, and deposit runs at some U.S. banks triggered a financial crisis followed by a severe U.S. recession. During 2008Q3-2009Q2, U.S. output contracted by 4.0 percent—more than in any other U.S. recession since World War II. Given the size and international connectedness of the U.S. economy, the spillovers to the rest of the world were sizeable. Although the global financial crisis originated in the United States, EMDEs were adversely affected by the collapse in global trade and finance. On the whole, however, EMDEs weathered the crisis relatively well: EMDE growth slowed to 1.6 percent in 2009, but output did not contract.

Some EMDEs withstood the crisis better than others. Countries that were less dependent on external trade and finance, had stronger precrisis fundamentals, and were able to implement swifter and more aggressive stimulus policies suffered milder growth slowdowns. China and India were among the fastest to recover, in part because of swift policy responses. LICs were also resilient because foreign aid, remittances, and FDI flows remained broadly stable. In contrast, EMDEs that were heavily dependent on short-term and potentially volatile capital flows—such as portfolio investment and cross-border bank lending—fared less well, especially those in ECA.

---

[19] These structural factors have also been postulated as the drivers of the "secular stagnation" in global growth (see Bernanke 2015; Eggertsson, Lancastre, and Summers 2018; Eggertsson, Mehrotra, and Robbins 2019; Rachel and Summers 2019; Rogoff 2015; and Summers 2014). The "secular stagnation" theory further posits that with historically low global real interest rates (negative in many advanced economies, including Japan, Sweden, Switzerland, and the euro area), expansionary monetary policy has limited effectiveness in stimulating aggregate demand.

Since the 2009 global recession, EMDE growth has slowed, from a peak of 6.5 percent in 2011 to a trough of 3.8 percent in 2015, continuing at a moderate 4.3 percent during 2017-19. This still-robust, albeit slowing, growth in EMDEs, combined with the sluggish postrecession recovery in advanced economies, has resulted in a growing role of EMDEs in the global economy. By 2018, the share of EMDEs increased to 39 percent of global GDP, compared with 31 percent in 2007. Given the increasing importance and international connectedness of EMDEs, an adverse shock originating in any part of the world economy could generate greater spillovers to EMDEs than those associated with the 2009 global recession.

The global recession was a reminder of the importance of resilience during times of severe financial stress, as well as the importance of early policy intervention, in international policy coordination, to dampen global shocks. Measures to strengthen resilience include improving debt management, maintaining adequate reserves, designing appropriate macroprudential policies, diversifying export and financing structures, and strengthening monetary and fiscal frameworks. Framework-strengthening measures include enhancing central bank credibility, adopting more flexible exchange rate regimes where appropriate, and ensuring sustainable public finances through fiscal rules. The window of opportunity for rebuilding resilience before the next shock materializes may be narrowing. Separately, that the global economy remains weak postcrisis despite unprecedented policy stimulus illustrates the limitations of cyclical stimulus. It is a reminder of the need for reforms that foster growth led by the private sector and driven by productivity.

References

Aizenman, J., and J. Lee. 2007. "International Reserves: Precautionary Versus Mercantilist Views, Theory and Evidence." *Open Economies Review* 18 (2): 191-214.

Akin, C., and M. A. Kose. 2007. "Changing Nature of North-South Linkages: Stylized Facts and Explanations." IMF Working Paper 07/280, International Monetary Fund, Washington, DC.

Allen, F., and G. Giovannetti. 2011. "The Effects of the Financial Crisis on Sub-Saharan Africa." *Review of Development Finance* 1 (1): 1-27.

Araujo, J., A. David, C. van Hombeeck, and C. Papageorgiou. 2015. "Non-FDI Capital Flows in Low-Income Developing Countries: Catching the Wave?" IMF Working Paper 15/86, International Monetary Fund, Washington, DC.

Arestis, P., and E. Karakitsos. 2013. *Financial Stability in the Aftermath of the "Great Recession."* London: Palgrave Macmillan.

Arteta, C., M. A. Kose, F. Ohnsorge, and M. Stocker. 2015. "The Coming U.S. Interest Rate Tightening Cycle: Smooth Sailing or Stormy Waters?" Policy Research Note 2, World Bank, Washington, DC.

Baffes, J., M. A. Kose, F. Ohnsorge, and M. Stocker. 2015. "The Great Plunge in Oil Prices: Causes, Consequences, and Policy Responses." Policy Research Note 1, World Bank, Washington, DC.

Baffes, J., A. Kabundi, P. Nagle, and F. Ohnsorge. 2018. "The Role of Major Emerging Markets in Global Commodity Demand." Policy Research Working Paper 8495, World Bank, Washington, DC.

Balakrishnan, R., S. Danninger, S. Elekdag, and I. Tytell. 2009. "The Transmission of Financial Stress from Advanced to Emerging Economies." IMF Working Paper 09/133, International Monetary Fund, Washington, DC.

Ball, L. 2014. "Long-Term Damage from the Great Recession in OECD Countries." NBER Working Paper 20185, National Bureau of Economic Research, Cambridge, MA.

Banerji, A., D. Newhouse, P. Paci, and D. Robalino. 2014. *Working Through the Crisis: Jobs and Policies in Developing Countries During the Great Recession*. Directions in Development. Washington, DC: World Bank.

Berkmen, S., G. Gelos, R. Rennhack, and J. Walsh. 2012. "The Global Financial Crisis: Explaining Cross-Country Differences in the Output Impact." *Journal of International Money and Finance* 31 (1): 42–59.

Bernanke, B. S. 2005. "The Global Saving Glut and the U.S. Current Account Deficit." Speech 77, Board of Governors of the Federal Reserve System.

Bernanke, B. S. 2015. "Why Are Interest Rates So Low, Part 2: Secular Stagnation." Brookings Institution (blog), March 31. https://www.brookings.edu/blog/ben-bernanke/2015/03/31/why-are-interest-rates-so-low-part-2-secular-stagnation/.

Bernanke, B. S. 2018. "The Real Effects of Disrupted Credit: Evidence from the Global Financial Crisis." Brookings Papers on Economic Activity Conference Drafts September 13-14 2018, Brookings Institution, Washington, DC

Binici, M., and M. Yörükoğlu. 2011. "Capital Flows in the Post-Global Financial Crisis Era: Implications for Financial Stability and Monetary Policy." BIS Papers 57, Bank for International Settlements, Basel.

BIS (Bank for International Settlements). 2009. *79th Annual Report, 2008/09*. Basel: Bank for International Settlements.

Bitler, M., H. Hoynes, and E. Kuka. 2017. "Child Poverty, the Great Recession, and the Social Safety Net in the United States." *Journal of Policy Analysis and Management* 36 (2): 358-89.

Blanchard, O., H. Faruqee, and M. Das. 2010. "The Initial Impact of the Crisis on Emerging Market Countries." *Brooking Papers on Economic Activity* 41 (1): 263–23.

Blinder, A. 2013. *After the Music Stopped: The Financial Crisis, the Response, and the Work Ahead.* London: Penguin Press.

Bolt, J., R. Inklaar, H. de Jong, and J. L. van Zanden. 2018. "Rebasing 'Maddison': New Income Comparisons and the Shape of Long-Run Economic Development." Maddison Project Working Paper 10, Groningen Growth and Development Centre, Groningen, Netherlands.

Carstens, A. 2019. "Monetary Policy: 10 Years after the Financial Crisis." Speech to the Basler Bankenforum, Basel, September 5. https://www.bis.org/speeches/sp190905b.htm.

Celasun, O., F. Grigoli, K. Honjo, J. Kapsoli, A. Klemm, B. Lissovolik, J. Luksic, M. Moreno-Badia, J. Pereira, M. Poplawski-Ribeiro, B. Shang, and Y. Ustyugova. 2015. "Fiscal Policy in Latin America: Lessons and Legacies of the Global Financial Crisis." IMF Staff Discussion Note 15/06, International Monetary Fund, Washington, DC.

Chen, W., M. Mrkaic, and M. Nabar. 2019. "The Global Economic Recovery 10 Years after the 2008 Financial Crisis." IMF Working Paper 19/83, International Monetary Fund, Washington, DC.

Chinn, M., and H. Ito. 2006. "What Matters for Financial Development? Capital Controls, Institutions, and Interactions." *Journal of Development Economics* 81 (1): 163-92.

Constantinescu, C., A. Mattoo, and M. Ruta. 2016. "Does the Global Trade Slowdown Matter?" Policy Research Working Paper 7673, World Bank, Washington, DC.

Dadush, U., and B. Stancil. 2011. "Why Are Reserves so Big?" VoxEU.org, CEPR Policy Portal, May 9. https://voxeu.org/article/why-are-reserves-so-big-and-who-blame.

Davis, S. 2016. "An Index of Global Economic Policy Uncertainty." NBER Working Paper 22740, National Bureau of Economic Research, Cambridge, MA.

De, S., E. Islamaj, M. A. Kose, and S. Yousefi. 2019. "Remittances over the Business Cycle: Theory and Evidence." *Economic Notes* 48 (3): 1-18.

De Gregorio, J. 2014. *How Latin America Weathered the Global Financial Crisis.* Washington, DC: Peterson Institute for International Economics.

Didier, T., M. A. Kose, F. Ohnsorge, and L. Ye. 2015. "Slowdown in Emerging Markets: Rough Patch or Prolonged Weakness?" Policy Research Note 4, World Bank, Washington, DC.

Dooley, Mi, D. Folkerts-Landau, and P. Garber. 2003. "An Essay on the Revived Bretton Woods System." NBER Working Paper 9971, National Bureau of Economic Research, Cambridge, MA.

Doraisami, A. 2011. "The Global Financial Crisis: Countercyclical Fiscal Policy Issues and Challenges in Malaysia, Indonesia, the Philippines, and Singapore." ADBI Working Paper 288, Asian Development Bank Institute, Tokyo.

Duffie, D. 2019. "Prone to Fail: The Pre-Crisis Financial System." *Journal of Economic Perspective* 33 (1): 81-106.

ECB (European Central Bank). 2010. "The Impact of the Financial Crisis on the Europe and Central Asian Countries." *Monthly Bulletin,* July, European Central Bank, Frankfurt.

Eichengreen, B., P. Gupta, and O. Masetti. 2017. "Are Capital Flows Fickle? Increasingly? And Does the Answer Still Depend on Type?" Policy Research Working Paper 7972, World Bank, Washington, DC.

Eggertsson, G., M. Lancastre, and L. Summers. 2018. "Aging, Output Per Capita and Secular Stagnation." NBER Working Paper 24902, National Bureau of Economic Research, Cambridge, MA.

Eggertsson, G., N. Mehrotra, and J. Robbins. 2019. "A Model of Secular Stagnation: Theory and Quantitative Evaluation." *American Economic Journal: Macroeconomics* 11 (1): 1-48.

Gertler, M., and S. Gilchrist. 2018. "What Happened: Financial Factors in the Great Recession." *Journal of Economic Perspectives* 32 (3): 3-30.

Ghosh, A. R., J. D. Ostry, and C. Tsangarides. 2012. "Shifting Motives: Explaining the Buildup in Official Reserves in Emerging Markets since the 1980s." IMF Working Paper 12/34, International Monetary Fund, Washington, DC.

Goldstein, M., and D. Xie. 2009. "The Impact of the Financial Crisis on Emerging Asia." In *Asia and the Global Financial Crisis,* edited by R. Glick and M. Spiegel. San Francisco, CA: Federal Reserve Bank of San Francisco.

Habib, B., A. Narayan, S. Olivieri, and C. Sanchez. 2010. "The Impact of the Financial Crisis on Poverty and Income Distribution: Insights from Simulations in Selected Countries." *Economic Premise* 7, World Bank, Washington, DC.

Hall, R. 2017. "Low Interest Rates: Causes and Consequences." *International Journal of Central Banking* 13 (3): 103-17.

Huidrom, R., M. A. Kose, H. Hideaki, and F. Ohnsorge. 2019. "How Important Are Spillovers from Major Emerging Markets?" *International Finance* 23 (1): 47-63.

Imbs, J. 2010. "The First Global Recession in Decades." *IMF Economic Review* 58 (2): 327-54.

IMF (International Monetary Fund). 2007. *World Economic Outlook: Spillovers and Cycles in the Global Economy*. April. Washington, DC: International Monetary Fund.

IMF (International Monetary Fund). 2009a. *India: Staff Report for the 2009 Article IV Consultation*. Washington, DC: International Monetary Fund.

IMF (International Monetary Fund). 2009b. *Mexico: Staff Report for the 2009 Article IV Consultation*. Washington, DC: International Monetary Fund.

IMF (International Monetary Fund). 2009c. *Indonesia: Staff Report for the 2009 Article IV Consultation*. Washington, DC: International Monetary Fund.

IMF (International Monetary Fund). 2009d. *Russian Federation: Staff Report for the 2009 Article IV Consultation*. Washington, DC: International Monetary Fund.

IMF (International Monetary Fund). 2010a. *People's Republic of China: Staff Report for the 2010 Article IV Consultation*. Washington, DC: International Monetary Fund.

IMF (International Monetary Fund). 2010b. *Turkey: Staff Report for the 2010 Article IV Consultation*. Washington, DC: International Monetary Fund.

IMF (International Monetary Fund). 2018. *World Economic Outlook: Challenges to Steady Growth*. October. Washington, DC: International Monetary Fund.

Kee, H. L., and H. Tang. 2016. "Domestic Value Added in Exports: Theory and Firm Evidence from China." *American Economic Review* 106 (6): 1402-36.

Khan, T., T. Nguyen, F. Ohnsorge, and R. Schodde. 2016. "From Commodity Discovery to Production." Policy Research Working Paper 7823, World Bank, Washington, DC.

Kose, M. A., F. Ohnsorge, L. S. Ye, and E. Islamaj. 2017. "Weakness in Investment Growth: Causes, Implications and Policy Responses." Policy Research Working Paper 7990, World Bank, Washington, DC.

Kose, M. A., and E. Prasad. 2010. *Emerging Markets: Resilience and Growth amid Global Turmoil* Washington, DC: Brookings Institution Press.

Kose, M. A., and M. Terrones. 2015. *Collapse and Revival: Understanding Global Recessions and Recoveries*. Washington, DC: International Monetary Fund.

Kumar, R., and P. Vashisht. 2009. "The Global Economic Crisis: Impact on India and Policy Responses." ADBI Working Paper 164, Asian Development Bank Institute, Tokyo.

Laborde, D., Lakatos, C., and W. Martin. 2019. "Poverty Impact of Food Price Shock and Policies." Policy Research Working Paper 8724, World Bank, Washington, DC.

Lakatos, C., and F. Ohnsorge. 2017. "Arm's-Length Trade: A Source of Post-Crisis Trade Weakness." Policy Research Working Paper 8144, World Bank, Washington, DC.

Lin, J. 2008. "The Impact of the Financial Crisis on Developing Countries." Paper presented at the Korea Development Institute, Seoul, October 31.

Lin, J., and T. Volker. 2012. "The Crisis in the Euro Zone: Did the Euro Contribute to the Evolution of the Crisis?" Policy Research Working Paper 6127, World Bank, Washington, DC.

Louis, K., N. Léonce, and R. Taoufik. 2009. "Impact of the Global Financial and Economic Crisis on Africa." Working Paper 96, African Development Bank, Tunis, Tunisia.

Mishkin, F. 2011. "Over the Cliff: From the Subprime to the Global Financial Crisis." *Journal of Economic Perspectives* 25 (1): 49-70.

Obstfeld, M. 2015. "The World Economy After the Global Financial Crisis." In *Policy Challenges in a Diverging Global Economy*, edited by R. Glick and M. Spiegel, 27-80. San Francisco, CA: Federal Reserve Bank of San Francisco.

Ocampo, J. A. 2009. "Latin America and the Global Financial Crisis." *Cambridge Journal of Economics* 33 (4): 703-24.

Ohnsorge, F., and S. Yu. 2016. "Recent Credit Surge in Historical Context." Policy Research Working Paper 7704, World Bank, Washington, DC.

Ohnsorge, F., and S. Yu. 2017. "Recent Credit Surge in Historical Context." *Journal of International Commerce, Economics and Policy* 8 (1): 1-20.

Osakwe, P. N. 2010. "Africa and the Global Financial and Economic Crisis: Impacts, Responses and Opportunities." In *The Financial and Economic Crisis of 2008-2009 and Developing Countries*, edited by S. Dullien, D. J. Kotte, A. Márquez, and J. Priewe, 203-22. Geneva: United Nations.

Perri, F., and V. Quadrini. 2018. "International Recessions." *American Economic Review* 108 (4-5): 935-84.

Ponomarenko, A., and S. Vlasov. 2010. "Russian Fiscal Policy During the Financial Crisis." BOFIT Discussion Papers 12/2010, Bank of Finland, Helsinki.

Portes, R. 2010. "Currency Wars and the Emerging-Market Countries." VoxEU.org, CEPR Policy Portal, November 4, https://voxeu.org/article/currency-wars-and-emerging-markets.

Rachel, L., and L. H. Summers. 2019. "On Secular Stagnation in the Industrialized World." NBER Working Paper 26198, National Bureau of Economic Research, Cambridge, MA.

Ranciere, R., A. Tornell, and A. Vamvakidis. 2010. "A New Index of Currency Mismatch and Systemic Risk." IMF Working Paper 10/263, International Monetary Fund, Washington, DC.

Ratha, D., S. Mohapatra, and A. Silwal. 2011. *Migration and Remittances Factbook 2011*. Washington, DC: World Bank.

Ravallion, M. 2009. "The Developing World's Bulging (but Vulnerable) Middle Class." Policy Research Working Paper 4816, World Bank, Washington, DC.

Ravallion, M., and S. Chen. 2009. "The Impact of the Global Financial Crisis on the World's Poorest." VoxEU.org, CEPR Policy Portal, April 30, https://voxeu.org/article/impact-global-financial-crisis-world-s-poorest.

Rawdanowicz, L. 2010. "The 2008-09 Crisis in Turkey: Performance, Policy Responses and Challenges for Sustaining the Recovery." OECD Economics Department Working Paper 819, Organisation for Economic Co-operation and Development, Paris.

Rhee, C., and A. S. Posen. 2013. *Responding to Financial Crisis: Lessons from Asia Then, the United States and Europe Now*. Washington, DC: Peterson Institute for International Economics.

Rogoff, K. 2015. "Debt Supercycle, Not Secular Stagnation." VoxEU.org, CEPR Policy Portal, April 22, https://voxeu.org/article/debt-supercycle-not-secular-stagnation.

Schwandt, H., and T. von Wachter. 2019. "Unlucky Cohorts: Estimating the Long-Term Effects of Entering the Labor Market in a Recession in Large Cross-Sectional Data Sets." *Journal of Labor Economics* 37 (S1): S161-S198.

Seeman, T., D. Thomas, S. S. Merkin, K. Moore, K. Watson, and A. Karlamangla. 2018. "The Great Recession Worsened Blood Pressure and Blood Glucose Levels in American Adults." *Proceedings of the National Academy of Sciences* 115 (13): 3296-301.

Stocker, M., J. Baffes, Y. M. Some, D. Vorisek, and C. M Wheeler. 2018. "The 2014-16 Oil Price Collapse in Retrospect: Sources and Implications." Policy Research Working Paper 8419, World Bank, Washington, DC.

Summers, L. H. 2014. "Reflections on the 'New Secular Stagnation Hypothesis.'" In *Secular Stagnation: Facts, Causes and Cures*, edited by C. Teulings and R. Baldwin. London: CEPR Press.

Tong, H., and S.-J. Wei. 2009. "The Composition Matters: Capital Inflows and Liquidity Crunch During a Global Economic Crisis." IMF Working Paper 09/64, International Monetary Fund, Washington, DC.

UNCTAD (United Nations Conference on Trade and Development). 2010. *International Trade After the Economic Crisis: Challenges and New Opportunities*. Geneva: United Nations Conference on Trade and Development.

UNCTAD (United Nations Conference on Trade and Development). 2018. *World Investment Report 2018: Investment and New Industrial Policies*. Geneva: United Nations Conference on Trade and Development.

Vashakmadze, E., G. Kambou, D. Chen, B. Nandwa, Y. Okawa, and D. Vorisek. 2017. "Regional Dimensions of Recent Weakness in Investment: Drivers, Investment Needs and Policy Responses." Policy Research Working Paper 7991, World Bank, Washington, DC.

World Bank. 2009a. *Global Monitoring Report: A Development Emergency*. Washington, DC: World Bank.

World Bank. 2009b. *East Asia and Pacific Economic Update: Transforming the Rebound into Recovery*. November. Washington, DC: World Bank.

World Bank. 2010a. *South Asia Economic Update: Moving Up, Looking East*. June. Washington, DC: World Bank.

World Bank. 2010b. *MENA Regional Economic Update: Recovering from the Crisis*. April. Washington, DC: World Bank.

World Bank. 2011. *Emerging Europe and Central Asia Economic Update*. April. Washington, DC: World Bank.

World Bank. 2015a. *Global Economic Prospects: Having Fiscal Space and Using It*. January. Washington, DC: World Bank.

World Bank. 2015b. *Global Economic Prospects: The Global Economy in Transition.* June. Washington, DC: World Bank.

World Bank. 2015c. *Commodity Markets Outlook.* July. Washington, DC: World Bank.

World Bank. 2015d. *Africa's Pulse.* October. Washington, DC: World Bank.

World Bank. 2016a. *Global Economic Prospects: Divergences and Risks.* June. Washington, DC: World Bank.

World Bank. 2016b. *Poverty and Shared Prosperity 2016: Taking on Inequality.* Washington, DC: World Bank.

World Bank. 2016c. *Global Economic Prospects: Spillovers amid Weak Growth.* January. Washington, DC: World Bank.

World Bank. 2017. *Global Economic Prospects: Weak Investment in Uncertain Times.* January. Washington, DC: World Bank.

World Bank. 2018a. *Global Economic Prospects: Broad-Based Upturn, but for How Long?* January. Washington, DC: World Bank.

World Bank. 2018b. *Europe and Central Asia Economic Update.* April. Washington, DC: World Bank.

World Bank. 2018c. *Commodity Markets Outlook: Oil Exporters: Policies and Challenges.* April. Washington, DC: World Bank.

World Bank. 2019a. *Global Economic Prospects: Heightened Tensions, Subdued Investment.* June. Washington, DC: World Bank.

World Bank. 2019b. "Long-Term Growth Challenges in Emerging Market and Developing Economies: Implications for Achieving the Twin Goals." Development Committee Ministerial Lunch Discussion Paper, World Bank, Washington, DC.

WTO (World Trade Organization). 2018. *Report to the TPRB from the Director-General on Trade -Related Developments.* Geneva: World Trade Organization.

Yang, L., and C. Huizenga. 2010. "China's Economy in the Global Economic Crisis: Impact and Policy Responses." In *The Financial and Economic Crisis of 2008-2009 and Developing Countries,* edited by S. Dullien, D. J. Kotte, A. Márquez, and J. Priewe, 119-47. Geneva: United Nations.

With hindsight, it has become clear that there was in fact no coherent growth story for most emerging markets. Scratch the surface, and you found high growth rates driven not by productive transformation but by domestic demand, in turn fueled by temporary commodity booms and unsustainable levels of public or, more often, private borrowing.

Dani Rodrik (2015)
Professor of International Political Economy
Harvard University

CHAPTER 4

Financial Market Developments

The global financial crisis and subsequent global recession led to only a modest deceleration of credit in emerging market and developing economies (EMDEs), partly reflecting a general reliance of EMDE banks on local funding bases, limited exposure to sophisticated derivative financial products that suffered stress, strengthened macroeconomic policy frameworks, and improved supervision and regulation. A number of EMDEs, however, experienced credit crunches amid a loss of access to external funding—especially in Europe and Central Asia, as foreign banks that operated local subsidiaries and branches deleveraged. Following the global recession, many EMDEs have experienced a rapid buildup of debt and a shift toward lightly regulated nonbank financial intermediaries, which have heightened their vulnerability to financial disruption. These trends underscore the importance of an effective system of regulation and supervision, including appropriate macroprudential tools, to help contain systemic financial stability risks. The increasing regional role of EMDE banks also calls for close cooperation between home and host country regulators.

Introduction

Across emerging market and developing economies (EMDEs), robust economic growth before the 2009 global recession was accompanied by increasing financial deepening. The ratio of domestic banks' assets to gross domestic product (GDP) in the median EMDE increased from 26 percent at end-2002 to 31 percent at end-2007.[1] By the onset of the global recession, EMDE banks were the main source of domestic private sector credit and were mostly funded by local deposits, which limited funding risks for banks and nonfinancial corporations.

This funding pattern—as well as minimal exposure to financial derivatives, especially those related to the housing sector in the United States—limited the spillovers from the global financial crisis to EMDEs. The resilience of EMDE financial systems was also buttressed by earlier efforts to strengthen macroeconomic policy and financial oversight frameworks, and by the financial buffers that were built in response to previous financial crises.[2]

Note: This chapter was prepared by Carlos Arteta and Sergiy Kasyanenko.

[1] A large and growing literature addresses the trade-off between financial development and financial stability. Substantial heterogeneity in this trade-off has been found, depending on the level of financial development, country attributes, and characteristics of financial systems (Loayza, Ouazad, and Ranciere 2017). Nonetheless, a broad consensus has emerged that a rapid acceleration of financial deepening may elevate crisis risks. For a detailed discussion of the role financial systems play in development, see World Bank (2012).

[2] For example, in the median EMDE, the ratio of foreign exchange reserves to GDP increased by 6 percentage points from about 10 percent during the Asian financial crisis, reflecting a broad-based buildup of reserves across all EMDE regions, but especially in Asia. Policy reforms that boosted the role of the private sector and gradually liberalized financial markets, interest rates, and exchange rates may also have helped EMDEs to absorb external shocks, with fewer disruptions compared to previous crises (Wise, Armijo, and Katada 2015).

As a result, EMDE financial systems were less affected by the global shocks of 2008-09 than in previous episodes of financial distress. Following a brief period of slowing financial system growth, several EMDEs went through credit booms after the global recession, spurred by supportive macroeconomic policies, large capital inflows, and accommodative global financial conditions.

Unfortunately, credit booms in recent years have left a legacy of elevated debt among many EMDEs, which may have raised their risk of financial instability. Private sector credit in percent of GDP more than doubled in one-tenth of EMDEs in the decade to end-2018, whereas in over a quarter it increased by more than half. In the past, such private credit booms were often associated with costly macroeconomic and financial adjustments (Ohnsorge and Yu 2016). Meanwhile, a buildup of government debt—in nearly 30 percent of EMDEs, government debt in percent of GDP doubled over the past decade—makes some EMDEs more vulnerable to sovereign debt crises. Elevated levels of government debt may also constrain the scope and effectiveness of countercyclical fiscal policies (World Bank 2019a). As a result of rising debt burdens, EMDE financial systems look more fragile than at the onset of the global recession, and this fragility may amplify an economic downturn.

Systemic risks among EMDEs are also exacerbated by their increased inter-connectedness. These economies have increased their reliance on capital inflows, including from other EMDEs, and in many cases foreign portfolio investors play a much larger role in domestic bond markets. As a result, these EMDEs are now more susceptible to shocks to international capital markets, shifts in global investor sentiment, or contagion from other EMDEs.

Against this backdrop, this chapter considers the following questions:

- How were EMDE financial markets affected by the global recession?
- How have financial markets in EMDEs evolved since the global recession?
- What implications do these changes have for financial stability and policies in EMDEs?

Contributions. The chapter expands the existing literature on the topic in several directions. In particular, it documents the extent to which the global financial crisis and subsequent global recession affected financial systems in EMDEs across a much larger sample of economies and broader dimensions compared to what has been done in similar exercises. Previous studies have focused on financial systems in advanced economies and associated global financial regulation, or have focused on developments in EMDE banking systems, with limited integration of the discussion into the broader context of changes in international capital markets after the global recession. For example, World Bank (2016, 2019a) show how private credit booms and increasing government debt can amplify financial stability risks. World Bank (2018a) argues that international banking may lead to increased exposure to volatile capital inflows and sudden stops in cross-border lending as well as facilitate the propagation of shock within regions. IMF (2019a) and FSB (2018a) point to increasing complexity of EMDE financial systems and new shock amplification mechanisms and propagation channels that this complexity may create. Other research on these topics typically focuses on a narrow set of questions, such as the impact of financial integration on spillovers from global financial shocks (Bräuning and Ivashina 2019), and usually covers small samples of EMDEs. This study brings these different strands together into an overall assessment of EMDE financial systems over the past decade.

Main findings and lessons. This chapter documents the following findings. First, during the global recession, private sector deleveraging in EMDEs was milder than in previous episodes of financial distress. In 2009-10, nonfinancial private sector debt in EMDEs was little changed as a percent of GDP, compared to large decreases after past crises. The most severe credit crunches occurred in economies where precrisis credit booms were funded by large capital flows and where banks had a narrow deposit base, such as some economies in Europe and Central Asia (ECA) region (Feyen et al. 2014).

Second, credit growth and capital flows resumed in many EMDEs following a brief pause after the global recession, as benign international financial conditions encouraged EMDE corporate sector and governments to access international capital markets (Feyen et al. 2015). Many EMDEs witnessed credit booms during 2011-16. Although these booms have largely subsided, they have left a legacy of high private sector debt that makes corporations more vulnerable to financing shocks (World Bank 2019b). Over the decade to end-2018, private sector debt nearly doubled, reaching 118 percent of GDP on average, which contributed to total debt in EMDEs surging to 169 percent of GDP on average from 98 percent of GDP at end-2007.

In several EMDEs, greater borrowing in international capital markets has also increased debt denominated in foreign currency. On average, foreign currency-denominated corporate debt rose from 21 percent of GDP in 2007 to 28 percent of GDP in 2018, increasing the risk that the EMDE corporate sector and banks will be unable to meet these obligations in the event of large currency depreciation. The risks associated with elevated debt, and especially foreign currency-denominated debt, have been apparent in several large EMDEs.

Third, tighter regulations and a retrenchment by crisis-hit global banks have significantly curtailed foreign bank credit in several EMDE regions—most notably ECA and, to a lesser degree, Latin America and the Caribbean (LAC) and Sub-Saharan Africa (SSA)—where lending by international banks was an important source of finance for the government and the private sector (IMF 2016, 2017; World Bank 2018b). The retrenchment of global banks has opened space for the rapid expansion of EMDE-headquartered banks in some regions, such as SSA.[3]

[3] More than 80 percent of high-income countries have already adopted Basel III regulations (World Bank 2019c). Stricter regulatory frameworks, introduced through the Basel III, have generally strengthened the global banking system (Adrian, Kiff, and Shin 2018). These postcrisis reforms of bank regulation and supervision may have also contributed to the decline in riskier cross-border activities of international banks, which may have a lasting negative impact on cross-border lending to EMDEs (CGD 2019). Spillovers from these regulatory reforms in advanced economies have yet to be felt across EMDEs but can be mitigated if new rules are consistently applied across jurisdictions and countries cooperate better when they design and implement financial system regulations (Briault et al. 2018).

Finally, financial intermediation in EMDEs with systemically important financial sectors is now larger and more complex, opaque, and interconnected than at the onset of the crisis, which raises new regulatory challenges.[4] For example, in several large economies, especially China, the nonbank financial sector—which is often less regulated than banks—is playing an increasing role in supplying credit to corporate borrowers (Ehlers, Kong, and Zhu 2018). A postcrisis buildup of liquidity and maturity mismatches in nonbank financial institutions, and their strong links to banks, may substantially magnify the impact of financial shocks on credit intermediation in EMDEs (IMF 2019a).

The rest of this chapter proceeds as follows. The next two sections briefly discuss developments of EMDE financial systems and the growth of private credit before and during the 2009 global recession. A surge in capital inflows to EMDEs after the global recession and its contribution to credit booms and growing indebtedness are covered in the subsequent section. The chapter then highlights several new features of the financial systems in EMDEs, including diminishing role of international banks, growing EMDE-to-EMDE cross-border lending, and increasing reliance of EMDE borrowers on international capital markets. The last section presents concluding remarks and policy implications.

Before the global recession: Expansion and strengthening

Expansion of EMDE financial systems. EMDE financial systems expanded rapidly during 2002-07 in response to strong economic growth and a trend toward financial deepening. In particular, the ratio of banks' assets to GDP in the median EMDE increased from 26 percent at end-2002 to 31 percent of GDP at end-2007 (figure 4.1). Despite this increase, banks maintained healthy balance sheets, partly as a result of improvements in financial regulation. At the onset of the global recession, the ratio of Tier 1 capital to risk-weighted assets stood at about 14 percent in the median EMDE, and residential housing loans represented only a 10th of all bank lending.

The rapid expansion of bank balance sheets was primarily financed with local deposits—in all EMDE regions except ECA, bank credit continued to be predominantly deposit-financed. The average EMDE loan-to-deposit ratio was 80 percent at end-2007 despite an uptick before the global recession (figure 4.1), reflecting little exposure of EMDE banks to less stable wholesale funding.

In many large EMDEs, the growing role of nonbank financial institutions such as pension funds and insurance companies also helped to broaden the domestic base for financial intermediation. Total assets of financial institutions (other than central banks) in large EMDEs, excluding China, rose by almost 10 percentage points of GDP, to 62.5 percent of GDP at end-2007 (figure 4.1). The role of financial institutions other than

[4] The International Monetary Fund designates Brazil, China, India, Mexico, the Russian Federation, and Turkey as EMDEs having systemically important financial sectors (IMF 2018a).

FIGURE 4.1 EMDE financial markets before the global recession

EMDE banks expanded rapidly during 2002-07, primarily relying on local deposits. This expansion was also accompanied by strengthening prudential regulations and oversight, and by increasing competition.

A. Banks' assets

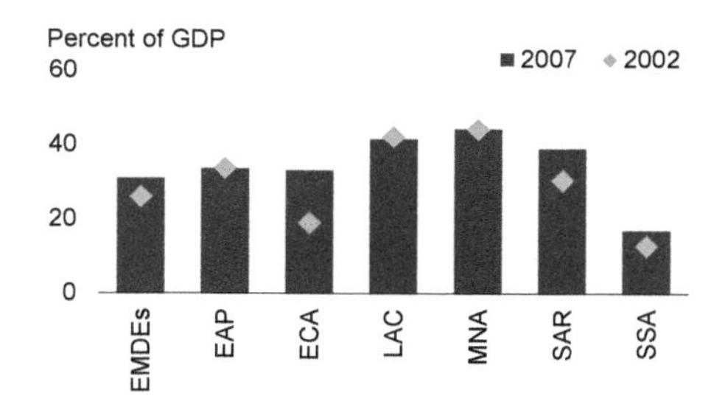

B. Loan-to-deposit ratios

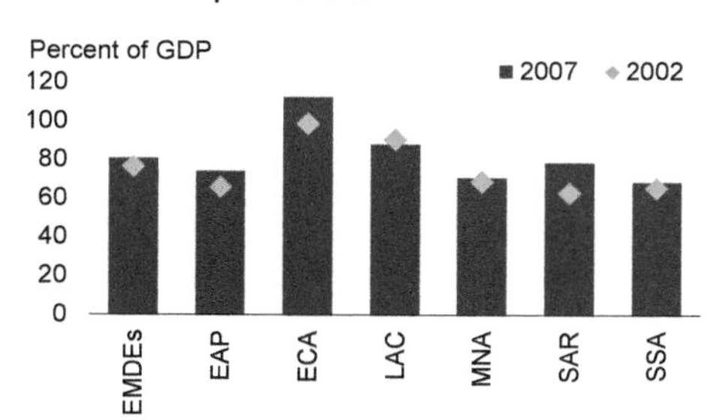

C. Financial system assets

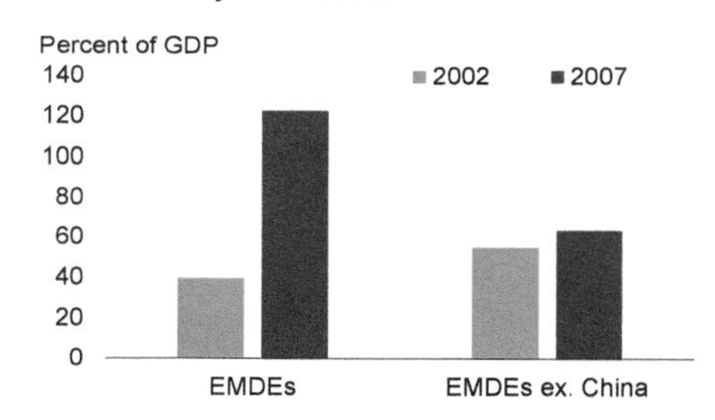

D. Macroprudential supervision: 2002 vs. 2007

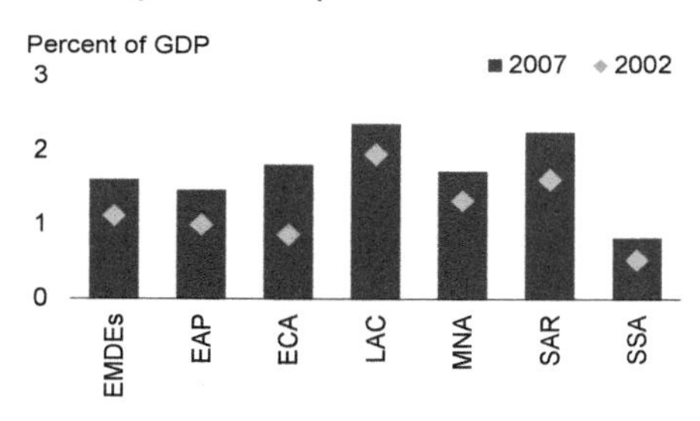

E. Concentration in banking sectors

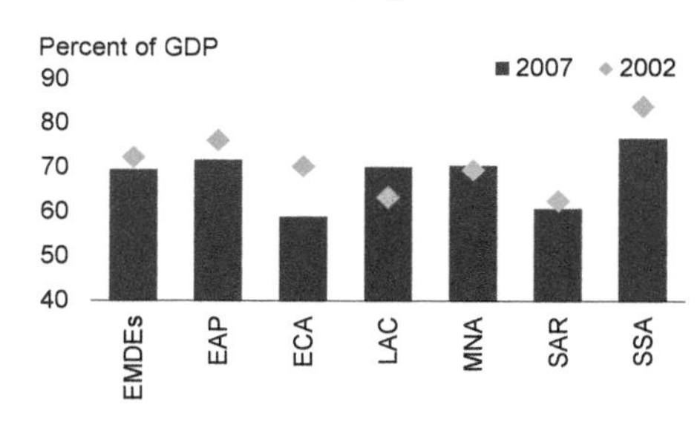

F. Cross-border bank lending to EMDEs

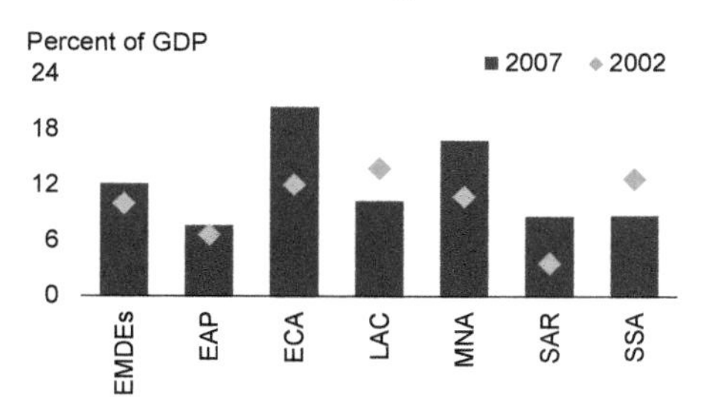

Sources: Bank for International Settlements; Cerutti, Claessens, and Laeven (2017); Čihák et al. (2012); Haver Analytics; International Monetary Fund; World Bank.

Note: Offshore financial centers are excluded. EAP = East Asia and Pacific; ECA = Europe and Central Asia; EMDEs = emerging market and developing economies; LAC = Latin America and the Caribbean; MNA = Middle East and North Africa; SAR = South Asia; SSA = Sub-Saharan Africa.

A.B.E. Data are from the Financial Structure Dataset (Čihák et al. 2012).

A. Median. Based on data for 141 EMDEs in 2002 and 144 in 2007.

B. Banks' loans to the private sector as a ratio of the sum of their demand, time, and savings deposits.

C. Excluding assets of central banks; based on data for 10 EMDEs—Argentina, Brazil, Chile, China, India, Indonesia, Mexico, the Russian Federation, South Africa, and Turkey—which jointly account for about 71 percent of total EMDE output in 2018. Ratios shown are total financial assets across the 10 EMDEs divided by their total GDP.

D. Sample comprises 123 EMDEs; each bar shows unweighted averages of the Macroprudential Policy Index of Cerutti, Claessens, and Laeven (2017).

E. Assets of three largest commercial banks as a share of total commercial banking assets. Data are available for 8 economies in EAP, 20 in ECA, 25 in LAC, 14 in MNA, 5 in SAR, and 28 in SSA.

F. Sample comprises 140 EMDEs, ratios shown are the total stock of cross-border bank claims on the region divided by regional GDP aggregates.

banks, pension funds, and insurance companies—for example, money market funds, investment funds, hedge funds, structured finance vehicles, and trust companies—remained relatively small (only 17 percent of GDP at end-2007 in the median EMDE, roughly half the ratio in advanced economies).[5] The more limited exposure of EMDEs to these relatively lightly regulated entities also insulated them from financial stress ahead of the crisis (FSB 2017a).

Strengthening frameworks. The expansion of EMDE financial systems before the global recession was also accompanied by strengthening prudential regulations and oversight, especially in ECA and LAC (figure 4.1; Cerutti, Claessens, and Laeven 2017), and by increasing competition (for example, in ECA and SSA). Banking systems became more diversified, with a smaller market share of the largest banks in over 60 percent of EMDEs (figure 4.1), partly due to increased competition after the entry of foreign banks in many EMDEs (Claessens and van Horen 2015).[6]

In general, financial systems in EMDEs had limited exposure to sophisticated derivative financial products linked to housing markets in advanced economies. As a result, those systems were largely spared a severe disruption to credit intermediation during the global financial crisis. More fundamentally, the resilience of EMDE financial systems can be attributed to well-capitalized banks, mostly funded with local deposits, and primarily focused on supplying credit to their domestic corporate sectors.

During the global recession: General resilience, with exceptions

Resilience of private credit. The global financial crisis, which triggered severe economic downturns and private sector deleveraging in advanced economies, had only a modest and brief impact on EMDE financial systems. Limited exposure to financial products and markets where the crisis originated, the general reliance of EMDE banks on domestic funding, and, in some regions, moderate levels of overall integration with global financial markets protected most EMDEs from the financial shocks emanating from advanced economies. This resilience contrasts sharply with previous episodes of global financial distress (such as the 1998 Asian financial crisis) when reversals of private capital flows caused sizable disruptions to credit intermediation across several large EMDEs.

The generally solid balance sheets of EMDE banks—and, in some EMDEs, macroeconomic policy stimulus—supported private sector credit during the 2009 global

[5] These nonbank financial institutions are often referred to as the "shadow banking system" and are often used by regulated financial institutions to engage in unregulated activities. Among advanced economies, these institutions were found to have taken on excessive leverage, as well as maturity and liquidity mismatches.

[6] The degree of competition in the banking sector is just one of the attributes of the financial architecture that may influence financial stability and development (see World Bank 2012 for a detailed discussion). Cross-country studies show that more competitive banking systems have a lower incidence of systemic banking crises (Beck, Demirgüç-Kunt, and Levine 2006) because banks tend to have higher capital ratios in more competitive markets (Schaeck and Čihák 2012).

recession.[7] Average EMDE private credit growth as percent of GDP declined only moderately, and it was considerably more stable than in EMDEs that experienced episodes of financial distress in the past (figure 4.2). In the three-year window centered around the 2009 global recession, average private credit to GDP in EMDEs (excluding China) declined by only about 0.7 percentage point.[8] This moderate drop contrasts markedly with other episodes of financial crises over the past three decades, when the average decline from the year before these events and the year after was 3.5 percentage points. Consistent with the mild decline in private sector credit to GDP, EMDE nonfinancial private sectors deleveraged by considerably less than during previous episodes of financial crises.

Overall, average EMDE nonfinancial private sector debt as percent of GDP was little changed in 2009-10 after having risen by 1.3 percent of GDP per year, on average, during 2002-07 (figure 4.2). This constancy contrasts with previous financial crises in EMDEs. For example, the deleveraging across EMDEs during the global recession was less severe than during the Asian financial crisis, when average EMDE private debt contracted by over 2 percentage points of GDP the year after the crisis started (figure 4.2).

Credit crunches in some EMDEs during and after the global recession. Despite the general resilience of private sector credit, the global financial crisis and subsequent euro area crisis of 2010-12 did trigger credit crunches in over one-fifth of EMDEs, especially those with fragile financial systems and heavy reliance before the crisis on cross-border lending that financed earlier credit booms.[9] These EMDEs faced a decline in external funding, experienced a sharp increase in nonperforming loans amid currency depreciations and slower economic growth, and were forced to deleverage, markedly curtailing credit supply. On average during these credit crunches, private sector credit declined by about 13 percentage points of GDP (peak to trough; figure 4.2).

Credit crunches were most pronounced in ECA and, to a lesser extent, the Middle East and North Africa (MNA)—regions that, to varying degrees, relied on cross-border lending, had a relatively narrow domestic deposit base, or had weak and highly leveraged banking systems (figure 4.2).[10] Credit crunches were particularly severe and widespread across countries in ECA, as stressed euro area banks curtailed their cross-border lending. In MNA, the 2008-09 oil price collapse led to a sharp drop in asset prices and tighter external funding conditions for the corporate sector in several economies, putting an end

---

[7] Direct interventions in individual institutions (for example, through capital injections or nationalization of banks), were much less common in EMDEs than in advanced economies (Igan et al. 2019).

[8] These financial crisis episodes include currency crises, systemic banking crises, and sovereign debt crises and restructuring, as identified by Laeven and Valencia (2018).

[9] A credit crunch is defined as a peak-to-trough phase of a credit cycle that lasts at least five years, featuring a decline in the credit-to-GDP ratio of at least 7 percentage points of GDP (the median decline in the credit-to-GDP ratio in the full sample of EMDEs). The peak of the credit cycle is defined as the year immediately before the private sector credit-to-GDP ratio begins to decline. The trough is defined as the year before this ratio begins to rise. During 1990-2018, 82 credit crunches were identified in 60 EMDEs (where population exceeds 2.5 million) with 24 credit crunches still ongoing. Thirty-three of these credit crunches started in 2008-16.

[10] Feyen et al. (2014) show that high loan-to-deposit ratios and a strong reliance on foreign funding make bank credit growth to the private sector in EMDEs particularly sensitive to shocks in cross-border lending.

FIGURE 4.2 EMDE bank credit and private debt

During the global recession, EMDE nonfinancial private sectors deleveraged by considerably less than during previous episodes of financial distress. Some EMDEs, however, experienced deep and widespread credit crunches, in part due to above-average reliance on cross-border bank lending.

A. Change in bank credit to the private sector during financial crises

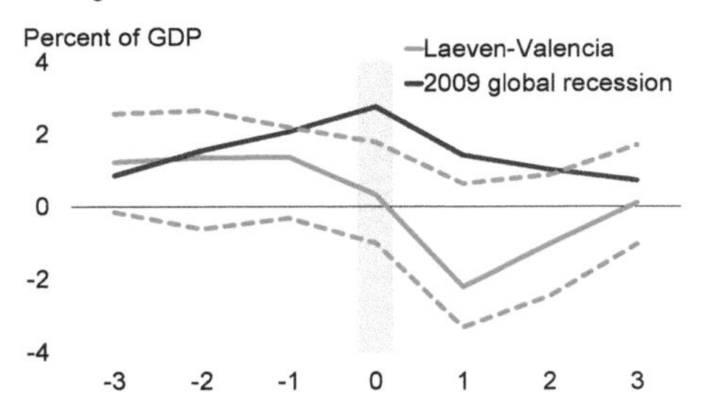

B. Private debt and bank credit in EMDEs

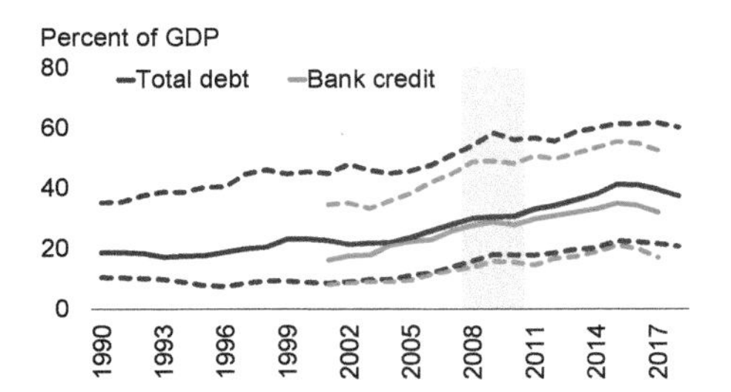

C. Change in total private debt in EMDEs

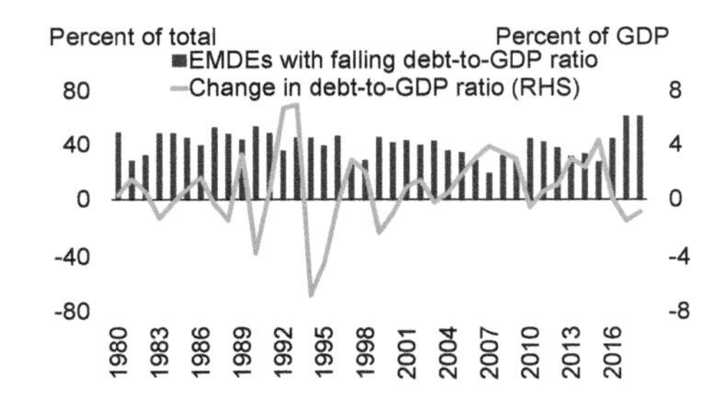

D. Peak-to-trough change in credit during postcrisis credit crunches

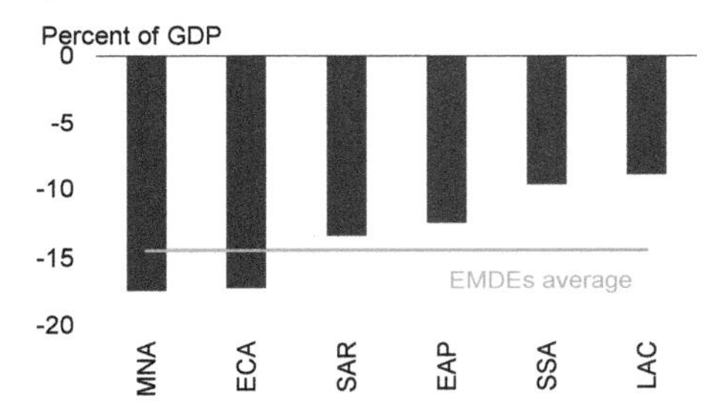

E. Credit crunches by region

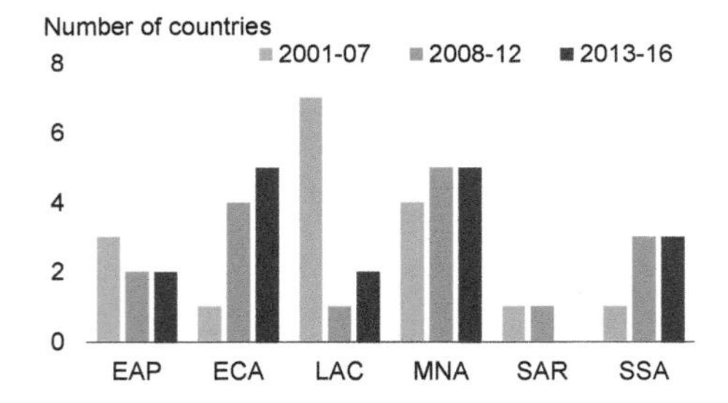

F. Bank credit in total private sector debt

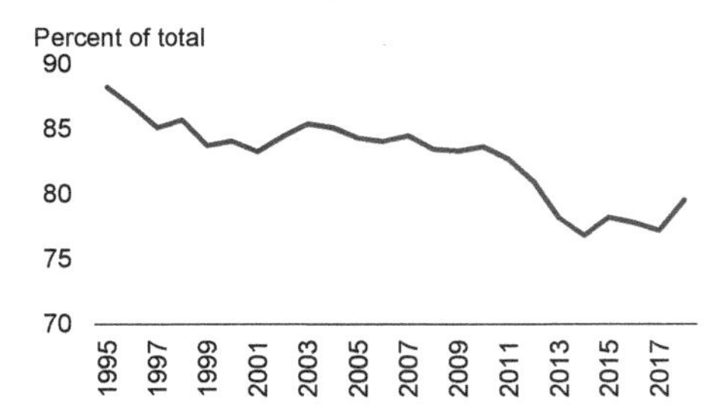

Sources: Bank for International Settlements; Haver Analytics; International Monetary Fund; World Bank.

Note: Offshore financial centers are excluded; dashed lines indicate interquartile ranges. EAP = East Asia and Pacific; ECA = Europe and Central Asia; EMDEs = emerging market and developing economies; LAC = Latin America and the Caribbean; MNA = Middle East and North Africa; SAR = South Asia; SSA = Sub-Saharan Africa.

A. The year a crisis started is marked as t = 0 (about 73 crises from 1990 to 2017; Laeven and Valencia 2018). "2009 global recession" denotes averages across all EMDEs, with the three-year window centered on 2008-09.

B. Unweighted averages. Sample includes about 120 EMDEs (bank credit) and 140 EMDEs (total private debt).

C. Excluding China; GDP-weighted average change in debt-to-GDP ratios.

D.E. Identification of credit crunches follows Claessens, Kose, and Terrones (2011) and uses the Harding and Pagan (2002) method to identify cyclical turning points in private credit-to-GDP ratios.

D. Postcrisis credit crunches are credit crunches that started in 2008-16.

E. Number of countries where a credit crunch started during the period.

F. Sample includes total debt and bank credit of the nonfinancial private sector in Argentina, Brazil, Chile, China, Colombia, Hungary, India, Indonesia, Malaysia, Mexico, Thailand, Poland, the Russian Federation, South Africa, and Turkey.

to precrisis credit booms (IMF 2010). In other regions, credit crunches were less widespread, occurred later, and in many cases were associated with weakening commodity prices in 2014-16.

The deep and widespread credit crunches in ECA during the global financial crisis and subsequent euro area crisis largely reflected above-average precrisis reliance on cross-border lending, especially from European Union (EU) banks.[11] At their prerecession peak, cross-border bank loans to EMDEs in ECA ranged from 17 percent of GDP in Kazakhstan to 72 percent of GDP in Croatia. Many ECA economies benefitted from cross-border bank lending as their financial systems expanded, the private sector gained access to more affordable credit, and the quality of financial services improved. The ensuing credit booms and a slow development of local funding markets, however, led to a buildup of substantial vulnerabilities, such as excessive reliance on parent banks for funding and currency mismatches in the banking systems.[12]

As EU banks came under stress during the euro area crisis and retrenched from noncore activities, many banks in ECA lost access to cross-border lending. Cross-border lending to ECA declined by about 10 percentage points of GDP on average between mid-2008 and end-2012. In Central Europe, the ratio of bank private credit to GDP, which had increased from an average of 24 percent in 2003 to about 55 percent in 2008, subsequently stalled.[13] This situation coincided with deep recessions or sharp slowdowns in many ECA economies, with GDP contracting, on average, by 2 percent a year in 2009-10 compared to average annual expansions of 5.3 percent during the credit booms of 2003-08.[14] This rapid precrisis buildup of risks associated with international banking in ECA may also be attributed to lapses in financial oversight, as regulators in home and host countries failed to properly assess financial stability risks arising from the elevated exposure to foreign bank claims (Allen et al. 2011).

This experience suggests the importance of effective coordination between host and home country banking regulators to mitigate risks of sudden stops in cross-border lending, especially when substantial differences in regulatory standards exist (Claessens 2017). In 2009, a major policy initiative was launched—the Vienna Initiative—to coordinate the responses of pan-European banks, macroprudential authorities, and international organizations to ensure that bank subsidiaries in host countries remain well

---

[11] Bank conditions in the euro area and the United Kingdom are generally significant determinants of cross-border bank flows (Cerutti, Claessens, and Ratnovski 2017). For example, a retrenchment of Austrian and Italian banks had significantly curtailed cross-border funding for ECA economies (Feyen and del Mazo 2013). That said, spillovers from the euro area crisis were less pronounced in EMDEs where European banks had a greater reliance on local deposit base for funding, such as Spanish banks in LAC.

[12] Before the global recession, banks in several ECA economies aggressively expanded lending by issuing loans denominated in foreign currencies. For example, in Ukraine and Romania, the share of foreign currency-denominated loans in total domestic credit rose substantially, reaching about 60 percent at end-2007.

[13] EMDEs in Central Europe are Bulgaria, Croatia, Hungary, Poland, and Romania. EMDEs in Central Asia are Kazakhstan, the Kyrgyz Republic, Tajikistan, Turkmenistan, and Uzbekistan.

[14] The Baltic states also experienced sharp declines in credit and economic activity after Scandinavian banks withdrew from the region. Cumulative output declines during the crisis reached 20-25 percent from peak levels in Estonia, Latvia, and Lithuania (Purfield and Rosenberg 2010). From 2008 to 2012, cross-border claims on the Baltic states shrank by 24 percent of GDP, on average.

capitalized and cross-border exposures are maintained in five ECA economies (Bosnia and Herzegovina, Hungary, Latvia, Romania, Serbia). Multinational banks that participated in this initiative were more stable lenders in the aftermath of the global recession than domestic and foreign banks that did not sign country-specific commitments to maintain exposures to their subsidiaries in the ECA region (de Haas et al. 2012).

Limited impact on low-income countries (LICs). Compared to the financial systems in other EMDEs, those in many LICs were more bank dominated, less complex, and less integrated into global financial markets at the onset of the global recession. Also, LIC banking systems were smaller: at end-2007, bank credit to the private sector stood at only about 12 percent of GDP in a median LIC compared to about a third of GDP in a median non-LIC EMDE. As a result, domestic financial systems in many LICs were not strongly affected by the global financial crisis (IMF 2009). In commodity-producing LICs, however, credit growth slowed as investments in mining and commodity-related infrastructure were postponed in response to falling commodity prices (for example, Chad, Guinea, Liberia, Sierra Leone, Uganda). Of note, in many LICs, banks shifted from making riskier loans to nonfinancial corporations to holding government securities, which increased sovereign-bank linkages and, therefore, the exposure of LIC banks to domestic fiscal policy shocks (IMF 2019c; see also chapter 6).

Notwithstanding the resilience of domestic financial systems in many LICs, financial stress in global credit markets did reduce LICs' access to global capital markets. Several LICs with solid macroeconomic fundamentals, which had gained access to international debt markets prior to the crisis, had to postpone or cancel the issuance of new bonds (Tanzania, Uganda). LICs with a substantial presence of foreign lenders (Mozambique, Togo) experienced a withdrawal of cross-border lending owing to the retrenchment of international commercial banks.

After the global recession: Growing debt and heightened vulnerabilities

After a sharp reversal in 2008-09, capital inflows to EMDEs staged a marked rebound in the context of low global interest rates, sustained by large-scale quantitative easing in major advanced economies, and search for yield; however, they have remained below precrisis averages (figure 4.3). Following the initial rebound, the period after the global recession has been marked by bouts of global financial turbulence and periodic declines in capital inflows, generating exchange rate volatility (figure 4.3).

Nevertheless, the incidence of sudden stops in foreign capital inflows tipping countries into financial distress has been about half of that prior to 2008 (figure 4.3).[15] This reduction suggests that EMDEs have improved their capacity to manage capital flow volatility, partly thanks to more flexible exchange rate regimes and accumulations of foreign currency reserves.

[15] Dates for sudden stops are from Eichengreen and Gupta (2016). Crises dates are from Laeven and Valencia (2018).

FIGURE 4.3 Capital inflows to EMDEs after the global recession

Spurred by accommodative monetary policy and a search for yield, capital flows to EMDEs rebounded after the global recession but remained below precrisis averages. Meanwhile, a sharp drop in cross-border bank lending during and following the global recession has been accompanied by growth in portfolio flows.

A. Gross capital inflows

B. Gross portfolio inflows and exchange rate volatility

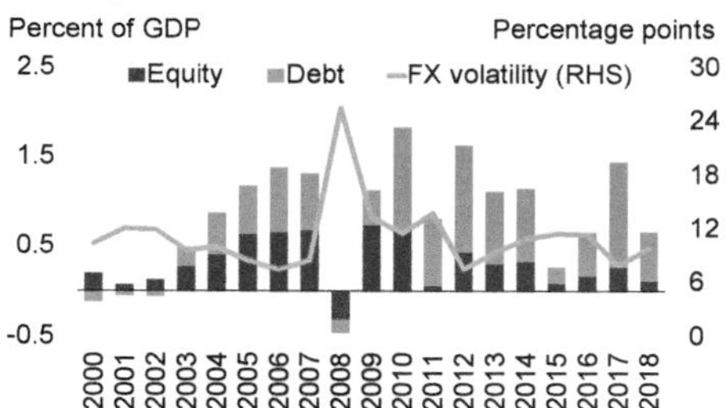

C. Share of EMDEs in a financial crisis following a sudden stop in capital flows

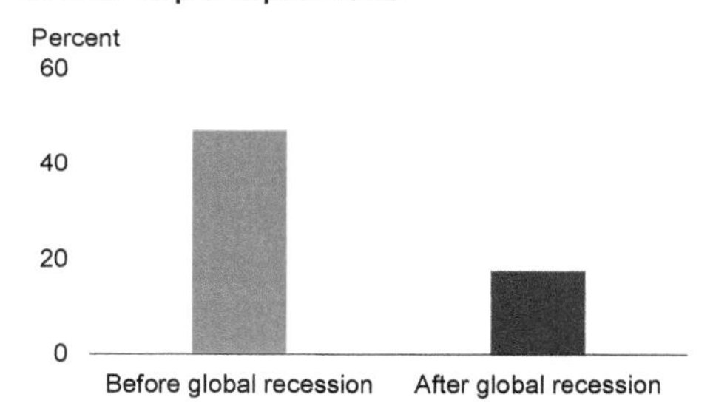

D. Composition of gross capital inflows

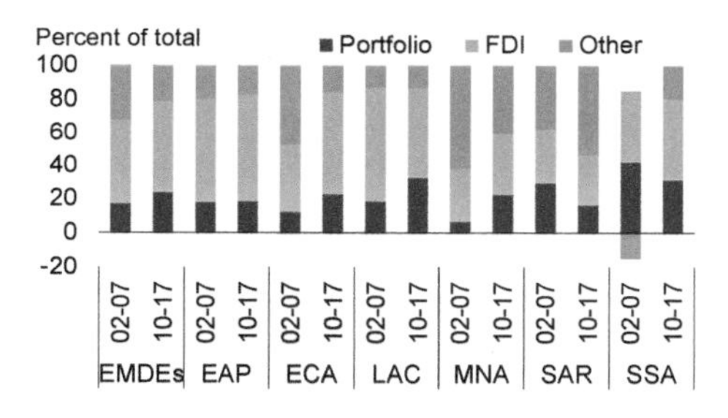

E. Share of portfolio liabilities in total external liabilities

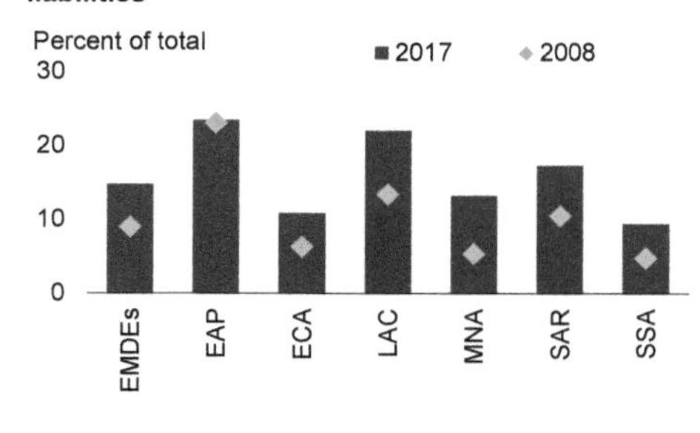

F. Change in cross-border bank lending to EMDEs during episodes of financial distress

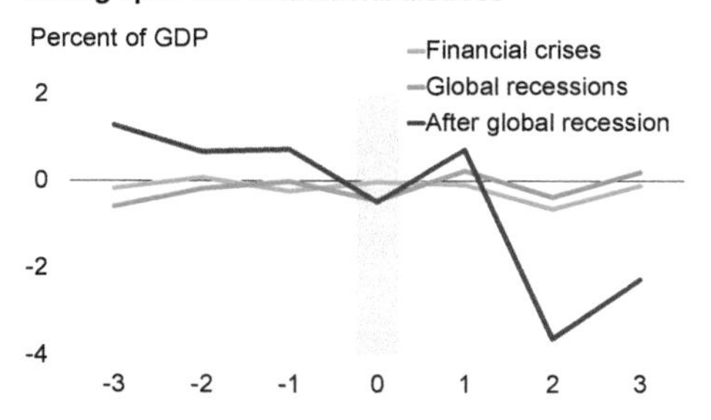

Sources: Bank for International Settlements; Bloomberg; International Monetary Fund; World Bank.

Note: EAP = East Asia and Pacific; ECA = Europe and Central Asia; EMDEs = emerging market and developing economies; FDI = foreign direct investment; FX = foreign exchange; LAC = Latin America and the Caribbean; MNA = Middle East and North Africa; SAR = South Asia; SSA = Sub-Saharan Africa.

A. Total gross inflows of foreign direct investments, portfolio investments, and other investments for about 120 EMDEs.

B. Based on data for about 90 EMDEs. FX volatility is the J.P. Morgan VXY Global index for 23 U.S. dollar currency pairs.

C. Share of economies in a financial crisis within two years of a sudden stop. Dates for sudden stops are from Eichengreen and Gupta (2016); dates for financial crises are from Laeven and Valencia (2018).

D. Aggregate flows; based on a balanced panel for 76 EMDEs.

E. Unweighted averages; end-of-period stocks of external liabilities for EMDEs with data available in 2008.

F. t = 0 indicates the year when a crisis started. Global recession years are 1982 and 1991. "Financial crises" denotes averages for EMDEs that went through a systemic banking crisis before the 2009 global recession (99 crises from 1980 to 2003). "After global recession" denotes averages for EMDEs that went through a systemic banking crisis after the global financial crisis (seven crises in 2008-14).

Changing composition of capital flows. A rebound of capital flows after the global recession was accompanied by a shift in their composition. A sharp drop in cross-border lending during and following the global recession has been followed by growth in portfolio flows (figure 4.3). During 2010-17, cumulative portfolio flows accounted for over 24 percent of all capital flows to EMDEs, up from 17 percent in 2002-07 on average. As a result, at end-2017, portfolio liabilities accounted for over 13 percent of EMDE external liabilities, on average, compared to 8 percent at end-2008 (figure 4.3). The share of portfolio liabilities in external liabilities increased in all EMDE regions except East Asia and Pacific (EAP).[16] In contrast, the share of other liabilities, which include direct cross-border lending, declined in all regions, with the biggest decreases in LAC, MNA, and SSA; however, it remained generally stable in South Asia (SAR).

The inclusion of some EMDEs in major benchmark bond indexes has contributed to increasing portfolio inflows, particularly to smaller markets for which membership in an index may have attracted foreign investors. By linking economies with different fundamentals into the same portfolio, this inclusion may have also heightened the exposure of EMDEs in benchmark indexes to shocks and fluctuations in international capital markets (Arslanalp and Tsuda 2015; IMF 2019a; Miyajima and Shim 2014).[17]

Volatility of capital inflows back at its precrisis level. The volatility of capital inflows to EMDEs spiked in 2009-10. After the global recession, it returned to its 2002-07 level, with bouts of volatility flaring up during periods of heightened risk aversion such as the 2013 taper tantrum (figure 4.4). This variation reflects the impact of global financial shocks such as a tightening of international liquidity, which are often accompanied by increases in capital inflow volatility (Pagliari and Hannan 2017).

Country-specific factors, including the level of foreign reserves and domestic financial sector development, may reduce the volatility of certain capital inflows (Aghion, Bacchetta, and Banerjee 2004; Broto, Díaz-Cassou, and Erce 2011). After the global recession, however, the sensitivity of capital inflows—in particular, portfolio inflows—to global shocks has increased (Ahmed and Zlate 2014; Fratzscher 2012; IMF 2019b). This increased sensitivity suggests that, if global risk sentiment were to suddenly deteriorate, some EMDEs may encounter increased swings in inflows.

Trends in the volatility of aggregate capital inflows to EMDEs mask cross-country heterogeneity. In about a third of EMDEs, the average volatility of inflows that were not foreign direct investment (FDI) during 2011-18 was at least 10 percent higher than the average volatility in 2002-07.[18] Cross-country differences in capital inflow volatility have largely reflected the different roles of push and pull factors and their interaction, as well

[16] Foreign direct investment continues to be the principal source of external funding for EAP economies, representing over 55 percent of all external liabilities in that region.

[17] For example, Cerutti, Claessens, and Puy (2019) show that a higher reliance on global mutual funds increases the exposure of EMDEs to shifts in global financing conditions transmitted through capital flows.

[18] Capital inflows volatility refers to country-by-country GARCH (generalized autoregressive conditional heteroskedasticity) estimates of the conditional variance of gross non-FDI inflows adjusted by the level of GDP. Non-FDI inflows are portfolio inflows and other investments. Other investments include cross-border bank lending.

FIGURE 4.4 EMDE capital inflow volatility after the global recession

The volatility of aggregate EMDE capital inflows has returned to its precrisis level, notwithstanding some risk-off episodes. Relative to FDI, portfolio inflows continue to exhibit greater swings, as do other inflows such as cross-border bank lending.

A. Volatility of non-FDI capital inflows

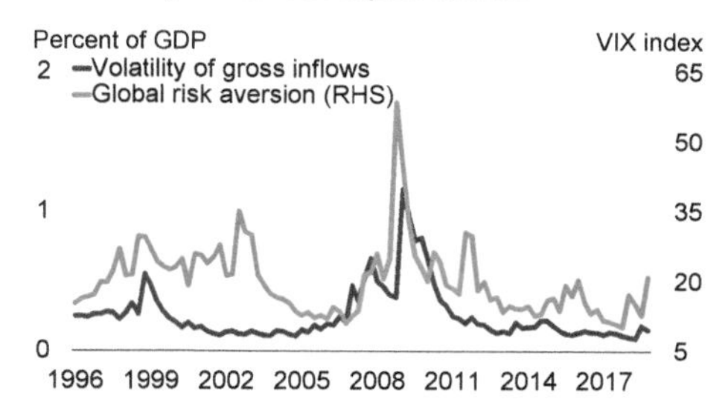

B. Average volatility of capital inflows

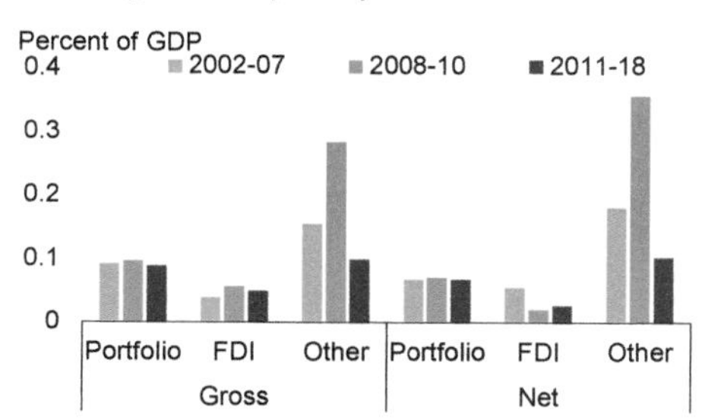

Sources: Bloomberg; International Monetary Fund; World Bank.

Note: Capital flows volatility refers to GARCH (generalized autoregressive conditional heteroskedasticity) estimates of the conditional variance of non-FDI inflows adjusted by the level of GDP. Estimates are based on aggregate inflows to 29 EMDEs with quarterly data from 1996Q1 to 2018Q4; China is not included. Non-FDI inflows are portfolio inflows and other investments; other investments include cross-border bank lending. EMDEs = emerging market and developing economies; FDI = foreign direct investment; VIX = Volatility Index.

A. Non-FDI inflows include portfolio inflows and other investments. Global risk aversion refers to the volatility measured by the VIX implied volatility index of option prices on the U.S. S&P 500.

as country-specific composition of inflows and the types of borrowers and lenders (Avdjiev et al. 2017; Cerutti, Claessens, and Puy 2019; Hannan 2018; Koepke 2019). Furthermore, in several EMDEs, vulnerability to the volatility of capital inflows grew after the global recession because of higher reliance on market-based finance and increased issuance of foreign currency-denominated bonds.

Reemergence of credit booms in EMDEs. More than one-quarter of EMDEs experienced private sector credit booms in at least one year during 2011-18 (figure 4.5).[19] Unlike previous episodes of rapid credit growth in EMDEs, however, many of these credit booms were not accompanied by investment surges, because they primarily boosted consumption (box 4.1). The credit booms were fueled by large capital flows to EMDEs amid historically unprecedented monetary policy accommodation in major advanced economies, including negative interest rate policies (box 4.2), and monetary policy loosening in EMDEs (Arteta et al. 2015, Arteta et al. 2018).

As in advanced economies, many EMDE central banks reduced, and then maintained, their monetary policy rates at historic lows. During 2009-16, most EMDEs (with the exception of Brazil) maintained real policy rates below the 2002-07 average of about 4 percent (figure 4.5). A growth rebound in EMDEs supported investor confidence and increased credit demand from nonfinancial corporations (Ohnsorge and Yu 2016;

[19] About half of all credit booms are followed by at least a mild deleveraging within three years (Ohnsorge and Shu 2016).

FIGURE 4.5 EMDE bank credit to the private sector after the global recession

More than a quarter of EMDEs experienced private sector credit booms after the global recession. By end-2016, these credit booms began to recede, because EMDE borrowing costs started to increase, the U.S. Federal Reserve raised policy interest rates, and several EMDEs adopted stricter macroprudential tools to rein in excessive credit growth.

A. Number of EMDEs in credit booms and credit crunches

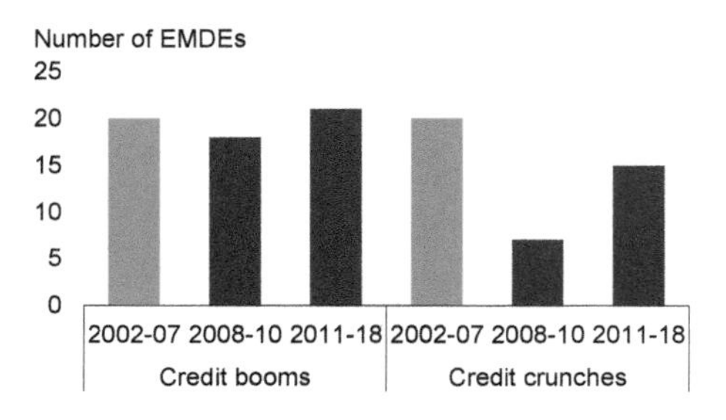

B. Monetary policy rates in EMDEs

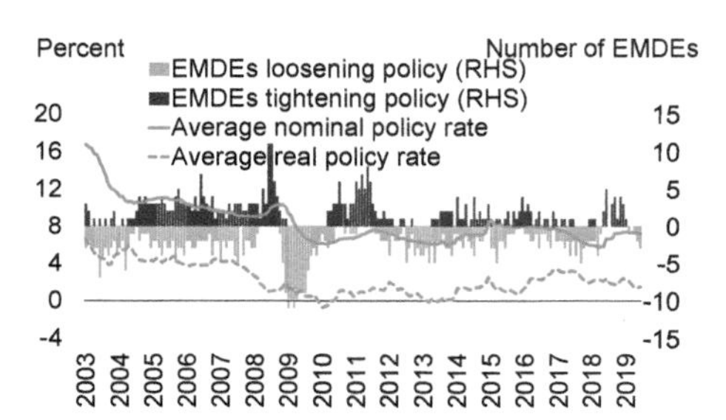

C. Global financing conditions

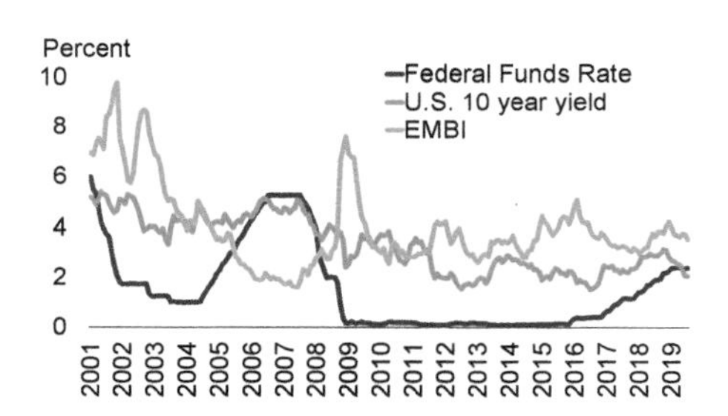

D. Macroprudential policies: Use of borrower-targeted instruments

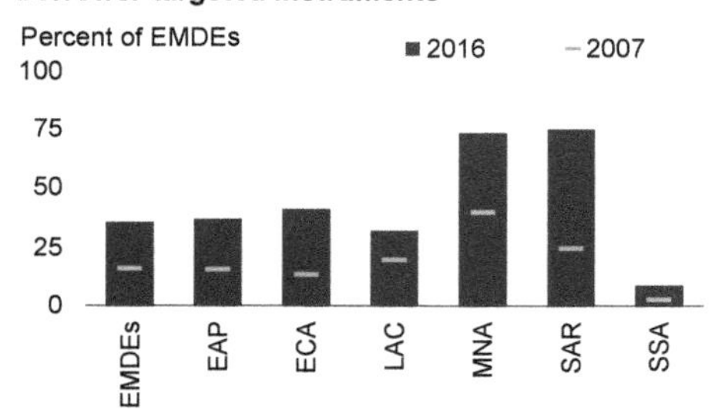

E. Macroprudential policies: Use of financial institution-targeted instruments

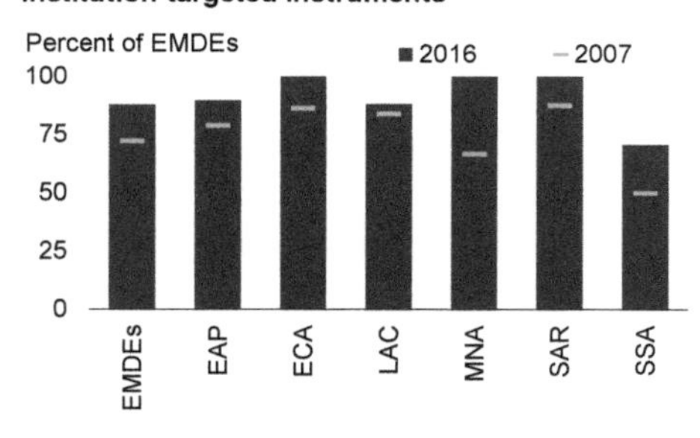

F. Domestic credit to the private sector

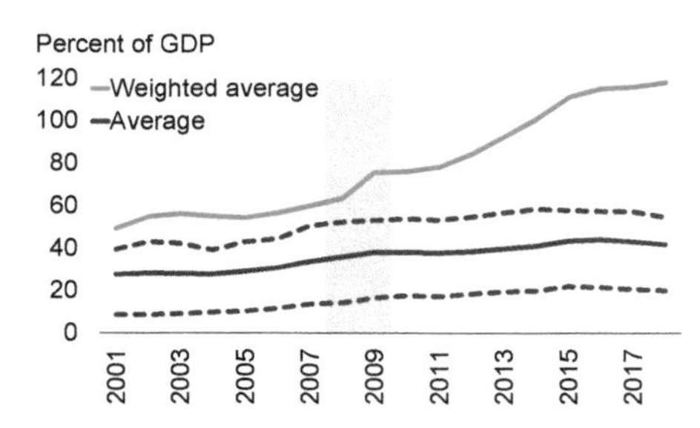

Sources: Bank for International Settlements; Haver Analytics; International Monetary Fund; World Bank.

Note: EAP = East Asia and Pacific; ECA = Europe and Central Asia; EMDEs = emerging market and developing economies; LAC = Latin America and the Caribbean; MNA = Middle East and North Africa; SAR = South Asia; SSA = Sub-Saharan Africa.

A. Sample includes about 85 EMDEs. Credit booms (crunches) are episodes when private credit-to-GDP exceeds (falls below) its long-term trend by 1.65 standard deviations of a cyclical component obtained with the Hodrick-Prescott filter. Each bar indicates the number of EMDEs that spent at least one year in a boom (crunch) during the period.

B. Red solid line indicates GDP-weighted average of nominal policy rates of Brazil, Chile, Colombia, Hungary, Indonesia, India, Mexico, Malaysia, Peru, the Philippines, Poland, the Russian Federation, Thailand, Turkey, and South Africa. Orange bars show the number of EMDEs cutting policy rates, and blue bars show the number of EMDEs raising policy rates. Dashed line indicates inflation-adjusted GDP-weighted average policy rate.

C. EMBI = J.P. Morgan's Emerging Market Bond Index.

D.E. Each bar represents share of EMDEs using at least one macroprudential tool (Cerutti, Claessens, and Laeven 2017).

F. Sample includes about 140 EMDEs. Weighted average is calculated using nominal GDP as weights. Dashed lines indicate interquartile range.

World Bank 2016). In addition, weak commodity prices during 2011-16 increased corporate borrowing needs in commodity-exporting EMDEs.

The rapid credit growth after the global recession was accompanied by some deterioration in asset quality and an increased reliance on short-term wholesale funding. Nonperforming loan ratios and loan-to-deposit ratios edged up (especially in SSA and SAR), although the latter still remained well below 100 percent, on average.

Toward the end of 2016, however, these credit booms began to recede. EMDE borrowing costs started to increase at the same time that the U.S. Federal Reserve raised policy interest rates in late 2015 (figure 4.5). These increases coincided with the adoption by more EMDEs of stricter macroprudential tools to cool credit booms, EMDE monetary policy tightening and a sharp slowdown of output growth in commodity exporters during 2014-16 (figure 4.5; chapter 5 explores financial sector regulatory reforms in EMDEs after the global recession).

Expectations of additional policy easing by major central banks have accompanied an easing of global financing conditions in 2019, as manifested by a significant decline in global bond yields and growing share of negative-yielding debt. These developments have not, however, resulted in a sustained, broad-based recovery in capital flows to EMDEs, amid heightened risk aversion and flight to safety, in the context of a deteriorated global growth outlook and heightened trade policy uncertainty. In contrast to the broad-based rebound in the aftermath of the global recession, fewer EMDEs have been experiencing increased capital inflows, primarily in the form of portfolio debt inflows (IIF 2019a).

Rising levels of private sector debt in EMDEs. Credit booms have contributed to a rapid buildup of private sector debt in EMDEs, increasingly owed to nonresident creditors and in the form of local currency-denominated debt securities (figure 4.6; Agur et al. 2018). Despite the deceleration in credit growth since 2016, at end-2017 bank credit to households and nonfinancial corporations in the average EMDE amounted to 39 percent of GDP, 9 percentage points higher than at end-2007.

In China alone, credit to nonfinancial corporations and households, as percent of GDP, nearly doubled in the decade to end-2018, to 204 percent. Most of this increased credit was to corporations, rather than households (Bruno and Shin 2014; IMF 2015a; World Bank 2018c). More generally, in the 15 largest EMDEs for which Bank for International Settlements data on credit to nonfinancial corporations and households are available, average bank credit to nonfinancial corporations rose to about 55 percent of GDP by end-2018, nearly 12 percentage points higher than at end-2007. Again, this increase was especially pronounced in China, where corporate debt constituted almost 152 percent of GDP in 2018, 54 percentage points higher than in 2007. Excluding China, from end-2007 to end-2018, credit to nonfinancial corporations in EMDEs rose by about 10 percentage points of GDP, on average, to just under 50 percent of GDP (figure 4.6).

There is, however, substantial variation across countries. Nonfinancial corporations deleveraged in Argentina and Hungary—credit declined by 1.4 percent of GDP and 11

FIGURE 4.6 EMDEs: Financing of debt after the global recession

Credit booms have contributed to a rapid buildup of private sector debt, especially in the nonfinancial corporate sector. Issuance of debt denominated in local currency has grown, partly because of the increasing role of nonresident creditors in local bond markets.

A. Foreign ownership of government debt

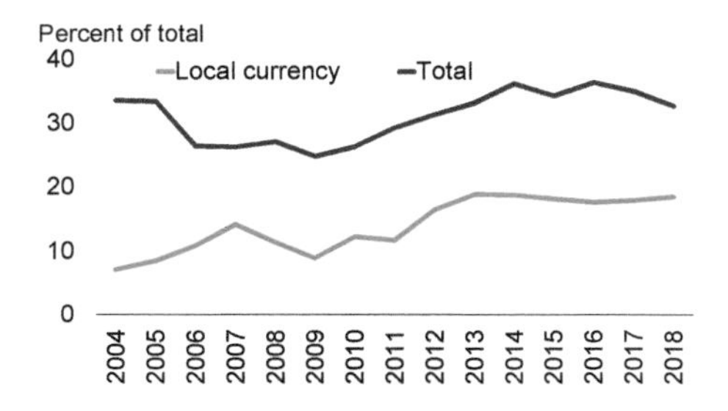

B. Total credit to nonfinancial corporations

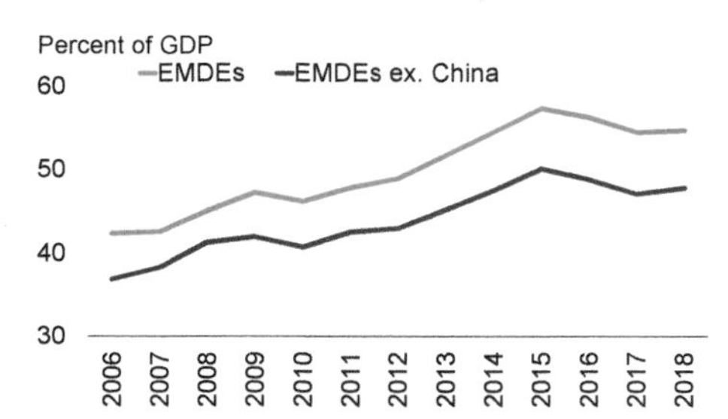

C. Local currency debt

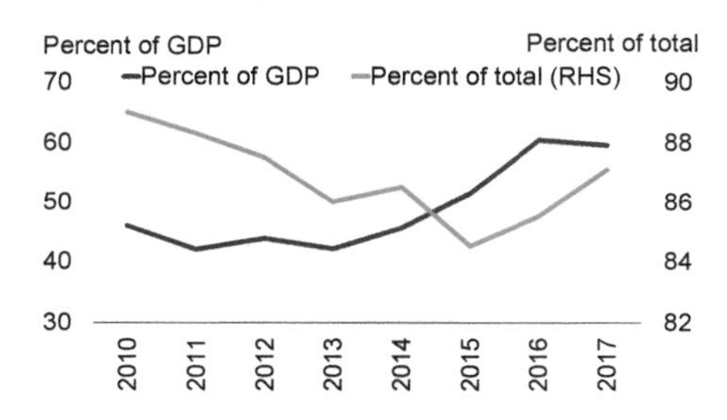

D. Claims on private nonfinancial sector

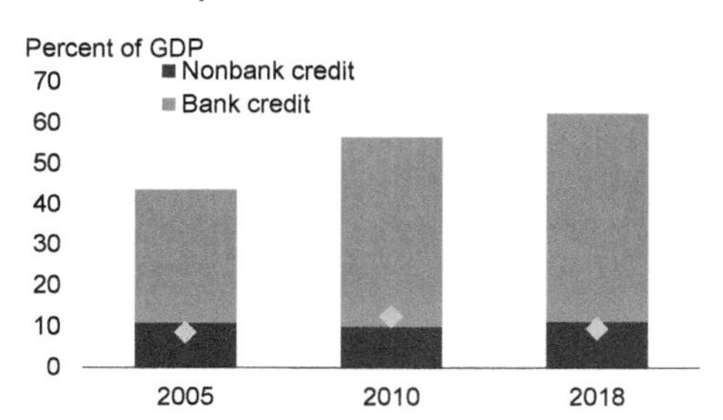

E. Reliance on foreign banks by sector

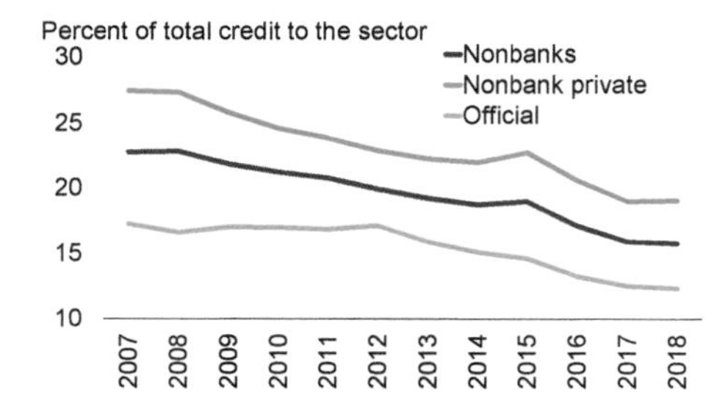

F. Government bonds owned by domestic banks

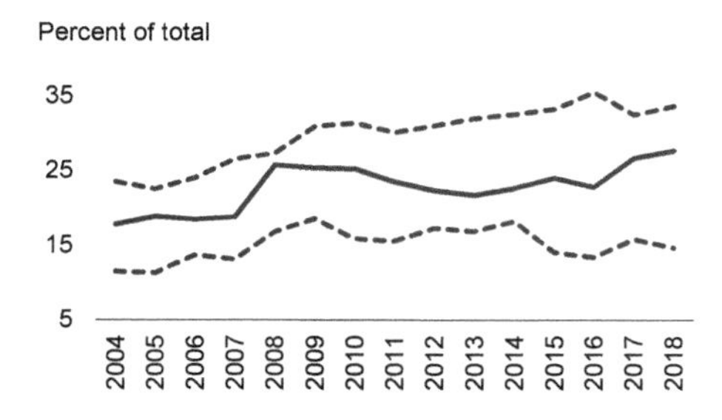

Sources: Bank for International Settlements; Institute of International Finance; International Monetary Fund; World Bank.

Note: Unweighted averages. Dashed line indicates interquartile range. EMDEs = emerging market and developing economies.

A.F. Medians for 21 EMDEs: Argentina, Brazil, Bulgaria, Chile, Colombia, the Arab Republic of Egypt, Hungary, India, Indonesia, Malaysia, Mexico, Peru, the Philippines, Poland, Romania, the Russian Federation, South Africa, Thailand, Turkey, Ukraine, and Uruguay.

B. The sample includes Argentina, Brazil, Chile, China, Colombia, Hungary, Indonesia, India, Mexico, Malaysia, Poland, Russia, Thailand, Turkey, and South Africa.

C. Local currency-denominated debt as share of total debt of the general government and nongovernment sectors. Nongovernment sector debt includes debt of financial corporations (including banks) and nonfinancial corporations.

D.E. Sample includes Argentina, Brazil, Chile, Colombia, Hungary, India, Indonesia, Mexico, Malaysia, Poland, Russia, Thailand, Turkey, and South Africa. Claims by foreign banks (on an ultimate risk basis) are a sum of cross-border lending and credit extended by local subsidiaries of foreign banks.

E. Average foreign bank reliance (FBR) measure across the sample of 15 EMDEs with Bank for International Settlements data on total credit; sample excludes Saudi Arabia. Sector-specific FBR measure is calculated as a ratio of cross-border lending and local claims by subsidiaries of foreign banks divided by total credit to the sector (see BIS 2019a for details).

BOX 4.1 Credit booms without investment booms

Following the 2009 global recession, private credit rose sharply in several emerging market and developing economies (EMDEs). Unlike in previous such episodes, these credit booms have not, in most cases, been accompanied by investment booms. The absence of investment booms during postcrisis credit booms is associated with lower economic growth once the credit boom unwinds.

Introduction

During the recent wave of credit booms in EMDEs, investment growth in many slowed despite rapidly rising credit to the nonfinancial private sector. By contrast, in episodes before the 2009 global recession, credit booms often financed rapid investment growth, with investment subsequently stalling. Against this background, this box addresses the following questions:

- How has investment evolved during credit booms and deleveraging episodes?
- How often have credit booms been accompanied by investment booms?
- How has output growth evolved during credit booms and deleveraging episodes?

The results indicate that, whereas investment often grew rapidly during previous credit booms, this has not been the case since 2010. In the recent wave of credit surges in EMDEs, growing credit mainly financed a rise in consumption. This is of concern because, as highlighted by recent studies, when credit booms unwind, economic growth tends to contract more if the credit boom was not accompanied by an investment surge.

Data and methodology

Credit to the nonfinancial private sector consists of claims—including loans and debt securities—on households and nonfinancial corporations by the domestic financial system and external creditors (Ohnsorge and Yu 2016). A credit boom is defined as an episode during which the ratio of private sector credit to gross domestic product (GDP) is more than 1.65 standard deviations above its Hodrick-Prescott filtered trend in at least one year (Ohnsorge and Yu 2016; World Bank 2016). The start of such a boom is defined as when the credit-to-GDP ratio rises above its trend by one standard deviation and the end as when the ratio begins to fall. Conversely, a deleveraging episode is defined as a period during which the private sector credit-to-GDP ratio is more than 1.65 standard deviations below trend in at least one year. The deleveraging episode starts when the ratio falls more than one standard deviation below trend and ends when the credit-to-GDP ratio begins to climb.

Note: This box was prepared by Shu Yu.

BOX 4.1 Credit booms without investment booms *(continued)*

Investment surges are defined as episodes in which the investment-to-GDP ratio rises to at least one standard deviation above its long-term Hodrick-Prescott filtered trend (or 1.65 standard deviation above trend for investment booms). Similarly, investment slowdowns are defined as episodes in which the investment-to-GDP ratio declines to at least one standard deviation below its Hodrick-Prescott filtered trend.[a]

Credit booms and deleveraging episodes are studied within a seven-year event window centered on either peak or trough years (t = 0). In the sample used here, there were 64 credit booms and 27 deleveraging episodes in EMDEs. A typical credit boom lasted 2.2 years, and an average deleveraging episode lasted 2.4 years.

Investment behavior during credit booms and deleveraging episodes

Credit booms have typically been associated with rising investment. During the median credit boom over the past two to three decades, the ratio of real investment to real GDP increased by 1 percentage point above its long-term (Hodrick-Prescott filtered) trend until the peak of the credit boom. In a quarter of previous credit booms, the investment-to-GDP ratio dropped by about 2 percentage points below its long-term (Hodrick-Prescott filtered) trend over the two years after the peak. Investment swung sharply in the most severe credit boom and bust episodes. For example, during the Asian financial crisis of the late 1990s, in the median affected EMDE, investment contracted by 6.5 percentage points of GDP in 1998 and by 8.6 percentage points of GDP in 1999.

Similarly, investment growth slowed during deleveraging episodes. Real investment dropped below its long-term trend by about 2 percentage points of GDP until the trough of a median deleveraging episode. From that trough, real investment bounced back within a year to 1 percent of GDP above its long-term trend.

Credit and investment booms together

Although investment growth has tended to rise during credit booms, not all credit booms have been associated with investment booms. For instance, Mendoza and Terrones (2012) find that the coincidence between investment booms and credit booms in EMDEs is about 34 percent. The only partial coincidence of credit booms and investment booms may reflect the fact that some credit booms have mainly fueled consumption.[b] In past credit booms, consumption on average rose above its Hodrick-Prescott filtered trend by about 0.3 percentage point of GDP at the peak of the boom and fell below trend by about 1 percentage point of GDP during the deleveraging episode (figure B4.1.1). Whereas consumption expansions

a. The results are similar when investment growth, instead of the investment-to-GDP ratio, is used.

b. See, for instance, Mendoza and Terrones (2008) and Elekdag and Wu (2011).

BOX 4.1 Credit booms without investment booms *(continued)*

FIGURE B4.1.1 Investment and consumption during credit booms and deleveraging episodes

In the median EMDE credit boom, investment rose by about 1 percentage point of GDP above its long-term trend until the credit boom peaked. It dropped below its long-term trend by 1-2 percentage points of GDP before deleveraging episodes reached their troughs. In the recent wave of credit surges in EMDEs, credit booms fueled more household consumption than did average credit booms in the past.

A. Change in investment during credit booms

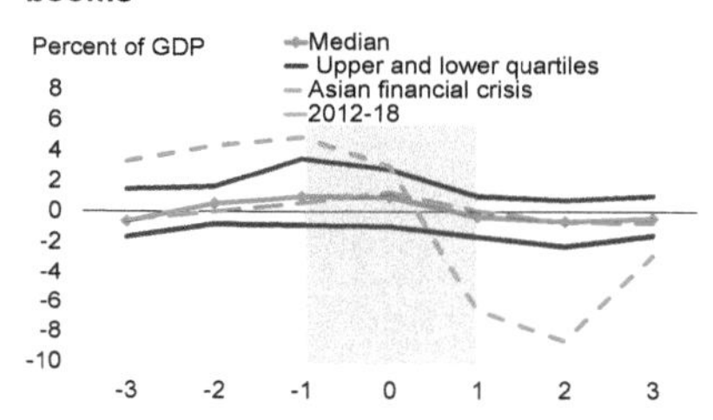

B. Change in investment during deleveraging episodes

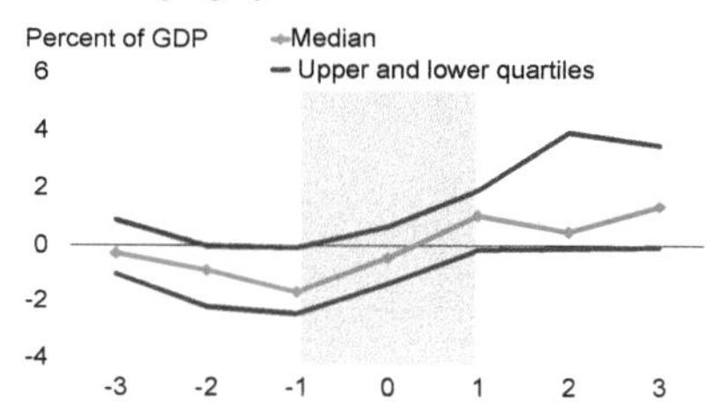

C. Change in consumption during credit booms

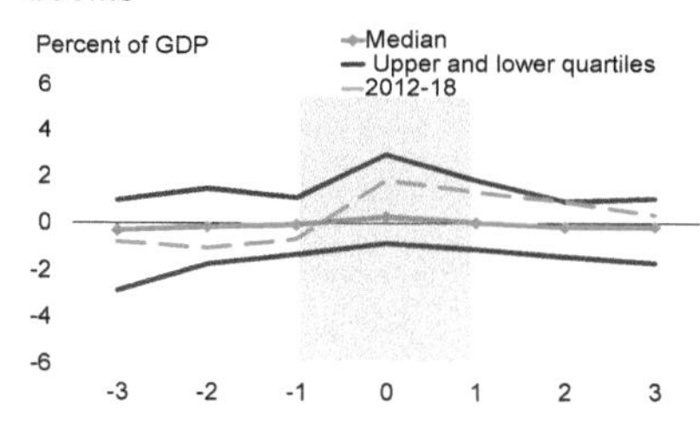

D. Change in consumption during deleveraging episodes

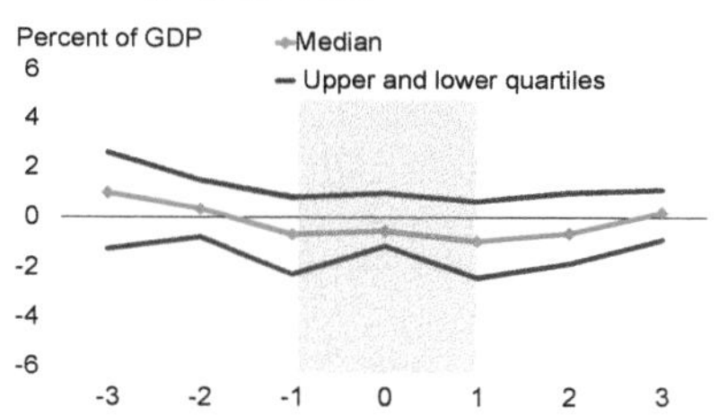

Sources: Bank for International Settlements; Haver Analytics; International Monetary Fund (International Financial Statistics and World Economic Outlook); World Bank (World Development Indicators).

Note: The red lines show sample medians; the blue lines show the corresponding upper and lower quartiles. A credit boom is defined as an episode during which the cyclical component of the nonfinancial private sector credit-to-GDP ratio (derived by Hodrick-Prescott filter) is larger than 1.65 times its standard deviation in at least one year. The episode starts when the cyclical component first exceeds one standard deviation and ends in a peak year ("0") when the nonfinancial private sector credit-to-GDP ratio declines in the following year. A deleveraging episode is defined correspondingly. To address the end-point problem of a Hodrick-Prescott filter, the dataset is expanded by setting the data for 2019-2021 to be equal to the data in 2018. In the case of China, the data for credit-to-GDP ratios in 2019-2021 will follow the declining trend between 2017-2018. Data are not available for Argentina until 1994, Brazil until 1993, China until 1984, Hungary until 1989, Poland until 1992, the Russian Federation until 1995, Saudi Arabia until 1993, and Turkey until 1986. EMDEs = emerging market and developing economies.

A.B. The cyclical component of investment in percent of GDP (derived by Hodrick-Prescott filter). The yellow dashed line is the median cyclical component of investment in percent of GDP in the six EMDEs that were affected by the 1997-98 Asian financial crisis (year 1997 is set as t = 0). The light blue dashed line in A shows the sample median for the 18 countries that were in a credit boom in 2015 during 2012-18.

C.D. The cyclical component of consumption in percent of GDP (derived by Hodrick-Prescott filter). In C, the light blue dashed line for 2012-18 shows the sample median for the 18 countries that were in a credit boom in 2015.

BOX 4.1 Credit booms without investment booms *(continued)*

FIGURE B4.1.2 Coincidence between investment surges and credit booms

Before the global recession, half of all credit booms in EMDEs were accompanied by investment surges around the credit boom's peak years. Since 2010, the share of credit booms accompanied by investment surges has dropped below the levels before the global financial crisis.

A. Investment surges during past booms in EMDEs

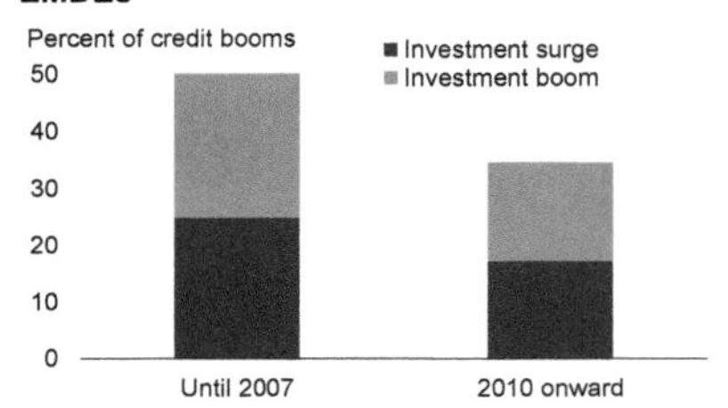

B. Investment surges during recent credit booms in EMDEs

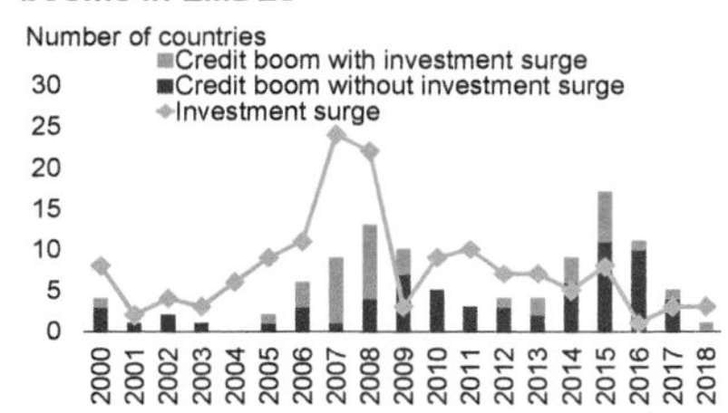

Sources: Bank for International Settlements; Haver Analytics; International Monetary Fund (International Financial Statistics); World Bank (World Development Indicators).

Note: A credit boom is defined as an episode during which the cyclical component of the nonfinancial private sector credit-to-GDP ratio (derived by Hodrick-Prescott filter) is larger than 1.65 times its standard deviation in at least one year. The episode starts when the cyclical component first exceeds one standard deviation and ends in a peak year ("0") when the nonfinancial private sector credit-to-GDP ratio declines in the following year. Investment surge is defined as years when the cyclical component of the investment-to-GDP ratio is at least one standard deviation (1.65 for investment booms) above the Hodrick-Prescott filtered trend; investment slowdown is a year when the cyclical component of the investment-to-GDP ratio is at least one standard deviation below the Hodrick-Prescott filtered trend. Data are not available for Argentina until 1994, Brazil until 1993, China until 1984, Hungary until 1989, Poland until 1992, the Russian Federation until 1995, Saudi Arabia until 1993, and Turkey until 1986. EMDEs = emerging market and developing economies.

A. Investment surges during the peak year (t = 0) or the following year.

during credit booms have not continued for long, consumption contractions during a typical deleveraging episode have tended to last for three to four years.

After the global financial crisis, the coincidence between credit booms and investment surges around the peak year of a credit boom dropped significantly in EMDEs (figure B4.1.2). Before 2008, half of credit booms were accompanied by investment surges or booms. After the global recession, however, the share of credit booms coinciding with investment surges or booms dropped to one-third.

In EMDEs, the number of investment surges peaked before the global recession, whereas the wave of credit booms in EMDEs reached its peak in 2015. The number of EMDEs in a credit boom increased from 3 in 2011 to 18 in 2015, subsequently falling to just 2 in 2018. Meanwhile, the number of EMDEs in an investment surge dropped from 10 in 2011 to 1 in 2016. In 2018, the number of EMDEs in an investment surge remained low.

In several countries, rapid credit growth fueled above-average consumption growth but no investment surge or boom. In EMDEs where a credit boom occurred in

BOX 4.1 Credit booms without investment booms (*continued*)

FIGURE B4.1.3 Output growth during credit booms and deleveraging episodes

In EMDEs, output on average rose above its trend by about 2.5 percent during credit booms and fell below trend by 2.0 percent during deleveraging episodes. Output growth during credit booms and in the run-up to deleveraging episodes tended to be stronger when accompanied by investment surges. During deleveraging episodes, declines were deeper when accompanied by investment slowdowns.

A. GDP during credit booms

Percent deviation from trend

All
With investment surge
Without investment surge
2012-18

5
4
3
2
1
0
-1
-2
-3

-3 -2 -1 0 1 2 3

B. GDP during deleveraging episodes

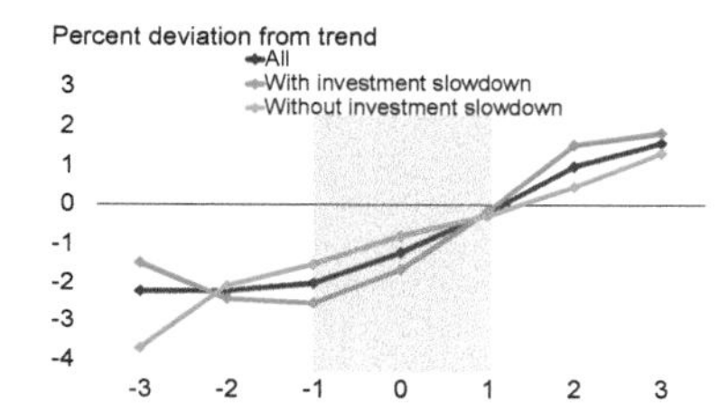

Sources: Bank for International Settlements; Haver Analytics; International Monetary Fund (International Financial Statistics); World Bank (World Development Indicators).

Note: A credit boom is defined as an episode during which the cyclical component of the nonfinancial private sector credit-to-GDP ratio (derived by Hodrick-Prescott filter) is larger than 1.65 times its standard deviation in at least one year. The episode starts when the cyclical component first exceeds one standard deviation and ends in a peak year ("0") when the nonfinancial private sector credit-to-GDP ratio declines in the following year. A deleveraging episode is defined correspondingly. Investment surge is defined as years when the cyclical component of the investment-to-GDP ratio is at least one standard deviation (1.65 for investment booms) above the Hodrick-Prescott filtered trend; investment slowdown is a year when the cyclical component of the investment-to-GDP ratio is at least one standard deviation below the Hodrick-Prescott filtered trend. Data are not available for Argentina until 1994, Brazil until 1993, China until 1984, Hungary until 1989, Poland until 1992, the Russian Federation until 1995, Saudi Arabia until 1993, and Turkey until 1986. EMDEs = emerging market and developing economies.

A. Group means for the cyclical components of GDP in percent of its trend (derived using a Hodrick-Prescott filter) for all credit booms (in blue), credit booms with investment surge (occurred in 1 year around t = 0, in red), and credit booms without investment surge (in yellow). The mean cyclical components of GDP in percent of its Hodrick-Prescott filtered trend for the 18 countries that were in a credit boom in 2015.

B. Group means for the cyclical components of GDP in percent of its trend (derived using a Hodrick-Prescott filter) for all deleveraging episodes (in blue), deleveraging episodes with investment slowdown (occurred in 1 year around t = 0, in red), and deleveraging episodes without investment slowdown (in orange).

2015, consumption was about 2 percentage points of GDP above trend—above its median expansion during previous credit boom episodes (1.5 percentage points).

Output during credit booms and deleveraging episodes

In general, output has expanded during credit booms, but by less than investment (Mendoza and Terrones 2008, 2012). Before a typical credit boom peaked, output increased, on average, by 3 percent above trend when the boom was accompanied by an investment surge, but by only 1 percent above trend when there was no investment surge (figure B4.1.3). Two years after the peak credit-to-GDP level, output was typically below trend by more than 2 percent in the absence of investment surges, but by only one-third as much following booms

BOX 4.1 Credit booms without investment booms *(continued)*

accompanied by investment surges. The larger output loss in the aftermath of credit booms without investment surges may reflect the lack of a boost to potential output from capital accumulation that could have been created by an investment surge. In the recent postcrisis wave of credit surges, EMDE output has evolved similarly to that of an average past credit boom, largely supported by rising consumption around the peak of the boom.

During a typical deleveraging episode, output fell, on average, to a level almost 2 percent below trend. If accompanied by an investment slowdown, the decline in output was sharper as output fell from near trend in the run-up to the deleveraging to about 3 percent below trend at its trough. Output remained below trend one year after reaching the trough of a deleveraging episode and moved back to its trend shortly afterward.

Conclusion

Since the global recession, several EMDEs have experienced rapid private sector credit growth. In contrast to many precrisis episodes, these credit surges have typically not been accompanied by investment surges and have largely fueled consumption in some EMDEs. In the past, output contracted as credit booms unwound and it contracted more when credit booms occurred without investment surges.

percent of GDP, respectively, in the decade leading up to end-2018. Meanwhile, credit to the nonfinancial corporate sector surged in Turkey—by nearly 40 percent of GDP, to 70 percent—and Chile—by 33 percent of GDP, to 99 percent. Households in EMDEs have been accumulating debt at a somewhat slower pace compared to the corporate sector. At the end of 2018, average credit to households stood at 29 percent of GDP. Household debt remains modest in Argentina, India, and Turkey (at 7 percent, 11 percent, and 15 percent of GDP, respectively). In Malaysia and Thailand, however, household debt now accounts for two-thirds of GDP.

Riskier composition of private debt. This rapid increase in private debt was accompanied by a shift toward riskier borrowing, at least in some EMDEs (Alfaro et al. 2019; Beltran, Garud, and Rosenblum 2017; Feyen et al. 2017; IMF 2018b; World Bank 2018a). On average across the 21 EMDEs with available data, foreign currency-denominated corporate debt rose from 21 percent of GDP in 2007 to 28 percent in 2018, although its share of total corporate debt remained around 40 percent over this period (IIF 2019b). By end-2018, one-third of the 21 EMDEs with available data had foreign currency-denominated corporate debt above 20 percent of GDP.

This rise in foreign currency-denominated corporate debt between 2007 and 2018 was mainly concentrated in LAC, where it rose by 15 percentage points to 50 percent of total corporate debt and its ratio to GDP rose by 19 percentage points on average. In contrast, in ECA and EAP (excluding China), the share of foreign currency-denominated corporate debt has declined since 2007 by about 5 percentage points, to 25 and 13 percent of GDP in the two regions, respectively.

Moreover, a greater share of corporate debt than before the global financial crisis is held by firms with riskier financial profiles, because supportive financing conditions have allowed firms to issue more debt with weaker credit quality (Beltran and Collins 2018; Feyen et al. 2017; IMF 2015a). The postcrisis decline in syndicated lending from advanced economies has also reduced the supply of long-term finance to corporate borrowers in EMDEs. Increased reliance on short-term debt has raised rollover risks and reduced the scope to undertake long-term investments such as infrastructure projects (World Bank 2015). In some EMDEs, the investor base has broadened, and the liquidity of local bond markets has increased. The continued reliance on bank credit, high costs and risks associated with issuing local bonds, and insufficient market infrastructure still limit the scale and sophistication of domestic debt markets in many economies (Goswami and Sharma 2011).

Rising external private debt and foreign exchange risks. After the global recession, the low cost of international borrowing prompted many EMDE corporations to finance the accumulation of local currency-denominated assets with proceeds from international bond issuance (Bruno and Shin 2018). Increasing issuance of foreign currency-denominated debt in EMDEs has contributed to rising currency mismatches and heightened the risks of financial distress in the corporate sector and the banking system. U.S. dollar appreciation could substantially increase the local currency cost of servicing foreign debts, raise corporate defaults, and weaken banks' balance sheets, threatening their capacity to provide domestic credit.[20]

It is increasingly apparent that the appreciation of local currencies against the U.S. dollar is associated with increased portfolio flows into EMDEs, and that outflows often occur when currencies depreciate (BIS 2019b; Hofmann, Shim, and Shin 2016). This means that local currency depreciations may significantly amplify the negative impact of tighter global liquidity on EMDEs' borrowing costs and access to external financing (BIS 2018a; Hofmann, Shim, and Shin 2019).

The U.S. dollar is also an indicator of global risk appetite and can therefore influence real investment activity in EMDEs. A stronger U.S. dollar can be associated with increased risk aversion and a reduced willingness of global banks to extend cross-border loans to EMDEs, which in turn can weaken local credit supply and investment activity (Avdjiev et al. 2018).

Greater shadow banking activities. Shadow banking refers to nonbank financial intermediation that takes place outside of the regulated financial system and may provide credit to riskier borrowers who often lack access to bank credit. Shadow banking

[20] This appreciation could be triggered, for example, by reversals of capital flows to EMDEs on heightened global risk aversion.

BOX 4.2 Negative interest rate policies: Implications for emerging market and developing economies

A number of central banks in advanced economies have implemented negative interest rate policies (NIRPs) in recent years as part of their unconventional monetary policy toolkit. Although their implications for advanced economies and EMDEs are broadly similar to the implications of other unconventional expansionary monetary policies, NIRPs could pose new risks. These risks include an erosion of profitability for banks and other financial intermediaries, as well as excessive risk-taking by investors in advanced economies, which can contribute to higher volatility of capital flows to EMDEs. Macroprudential policies, along with strong supervisory and regulatory frameworks, can mitigate such risks and reduce the volatility of financial cycles.

Introduction

In recent years, a number of central banks in advanced economies—including in Denmark, Japan, Sweden, Switzerland, and the euro area—have adopted negative interest rate policies (NIRPs) to provide additional monetary policy stimulus. The central banks implementing NIRPs are charging (instead of paying) commercial banks for their excess reserves, effectively taxing banks for hoarding cash and potentially encouraging them to boost lending.

In principle, cutting policy rates slightly below zero should lead to lower market interest rates and encourage lending. Given the downward rigidity of deposit rates arising from the guaranteed zero nominal yield on cash, however, NIRPs tend to shrink banks' interest margins and reduce their profitability, potentially posing a financial stability risk. Weaker profits of banks in advanced economies can affect EMDEs through cutbacks in banks' cross-border operations.

At the same time, profit erosion due to NIRPs and an increasing volume of negative-yielding bonds can accelerate search for higher yields, including through capital inflows to EMDEs, leading to their increasing exposure to the volatility of capital flows. These potential spillovers of NIRPs to EMDEs highlight the importance of having an appropriate policy framework to mitigate risks.

On the basis of the findings of a recent comprehensive study (Arteta et al. 2018), this box addresses the following questions regarding NIRPs:

- How can NIRPs affect financial markets?
- How can NIRPs affect financial stability?
- What policies can EMDEs use to mitigate the associated risks?

Impact on financial markets

NIRPs have important transmission channels that affect financial markets in advanced economies (Eggertsson et al. 2019). In particular, negative policy rates

Note: This box was prepared by Carlos Arteta and Temel Taskin.

BOX 4.2 Negative interest rate policies: Implications for emerging market and developing economies *(continued)*

can be expected to reduce the rates at which financial intermediaries borrow and lend, which should lead to an increase in private sector demand for other assets such as equities, resulting in rising stock prices. Banks are encouraged to expand lending to avoid negative returns on their excess reserves at central banks. Households and nonfinancial corporations enjoy a lower external finance premium through strengthening balance sheets, and hence demand more credit.

Despite the potential benefits of NIRPs, associated complications could limit their effectiveness in boosting financial intermediation, particularly if they have adverse effects on the financial sector. For example, in order to prevent a loss of their deposit base, commercial banks may hesitate to impose negative rates on depositors (Heider, Saidi, and Schepens 2019). This may either limit the pass-through to lending rates, as banks seek to maintain interest margins, or adversely affect profitability, which could weaken the transmission of monetary policy (Erikson and Vestin 2019; Ulate Campos 2019; Waller 2016).

By affecting the profitability of banks in advanced economies, NIRPs can also have implications for financial markets in EMDEs.[a] Lower profits of banks in advanced economies can spill over to EMDEs through the reduction in cross-border operations. An additional reduction would exacerbate the retrenchment of a number of major global banks from EMDEs that has already taken place in recent years.

NIRPs have also generally been associated with a downward shift in the yield curve—a broad-based decline in interest rates, with most short-term government bond yields and some longer-term yields having turned negative in NIRP countries. The impact of NIRPs on bond yields appears to reflect primarily a downward shift in expectations about the future path of policy rates, rather than a further compression of term premia from already low levels.

Impact on financial stability

NIRPs could pose specific risks to financial stability in the advanced economies implementing them, particularly if rates go substantially below zero or if NIRPs are employed for a protracted period of time. A decade of record low interest rates has compressed banks' net interest margins (Claessens, Coleman, and Donnelly 2018). Some bank surveys also indicate a perception that NIRPs have had an adverse impact on bank profits (figure B4.2.1). Investors may be encouraged by negative policy rates and low or negative bond yields to take excessive risk, leading to asset bubbles (Arteta et al. 2018).

a. Molyneux, Reghezz, and Xie (2019) find that bank margins and profits fell in countries that adopted NIRPs compared to countries where this policy was not implemented.

BOX 4.2 Negative interest rate policies: Implications for emerging market and developing economies *(continued)*

FIGURE B4.2.1 Bank profitability and government bond yields

Survey results indicate a perception that NIRPs have an adverse impact on euro area bank profits. Government bond yields have fallen into negative territory in NIRP economies, encouraging investors to search for higher yield in EMDEs.

A. Impact of ECB's NIRP on banks

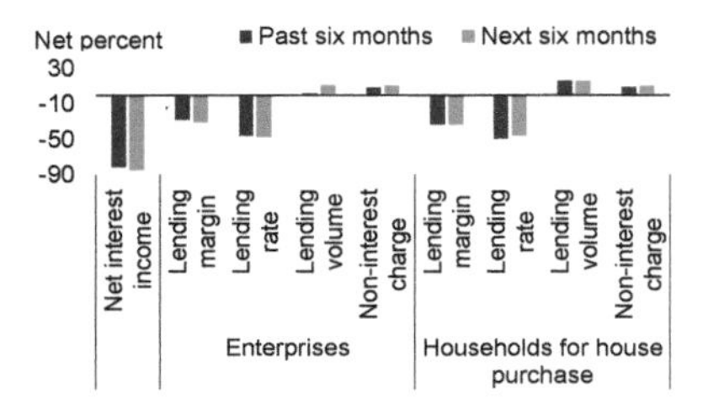

B. Two-year government bond yields

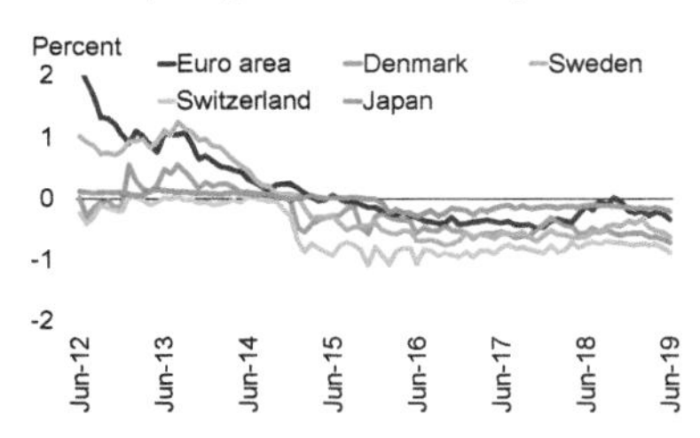

Sources: Arteta et al. (2018); Bloomberg; European Central Bank; World Bank.

Note: ECB = European Central Bank; EMDEs = emerging market and developing economies; NIRP = negative interest rate policy.

A. Results from ECB's Bank Lending Survey in April 2016. Questions start: "Given the ECB's negative deposit facility rate, did or will this measure, either directly or indirectly, contribute to…" Net percent is calculated as the difference between the sum of responses mentioning "increased considerably" and "increased somewhat" and the sum of responses mentioning "decreased somewhat" and "decreased considerably," divided by the number of responding banks that did not reply "not applicable."

B. "Euro area" yield is the European Central Bank's euro area two-year government benchmark bond yield estimation. Last observation is June 2019.

NIRPs could also have financial stability implications for EMDEs, by potentially triggering excessive capital inflows and exacerbating volatility. Under persistently low or negative government bond yields in advanced economies, investors may divert funds to EMDEs in search of higher yield. Negative policy rates and bond yields were accompanied by a rebound in capital flows to EMDEs in 2016-17. In recent months, however, capital flows have moderated, reflecting heightened risk aversion and flight to safety amid deteriorating global growth prospects.

More generally, the significant increase in portfolio flows to EMDEs after the global recession, including in the period of NIRPs, has already contributed to elevated corporate debt in EMDEs, heightening the risk of abrupt deleveraging. Capital inflow surges to EMDEs are usually followed by credit booms, as extensively documented in the literature. Credit booms, if not accompanied by appropriate prudential policies, could increase financial risks and eventually lead to credit busts and financial crises. Credit booms that are not accompanied by investment booms can be particularly problematic, because they are associated with slower economic growth after the boom episodes (box 4.1).

BOX 4.2 Negative interest rate policies: Implications for emerging market and developing economies *(continued)*

This box employs event studies (similar to Chen et al. 2011 and Gagnon 2016) to assess the immediate impact of NIRP announcements on financial market developments across EMDEs, which can be interpreted as providing information about market participants' expectations of the longer-run effects of NIRPs on EMDEs. The event study tracks three major EMDE variables: exchange rates, EMBI spreads, and equity prices on the day of rate cuts into or within negative territory by central banks in advanced economies.

On average, the response of EMDE assets is broadly consistent with prior estimates and the previous literature. EMDE currencies appreciated, bond spreads narrowed, and equity prices in EMDEs increased on the day of NIRP announcements (figure B4.2.2). The average impact on EMDEs is directionally consistent with previous estimates for other unconventional monetary policies by major advanced economies. The reaction of asset prices varies across countries, which likely reflects domestic developments or other changes in international financial markets on the day of the announcements (figure B4.2.2).

The immediate reaction of EMDE assets, reflected in declining bond yields, rising equity prices, and appreciating currencies, is also consistent with the longer-term trends in EMDE financial markets in the postcrisis period. In particular, surges in capital inflows to EMDEs have been accompanied by significant upswings in private sector debt amid favorable funding costs, as well as increases in foreign currency-denominated corporate debt.

Policies to mitigate risks

In an environment of weak growth, depressed real interest rates, and low inflation expectations, NIRPs can help provide additional monetary policy stimulus in the economies implementing them—as long as policy interest rates are only modestly negative and do not stay negative for too long, so that lasting adverse effects on the financial sector can be avoided. Shrinking interest margins, accompanied by negative bond yields, can lead to the erosion of bank profitability in NIRP economies. Thus, although negative policy interest rates have a place in a policy maker's toolkit, they need to be handled with care in order to secure their benefits and mitigate their risks.

Because NIRPs and other unconventional monetary policies tend to lower interest rates in advanced economies, they can trigger capital inflows to EMDEs as investors search for higher yields. Given the risks associated with high capital flow volatility, macroprudential policies should be employed to mitigate systemic risks and reduce the procyclicality of domestic credit supply. Such policies can include a range of instruments, including caps on loan-to-value or debt-to-income ratios, dynamic provisioning, and credible stress tests. Banks and nonfinancial

BOX 4.2 Negative interest rate policies: Implications for emerging market and developing economies *(continued)*

FIGURE B4.2.2 EMDEs: Consequences of NIRPs

An event study of EMDE financial variables indicates that currencies appreciated, bond spreads declined, and equity prices increased in EMDEs, on average, on the day of a NIRP announcement. This finding is consistent with market expectations of increased net capital inflows to EMDEs.

A. Change in indexes

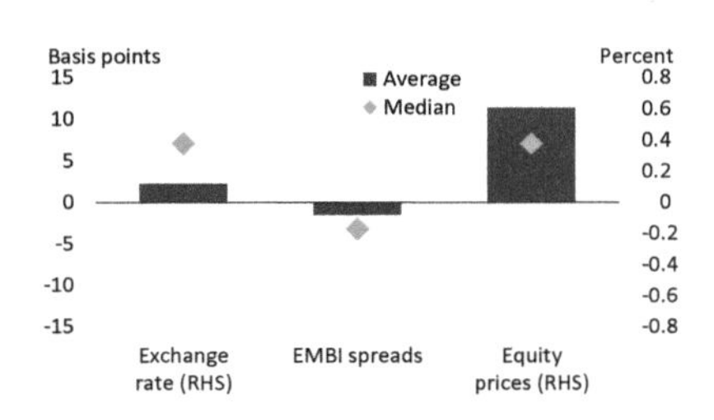

B. Changes in nominal effective exchange rates

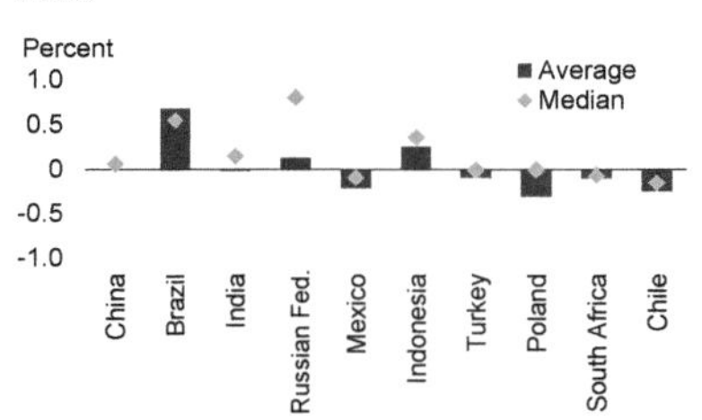

C. Changes in equity market indexes

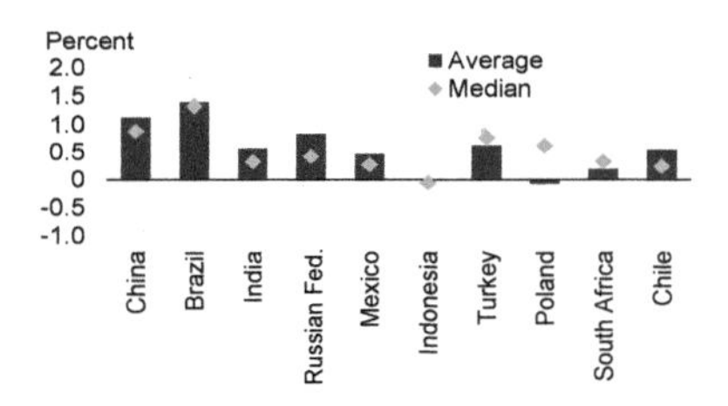

D. Changes in 10-year government bond yields

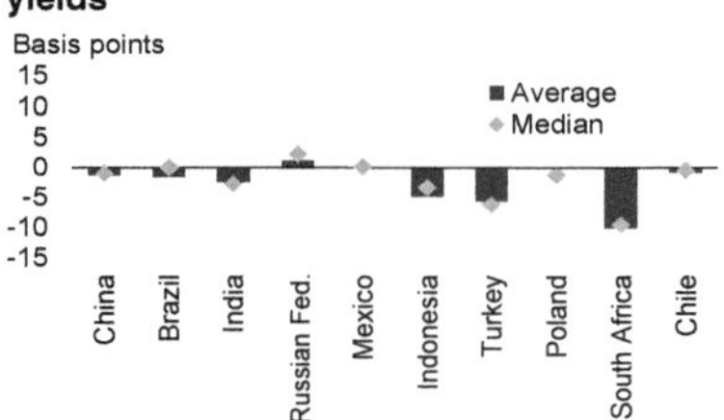

Sources: Bloomberg; Haver Analytics; J.P. Morgan; Morgan Stanley Capital International; World Bank.

Note: BoJ = Bank of Japan; ECB = European Central Bank; EMBI = J.P. Morgan's Emerging Market Bond Index; EMDEs = emerging market and developing economy; MSCI = Morgan Stanley Capital International; NIRP = negative interest rate policy; Russian Fed. = Russian Federation; SNB = Swiss National Bank.

A. Basis points or percent change between closing values on the day before the NIRP announcement and closing values on the day of the announcement. NIRP announcements are those of the ECB (on June 5 and September 4, 2014, December 3, 2015, and March 10, 2016), the BoJ (on January 29, 2016), and the SNB (on January 15, 2015, to abandon the Swiss franc's floor against the euro). Announcements were made by ECB on June 5 and September 4, 2014, December 3, 2015, March 10, 2016; by SNB on January 15, 2015; and by BoJ on January 29, 2016. For emerging market indexes, exchange rate is the J.P. Morgan EM Foreign Exchange Index, EMBI spread is calculated as the average premium paid over a U.S. government bond with comparable 10-year maturity, and equity prices are the MSCI Emerging and Frontier Index.

B. A decrease indicates depreciation of the domestic currency.

C. Equities are the main stock market index for each country, expressed in local currency.

D. Bond yields are for 10-year government bonds.

corporations with elevated foreign currency mismatches or significant reliance on short-term debt will require close monitoring.

In principle, NIRPs in advanced economies can provide some additional room to maneuver for EMDE monetary policy through their generally benign effects on

BOX 4.2 Negative interest rate policies: Implications for emerging market and developing economies *(continued)*

global financing conditions. Low global interest rates may not necessarily translate into a commensurate decline in EMDE bond yields and spreads, however, particularly in the more vulnerable economies. Adverse financial developments, such as sharp currency depreciations, can constrain the ability of EMDEs to pursue monetary policy accommodation.

The availability of fiscal policy buffers as a countercyclical tool thus remains important for EMDEs. On the one hand, downward pressure from NIRPs on global interest rates can help contain borrowing costs in many EMDEs and create some fiscal space to maneuver, if needed. On the other hand, fiscal policy can lean against temporary capital inflows associated with exceptionally accommodative monetary policies in advanced economies, including NIRPs, and rebuild buffers before global financing conditions eventually tighten (Arteta et al. 2015, 2018).

Conclusion

A number of central banks in advanced economies have employed NIRPs to provide additional monetary policy stimulus over the past few years. Countries with short-term policy rates in negative territory now account for one-fourth of world GDP. NIRPs have been accompanied by a decline in advanced economy bond yields, sometimes into negative territory. The global economy has never before witnessed negative interest rates on such a large scale. The unprecedented step of deploying NIRPs in multiple countries has implications for both advanced economies and EMDEs.

In principle, rate cuts into negative territory can be expected to reduce the rates at which financial intermediaries conduct their borrowing and lending activities. Using NIRPs, however, may result in complications that limit policy effectiveness, particularly if they have adverse effects on financial institutions. In particular, downward rigidity in deposit rates, due to the guaranteed zero nominal yield on cash, tends to shrink interest margins and reduce the profitability of banks.

By affecting bond yields and the profitability of banks, NIRPs can have spillovers to EMDEs. Specifically, investors are encouraged to search for yield amid negative yields in advanced economies, potentially resulting in capital flow surges into EMDEs. The debt overhang in EMDEs, following the credit booms in the postcrisis period, makes them vulnerable to global and regional shocks. Moreover, debt accumulation threatens to reduce the asset quality of banks in some EMDEs. In this context, macroprudential policies should be used appropriately against excessive capital flows to avoid credit boom/bust cycles and financial crises, while supervisory and regulatory frameworks should be strengthened to reduce the associated risks.

systems, which were small before the global recession, have expanded rapidly in a number of EMDEs, particularly in large economies such as China and India (IMF 2014). In these two countries, assets of nonbank financial institutions now represent over a third of total financial system assets. In China alone, this share has more than doubled over the last decade, and the size and complexity of its nonbank financial sector is becoming comparable to those of advanced economies (Ehlers, Kong, and Zhu 2018).

A decade of relatively light regulation and rapid growth has increased maturity mismatches and credit risks in shadow banking (IMF 2019a). Financial stress in shadow banking may quickly propagate to the rest of the financial system, owing to its interconnectedness with banks. A recent shift toward stricter regulations and supervision of shadow banking in China and a default of one of the largest nonbank lenders in India have already created tighter financial conditions for the private sector in those economies (IMF 2019d).

Rising private debt in LICs. Private sector credit in LICs, which stalled in the aftermath of the global recession, resumed growing markedly in 2011. Average credit to the private sector in LICs increased to 19 percent of GDP in 2017, from 12 percent in 2007. The rise in credit was most pronounced in West Africa, where pan-African banks became more active after the onset of the global recession. For example, between 2007 and 2017, the ratio of private sector credit to GDP in Burkina Faso, Senegal, Mali, and Togo almost doubled—to 30, 29, 26, and 41 percent, respectively. Such a rapid acceleration of credit has created regulatory challenges in LICs (Arena et al. 2015). In many of these countries, financial oversight infrastructure tends to be weaker and less developed, and incomplete disclosure of information by financial institutions impedes proper assessment and mitigation of financial stability risks.

Less robust financial system balance sheets in EMDEs. In the past, unsustainable and inadequately supervised acceleration of credit has sometimes precipitated sharp slowdowns in economic growth, accompanied and followed by prolonged deleveraging (see Albanesi, De Giorgi, and Nosal 2017; Bernanke 2018; Cerutti, Dell'Ariccia, and Dagher 2017; Duffie 2019; Gertler and Gilchrist 2018; Mian, Sufi, and Verner 2017). The recent rapid rise in credit growth among EMDEs has led to similar concerns about the health and resilience of their financial sector balance sheets.

- *Asset quality.* In nearly two-thirds of EMDEs, asset quality has deteriorated since the crisis (figure 4.7). Between 2007 and 2017, nonperforming loan ratios rose in 57 percent of the EMDEs with available data. The asset quality deterioration has been particularly pronounced in smaller state-controlled banks in SAR and commodity-exporting ECA economies as a result of a growth slowdown during 2015-16 and allocative inefficiencies among public sector banks. Meanwhile, bank exposures to governments have increased steadily since the crisis, exacerbating the risks to bank asset quality should sovereign creditworthiness deteriorate (figure 4.7)

- *Funding stability.* The funding models of some EMDE banking systems may have become more fragile, because some banks have increased their reliance on short-term wholesale funding, albeit from a low base, in response to improved access to

FIGURE 4.7 EMDEs: Banking system health after the global recession

In many EMDE banking systems, asset quality has deteriorated, and banks have increased their reliance on less stable, nondeposit funds. Bank profitability has generally declined.

A. Nonperforming loans and loan-to-deposit ratios

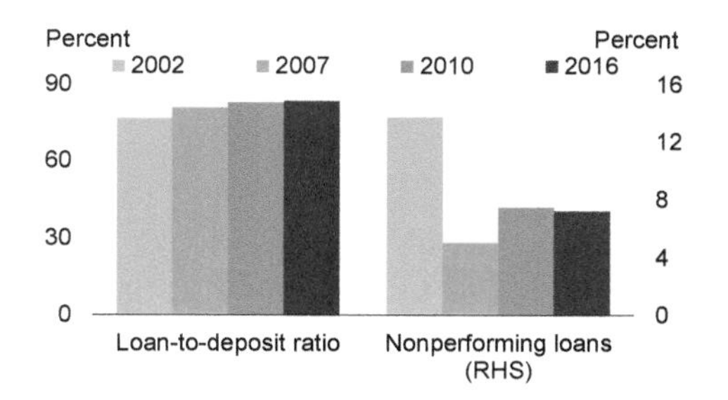

B. Nonperforming loans, by region

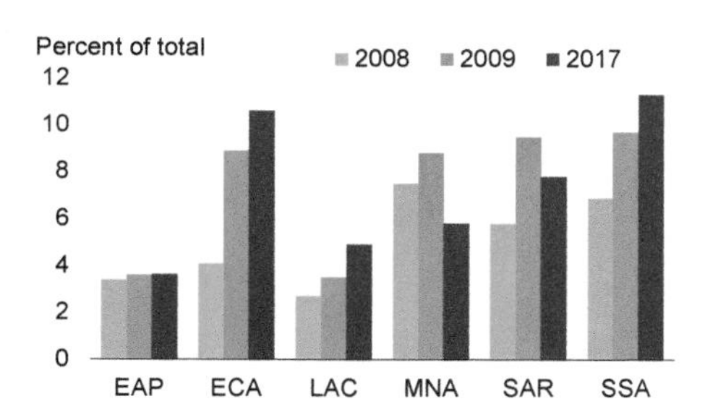

C. Bank claims on government and other public sector nonfinancial entities

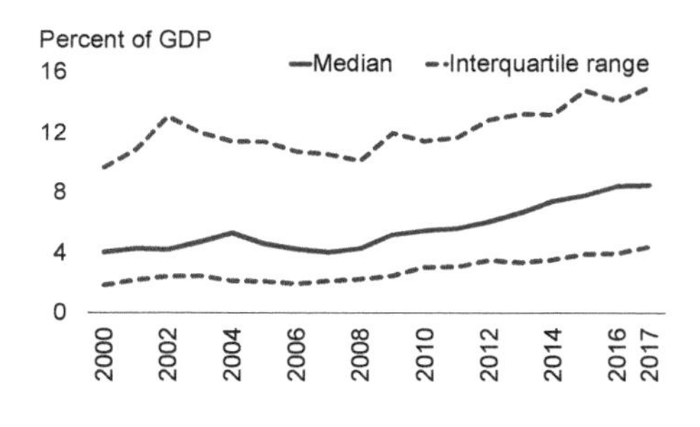

D. Loan-to-deposit ratios, by region

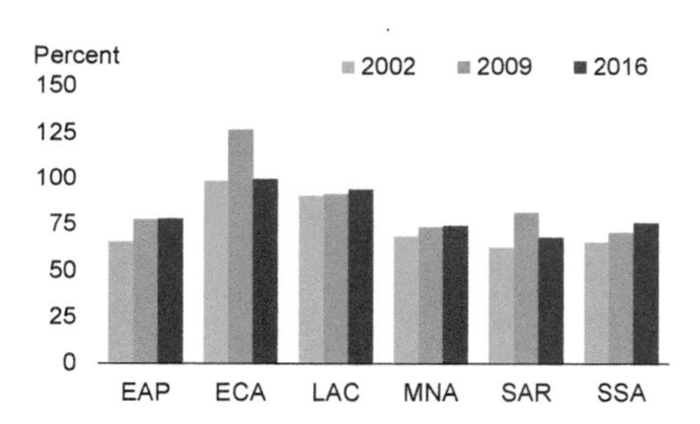

E. Bank profitability

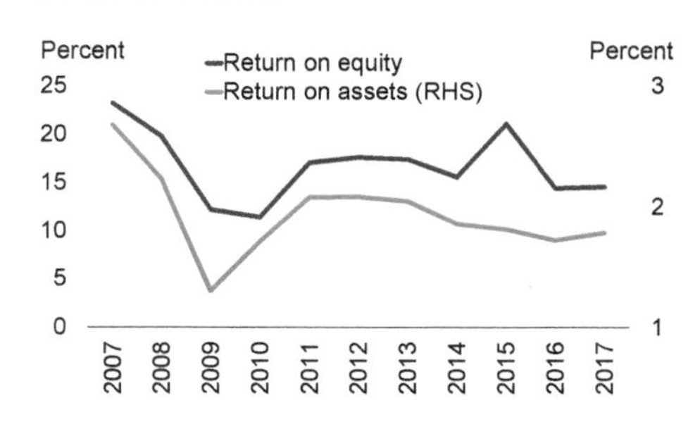

F. Return on equity, by region

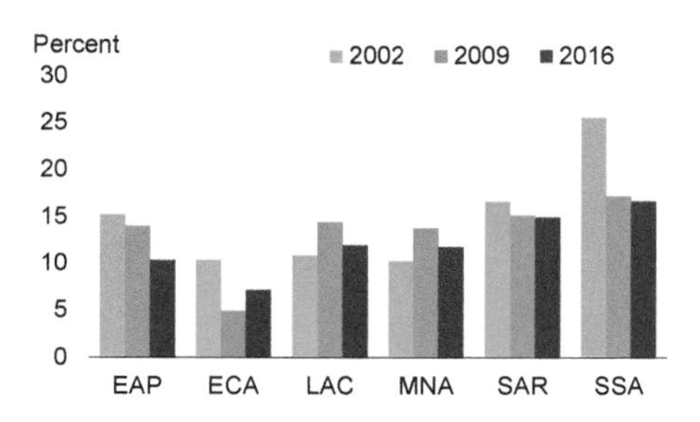

Sources: Čihák et al. (2012); International Monetary Fund; World Bank.

Note: Latest data available; unweighted averages. EAP = East Asia and Pacific; ECA = Europe and Central Asia; EMDEs = emerging market and developing economies; LAC = Latin America and the Caribbean; MNA = Middle East and North Africa; SAR = South Asia; SSA = Sub-Saharan Africa.

A.B. Loan-to-deposit ratios are from the Financial Structure Database (Čihák et al. 2012). Nonperforming loans ratios are from the Global Financial Development Database (Čihák et al. 2012).

D.E. Data from the Financial Soundness Indicators Dataset (IMF).

F. Financial Structure Dataset (Čihák et al. 2012).

capital markets and continued growth of private sector credit. In the average EMDE, the loan-to-deposit ratio edged up to 86 percent in 2017 from 80 percent in 2007, but with notable regional variations (figure 4.7).

- *Profitability.* Banks' returns on assets and equity in EMDEs have generally declined since the onset of the global recession (figure 4.7). In some EMDEs, bank profitability has weakened more recently as postrecession credit booms receded, economic growth slowed, and loan quality deteriorated (BIS 2018b).

Changes in financial markets

Domestic banks—particularly state-owned banks in some large EMDEs such as China and India—remain the primary source of private credit in EMDEs.[21] EMDE private sector borrowing from international capital markets, however, has increased since the global recession. Moreover, the role of regional banks has increased, following the retrenchment of large international banks.

Retrenchment of EU- and U.S.-headquartered banks. EU- and U.S.-headquartered banks have downsized their EMDE operations—especially in ECA, and, to a lesser extent, in LAC and SSA—partly as a response to stricter financial regulations in advanced economies.[22] In some cases, government bailouts required an exit from noncore activities abroad (BIS 2018b; Cetorelli and Goldberg 2011; Claessens and Van Horen 2015; McCauley et al. 2017; World Bank 2018b). Several global, systemically important financial institutions have sharply reduced their foreign operations, triggering a sharp contraction of cross-border bank lending to some EMDEs (figure 4.8).[23] After the global recession, a number of banking systems in advanced economies, especially in the euro area, have suffered from weak profitability, reflecting lackluster growth and persistently low—and even negative—interest rates (BIS 2019b; box 4.2). These profitability issues may have contributed to weak cross-border bank lending from advanced economies to some EMDE regions.

Increasing regional concentration of EMDE banks. As large international banks retrenched, cross-border bank lending to EMDEs shifted to EMDE-headquartered

[21] In several EMDEs, large state-owned banks (and in particular state-owned development banks in Brazil, China, and Mexico) played a countercyclical role in stabilizing credit by expanding their loan portfolios and through various credit guarantee schemes. Several studies show that credit provision by state-owned banks is less procyclical compared to credit extended by private banks, which may help mitigate credit cycles. Countercyclical lending by state-owned banks, however, crowds out lending by private banks and results in long-term fiscal and economic costs in the form of contingent government liabilities and misallocation of credit (see World Bank 2012 for a detailed discussion and literature review).

[22] The postcrisis overhaul of financial regulations in advanced economies has greatly strengthened crisis prevention measures, including stricter liquidity and capital requirements. Meanwhile, new resolution mechanisms gave regulators more powers to dismantle and liquidate systemically important financial institutions, including large international banks (Metrick and Rhee 2018).

[23] For example, since 2016, Barclays has reduced its stake in Barclays Africa Group Ltd. (an important lender in Kenya, Botswana, Tanzania, Ghana, and South Africa) and ended entirely its nearly 100-year presence in SSA in mid-2018. HSBC reduced the number of its countries of operation to 67 from 88, especially in EAP, LAC, and SAR. U.K.-based Standard Chartered sold its retail operations in Thailand in 2016. U.S.-headquartered Citi has withdrawn from retail banking in Argentina, Brazil, and Colombia.

FIGURE 4.8 EMDEs: Changes in financial intermediation

As EU- and U.S.-headquartered banks have downsized their EMDE operations, cross-border bank lending to EMDEs shifted to EMDE-headquartered banks. EMDE corporate and sovereign borrowers have increasingly turned to capital markets to raise new debt.

A. Cross-border bank lending to EMDEs

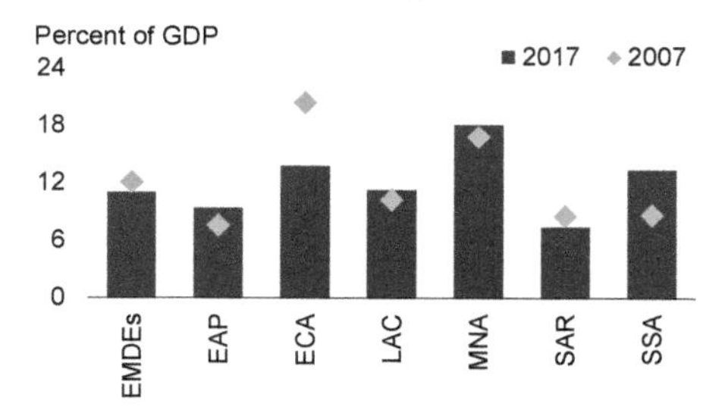

B. Changing sources of cross-border bank loans

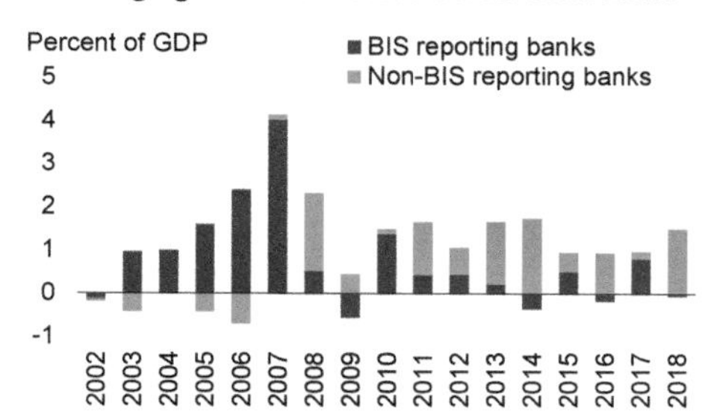

C. Panregional banks

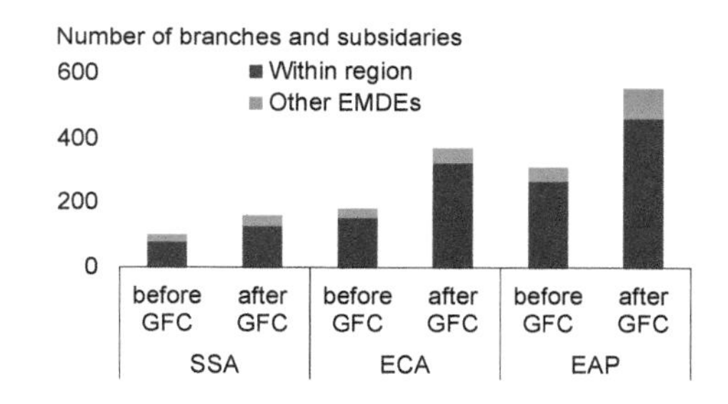

D. Global assets of 10 largest G-SIBs by bank domicile

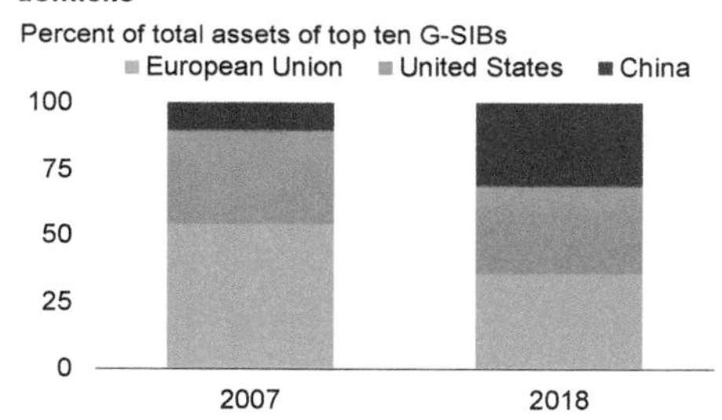

E. Debt issuance, EMDEs excluding China

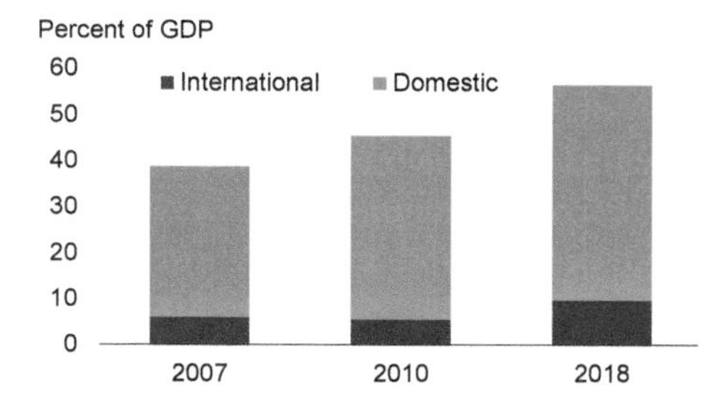

F. Claims on the official sector

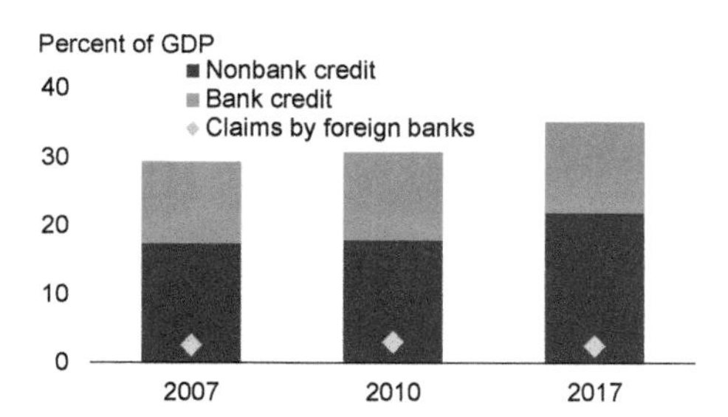

Sources: Bank for International Settlements (BIS); International Monetary Fund (IMF); World Bank.

Note: EAP = East Asia and Pacific; ECA = Europe and Central Asia; EMDEs = emerging market and developing economies; GFC = global financial crisis; G-SIBs = global systemically important banks; LAC = Latin America and the Caribbean; MNA = Middle East and North Africa; SAR = South Asia; SSA = Sub-Saharan Africa.

A. Sample has 140 EMDEs; ratios of the total stock of cross-border bank claims on the region to its aggregate GDP.

B. Sample includes 115 EMDEs excluding China (data for only 77 EMDEs in 2018). Lending by non-BIS banks is estimated as total bank loans and deposits from the IMF Balance of Payment Statistics (excluding central banks) minus cross-border lending by BIS reporting banks. This difference mostly accounts for the banking flows originating from non-BIS reporting countries (IIF 2016).

C. Based on annual bank statements; before the GFC—2008 or 2009 depending on data availability; after GFC—2018, or latest data available.

D. Based on the Financial Stability Board 2018 list of G-SIBs.

E. Debt securities outstanding. Data for Argentina, Brazil, Colombia, India, Indonesia, Malaysia, Mexico, Philippines, the Russian Federation, South Africa, Thailand, and Turkey.

F. Data on EMDE aggregates are from BIS (2019a). BIS estimates of the claims by foreign banks on official sector; sample comprises Argentina, Brazil, Chile, Colombia, Hungary, India, Indonesia, Israel, Mexico, Malaysia, Poland, Russia, Thailand, Turkey, South Africa, and Republic of Korea. BIS estimates of claims by foreign banks are available from 2006.

banks, which greatly expanded their regional presence, most notably in SSA (Cerutti and Zhou 2017, 2018; IMF 2015b; World Bank 2018b; figure 4.8). Chinese banks accounted for two-thirds of EMDE-to-EMDE lending between 2013 and 2017—and for most of the doubling in cross-border claims on SSA economies in the same period, to over 10 percent of GDP on average (Cerutti, Koch, and Pradhan 2018; Dollar 2016). Other EMDE banks have also increased their presence in EMDEs within their respective regions. In all, the share of assets held by banks headquartered outside Organisation for Economic Co-operation and Development countries in 2013 more than doubled compared to 2007, to 11 percent of all foreign bank assets, highlighting that foreign bank presence is now more regionally focused (Claessens and van Horen 2015).

In SSA, banks headquartered in Nigeria, South Africa, and Togo have expanded rapidly to other EMDEs in the region (Arizala et al. 2018; IMF 2015c). In ECA, Russian Federation banks initially expanded within the region after the crisis, as Western European banks withdrew.[24] LAC was an exception. Domestic banks expanded by acquiring assets from exiting foreign lenders, whereas banks from elsewhere in the region played a limited role (IMF 2017).

Despite the large presence of foreign-owned banks in the financial systems of many EMDEs, few EMDEs have put in place regulatory frameworks to deal with the resolution of international banks (World Bank 2019c). The regional expansion of EMDE banks points to the urgency of establishing an effective set of rules for cross-border resolution of global and regional banks. These rules are particularly important during crises, when cross-jurisdictional cooperation could become more challenging because of political constraints.

Increasing EMDE reliance on capital markets. Both corporate and sovereign borrowers have increasingly accessed capital markets, in some regions following the retrenchment of large international banks. Foreign portfolio investors are also becoming more active in local bond markets, accounting for an increasing share of local currency-denominated sovereign bonds. As a result, EMDE financial markets are now more tightly integrated into the global financial system, which could in some circumstances facilitate the contagion of global financial shocks both to foreign currency and, to a lesser extent, local currency debt markets (Agur et al. 2018).

Nonfinancial corporations in many EMDEs have reduced, in varying degrees, their dependence on bank credit after the global recession (CGFS 2019). The share of corporate debt financed by debt securities on average rose from 16 percent to 25 percent of total lending between end-2007 and end-2018. This increase included issuance on both international and domestic debt markets. The volume of international debt securities issued by EMDEs increased by more than three times between 2007 and 2018. Domestic debt issuance excluding China increased from 33 percent of GDP in 2007 to 47 percent of GDP in 2018 (figure 4.8).

[24] For example, Russia's largest lender, Sberbank, acquired Volksbanken's VBI Eastern European operations in 2012.

EMDE sovereign borrowers are also relying more heavily on capital markets. Since 2007, government debt in EMDEs has risen rapidly—by 17 percentage points of GDP—to a weighted average of 50 percent of GDP in 2018, with debt issuances playing an increasing role. From 2007 to 2017, debt securities issued by EMDE governments increased by 4.4 percentage points of GDP on average, to 22 percent of GDP. Sovereign debt issuance has grown particularly rapidly in domestic bond markets, especially in EAP (G20 2018a; figure 4.8). In some EMDEs, the share of nonresident investors in local currency sovereign bond holdings exceeds 30 percent, which makes these economies more vulnerable to sudden shifts in investor confidence (G20 2018a).

Increasing role of financial technology and mobile banking in EMDEs. In many EMDEs, digital technology, such as nonbank payment systems, has greatly expanded access to financial services for unbanked and underbanked firms and households. For example, in SSA one in five adults has a mobile money account—the highest penetration rate of mobile banking across EMDEs (World Bank 2018d). SSA is home to all 10 economies worldwide in which more adults have a mobile money account than a bank account.[25]

A broader adoption of technological innovations in finance in EMDEs, such as mobile banking and payments, makes it easier and less expensive for people to use financial services (World Bank 2014). Better access to financial services improves financial literacy, permits more efficient use of domestic savings, and reduces the costs of acquiring and sharing credit information, reinforcing the development of deeper and more inclusive financial systems.

The financial systems in EMDEs will continue to evolve as new financial and information technologies are more widely adopted, supporting innovation and expanding access to finance. This evolution, however, will also present new challenges to financial regulators. For example, new financial technologies will enable the provision of financial services by unregulated nonbank institutions. Data privacy and cybersecurity risks arising from the spread of digital technologies in finance are also a potential concern (FSB 2017b). Regulators will need to address gaps in the current monitoring and supervisory frameworks, as well as develop a better understanding of how technological innovations in finance reshape linkages and shock propagation channels across markets (Claessens et al. 2018; IMF and World Bank Group 2019).

New forms of infrastructure finance. Infrastructure finance, which remains predominantly bank-based, has declined in EMDEs following the sharp reduction in cross-border lending and stricter postcrisis regulations in the financial sector (FSB 2018b; G20 2013).[26] In many EMDEs, infrastructure bonds also remain rare because of

[25] The benefits of this trend are exemplified by Kenya's experience: About 75 percent of adults in that country own a mobile money account, and increased access to financial services has helped reduce poverty and improved economic outcomes for women (Suri and Jack 2016).

[26] Grants and concessional loans are the primary source of infrastructure finance in LICs, with bank lending providing a complementary source of funding only in a small number of countries (Gurara et al. 2017).

shallow capital markets, regulatory risks, weak institutions, poor design of concession contracts, and, outside of several large EMDEs, lack of data and experience with project finance to perform project evaluation. As a result, institutional investors account for less than 1 percent of all EMDE investment in infrastructure (World Bank 2018e). A number of recent initiatives, backed by multilateral development banks, aim to bring institutional investors to EMDE infrastructure finance through co-lending programs.[27]

Conclusion

During the global recession, private sector credit growth in the average EMDE slowed only moderately, resuming apace in 2011-16. Some EMDE regions experienced deep credit crunches, especially those, such as ECA, with heavy reliance on cross-border lending before the crisis.

During 2011-16, large capital inflows, supported by accommodative global financial conditions, fueled credit booms in nearly a quarter of all EMDEs with available data. By the end of 2016, some of these credit booms had started to recede because of higher EMDE borrowing costs, monetary policy tightening in some advanced economies, stricter macroprudential regulations, and weakening commodity prices and slowing growth in commodity producers. Although financial deepening can improve capital allocation and long-run growth prospects, the credit booms following the global recession have left a legacy of high debt that makes private sectors more vulnerable to increases in borrowing cost.

In addition, changes in EMDE financial systems since the global recession may have created new fragilities. Compared to 2007, EMDEs now rely more on international bond markets, which may amplify the impact of sudden stops of capital flows and adverse shocks to global sentiment. Growing cross-border bank lending between EMDEs may have reduced exposure to financial shocks originating in the banking systems of advanced economies; however, it has also made financial links among EMDEs stronger and increased the potential for inter-EMDE contagion of adverse shocks. Inflows from international capital markets since the global recession may thus exacerbate vulnerabilities to rollover risk or borrowing cost increases. This possibility underscores the importance of developing a strong domestic institutional base to mitigate large fluctuations in a country's ability to access external finance.

Finally, there are signs that rapid credit growth and the accumulation of risks in lightly regulated segments of financial systems have created pressures on the health of financial sector balance sheets in some EMDEs, as suggested by deteriorating asset quality, increased reliance on short-term wholesale funding, declining bank profitability, and increasing exposure to sovereign debt. These developments raise concerns that future financial shocks could be more disruptive to financial systems in EMDEs than those that took place during the global recession.

[27] For example, the International Finance Corporation's Managed Co-Lending Portfolio Program (MCPP) for Infrastructure was created to facilitate access by institutional investors to infrastructure debt in EMDEs.

In this environment of elevated financial vulnerabilities, financial regulators have become increasingly aware of the urgency to identify and mitigate systemic risks to financial stability. Regulators in some countries were caught off guard by the scale and magnitude of financial disruptions during the global recession, which exposed policy challenges arising from complications related to measuring and mitigating financial cycles (Stellinga 2019). Financial regulations have since been overhauled and strengthened in both advanced economies and EMDEs, and regulatory agencies are now generally better equipped to detect and resolve systemic financial stability risks.

Despite these improvements, the resilience of this new regulatory infrastructure has yet to be tested—especially in EMDEs, where macroprudential policies are a relatively recent addition to their macroeconomic policy toolkits. Governments in EMDEs need to accelerate the appropriate reform of regulatory and monitoring frameworks in the financial sector, as well as implement macroprudential instruments that can adapt to the rapidly changing nature of financial systems.

Finally, as EMDEs become more deeply integrated both through global capital markets and regional cross-border lending, coordination of policy responses across countries will be needed to limit the contagion of financial shocks. For example, new regional financing arrangements can be set up to reflect the increasing role of EMDE-to-EMDE financial flows. Cooperation between various regional and international organizations needs to be enhanced to ensure that all layers of the global financial safety nets are effectively deployed during episodes of financial stress (ECB 2018; G20 2018b).

References

Adrian, T., J. Kiff, and H. S. Shin. 2018. "Liquidity, Leverage, and Regulation 10 Years After the Global Financial Crisis." *Annual Review of Financial Economics* 10 (1):1-24.

Aghion, P., P. Bacchetta, and A. Banerjeee. 2004. "Financial Development and The Instability of Open Economies." *Journal of Monetary Economics* 51 (6): 1077-106.

Agur, I., M. Chan, M. Goswami, and S. Sharma. 2018. "On International Integration of Emerging Sovereign Bond Markets." IMF Working Paper 18/18, International Monetary Fund, Washington, DC.

Ahmed, S., and A. Zlate. 2014. "Capital Flows to Emerging Market Economies: A Brave New World?" *Journal of International Money and Finance* 48 (B): 221-48.

Albanesi, S., G. De Giorgi, and J. Nosal. 2017. "Credit Growth and The Financial Crisis: A New Narrative." NBER Working Paper 23740, National Bureau of Economic Research, Cambridge, MA.

Alfaro, L., G. Asis, A. Chari, and U. Panizza. 2019. "Corporate Debt, Firm Size and Financial Fragility in Emerging Markets." NBER Working Paper 25459, National Bureau of Economic Research, Cambridge, MA.

Allen, F., T. Beck, E. Carletti, P. Lane, D. Schoenmaker, and W. Wagner. 2011. *Cross-Border Banking in Europe: Implications for Financial Stability and Macroeconomic Policies*. London: Centre for Economic Policy Research.

Arena, M., S. Bouza, E. Dabla-Norris, K. Gerling, and L. Njie. 2015. "Credit Booms and Macroeconomic Dynamics: Stylized Facts and Lessons for Low-Income Countries." IMF Working Paper 15/11, International Monetary Fund, Washington, DC.

Arizala, F., M. Bellon, M. MacDonald, M. Mlachila, and M. Yenice. 2018. "Regional Spillovers in Sub-Saharan Africa: Exploring Different Channels." *Spillover Notes* 18/01, International Monetary Fund, Washington, DC.

Arslanalp, S., and T. Tsuda. 2015. "Emerging Market Portfolio Flows: The Role of Benchmark-Driven Investors." IMF Working Paper 15/263, International Monetary Fund, Washington, DC.

Arteta, C., M. A. Kose, F. Ohnsorge, and M. Stocker. 2015. "The Coming U.S. Interest Rate Tightening Cycle: Smooth Sailing or Stormy Waters?" Policy Research Note 2, World Bank, Washington, DC.

Arteta, C., M. A. Kose, M. Stocker, and T. Taskin. 2018. "Implications of Negative Interest Rate Policies: An Early Assessment." *Pacific Economic Review* 23 (1): 8-26.

Avdjiev, S., V. Bruno, C. Koch, and H. Shin. 2018. "The Dollar Exchange Rate as a Global Risk Factor: Evidence from Investment." BIS Working Papers 695, Bank for International Settlements, Basel, Switzerland.

Avdjiev, S., L. Gambacorta, L. Goldberg, and S. Schiaffi. 2017. "The Shifting Drivers of Global Liquidity." BIS Working Paper 644, Bank for International Settlements, Basel.

Beck, T., A. Demirgüç-Kunt, and R. Levine. 2006. "Bank Concentration, Competition and Crises: First Results." *Journal of Banking and Finance* 30 (5): 1581-603.

Beltran, D., and C. Collins. 2018. "How Vulnerable Are EME Corporates?" IFDP Notes, Board of Governors of the Federal Reserve System, Washington, DC.

Beltran, D., K. Garud, and A. Rosenblum. 2017. "Emerging Market Nonfinancial Corporate Debt: How Concerned Should We Be?" International Finance Discussion Paper Note, Board of Governors of the Federal Reserve System, Washington, DC.

Bernanke, B. 2018. "The Real Effects of Disrupted Credit. Evidence from the Global Financial Crisis." *Brookings Papers on Economic Activity*, conference draft, September 13-14.

BIS (Bank for International Settlements). 2018a. *Annual Economic Report.* Basel: Bank for International Settlements.

BIS (Bank for International Settlements). 2018b. "Structural Changes in Banking After the Crisis." CGFS Paper 60, Committee on the Global Financial System, Bank for International Settlements, Basel.

BIS (Bank for International Settlements). 2019a. BIS *Quarterly Review: International Banking and Financial Market Development.* March. Basel: Bank for International Settlements.

BIS (Bank for International Settlements). 2019b. *Annual Economic Report.* Basel: Bank for International Settlements.

Bräuning, F., and V. Ivashina. 2019. "U.S. Monetary Policy and Emerging Market Credit Cycles." *Journal of Monetary Economics.* Advance online publication. https://doi.org/10.1016/j.jmoneco.2019.02.005.

Briault, C., E. Feyen, I. Gonzalez Del Mazo, J. Rademacher, B. Kwok Chung Yee, and I. Skamnelos. 2018. "Cross-Border Spillover Effects of the G20 Financial Regulatory Reforms:

Results from a Pilot Survey." Policy Research Working Paper 8300, World Bank, Washington, DC.

Broto, C., J. Díaz-Cassou, and A. Erce. 2011. "Measuring and Explaining the Volatility of Capital Flows to Emerging Countries." *Journal of Banking & Finance* 35 (8): 1941-53.

Bruno, V., and H. Shin. 2014. "Globalization of Corporate Risk Taking." Journal *of International Business Studies.* 45 (7): 800-20.

Bruno, V., and H. Shin. 2018. "Currency Depreciation and Emerging Market Corporate Distress." BIS Working Paper 753, Bank for International Settlements, Basel.

Cerutti, E., S. Claessens, and L. Laeven. 2017. "The Use and Effectiveness of Macroprudential Policies: New Evidence." *Journal of Financial Stability* 28 (February): 203-24.

Cerutti, E., S. Claessens, and D. Puy. 2019. "Push Factors and Capital Flows to Emerging Markets: Why Knowing Your Lender Matters More Than Fundamentals." *Journal of International Economics* 119 (C): 133-49.

Cerutti, E., S. Claessens, and L. Ratnovski. 2017. "Global Liquidity and Cross-Border Bank Flows." *Economic Policy* 32 (89): 81-125.

Cerutti, E., G. Dell'Ariccia, and J. Dagher. 2017. "Housing Finance and Real Estate Booms: A Cross-country Perspective." *Journal of Housing Economics* 38 (December): 1–13.

Cerutti, E., C. Koch, and S. Pradhan. 2018. "The Growing Footprint of EME Banks in the International Banking System." In *BIS Quarterly Review*. December. Basel: Bank for International Settlements.

Cerutti, M., and H. Zhou. 2017. "The Global Banking Network in the Aftermath of the Crisis: Is There Evidence of De-globalization?" IMF Working Paper 17/232, International Monetary Fund, Washington, DC.

Cerutti, M., and H. Zhou. 2018. "The Global Banking Network: What Is Behind the Increasing Regionalization Trend?" IMF Working Paper 18/46, International Monetary Fund, Washington, DC.

Cetorelli, N., and L. Goldberg. 2011. "Global Banks and International Shock Transmission: Evidence from the Crisis." *IMF Economic Review* 59 (1): 41-76.

CGD (Center for Global Development). 2019. *Making Basel III Work for Emerging Markets and Developing Economies.* A CGD Task Force Report. Washington, DC: Center for Global Development.

CGFS (Committee on the Global Financial System). 2019. "Establishing Viable Capital Markets." CGFS Papers 62, Bank for International Settlements, Basel.

Chen, Q., A. Filardo, D. He, and F. Zhu. 2011. "International Spillovers of Central Bank Balance Sheet Policies." BIS Working Papers 66, Bank for International Settlements, Basel.

Čihák, M., A. Demirgüç-Kunt, E. Feyen, and R. Levine. 2012. "Benchmarking Financial Systems around the World." Policy Research Working Paper 6175, World Bank, Washington, DC.

Claessens, S. 2017. "Global Banking: Recent Developments and Insights from Research." *Review of Finance* 21 (4): 1513-55.

Claessens, S., N. Coleman, and M. Donnelly. 2018. "Low-For-Long" Interest Rates and Banks' Interest Margins and Profitability: Cross-Country Evidence." *Journal of Financial Intermediation* 35 (A): 1-16.

Claessens, S., J. Frost, G. Turner, and F. Zhu. 2018. "Fintech Credit Markets Around the World: Size, Drivers and Policy Issues." In *BIS Quarterly Review*. September. Basel: Bank for International Settlements.

Claessens, S., M. A. Kose, and M. Terrones. 2011. "How Do Business and Financial Cycles Interact?" IMF Working Paper 11/88, International Monetary Fund, Washington, DC.

Claessens, S., and N. van Horen. 2015. "The Impact of the Global Financial Crisis on Banking Globalization." *IMF Economic Review* 63 (4): 868-918.

De Haas, R., Y. Korniyenko, E. Loukoianova, and A. Pivovarsky. 2012. "Foreign Banks and the Vienna Initiative: Turning Sinners into Saints?" IMF Working Paper 12/117, International Monetary Fund, Washington, DC.

Dollar, D. 2016. *China's Engagement with Africa: From Natural Resources to Human Resources.* Washington, DC: Brookings Institution.

Duffie, D. 2019. "Prone to Fail: The Pre-Crisis Financial System." *Journal of Economic Perspective* 33 (1): 81-106.

ECB (European Central Bank). 2018. "Strengthening the Global Financial Safety Net." Occasional Paper Series 207, European Central Bank, Frankfurt, Germany.

Eggertsson, J., R. Juelsrud, L. Summers, and E. Wold. 2019. "Negative Nominal Interest Rates and the Bank Lending Channel." NBER Working Paper 25416, National Bureau of Economic Research, Cambridge, MA.

Ehlers, T., S. Kong, and F. Zhu. 2018. "Mapping Shadow Banking in China: Structure and Dynamics." BIS Working Paper 701, Bank for International Settlements, Basel.

Eichengreen, B., and P. Gupta. 2016. "Managing Sudden Stops." Policy Research Working Paper 7639, World Bank, Washington, DC.

Elekdag, S., and Y. Wu. 2011. "Rapid Credit Growth: Boon or Boom-Bust?" IMF Working Paper 11/241, International Monetary Fund, Washington, DC.

Erikson, H., and D. Vestin. 2019. "Pass-through at Mildly Negative Policy Rates: The Swedish Case." VoxEU.org, CEPR Policy Portal, January 22.

Feyen E., N. Fiess, I. Zuccardi Huertas, and L. Pillonca. 2017. "Which Emerging Markets and Developing Economies Face Corporate Balance Sheet Vulnerabilities? A Novel Monitoring Framework." Policy Research Working Paper 8198, World Bank, Washington, DC.

Feyen E., S. Ghosh, K. Kibuuka, and S. Farazi. 2015. "Global Liquidity and External Bond Issuance in Emerging Markets and Developing Economies." Policy Research Working Paper 7363, World Bank, Washington, DC.

Feyen E., and I. Gonzalez del Mazo. 2013. "European Bank Deleveraging and Global Credit Conditions: Implications of a Multi-Year Process on Long-Term Finance and Beyond." Policy Research Working Paper 6388, World Bank, Washington, DC.

Feyen, E., R. Letelier, I. Love, S. Maimbo, and R. Rocha. 2014. "The Impact of Funding Models and Foreign Bank Ownership on Bank Credit Growth: Is Central and Eastern Europe Different?"

Policy Research Working Paper 6783, World Bank, Washington, DC.

Fratzscher, M. 2012. "Capital Flows, Push Versus Pull Factors and The Global Financial Crisis." *Journal of International Economics* 88 (2): 341-56.

FSB (Financial Stability Board). 2017a. *Assessment of Shadow Banking Activities, Risks and The Adequacy of Post-Crisis Policy Tools to Address Financial Stability Concerns.* Basel: Financial Stability Board.

FSB (Financial Stability Board). 2017b. "Financial Stability Implications from FinTech: Supervisory and Regulatory Issues that Merit Authorities' Attention." Financial Stability Board, Basel.

FSB (Financial Stability Board). 2018a. *Global Monitoring Report on Non-Bank Financial Intermediation 2018.* Basel: Financial Stability Board.

FSB (Financial Stability Board). 2018b. *Evaluation of the Effects of Financial Regulatory Reforms on Infrastructure Finance.* Basel: Financial Stability Board.

Gagnon, J. 2016. "Quantitative Easing: An Underappreciated Success." *Policy Brief* 16-4, Peterson Institute for International Economics, Washington, DC.

G20 (Group of 20). 2013. "Long-Term Investment Financing for Growth and Development: Umbrella Paper."

G20 (Group of 20). 2018a. "Recent Development of Local Currency Bond Markets in Emerging Economies." Staff Note, International Financial Architecture Working Group.

G20 (Group of 20). 2018b. "Making the Global Financial System Work for All." Report of the G20 Eminent Persons Group on Global Financial Governance, October. https://www.globalfinancialgovernance.org/assets/pdf/G20EPG-Full%20Report.pdf.

Gertler, M., and S. Gilchrist. 2018. "What Happened: Financial Factors in the Great Recession." *Journal of Economic Perspectives* 32 (3): 3-30.

Goswami, M., and S. Sharma. 2011. "The Development of Local Debt Markets in Asia" IMF Working Paper 11/132, International Monetary Fund, Washington, DC.

Gurara, D., V. Klyuev, N. Mwase, A. Presbitero, X. Xu, and G. Bannister. 2017. "Trends and Challenges in Infrastructure Investment in Low-Income Developing Countries." IMF Working Paper 17/233, International Monetary Fund, Washington, DC.

Hannan, S. 2018. "Revisiting the Determinants of Capital Flows to Emerging Markets-A Survey of the Evolving Literature." IMF Working Paper 18/214, International Monetary Fund, Washington, DC.

Harding, D., and A. Pagan. 2002. "Dissecting the Cycle: A Methodological Investigation." Journal of Monetary Economics 49 (2): 365-81.

Heider, F., F. Saidi, and G. Schepens. 2019. "Life below Zero: Bank Lending under Negative Policy Rates." *The Review of Financial Studies* 32 (10): 3728-61.

Hofmann, B., I. Shim, and H. Shin. 2016. "Sovereign Yields and the Risk-Taking Channel of Currency Appreciation." BIS Working Papers 538, Bank for International Settlements, Basel.

Hofmann, B., I. Shim, and H. Shin. 2019. "Bond Risk Premia and the Exchange Rate." BIS Working Papers 775, Bank for International Settlements, Basel.

Igan, D., H. Moussawi, A. Tieman, A. Zdzienicka, G. Dell'Ariccia, and P. Mauro. 2019. "The Long Shadow of the Global Financial Crisis: Public Interventions in the Financial Sector." IMF Working Paper 19/164, International Monetary Fund, Washington, DC.

IIF (International Institute of Finance). 2016. "EM Cross-border Bank Flow-New Patterns, New Vulnerabilities." June. International Institute of Finance, Washington, DC.

IIF (International Institute of Finance). 2019a. "Capital Flows Report. The EM Positioning Overhang." April. International Institute of Finance, Washington, DC.

IIF (International Institute of Finance). 2019b. "Nonfinancial Corporate Debt Database." International Institute of Finance, Washington, DC. Database available at https://www.iif.com/.

IMF (International Monetary Fund). 2009. *The Implications of the Global Financial Crisis for Low-Income Countries.* Washington, DC: International Monetary Fund.

IMF (International Monetary Fund). 2010. *Impact of the Global Financial Crisis on the Gulf Cooperation Council Countries and Challenges Ahead.* Washington, DC: International Monetary Fund.

IMF (International Monetary Fund). 2014. *Global Financial Stability Report: Risk Taking, Liquidity, and Shadow Banking.* October. Washington, DC: International Monetary Fund.

IMF (International Monetary Fund). 2015a. *Global Financial Stability Report: Vulnerabilities, Legacies, and Policy Challenges - Risks Rotating to Emerging Markets.* October. Washington, DC: International Monetary Fund.

IMF (International Monetary Fund). 2015b. *Global Financial Stability Report: Navigating Monetary Policy Challenges and Managing Risks.* April. Washington, DC: International Monetary Fund.

IMF (International Monetary Fund). 2015c. *Pan-African Banks: Opportunities and Challenges for Cross-Border Oversight.* Washington, DC: International Monetary Fund.

IMF (International Monetary Fund). 2017. *Financial Integration in Latin America: A New Strategy for a New Normal.* Washington, DC: International Monetary Fund.

IMF (International Monetary Fund). 2018a. "Financial Sector Assessment Program (FSAP): Factsheet." International Monetary Fund, Washington, DC.

IMF (International Monetary Fund). 2018b. *Global Financial Stability Report. A Decade after the Global Financial Crisis: Are We Safer?* Washington, DC: International Monetary Fund.

IMF (International Monetary Fund). 2019a. *Global Financial Stability Reports. Vulnerabilities in a Maturing Credit Cycle.* April. Washington, DC: International Monetary Fund.

IMF (International Monetary Fund). 2019b. *Global Financial Stability Report: Lower for Longer.* October. Washington, DC: International Monetary Fund.

IMF (International Monetary Fund). 2019c. *Sub-Saharan Africa. Sub-Saharan Africa Regional Economic Outlook: Recovery Amid Elevated Uncertainty.* Washington, DC: International Monetary Fund.

IMF (International Monetary Fund). 2019d. "People's Republic of China Article IV Consultation Staff Report." International Monetary Fund, Washington, DC.

IMF (International Monetary Fund) and World Bank. 2019. "Fintech: The Experience So Far." IMF Policy Paper 19/024, International Monetary Fund and World Bank, Washington, DC.

Koepke, R. 2019. "What Drives Capital Flows to Emerging Markets? A Survey of The Empirical Literature." *Journal of Economic Surveys* 33 (2): 516-40.

Laeven, L., and F. Valencia. 2018. "Systematic Banking Crises Revisited." IMF Working Paper 18/206, International Monetary Fund, Washington, DC.

Loayza, N., A. Ouazad, and R. Ranciere. 2017. "Financial Development, Growth, and Crisis. Is There a Trade-Off?" Policy Research Working Paper 8237, World Bank, Washington, DC.

McCauley, R., A. Bénétrix, P. McGuire, and G. von Peter. 2017. "Financial Deglobalization in Banking?" BIS Working Paper 650, Bank for International Settlements, Basel.

Mendoza, E., and M. Terrones. 2008. "An Anatomy of Credit Booms: Evidence from Macro Aggregates and Micro Data." NBER Working Paper 14049, National Bureau of Economic Research, Cambridge, MA.

Mendoza, E., and M. Terrones. 2012. "An Anatomy of Credit Booms and their Demise" NBER Working Paper 18379, National Bureau of Economic Research, Cambridge. MA.

Metrick, A., and J. Rhee. 2018. "Regulatory Reform." *Annual Review of Financial Economics* 10 (November): 153-72.

Mian, A., A. Sufi, and E. Verner. 2017. "Household Debt and Business Cycles Worldwide." *The Quarterly Journal of Economics* 132 (4): 1755-817.

Miyajima, K., and I. Shim. 2014. "Asset Managers in Emerging Market Economies." *BIS Quarterly Review* (September): 19-34.

Molyneux, P., A. Reghezz, and R. Xie. 2019. "Bank Margins and Profits in a World of Negative Rates." *Journal of Banking and Finance* 107 (October). Advance online publication. https://doi.org/10.1016/j.jbankfin.2019.105613.

Ohnsorge, F., and S. Yu. 2016. "Recent Credit Surge in Historical Context." Policy Research Working Paper 7704, World Bank, Washington, DC.

Pagliari, M., and S. Hannan. 2017. "The Volatility of Capital Flows in Emerging Markets: Measures and Determinants." IMF Working Paper 17/41, International Monetary Fund, Washington, DC.

Purfield, C., and C. Rosenberg. 2010. "Adjustment Under a Currency Peg : Estonia, Latvia and Lithuania During the Global Financial Crisis 2008-09." IMF Working Paper 10/213, International Monetary Fund, Washington, DC.

Rodrik, D. 2015. "Back to Fundamentals in Emerging Markets." *Project Syndicate*, August 13. https://www.project-syndicate.org/commentary/emerging-market-growth-by-dani-rodrik-2015-08.

Schaeck, K., and M. Čihák. 2012. "Banking Competition and Capital Ratios." *European Financial Management* 18 (5): 836-66.

Stellinga, B. 2019. "The Open-Endedness of Macroprudential Policy - Endogenous Risks as an Obstacle to Countercyclical Financial Regulation." *Business and Politics* (August), 1-28.

Suri, T., and W. Jack. 2016. "The Long-Run Poverty and Gender Impacts of Mobile Money." *Science* 354 (6317): 1288-92.

Ulate Campos, M. 2019. "Going Negative at the Zero Lower Bound: The Effects of Negative Nominal Interest Rates." Federal Reserve Bank of San Francisco Working Paper 2019-21.

Waller, C. J. 2016. "Negative Interest Rates: A Tax in Sheep's Clothing." *On the Economy* (blog), Federal Reserve Bank of St. Louis. May 2.

Wise C., L. Armijo, and S. Katada, eds. 2015. *Unexpected Outcomes: How Emerging Economies Survived the Global Financial Crisis.* Washington, DC: Brookings Institution Press.

World Bank. 2012. *Global Financial Development Report 2013: Rethinking the Role of the State in Finance.* Washington, DC: World Bank.

World Bank. 2014. *Global Financial Development Report 2014: Financial Inclusion.* Washington, DC: World Bank.

World Bank. 2015. *Global Financial Development Report 2015/2016: Long-Term Finance.* Washington, DC: World Bank.

World Bank. 2016. *Global Economic Prospects: Divergences and Risks.* June. Washington, DC: World Bank.

World Bank. 2018a. *Global Economic Prospects: The Turning of the Tide?* June. Washington, DC: World Bank.

World Bank. 2018b. *Global Financial Development Report 2017/2018: Bankers Without Borders.* Washington, DC: World Bank..

World Bank. 2018c. *Global Economic Prospects: Broad-Based Upturn, but for How Long?* January. Washington, DC: World Bank.

World Bank. 2018d. *The Global Findex Database 2017: Measuring Financial Inclusion and the Fintech Revolution.* Washington, DC: World Bank.

World Bank. 2018e. *Contribution of Institutional Investors Private Investment in Infrastructure 2011-H1 2017.* Washington, DC: World Bank.

World Bank. 2019a. *Global Economic Prospects: Heightened Tensions, Subdued Investments.* June. Washington, DC: World Bank.

World Bank. 2019b. *Global Economic Prospects: Darkening Skies.* January. Washington, DC: World Bank.

World Bank. 2019c. *Global Financial Development Report 2019/2020: Bank Regulation and Supervision a Decade after the Global Financial Crisis.* Washington, DC: World Bank.

The challenge for government will be to find ways to finance the deficit in a growth-positive manner, and at the same time convey a credible commitment to structural reforms that can raise the potential growth of the economy.

Lesetja Kganyago (2018)

Governor

South African Reserve Bank

CHAPTER 5

Macroeconomic and Financial Sector Policies

Unprecedented monetary policy accommodation in advanced economies and a large, coordinated fiscal stimulus by Group of Twenty countries helped to support a solid rebound in global output in 2010. Global growth subsequently slowed to a sluggish pace by prerecession standards, however, and many emerging market and developing economies have been struggling to unwind their fiscal stimulus and contain a buildup of debt. The experience of the 2009 global recession highlights not only the need for well-timed, appropriately calibrated domestic stabilization policies but also the benefits of international cooperation and coordination in support of strong and sustained global growth and financial system stability. Sound policy frameworks can help create room for stabilization policies, such as fiscal rules to safeguard fiscal sustainability or macroprudential policies and capital flow management measures to better manage systemic risks.

Introduction

In 2009, the global economy experienced the deepest recession since the Great Depression of the 1930s. Yet global growth rebounded within a year, reflecting in part the use of macroeconomic stabilization policies in many advanced economies, as well as in emerging market and developing economies (EMDEs). For the first time during a major global crisis, EMDEs actively employed a wide range of countercyclical monetary and fiscal policies to stem contagion and boost postcrisis recovery. Many EMDEs lowered policy interest rates, intervened heavily in foreign exchange markets to maintain exchange rate stability, and implemented fiscal stimulus packages.

Robust growth before the 2009 global recession had allowed EMDEs to improve their fiscal and external positions, and to strengthen their macroeconomic policy frameworks. Policy space had widened in several dimensions. Lower inflation created room for expansionary monetary policies. Fiscal balances had improved, from a deficit of 0.8 percent of gross domestic product (GDP) in 2002, on average, to a surplus of 2.4 percent in 2007. EMDEs had strengthened external buffers, too, because their foreign exchange reserves had increased substantially—70 percent of EMDEs increased their international reserves by more than 10 percentage points of external debt, while one-quarter of EMDEs increased them by more than 50 percentage points.[1]

Note: This chapter was prepared by Wee Chian Koh and Shu Yu.

[1] Some suggest that global current account imbalances are a key factor contributing to the financial crisis (for example, Bernanke 2009; Portes 2009). They argue that excessive saving in EMDEs, reflected in current account surpluses (termed as "global saving glut"), put downward pressure on world interest rates and fueled a credit boom and risk-taking in major advanced economies, particularly in the United States, sowing the seeds of the global financial crisis.

Since the global recession, however, EMDEs have mostly depleted their policy buffers. This depletion is partly due to sluggish global growth and low commodity prices. EMDEs, as a group, have not yet fully unwound their fiscal and monetary stimulus, and they face elevated fiscal and current account deficits, and growing debt. As a consequence, many EMDEs are now less resilient to adverse shocks than they were in 2007.

The global recession highlighted several shortcomings in the financial sector policies of EMDEs. For example, precrisis financial regulation and supervision tended to focus on microprudential policies, aimed at the stability of individual financial institutions, rather than on the stability of the financial system as a whole. Furthermore, the risk-weighted capital requirements of Basel II have tended to be procyclical because requirements decline as risk ratings of bank loans improve, whereas during a contraction requirements tend to rise (Admati and Hellwig 2014; Gordy and Howells 2006).

Since the global recession, financial sector policies have undergone a major transformation. They now aim more explicitly at mitigating system-wide risks in order to safeguard financial stability. Prudential supervision shifted toward a more macroprudential focus, targeting the stability of the financial system as a whole. Restrictions on capital flows, a controversial policy measure before the global recession, have since been viewed more favorably from a macroprudential perspective.

Against this backdrop, this chapter examines the following questions:

- What macroeconomic and financial sector policies characterized EMDEs prior to the global recession?
- How have EMDE macroeconomic and financial sector policies evolved since the global recession?

Contribution to the literature. Chapter 5 constitutes the first extensive stocktaking of the evolution of macroeconomic policies used by EMDEs before, during, and after the global recession. Previous studies focused on subsets of policies, such as monetary policies or fiscal policies (Cukierman 2013; de Haan et al. 2018; Ramey 2019); policies during or shortly after the global recession (Akerlof et al. 2014; Blanchard et al. 2016; Taylor 2014); or macrofinancial linkages that propagated the financial crisis (Blanchard, Faruqee, and Das 2010; Claessens and Kose 2018). Most of these existing studies do not distill policy lessons specifically for EMDEs. The chapter also provides a detailed overview of financial sector policies in EMDEs, whereas the previous literature on such policies focuses on advanced economies (IMF 2018a). The chapter distills lessons from the global recession that are relevant to EMDE policy makers today.

Main findings. This chapter reports the following findings. First, during the global recession, unprecedented coordinated monetary stimulus (in advanced economies) and fiscal stimulus (in advanced economies and EMDEs) supported a rapid rebound in global growth. Three-fifths of EMDEs with floating exchange rates had lowered their policy interest rates by the first quarter of 2009. EMDEs also made use of other measures to encourage bank lending, such as reducing reserve requirements; accepting a broader range of collateral as lender of last resort; injecting liquidity into, and recapitalizing, domestic banks; and channeling government-supported lending through development banks. In addition, the fiscal policy response was unprecedented, with large spending packages implemented by Group of Twenty (G20) economies.

Second, since the global recession, monetary policy has remained accommodative and fiscal stimulus has not been fully unwound in many EMDEs. By 2018, fiscal balances had returned to 2007 levels in only one-quarter of EMDEs and real interest rates had returned to 2007 levels in only one-half of them. Most of the EMDEs that have unwound their crisis-related fiscal stimulus were commodity importers. Many commodity-exporting EMDEs implemented procyclical policy tightening in response to the steep commodity price decline of 2011-16. Rising external, corporate, household, and government debt stocks, combined with wider fiscal and current account deficits, have increased the vulnerabilities of EMDEs to shocks.

Third, since the global recession, all advanced economies and about 70 percent of EMDEs have strengthened their macroprudential policy frameworks and the resilience of their financial systems. Several new instruments have been implemented under the Basel III framework to reduce systemic risk. EMDEs have been more aggressive than advanced economies in their use of macroprudential tools like foreign exchange and liquidity policies (for instance, limits on foreign currency loans and foreign exchange countercyclical reserve requirements) to mitigate their exposure to volatile capital inflows.

Fourth, the use of capital flow management measures as a tool to promote financial stability in appropriate circumstances has gained greater acceptance. During the global recession, many EMDEs strengthened existing capital flow management measures whereas others introduced new ones. Measures such as reserve requirements on foreign investment, taxes on currency outflows, taxes on interest and capital gains earned by nonresidents, minimum term requirements for holdings of central bank securities, and limits on foreign currency positions have often been used by EMDEs over the past decade.

Fifth, the global recession offers important lessons for policy priorities. Fiscal and monetary policy can be effective stabilization tools if they are implemented swiftly and, especially, if they are coordinated in response to global shocks. Policy stimulus, however, can have the unintended consequence of sowing the seeds for the next crisis if the stimulus is not unwound in a timely manner and if financial sector supervision and regulation are inadequate.

The rest of the chapter is structured as follows. First, the chapter describes the macroeconomic policies used by EMDEs before, during, and after the global recession. Second, it focuses on financial sector policies, including the emerging interest in complementing microprudential policies with macroprudential policies, and the renewed interest in capital flow management policies. Finally, it concludes and distills policy lessons.

Macroeconomic policies

Before the global recession: Growing policy space in EMDEs

Strong growth during 2002-07 widened policy space in many EMDEs. Lower inflation created room for monetary policy to ease substantially without undermining the credibility of central bank commitments to inflation control. Budget deficits narrowed and government debt declined, which provided governments the space to raise spending or cut taxes. Improved current account balances and rising international reserves strengthened the buffers against external shocks and boosted the confidence of investors.

Monetary buffers. Inflation remained in single digits in 82 percent of EMDEs during 2002-07, compared to only 35 percent in the preceding decade (box 5.1). Even in Latin America and the Caribbean (LAC), which had been plagued by persistently high inflation during the 1980s and 1990s, inflation was brought down to an average of 4.6 percent in 2002-07. In a notable case, Brazil's inflation rate in 2007 had fallen to 3.6 percent, compared to an average of more than 1,000 percent in the early 1990s. This broad-based disinflation reflected the strengthening by many EMDEs of their macroeconomic policy frameworks, including granting greater independence to their central banks over the conduct of monetary policy and moving toward more flexible exchange rate regimes (Ha, Kose, and Ohnsorge 2019; box 5.1).

Fiscal buffers. The fiscal position of many EMDEs improved as robust growth buoyed government revenues and lightened real debt burdens. Fiscal balances in EMDEs improved on average from a deficit of 0.8 percent of GDP in 2002 to a surplus of 2.4 percent in 2007. Government debt declined sharply from 76 percent of GDP in 2002 to 45 percent in 2007. The improvements were most pronounced in commodity exporters, which benefitted from the commodity price boom of the mid-2000s.

External buffers. Export-driven growth generated smaller current account deficits in EMDEs (up from 3.5 percent of GDP in 2001 to 1.2 percent in 2007), allowing a considerable accumulation of foreign exchange reserves (Goldstein and Xie 2009; Ocampo 2009). In about 70 percent of EMDEs, reserves increased by more than 10 percentage points of external debt between 2002 and 2007 and, in one-quarter of EMDEs, increased by more than 50 percentage points of external debt. The reserve buildup was most pronounced in the East Asia and Pacific (EAP) region, where reserves increased to 250 percent of external debt in 2007 (figure 5.1). China, with reserves of more than four times external debt in 2007, accounted for most of this increase. Among other major EMDEs, Brazil accumulated foreign reserves equivalent to 75 percent of external debt. The increases in current account surpluses and accumulation of international reserves were partly a reflection of exchange rate policies, because several countries intervened in foreign exchange markets to contain appreciation of their currencies, which both increased their reserves and helped maintain or improve their international competitiveness.

During the global recession: Stimulus

Unprecedented coordination of monetary and fiscal stimulus, in the largest advanced economies and EMDEs alike, supported a strong rebound of global output in 2010.

FIGURE 5.1 Monetary policy since the global recession

Unprecedentedly coordinated monetary policy accommodation in advanced economies supported a rebound in global growth. EMDE central banks also loosened their monetary policies, in contrast to previous crises. During the global financial crisis, a large number of EMDEs intervened in foreign exchange markets to support their currencies and to ensure an orderly financial system.

A. Monetary policy in advanced economies

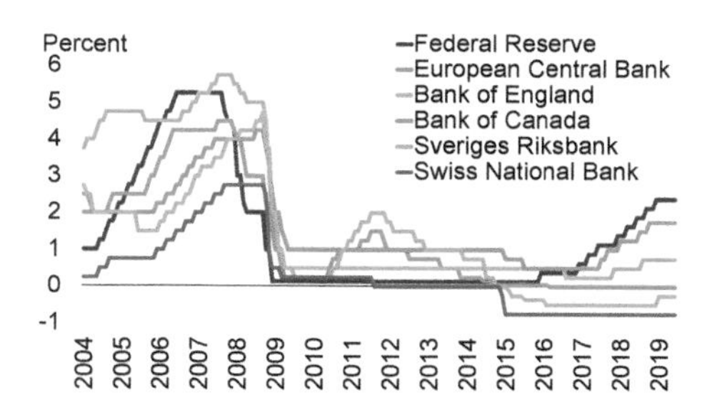

B. EMDE policy interest rates around previous crises

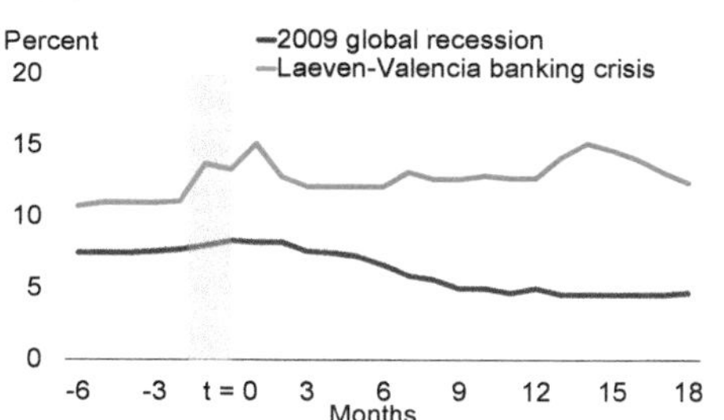

C. Nominal effective exchange rates in EAP around crises

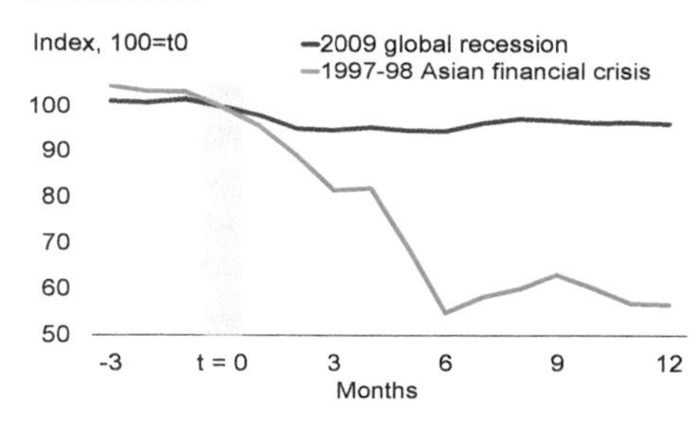

D. Foreign reserves

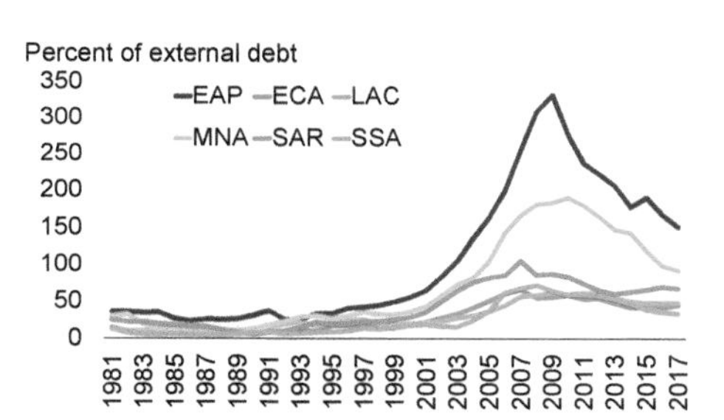

Sources: Bank for International Settlements; Darvas (2012); Laeven and Valencia (2018); Haver Analytics; World Bank.
Note: EAP = East Asia and Pacific; ECA = Europe and Central Asia; EMDEs = emerging market and developing economies; LAC = Latin America and the Caribbean; MNA = Middle East and North Africa; SAR = South Asia; SSA = Sub-Saharan Africa.
B. Median policy rates. The country sample (based on data availability) in the Laeven-Valencia banking crisis episodes consists of Argentina, Bulgaria, Colombia, Croatia, Czech Republic, Hungary, Malaysia, Philippines, the Russian Federation, and Vietnam. The starting dates (t = 0) are defined by Laeven and Valencia (2018). The country sample in the 2009 global recession consists of 26 EMDEs. t = 0 for the 2009 global recession is September 2008.
C. A decline denotes nominal effective depreciation. The East Asian countries are Indonesia, the Republic of Korea, Malaysia, Philippines, Singapore, and Thailand. t = 0 for the crisis episodes (and global recession) are July 1997 and September 2008.

EMDE central banks, having accumulated large foreign reserves and tamed inflation before the crisis, were able to intervene heavily in foreign exchange markets in support of their currencies and lower policy interest rates. In addition, EMDE governments announced fiscal packages that included infrastructure investment, tax cuts, and social protection programs.

Monetary stimulus in advanced economies. In response to slowing output growth and escalating threats to financial stability, six major central banks—the U.S. Federal Reserve, the Bank of Canada, the Bank of England, the European Central Bank (ECB), the Sveriges Riksbank, and the Swiss National Bank—announced policy rate cuts simultaneously in October 2008 (figure 5.1). It was the first-ever coordinated monetary policy response to a financial crisis or recession (BIS 2009).[2] By May 2009, policy rates of the major central banks had been reduced to nearly zero, except for the ECB and Bank of Canada, which stopped their rate cuts well before reaching the zero lower bound (Arteta et al. 2015). In several advanced economies, rate cuts were complemented with capital injections or emergency funding for financial institutions (U.S. Department of Treasury 2013).

Despite lower funding costs, banks globally tightened credit standards, so financial conditions faced by borrowers did not ease by nearly as much as the cuts in policy rates might indicate. To boost credit availability, major central banks subsequently broadened the scope of their policy to include quantitative easing programs—large-scale purchases of government bonds and private sector assets and credit provision—and forward guidance on monetary policy, both aimed at lowering longer-term rates (Carstens 2019). The asset purchases resulted in substantial changes in the size and composition of the balance sheets of central banks.[3]

The U.S. Federal Reserve also coordinated swap arrangements with other major central banks to address the shortage of U.S. dollar funding among non-U.S. banks. By the end of 2008, the U.S. Federal Reserve had extended swap lines to all major central banks as well as to Australia, Brazil, Denmark, the Republic of Korea, Mexico, New Zealand, Norway, and Sweden. Within Europe, central banks had similar swap arrangements for short-term funding in the euro and Swiss franc.

Although these policy responses addressed the immediate funding needs of banks and succeeded in averting a collapse of the financial system, the bankruptcy of Lehman Brothers in September 2008 caused serious concerns about the solvency of many systematically important financial institutions. As a result, additional measures were undertaken by governments in advanced economies to stabilize markets and institutions, including providing deposit and debt guarantees, capital injections to increase bank solvency, and asset purchases.

Monetary stimulus in EMDEs. Against the backdrop of a decade of low inflation, improved policy frameworks, and high international reserves, EMDEs also pursued monetary policy accommodation. Three-fifths of central banks in EMDEs with floating exchange rates lowered policy rates by the first quarter of 2009 (Ha, Kose, and Ohnsorge 2019).[4] Some low-income countries (LICs), mostly in Sub-Saharan Africa (SSA), eased

---

[2] The Bank of Japan, with a policy rate already very low, at 0.5 percent, did not ease, but expressed strong support for the coordinated policy action.

[3] The U.S. Federal Reserve began its quantitative easing program in November 2008, the Bank of England in March 2009, and the ECB in May 2009. These programs of large-scale purchases of longer-term assets were intended mainly to lower longer-term interest rates, partly through a "signaling effect" (that is, by boosting investor confidence in these assets) and, more important, through a "portfolio balance effect" through which the asset purchases would reduce the availability of such assets to the private sector, thus raising their prices and lowering their yields.

[4] Based on 39 EMDEs with available data on exchange rate regimes and monetary policy rates. In the early stages of the crisis, EMDEs increased policy rates to stem rising inflation because growth remained robust, whereas in advanced economies growth had weakened. EMDEs started to cut rates in late 2008 and early 2009.

BOX 5.1 Disinflation in emerging market and developing economies

Emerging market and developing economies (EMDEs) have achieved a remarkable decline in inflation, from a median rate over 17 percent in 1974 to about 3 percent in 2018. This achievement has coincided with an even sharper decline in inflation in advanced economies. What may be called the "great disinflation" in EMDEs has been accompanied by growing inflation synchronization as evidenced by the emergence of a global inflation cycle. It has been supported by long-term trends such as the widespread adoption of robust monetary policy frameworks and strengthening of global trade and financial integration. The 2009 global recession also contributed to the decline in inflation. If the wave of structural and policy-related factors that have driven disinflation since the 1970s loses momentum or is reversed, however, policy makers may find that maintaining low inflation can be as great a challenge as achieving it.

Introduction

Emerging market and developing economies (EMDEs) have achieved a remarkable decline in inflation since the mid-1970s (Ha, Kose, and Ohnsorge 2019).[a] Median annual national consumer price index (CPI) inflation in EMDEs fell from stubbornly persistent double-digit rates during the 1970s to about 3 percent in 2018 (figure B5.1.1). By 2018, inflation was within or below central bank target ranges in three-quarters of the EMDEs that had adopted inflation targeting. The decline in inflation began in the mid-1980s in advanced economies and in the mid-1990s in EMDEs. By 2000, global inflation had stabilized at historically low levels.

Low and stable inflation has historically been associated with steady and faster economic growth and better development outcomes. But it remains to be seen whether EMDEs can continue to enjoy low inflation if the confluence of structural and policy-related factors that have fostered global disinflation over recent decades is not sustained.

Against this backdrop, this box addresses the following questions:

- How has EMDE inflation evolved?
- How important is global inflation in explaining national inflation in EMDEs?
- Can EMDEs sustain low inflation?

Evolution of inflation: A remarkable conquest

Disinflation. EMDEs have witnessed a significant decline in inflation since the mid-1970s, with median annual national CPI inflation down from a peak of 17.6

Note: This box was prepared by Jongrim Ha.

a. The "near-universal" character of the decline in inflation since the mid-1970s was recognized at an early stage by Rogoff (2003).

BOX 5.1 Disinflation in emerging market and developing economies *(continued)*

FIGURE B5.1.1 Inflation and inflation expectations

EMDE inflation remains near the historic lows of 2015 despite a recent normalization in inflation in some advanced economies. Inflation is now below inflation targets (or within target ranges) in most EMDEs.

A. Median annual CPI inflation, by country group

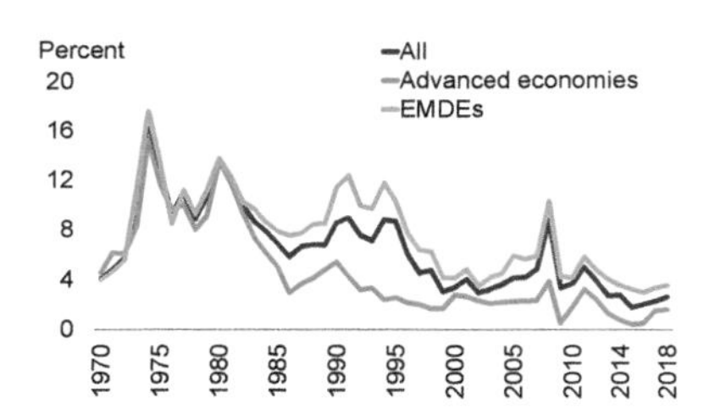

B. Shares of advanced economies and EMDEs with inflation below targets (or within target ranges)

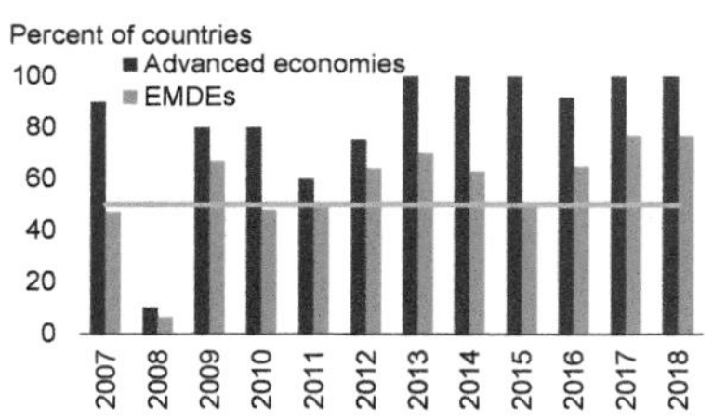

Sources: Bloomberg; Consensus Economics; Haver Analytics; World Bank.

Note: CPI = consumer price index; EMDEs= emerging market and developing economies; LICs = low-income countries.

A. Median year-on-year change in CPI for 29 advanced economies and 126 EMDEs (including 29 LICs).

B. All inflation rates refer to year-on-year inflation. Share of inflation-targeting countries with inflation below target (or within target range). Horizontal line indicates 50 percent.

percent in 1974 to 3.5 percent in 2018. Disinflation over recent decades has been broad-based across regions and country groups.[b] For example, disinflation occurred across all EMDE regions, including those with a history of persistently high inflation, such as Latin America and the Caribbean, and Sub-Saharan Africa (figure B5.1.2).[c] Even among low-income countries (LICs), inflation fell sharply between the mid-1970s (about 15 percent a year) and 2018 (3.9 percent), although there is larger variability in national inflation rates among LICs than among other EMDEs.

EMDE disinflation occurred against the backdrop of even sharper disinflation among advanced economies, where median inflation dropped from its highest rate in 60 years in 1974 (15.0 percent) to its lowest in 2015 (0.4 percent). Since 2015, it has risen somewhat to 1.6 percent in 2018 but remains below the median inflation target of advanced economy central banks. After 2008, below-target inflation and, in some cases, deflation became pervasive across advanced economies: for example, in 2015, inflation was negative in more than half of

b. Disinflation is a decline in inflation rates, regardless of inflation being negative (deflation) or positive.

c. But inflation remains in double-digits in the Arab Republic of Egypt, the Islamic Republic of Iran, Nigeria, and Turkey, often reflecting currency depreciation.

BOX 5.1 Disinflation in emerging market and developing economies *(continued)*

FIGURE B5.1.2 Factors associated with disinflation

Inflation has declined in all EMDE regions and low-income countries. In most EMDEs, annual inflation is now below 5 percent. Lower inflation is associated with greater trade and financial openness. Inflation also tends to be lower in countries that employ inflation targeting and have more independent and transparent central banks.

A. Median CPI inflation, by region

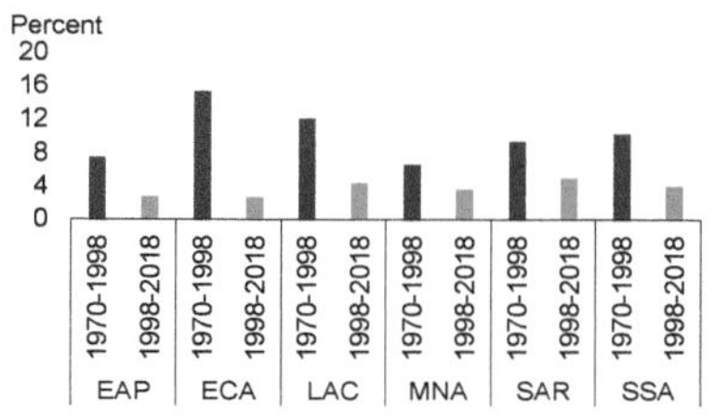

B. Inflation in low-income countries

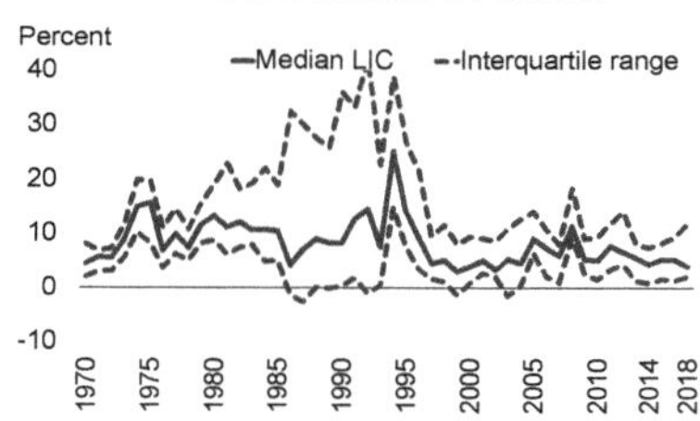

C. Distribution of inflation in EMDEs

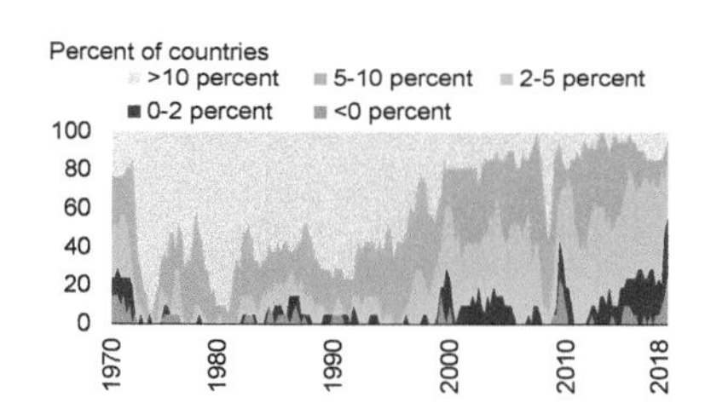

D. Inflation, by trade and financial openness

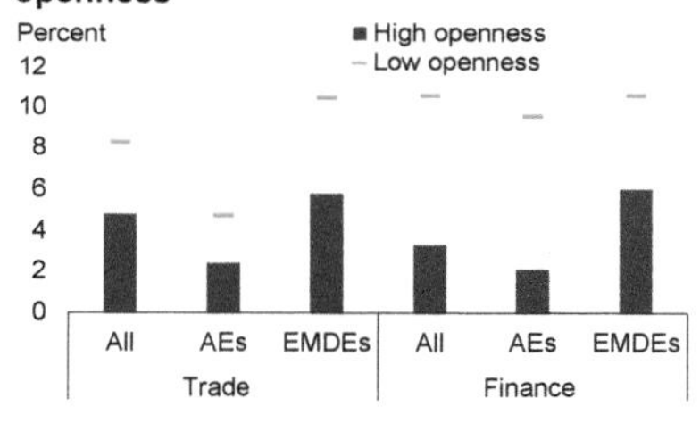

E. Inflation, by index of central bank independence and transparency

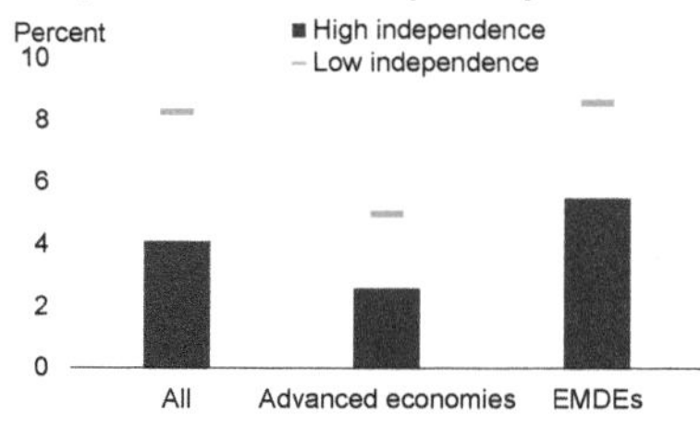

F. Inflation, by monetary policy regime

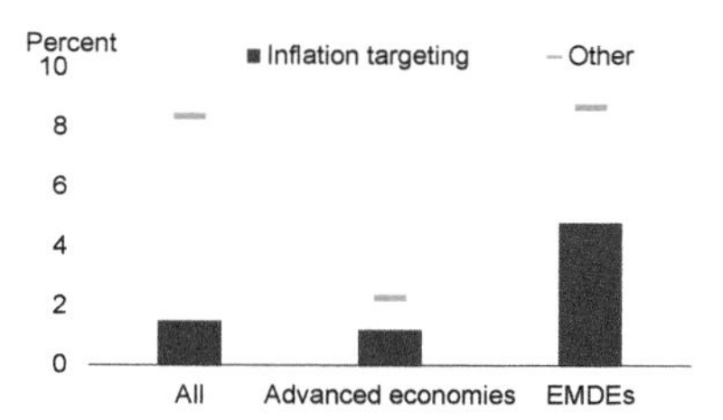

Sources: Ha, Kose, and Ohnsorge (2019); Haver Analytics; International Monetary Fund; Organisation for Economic Co-operation and Development.

Note: Median headline CPI (consumer price index) inflation of 29 advanced economies (AEs) and 123 EMDEs. EAP = East Asia and Pacific; ECA = Europe and Central Asia; EMDEs = emerging market and developing economies; LAC = Latin America and the Caribbean; LICs = low-income countries; MNA = Middle East and North Africa; SAR = South Asia; SSA = Sub-Saharan Africa.

B. Solid line shows median inflation and dotted lines refer to interquartile ranges, based on 29 LICs.

C. Inflation refers to quarter-on-quarter annualized inflation. Sample includes 50 EMDEs.

D. Columns indicate median inflation in countries with high trade-to-GDP ratios ("Trade") or high levels of financial assets and liabilities relative to GDP ("Finance") in the top quartile ("high openness") of 175 economies during 1970 -2017. Horizontal bars indicate countries in the bottom quartile ("low openness").

E.F. Columns indicate median inflation in country-year pairs with a central bank transparency index in the top quartile (E) or with inflation targeting monetary policy regimes (F). Horizontal bars denote medians in the bottom quartile (E) or with monetary policy regimes that are not inflation targeting (F).

D.-F. Differences are significant at the 5 percent level.

BOX 5.1 Disinflation in emerging market and developing economies *(continued)*

advanced economies. Some advanced economy central banks have struggled to lift inflation back to their inflation targets over the past decade.

Drivers of low inflation. Although the global financial crisis played a major role in pushing inflation down around the world over the past decade, a wide range of structural changes has supported the longer-term trend of disinflation. The most significant of these changes have been the widespread adoption of more effective and transparent monetary, exchange rate, and fiscal policy frameworks as well as globalization (figure B5.1.2).[d]

- *Macroeconomic policies.* In the second half of the 1980s and during the 1990s, many EMDEs implemented programs of macroeconomic stabilization and structural reform, and gave their central banks greater independence and clearer mandates to achieve and maintain low inflation. The adoption of more resilient policy frameworks has facilitated more effective control of inflation (Fischer 2015; Taylor 2014). Twenty-four EMDEs have introduced inflation-targeting monetary policy frameworks since the late 1990s; in the median EMDE, the Dincer-Eichengreen index of central bank independence and transparency rose more than 150 percent between 1990 and 2014. Inflation tends to be lower in countries that employ an inflation-targeting framework and that have more independent and transparent central banks. Changes in fiscal policy frameworks have also contributed: fiscal rules have been adopted in 88 countries, including 49 EMDEs (Ha et al. 2019). Other reforms, including labor market and product market liberalization, and the removal or easing of foreign exchange market controls, also assisted the disinflation process.
- *International trade and financial integration.* Inflation tends to be lower in economies that are more open to trade and financial flows. With regard to trade, in both the median EMDE and the median advanced economy, the ratio of trade (exports plus imports) to gross domestic product (GDP) increased by half between 1970 and 2017, to 75 percent of GDP in the case of EMDEs. Increasing international integration of product markets has contributed to lower inflation partly because increased openness to imports in consumption and production has increased competition in domestic markets. In addition, the growth of manufacturing production and exports in EMDEs (particularly China, where labor costs are relatively low) has played an important role in lowering CPI inflation worldwide. Increased financial integration has helped discipline macroeconomic policies: more financially

d. Other structural changes have also been important (Ha et al. 2019). For example, technological advances, including the digitalization of services and automation of manufacturing, have transformed production processes that attenuated inflation pressures. Population aging may also have contributed.

BOX 5.1 Disinflation in emerging market and developing economies *(continued)*

FIGURE B5.1.3 Inflation synchronization

Inflation has become increasingly globally synchronized. The "global factor" accounts for a greater share of inflation variance in advanced economies than in EMDEs, and is more important in explaining the variance of price indexes with a greater tradable goods and services content.

A. Contribution of global factor to inflation variation

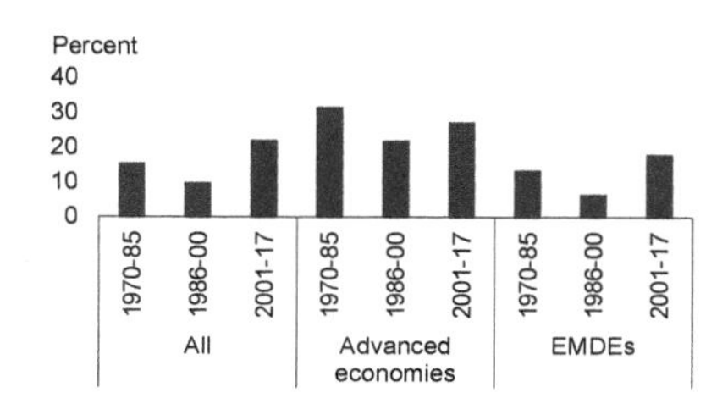

B. Contributions of global factors to inflation variation, by inflation measure

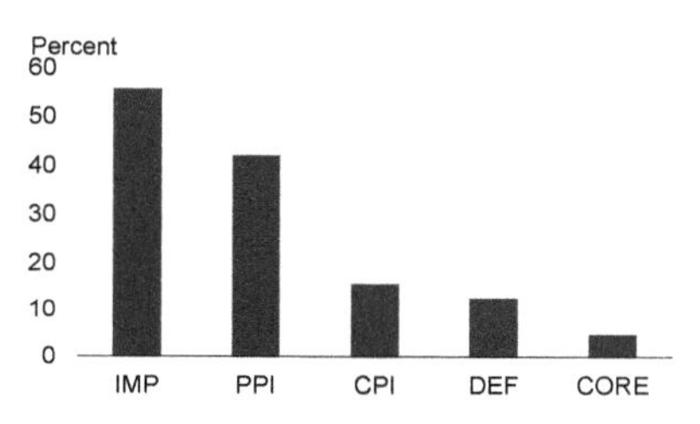

Sources: Ha, Kose, and Ohnsorge (2019); World Bank.

A. The results are based on a two-factor dynamic factor model with inflation using a sample of 99 economies (25 advanced economies and 74 emerging market and developing economies (EMDEs) for 1970-2017. The model includes global and group inflation factors. All numbers refer to median variance shares of total inflation variance accounted for by the global factor.

B. Global inflation factors are estimated with two-factor dynamic factor models for annual inflation for each measure in 38 countries (25 advanced economies and 13 EMDEs) for the period 1970-2016, the size of the sample being constrained by data availability. CORE = core consumer price index; CPI = headline consumer price index; DEF = GDP deflator; IMP = import price index; PPI = producer price index.

integrated economies are more likely to implement monetary policies targeting low and stable inflation (Kose et al. 2010). In EMDEs, international assets and liabilities tripled (although they remain only half the level of advanced economies).

Global inflation cycle: Getting stronger

A critical feature of the international inflation experience of the past four to five decades has been the emergence of a "global inflation cycle" (Ciccarelli and Mojon 2010). This cycle is reflected in a growing contribution of a common "global factor" to the variation in country-level inflation rates. To analyze its importance, a dynamic factor model is estimated for annual CPI inflation rates in 25 advanced economies and 74 EMDEs during 1970-2017 (Ha, Kose, and Ohnsorge 2019). The model includes a common global factor as well as group factors specific to advanced economies and EMDEs, respectively. The presence of group factors allows the model to account for the large differences in country characteristics between advanced economies and EMDEs.

BOX 5.1 Disinflation in emerging market and developing economies *(continued)*

Global inflation factor. Inflation has become increasingly globally synchronized (figure B5.1.3). The contribution of the global factor to inflation variation has grown over time: since 2001, it has almost doubled, and it now accounts for 22 percent of inflation variation (Ha, Kose, and Ohnsorge 2019). In this period, it explains about one-fifth and one-quarter, respectively, of inflation variation in EMDEs and advanced economies. Over the past four decades, the EMDE-specific factor has also become more important. The rising importance of these global and group-specific factors indicates that inflation synchronization has become more broad-based over time.

Tradables versus nontradables. The role of the global factor has been more prominent in price baskets with a larger tradables content. The global factor's contribution to inflation variation was largest for import prices (54 percent in the median country) and smallest for core CPI inflation (5 percent). Between these two extremes, the global factor's contribution to variation in producer price index inflation was 42 percent and that for GDP deflator growth was 13 percent and comparable to that for headline CPI inflation.

Maintaining low inflation: A challenge

The future maintenance of low inflation cannot be taken for granted (Carstens 2018; Draghi 2015; Rogoff 2014). If cyclical and structural forces become less disinflationary over the next decade than they have been over the past five decades, inflation could rise globally. The strengthening global inflation cycle could put upward pressure on EMDE inflation. More important, structural and policy-related factors that have helped lower inflation over the past several decades may lose momentum or be reversed amid mounting populist sentiment.

- *Slowing globalization.* The rising protectionist sentiment of recent years may slow the pace of globalization or put it into reverse. New tariffs and import restrictions have been put in place in advanced economies and EMDEs since 2017. The risk of further escalation in trade restrictions by major economies remains elevated.

- *Weakening monetary policy frameworks.* A shift from a strong mandate of inflation control to objectives related to the financing of government would undermine the credibility of monetary policy frameworks and raise inflation expectations. In the past, declines in EMDE central bank independence and transparency have been associated with significantly less well-anchored inflation expectations and greater pass-through of exchange rate movements to inflation.

- *Weakening fiscal policy frameworks.* Growing populist sentiment or persistently weak economic growth could trigger a move away from rules-based, or otherwise disciplined, fiscal policies. Fiscal rules can become ineffective once

BOX 5.1 Disinflation in emerging market and developing economies *(continued)*

FIGURE B5.1.4 Low inflation episodes

Global inflation has been low and stable before: during most of the 1950s and 1960s under the Bretton Woods fixed exchange rate system and during the gold standard of the early 1900s.

Global inflation

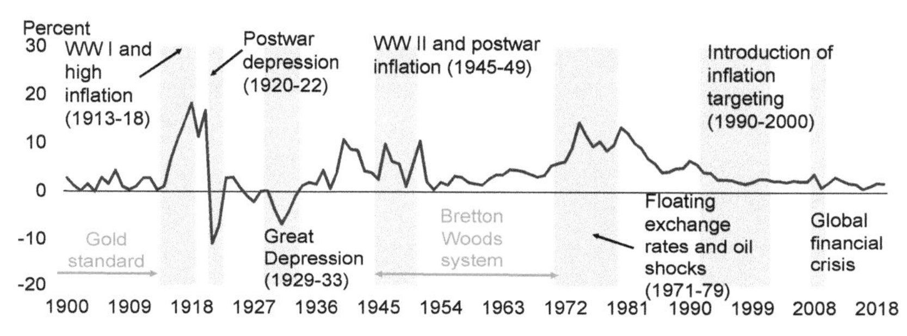

Source: World Bank.
Note: Median of annual average inflation in a sample of 24 economies for which data are available across the full period.

commitment to them falters (Wyplosz 2013). Mounting public and private debt in EMDEs could also weaken commitments to strong fiscal and monetary policy frameworks. Government or private sector debt (or both) has risen in more than half of EMDEs since 2012, including in many LICs (World Bank 2018b). EMDE sovereign credit ratings have continued to deteriorate, with some falling below investment grade, reflecting concerns about rising government debt and deteriorating growth prospects.

If unwanted inflation makes a comeback, policy frameworks may be tested in EMDEs: inflation expectations in these economies are generally less well-anchored than in advanced economies, and the absence of strong monetary policy frameworks in many of them means that inflation is sensitive to exchange rate movements (Ha, Stocker, and Yilmazkuday 2019; Kose et al. 2019). Growing inflation synchronization also increases the risk of policy errors when the appropriate response depends on the origin of the underlying inflation shock (IMF 2018b).[e] EMDE central banks may struggle to contain inflationary pressures and may not receive adequate support from fiscal policy.

e. Major advanced economy central banks have also acknowledged the need to consider the global environment in setting monetary policy in light of the highly synchronized nature of global inflation (Bernanke 2007; Carney 2015; Draghi 2015).

BOX 5.1 Disinflation in emerging market and developing economies *(continued)*

History teaches us that it is difficult to sustain low inflation. For example, the 1950s and 1960s under the Bretton Woods fixed exchange rate system and the period of the gold standard in the early 1900s were followed by sharply rising inflation (figure B5.1.4). The steep increase in oil prices in 1973-74 led to a rapid acceleration in global inflation, accompanied by sharp declines in growth in many countries (Kose and Terrones 2015). Global inflationary pressures also led to significant increases in domestic inflation in developing economies, including those that had experienced relatively low and stable inflation in the late 1960s and early 1970s (Cline 1981). All three episodes of sustained low inflation are characterized by inflation below 5 percent for an extended period. Such experiences illustrate the fact that maintaining low inflation can be as great a challenge as achieving low inflation.

EMDE policy makers need to recognize the increasing role of the global inflation cycle in driving domestic inflation. Options to help insulate economies from the impact of global shocks include strengthening institutions, including central bank independence, and establishing fiscal frameworks that can both ensure long-run debt sustainability and provide room for effective countercyclical policies.

monetary policy when inflation pressures subsided amid lower energy and food prices (IMF 2010a). The monetary easing during the crisis stands in sharp contrast to, for example, the 1997-98 Asian financial crisis when many of the affected countries had exchange rate targets, and raised policy rates in attempts to prevent large currency depreciations (figure 5.1).

EMDEs adopted a wide range of additional monetary instruments during this period. Central banks in EAP (China, Malaysia), LAC (Brazil, Colombia, Peru), and South Asia (SAR; India) reduced reserve requirements whereas others accepted a broader range of collateral as lender of last resort (Argentina, Chile, the Czech Republic).[5] Some central banks in the Middle East and North Africa (MNA) and SSA injected liquidity into domestic banking systems (Nigeria, Tunisia) or recapitalized domestic banks (Algeria, Kenya, Mali). Brazil, China, Colombia, and the Philippines also loosened financial conditions by increasing government-financed lending, channeled through their development banks. During 2007-09, the combined loan portfolio of development banks increased by 36 percent, well above the 10 percent increase in commercial bank credit (de Luna-Martínez and Vicente 2012).

[5] In the run-up to and in the wake of the global financial crisis, several EMDEs such as Brazil, Colombia, Indonesia, and Thailand introduced capital controls and other measures to manage exchange rate pressures (Gallagher 2015; IMF 2012; World Bank 2009). Some EMDEs also implemented unconventional monetary policy (García-Cicco and Kawamura 2014).

Foreign exchange market support. In addition to injecting monetary policy stimulus, many EMDE central banks used a variety of tools to ease downward pressures on their exchange rates.[6] In 2009, about one-fifth of EMDEs intervened in foreign exchange markets to support their currencies and, on average, these countries used 15 percent of their international reserves (figure 5.1). Such operations included selling foreign currency in the spot market (Brazil, India, Mexico) and engaging in swap market auctions (Brazil, Hungary, Poland). Other measures included setting up repo facilities (Argentina, Brazil, the Philippines), providing guarantees on currency deposits (India, Malaysia, Turkey), and changing regulations to facilitate foreign borrowing (Chile, India). Some central banks established loan facilities.[7] In the fourth quarter of 2008, the U.S. Federal Reserve extended swap lines to Brazil, Korea, Mexico, and Singapore; while the ECB and the Swiss National Bank provided support to Hungary and Poland through swap and repurchase agreements.[8]

Fiscal stimulus during the crisis. Beginning in late 2008, concerns that monetary stimulus would not be sufficient to avert sharp output contractions led to an unprecedented use of countercyclical fiscal policy responses by major economies (figure 5.2). G20 countries concurrently introduced fiscal stimulus packages, equivalent to 1.4 percent of global GDP (IILS 2011).[9] Among advanced economies, the packages adopted in the United States, euro area, and Japan amounted to 5.6, 2.0, and 7.9 percent of annual GDP, respectively (Cottarelli, Gerson, and Senhadji 2014; ECB 2010; OECD 2009).[10] China adopted the largest stimulus package, equivalent to 12.7 percent of GDP. Other G20 EMDEs, such as India, the Russian Federation, Saudi Arabia, South Africa, and Turkey, also implemented large fiscal stimulus packages.

Outside the G20, several countries (the Arab Republic of Egypt, the Philippines, Singapore, Vietnam) also announced large fiscal stimulus packages (more than 4 percent of GDP; Nanto 2009). Several commodity exporters that had accumulated large sovereign wealth funds during the 2002-07 commodity price boom (Kuwait, Qatar, the United Arab Emirates) implemented countercyclical fiscal stimulus (IMF 2010b). Governments in several LICs, such as Kenya and Tanzania, also increased government spending, mostly on infrastructure and other public investments (Osakwe 2010).[11] In contrast, many Europe and Central Asia (ECA) countries could not adopt sizable fiscal stimulus programs because of severely constrained government finances. Several

[6] China faced upward pressures instead; the central bank accumulated foreign reserves until mid-2014.

[7] Many EMDEs with less developed financial systems lack the administrative capacity or policy credibility to implement effective countercyclical measures (Allen and Giovannetti 2011). Monetary policy in these countries has therefore focused on boosting credit supply by using non-interest rate instruments (Binici and Yörükoğlu 2011).

[8] Colombia, Mexico, and Poland also obtained access to the International Monetary Fund's Flexible Credit Line for countries with sound fundamentals.

[9] At the November 2008 G20 Summit in Washington, DC, leaders of the G20 countries pledged rapid action to use fiscal measures to stimulate domestic demand.

[10] Estimating the size of fiscal stimulus packages is complicated by an often unclear breakdown of old and new spending and an uncertain time frame for implementation. Hence, estimates from different sources may differ substantially (Cottarelli, Gerson, and Senhadji 2014).

[11] Kenya graduated to middle-income status in 2016.

FIGURE 5.2 Fiscal policy since the global recession

Fiscal stimulus in the largest advanced economies and EMDEs supported a swift recovery in global output. Advanced economies have gradually unwound their fiscal stimulus since the crisis, but fiscal stimulus has not been fully unwound in many EMDEs and policy buffers have deteriorated.

A. Share of EMDEs with debt on rising trajectories

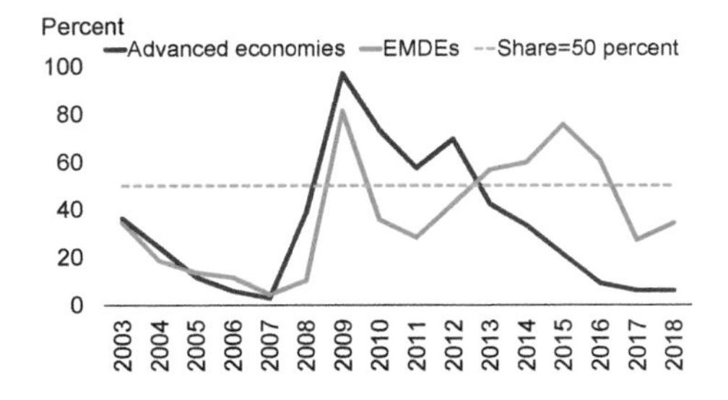

B. Fiscal balance

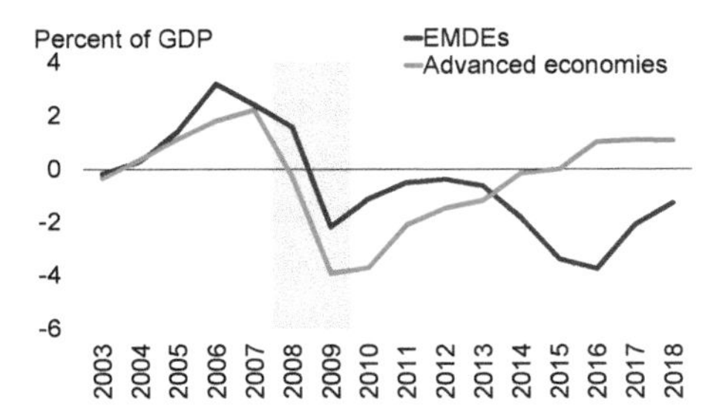

C. Fiscal balance in selected major advanced economies

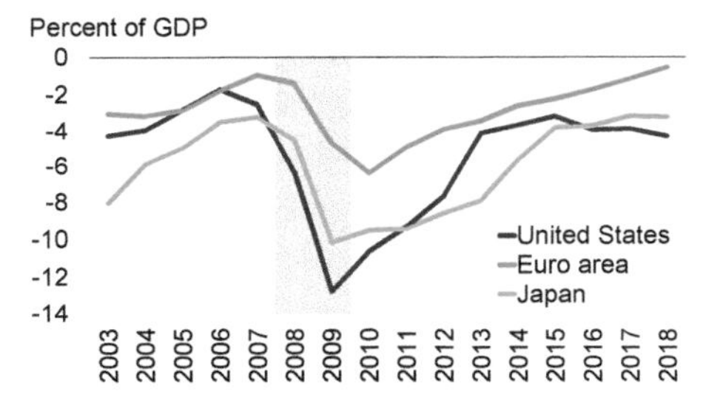

D. Fiscal balance in selected major EMDEs

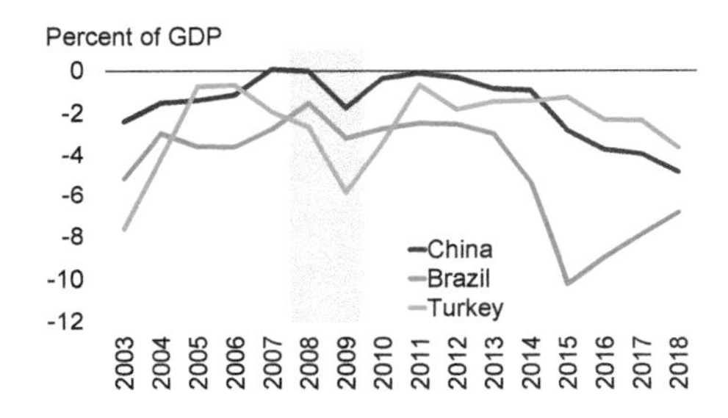

Sources: European Central Bank; Kose et al. (2017); World Bank.

A. Share of emerging market and developing economies (EMDEs) with sustainability gaps below -1 percent of GDP, that is, government debt on a clearly rising trajectory even at current low interest rates. Lines reflect GDP-weighted averages for corresponding country groups. The sustainability gap is the difference between the actual primary balance and the debt-stabilizing primary balance at current interest and growth rates.

B. Lines show simple averages for corresponding country groups.

economies in this region (Hungary, Kyrgyz Republic, Ukraine) sought emergency lending from the International Monetary Fund.

The composition of the fiscal stimulus packages varied widely. In the United States and the euro area, the measures consisted mainly of tax cuts and increases in transfers, which tend to have lower fiscal multipliers (Ramey 2019). In contrast, China's fiscal stimulus package focused primarily on infrastructure investment, which tends to have large multipliers (Leduc and Wilson 2014). Given the high import content of investment spending, this package also benefitted regions with close trade links to China (SAR for manufacturing and LAC, MNA, and SSA for commodities). Other EMDEs, such as India, Mexico, and South Africa, also channeled their stimulus into infrastructure investment to close infrastructure gaps. Some countries introduced new social protection programs, such as conditional cash transfer schemes (CCTs) in

2008-09; others either expanded existing coverage of CCTs or increased benefits (Fiszbein, Ringold, and Srinivasan 2011).[12]

During the global recession, most EMDEs implemented discretionary fiscal stimulus on a larger scale than in earlier global contractions and allowed automatic fiscal stabilizers to operate unimpeded (World Bank 2015). Economies with relatively wide fiscal space (that is, with government debt below 40 percent of GDP) were able to implement greater fiscal stimulus than more indebted governments with narrower fiscal space (box 5.2; figure 5.2). Widening fiscal deficits, however, were reflected in rapidly rising debt.

After the global recession: Partial policy tightening

Countries have by and large not fully reversed the postcrisis policy stimulus, in part because of protracted weakness in postcrisis growth. Since the global recession, monetary policy has remained highly accommodative in advanced economies and EMDEs. Although the postcrisis plunge in commodity prices forced a policy tightening in commodity exporters, EMDE fiscal and external positions have generally worsened.

Gradual unwinding of fiscal stimulus in advanced economies. Early this decade, large government fiscal deficits and rising debt in advanced economies, resulting partly from the fiscal stimulus and financial rescue packages, raised concerns about fiscal sustainability. Some euro area countries with large deficits at times faced acute market concerns about sovereign risk. Despite austerity measures in Greece, Ireland, Italy, Portugal, and Spain, these market concerns spilled into the banking sector, which had accumulated sizable government debt holdings. A series of bailout packages organized under new standing facilities backed by the European Union and the International Monetary Fund, as well as expanded bond purchases by the ECB, provided crucial support to these economies.

The euro area's fiscal balance has gradually improved since 2011, and the deficit-to-GDP ratio had almost returned to its 2007 level by 2018 (figure 5.2). The fiscal deficit of the United States fell from about 13 percent of GDP in 2009 to just over 3 percent in 2015, but has since risen to over 4 percent in 2018. Japan maintained an expansionary fiscal stance on reconstruction efforts following the 2011 earthquake, but fiscal deficits have gradually declined.

Slow withdrawal of monetary accommodation in advanced economies. Since the crisis, monetary policy in the major advanced economies has remained highly accommodative (Arteta et al. 2018; box 4.2). In part, it has reflected concerns about the possibility of secular stagnation, which posits that chronic demand weakness lowers potential growth

[12] As shown in Fiszbein, Ringold, and Srinivasan (2011), examples of new CCT programs implemented between 2008 and 2009 include Indonesia's Bantuan Langsung Tunai (existed in 2005 and started again in 2008 as a one-off program) and Senegal's Social Cash Transfer and Nutritional Security (lasted for 6 months in 2009). Kenya's Orphan and Vulnerable Children program (launched in 2004 with the scaled-up program rolled out in 2010, still operating) and the Philippines' Pantawid Pamilyang Pilipino Program have been scaled up (carried out in 2008, still operating). In 2008, Brazil's Bolsa Familia (created in 2003, still running) and Mexico's Oportunidades (created in 1997, still running), have expanded their coverage and increased the amount of household transfers.

(Summers 2014). During the recovery, major central banks have kept policy rates at, or a little above, the historically low levels attained after the crisis. The U.S. Federal Reserve started to raise the federal funds rate from close to zero in December 2015, and its target range for the rate reached 2.25-2.50 percent in late 2018 before being reduced by 25 basis points one year later. But, a decade after the global recession, euro area and Japanese policy rates remain negative.

In addition, central banks continued their large-scale asset purchases well after the global financial crisis. To boost the sluggish recovery, the U.S. Federal Reserve undertook several rounds of such asset purchases between late 2008 and October 2014. The ECB announced several asset purchase facilities during 2011-16, including an expanded asset purchase program in March 2015. Although the program was due to be phased out after December 2018, the weakness of the euro area economy in the following year has prompted the ECB to announce preparations for an additional round of purchases. The Bank of Japan, over the same period, also introduced new asset purchase programs. Despite slowing its quantitative easing program in December 2018, it has maintained a highly accommodative policy stance.

Delayed unwinding of stimulus in most EMDEs. Several EMDEs that had introduced fiscal and monetary stimulus in 2009-10 gradually, but only partially, unwound this stimulus starting in 2010. By 2018, only one-quarter of EMDEs had returned their fiscal deficit-to-GDP ratios to 2007 levels, and about one-half had returned their real interest rates to 2007 levels (figure 5.3). Most of the EMDEs that fully unwound their crisis-related fiscal stimulus were commodity importers.

Several large EMDEs have not reversed their fiscal stimulus at all since 2011. In China, to deal with potential financial stability risks, the government reined in investment by local governments, discouraged financing through the nonbank system, tightened housing market regulations, and slowed the growth of bank lending (World Bank 2014).[13] The government subsequently embarked on additional rounds of stimulus spending in 2015-16 and 2018-19. Similarly, in India, fiscal and monetary stimulus by the central government was only partially unwound until 2016, when policy loosening resumed.[14] In Brazil, the unwinding of crisis-related fiscal stimulus was also delayed.[15] Turkey has struggled to unwind its spending increases and its policy interest rates remained negative in real terms despite double-digit inflation and rapid credit growth since 2017 (Gürkaynak et al. 2015). The persistence of large budget deficits has meant that EMDE debt sustainability indicators have steadily deteriorated since 2011. In more

[13] The People's Bank of China raised its policy interest rate by 1.25 percentage points between October 2010 and May 2012, but subsequently pursued a more accommodative monetary policy, including a reduction of the required reserve ratio.

[14] The general government deficit declined from 9.5 percent of GDP in 2009 to 6.9 percent in 2019, despite a large stimulus package carried out in 2017 to support the ailing banking sector and to boost infrastructure investment. The Reserve Bank of India raised policy rates by 3.75 percentage points between February 2010 and October 2011 but has since lowered them.

[15] Brazil's fiscal deficit deteriorated from 3.2 percent of GDP in 2009 to 10.2 percent of GDP in 2015, before a slight improvement in 2016-18.

FIGURE 5.3 Fiscal vulnerabilities in EMDEs since the global recession

Fiscal positions in many EMDEs have deteriorated compared to precrisis positions. In addition to rising government debt, the stocks of external, corporate, and household debt have also risen.

A. Fiscal balance

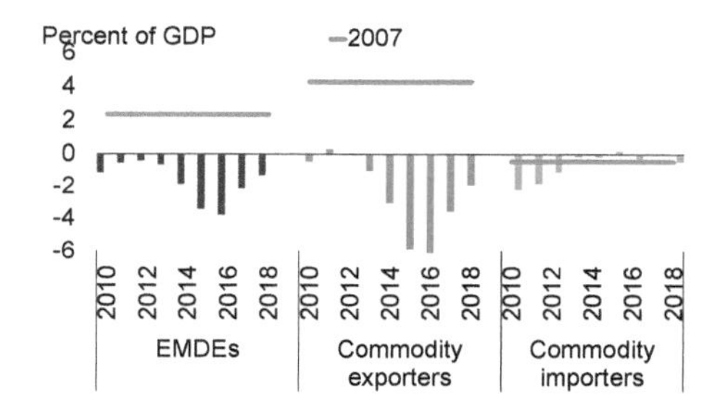

B. Nonresident share of local government bonds

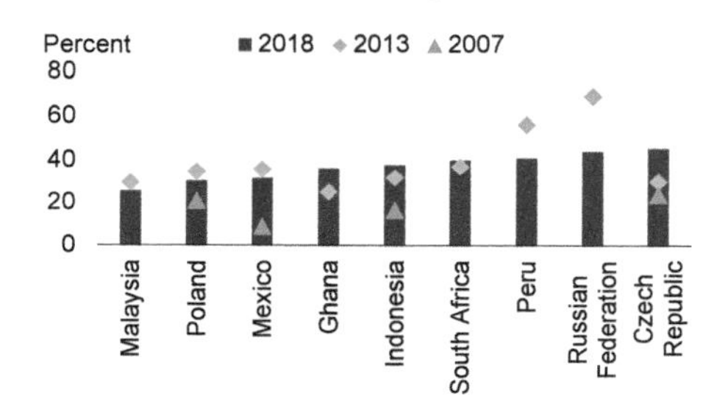

C. Government debt

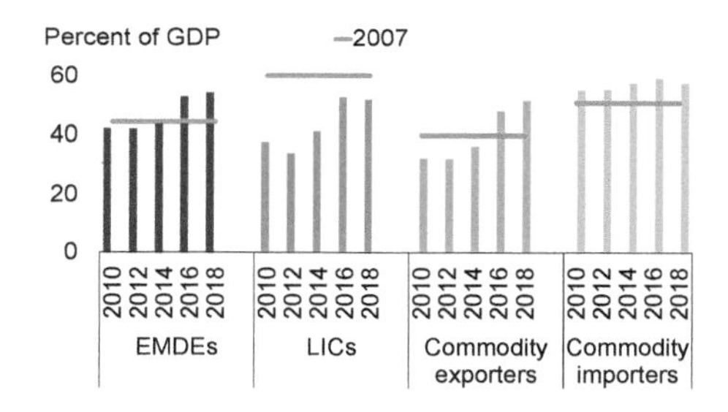

D. EMDE corporate and household debt

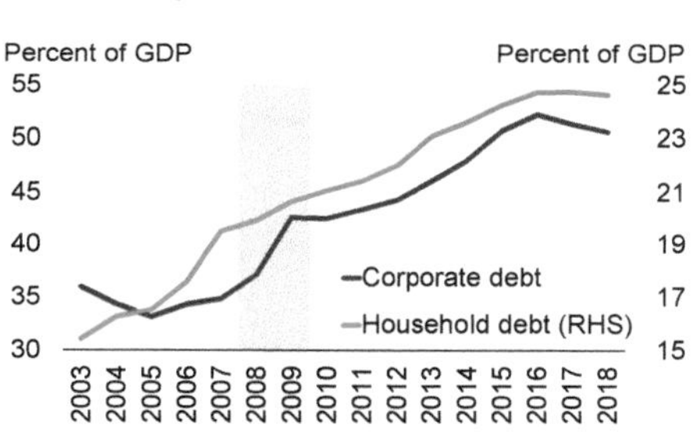

Sources: AsianBondsOnline; Haver Analytics; Institute of International Finance; World Bank.
Note: Unweighted averages. EMDEs = emerging market and developing economies; LICs = low-income countries.

than one-third of EMDEs, widening deficits are setting government debt on firmly rising trajectories, especially in LICs (Kose et al. 2017; World Bank 2017; figure 5.3).[16]

Procyclical policy tightening in commodity-exporting EMDEs. Many commodity-exporting EMDEs were required to enact procyclical policy tightening during the commodity price slide of 2011-16, despite being in the midst of recessions or sharp slowdowns (World Bank 2018a). Two-thirds of commodity exporters tightened fiscal policy in 2014-16, even in the face of slowing growth. One-half of commodity exporters with flexible exchange rates raised policy rates in 2014-16, in response to above-target inflation and strong depreciation pressures. Under exchange market pressure, several EMDEs allowed more exchange rate flexibility. Russia, which had been operating on a managed floating exchange rate regime since 1999, transitioned to a flexible rate in November 2014. Azerbaijan, Kazakhstan, and Nigeria also began to allow greater

[16] The average fiscal deficit of LICs peaked at 5.2 percent of GDP in 2015 compared to 1.8 percent of GDP in 2007. Government debt, although lower than before the crisis, increased by 17 percentage points of GDP between 2012 and 2018.

BOX 5.2 Fiscal space and financial crisis

The availability of fiscal policy as an effective instrument to support demand and activity in economic downturns depends on the amount of budget resources available to raise spending or lower taxes without jeopardizing fiscal sustainability. This resource availability is often called fiscal space. Since the 2009 global recession, fiscal space in emerging market and developing economies has narrowed, which makes them more vulnerable to economic downturns and sudden spikes in financing costs, and limits their ability to counteract adverse shocks.

Introduction

In many emerging market and developing economies (EMDEs), public debt levels have increased and market perceptions of sovereign credit quality have deteriorated. Such developments may limit the budgetary resources available for governments to stimulate demand and activity and boost employment in future economic downturns. They may similarly restrict the ability of government to use fiscal policy as a tool for macroeconomic management in the event of adverse shocks, such as natural disasters. The availability of budgetary resources for the conduct of effective fiscal policy is often called "fiscal space" (Kose et al. 2017; Kose, Ohnsorge, and Sugawara 2020).

Although fiscal space is difficult to measure, a critical component is debt service capacity. Kose et al. (2017) distinguish four broad components of this capacity: government debt sustainability, balance sheet composition, external and private sector debt, and market perception of sovereign risk. Government debt sustainability captures the longer-term capacity of the government to finance its obligations. The composition of the public sector balance sheet can provide a metric for the government's exposures to sudden changes in financial market conditions. External and private sector debt may involve contingent liabilities of the government, including debt that is only implicitly government-guaranteed. Finally, market perception of sovereign risks reflects a government's ability to tap markets and service its obligations.

Using a cross-country database prepared by Kose et al. (2017), this box addresses the following questions:

- How has fiscal space in EMDEs evolved over time?
- How does fiscal space typically behave during episodes of financial stress?
- How can fiscal space be increased?

Evolution of fiscal space over time

Fiscal space increased during 2000-07, but has shrunk around the world since the 2009 global recession. As illustrative examples, figure B5.2.1 shows the evolution of

Note: This box was prepared by Naotaka Sugawara.

BOX 5.2 Fiscal space and financial crisis *(continued)*

FIGURE B5.2.1 Fiscal space

Different measures of fiscal space suggest that it has narrowed in both advanced economies and EMDEs since the global recession.

A. Government and private debt

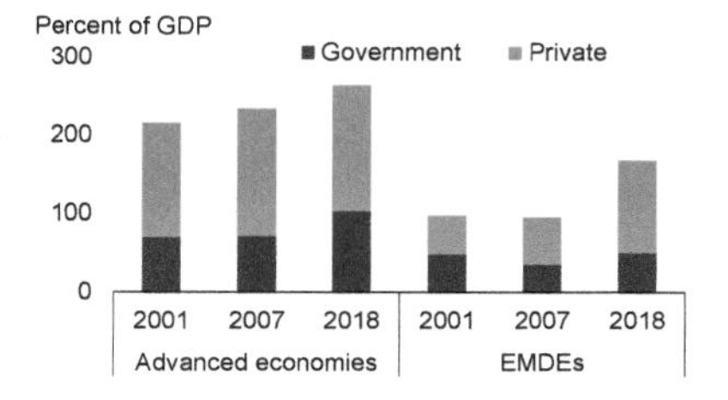

B. Government debt held by nonresidents

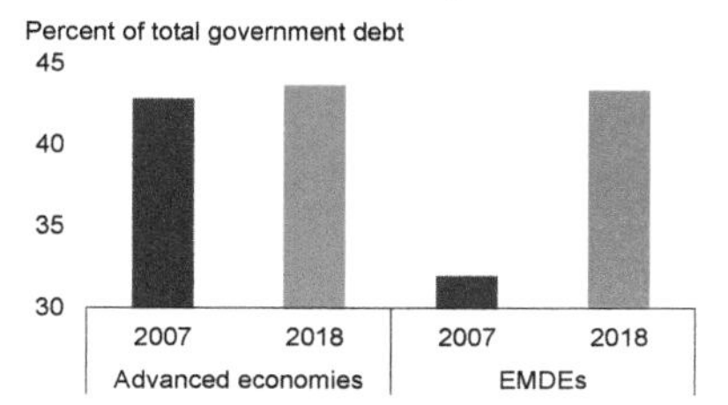

C. External debt

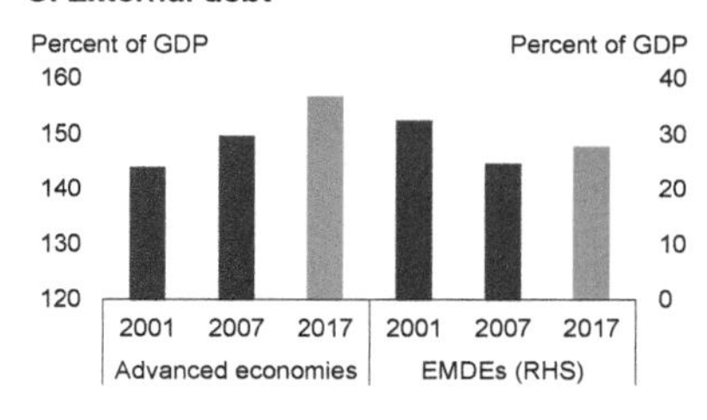

D. Sovereign debt ratings

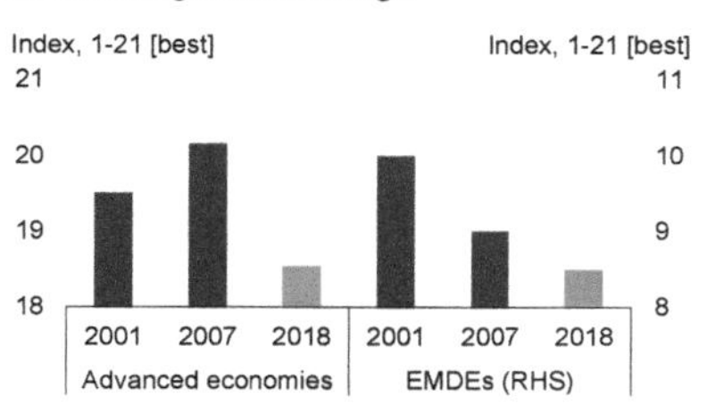

Source: Kose et al. (2017).

A.C. Averages computed with current U.S. dollar GDP as a weight, based on 38 advanced economies and 154 emerging market and developing economies (EMDEs; panel A) and 35 advanced economies and 137 EMDEs (panel C).

B.D. Median of 29 advanced economies and 43 EMDEs (panel B) and median of 40 advanced economies and 108 EMDEs (panel D), though the sample size varies by year.

D. The sovereign debt ratings are converted to a numerical scale ranging from 1 to 21 (higher number, better rating). An index value of 12 is the border between investment grade and non-investment grade.

some measures of the four components of debt service capacity mentioned above. The measures used are for illustrative purposes but are fairly representative of the concepts. The improving trend before the crisis was widely shared, because virtually all indicators of fiscal space improved in more than half of EMDEs and most indicators improved in more than half of advanced economies. After the global recession, however, debt sustainability indicators, including government debt, have deteriorated in at least three-quarters of all countries. External and private debt stocks have increased in more than half of all countries and market perceptions of sovereign credit risks have also worsened.

Before the global recession, measures of government debt sustainability improved significantly in EMDEs, and to a considerably lesser extent in advanced economies,

BOX 5.2 Fiscal space and financial crisis *(continued)*

because rapid growth reduced deficits and helped to reduce debt stocks in relation to gross domestic product (GDP; Kose, Ohnsorge, and Sugawara 2018). In low-income countries, debt relief initiatives such as the Heavily Indebted Poor Countries Initiative and Multilateral Debt Relief Initiative helped reduce debt burdens. These improvements contributed to a decline in EMDE general government gross debt by 13 percentage points of GDP over 2001-07, to 36 percent of GDP. By contrast, government debt in advanced economies stabilized at about 70 percent of GDP.

Other trends were less favorable. Although by 2007 external debt-to-GDP ratios were below the levels of the early 2000s in three-quarters of EMDEs, external debt had become increasingly short-term. Still well below that of advanced economies, on average, private debt in EMDEs rose over 2001-07.

Since the global recession, fiscal space has shrunk in EMDEs. Partly as a result of steep revenue losses in commodity-exporting EMDEs, sustainability gaps and fiscal deficits have widened in EMDEs. Government debt has risen to 54 percent of GDP, on average, in 2018. It now exceeds 2000 levels in more than one-third of EMDEs and is increasingly held by nonresidents.

Moreover, external and private sector debt has increased from 2007 levels in most EMDEs. A rapid increase in private sector debt, especially for corporations, since the global recession has been accompanied by weaker corporate solvency and profitability (Alfaro et al. 2017; World Bank 2018b).

Fiscal space during financial crises

Figure B5.2.2 illustrates how fiscal space has changed during financial crises. It employs event study analysis to examine the behavior of selected indicators of fiscal space around financial crises since 1990—including banking, currency, and debt crises—and to compare these events against recent developments.

In the run-up to and during these crisis episodes, fiscal space typically deteriorated as government debt increased and fiscal balances weakened. This deterioration largely reflects the budgetary cost to support banking systems (Tagkalakis 2013) and the increased cost of government debt denominated in foreign currency following exchange rate depreciations. Increasing government debt coincided with worsening long-term sovereign debt ratings; however, within two years of financial crises, government debt and sovereign ratings returned to stable paths. This improvement may reflect debt restructuring and losses of access to financing that forced governments to rein in spending or raise revenues. During crises, deleveraging reduced private debt. Prior to crises, the median ratio of private sector debt to GDP tended to remain stable, but, in the year following crises, median private debt declined by more than 3 percentage points of GDP.

BOX 5.2 Fiscal space and financial crisis *(continued)*

FIGURE B5.2.2 Fiscal space around financial crises and in 2018

Fiscal space has deteriorated during financial crises in EMDEs. Within two years of such episodes, government debt and sovereign ratings typically return to stable paths.

A. Government debt

Percent of GDP
—Median
--Interquartile range
—Current (t=2018)
100
80
60
40
20
t-2 t-1 t t+1 t+2

B. Private debt

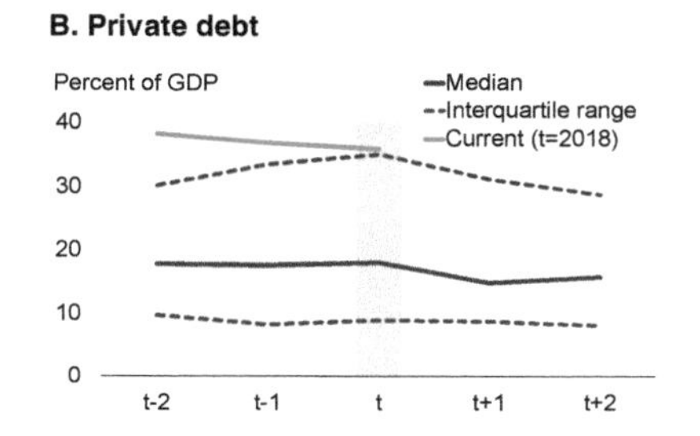

C. External debt

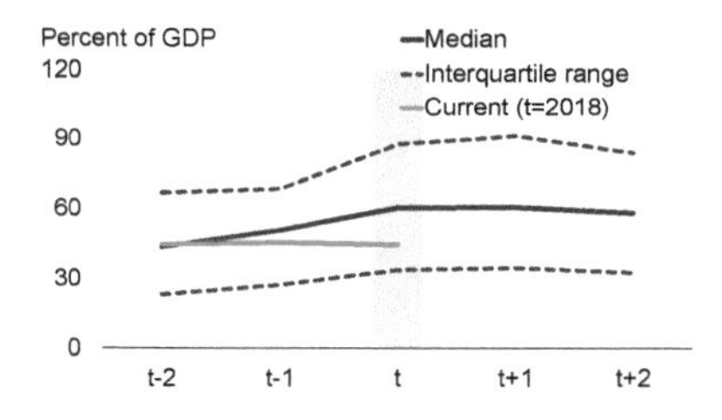

D. Sovereign debt ratings

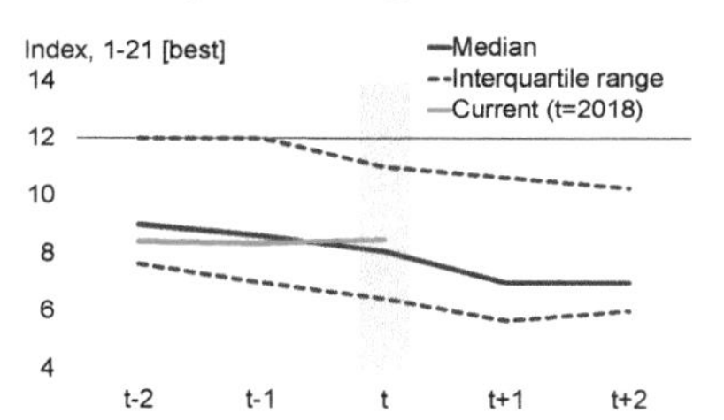

Sources: Kose et al. (2017); Laeven and Valencia (2018).

Note: Year "t" refers to the year of onset of financial crises in emerging market and developing economies (EMDEs). Medians, as well as interquartile ranges, are based on balanced samples. Crises consider banking, currency, and debt crises, as defined in Laeven and Valencia (2018). When multiple crises are identified within five years, the one with the lowest real GDP growth is counted as an event. Sample includes 80 crisis episodes (panel A), 127 episodes (panel B), 122 episodes (panel C), and 56 episodes (panel D). The red line is based on all EMDEs, though it is not a crisis episode.

D. The sovereign debt ratings are converted to a numerical scale ranging from 1 to 21 (higher, better rating). The horizontal line at an index value of 12 is the border between investment grade (above the line) and non-investment grade (below the line).

Several indicators suggest that EMDE fiscal space is more limited than before previous crises. In particular, the government debt ratio in the median EMDE was as high at end-2018 as levels during previous financial crises, and private debt was higher, and outside the range of past crisis episodes. In addition, sovereign ratings were as low as ratings during past crisis episodes.

Policy frameworks to improve fiscal space

Fiscal space is critical for the use of fiscal policy to manage aggregate demand and to reduce vulnerabilities to adverse shocks, such as natural disasters. With fiscal space having narrowed since the global recession, policy measures to shore up fiscal sustainability have become a priority for EMDEs.

BOX 5.2 Fiscal space and financial crisis *(continued)*

Fiscal sustainability could be improved by increasing the efficiency of revenue collection and spending. Measures to strengthen revenue collection could include broadening tax bases, removing loopholes for higher-income households or profitable corporations, and strengthening tax administration (Akitoby 2018). In countries with high levels of informality, increasing the revenue raised from the informal sector—for example, by promoting a change in payment methods to noncash transactions and facilitating collective bargaining and agreement with informal sector associations on taxation—could help increase revenues directly, as well as indirectly, by encouraging informal firms to join the formal sector, which would enhance their growth prospects (Awasthi and Engelschalk 2018; Joshi, Prichard, and Heady 2014).

On the spending side, governments should seek to change the composition of expenditures away from unproductive and inefficient outlays, such as broad-based subsidies, toward productive and growth-enhancing ones, such as public investment and well-targeted income support (Gemmell, Kneller, and Sanz 2016). More efficient public investment management could increase the returns and contain the cost of public investment. Well-designed pension reforms can also support fiscal sustainability.

In addition, credible and well-founded institutional mechanisms can help support fiscal discipline and strengthen fiscal space. Three such mechanisms have been widely introduced: fiscal rules, stabilization funds, and medium-term expenditure frameworks.

Fiscal rules impose numerical constraints on budgetary aggregates or balances—debt, overall balance, expenditures, or revenues. Rules often allow some flexibility in meeting targets to take into account cyclical deviations, estimated, for example, in terms of an output gap, or structural adjustments. Fiscal rules, and in particular cyclically adjusted or structural balance rules, have been increasingly employed in EMDEs, especially since the global financial crisis (Schaechter et al. 2012). Implementation of fiscal rules can be improved by the establishment of a simple enforcement structure and strict limits on off-budget government guarantees. Transparency and oversight arrangements, such as fiscal councils, can allow governments some flexibility to respond to events while maintaining the credibility of the framework (Debrun and Kinda 2017). Chile's use of a technical fiscal council and fiscal rule with a set target for the structural balance is a good example of a well-designed, credible, and successfully operated fiscal rule system.

Stabilization funds set aside receipts from natural resource revenues, or from other income that might not be long-lasting. Amounts saved during favorable times may be released to cushion revenue shortfalls and to mitigate negative shocks to government expenditures resulting from drops in revenues. Such funds were adopted widely in the 2000s when high oil prices, along with the discovery of oil

BOX 5.2 Fiscal space and financial crisis *(continued)*

in a number of EMDEs, swelled government revenues. Many stabilization funds are integrated with the budget, with clear rules to guide the accumulation and withdrawal of fund resources. The effective use of stabilization funds requires a government commitment to fiscal discipline and macroeconomic management (Gill et al. 2014). Proper design and strong institutional environments that support their operations are crucial factors for their success, as in the cases of Chile and Norway (Schmidt-Hebbel 2012; Stone and Truman 2016).

Medium-term expenditure frameworks are intended to establish or improve credibility in the budgetary process. Such frameworks seek to ensure a transparent budgetary process, where government agencies allocate public resources based on strategic priorities. Robust implementation is closely related to linkages with broader economic and social policy objectives, to the reliability of the relevant data, and to the forecasting capability of the authorities (Allen et al. 2017). In South Africa, such a framework was introduced in the context of high government debt and a combination of underspending by the central government and overspending by provincial governments. Underspending and overspending were both reduced following the introduction of the medium-term framework (World Bank 2013).

Conclusion

Fiscal space has been shrinking in EMDEs since the global recession, narrowing to levels typically seen before past financial crises. Adequate space is critical for fiscal policy to be available to help manage aggregate demand and to reduce vulnerabilities to adverse shocks. Hence, policy measures to shore up fiscal sustainability are now a priority for EMDEs. Credible and well-designed policy frameworks, with clear objectives, help implement and sustain such measures.

exchange rate flexibility in 2015-16. Oil-exporting countries with fixed exchange rate regimes were less able to avoid procyclical fiscal policies, reducing government spending by 8 percentage points of GDP more than those with flexible exchange rate regimes.

Legacy of the global recession: Higher vulnerabilities than before the recession. Since the global recession, rising external, corporate, household, and government debt stocks, and deteriorations in fiscal and current account balances, have increased the vulnerabilities of EMDEs to external shocks.[17] As a result, EMDE policy makers have

[17] There has been an intense debate about whether the rapid increase in debt is cause for concern, given historically low interest rates. Blanchard (2019) and Furman and Summers (2019) provide reasons for additional borrowing, but Auerbach, Gale, and Krupkin (2019) caution against adding to debt. A detailed discussion on the benefits and costs of debt accumulation is provided in Kose, Ohnsorge, and Sugawara (2020) and World Bank (2019a).

less room than they had in 2007 to support domestic demand and activity in the event of future financial or economic stress.

- *External positions.* On average, external debt in EMDEs has increased sharply, to 57 percent of GDP in 2018 from 43 percent of GDP in 2007. Although still above 1990s averages, international reserves have fallen relative to external debt in more than two-thirds of EMDEs, and in some EMDEs more than halved, since 2007.

- *Fiscal positions.* On average, EMDE fiscal surpluses of 2.4 percent of GDP in 2007 have turned into deficits of 2.7 percent in 2018 (figure 5.3). Because of the sharp decline in commodity prices, the deterioration has been particularly severe in commodity exporters, from a surplus of 3.5 percent of GDP in 2007 to a deficit of 3.3 percent of GDP in 2018. EMDE government debt has increased to 54 percent of GDP in 2018, from 45 percent of GDP in 2007; in more than one-third of EMDEs, government debt rose by more than 20 percentage points of GDP. Deteriorating public debt sustainability has also been reflected in sovereign credit rating downgrades.

- *Nonresident exposures.* In some EMDEs, the share of nonresident holdings in local currency bond markets has grown to more than 30 percent, exposing these countries to the risk of sharp market displacements in the event of swings of global risk sentiment (Agur et al. 2018; figure 5.3).

- *LIC government debt.* In LICs, average government debt relative to GDP is less than it was in 2007, but it has risen sharply, by 17 percentage points of GDP from a low in 2012 to 51 percent of GDP in 2018 (World Bank 2019b; figure 5.3).[18] As a result, interest payments have absorbed a growing share of government revenues. Debt has been increasingly owed to nonconcessional and private creditors, heightening the vulnerability of LICs to financial market disruptions.

- *Corporate debt.* In non-LIC EMDEs, rapid credit growth fueled an increase in corporate debt, on average by 16 percentage points of GDP since 2007 to 50 percent of GDP in 2018 (figure 5.3). Although the largest corporate debt increase (54 percentage points of GDP) occurred in China, several other EMDEs (Chile, the Philippines, Turkey, and the United Arab Emirates) experienced increases in excess of 30 percentage points of GDP (Borensztein and Ye 2018; Ohnsorge and Yu 2016).

- *Household debt.* EMDE household debt has increased on average by 5 percentage points of GDP since 2007 to 25 percent of GDP in 2018. In some EMDEs (Brazil, Chile, Colombia, Czech Republic, Malaysia, Poland), household debt has risen by more than 10 percentage points of GDP. The largest increases occurred in China and Thailand, where household debt swelled by 32 and 24 percentage points of GDP, respectively.

[18] Debt relief under the Heavily Indebted Poor Countries initiative and the Multilateral Debt Relief Initiative helped to reduce average public debt in LICs from a debt-to-GDP ratio of 115 percent in the early 2000s to 35 percent in 2012.

Financial sector policies

The crisis triggered a major shift in financial sector policies. Prudential regulation and supervision have evolved from a focus on the stability of individual financial institutions toward a focus on the stability of the financial system as a whole. Restrictions on capital flows, a controversial policy measure before the crisis, have come to be viewed more favorably from a macroprudential perspective.

Prudential policies

Before the global recession: stability of individual institutions. Before the global financial crisis, the financial regulatory framework and supervision practices focused mainly on monitoring prudential risks at individual institutions. For example, in 2006, following this traditional microprudential approach, the U.S. Federal Deposit Insurance Corporation claimed that more than 99 percent of U.S. insured institutions met or exceeded the requirements of the highest regulatory capital standards, giving no indication of the large-scale vulnerabilities that were building up.

The crisis highlighted several shortcomings of this microprudential approach.

- The regulatory perimeter had mainly encompassed banks, with much less attention paid to the buildup of systemic risk in the nonbank sector. In the United States and other advanced economies, lightly regulated nondeposit institutions had steadily grown in size and complexity.

- The microprudential regulatory regime tended to have procyclical effects on bank behavior (Gordy and Howells 2006). In particular, the risk-weighted capital requirements of Basel II tended to decline in the expansionary phase of the business cycle as risk ratings improved, and they tended to rise during the contractionary phase. As a result, despite meeting the Basel II requirements, banks in advanced economies and some EMDEs—especially in Europe—had high leverage, which posed risks to financial stability (Bruno and Shin 2015).

- Fair-value accounting—using current market values as the basis for valuation—lent a further procyclical impulse because it encouraged balance sheet expansion as asset prices increased in economic upswings, and it encouraged deleveraging in downswings.

After the global recession: stability of the financial system. The crisis brought about a rethinking of prudential regulation, which led to a rising interest in complementing microprudential policies that regulate the risk of individual institutions with macroprudential policies aimed at minimizing system-wide risk and at ensuring that the financial system does not create or amplify shocks that could lead to economic downturns (Claessens 2014; World Bank 2019c; Zeev 2017).[19] An illustration of this new focus is the rapid increase in the use of the term "macroprudential" since 2008

[19] Despite the rising interest in macroprudential policies, there are many challenges in designing and implementing them, especially in EMDEs. See details in Dijkman (2015) and Krishnamuti and Lee (2014).

FIGURE 5.4 Macroprudential policy since the global recession

The global financial crisis and subsequent global recession led to an increased emphasis on macroprudential policy, which focuses on minimizing systemic risk. Most countries have strengthened the resilience of their financial systems. Advanced economies tend to use macroprudential tools aimed at borrowers, whereas EMDEs favor both borrower- and foreign exchange-related tools.

A. Google search term "macroprudential"

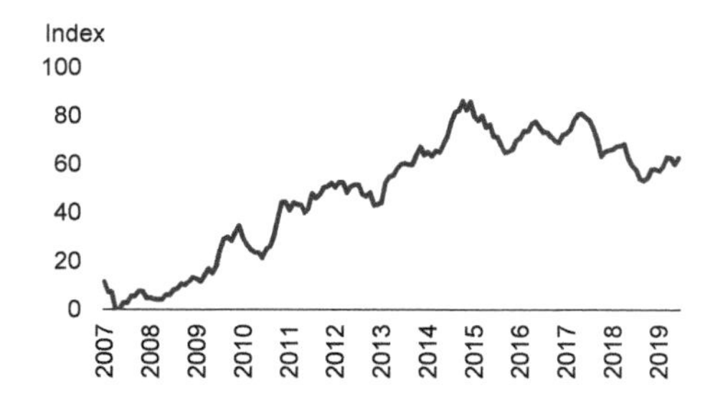

B. Average number of macroprudential tools in EMDEs

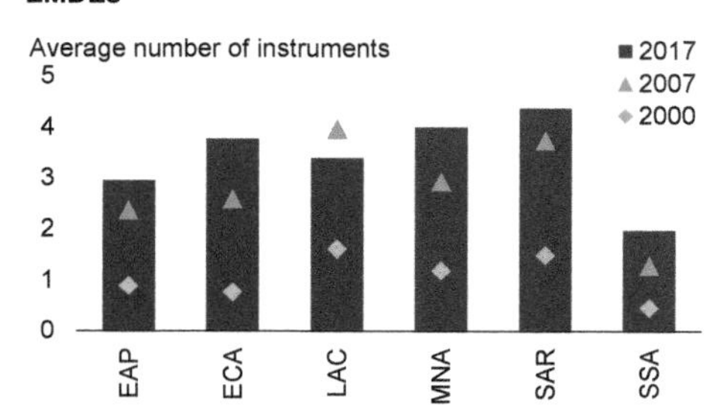

C. Use of macroprudential tools

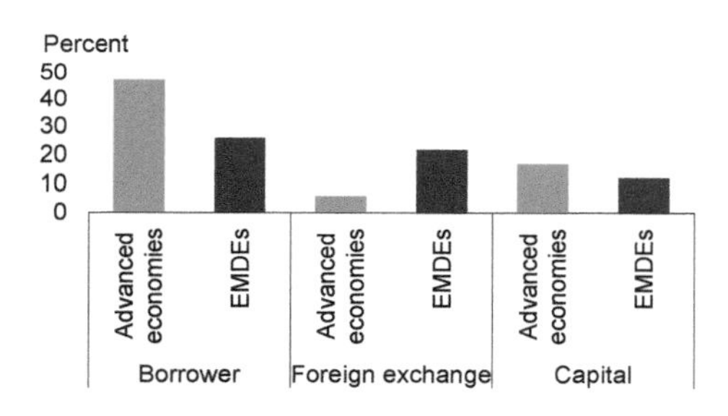

D. Countries that used at least five macroprudential tools between 2007 and 2017

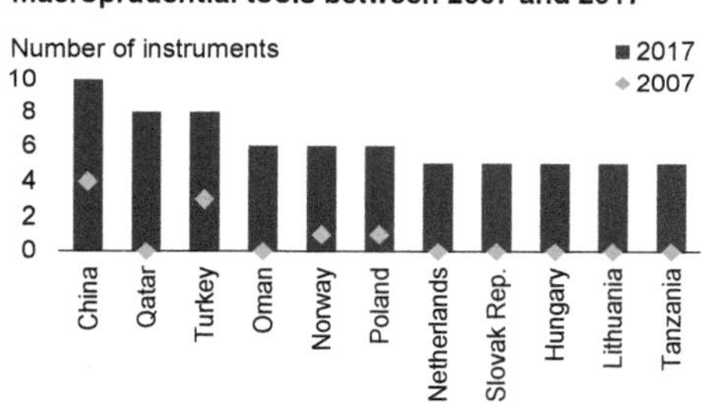

Sources: Cerutti, Claessens, and Laeven (2017); Google Trends; World Bank.

Note: EAP = East Asia and Pacific; ECA = Europe and Central Asia; EMDEs = emerging market and developing economies; LAC = Latin America and the Caribbean; MNA = Middle East and North Africa; SAR = South Asia; Slovak Rep. = Slovak Republic; SSA = Sub-Saharan Africa.

A. Google trends data based on worldwide interest relative peak popularity (100) in the observed period. Six-month moving average.

B. Bars show the average number of macroprudential tools per country in each EMDE region for 2017, with diamonds showing the number for 2000 and triangles for 2007.

C. Bars show the percent of countries in each country group that use certain macroprudential tools. Borrower-targeted tools include debt-to-income ratio and loan-to-value ratio; Foreign exchange-related tools include limits on foreign lending and foreign exchange reserve requirements; Capital-related tools include countercyclical capital requirements and dynamic loan loss provisioning.

D. Bars show the number of macroprudential tools in effect in 2017, whereas diamonds show the number of macroprudential tools in effect in 2007.

(Cukierman 2013; Ostry et al. 2010; figure 5.4). A key objective of macroprudential policy is to minimize systemic risk by limiting boom-bust credit cycles. Several new instruments have been developed under the Basel III framework specifically to promote this objective. These instruments include countercyclical capital requirements and dynamic provisioning to build up capital or liquidity buffers during good times, maximum leverage ratios to capture both on- and off-balance sheet exposures, and capital surcharges on systemically important financial institutions.

Macroprudential instruments have increasingly become an integral part of the toolkit of many central banks and other financial regulators since the crisis. Macroprudential indexes derived from a dataset for 36 advanced economies and 124 EMDEs suggest that all advanced economies, and about 70 percent of EMDEs, have used these instruments to strengthen the resilience of their financial systems (Cerutti, Claessens, and Laeven 2017). EMDEs have more actively used macroprudential instruments—often on an ad hoc or experimental basis—partly reflecting the fact that they are more exposed to volatile capital flows and have less liberalized financial systems (Claessens 2014). These instruments have been used to reduce the growth of credit to nonfinancial corporations and households, and to help restrain asset price inflation, especially in the housing sector (Budnik and Kleibl 2018; Kuttner and Shim 2013, Vandenbussche, Vogel, and Detragiache 2015; Zhang and Zoli 2016).

In ECA, more than four-fifths of EMDEs have increased the use of macroprudential tools, whereas in SSA the share is only about one-half (figure 5.4). The use of different tools has reflected different structural characteristics among countries. ECA has had relatively high financial integration internationally with a large presence of foreign banks that had experienced difficulties, and at the same time high public debt, which reduced the scope for countercyclical fiscal policies. Conversely, SSA, which has less open capital accounts and faced fewer banking sector challenges, has relied less on such tools.

Use of macroprudential tools. Since the global recession, macroprudential measures aimed at borrowers, such as caps on the loan-to-value ratio and the debt-to-income ratio, have been more extensively used in advanced economies. These instruments can be effective in reducing the amplitude of credit cycles, partly because they may be easier to enforce and calibrate than policies aimed at institutions (Epure et al. 2018; Fendoğlu 2017). Macroprudential increases in capital requirements have been associated with slower lending in U.K. banks, and dynamic provisioning has been associated with smoother credit cycles in Spain (Aiyar, Calomiris, and Wieladek 2016; Jiménez et al. 2017). In contrast, foreign exchange and liquidity policies, such as limits on foreign currency loans and foreign exchange countercyclical reserve requirements, have been more often used in EMDEs in efforts to reduce exposures to volatile capital inflows (figure 5.4). This effort is especially the case in ECA, which had been plagued by currency mismatches in the balance sheets of households and firms (Ben Naceur, Hosny, and Hadjian 2019; Fidrmuc, Hake, and Stix 2013; Ranciere, Tornell, and Vamvakidis 2010).

China has implemented a wide range of macroprudential policies since the crisis (figure 5.4). A priority goal has been to contain the growth of corporate debt, especially of state-owned enterprises, through limits on the exposures of banks. Other macroprudential measures have aimed at curbing real estate speculation through sector-specific lending limits and higher mortgage down payment requirements. In India, macroprudential policy has focused on preventing excessive credit growth by increasing the capital that banks are required to hold against riskier loans and increasing the rate at which banks are required to provision against loan losses for specific sectors. Macroprudential measures have also been used in economic downturns; for example, Brazil lowered reserve requirements in 2017 to help counter its protracted economic slowdown.

Interaction between financial sector and macroeconomic policies. The experience of the global financial crisis kindled interest in the impact of monetary and fiscal policy on financial stability and, conversely, the impact of prudential decisions on monetary conditions.[20]

- *Prudential policies and monetary conditions.* The impact of prudential policies on monetary conditions is explored in a small body of literature that is constrained by prudential data requirements. Among U.K. banks, higher capital requirements have been found to lower bank lending abroad and domestically (Aiyar et al. 2014; Meeks 2017). For large banks, their domestic lending response to capital requirements was stronger than their response to monetary policy (Aiyar, Calomiris, and Wieladek 2016).

- *Monetary policy and financial stability.* The main instrument of monetary policy—the short-term interest rate—is generally a weaker instrument for the promotion of financial stability than are regulatory instruments (Adrian, Laxton, and Obstfeld 2018; Lane 2016). The latter can be focused on specific issues in institutions or markets and on lenders or borrowers whereas monetary policy cannot. That said, sound monetary policy contributes to financial stability. In times of severe stress, such as 2008-09, central banks inject liquidity into the system on a large scale and stand ready to act as lender of last resort. In normal times, central banks provide support to financial stability, for example, through oversight of payment systems, monitoring of risks and vulnerabilities, and the maintenance of foreign reserves to defend their currencies against short-term speculative attacks (Cheung and Qian 2009; Jara, Moreno, and Tovar 2009).

- *Fiscal policy and financial stability.* Sound fiscal policy also contributes to financial stability. For example, by removing tax incentives to borrowing by the corporate sector, allowing a more balanced tax treatment of equity financing, and reducing tax exemptions of interest payments on mortgages, fiscal authorities can help curb credit growth and increases in housing prices.

Overhauling the regulatory framework. The increase in emphasis on systemic risk and macroprudential policy led to the establishment of the Financial Stability Board (FSB) in 2009, with the endorsement of the G20, to promote the reform of international financial regulation and supervision. Several countries have improved their system-wide regulatory architecture to meet goals set by the FSB. Improvements include enhancing the capacity to use macroprudential tools, strengthening international coordination among entities that share the financial stability mandate (especially in the cases of

[20] Nevertheless, the consensus among central bankers and economists remains that monetary policy is best aimed at controlling inflation and that it cannot take primary responsibility for financial stability (Yellen 2014). There are, however, exceptions to this general proposition (IMF 2019, Lane 2016, Mishkin 2011, Yellen 2014). For example, a large-scale, credit-fueled, asset price boom may pose an obvious risk to financial and economic stability, and justify an increase in the policy rate beyond the normal requirements of the inflation objective (Gourio, Kashyap, and Sim 2018). An entirely alternative view is that monetary policy should systematically focus on financial stability as well as on macroeconomic goals (Borio 2014; Collard et al. 2017; Stems 2013; Svensson 2017).

potential cross-border spillovers), and improving governance, transparency, and accountability. In general, economies that were harder-hit by the crisis—such as the European Union, the United Kingdom, and the United States—have been somewhat more proactive in addressing regulatory weaknesses (Lombardi and Moschella 2017; Lombardi and Siklos 2016).

Since the crisis, several EMDEs with FSB memberships have established national financial stability councils or committees (Brazil, China, India, Mexico, Russia, Turkey), and incorporated new mandates for the central bank to exercise macroprudential supervision (Indonesia, Russia, South Africa; FSB 2018, 2019). Most of these EMDEs have made progress in implementing reforms, especially to meet Basel III capital and liquidity requirements and implement over-the-counter derivatives reforms (FSB 2018). EMDEs that are also members of the Basel Committee on Banking Supervision, including Brazil, China, Russia, and South Africa, have put in place risk-based capital rules, liquidity coverage ratio regulations, and capital conservation buffers (BCBS 2019).

The financial regulatory agenda set out by the G20 has several implications in EMDEs. Regulatory tightening in advanced economies has contributed to the withdrawal of major banks from EMDEs (chapter 4). The Basel III recommendations are, like their predecessors, calibrated primarily for advanced economies, making some EMDEs hesitant to adopt those regulations to avoid potential new challenges associated with these new standards (Beck and Rojas-Suarez 2019). A recent survey suggests that the financial sector agenda set out by the G20 may have unintended economic costs for individual EMDEs (Briault et al. 2018). For example, the introduction of creditor-funded recapitalization, known as "bail in," wipes out senior claims on the bank during bank resolution; however, most of the depositors on the liability side of banks in many EMDEs are small depositors. Bailing in those depositors would only intensify a financial crisis by eroding the credibility of the financial system. Additionally, these EMDEs typically lack sufficiently developed financial markets for banks to issue debt securities that can be bailed in (Feyen and Zuccardi 2019).

Challenges of macroprudential policy. Although the importance of macroprudential policy is now widely accepted, it is still not clear which tools are best suited to different circumstances and how they should be adapted to country characteristics. There are also questions on the appropriate design of policy institutions, in particular whether such policies should be under the purview of the central bank, a new financial stability agency, an existing market supervisory agency, or a committee comprising various institutions.

Capital flow management policies

Before the global recession: Limited role for capital flow management

Capital flow management measures (CFMs) were widespread under the Bretton Woods regime of pegged exchange rates, when they provided countries with a degree of independence in monetary policy. After the collapse of the regime in the early 1970s, advanced economies began to shun restrictions on capital flows. They opened their capital accounts and financial markets to the international economy. EMDEs started to open their capital accounts later, during the 1980s and 1990s. This move reflected the view that, by liberalizing international capital flows, EMDEs would potentially benefit from access to credit and investment from advanced economies, hence promoting growth and development. The experiences of several countries during the 1997-98 Asian financial crisis, however, highlighted the risk of too rapid an opening of the capital account and of the importance of coordinating capital account liberalization with stronger financial regulation and supervision.

Capital flow management measures during the global recession

Many EMDEs deployed capital management measures during and following the global recession, mainly in response to capital flow volatility (Gallagher 2011; IMF 2012, 2018a; Rey 2015). Early in the crisis, EMDEs experienced heavy outflows, in a flight to safety (figure 5.5).[21] The recovery of capital inflows in 2009-11 reflected the widening of interest rate differentials in favor of EMDE assets and was induced by unprecedented monetary policy accommodation in advanced economies. Concerns that heavy inflows might result in currency appreciation, asset bubbles, inflationary pressures, and financial instability more broadly led to the use of capital flow management measures on inflows, whereas the risk of a resurgence of capital flight underlay increased controls on outflows.

Some EMDEs strengthened existing controls while others introduced new measures (Gallagher 2011; Ghosh, Ostry, and Qureshi 2017). These CFMs included a wide range of price-based and quantity-based controls, for example, reserve requirement taxes on foreign investment (Brazil, Ecuador, Indonesia, Peru, Uruguay), taxes on currency outflows (Argentina, Ecuador, República Bolivariana de Venezuela), taxes on interest earned and capital gains on nonresidents (Thailand), minimum term requirements for holding central bank securities (Indonesia), and limits on foreign currency positions (the Philippines). Some of these measures were subsequently eased when the inflow surge abated after 2012 (IMF 2016).

Not all countries responded to the pressures of capital inflows with CFMs—some could not impose CFMs because of bilateral or multilateral trade and investment treaties (Abdelal 2007; Gallagher 2011). For example, the European Union enforces open capital accounts across the union (Article 63 of the Lisbon Treaty; EU 2007), the North American Free Trade Agreement considers capital controls an actionable offense, and the Organisation for Economic Co-operation and Development (OECD) has a code (although not actionable) on liberalization of capital movements. Some countries bound

[21] Brazil, for example, imposed a series of CFMs between October 2009 and August 2011. The measures included taxes on inward portfolio investment (2 percent in October 2009, 6 percent in October 2010), taxes on American Depositary Receipts (1.5 percent in November 2009), an increase in reserve requirements on capital inflows (January 2011), taxes on repatriated funds (6 percent in March 2011), and taxes on derivatives (1 percent in August 2011). In advanced economies, Iceland imposed CFMs in November 2008 amid a severe banking crisis. To prevent capital flight and a collapse of the exchange rate, the Central Bank of Iceland restricted foreign currency outflows and froze offshore holdings of krona-denominated assets. Restrictions on capital outflows were lifted in March 2017, but those on inflows have been tightened, primarily to prevent currency speculation.

FIGURE 5.5 Capital flow management policies since the global recession

Historically low interest rates in advanced economies in the wake of the crisis led to a resurgence of capital flows to EMDEs. Controls on both inflows and outflows were increasingly deployed to contain exchange rate volatility and to stem credit-fueled asset price inflation.

A. Capital flows to EMDEs

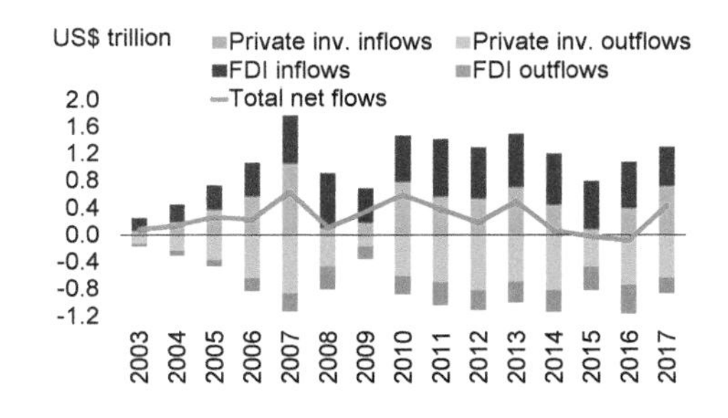

B. Interest rate differential between EMDEs and the United States

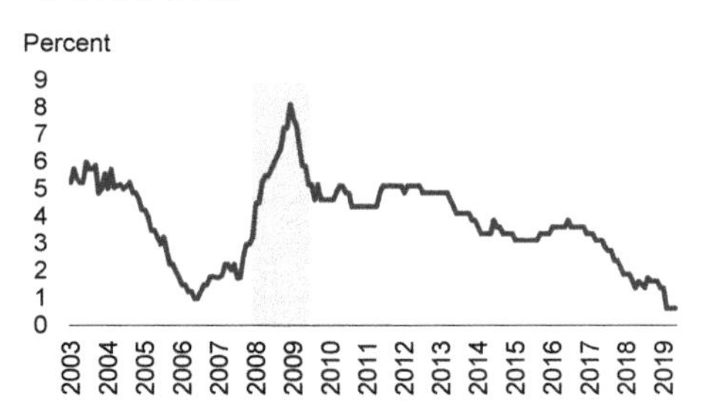

C. Capital controls on inflows

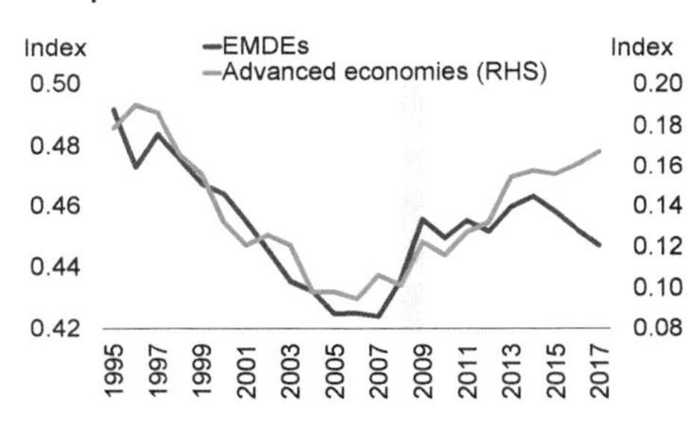

D. Capital controls on outflows

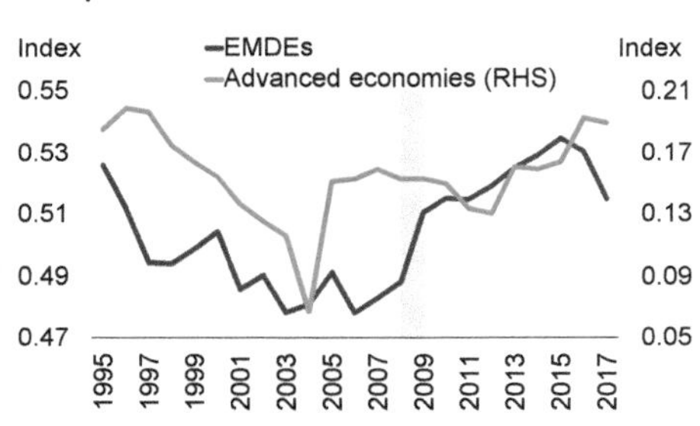

Sources: Araujo et al. (2015); Bank for International Settlements; Fernández et al. (2016); International Monetary Fund; World Bank.
Note: Shaded area in B shows the period of the global financial crisis, but it captures the 2009 global recession in C and D. EMDEs = emerging market and developing economies; FDI = foreign direct investment.
A. Private investment flows include portfolio investment, other investment, and financial derivatives.
B. The line shows the differential between the central bank policy rates in EMDEs (group median) and in the United States.
C. Lines show the overall inflow restrictions index (all asset categories), with a higher value suggesting more controls.
D. Lines show the overall outflow restrictions index (all asset categories), with a higher value suggesting more controls.

by trade and investment agreements reframed capital controls as macroprudential policies or as quasi-controls (Indonesia, Korea, Peru, and Uruguay; Grabel 2015).

After the global recession: Rising role for capital flow management

The crisis triggered a rethinking of the role, benefits, and costs of financial liberalization, especially in light of the role of cross-border capital flows during the financial crises (Reinhart and Rogoff 2008). There is now an emerging consensus that CFMs can play a legitimate role in a framework of rules to promote macroeconomic and financial stability. This consensus has been supported by successes in stabilizing financial markets by reining in large capital flows (Brazil), and by development models built on measured capital account opening (China, India). The institutional views of major international organizations have evolved to admit the possibility of a role for managing capital flows, which can include CFMs as part of broad coordinated policy packages (for example, FSB, IMF, and BIS 2011; Ghosh, Ostry, and Qureshi 2017; IMF 2012, 2018a; Ostry et al. 2010, 2011).

Since 2013, however, global capital flows have been more subdued than in the precrisis period. Thus, in practice, despite the increased availability of capital flow management measures, countries that have experienced episodes of large-scale inflows have dealt with the associated concerns about currency appreciation mainly through monetary easing and foreign exchange intervention (Colombia, India, Indonesia, Thailand, Turkey). These responses indicate that CFMs may play a useful role during capital-inflow surges in certain situations (IMF 2018a).[22] During periods of financial stress, CFMs can provide effective support to other instruments (IMF 2016). For example, CFMs have been used complementarily with macroeconomic policies, as well as with structural and financial sector reforms, to moderate financial stress episodes in Belarus, Cyprus, Greece, Iceland, and Ukraine. Outside crisis episodes, CFMs have been employed to address country-specific financial sector vulnerabilities (China, North Macedonia, Peru, Russia). In some cases, macroprudential measures have been used to discourage borrowing in foreign currency (Korea, Peru).

Challenges of capital flow management

Whether capital flows are to be welcomed or represent a problem to be tackled may be difficult to determine. Policy makers thus face challenges in understanding the underlying causes, and determining whether the flows will cause undue damage to competitiveness or threaten financial stability. A CFM intended to address a specific component of capital flows could merely shift the composition of flows toward unregulated segments of the financial system. Widespread CFMs could have cross-border spillover effects, for example, if they strongly affect exchange rate valuations and trade competitiveness.

Conclusion

Following the global financial crisis and the 2009 global recession, the largest advanced economies and EMDEs enacted unprecedented and coordinated macroeconomic stimulus. This stimulus provided crucial support to the international financial system and staved off a deeper global recession. For the first time during a major crisis, EMDEs were also able to employ a wide range of countercyclical monetary and fiscal policies to stem contagion and boost the postcrisis recovery. Numerous EMDEs lowered policy interest rates, intervened heavily in foreign exchange markets, and implemented fiscal stimulus packages. Three-fifths of EMDEs with floating exchange rates had lowered policy rates by the first quarter of 2009 and made use of other stimulus measures, such

[22] During capital inflow surges, CFMs may play a useful role particularly in any or all of the following situations: the room for adjusting macroeconomic policies is limited, appropriate policies require time to take effect, the inflow surge contributes to systemic financial risks; and there is heightened uncertainty about the underlying economic stance due to the capital inflow surge (Adrian 2018; IMF 2018a).

as reducing reserve requirements, injecting liquidity into and recapitalizing domestic banks, and channeling lending through development banks.

The crisis also ushered in a rethinking of financial sector policies. The emphasis of prudential regulation and supervision has shifted from a sole focus on the regulation and supervision of individual institutions (involving microprudential tools) toward a more balanced view on containing both individual risks and system-wide risks (involving macroprudential measures). At the same time, the appropriate use of capital controls as part of a package of policies to promote financial stability has gained greater acceptance.

Despite the successful manner in which EMDEs navigated the global financial crisis and its aftermath, as a group, they now appear more vulnerable to external financial or trade shocks than they were in 2007. This vulnerability could be compounded by other pressures if there is a broader retreat from global cooperation and multilateralism. The crisis-related fiscal stimulus in many EMDEs has still not been fully unwound; by 2018, fiscal balances have returned to 2007 levels in only one-quarter of EMDEs. Rising external, corporate, household, and government debt stocks, combined with wider fiscal and current account deficits, have increased the vulnerabilities of EMDEs to shocks compared with their vulnerabilities in 2007.

The crisis and its aftermath provide a reminder that countercyclical fiscal and monetary policies can be crucial during periods of severe financial and economic stress. The 2008-09 experience also demonstrates that international cooperation and coordination enhance the credibility, and hence the overall positive impact, of stimulative policies. At the same time, the postcrisis experience illustrates the difficulties of unwinding a large stimulus and the danger that this can leave countries with increased vulnerability to future shocks. EMDE policy makers therefore need to develop a coherent framework of policies that address these vulnerabilities and credibly target the objectives of price, output, and financial stability.

References

Abdelal, R. 2007. *Capital Rules: The Construction of Global Finance*. Cambridge, MA: Harvard University Press.

Admati, A., and M. Hellwig. 2014. *The Bankers' New Clothes: What's Wrong with Banking and What to Do about It?* Princeton, NJ: Princeton University Press.

Adrian, T. 2018. "Policy Responses to Capital Flows." Speech at LIII Meeting of Governors of Latin America, Spain and the Philippines at the IMF-World Bank Annual Meetings in Bali, Indonesia, October 11.

Adrian, T., D. Laxton, and M. Obstfeld. 2018. *Advancing the Frontiers of Monetary Policy*. Washington, DC: International Monetary Fund.

Agur, I., M. Chan, M. Goswami, and S. Sharma. 2018. "On International Integration of Emerging Sovereign Bond Markets." IMF Working Paper 18/18, International Monetary Fund, Washington, DC.

Aiyar, S., C. W. Calomiris, J. Hooley, Y. Korniyenko, and T. Wieladek. 2014. "The International Transmission of Bank Capital Requirements: Evidence from the UK." *Journal of Financial Economics* 113 (3): 368-82.

Aiyar, S., C. W. Calomiris, and T. Wieladek. 2016. "How Does Credit Supply Respond to Monetary Policy and Bank Minimum Capital Requirements?" *European Economic Review* 82 (December): 142-65.

Akerlof, G., O. Blanchard, D. Romer, and J. Stiglitz. 2014. *What Have We Learned? Macroeconomic Policy after the Crisis*. Cambridge, MA: MIT Press.

Akitoby, B. 2018. "Raising Revenue: Five Country Cases Illustrate How Best to Improve Tax Collection." *Finance & Development* 55 (1): 18-21.

Alfaro, L., G. Asis, A. Chari, and U. Panizza. 2017. "Lessons Unlearned? Corporate Debt in Emerging Markets." NBER Working Paper 23407, National Bureau of Economic Research, Cambridge, MA.

Allen, F., and G. Giovannetti. 2011. "The Effects of the Financial Crisis on Sub-Saharan Africa." *Review of Development Finance* 1 (1): 1-27.

Allen, R., T. Chaponda, L. Fisher, and R. Ray. 2017. "Medium-Term Budget Frameworks in Selected Sub-Saharan African Countries." IMF Working Paper 17/203, International Monetary Fund, Washington, DC.

Araujo, J., A. C. David, C. van Hombeeck, and C. Papageorgiou. 2015. "Non-FDI Capital Flows in Low-Income Developing Countries: Catching the Wave?" IMF Working Paper 15/86, International Monetary Fund, Washington, DC.

Arteta, C., M. A. Kose, F. Ohnsorge, and M. Stocker. 2015. "The Coming U.S. Interest Rate Tightening Cycle: Smooth Sailing or Stormy Waters?" Policy Research Note 2, World Bank, Washington, DC.

Arteta, C., M. A. Kose, M. Stocker, and R. Taskin. 2018. "Implications of Negative Interest Rate Policies: An Early Assessment." *Pacific Economic Review* 23 (1): 8-26.

Auerbach, A. W. Gale, and A. Krupkin. 2019. "If Not Now, When? New Estimates of the Federal Budget Outlook." Brookings Institution Working Paper, Washington, DC.

Awasthi, R., and M. Engelschalk. 2018. "Taxation and the Shadow Economy: How the Tax System Can Stimulate and Enforce the Formalization of Business Activities." Policy Research Working Paper 8391, World Bank, Washington, DC.

BCBS (Basel Committee on Banking Supervision). 2019. *Sixteenth Progress Report on Adoption of the Basel Regulatory Framework.* Basel: Basel Committee on Banking Supervision.

Beck, T., and L. Rojas-Suarez. 2019. *Making Basel III Work for Emerging Markets and Developing Economics. A CDG Task Force Report.* Washington, DC: Center for Global Development.

Bernanke, B. S. 2007. "Globalization and Monetary Policy," Speech at the Fourth Economic Summit, Stanford Institute for Economic Policy Research, Stanford, CA, March 2.

Bernanke, B. S. 2009. "Financial Reform to Address Systemic Risk." Speech at the Council on Foreign Relations, Washington DC, March 10.

Ben Naceur, S., A. Hosny, and G. Hadjian. 2019. "How to De-Dollarize Financial Systems in the Caucasus and Central Asia?" *Empirical Economics* 56 (6): 1979–99.

Binici, M., and M. Yörükoğlu. 2011. "Capital Flows in the Post-Global Financial Crisis Era:

Implications for Financial Stability and Monetary Policy." BIS Paper 57, Bank for International Settlements, Basel.

BIS (Bank for International Settlements). 2009. *79th Annual Report, 2008/09*. Basel: Bank for International Settlements.

Blanchard, O. 2019. "Public Debt and Low Interest Rates." *American Economic Review* 109 (4): 1197-229.

Blanchard, O., H. Faruqee, and M. Das. 2010. "The Initial Impact of the Crisis on Emerging Market Countries." *Brookings Papers on Economic Activity* 41 (1): 263-323.

Blanchard, O., R. Rajan, K. Rogoff, and L. Summers. 2016. *Progress and Confusion: The State of Macroeconomic Policy*. Cambridge, MA: MIT Press.

Borensztein, E., and L. S. Ye. 2018. "Corporate Debt Overhang and Investment: Firm-Level Evidence." Policy Research Working Paper 8553, World Bank, Washington, DC.

Borio, C. 2014. "Monetary Policy and Financial Stability: What Role in Prevention and Recovery?" BIS Working Papers 440, Bank for International Settlements, Basel.

Briault, C., E. Feyen, I. Gonzalez Del Mazo, J. Rademacher, B. Yee, and I. Skamnelos. 2018. "Cross-Border Spillover Effects of the G20 Financial Regulatory Reforms: Results from a Pilot Survey." Policy Research Working Paper 8300, World Bank, Washington, DC.

Bruno, V., and H. S. Shin. 2015. "Capital Flows and the Risk-Taking Channel of Monetary Policy." *Journal of Monetary Economics* 71 (April): 119-32.

Budnik, K., and J. Kleibl. 2018. "Macroprudential Regulation in the European Union in 1995-2014: Introducing a New Data Set on Policy Actions of a Macroprudential Nature." Working Paper 2123, European Central Bank, Frankfurt.

Carney, M. 2015. "Inflation in a Globalised World." Remarks at the Economic Policy Symposium, Federal Reserve Bank of Kansas City, Jackson Hole, August 29.

Carstens, A. 2018. Interview with Borsen-Zeitung financial newspaper, May 22. https://www.bis.org/speeches/sp180523.htm.

Carstens, A. 2019. Speech at the Basler Bankenforum, Basel, September 4.

Cerutti, E, S. Claessens, and L. Laeven. 2017. "The Use and Effectiveness of Macroprudential Policies: New Evidence." *Journal of Financial Stability* 28 (February): 203-24.

Cheung, Y., and X. Qian. 2009. "Hoarding of International Reserves: Mrs. Machlup's Wardrobe and the Joneses." *Review of International Economics* 17 (4): 824-43.

Ciccarelli, M., and B. Mojon. 2010. "Global Inflation." *The Review of Economics and Statistics* 92 (3): 524-35.

Claessens, S. 2014. "An Overview of Macroprudential Policy Tools." IMF Working Paper 14/214, International Monetary Fund, Washington, DC.

Claessens, S., and M. A. Kose. 2018. "Frontiers of Macrofinancial Linkages." BIS Papers 95, Bank for International Settlements, Basel.

Cline, W. R. 1981. *World Inflation and the Developing Countries*. Washington, DC: Brookings Institution.

Collard, F., H. Dellas, B. Diba, and O. Loisel. 2017. "Optimal Monetary and Prudential Policies." *American Economic Journal: Macroeconomics* 9 (1): 40–87.

Cottarelli, C, P. Gerson, and A. Senhadji. 2014. *Post-crisis Fiscal Policy*. Cambridge, MA: MIT Press.

Cukierman, A. 2013. "Monetary Policy and Institutions Before, During, and After the Global Financial Crisis." *Journal of Financial Stability* 9 (3): 373–84.

Darvas, Z. 2012. "Real Effective Exchange Rates for 178 Countries: A New Database." Bruegel Working Paper 2012/06, Brussels.

de Haan, J., C. Bodea, R. Hicks, and S. Eijffinger. 2018. "Central Bank Independence Before and After the Crisis." *Comparative Economic Studies* 60 (2): 183-202.

de Luna-Martínez, J. and Vicente, C.L., 2012. *Global Survey of Development Banks*. Washington, DC: World Bank.

Debrun, X., and T. Kinda. 2017. "Strengthening Post-Crisis Fiscal Credibility: Fiscal Councils on the Rise – A New Dataset." *Fiscal Studies* 38 (4): 667-700.

Dijkman, M. 2015. "Monitoring Financial Stability in Developing and Emerging Economies: Practical Guidance for Conducting Macroprudential Analysis." Policy Research Working Paper 7248, World Bank, Washington, DC.

Draghi, M. 2015. "Global and Domestic Inflation." Speech at the Economic Club of New York, December 4.

ECB (European Central Bank). 2010. "Euro Area Fiscal Policies and Crisis." Occasional Paper Series 109, European Central Bank, Frankfurt.

Epure, M., I. Mihai, C. Minoiu, and J. Peydró, 2018. "Household Credit, Global Financial Cycle, and Macroprudential Policies; Credit Register Evidence from an Emerging Country." IMF Working Paper 18/13, International Monetary Fund, Washington, DC.

EU (European Union). 2007. *Treaty of Lisbon Amending the Treaty on European Union and the Treaty Establishing the European Community*. Lisbon.

Fendoğlu, S. 2017. "Credit Cycles and Capital Flows: Effectiveness of the Macroprudential Policy Framework in Emerging Market Economies." *Journal of Banking and Finance* 79 (March): 110-28.

Fernández, A., M. W. Klein, A. Rebucci, M. Schindler, and M. Uribe. 2016. "Capital Control Measures: A New Dataset." *IMF Economic Review* 64 (3): 548-74.

Feyen, E., and I. Zuccardi. 2019. "The Sovereign-Bank Nexus in EMDEs: What Is It, Is It Rising and What Are the Policy Implications?" Policy Research Working Paper 8950, World Bank, Washington, DC.

Fidrmuc, J., M. Hake, and H. Stix. 2013. "Households' Foreign Currency Borrowing in Central and Eastern Europe." *Journal of Banking & Finance* 37 (6): 1880–97.

Fischer, S. 2015. "The Transmission of Exchange Rate Changes to Output and Inflation." Speech at Monetary Policy Implementation and Transmission in the Post-Crisis Period, a research conference sponsored by the Board of Governors of the Federal Reserve System, Washington, DC, November 12.

Fiszbein, A., D. Ringold, and S. Srinivasan. 2011. "Cash Transfers, Children, and the Crisis: Protecting Current and Future Investments." Social Protection Discussion Paper 1112, World Bank, Washington, DC.

FSB (Financial Stability Board). 2018. "Implementation and Effects of the G20 Financial Regulatory Reforms: Fourth Annual Report." Financial Stability Board, Basel.

FSB (Financial Stability Board). 2019. "Implementation of G20/FSB Financial Reforms in Other Areas: Summary of Key Findings Based on the 2018 FSB Implementation Monitoring Network (IMN) Survey." Financial Stability Board, Basel.

FSB, IMF, and BIS (Financial Stability Board, International Monetary Fund, and Bank for International Settlements). 2011. "Macroprudential Tools and Frameworks." Update to G20 Finance Ministers and Central Bank Governors.

Furman, J., and L. Summers. 2019. "Who's Afraid of Budget Deficits: How Washington Should End Its Debt Obsession." *Foreign Affairs* 2019 (March/ April).

Gallagher, K. 2011. "Losing Control: Policy Space for Capital Controls in Trade and Investment Agreements." *Development Policy Review* 29 (4): 387-413.

Gallagher, K. 2015. *Ruling Capital: Emerging Markets and the Reregulation of Cross-Border Finance*. New York: Cornell University Press.

García-Cicco, J., and E. Kawamura. 2014. "Central Bank Liquidity Management and 'Unconventional' Monetary Policies." *Economía* 15 (1): 39-87.

Gemmell, N., R. Kneller, and I. Sanz. 2016. "Does the Composition of Government Expenditure Matter for Long-Run GDP Levels?" *Oxford Bulletin of Economics and Statistics* 78 (4): 522-47.

Ghosh, A., J. Ostry, and M. Qureshi. 2017. *Taming the Tide of Capital Flows*. Cambridge, MA: MIT Press.

Gill, I. S., I. Izvorski, W. van Eeghen, and D. De Rosa. 2014. *Diversified Development: Making the Most of Natural Resources in Eurasia*. Washington, DC: World Bank.

Goldstein, M., and D. Xie. 2009. "The Impact of the Financial Crisis on Emerging Asia." In *Asia and the Global Financial Crisis*, edited by R. Glick and M. Spiegel, 27-80. Federal Reserve Bank of San Francisco.

Gordy, M., and B. Howells. 2006. "Procyclicality in Basel II: Can We Treat the Disease without Killing the Patient?" *Journal of Financial Intermediation* 15 (3): 395-417.

Gourio, F., A. Kashyap, and J. Sim. 2018. "The Trade Offs in Leaning Against the Wind." *IMF Economic Review* 66 (1): 70–115.

Grabel, I. 2015. "The Rebranding of Capital Controls in an Era of Productive Incoherence." *Review of International Political Economy* 22 (1): 7-43.

Gürkaynak, R. S., Z. Kantur, M. A. Taş, and S. Yildrim. 2015. "Monetary Policy in Turkey After Central Bank Independence." CESifo Working Paper 5582, Center for Economic Studies and Ifo Institute, Munich.

Ha, J., A. Ivanova, F. Ohnsorge, and F. Unsal. 2019. "Inflation: Concepts, Evolution and Correlates." In *Inflation in Emerging and Developing Economies: Evolution, Drivers and Policies*, edited by J. Ha, M. A. Kose, and F. Ohnsorge. Washington, DC: World Bank.

Ha, J., M. A. Kose, and F. Ohnsorge, eds. 2019. *Inflation in Emerging and Developing Countries: Evolution, Drivers, and Policies*. Washington, DC: World Bank.

Ha, J., M. Stocker, and H. Yilmazkuday. 2019. "Inflation and Exchange Rate Pass-Through." In *Inflation in Emerging and Developing Economies: Evolution, Drivers and Policies*, edited by J. Ha, M. A. Kose, and F. Ohnsorge. Washington, DC: World Bank.

IILS (International Institute for Labour Studies). 2011. "A Review of Global Fiscal Stimulus." EC-IILS Joint Discussion Paper Series 5, International Institute for Labour Studies, Geneva.

IMF (International Monetary Fund). 2010a. *Coping with the Global Financial Crisis: Challenges Facing Low-Income Countries.* Washington, DC: International Monetary Fund.

IMF (International Monetary Fund). 2010b. *Impact of the Global Financial Crisis on the Gulf Cooperation Council Countries and Challenges Ahead.* Washington, DC: International Monetary Fund.

IMF (International Monetary Fund). 2012. *The Liberalization and Management of Capital Flows: An Institutional View.* Washington, DC: International Monetary Fund.

IMF (International Monetary Fund). 2016. "Capital Flows—Review of Experience with the Institutional View." Policy Paper, International Monetary Fund, Washington, DC.

IMF (International Monetary Fund). 2018a. *The IMF's Institutional View on Capital Flows in Practice.* Washington, DC: International Monetary Fund.

IMF (International Monetary Fund). 2018b. "Challenges for Monetary Policy in Emerging Markets as Global Financial Conditions Normalize." Chapter 3 in *World Economic Outlook,* October. Washington, DC: International Monetary Fund.

IMF (International Monetary Fund). 2019. "Frontier Issues in Central Banking—An Assessment of IMF Contributions." Independent Evaluation Office Background Paper 19-01/07, International Monetary Fund, Washington, DC.

Jara, A., R. Moreno, and C. E. Tovar. 2009. "The Global Crisis and Latin America: Financial Impact and Policy Responses." *BIS Quarterly Review,* Bank of International Settlement, Basel.

Jiménez, G., S. Ongena, J. L. Peydró, and J. Saurina. 2017. "Macroprudential Policy, Countercyclical Bank Capital Buffers, and Credit Supply: Evidence from the Spanish Dynamic Provisioning Experiments." *Journal of Political Economy* 125 (6): 2126-77.

Joshi, A., W. Prichard, and C. Heady. 2014. "Taxing the Informal Economy: The Current State of Knowledge and Agendas for Future Research." *Journal of Development Studies* 50 (10): 1325-47.

Kganyago, L. 2018. "Statement of the Monetary Policy Committee." South African Reserve Bank, Pretoria, January.

Kose, M. A., S. Kurlat, F. Ohnsorge, and N. Sugawara. 2017. "A Cross-Country Database of Fiscal Space." Policy Research Working Paper 8157, World Bank, Washington, DC.

Kose, M. A., H. Matsuoka, U. Panizza, and D. Vorisek. 2019. "Inflation Expectations: Review and Evidence." In *Inflation in Emerging and Developing Economies: Evolution, Drivers and Policies,* edited by J. Ha, M. A. Kose, and F. Ohnsorge. Washington, DC: World Bank.

Kose, M. A., F. Ohnsorge, and N. Sugawara. 2018. "Fiscal Space: Concept, Measurement, and Policy Implications," Research and Policy Brief 132195, World Bank, Washington, DC.

Kose, M. A., F. Ohnsorge, and N. Sugawara. 2020. "Benefits and Costs of Debt: The Dose Makes the Poison." Policy Research Working Paper 9166, World Bank, Washington, DC.

Kose, M. A., E. Prasad, K. Rogoff, and S.-J. Wei. 2010. "Financial Globalization and Economic Policies." In *Handbook of Development Economics 5,* edited by D. Rodrik and M. Rosenzweig. Amsterdam: North-Holland.

Kose, M. A., and M. E. Terrones. 2015. *Collapse and Revival. Understanding Global Recessions and Recoveries.* Washington, DC: International Monetary Fund.

Krishnamurti, D., and Y. Lee. 2014. *Macroprudential Policy Framework: A Practice Guide.* Washington, DC: World Bank.

Kuttner, K., and I. Shim. 2013. "Can Non-Interest Rate Policies Stabilize Housing Markets? Evidence from a Panel of 57 Economies." BIS Working Paper 433, Bank for International Settlements, Basel.

Laeven, L., and F. Valencia. 2018. "Systematic Banking Crises Revisited." IMF Working Paper 18/206, International Monetary Fund, Washington, DC.

Lane, T. 2016. "Monetary Policy and Financial Stability—Looking for the Right Tools." Speech by the Deputy Governor of the Bank of Canada, Montreal.

Leduc, S., and D. Wilson. 2014. "Infrastructure Spending as Fiscal Stimulus: Assessing the Evidence." *Review of Economics and Institutions* 5 (1): 1-24.

Lombardi, D., and M. Moschella. 2017. "The Symbolic Politics of Delegation: Macroprudential and Independent Regulatory Authorities." *New Political Economy* 22 (1): 92-108.

Lombardi, D., and P. L. Siklos. 2016. "Benchmarking Macroprudential Policies: An Initial Assessment." *Journal of Financial Stability* 27 (December): 35-49.

Meeks, R. 2017. "Capital Regulation and the Macroeconomy: Empirical Evidence and Macroprudential Policy." *European Economic Review* 95 (June): 125-41.

Mishkin, F. S. 2011. "Monetary Policy Strategy: Lessons from the Crisis." In *Monetary Policy Revisited: Lessons from the Crisis*, edited by M. Jorocinski, F. Smets, and C. Thimann, 67-118. Frankfurt: European Central Bank.

Nanto, D. K. 2009. *The Global Financial Crisis: Analysis and Policy Implications.* Washington, DC: Congressional Research Service.

Ocampo, J. A. 2009. "Latin America and the Global Financial Crisis." *Cambridge Journal of Economics* 33 (4): 703-24.

OECD (Organisation for Economic Co-operation and Development). 2009. *OECD Economic Outlook Interim Report.* Paris: OECD.

Ohnsorge, F., and S. Yu. 2016. "Recent Credit Surge in Historical Context." Policy Research Working Paper 7704, World Bank, Washington, DC.

Osakwe, P. N. 2010. "Africa and the Global Financial and Economic Crisis: Impacts, Responses and Opportunities." In *The Financial and Economic Crisis of 2008-2009 and Developing Countries*, edited by S. Dullien, D. J. Kotte, A. Márquez, and J. Priewe, 203-22. Geneva: United Nations.

Ostry, J., A. Ghosh, K. Habermeier, M. Chamon, M. Qureshi, L. Laeven, and A. Kokenyne. 2011. "Managing Capital Inflows: What Tools to Use?" IMF Staff Discussion Note 11/06, International Monetary Fund, Washington, DC.

Ostry, J., A. Ghosh, K. Habermeier, M. Chamon, M. Qureshi, and D. Reinhardt. 2010. "Capital Inflows: The Role of Controls." IMF Staff Position Note 10/04, International Monetary Fund, Washington, DC.

Portes, R. 2009. "Global Imbalances." In *Macroeconomic Stability and Financial Regulation: Key Issues for the G20*, edited by M. Dewatripont, X. Freixas, and R. Portes. London: Centre for Economic Policy Research.

Ramey, V. 2019. "Ten Years After the Crisis: What Have We Learned from the Renaissance in Fiscal Research?" *Journal of Economic Perspectives* 33 (2): 89-114.

Ranciere, R., A. Tornell, and A. Vamvakidis. 2010. "A New Index of Currency Mismatch and Systemic Risk." IMF Working Paper 10/263, International Monetary Fund, Washington, DC.

Reinhart, C. M., and K. S. Rogoff. 2008. "Is the 2007 US Sub-Prime Financial Crisis So Different? An International Historical Comparison." *American Economic Review: Papers & Proceedings* 98 (2): 339-44.

Rey, H. 2015. "Dilemma Not Trilemma: The Global Financial Cycle and Monetary Policy Independence." NBER Working Paper 21162, National Bureau of Economic Research, Cambridge, MA.

Rogoff, K. 2003. "Globalization and Global Disinflation." *Federal Reserve Bank of Kansas City Economic Review* 88 (4): 45-78.

Rogoff, K. 2014. "The Exaggerated Death of Inflation." *Project Syndicate,* Prague, Czech Republic. September 2.

Schaechter, A., T. Kinda, N. Budina, and A. Weber. 2012. "Fiscal Rules in Response to the Crisis—Toward the "Next-Generation" Rules. A New Dataset." IMF Working Paper 12/187, International Monetary Fund, Washington, DC.

Schmidt-Hebbel, K. 2012. "Fiscal Institutions in Resource-Rich Economies: Lessons from Chile and Norway." Institute of Economics Working Paper 416, Pontifical Catholic University of Chile, Santiago.

Stems, F. 2013. "Financial Stability and Monetary Policy: How Closely Interlinked?" *Sveriges Riksbank Economic Review* 3: 121–60.

Stone, S. E., and E. M. Truman. 2016. "Uneven Progress on Sovereign Wealth Fund Transparency and Accountability." PIIE Policy Brief 16-18, Peterson Institute for International Economics, Washington, DC.

Summers, L. 2014. "Reflections on the 'New Secular Stagnation Hypothesis.'" In *Secular Stagnation: Facts, Causes and Cures,* edited by C. Teulings and R. Baldwin. London: CEPR Press.

Svensson, L. 2017. "Cost-Benefit Analysis of Leaning against the Wind." *Journal of Monetary Economics* 90 (October): 193-213.

Tagkalakis, A. 2013. "The Effects of Financial Crisis on Fiscal Positions." *European Journal of Political Economy* 29 (March): 197-213.

Taylor, J. 2014. "The Role of Policy in the Great Recession and the Weak Recovery." *American Economic Review* 104 (5): 61–66.

U.S. Department of Treasury. 2013. "The Financial Crisis: Five Years Later—Response, Reform and Progress. "Washington DC: U.S. Department of Treasury.

Vandenbussche, J., U. Vogel, and E. Detragiache. 2015. "Macroprudential Policies and Housing Prices: A New Database and Empirical Evidence for Central, Eastern, and Southeastern Europe." *Journal of Money, Credit and Banking* 47 (S1): 343-77.

World Bank. 2009. *Global Monitoring Report: A Development Emergency.* Washington, DC: World Bank.

World Bank. 2013. *Beyond the Annual Budget: Global Experience with Medium-Term Expenditure Frameworks*. Washington, DC: World Bank.

World Bank. 2014. *China Economic Update*. October. Washington, DC: World Bank.

World Bank. 2015. *Global Economic Prospects: Having Fiscal Space and Using it.* January. Washington, DC: World Bank.

World Bank. 2017. *Global Economic Prospects: A Fragile Recovery*. January. Washington, DC: World Bank.

World Bank. 2018a. *Commodity Markets Outlook: Oil Exporters: Policies and Challenges*. April. Washington, DC: World Bank.

World Bank. 2018b. *Global Economic Prospects: The Turning of the Tide?* June. Washington, DC: World Bank.

World Bank. 2019a. *Global Economic Prospects: Heightened Tensions, Subdued Investment.* June. Washington, DC: World Bank.

World Bank. 2019b. *Global Economic Prospects: Darkening Skies.* January. Washington, DC: World Bank.

World Bank. 2019c. *Global Financial Development Report 2019/2020: Bank Regulation and Supervision A Decade After the Global Financial Crisis.* Washington, DC: World Bank.

Wyplosz, C. 2013. "Fiscal Rules: Theoretical Issues and Historical Experiences." In *Fiscal Policy After the Financial Crisis,* edited by A. Alesina and F. Giavazzi. University of Chicago Press: Chicago, IL.

Yellen, J. L. 2014. "Monetary Policy and Financial Stability." Speech by Chair of the Federal Reserve Board of Governors, Michel Camdessus Central Banking Lecture, International Monetary Fund, Washington, DC.

Zeev, N. 2017. "Capital Controls as Shock Absorbers." *Journal of International Economics* 109 (November): 43–67.

Zhang, L., and E. Zoli. 2016. "Leaning Against the Wind: Macroprudential Policy in Asia." *Journal of Asian Economics* 42 (February): 33-52.

PART III

Looking Ahead

While recessions are, by their very nature, unpredictable, the greatest near-term threat to the economy is not rising interest rates or various financial excesses, but, instead, unforeseen actions in areas like trade or geopolitics.

Raghuram G. Rajan (2019)

Professor of Finance

University of Chicago Booth School of Business

CHAPTER 6

Prospects, Risks, and Vulnerabilities

Growth in emerging market and developing economies (EMDEs) has generally disappointed since the 2009 global recession, with sizable forecast downgrades in most years, and 2019 is no different. EMDEs also face downside risks to this subdued growth outlook, which include heightened global policy uncertainty, trade tensions, spillovers from weaker-than-expected growth in major economies, and disorderly financial market developments. These risks are accompanied by region-specific risks, including geopolitical tensions, armed conflict, and severe weather events. If risks materialize, their impact on EMDEs depends on the magnitude of spillovers and domestic vulnerabilities. Since the 2009 global recession, external, corporate sector, and sovereign vulnerabilities have risen in most EMDEs, leaving them less well-prepared for future shocks. Low-income countries, in particular, face elevated vulnerabilities: about 40 percent of them are currently in debt distress. Over the longer run, EMDEs also face weakening potential growth, reflecting decelerations in capital accumulation and productivity growth, as well as demographic headwinds. These constraints are likely to hamper growth in the next decade unless they are mitigated by ambitious and credible reform agendas.

Introduction

Following the global recession of 2009, most analysts expected growth in emerging market and developing economies (EMDEs) to return to precrisis rates (chapter 3). After a strong rebound in 2010, subsequent growth outcomes, however, have generally disappointed. Comparing consensus forecasts prepared in January and June since 2009, over 70 percent of aggregated EMDE forecasts were downgrades and on average growth has been revised down by 0.2 percentage point. This year is no different, with a cumulative downgrade of 0.6 percentage point since January 2018. Growth for the year is now forecast to be at its weakest pace since 2015 and over a percentage point slower than average growth from 2000 to 2018. In addition to these repeated growth disappointments and forecast downgrades, downside risks to the outlook are rising.

Against this background this chapter addresses the following questions:

- What are EMDEs' growth prospects?
- What are the main global and regional risks to growth faced by EMDEs?
- How have external and domestic vulnerabilities evolved over the past decade and how do they compare to developments following previous crises?

Note: This chapter was prepared by Franz Ulrich Ruch.

Contributions to the literature. This chapter provides an up-to-date and comprehensive overview of the growth prospects, risks, and vulnerabilities facing EMDEs, including low-income countries (LICs). It contributes to the existing literature in several dimensions. First, the chapter updates earlier World Bank Group work on short- and long-term growth prospects, with granular regional and group perspectives (IMF 2019, World Bank 2018a). Second, it provides a comprehensive overview of vulnerabilities for the largest sample of EMDEs yet. Existing studies (for example, Chitu and Quint 2018, Dahlhaus and Lam 2018, IMF 2019, and Rojas-Saurez 2015) limit their analysis to a few, mainly large, EMDEs. In addition, this chapter is the first study that compares specific domestic and external vulnerabilities across a comprehensive list of almost 300 previous EMDE crises since 1980, building on the work of Laeven and Valencia (2018).[1]

Main findings. The chapter presents the following findings. First, EMDE growth has generally disappointed in the past decade, with repeated and significant forecast downgrades—and 2019 is no different. Almost 40 percent of EMDEs are now expected to grow more slowly in 2019 than in 2018.

Sustained and robust per capita income growth, however, is needed for EMDEs to meaningfully reduce poverty, improve shared prosperity, and converge to advanced economy levels. Income gaps with advanced economies are expected to widen in 2019 in one-third of EMDEs, with more economies affected in the Middle-East and North Africa (MNA), Sub-Saharan Africa (SSA), and Latin America and the Caribbean (LAC). The prospects of today's LICs, which are increasingly clustered in SSA, for progression to middle-income levels are dimmer than before the global recession, in part because of a rising number of countries affected by fragility, conflict, and violence; the prospect of weaker demand for primary commodities; and higher vulnerability to extreme weather, especially in agriculture-dependent economies (World Bank 2019b).

Second, although a cyclical upturn is expected over the next two years, near- and long-term growth prospects will likely remain subdued, and growth is expected to be slower than in recent decades. Long-term growth prospects are weakening, as fundamental drivers lose momentum. In the mid-2000s, potential growth in EMDEs was 5.9 percent a year; however, it slowed to 4.7 percent a year in 2013-18 and, on current trends, is expected to decelerate further over the next decade. This slowdown reflected a sharp deterioration in capital accumulation and productivity growth amid pronounced investment weakness, and demographic headwinds. Weakening growth prospects do not bode well for poverty reduction efforts in EMDEs, with evidence that poverty reduction has already started to slow. To improve prospects for potential growth, EMDE policy makers need to undertake ambitious and credible reforms that boost human and physical capital accumulation, ensure appropriate factor allocation, and raise productivity.

[1] This chapter links both to the literature on quantifying vulnerabilities (for example, Ahmed, Coulibaly, and Zlate 2017; Dahlhaus and Lam 2018; Feyen et al. 2017; Fisher and Rachel 2017; Ghosh 2016; IMF 2018; Lee, Posenau, and Stebunovs 2017) and to the literature on early warning indicators of crises. See Chamon and Crowe (2012) and Frankel and Saravelos (2012) for extensive literature reviews, and Aziz and Shin (2015) or Berg et al. (1999) as examples.

Third, near-term risks to the growth outlook for EMDEs are tilted to the downside. At the global level, EMDEs face risks related to trade tensions between the United States and other major economies, especially China; broader threats to the international trade system; the risk of a disorderly exit process of the United Kingdom from the European Union (EU); and the possibility of financial market disruptions. At the regional level, some EMDEs face risks related to security, geopolitical tensions, and severe weather events.

Fourth, the vulnerabilities of EMDEs to adverse events have risen since the 2009 global recession. EMDEs that are most vulnerable to spikes in borrowing cost are those that are highly indebted, especially those with elevated foreign-currency-denominated debt, and those that rely on potentially volatile portfolio and bank flows to finance large current account deficits. Today's average EMDE also has higher government and private debt, wider fiscal deficits, and only slightly smaller current account deficits than the average EMDE before past financial crises. These vulnerabilities may be partly mitigated by greater exchange rate flexibility and more robust monetary, prudential, and fiscal policy frameworks, compared to previous crises, as well as by financial sector reforms and the expansion of country-specific, regional, and multilateral financial safety nets since the global recession.

Prospects for growth

A decade of disappointing growth. Since 2009, January and June consensus forecasts for global growth in the same year have been downgraded by an average of 0.1 percentage point at each forecast (figure 6.1). Almost 60 percent of same-year growth forecasts have been downgrades.[2] Downgrades affected both advanced economies and EMDEs; however, in EMDEs, the growth forecast was revised down more frequently and by a greater margin. Since 2009, EMDE growth has been revised down by an average of 0.2 percentage point for the current year forecast, relative to the preceding projection. Over 70 percent of same-year forecasts for EMDEs have been downgraded.[3]

Projections for 2019 were no different. In January 2018, EMDE output was expected to grow by 4.6 percent in 2019. By the January 2019 forecast, this estimate was revised down to 4.2 percent and further to 3.9 percent in June 2019. Similarly, 10-year-ahead EMDE growth forecasts have been repeatedly downgraded. This pattern of downward revisions to both short- and long-term EMDE growth projections points to both cyclical and structural factors weighing on EMDE growth.

Since 2016, there have been consistent downward revisions to growth projections for all EMDE regions, except East Asia and Pacific (EAP; figure 6.1).[4] Regionally, the largest

[2] Forecasts published in the World Bank's *Global Economic Prospects* and the International Monetary Fund's *World Economic Outlook* showed more frequent downgrades to global growth.

[3] Forecasts for EMDEs by the International Monetary Fund, Consensus Forecasts, and the World Bank have seen a majority of forecasts downgraded in successive rounds, with the average revision since 2009 of similar magnitude.

[4] Based on data from the World Bank's *Global Economic Prospects*.

FIGURE 6.1 Growth forecast revisions since 2009

Revisions to global growth projections over the past decade have generally been downward. Growth projections for all EMDE regions, except East Asia and Pacific, have been revised down since 2016.

A. Global growth revisions

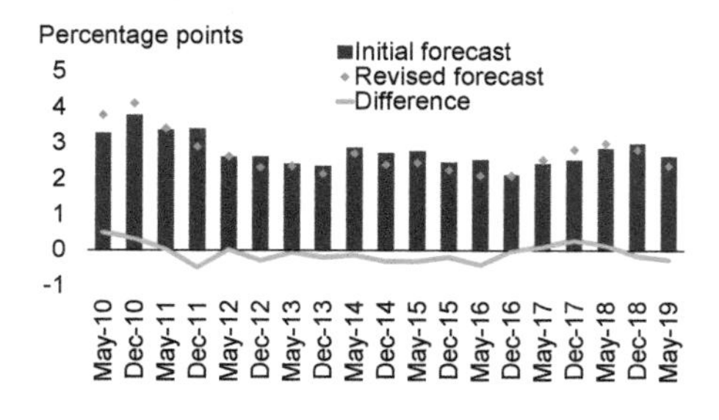

B. Advanced economy growth revisions

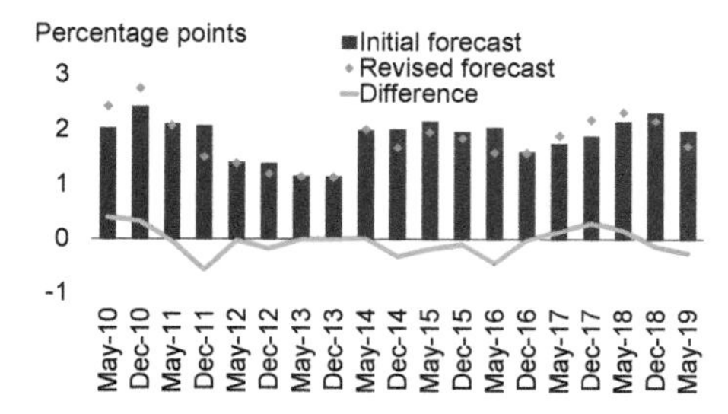

C. EMDE growth revisions

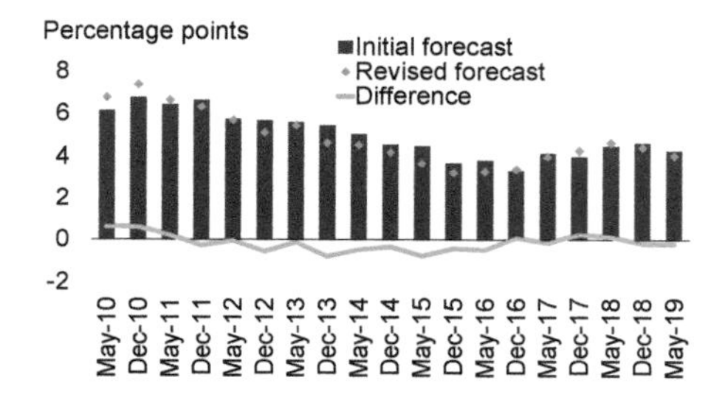

D. EMDE regional growth revisions

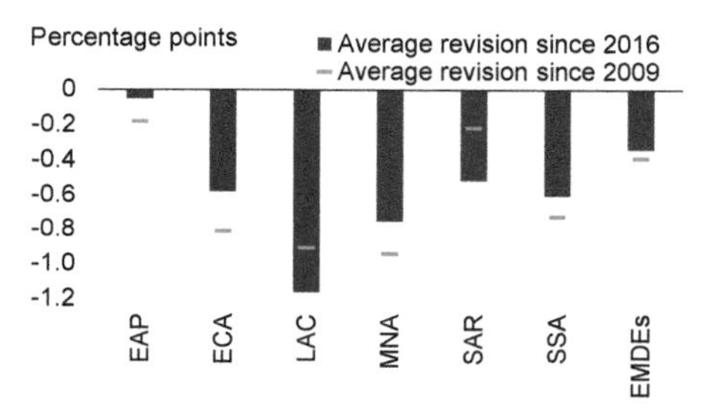

Sources: Consensus Economics; World Bank.

Note: EAP = East Asia and Pacific; ECA = Europe and Central Asia; EMDEs = Emerging market and developing economies; LAC = Latin America and the Caribbean; MNA = Middle East and North Africa; SAR = South Asia; SSA = Sub-Saharan Africa.

A-C. Output growth from the January and June consensus forecast publication of Consensus Economics since 2009. Revisions are the current forecast less the previous forecast for the current year. Weighted using constant 2010 U.S. dollar GDP for 2018.

D. Based on January and June forecasts of the World Bank's Global Economic Prospects, which achieves a better regional coverage than Consensus Economics.

revisions in this period have been to projections for LAC, with growth downgrades averaging 1.2 percentage points, amid falling commodity prices and recessions in some of LAC's largest economies in 2016 (World Bank 2019a). The second- and third-largest regional revisions since 2016 have been to growth in MNA and SSA, averaging 0.7 percentage point in both cases, with commodity-intensive countries suffering the largest downgrades.

In MNA, this downgrade reflected weak oil sector output and adjustments to lower oil prices, and more recently the intensification of U.S. sanctions on the Islamic Republic of Iran (World Bank 2019a). In SSA, oil exporters were also affected by the oil price fall whereas the region's largest economies struggled with idiosyncratic challenges. By contrast, downgrades since 2016 have been modest for South Asia (SAR), where growth has remained robust at or above its longer-term average rate since 1990 (World Bank

2019a). The absence of growth surprises in EAP reflects the steady slowing and rebalancing of growth in China, actively managed and broadly in line with official growth projections, and resilience of growth in Indonesia.

Subdued short-term outlook in EMDEs. EMDE growth is expected to stabilize at 4.4 percent over the forecast horizon (2019-21), marginally up from the average for 2016-18, but well below the more than 6 percent during 2000-08 (World Bank 2019a; figure 6.2). This outlook is premised on the dissipation of earlier financial pressures and policy uncertainties that have affected some large EMDEs and on global financing conditions remaining benign.

Many large commodity-exporting EMDEs face the lingering effects of recent financial stress and idiosyncratic headwinds (such as sanctions), postponing the expected recovery. As these effects fade, commodity-exporting EMDEs are expected to grow by 2.7 percent in 2019-21, significantly better than rates achieved in 2016-18 but still more than 1 percentage point below the average since 2000. In commodity-importing economies excluding China, growth is expected to slow to 4.7 percent in 2019-21, only slightly below the precrisis average although firmly below the average of the past three years (5.1 percent during 2016-18). Weakness among commodity importers has been most visible in Europe and Central Asia (ECA) where financial stress has undermined growth in Turkey, and binding domestic capacity constraints have particularly affected countries in Central Europe.

Still-robust prospects in low-income countries. LICs that export energy and metals commodities tend to have more volatile growth. Since 2016, they have enjoyed a recovery led by rising industrial metals prices, although it partially stalled in 2019. Other LICs have been able to maintain robust growth in a slowing global environment thanks to a combination of robust construction activity, urbanization, and expanding services sectors. For 2019-21, growth is forecast at 5.8 percent, somewhat higher than the 5.3 percent over 2016-18 (World Bank 2019a; figure 6.3). This forecast, however, represents a downgrade from earlier vintages, in part reflecting unexpectedly weak external demand from major trading partners, extreme weather events that dampened activity in several countries, and an earlier-than-expected normalization of agricultural production in some large LICs after strong recoveries from drought in previous years.

Several LIC economies are facing severe strains. LICs experiencing fragility, conflict, and violence have not seen any improvement in per capita incomes in 2016-18, which undermines efforts to reduce poverty (figure 6.3). Southern and East Africa were hit by two devastating tropical cyclones—Idai and Kenneth—in March and April 2019 that took a heavy human toll and caused severe damage to social and economic infrastructure in these economies.

Weaker longer-term growth prospects in EMDEs. Over the longer term, challenges relating to demographics, productivity growth, and investment point to weakening long-term growth in EMDEs (Diao, McMillan, and Rodrik 2019; McMillan, Rodick, and Sepúlveda 2016; World Bank 2018a; figure 6.4). Thus, potential output growth is

FIGURE 6.2 EMDE growth prospects

Following a further deceleration in 2019, output growth in EMDEs is expected to recover in 2020-21, because headwinds are assumed to dissipate in a number of key economies.

A. Growth

Percent

World | Advanced economies | EMDEs

B. Growth

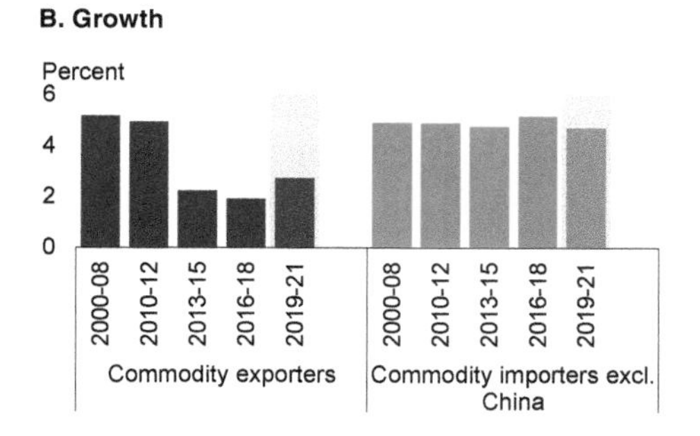

C. Growth

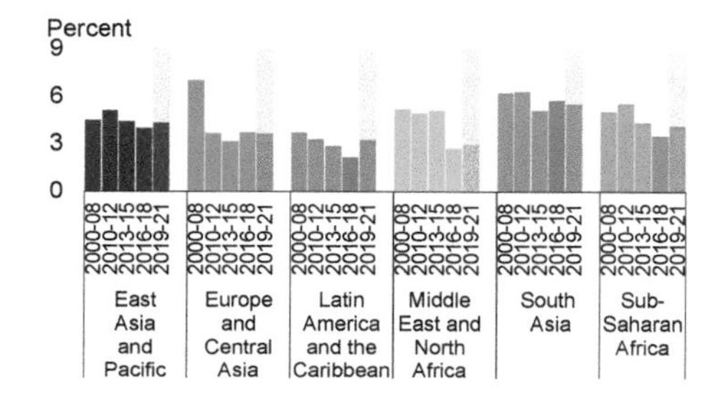

D. Per capita growth

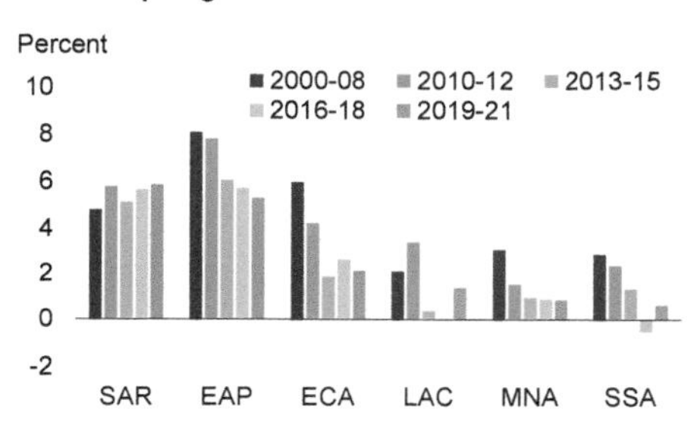

E. Per capita growth differential between EMDEs and advanced economies

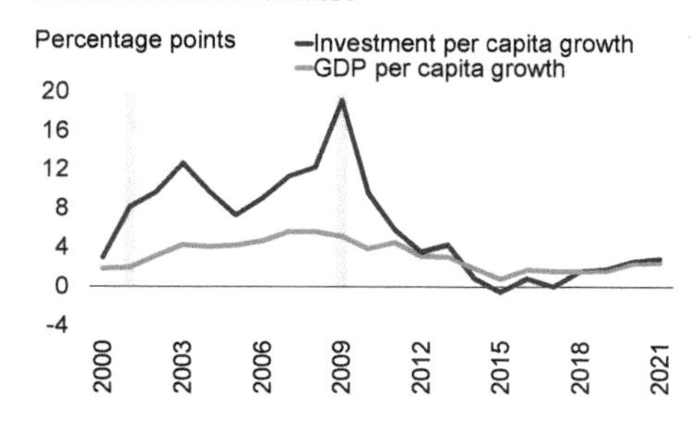

F. Share of EMDEs with widening per capita income gaps

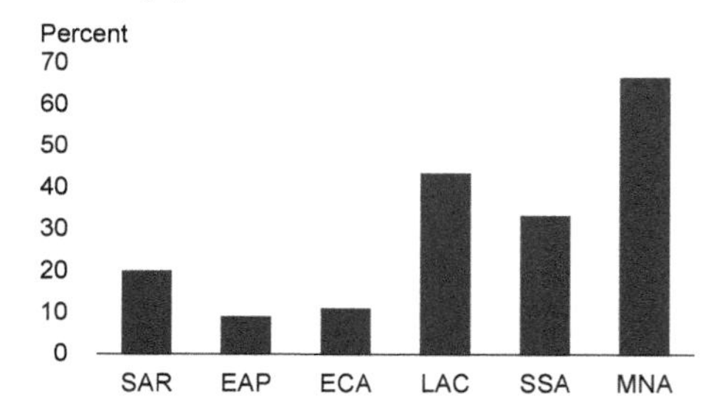

Source: World Bank.

Note: EAP = East Asia and Pacific; ECA = Europe and Central Asia; EMDEs = emerging market and developing economies; LAC = Latin America and the Caribbean; MNA = Middle East and North Africa; SAR = South Asia; SSA = Sub-Saharan Africa.

A.-D. Aggregate growth rates are calculated using constant 2010 U.S. dollar GDP weights. Shaded areas indicate forecasts.

C. Unweighted average regional growth is used to ensure broad reflection of regional trends across all countries in the region.

E. Weighted based on real GDP and investment in 2010 U.S. dollars. "Investment" refers to public and private real gross fixed capital formation. Sample consists of 50 EMDEs. Shaded areas indicate global recessions and slowdowns.

F. Economies with a widening income gap are those with per capita GDP growth that is at least 0.1 percentage point lower than advanced economy per capita GDP growth in 2019.

FIGURE 6.3 Growth prospects for low-income countries

Growth in LICs is expected to remain robust in 2019 and accelerate in 2020 as industrial-commodity-exporting LICs continue to recover from a low in 2016. Despite this expectation, per capita growth will not be sufficient to markedly reduce income gaps with advanced economies, which are likely to widen in LICs experiencing fragility, conflict, and violence.

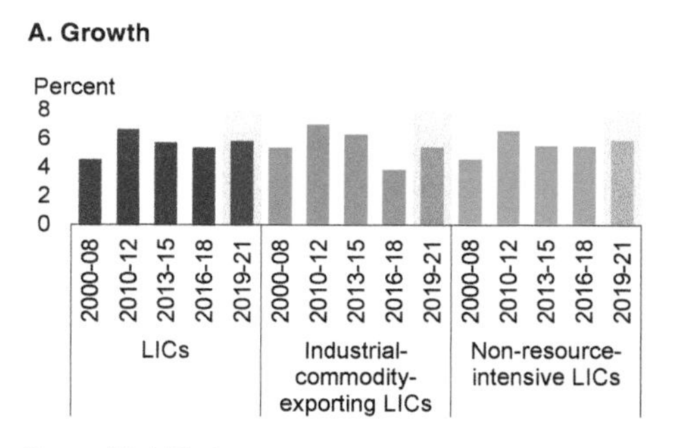

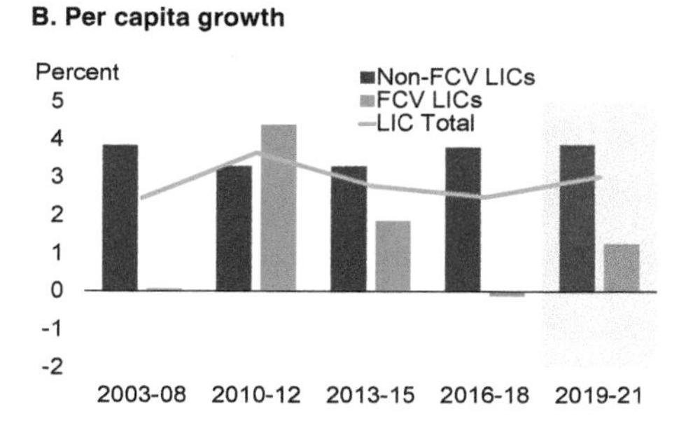

Source: World Bank.

Note: Based on low-income countries (LICs) as defined in 2018 and includes 28 economies. Shaded areas indicate forecasts.

A. Aggregate growth rates calculated using 2010 U.S. dollar GDP weights. Industrial commodity-exporting countries include energy and metal exporting-economies.

B. FCV = fragility, conflict, and violence. Weighted averages of country groups.

expected to decline to 4.3 percent a year on average in 2019-27, well below the 5.9 percent a year during 2003-07. Sixty percent of EMDEs are expected to experience a slowdown.

The slowdown is being driven by a combination of factors (box 6.1). Productivity growth has moderated as the growth of productivity-enhancing investment has slowed, precrisis gains in factor reallocation (notably including the migration of labor from agriculture to manufacturing and services activities) have been largely depleted, and growth in global value chains has moderated. Slower investment growth, partly driven by policy-guided rebalancing in China, has also tempered capital accumulation. Since 2010, the share of the working-age population has stabilized in the average EMDEs after more than four decades of rapid increases. Many of these factors will continue to constrain potential output growth in the period ahead. To counteract them, policy makers should undertake ambitious, credible reform agendas that boost human and physical capital accumulation and improve productivity. Sustained robust per capita income growth is needed for EMDEs to meaningfully reduce poverty (see Dollar, Kleineberg, and Kraay 2013; Dollar and Kraay 2002; Foster and Szekely 2008; Ravallion and Chen 1997; Santo, Dabus, and Delbianco 2019; World Bank 2018b, 2018c).

Slowing convergence with advanced economies. During 2000-08, per capita growth in EMDEs averaged 4.7 percent a year, up from 1 percent a year in the 1990s. Since the 2009 global recession, however, per capita growth has slowed, and is expected to reach 3.2 percent in 2019-21. Substantial differences, however, have been observed across regions (figure 6.2).

FIGURE 6.4 Long-term growth prospects of EMDEs

EMDE long-term growth and investment prospects slowed substantially in 2018 from the precrisis period. Potential growth is also expected to slow in the next decade.

A. Long-term consensus forecasts: Output growth

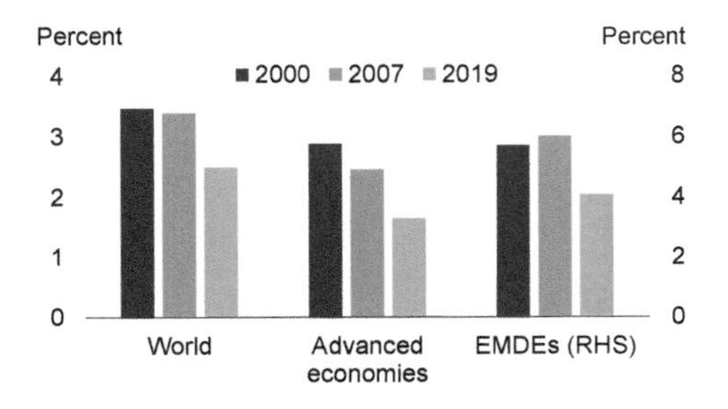

B. Long-term consensus forecasts: Investment growth

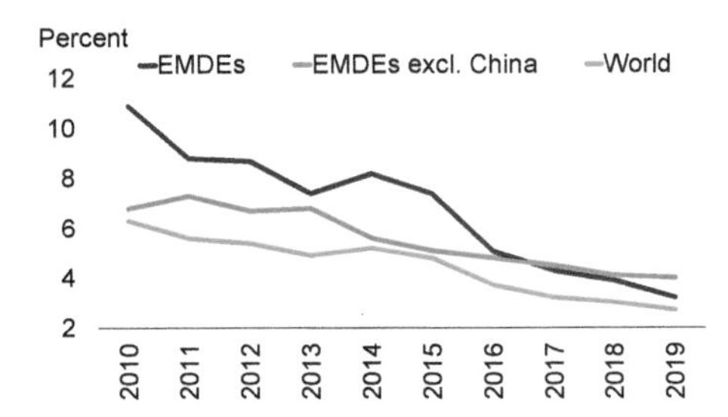

C. Potential output growth

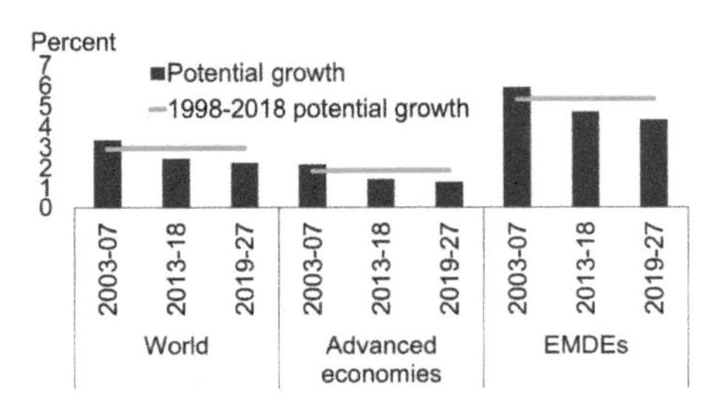

D. Potential per capita output growth

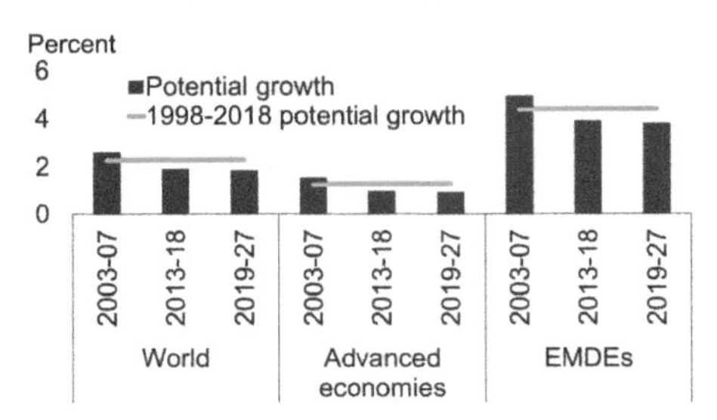

Sources: Consensus Economics; Haver Analytics; Penn World Table; UN Population Prospects; World Bank.

Note: EMDEs = emerging market and developing economies.

A. Bars show long-term (10 years ahead) average annual growth forecasts surveyed in respective years. Sample comprises 38 countries—20 advanced economies and 18 EMDEs—for which consensus forecasts are consistently available during 1998-2019. Aggregate growth rates calculated using constant 2010 U.S. dollar GDP weights.

B. 10-year-ahead forecasts surveyed in indicated year. Aggregate growth rates are calculated using constant 2010 U.S. dollar investment weights. Sample comprises 23 advanced economies and 20 EMDEs.

C.D. Period average of annual GDP-weighted averages. Estimates based on production function approach. World sample comprises 50 EMDEs and 30 advanced economies.

- *SAR and EAP.* Four of the five economies with the most rapid per capita growth were in SAR and EAP, where per capita growth averaged more than 5.7 percent in 2016-18 and is expected to remain above 5 percent growth in the next three years. SSA and LAC, however, lagged behind other regions.

- *SSA.* In SSA, where most of the world's poor live, average per capita output contracted in 2016-18 and is expected to remain near zero (0.6 percent) in 2019-21. SSA's three largest economies have witnessed negative per capita growth since 2015-16. Some metal exporters and countries affected by fragility, conflict, and violence have also had weak per capita growth. In contrast, other SSA economies have maintained robust per capita income growth.

BOX 6.1 Long-term growth prospects in emerging and developing economies

Since 2011, potential growth has slowed in emerging market and developing economies. This downward trend is expected to continue over the next decade. In the absence of a major reform push to reverse this trend, another crisis could cause further lasting damage to potential growth. This box looks at the sources of the potential growth slowdown and finds that it is due to weaker capital deepening and productivity growth, as well as a declining share of working-age population.

Introduction

Slowdown in potential growth. During 2013-18, emerging market and developing economies (EMDEs) growth averaged 4.2 percent a year, well below its average pace of 7.2 percent a year in 2003-07. Similarly, EMDE potential growth—the growth rate that can be sustained at full employment and full capacity—slowed to 4.7 percent a year on average during 2013-18, compared with 5.9 percent during 2003-07 (World Bank 2018a; figure B6.1.1). Postcrisis growth weakness in EMDEs is both cyclical and structural in nature. Structurally it reflects a sharp slowdown in capital accumulation and productivity growth amid pronounced weakness in investment, as well as demographic headwinds.

- *Weak productivity growth.* Precrisis gains from factor reallocation (notably including the migration of labor from agriculture to manufacturing and services) have increasingly been exhausted, the expansion of global value chains has moderated, and productivity-enhancing investment growth has slowed. In EMDEs, trend total factor productivity growth slowed to 1.9 percent a year in 2013-18, down from 2.5 percent a year in 2003-07, and below its long-term average of 2.2 percent.

- *Slow investment growth.* Several factors have weighed on investment growth: China's policy-guided rebalancing away from investment, declining commodity prices, lower foreign direct investment inflows, policy uncertainty, and lower long-term growth expectations. EMDE investment growth has slowed sharply from double-digit annual rates in the immediate wake of the global financial crisis to a decade-low 3.3 percent in 2015. Despite a recovery since 2016, investment growth remains subdued in commodity exporters and well below long-term averages among commodity importers.

- *Demographic headwinds.* In 2010, EMDEs as a whole passed a demographic turning point that advanced economies had already passed in the mid-1980s: after rising steadily for four decades, working-age population shares stabilized. As a result, working-age population growth has slowed since 2010, with the

Note: This box was prepared by Sinem Kilic Celik and Wee Chian Koh.

BOX 6.1 Long-term growth prospects in emerging and developing economies *(continued)*

FIGURE B6.1.1 Drivers of potential growth in EMDEs

Potential growth has slowed in many EMDEs and is expected to weaken further over the next decade as productivity growth declines further and demographic headwinds intensify. Long-term growth forecasts have consequently also been revised down.

A. Contributions to EMDE potential growth

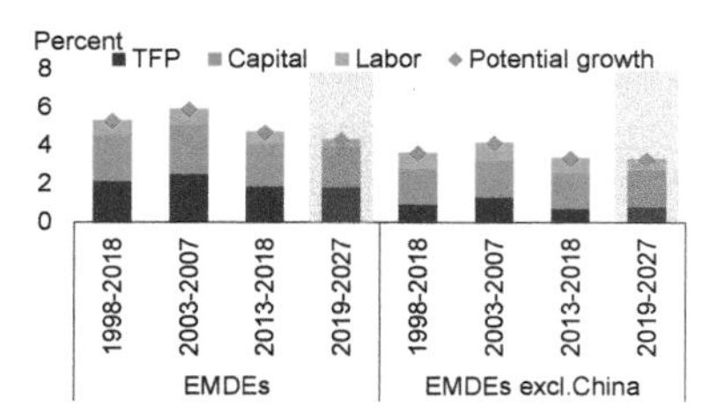

B. Contributions to EMDE potential growth

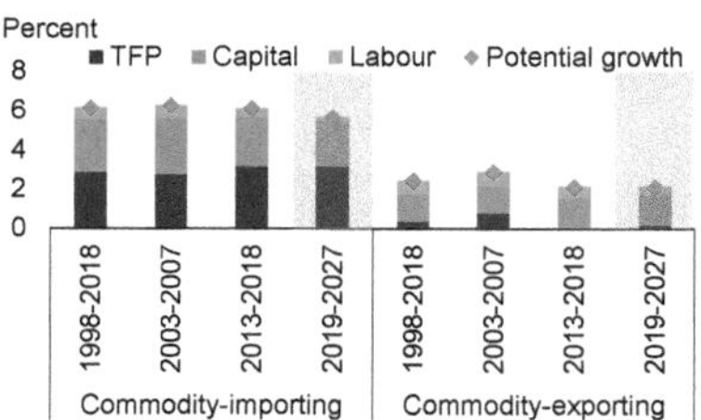

C. Contributions to EMDE regional potential growth

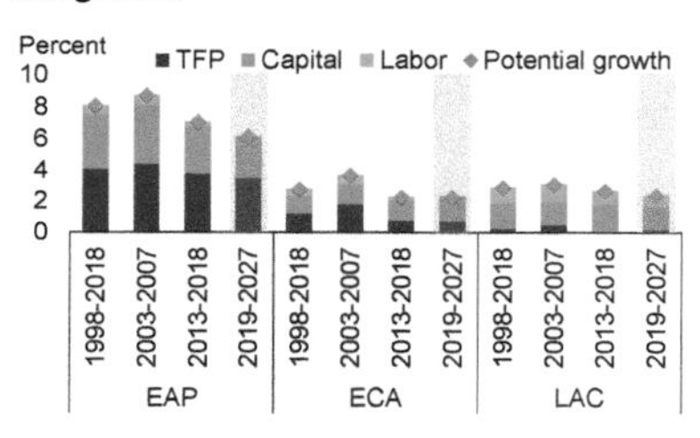

D. Contributions to EMDE regional potential growth

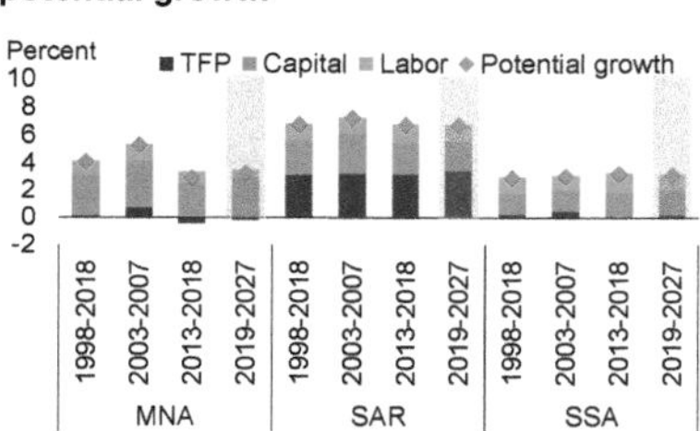

Sources: Penn World Table; United Nations; World Bank.

Note: Decomposition of the share of potential growth contributed by labor, capital, and total factor productivity (TFP). EAP = East Asia and Pacific; ECA = Europe and Central Asia; EMDEs = emerging market and developing economies; LAC = Latin America and the Caribbean; MNA = Middle East and North Africa; SAR = South Asia; SSA = Sub-Saharan Africa.

slowdown most pronounced in Eastern Europe and Central Asia and the Middle East and North Africa.

Prospects for long-term EMDE growth

Growth prospects over the next decade remain challenging for EMDEs. Potential growth is expected to decline further, to 4.3 percent a year in 2019-27 (World Bank 2018a). This slowdown is expected to be broad-based, affecting 60 percent of EMDEs, with potential growth likely to be below long-term averages in almost two-thirds of them. It is reflected in the continued downgrade of 10-year-ahead growth forecasts (Kose, Ohnsorge, and Sugawara, forthcoming).

BOX 6.1 Long-term growth prospects in emerging and developing economies *(continued)*

Many of the drivers of the potential growth slowdown in EMDEs are likely to persist over the next decade. In commodity exporters, weaker expectations for the long-term profitability of resource-based projects, amid a deceleration in global demand for industrial commodities as China's rebalancing continues, is expected to weigh on investment. Fading policy stimulus and tighter financing conditions will further weigh on investment growth and slow capital deepening, constrained by elevated public and private debt levels in many EMDEs. With the exception of South Asia and Sub-Saharan Africa, demographic trends are expected to turn from tailwinds to headwinds. Thus, over the next decade, countries with still-rising working-age population shares are expected to account for 38 percent of EMDE output, down from 98 percent in the mid-2000s. Many countries will have to contend with the fiscal cost of aging populations. The effects of climate change and new disruptive technologies could compound these challenges.

Ambitious, credible reform agendas that improve productivity and boost human and physical capital are needed to raise potential growth. Productivity-enhancing reforms entail removing barriers to the reallocation of resources toward higher-productivity firms and sectors, and stimulating the creation, innovation, and upgrades of individual firms. Investing in human capital and infrastructure could help unlock growth dividends and improve resilience to disruptive technologies and climate change.

Potential growth during contractions

Financial crises or severe economic contractions affect potential output in several ways: reduced productivity-enhancing research and development spending because of weak profitability; more limited funding for technology absorption because of reduced credit supply; less access to bank lending for creative firms; a legacy of obsolete capacity; self-fulfilling expectations of weak growth prospects; human capital loss and reduced job search activity among the long-term unemployed; and lower labor productivity after financial crises (World Bank 2018a).

Output contractions leave a legacy of weaker potential growth for at least the following half-decade. Two years following a contraction, potential annual growth is, on average, 1.2 percentage points less than in the year preceding the contraction. The effect is stronger in EMDEs than in advanced economies. Four to five years after the onset of the contraction, potential growth remains lower by about 1 percentage point a year. Over the past half-century, the global economy has been disrupted by a financial crisis of varying breadth and severity in every decade. If this pattern is repeated and if another crisis occurs in the near future, it would cause lasting damage to potential growth.

- *MNA*. Average per capita growth is expected to remain near zero (0.8 percent) over the next three years. In the region's two largest economies, the weakness of the last three years will remain. In the Islamic Republic of Iran, U.S. sanctions will weigh on growth. In Saudi Arabia, Organization of Petroleum Exporting Countries (OPEC) restrictions on oil production constrain prospects.

The weakness in EMDE growth in the past five years has set back convergence with per capita incomes in advanced economies. In 2019, per capita income gaps with advanced economies are expected to widen in about one-third of EMDEs overall, and in about two-thirds and one-half in MNA and LAC, respectively.

Poverty targets likely out of reach. The world has made significant strides in reducing the number of poor and the severity of poverty over the past two decades (World Bank 2018b). In 1999, 1.729 billion people lived on $1.90 or less per day (the international extreme poverty line), concentrated in EAP, SAR, and SSA (figure 6.5). In 2015, the latest available data point, their number had declined by more than half to 736 million. Much of the success in eradicating global poverty came from China and India. In China, the number of extreme poor fell from 503 million in 1999 to under 10 million by 2015. As a result, the share of extreme poor in EAP declined to just 2.3 percent of the population in 2015, from 38 percent of the population in 1999. In India, too, the number of people living in extreme poverty declined by 260 million to 176 million in 2015. As a result, the share of extreme poor in South Asia declined to 12.4 percent of the population in 2015 from 39 percent of the population in 1999.

In contrast, in MNA and SSA, rapid population growth has swelled the number of extreme poor, even though, in SSA, they now account for a smaller portion of the total population. In SSA, the number of poor rose by 14 million since 2008 and 32 million since 1999. The countries with the largest increases in the absolute number of extreme poor since 2008 are South Sudan, Madagascar, Nigeria, Malawi, and South Africa. In SSA, where 41 percent of the population live in extreme poverty, this share is five times as high as in other EMDEs, on average.

Since the global recession, there is evidence that the rate of poverty reduction has slowed further (World Bank 2018b).[5] Between 2011 and 2013, poverty declined by 1.25 percentage points per year but by only 0.6 percentage point between 2013 and 2015. Forecasts for these trends to 2018 suggest a further slowdown to 0.5 percentage point per year. The pace of reduction slowed particularly in ECA, which was hard-hit by the global recession and subsequent euro area crisis, and reversed in countries that experienced steep recessions (Habib et al. 2010; chapter 3).

In 2015, half of the 736 million people living in extreme poverty could be found in just five countries, two of which are classified as LICs: India, Nigeria, the Democratic

[5] Studies that looked at the negative impact of the global recession include Chen and Ravallion (2010); Development Committee (2010); Grosh, Bussolo, and Frejie (2014); Narayan and Sánchez-Páramo (2012); Tingson et al. (2010); World Bank (2009).

FIGURE 6.5 Poverty

The number of global poor has more than halved since 1999. In 2015, they were concentrated in a few countries, notably India, Nigeria, Bangladesh, and across low-income countries. Countries with slower growth see less poverty reduction, and current growth projections would be insufficient to achieve the goal of reducing global extreme poverty to 3 percent.

A. Global poor

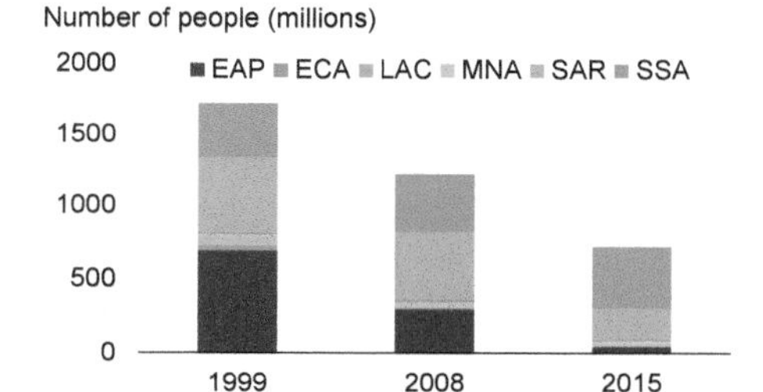

B. Poverty rates

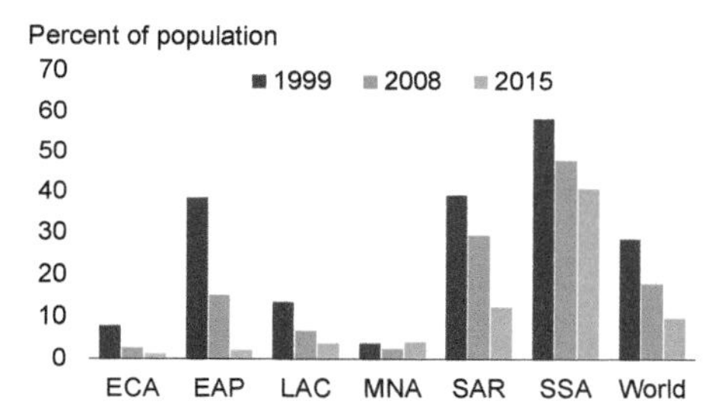

C. Shared prosperity

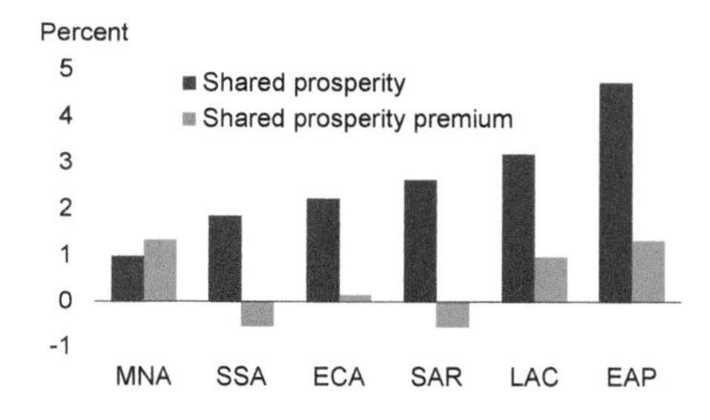

D. Change in poverty rates, by GDP growth

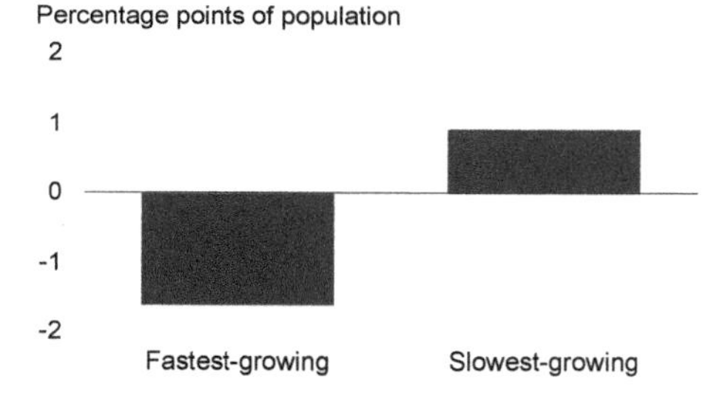

E. Projections of global extreme poverty

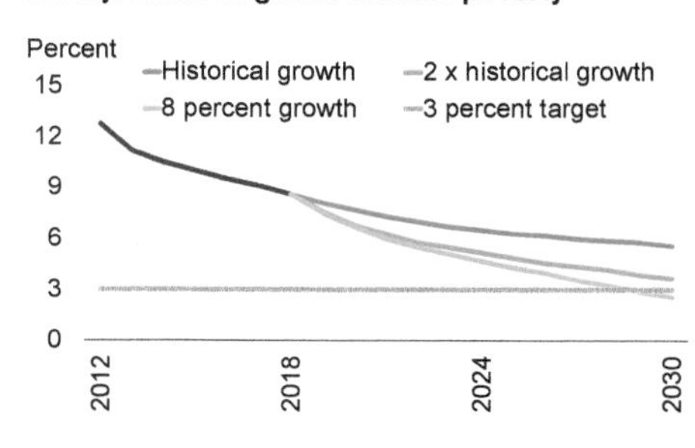

F. Distribution of poverty

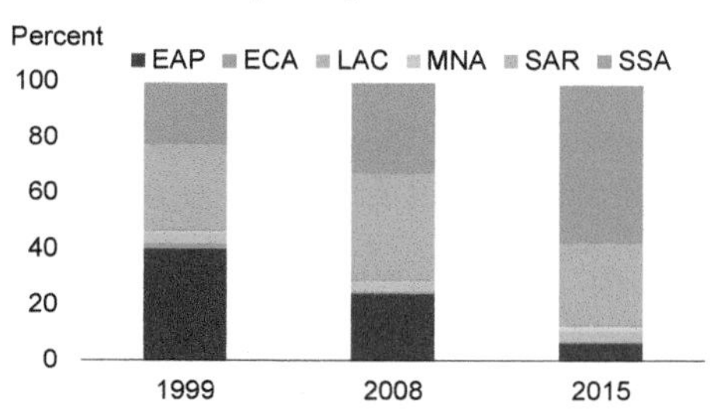

Sources: World Bank's PovcalNet.

Note: EAP = East Asia and Pacific; ECA = Europe and Central Asia; EMDEs = emerging market and developing economies; LAC = Latin America and the Caribbean; MNA = Middle East and North Africa; SAR = South Asia; SSA = Sub-Saharan Africa.

A.B.F. Regional aggregation based on 2011 purchasing power parity and $1.90 per day poverty line.

C. Shared prosperity is the average growth in household per capita income or consumption of the bottom 40 percent between 2010 and 2015. The shared prosperity premium measures the difference between income growth of the poorest 40 percent of households and the average household income growth.

D. Unweighted average of the average annual change in poverty headcount rates between two poverty estimates in each group of countries. "Fastest-growing" includes the quartile of EMDE country-year pairs with the highest average annual real GDP per capita growth between two poverty estimates; "slowest-growing" includes the quartile with the slowest average annual real GDP per capita growth. Based on data available from 1981.

E. Data based on global real per capita growth; 8 percent growth assumes average annual growth in per capita incomes of 6 percent for all countries, with incomes of the poorest 40 percent of households growing at 8 percent and those of the richest 60 percent growing at 4.7 percent.

Republic of Congo (LIC), Ethiopia (LIC), and Bangladesh.[6] Most of the other half are concentrated in other LICs, such as Kenya, Madagascar, Mozambique, Tanzania, and Uganda, each of which is home to at least 15 million people living in poverty. In total, LICs and four lower-middle-income countries (India, Nigeria, Bangladesh, and Indonesia) account for over 80 percent of global poverty. The countries with the highest poverty rates are all in Sub-Saharan Africa (and LICs): the Central African Republic (77), Madagascar (77 percent), Burundi (75 percent), South Sudan (73 percent), and the Democratic Republic of Congo (72 percent). Poverty rates are also rising in economies affected by fragility, conflict, and violence (World Bank 2019a).

Longer-run growth trends in EMDEs suggest that the 2030 poverty target is likely out of reach. Even if historical growth trends between 2005-15 are projected forward, the world will not be able to reach the 3 percent global poverty rate target set for 2030. If current trends continue, the share of global poor living in SSA will increase to 87 percent by 2030. In order to reach the 2030 goal of reducing the global poverty rate to 3 percent, SSA would need to grow by 6 percent per capita per year, with 8 percent income growth among the bottom 40 percent of the population. In contrast, during 2017-19, per capita growth in SSA has been near zero and only a small and declining proportion of EMDEs has achieved such growth in any year since 2009 (World Bank 2019a).

Shared prosperity. Rapid growth in incomes of the poorest 40 percent of households are key to "shared prosperity." During 2010-15, incomes of the poorest 40 percent of the population grew particularly rapidly (4.7 percent) in EAP but most slowly in MNA and SSA. In about half of EMDEs, incomes of the poorest 40 percent "caught up" by growing faster than average incomes since 2010. This catching up was particularly pronounced in EAP and MNA (1.3 percentage points faster)—in MNA notwithstanding slow income growth among the poorest 40 percent—and in LAC (1 percentage point faster; World Bank 2018b; figure 6.5). In contrast, in more than half of EMDEs in SSA, incomes of the poorest 40 percent have grown more slowly than average incomes, thus widening income inequality in the average SSA country (especially in Mozambique and Zambia)—with important exceptions such as Burkina Faso.

Global income inequality. Income inequality in EMDEs has fallen since the global financial crisis, continuing a trend that began in the late 1990s or early 2000s (Bourguignon 2017; World Bank 2016c, 2018a). In EMDEs, the average Gini coefficient declined from 41.4 in 2008 to 39.8 in 2017. The downward trend since the global recession has been broad-based: in more than half of EMDEs with available data for 2005-07 and 2015-17, the Gini coefficient has declined over the decade. On average, income distributions are most equal in ECA and least equal in LAC and SSA (World Bank 2016c).

Improving income inequality is about more than reducing extreme poverty because it affects the most vulnerable in society, women and children, and is associated with

[6] Some non-LIC countries in this list (Bangladesh, India, Nigeria) were LICs until recently. India became a lower-middle-income country in 2009, Nigeria in 2008, and Bangladesh in 2014.

greater fragility and instability (World Bank 2016c). For example, rich children are four times more likely to be enrolled in primary education, creating a significant gap in economic opportunity later in life. More equal societies are more conducive to political and institutional stability, and greater social cohesion helps mitigate threats from extremism. Inequality can therefore aggravate output volatility but can also rise with greater volatility (Atkinson and Morelli 2010; Fang, Miller, and Yeh 2015; Stiglitz 2012). Its impact on growth depends on the source of inequality.[7] Whereas income inequality can create incentives for productivity growth, inequality brought about by lack of opportunity—access to health care, credit, and education—stifles productivity growth.

Downside risks to growth prospects

EMDEs face significant downside risks to growth over the next few years, including policy uncertainty, trade tensions, financial market disruptions, spillovers from weaker-than-expected growth in major economies, and geopolitical risks. Some risks, if they materialize, could have profound repercussions for long-run growth prospects.

Policy uncertainty. Global policy uncertainty has risen to its highest level in over three decades in 2019 (Davis 2016; figure 6.6). This rise partly reflects heightened trade tensions between the United States and its largest trading partners, uncertainty related to the exit of the United Kingdom from the EU, and idiosyncratic developments in several large economies (including Brazil, France, and Italy). Heightened risks and uncertainty can lower growth and investment by depressing the expected value, and increasing the variance, of prospective future returns on long-term investment, and also by encouraging precautionary savings (Baker, Bloom, and Davis 2016; Jurado, Ludvigson, and Ng 2015; World Bank 2017a). For example, policy uncertainty in the euro area has been found to have had a statistically significant impact on investment outcomes in ECA EMDEs (World Bank 2017a).

Trade tensions. Much of the growth in trade since World War II has been due to the removal of protectionist measures including tariffs (Baier and Bergstrand 2001; Goldberg and Pavcnik 2016; Krugman, Cooper, and Srinivasan 1995). The commitment to trade liberalization and multilateralism has weakened recently amid growing trade restrictions. New import-restrictive measures imposed in the eight months to May 2019 were three-and-a-half times the average seen since May 2012 (WTO 2019).

Trade tensions between the Unites States and China have escalated, with import tariffs imposed in 2018 and raised in 2019 (figure 6.6). There are indications that recent tariff increases have reduced real incomes in both the United States and China, with the costs to consumers outweighing the additional government revenue (Amiti, Redding, and Weinstein 2019; Fajgelbaum et al. 2019). These trade tensions, combined with recent

[7] See Ferreira et al. (2014) and World Bank (2006) for a survey of the literature.

FIGURE 6.6 Risks to EMDE growth prospects: Policy uncertainty and trade tensions

Risks to the growth outlook for EMDEs are rising and mainly to the downside. They include heightened global policy uncertainty and trade disputes.

A. Global policy uncertainty

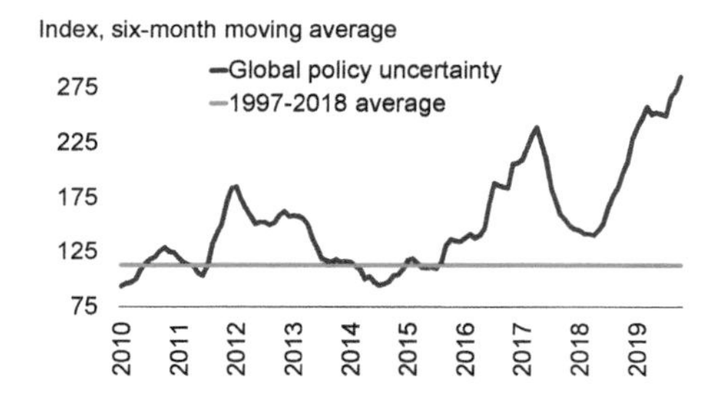

B. Impact of euro area policy uncertainty on investment in ECA

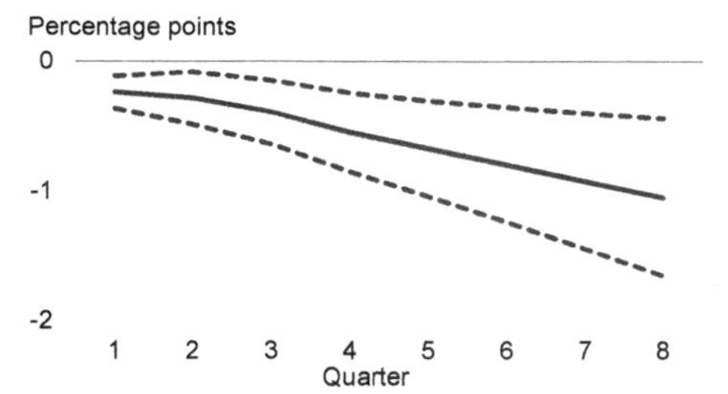

C. Import tariffs

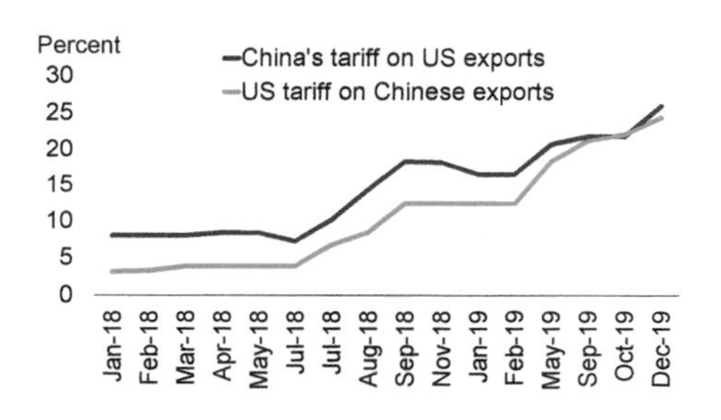

D. Goods trade, container shipping, and export orders

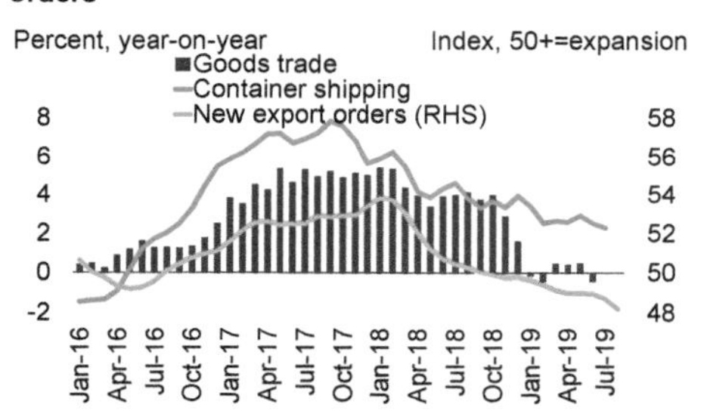

Sources: CPB Bureau for Economic Policy Analysis; China Ministry of Finance; Davis (2016); Freund et al. (2018); Haver Analytics; Institute of Shipping Economics and Logistics; International Trade Centre; United States Trade Representative; World Bank.

A. See Davis (2016) for details. Last observation is October 2019.

B. Vector autoregressions are used for estimation on a sample of aggregate emerging market and developing economy (EMDE) variables for 1998Q1-2016Q2. The model includes the Economic Policy Uncertainty for the euro area, emerging market stock price (euro area) index, emerging market bond index, aggregate real output and investment growth in six Europe and Central Asia (ECA) economies, with Group of Seven real GDP growth, U.S. 10-year bond yields, and Morgan Stanley Capital International World Index as exogenous regressors and estimated with two lags.

C. Trade-weighted average tariffs computed from product-level tariff and trade data, weighted by U.S. exports to the world and China's exports to the world in 2017.

D. Figure shows three-month moving averages. New export orders measured by Purchasing Managers' Index (PMI). PMI readings above 50 indicate expansion in economic activity; readings below 50 indicate contraction. Last observation is June 2019 for goods trade, July 2019 for container shipping, and August 2019 for new export orders.

cyclical headwinds, have weighed on global trade. In addition, the uncertainty created and the likely disruptions to global value chains will discourage firms from investing.

So far, the cost of trade tensions between the United States and China have been modest compared to the size of the economies involved. If trade tensions were to spread and worsen, however, the consequences for global growth could be sizable. If tariff rates on all bilateral U.S.-China trade flows were increased by 25 percentage points, the impact on world growth could be significant, especially if confidence were also to retreat (Freund et al. 2018). Similarly, if all World Trade Organization (WTO) members were to increase tariffs to legally allowed upper bounds, it could translate into a decline in global trade flows of about 9 percent, similar to the contraction seen during the global financial crisis in 2008-09 (Kutlina-Dimitrova and Lakatos 2017).

Weakening trade sets back global poverty reduction efforts, as the poorest EMDEs rely heavily on trade for economic growth, with advanced economies their main export destinations and capital imports driving investment (World Bank 2017c). Higher trade openness is associated with lower poverty and inequality, and with helping countries transition out of low-income status, provided other policies are implemented that target adjustment costs (Goldberg and Pavcnik 2004; Winters, McCulloch, and McKay 2004). Tariff reductions have also been found to proportionately increase the incomes of the poor (Dollar and Kraay 2002; Sachs and Warner 1995).

Financial market risks. Notwithstanding still-benign global financial conditions, rising indebtedness makes EMDEs vulnerable to disorderly financial market developments. Several events could trigger a materialization of this risk.

First, in advanced economies, deteriorating growth prospects could increase corporate default rates, especially in an environment where the share of low-rated corporate bonds and the use of less transparent leveraged loans and collateralized debt obligations have increased (figure 6.7).[8] High-yield debt markets, including those for leveraged loans, have grown rapidly since the financial crisis and now exceed precrisis levels (FSB 2019). The overall size of the leveraged loan market is estimated at $2.2 trillion to $2.4 trillion, mainly in the United States and the EU. The accumulation of this debt since 2009 has significantly outpaced growth in the earnings of the corporations taking on these loans. Debt is about five times earnings (before interest, tax, depreciation, and amortization) in the United States and EU and six times earnings in the rest of world, significantly above their precrisis levels (FSB 2019).

Second, large currency depreciations in EMDEs—possibly triggered by domestic vulnerabilities, shifts in U.S. monetary policy expectations, sharp commodity price movements, or changes in investor risk appetite—could lead to financial market disruptions, particularly through increases in the domestic currency value of debt denominated in foreign currencies. Some EMDEs have seen a rise in foreign ownership of local currency-denominated bonds, to over 30 percent of total, reducing immediate currency risks.

Unlike foreign direct investment, however, foreign participation in local bond markets can quickly reverse if investor sentiment changes. If a currency crisis ensues, EMDEs may experience output contractions, as occurred in half of EMDEs that faced previous crises (figure 6.7). Following a crisis and the accompanying jump in risk premia, debt service costs rise and real incomes fall, eroded by rising inflation and the required tightening of monetary policy. Sharp currency depreciations have been found to be

[8] Leveraged loans are loans to nonfinancial corporations that have high debt levels, below-investment grade credit ratings, or a spread at issuance higher than a certain threshold (FSB 2019).

FIGURE 6.7 Risks to EMDE growth prospects: Financial stress

Events that could trigger financial market disruptions include increasing high-yield debt, large currency depreciations in EMDEs, contagion from financial stress in other EMDEs, and shifts in investor risk perceptions.

A. Share of global bonds rated BBB or below

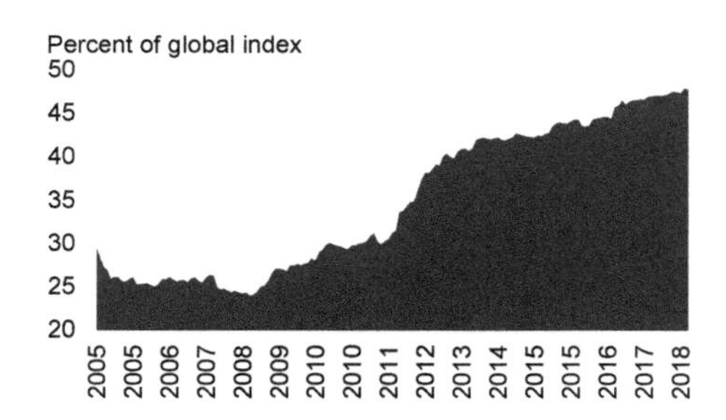

B. Share of EMDEs with negative growth around currency crises

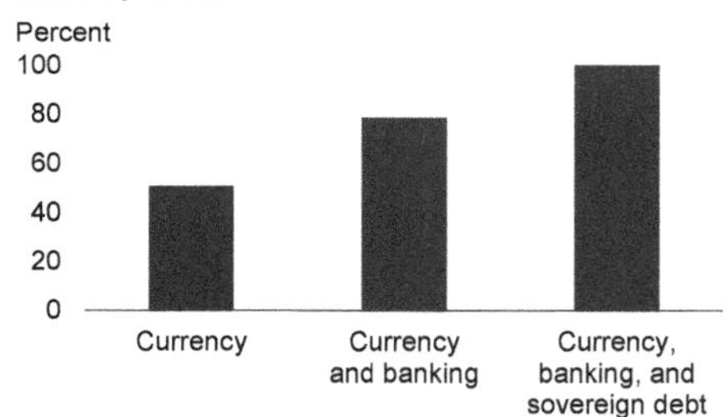

C. Number of countries with large currency depreciations

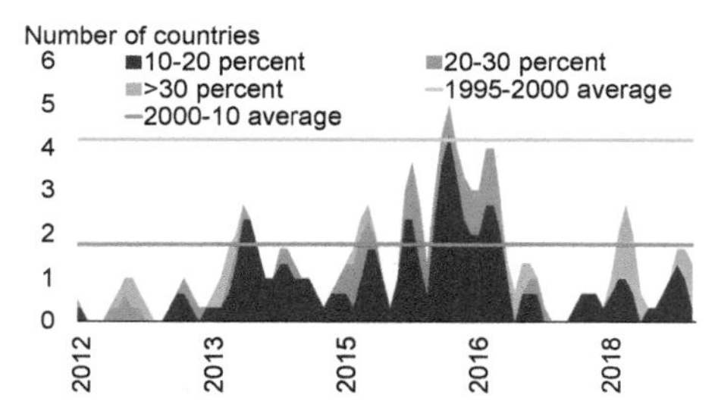

D. U.S. term premium

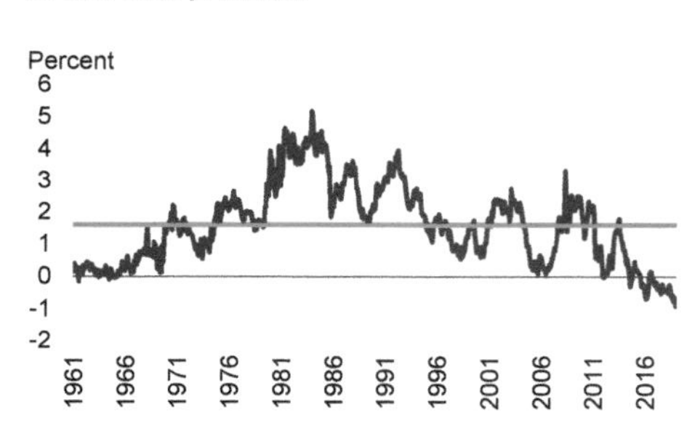

Sources: Dealogic; Federal Reserve Bank of New York; Laeven and Valencia (2018); World Bank.

Note: EMDEs = emerging market and developing economies.

A. Last observation is July 2018.

B. Share of countries that experienced negative growth in the current or next year following a currency crisis, a currency and banking crisis, or a currency, banking, and sovereign debt crisis between 1975 and 2017.

C. Figure shows three-month moving averages. Depreciations are defined as negative quarterly changes in the effective exchange rate. The sample comprises 138 EMDEs. Last observation is December 2018.

D. Based on Adrian, Crump, and Meonch (2013) model of the term premia at a 10-year maturity. Last observation is August 2019.

associated with significantly larger contractions in output when accompanied by banking sector and sovereign distress (Laeven and Valencia 2018).

Third, concerns about the possibility of contagion have resurfaced amid recent episodes of financial stress in some EMDEs. Financial stress in these economies has been accompanied by only mild exchange rate and equity market spillovers. Financial stress in the largest EMDEs might generate more sizable regional spillovers through trade and financial links (World Bank 2016a). Shifts in portfolio allocations across asset classes, in response to deteriorating investor sentiment, could also lead to contagion.

Fourth, U.S. term premia are negative and at record lows. Concerns about procyclical fiscal policy, intensifying wage pressures, or slowing foreign demand for U.S.

government debt could trigger a sudden upward adjustment in term premia and U.S. borrowing costs, as occurred during the taper tantrum of 2013.[9]

Spillovers from major economies. Weaker-than-expected growth in major economies could dampen activity in EMDEs through trade and financial links, as well as through confidence effects and commodity market movements (box 6.2). More than 80 percent of advanced economies are currently experiencing growth slowdowns (figure 6.8). Among them, the United States and the euro area are the most important sources of growth spillovers to EMDEs. A 1.0-percentage-point decline in U.S. annual growth is estimated to be associated with 0.6 percentage point lower EMDE growth after one year (Huidrom et al. 2019; Kose, Lakatos et al. 2017; World Bank 2016a). A 1-percentage-point decline in annual euro area growth is associated with a somewhat larger impact on EMDE growth (1 percentage point, broadly in line with the impact of China) in part because it has greater global trade integration than the United States and its close supply chain and financial links with EMDEs in ECA and EAP.

Among EMDEs, China is by far the most important source of growth spillovers to other EMDEs (Huidrom et al. 2019; figure 6.8).[10] A 1.0-percentage-point decline in China's growth is estimated to be associated with 0.5-percentage-point lower EMDE growth after one year (Huidrom et al. 2019). Because China is a major source of commodity demand, the adverse impact on commodity-exporting EMDEs is twice that on commodity importers (Baffes et al. 2018; World Bank 2016a). Growth fluctuations in some of the other seven largest EMDEs could also cause adverse spillovers to EMDEs in their regions. A synchronized growth slowdown in several major economies could severely set back EMDE growth. For example, a combined 1.0-percentage-point slowdown in growth in the United States, euro area, and China would depress global growth by almost 1.7 percentage points after a year and EMDE growth (excluding China) by 1.4 percentage points.

Region-specific risks. Region-specific risks have been rising, including geopolitical risks and risks relating to armed conflicts and climate change. Geopolitical risks remain high in MNA, SSA, and ECA. The number of armed conflicts in 2015-17 was significantly higher than the average of the past two decades (figure 6.8).[11] The economic costs of conflict can be substantial, through destruction of physical and human capital, reduced employment and investment, and capital outflows (Collier 2003; Goodhand 2001; World Bank 2005). In some cases, conflict can have global consequences. For example,

[9] During the 2013 taper tantrum, the estimated 10-year term premium rose by 160 basis points over a nine-month period (Adrian, Crump, and Moench 2013; Andolfatto and Spewak 2018; Crump, Eusepi, and Moench 2018; Kopp and Williams 2018). The U.S. 10-year term premium has been persistently negative since June 2017, compared to 1.6 percent on average from 1961 to June 2017.

[10] The past decade already featured major growth disappointments in China. For example, in 2012, China's growth was expected to average 7.4-10.1 percent during 2011-19 (World Bank 2012). Actual growth will average closer to 7.2 percent.

[11] The number of armed conflicts averaged 51 in 2015-17, compared to 35 in 2000-14 according to the Centre for the Study of Civil War at the Peace Research Institute Oslo. Conflicts are defined as developments that involve the use of armed force between two parties, of which at least one is the government of a state, and that result in at least 25 battle-related deaths in a calendar year.

FIGURE 6.8 Risks to EMDE growth prospects: Other adverse shocks

Weaker growth prospects in major economies present significant spillover risks to EMDEs. Region-specific risks include geopolitical developments in the Middle East and North Africa, conflict, and weather-related developments.

A. Share of countries with growth slowdowns

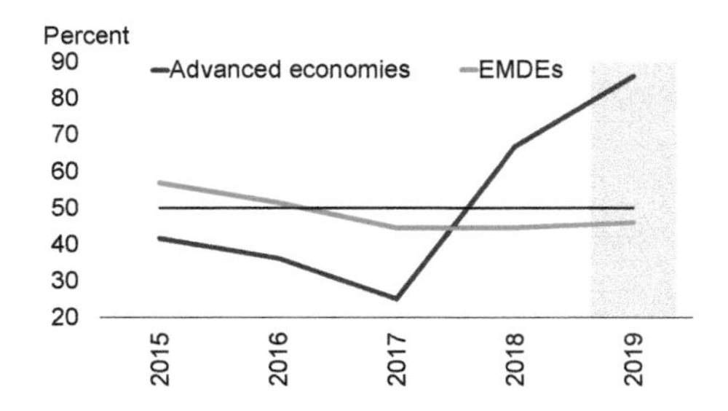

B. Spillovers from the United States, euro area and China

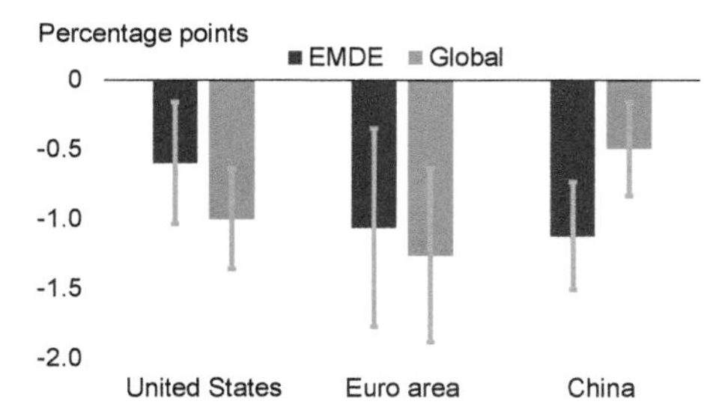

C. Spillovers from the seven largest EMDEs

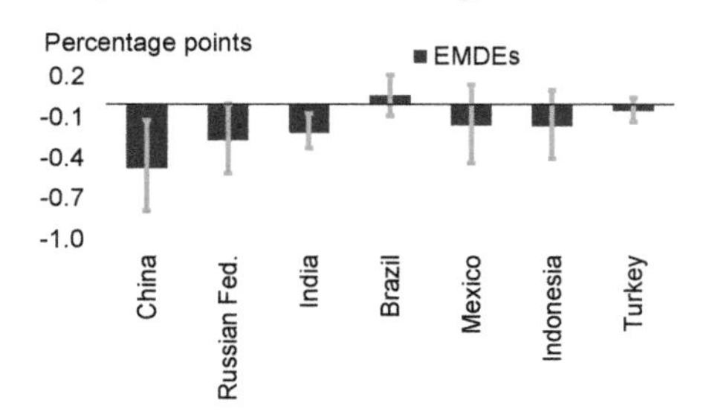

D. Number of armed conflicts

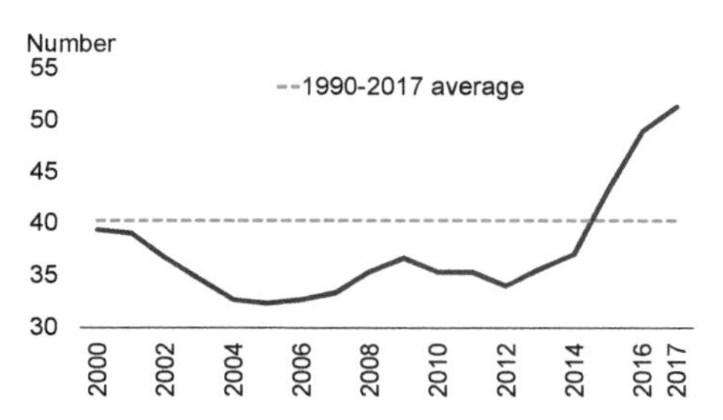

E. Oil production

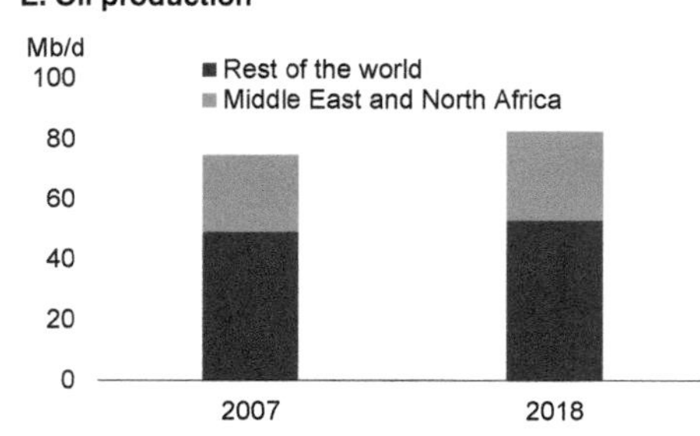

F. Weather-related events

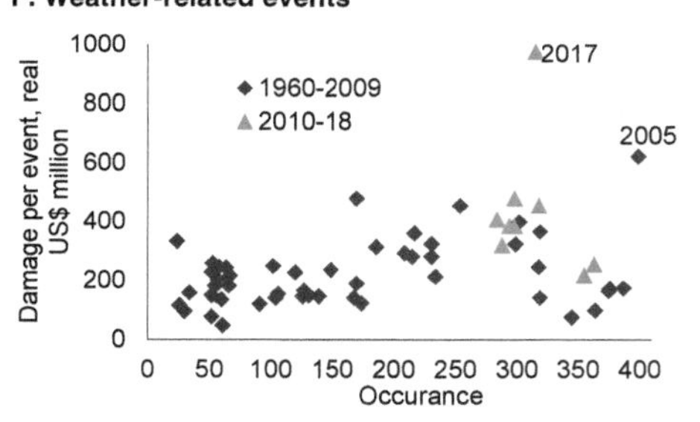

Sources: Centre for the Study of Civil War at the Peace Research Institute Oslo; Centre for Research on the Epidemiology of Disasters/ Office of U.S. Foreign Disaster Assistance International Disaster Database; Huidrom et al. (2019); International Energy Agency; World Bank.

A. Slowdowns of at least 0.1 percentage point in annual GDP growth. Data for 36 advanced economies and 146 emerging market and developing economies (EMDEs).

B. Median cumulative impulse response of EMDE and global GDP growth after one year to a 1-percentage-point decline in U.S. and euro area GDP growth. Based on vector autoregression of world GDP, output growth in the source country of the shock, the U.S. 10-year sovereign bond yield plus J.P. Morgan's Emerging Market Bond Index, output in EMDEs excluding China, and oil price as an exogenous variable. The "global" sample includes 22 advanced economies and 19 EMDEs for 1998Q1-2016Q2.

C. See Huidrom et al. (2019) for details. Cumulative impulse responses of EMDE growth after one year in response to a 1-percentage-point decline in growth in origin of shock. Russian Fed. = Russian Federation.

D. A state-based armed conflict is a contested incompatibility that concerns a government or territory where the use of armed force between two parties, of which at least one is the government of a state, results in at least 25 battle-related deaths in one calendar year. Three-year rolling average.

E. Mb/d stands for millions of barrels per day.

F. Observations each year. Weather events include drought, extreme temperature, floods, landslides, storms, and wildfires. Real cost deflated using U.S. GDP deflator in 2015 U.S. dollars. Last observation is 2018.

BOX 6.2 The global role of the United States and China

Economic developments in the United States and China, the world's two largest economies, can have effects far beyond their shores. A slowdown in these economies would result in considerably lower global growth transmitted through trade, financial, and commodity market channels. Easing U.S. financial conditions could reverberate across global financial markets, with pronounced effects on emerging market and developing economies that rely heavily on external financing. China's continued deceleration and rebalancing toward domestic consumption and services will likely put downward pressure on commodity prices worldwide and are expected to adversely affect commodity exporters. In addition, lingering uncertainty about the course of U.S. trade policy and an escalation of trade tensions between the United States and China could significantly dampen global growth prospects.

Introduction

The United States and China, the world's two largest economies, together account for close to 40 percent of global gross domestic product (GDP) and more than one -fifth of global trade and world population. Because of their size and international links in these two economies, developments in them are bound to have significant implications for the rest of the world. The United States, the world's largest economy (at market exchange rates), accounts for almost one-quarter of global output, about one-tenth of trade flows, close to one-fifth of remittances, and over a third of stock market capitalization. The United States plays a prominent role in virtually every global market, in international trade, financial and labor flows, and commodities (figure B6.2.1). China, the world's second-largest economy, accounts for about 16 percent of global output, one-tenth of global trade, and close to one-fifth of world population. China plays an important role in global commodity markets, accounting for virtually all of the increase in global consumption of metals and half of primary energy since 2000. China currently accounts for more than 50 percent of global consumption of coal and metals.

This box examines the role of the United States and China in the global economy by addressing the following questions:

- What are the main economic links between the United States and the world?
- What are the main economic links between China and the world?
- How large are global spillovers from shocks originating in the United States and China?

Links between the United States and the world economy

With an estimated nominal GDP of about $20.5 trillion in 2018, the United States is the world's largest economy and has the world's third-largest population.

Note: This box was prepared by Csilla Lakatos.

BOX 6.2 The global role of the United States and China *(continued)*

FIGURE B6.2.1 United States and China in the global economy

The United States and China, the world's two largest economies, together account for close to 40 percent of global GDP, and one-fifth of global trade and population.

A. Size of major economies

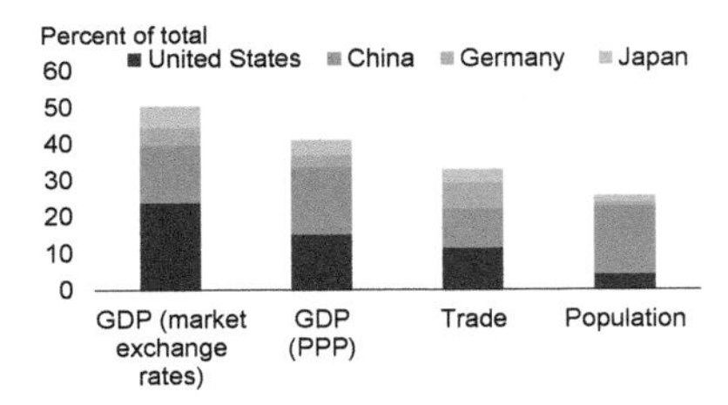

B. GDP and trade shares over time

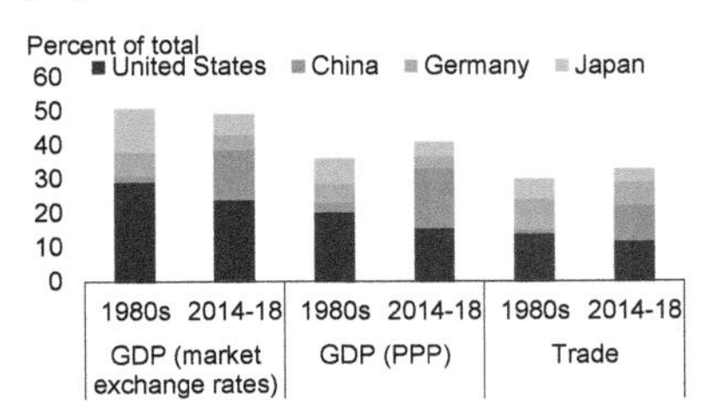

C. Share of global trade

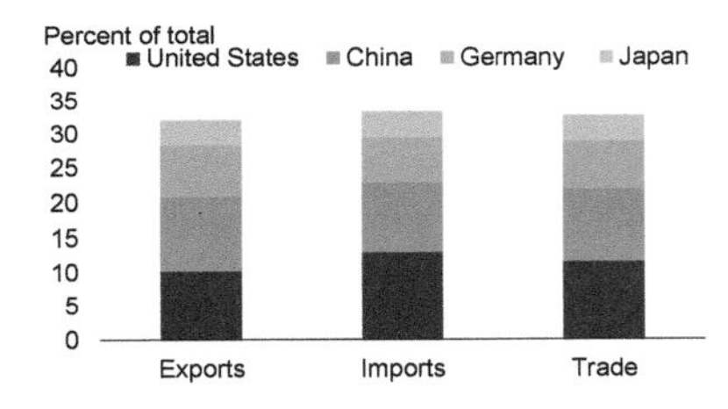

D. Share of regional trade

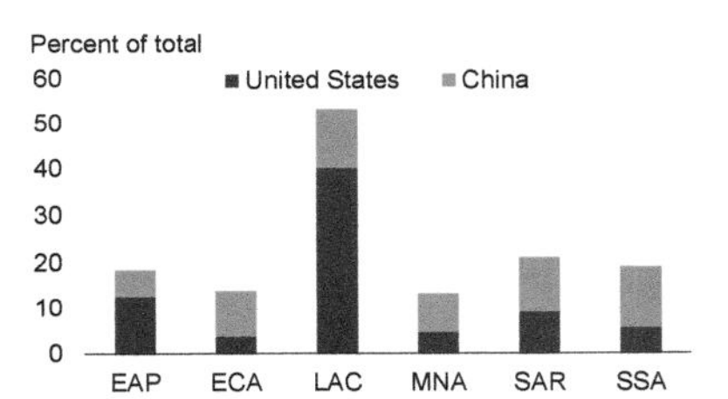

E. Trade openness over time

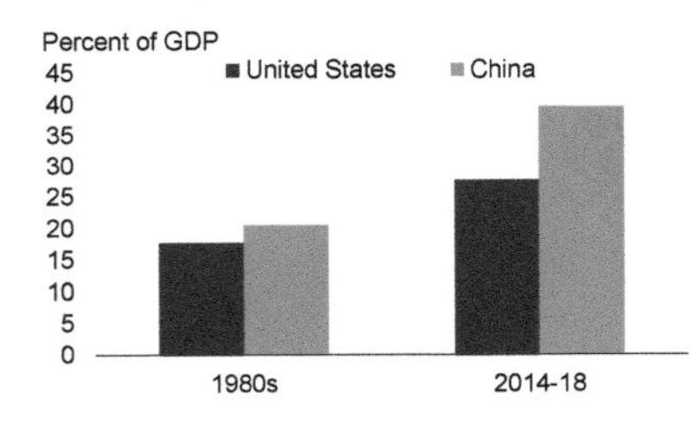

F. Share of commodity markets

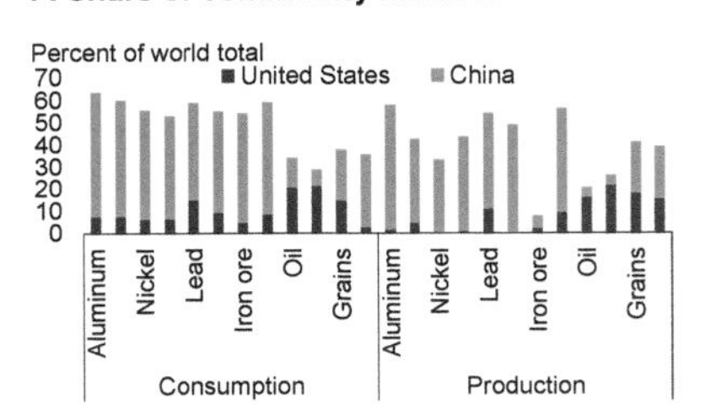

Source: World Bank.

Note: Trade represents the sum of exports and imports. EAP = East Asia and Pacific; ECA = Europe and Central Asia; LAC = Latin America and the Caribbean; MNA = Middle East and North Africa; PPP = purchasing power parity; SAR = South Asia; SSA = Sub-Saharan Africa.

A.F. Data for 2018.

C.D. Averages for 2014-2018.

D. Goods trade only.

BOX 6.2 The global role of the United States and China *(continued)*

The United States accounts for more than 24 percent of global GDP, 11 percent of global trade, 13 percent of bank foreign claims, and 44 percent of global stock market capitalization (figures B6.2.1 and B6.2.2).[a] The U.S. share of global output and trade has remained broadly stable since the 1980s, whereas the share of other major advanced economies has declined gradually. The United States is also the largest international creditor and debtor: it holds both the world's largest amount of foreign assets and liabilities and the largest net foreign asset position by a wide margin.

U.S. trade and financial integration with other advanced economies and emerging market and developing economies (EMDEs)—especially in Latin America and the Caribbean—runs deep. The countries most affected by developments in the U.S. economy are, directly, countries whose trade and financial ties are predominantly with the United States and, indirectly, those that are in general highly open to global trade and finance.

Trade linkages. Trade accounted for 28 percent of U.S. GDP in 2018, considerably less than the average for other advanced economies but 10 percentage points more than in the 1980s (18 percent). The United States is the world's largest importer of goods and services, and the largest exporter and importer of business services (figure B6.2.3). It accounts for 10 percent of global goods imports and 11 percent of global services imports.

Most U.S. imports are manufactured goods, accounting for more than three-quarters of goods imports. Oil imports make up most of the remainder despite a steady decline in oil imports since 2000. The most prominent imported product categories are motor vehicles, crude petroleum oil, data processing machines, and drugs. Until 2018, close to one-quarter of U.S. imports of goods came from China (22 percent) but this share is likely to have declined as a result of the increase in U.S.-China bilateral tariffs implemented during 2018-19. By the end of 2019, close to all U.S.-China bilateral trade flows were subject to additional tariffs, with average tariffs rising to nearly 25 percent. Other main sources of imports are the European Union (19 percent) and Mexico and Canada (together 26 percent).

The United States is the largest export destination for a quarter of the world's countries and is the primary export destination for countries in Latin America and the Caribbean, as well as a number of countries in other EMDE regions, especially those in East Asia and Pacific and South Asia. Mexico, Vietnam, Colombia, and many smaller Central American EMDEs rely particularly heavily on exports to the United States.

---

a. At purchasing power exchange rates, the United States is the world's second-largest economy (preceded by China as the world's largest), accounting for 15 percent of global GDP in 2018.

BOX 6.2 The global role of the United States and China *(continued)*

FIGURE B6.2.2 Links between the United States, China, and EMDE regions

The United States is a particularly important trading partner and source of finance for Latin America and the Caribbean. China's economic links are particularly prominent with East Asia and Pacific and Sub-Saharan Africa.

A. East Asia and Pacific

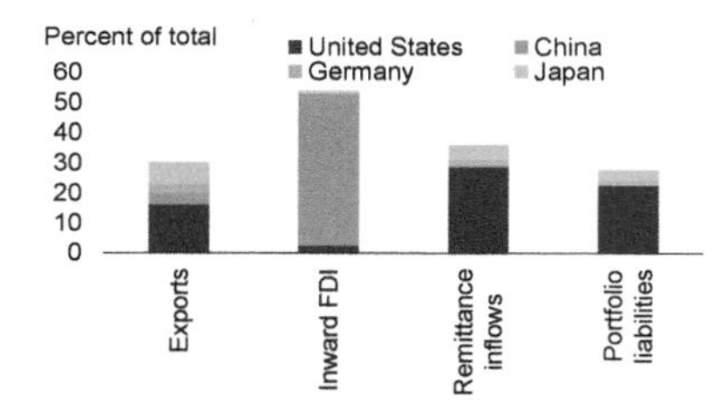

B. Europe and Central Asia

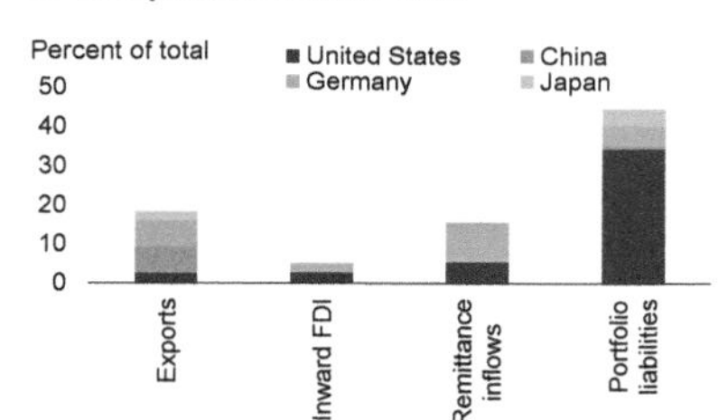

C. Latin America and the Caribbean

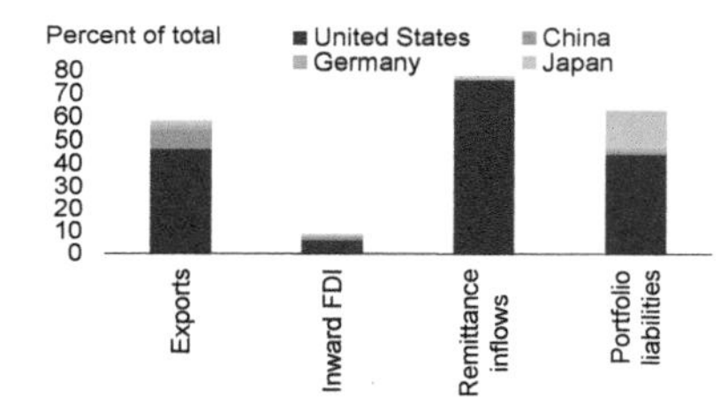

D. Middle East and North Africa

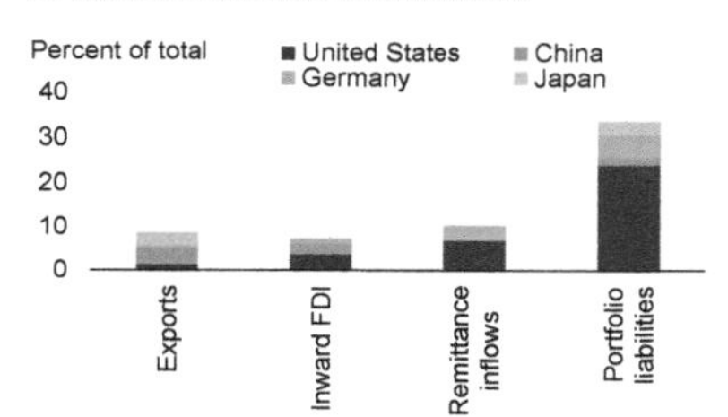

E. South Asia

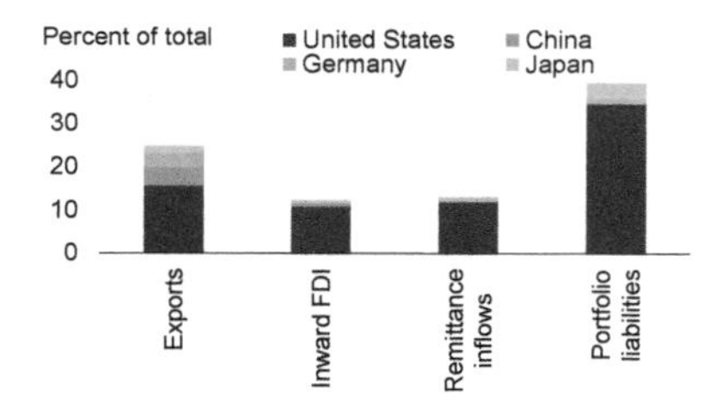

F. Sub-Saharan Africa

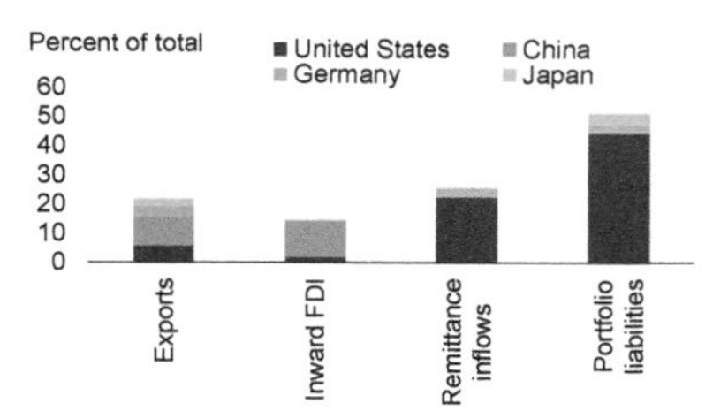

Sources: Bank for International Settlements; International Monetary Fund; World Bank.

Note: Trade data is based on 2014-18 averages. FDI and remittances data reflect inward FDI stocks and remittances in 2017 (latest available at the bilateral level). Portfolio liabilities reflect June 2019 data. In percent of total exports of each EMDE region, total inward FDI stocks in each EMDE region, total portfolio liabilities (derived from creditor data) in each EMDE region, total foreign claims of BIS-reporting banks on each EMDE region, and total remittance flows to each region. BIS = Bank for International Settlements; EMDEs = emerging market and developing economies; FDI = foreign direct investment.

BOX 6.2 The global role of the United States and China (continued)

FIGURE B6.2.3 U.S. trade flows: Composition and partners

The United States is the largest country destination of global exports of goods and services. Electronic and transport equipment account for the bulk of U.S. goods imports and are mostly imported from other North American Free Trade Agreement members, European Union countries, and China. The United States is a key export destination for economies in the LAC region and for some EMDEs in EAP.

A. U.S. share of global goods and services trade

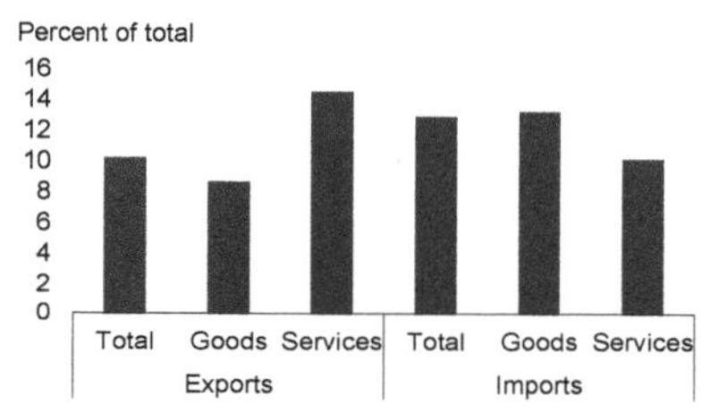

B. Composition of U.S. exports and imports

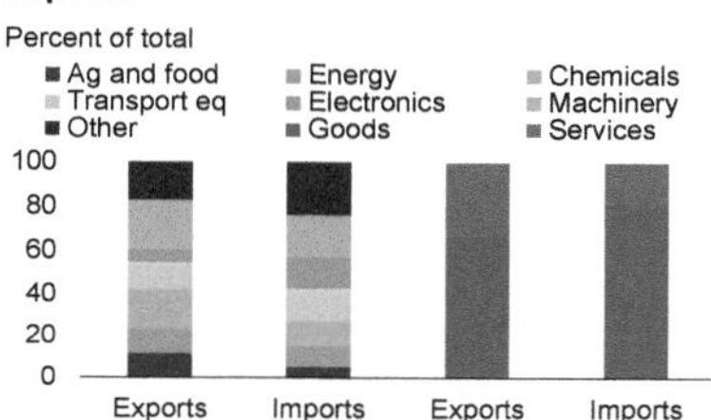

C. Main sources of U.S. imports

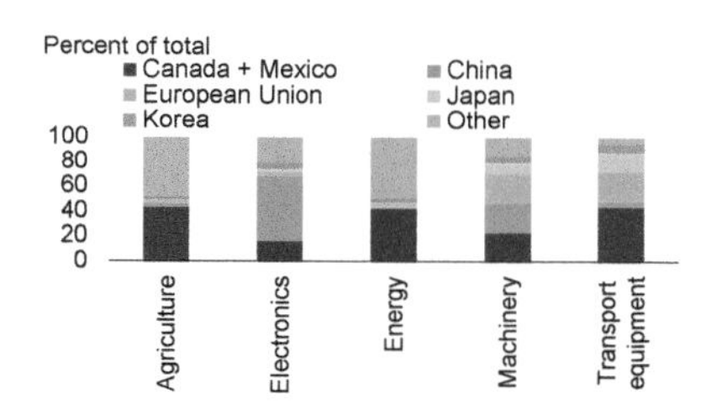

D. United States trade with EMDE regions

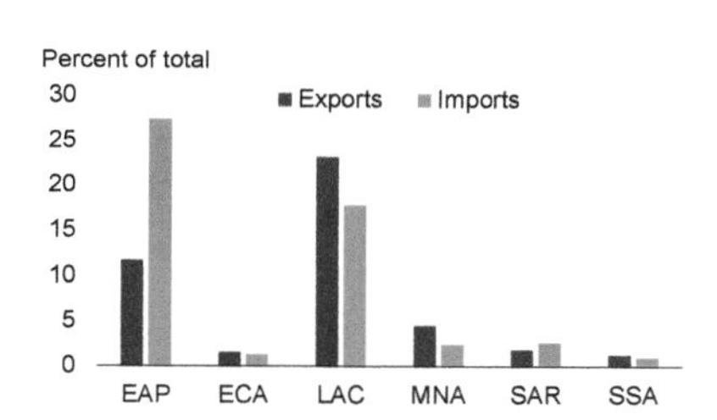

E. Selected EMDEs: Exports to the United States

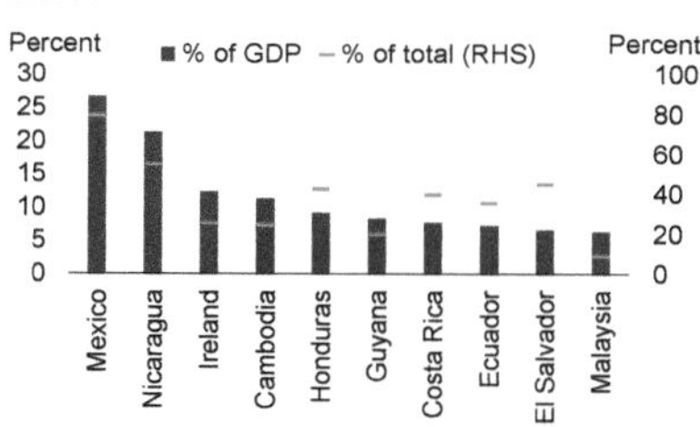

F. Selected EMDEs: Imports from the United States

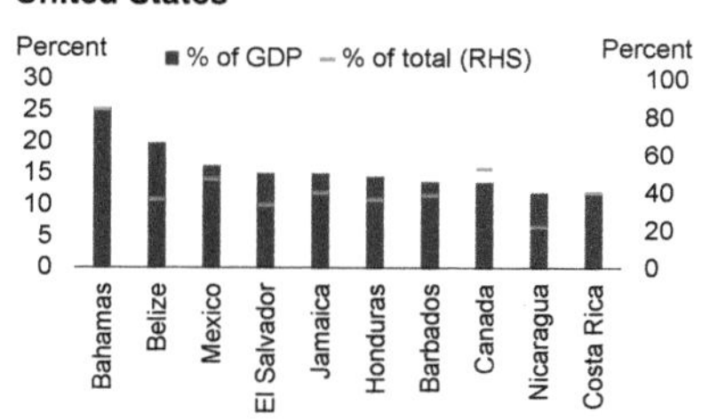

Sources: World Integrated Trade Statistics; World Bank.

Note: Averages for 2014-18 unless otherwise specified. EAP = East Asia and Pacific; ECA = Europe and Central Asia; EMDEs = emerging market and developing economies; LAC = Latin America and the Caribbean; MNA = Middle East and North Africa; SAR = South Asia; SSA = Sub-Saharan Africa.

B. U.S. exports/imports of goods or services in percent of total U.S. exports/imports of goods and services (purple bars); U.S. exports/imports in each sector in percent of total U.S. goods exports/imports (other bars).

C. Sectoral exports from Canada, China, the European Union, Japan, the Republic of Korea, Mexico, and other economies to the United States in percent of total U.S. imports in each sector.

E. Exports to the United States in percent of total exports or in percent of GDP.

F. Imports from the United States in percent of total imports or in percent of GDP.

BOX 6.2 The global role of the United States and China *(continued)*

The growth of trade links between the United States and other countries has been largely driven by its membership in the General Agreement on Trade and Tariffs (GATT) since 1948 and the World Trade Organization (WTO) since 1995, as well as 14 bilateral or regional trade agreements with 20 partner countries, which cover 18 percent of its imports.[b] The largest of these regional agreements is the North American Free Trade Agreement (NAFTA), in force since 1994. In 2018, NAFTA was renegotiated to be replaced by the United States-Mexico-Canada Agreement (USMCA), yet to be ratified by the United States and Canada. Imports from Sub-Saharan Africa have also grown rapidly following the preferential tariff scheme granted by the United States in 2000 to 34 African economies ("Africa Growth and Opportunities Act"; Frazer and Van Biesebroeck 2008; Mattoo, Roy, and Subramanian 2003).

Financial links. U.S. financial markets are highly integrated with global markets. U.S. international assets and liabilities were on average more than three times larger than GDP over 2010-18 period (figure B6.2.4). The United States remains the world's largest source and recipient of foreign direct investment (FDI) flows, accounting for about one-fifth of world FDI inflows and outflows in 2015. The European Union, Japan, Canada, and Switzerland together hold about 90 percent of their FDI assets in the United States, whereas the European Union and Canada are the largest recipients of U.S. FDI. EMDEs in Latin America and the Caribbean, in particular, Brazil, Chile and Mexico, are the most exposed to FDI inflows originating in the United States (figure B6.2.5). Reflecting the size and depth of its financial markets, the United States accounts for the largest share of portfolio assets in one-third of EMDEs.

The U.S. dollar is the most widely used currency in international trade and financial markets and is the world's preeminent reserve currency. More than 50 percent of cross-border bank flows to EMDEs are denominated in U.S. dollars. Europe and Central Asia is the only EMDE region where the U.S. dollar is surpassed by the euro as a currency of denomination for cross-border bank flows. A number of EMDEs use the U.S. dollar as their official currency (Ecuador, El Salvador, Panama), and 31 other EMDEs maintain exchange rate pegs against the U.S. dollar. A large share of foreign exchange reserves (61 percent of allocated reserves), deposits, and bonds held by central banks are dollar-denominated. The

b. For discussions of the implications of the North American Free Trade Agreement (NAFTA) and the Dominican Republic-Central America Free Trade Agreement (CAFTA-DR), see Kose, Meredith, and Towe (2005); Kose, Rebucci, and Schipke (2005); and Romalis (2007). Most U.S. trade is conducted under the most-favored nation (MFN) regime, with average tariffs at 3.5 percent, higher for agricultural products at 5.2 percent. The United States also grants unilateral preferences to a number of EMDEs through its Generalized System of Preferences (GSP) and African Growth Opportunity Act (AGOA), which cover about 3.3 percent of U.S. imports.

BOX 6.2 The global role of the United States and China (*continued*)

FIGURE B6.2.4 Role of the United States in global financial markets

The United States is the largest international creditor and debtor, and U.S. financial markets are highly integrated in global markets. The U.S. dollar is the most widely used currency in global trade and financial transactions.

A. Size in financial markets

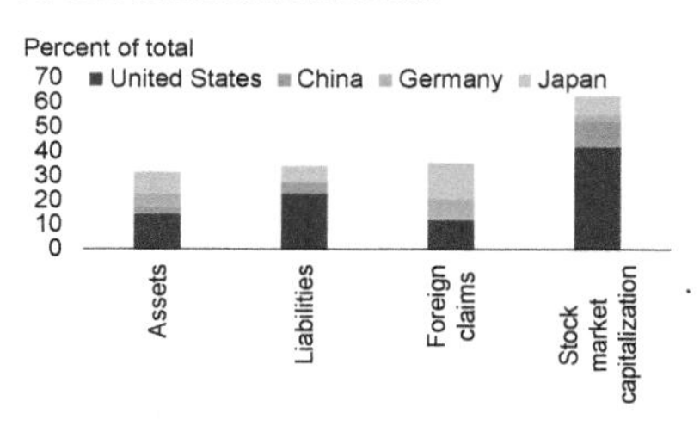

B. U.S. financial openness

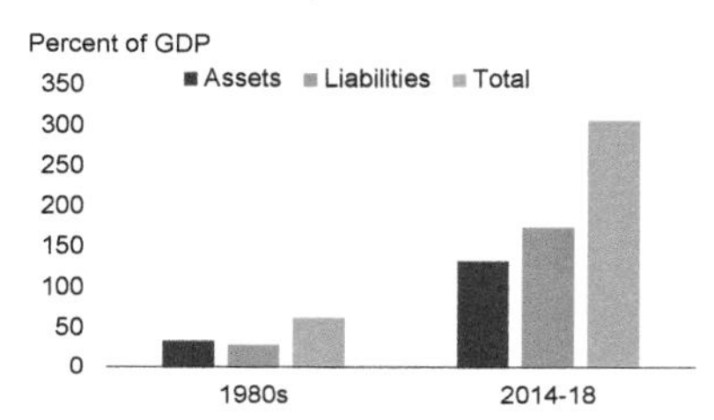

C. U.S. dollar-denominated transactions in financial markets, 2018

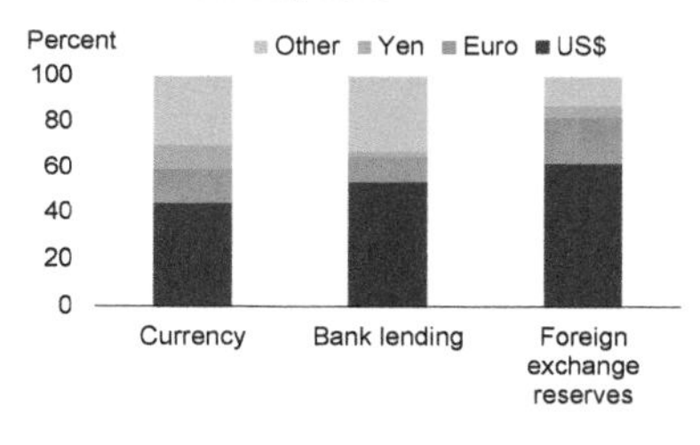

D. Capital inflows from the United States

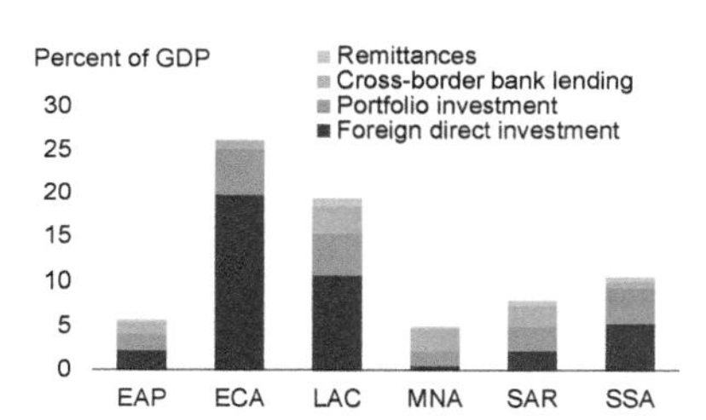

Sources: Bank for International Settlements; International Monetary Fund; Lane and Milesi-Ferretti (2007); World Bank; World Federation of Exchanges.

Note: BIS = Bank for International Settlements; EAP = East Asia and Pacific; ECA = Europe and Central Asia; LAC = Latin America and the Caribbean; MNA = Middle East and North Africa; SAR = South Asia; SSA = Sub-Saharan Africa.

A. Average share for 2014-18. Foreign claims are consolidated foreign claims of BIS-reporting banks headquartered in respective countries or locations. China is not a country where BIS-reporting banks are located (on a consolidated basis). Assets and liabilities are international positions.

B. Average shares in GDP over the periods of 1980-89 and 2014-18. Total is the sum of assets and liabilities.

C. Currency totals sum to 100 percent because each foreign exchange transaction involves two different currencies. "Euro" includes all legacy currencies of the euro as well as the European Currency Unit. Data for the center and right bars are for June 2016.

D. Capital flows refer to stocks of foreign direct investment (FDI), portfolio investment, and cross-border bank lending from the United States to emerging market and developing economy regions. Country coverage varies by capital flow component.

U.S. dollar is widely used in international trade transactions for invoicing of import and export transactions, accounting for about one-third of invoicing in Europe and two-thirds of invoicing in Asia (Goldberg and Tille 2008).

Commodity market links. The United States plays a significant role in global commodity markets as both a producer and consumer of commodities (figure

BOX 6.2 The global role of the United States and China *(continued)*

FIGURE B6.2.5 U.S. financial flows: Composition and partners

Because of its large financial system and economy, the United States is an important source of FDI, portfolio flows, remittances, and bank lending to EMDEs across the world.

A. FDI inflows from the United States

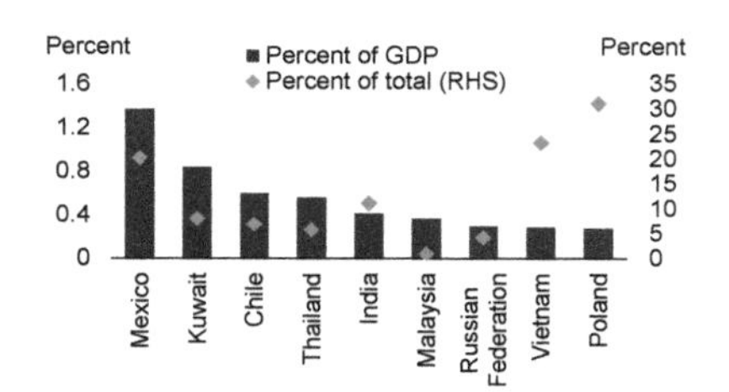

B. Portfolio inflows from the United States

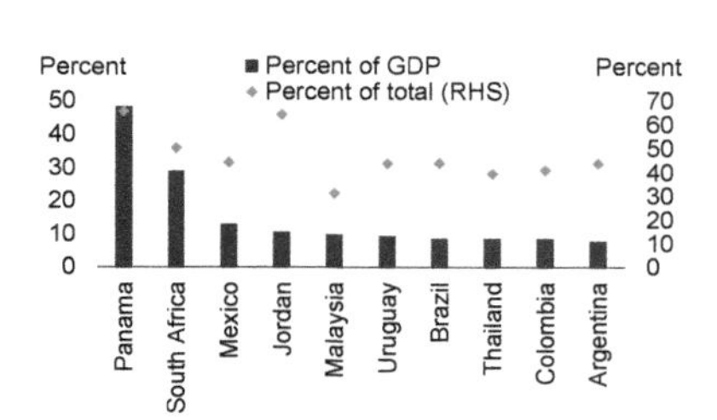

C. Cross-border bank claims of U.S. banks on selected EMDEs

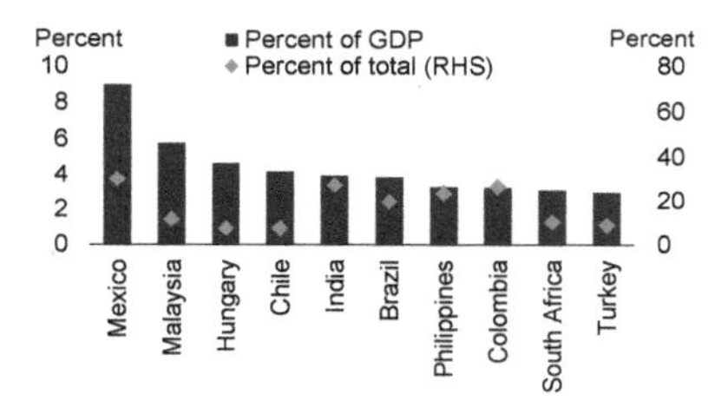

D. Remittance inflows from the United States

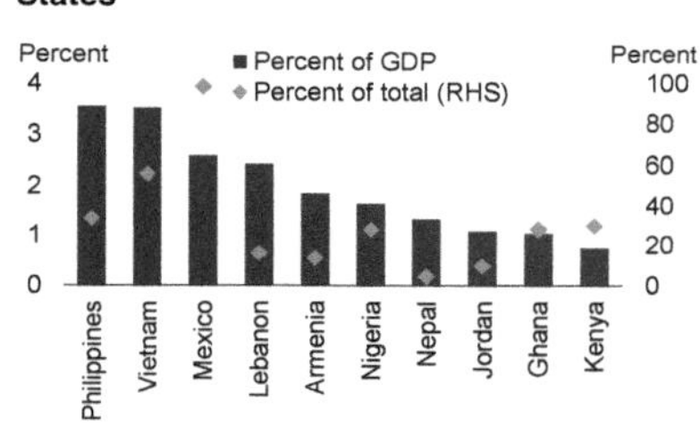

Sources: Bank for International Settlements; International Monetary Fund; World Bank.

Note: BIS = Bank for International Settlements; EMDEs = emerging market and developing economies; FDI = foreign direct investment.

A. Share of FDI inward stocks from United States in total FDI inward stocks into and as share of GDP of each country, average of 2013 to 2017.

B. Share of portfolio investment from United States in total portfolio inflows into and as share GDP of each EMDE in 2018.

C. Share of consolidated U.S.-headquartered BIS-reporting banks' claims on each EMDE region in total consolidated BIS-reporting banks' claims on and as share of GDP of each EMDE region, average of 2010 to 2015.

D. Share of remittances inflows from United States in total remittances inflows into and as share of GDP of each country in 2017.

B6.2.6). For example, in global energy markets, the United States has become the largest producer of oil since 2017 and natural gas since 2014. The United States now accounts for 16 percent of global oil production, exceeding the share in the early 1990s. Its oil and gas production is almost evenly split between natural gas and petroleum, in contrast to the predominantly petroleum-based production of other major hydrocarbon producers such as the Russian Federation and Saudi Arabia (EIA 2016). Because U.S. shale oil production, which tripled during 2009-

BOX 6.2 The global role of the United States and China (continued)

FIGURE B6.2.6 Role of the United States in commodity markets

The United States accounts for more than one-fifth of global consumption of oil and natural gas. In international crude oil and natural gas markets, the United States has recently become the largest producer.

A. U.S. share of global consumption

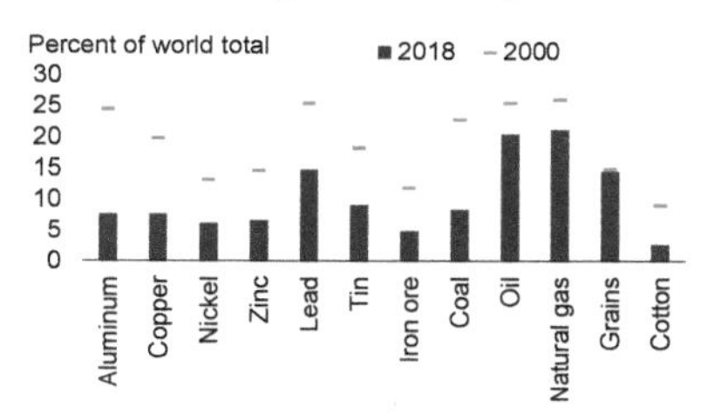

B. U.S. share of global production

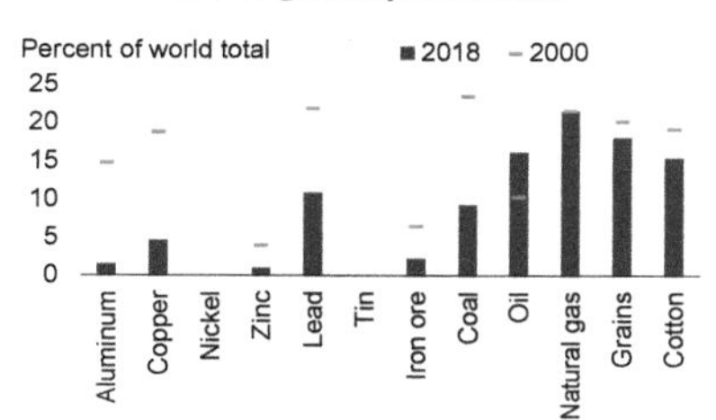

C. U.S. share of global crude oil consumption and production

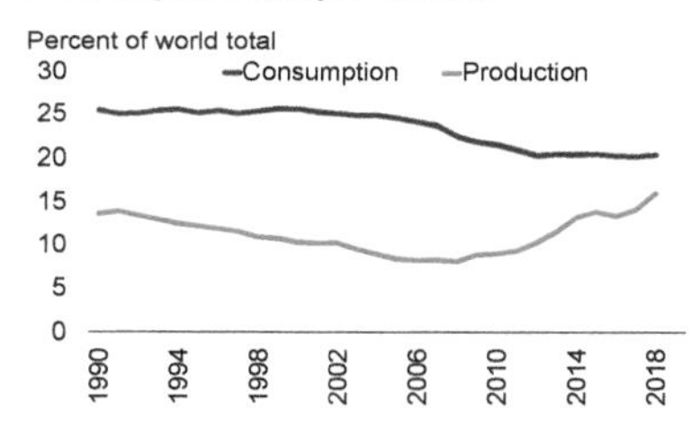

D. Oil and gas production

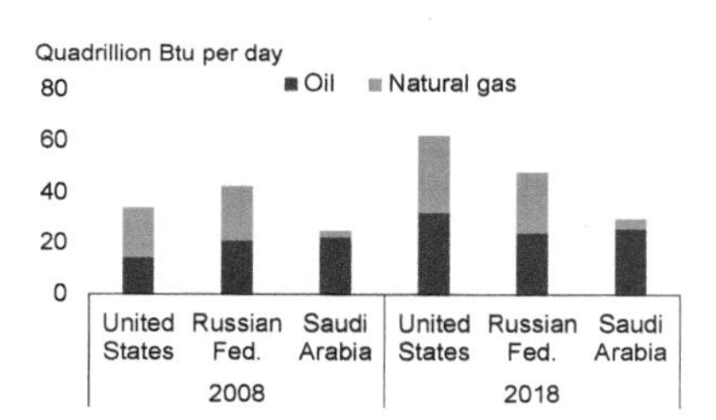

Sources: BP Statistical Review of World Energy Efficiency; Haver Analytics; U.S. Energy Information Administration; World Bank.

Note: Data for metals all represent refined consumption and production. Iron ore consumption is estimated with crude steel production. Grains include wheat, maize, and rice; edible oils include coconut oil, cottonseed oil, palm oil, palm kernel oil, peanut oil, rapeseed oil, and soybean oil. Oil includes inland demand plus international aviation and marine bunkers and refinery fuel and loss. Coal includes commercial solid fuels only, that is, bituminous coal and anthracite (hard coal), and lignite and brown (sub-bituminous) coal, and other commercial solid fuels. Natural gas excludes natural gas converted to liquid fuels but includes derivatives of coal as well as natural gas consumed in Gas-to-Liquids transformation.

D. Oil and natural gas production in British thermal units (Btu), assuming that 1 barrel of crude oil is equivalent to 5,729,000 Btu and 1 cubic foot of natural gas is equivalent to 1,032 Btu. Russian Fed. = Russian Federation.

14, requires little capital investment and can be brought onstream rapidly, it has become one of the most flexible sources of additional global oil supply that responds quickly to price changes (Baffes et al. 2015).

The United States is also the world's largest biofuel producer. U.S. biofuels account for four-tenths of global biofuel production and one-third of maize production. Rapid growth in maize-based U.S. biofuel production was encouraged

BOX 6.2 The global role of the United States and China *(continued)*

by the Renewable Fuel Standard (RFS), mandated by the Energy Policy Act of 2005 and Energy Independence and Security Act of 2007, which requires transportation fuel sold in the United States to contain a minimum volume of renewable fuels.

Historically, the United States has been a major consumer of agricultural, energy, and metals commodities. With the rise of large EMDEs, such as China and India, this role has diminished (World Bank 2015a); however, the United States is still the largest consumer of natural gas and oil, accounting for more than one-fifth of global oil and natural gas consumption and the second-largest consumer of a wide range of commodities, including aluminum, copper, lead, and coffee.

Links between China and the world economy

China's share in global GDP and in world trade has increased about 10-fold over the past four decades, to about 16 percent and 10 percent in 2018, respectively (figure B6.2.1). China is now the world's second-largest economy with GDP of $13.6 trillion in 2018, accounting for about one-third of global economic growth over the last seven years.

Trade links. Trade accounted for 40 percent of China's GDP in 2018, nearly twice as much as in the 1980s and considerably more than in the United States (27 percent). China's rising importance in international trade significantly benefitted from its accession to the WTO in 2001. In addition, China currently has 15 free trade agreements (FTAs) in force with a wide range of countries, including with members of the Association of Southeast Asian Nations and with Australia, the Republic of Korea, New Zealand, and Peru. Partly as a result of intraregional trade liberalization, China is especially highly integrated into production processes in countries in East Asia and Pacific (EAP; figure B6.2.7).

China is the destination of more than one-tenth of total exports of EMDEs in EAP and Sub-Saharan Africa (SSA). It accounts for more than half of exports of more than 17 EMDEs. Most of China's imports are manufactured goods accounting for more than three-quarters of goods imports, with oil and agricultural imports making up the remainder. Services account for one-fifth of total imports. The most prominent imported product categories are machinery and equipment, electronic equipment, and chemicals. Until 2018, close to one-tenth of China's imports came from the United States, but this share is likely to have declined as a result of the increase in U.S.-China bilateral tariffs in 2018-19. Other main sources of imports are Korea (11 percent), Japan (10 percent), and Germany, Australia, and Malaysia (together 15 percent).

Commodity market links. The rapid industrialization of China and its investment- and manufacturing-driven growth model resulted in a surge in

BOX 6.2 The global role of the United States and China (continued)

FIGURE B6.2.7 China's trade flows: Composition and partners

China accounts for one-tenth of global trade. Most of China's imports are manufactured goods, accounting for more than three-quarters of goods imports, with oil and agricultural imports making up the remainder. Services account for one-fifth of total imports and only 5 percent of exports. The most prominent imported product categories are machinery and equipment, electronic equipment, and chemicals.

A. China's share of global services and goods trade

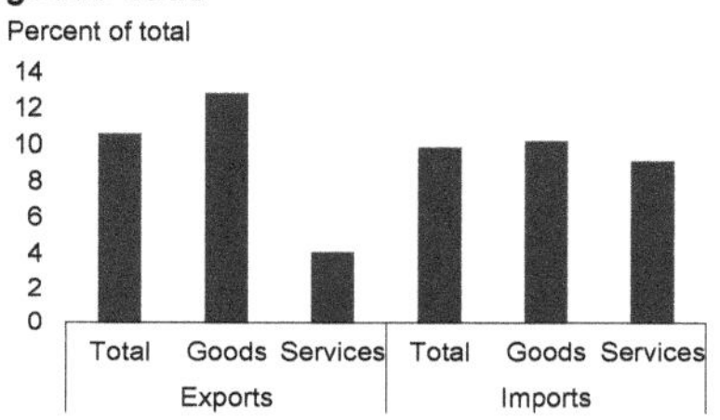

B. Composition of Chinese exports and imports

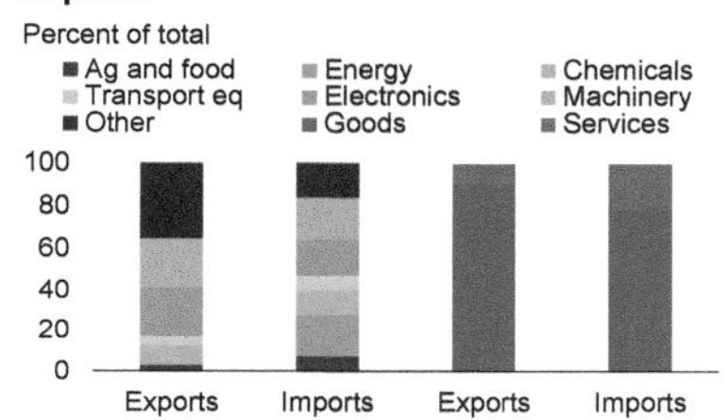

C. Main sources of China's imports

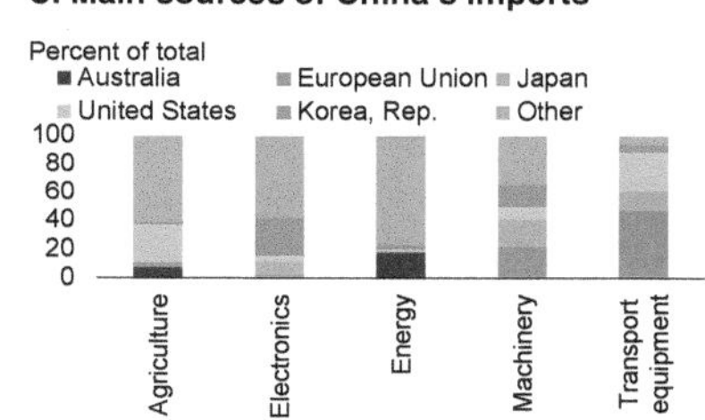

D. China's trade with EMDE regions

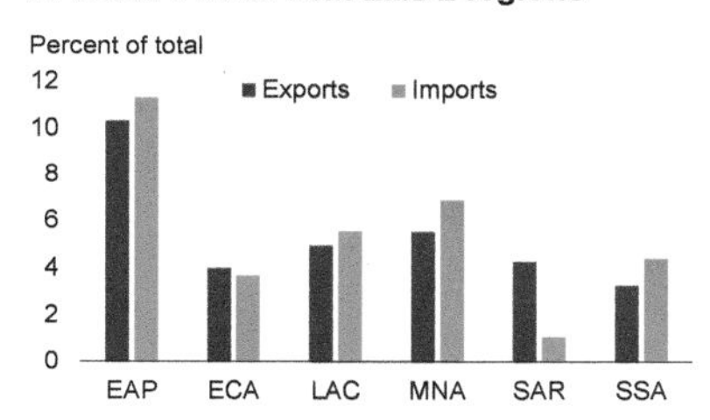

E. Selected EMDEs: Exports to China

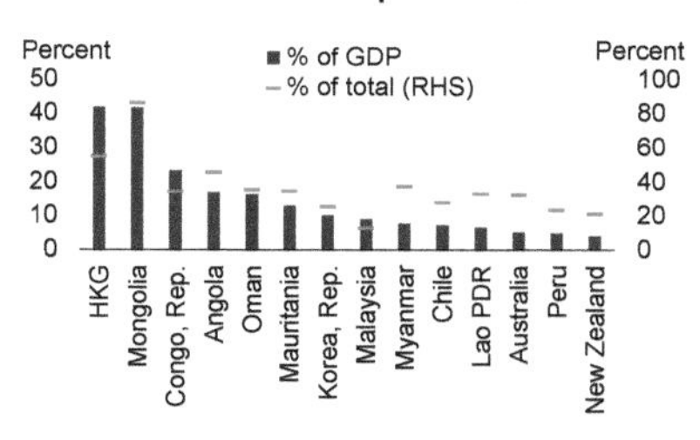

F. Selected EMDEs: Imports from China

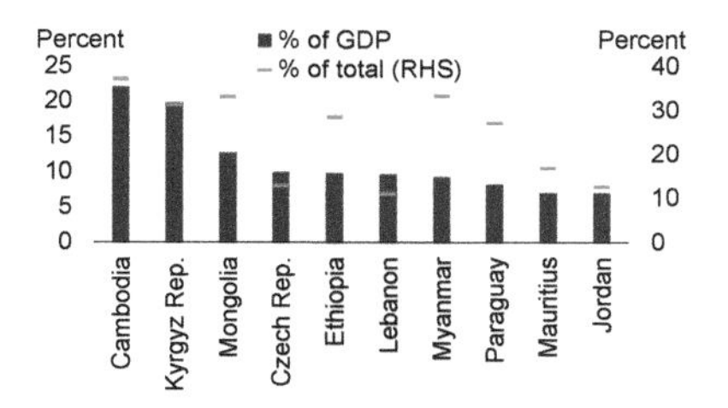

Source: World Bank.

Note: Averages for 2014-18 unless otherwise specified. EAP = East Asia and Pacific; ECA = Europe and Central Asia; EMDEs = emerging market and developing economies; LAC = Latin America and the Caribbean; MNA = Middle East and North Africa; SAR = South Asia; SSA = Sub-Saharan Africa.

B. China's exports/imports of goods or services in percent of total exports/imports of goods and services (purple bars); China's exports/imports in each sector in percent of total goods exports/imports (other bars).

C. Sectoral imports from Australia, the European Union, Japan, the Republic of Korea, the United States, and other economies as share of total imports in each sector.

E. Exports to China in percent of total exports or in percent of GDP of each EMDE. HKG = Hong Kong SAR, China.

F. Imports from China in percent of total imports or in percent of GDP of each EMDE. Czech Rep. = Czech Republic; Kyrgyz Rep. = Kyrgyz Republic.

BOX 6.2 The global role of the United States and China *(continued)*

demand for commodities from 2000. The expansion in demand contributed to a rapid increase in real energy and metals prices that marked a commodity "super cycle." China accounted for virtually all of the increase in global consumption of metals and half of primary energy over 2000-08, and again during 2010-18. It now accounts for about half of global consumption of coal and metals (figure B6.2.8). China's production of commodities has also risen sharply, with production of metals increasing 11-fold over the past two decades. China now accounts for about half of global coal and metals production, and is particularly dominant in aluminum. Commodity markets are highly sensitive to changes in China's growth. A 1 percent change in China's industrial production has been associated with a 5-7 percent change in metal and energy prices over the following year (Kolerus, N'Diaye, and Saborowski 2016).

Financial links. Although its financial ties are still limited, China is increasingly investing in other countries. China's combined cross-border assets and liabilities almost doubled to reach about 3 percent of world total between 2007 and 2016. Since 2014, China has been the world's largest destination for FDI inflows into the nonfinancial sector, surpassing 10.7 percent of total global inflows in 2018. China's FDI outflows increased more than fivefold between 2007 and 2018 to 12.8 percent of total global outflows. For example, China's direct investment in SSA has grown more than sixfold, and China's official development assistance to SSA expanded from $0.5 billion in 2000 to $3.2 billion in 2013.

Spillovers from the United States and China to the world economy

Economic developments in the United States and China can have significant impacts on the global economy, because shocks from these economies can be transmitted to the rest of the world through the wide range of channels documented. An acceleration in growth in each economy can lift growth in its trading partners directly, through an increase in import demand, and indirectly, by strengthening productivity spillovers embedded in trade (Eckmeier 2007; Jansen and Stockman 2004; Kose, Prasad, and Terrones 2004).[c] Given the sizable role of these economies in global commodity markets, an acceleration in growth could lift global commodity demand and raise prices, support activity, and ease balance of payments pressures in commodity exporters. Financial market developments in the United States can also have global implications. In addition, monetary and fiscal stimulus in the United States could boost domestic activity and generate cross-border spillovers through real and financial channels.

---

c. For a discussion of these channels, see Eckmeier (2007); Hirata, Kose, and Otrok (2013); and Jansen and Stockman (2004).

BOX 6.2 The global role of the United States and China *(continued)*

FIGURE B6.2.8 Role of China in commodity markets

China plays an important role in global commodity markets. China's production of commodities has risen sharply, with production of metals increasing 11-fold over the past 20 years. China now accounts for about half of global coal and metals production, and is particularly dominant in aluminum.

A. China's share of global consumption

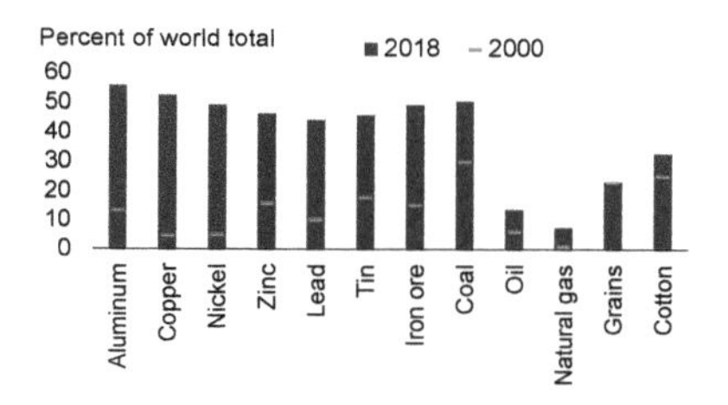

B. China's share of global production

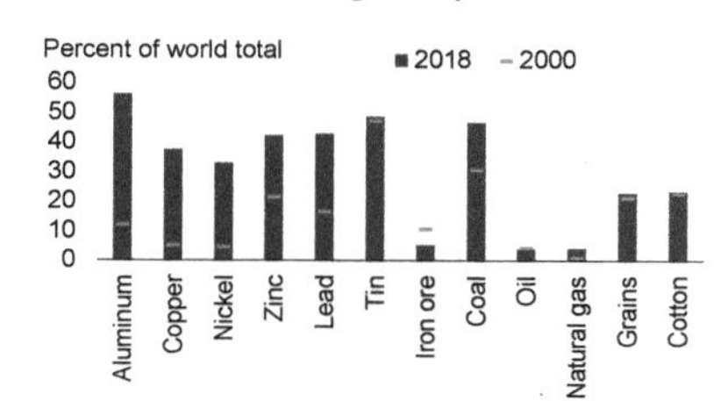

C. China's share of global coal consumption and production

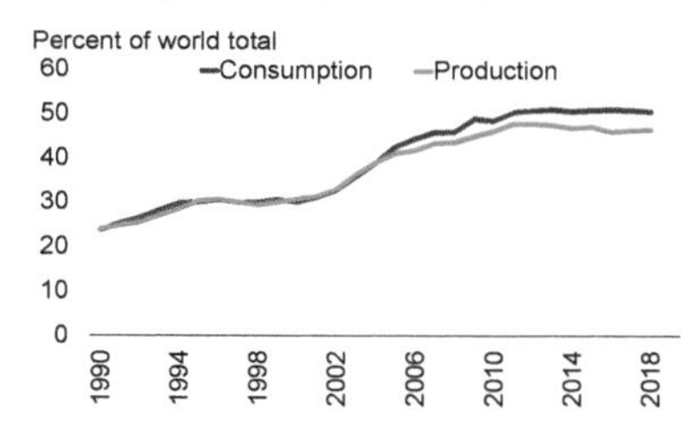

D. China's soybean imports and consumption

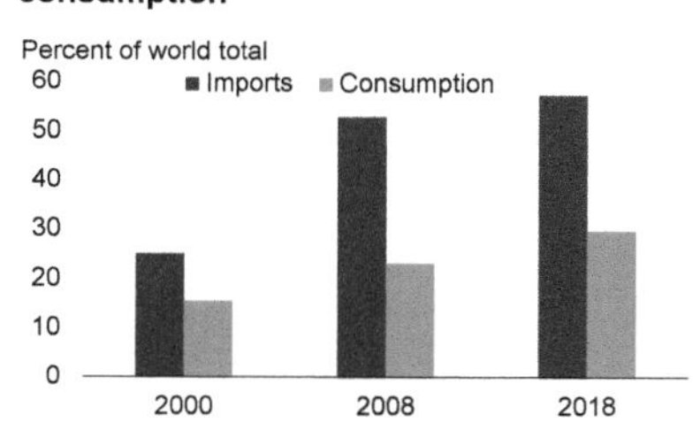

Sources: BP Statistical Review of World Energy Efficiency; Haver Analytics; U.S. Energy Information Administration; World Bank.

Note: Data for metals all represent refined consumption and production. Iron ore consumption is estimated with crude steel production. Grains include wheat, maize, and rice; edible oils include coconut oil, cottonseed oil, palm oil, palm kernel oil, peanut oil, rapeseed oil, and soybean oil. Oil includes inland demand plus international aviation and marine bunkers and refinery fuel and loss. Coal includes commercial solid fuels only, that is, bituminous coal and anthracite (hard coal), and lignite and brown (sub-bituminous) coal, and other commercial solid fuels. Natural gas excludes natural gas converted to liquid fuels but includes derivatives of coal as well as natural gas consumed in Gas-to-Liquids transformation.

In addition to growth shocks or policy or financial market developments, shocks to confidence in the United States and China can reverberate across borders and cause business cycle fluctuations elsewhere (Levchenko and Pandalai-Nayar 2018). Elevated uncertainty about changes in U.S. and Chinese policies can reduce incentives to commit to capital investment at home and abroad, which in turn could adversely affect long-term global growth prospects (Kose and Terrones 2015).

BOX 6.2 The global role of the United States and China *(continued)*

Spillovers from the U.S. economy

Growth spillovers. U.S. growth shocks—including those driven by fiscal stimulus—can have sizable effects on activity in the rest of the world.[d] A 1.0-percentage-point increase in U.S. growth could lift growth in both advanced economies and EMDEs by 0.8 and 0.6 percentage points after one year, respectively (figure B6.2.9).[e] The impact of such a U.S. growth shock on investment could be approximately twice as large. NAFTA members (Canada and Mexico) would particularly benefit from trade spillovers (Shen and Abeysinghe 2016). Commodity markets could be another transmission channel of a U.S. growth shock to EMDEs because such a shock could raise global oil prices given that the U.S. remains the world's largest consumer of crude oil (World Bank 2016b).

Financial market spillovers. The role of the United States in global financial markets goes well beyond direct capital flows to and from the United States (Berkmen et al. 2012; de Grauwe and Yi 2016; Frankel and Saravelos 2012). U.S. sovereign bond and equity markets are the largest and most liquid in the world (IMF 2007). Swings in U.S. sovereign bond yields—whether because of changing expectations of U.S. monetary policy or because of shifting risk sentiment—are often closely mirrored by sovereign bond yields in other large financial markets, including the euro area. The implications for EMDEs of actual or expected changes in U.S. monetary policy would likely depend on underlying drivers (Arteta et al. 2015; figure B6.2.10).[f] Financial stress associated with such a change could combine with domestic fragilities and increase the risks of sudden stops in capital flows among more vulnerable EMDEs (Ammer et al. 2016; Borio and Zhu 2012; Bowman, Londono, and Sapriza 2015; Bruno and Shin 2015b; Glick and Leduc 2013; Neely 2015). Similarly, cross-border spillovers from U.S. equity markets are large, regardless of the size of bilateral portfolio flows, depending instead on openness to the global economy (Ehrmann, Fratzscher and Rigobon

---

d. If U.S. fiscal stimulus leads to a higher U.S. public debt in the long term, it could also raise global interest rates and be a source of adverse cross-border spillovers by tightening financial conditions (Cardarelli and Kose 2004).

e. This estimate for advanced economies is in line with other estimates for Canada (Bayoumi and Swiston 2009). For Caribbean economies and Mexico with strong economic ties to the United States, considerably larger spillovers in excess of 1 percentage point have been estimated (Sun and Samuel 2009; Swiston and Bayoumi 2008).

f. If a rise in long-term U.S. yields is supported by prospects of a strengthening U.S. economy (a favorable "real shock"), the net effect for EMDEs could be positive. In particular, it could bolster equity valuations and activity, and lead to less pronounced currency pressures. Alternatively, if financial markets are surprised by prospects of a less accommodative stance of U.S. monetary policy that is not supported by strengthening growth, it could have adverse consequences for EMDEs through asset price and capital flow channels (an adverse "monetary shock").

BOX 6.2 The global role of the United States and China *(continued)*

FIGURE B6.2.9 Spillovers from U.S. growth shocks

A 1.0-percentage-point increase in U.S. growth could lift global growth by about 0.7 percentage point over the following year.

A. Output growth in other advanced economies

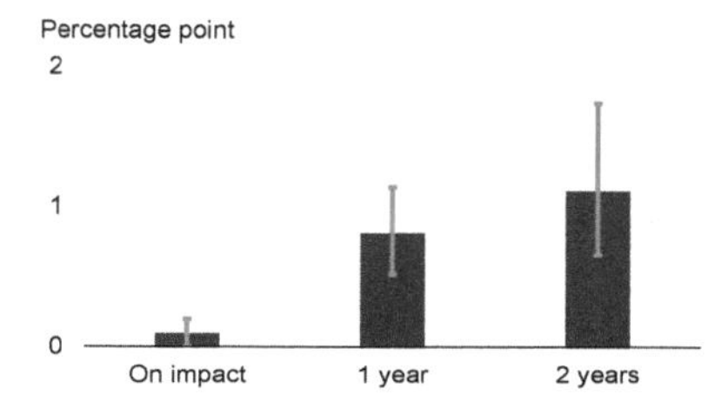

B. Output growth in EMDEs

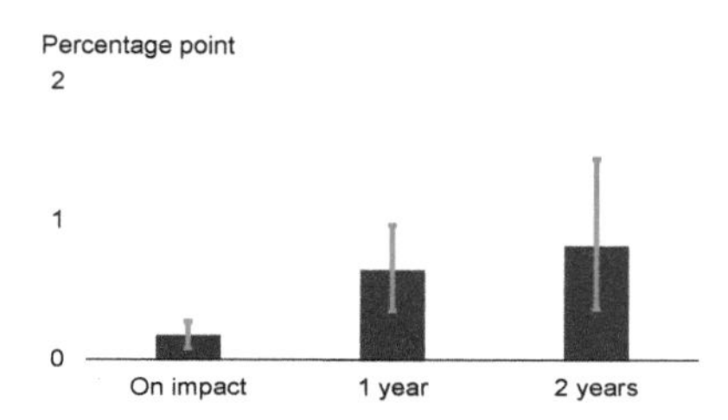

Sources: Haver Analytics; Organisation for Economic Co-operation and Development; World Bank.
Note: Cumulative impulse response of weighted average advanced economy (AE) and emerging market and developing economy (EMDE) output growth to a 1 percentage point decline in growth in real GDP in the United States. Growth spillovers to AE and EMDE based on a Bayesian vector autoregression of global GDP growth excluding the United States and AE or EMDE, U.S. GDP growth, the U.S. 10-year sovereign bond yield plus J.P. Morgan's Emerging Market Bond Index and AE or EMDE GDP growth or investment growth. The oil price is exogenous. Bars represent medians, and error bars 16-84 percent confidence bands. Sample for AE includes euro area (19 countries), Canada, Japan, and the United Kingdom, and 20 EMDEs for 1998Q1-2016Q2.

2011; Rose and Spiegel 2011). This makes U.S. monetary policy and investor confidence important drivers of global financial conditions (Arteta et al. 2015; Ehrmann and Fratzscher 2009; Rey 2015).

Because of the predominant use of the U.S. dollar in global trade and financial transactions, broadbased U.S. dollar exchange rate movements have global implications. Episodes of U.S. dollar appreciation tend to coincide with bank deleveraging, tighter global financial conditions, greater incidence of financial crises, and subdued EMDE growth (Abbate et al. 2016; Bruno and Shin 2015a, 2015b; Druck, Magud, and Mariscal 2015; IMF 2015a, 2015b). Although the average share of private and public debt denominated in foreign currency has declined since the 1990s, the exposure of some EMDEs to foreign currency movements is still high, especially in commodity exporters, and importers that have received large capital inflows after the global financial crisis (Arteta et al. 2016). As has happened in the past, if the U.S. dollar goes through a period of significant appreciation, EMDEs with substantial short-term dollar-denominated debt could become particularly vulnerable to rollover and interest rate risks and a drying up of foreign exchange liquidity (Chow et al. 2015; Chui, Fender, and Sushko 2014; McCauley, McGuire, and Sushko 2015).

BOX 6.2 The global role of the United States and China *(continued)*

FIGURE B6.2.10 U.S. interest rate shock spillovers to EMDEs

An increase in U.S. long-term yields, supported by a stronger U.S. economy (real shock), could lift EMDE equity prices and industrial production. In contrast, an increase in yields driven by a sudden reassessment of monetary policy expectations (monetary shock) could have a sizable adverse effect on EMDE equity markets, exchange rates, industrial production, and capital flows.

A. Impact of rising U.S. long-term yields on EMDE equity prices

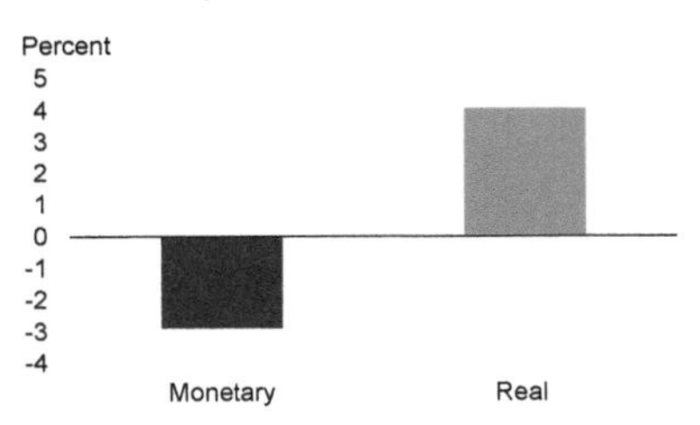

B. Impact of rising U.S. long-term yields on EMDE industrial production

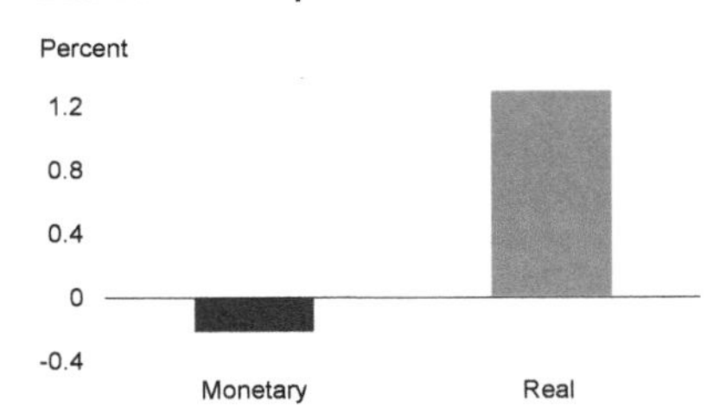

C. Impact of rising U.S. long-term yields on EMDE exchange rate

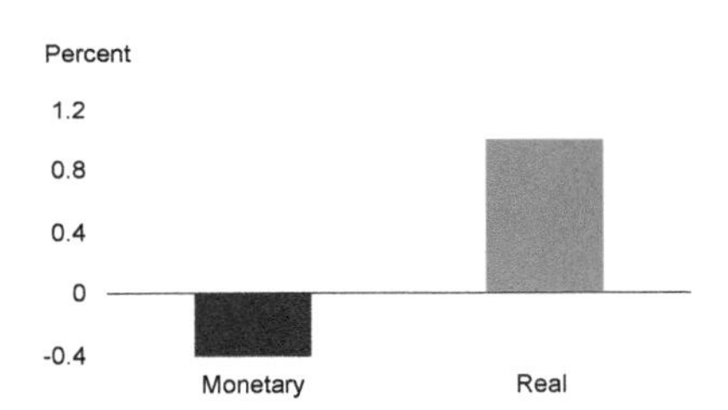

D. Impact of interest rate shocks in four major economies on EMDE capital flows

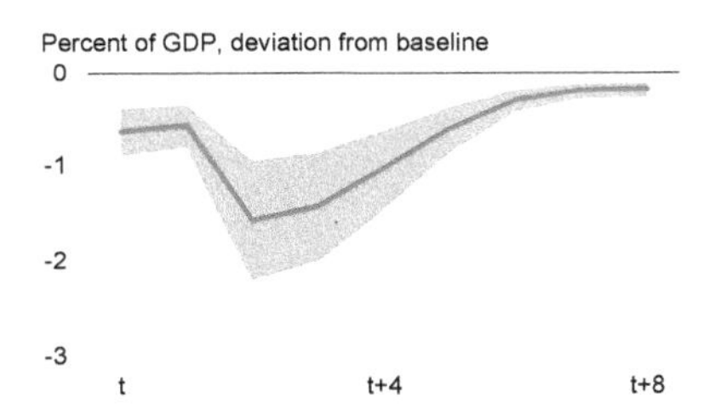

Sources: Bloomberg; Haver Analytics; World Bank estimates.

Note: Impulse responses after 12 months from a panel autoregressive model, including EMDE industrial production, long-term bond yields, stock prices, nominal effective exchange rates and bilateral exchange rates against the U.S. dollar, and inflation, with monetary and real shocks as exogenous regressors. Monetary and real shocks are defined as in box 1 of Arteta et al. (2015). All data are monthly or monthly averages of daily data, for January 2013-September 2015 for 23 EMDEs. For comparability, the size of the U.S. real and monetary shocks is normalized such that each shock raises EMDE bond yields by 100 basis points on impact. EMDEs = emerging market and developing economies.

Uncertainty spillovers. Increased uncertainty, driven by financial market volatility or ambiguity about the direction and scope of policies, could discourage investors—in the United States and elsewhere—who base their decisions about long-term investments on stable financing conditions and predictable policies. Sustained increases in financial market uncertainty would set back output and investment growth in the United States, other advanced economies, and EMDEs (Bloom 2009; Carrière-Swallow and Céspedes 2013). A 10 percent increase in the implied volatility of the U.S. stock market (VIX) would reduce average EMDE

BOX 6.2 The global role of the United States and China (continued)

FIGURE B6.2.11 U.S. uncertainty shock spillovers to EMDEs

A sustained increase in policy uncertainty or financial market volatility in the United States would significantly slow U.S. growth as well as output and investment growth in other advanced economies and EMDEs.

A. Impact of 10 percent rise in VIX on output growth

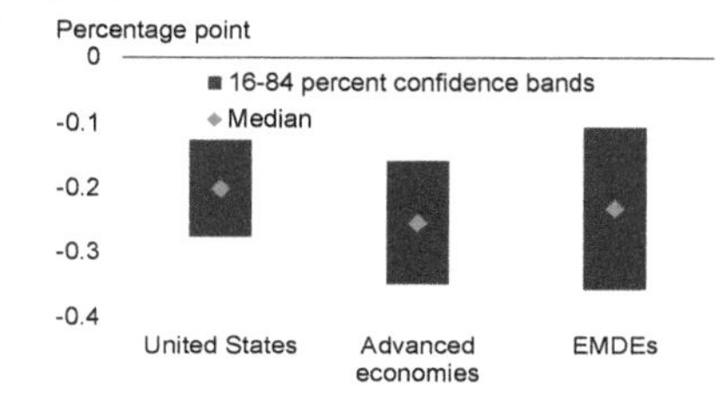

B. Impact of 10 percent rise in VIX on investment growth

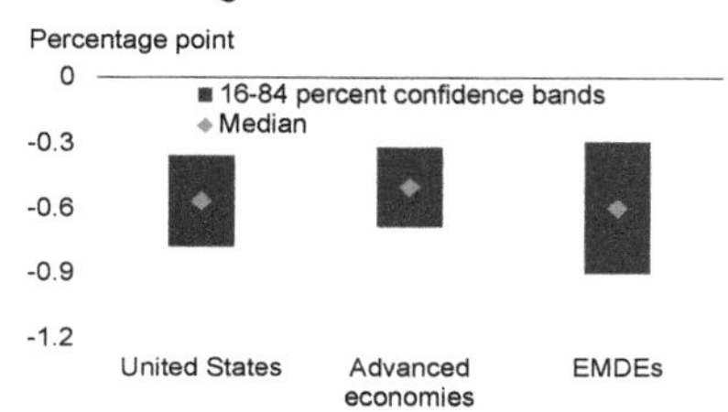

C. Impact of 10 percent rise in U.S. EPU on output growth

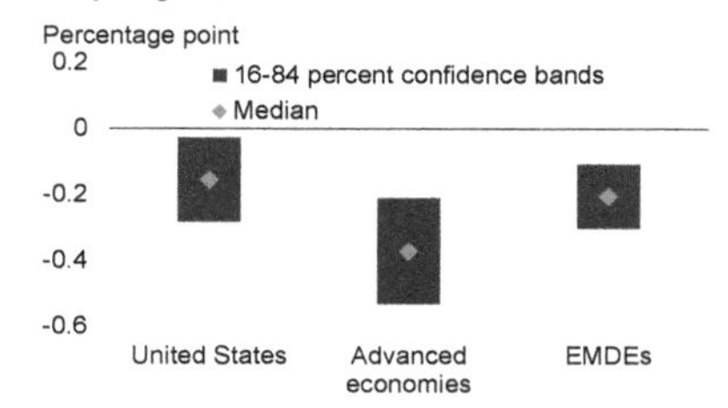

D. Impact of 10 percent rise in U.S. EPU on investment growth

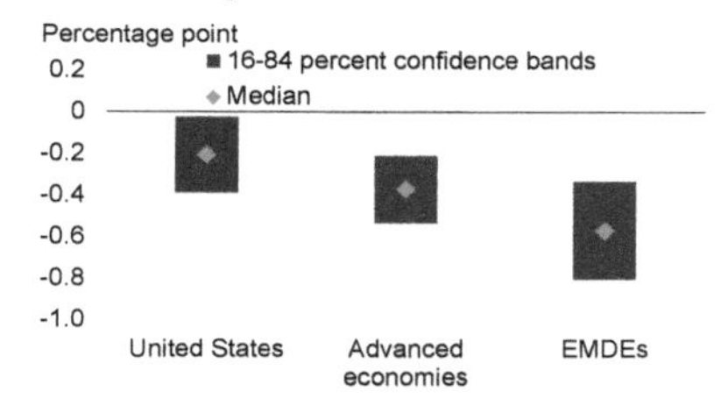

Sources: Haver Analytics; Organisation of Economic Co-operation and Development; World Bank estimates.
Note: Cumulative impulse responses after one year on output growth (A.C.) or investment growth (B.D.) in the United States, 23 other advanced economies (AEs), and 20 EMDEs to a 10 percent increase in volatility index (VIX, panels A and B) or in the U.S. Economic Policy Uncertainty index (EPU, panels C and D). Vector autoregressions are estimated for 1998Q1-2016Q2 with two lags. The model for the United States includes, in this order, uncertainty index (VIX or U.S. EPU), U.S. stock price index (S&P 500), U.S. 10-year bond yields, U.S. real GDP and investment growth. The model for AEs includes uncertainty index (VIX or U.S. EPU), Morgan Stanley Capital International (MSCI) index for advanced economies (MXGS), U.S. 10-year bond yields, aggregate real output and investment growth in 23 other AEs. The model for EMDEs includes uncertainty indexes (VIX or U.S. EPU), the MSCI emerging market equity price index, J.P. Morgan emerging market bond spreads (EMBIG), aggregate real output, and investment growth in 20 EMDEs. G7 real GDP growth, U.S. 10-year bond yields, and the MSCI world equity price index are added as exogenous regressors.

output growth by about 0.2 percentage point and EMDE investment growth by about 0.6 percentage point after one year (figure B6.2.11). The impact on other advanced economies would be broadly comparable.

Financial market volatility does not necessarily coincide with policy uncertainty, yet both appear to be detrimental to investment. Policy uncertainty is measured by the Economic Policy Uncertainty Index (EPU, a news-based measure of policy uncertainty; Baker, Bloom, and Davis 2016). A sustained 10 percent increase in

BOX 6.2 The global role of the United States and China *(continued)*

the index of U.S. economic policy uncertainty could reduce U.S. output growth by 0.15 percentage point, EMDE output growth by 0.2 percentage point, and EMDE investment growth by 0.6 percentage point after one year (figure B6.2.11).

Spillovers from China

Global growth spillovers from China are sizable and, in part because of China's larger economic size, much larger than those from other BRICS (Brazil, Russia, India, China, South Africa) economies (Huidrom et al. 2019). China's economy is twice as large as the other BRICS combined and five times as large as the next-largest BRICS economy (India); it has six times the trade of the next most open BRICS economy (Russia); and accounts for two times the commodity imports of the next-largest BRICS commodity importer (India). A 1.0-percentage-point increase in growth in China is estimated to contribute to global growth by 0.2 percentage point after two years, growth in emerging markets (excluding Brazil, Russia, India, and South Africa) by 0.5 percentage point, and in frontier markets by 1.0 percentage point after two years (figure B6.2.12). The impact on commodity-exporting EMDEs would be considerably larger than on commodity-importing ones. Spillovers from economic uncertainty in China could be significant. For example, variation in the macroeconomic uncertainty (MU) index in China constructed following Jurado, Ludvigson, and Ng (2015) explains 1.7 percent, 3.8 percent, 13 percent, and 4.3 percent of the fluctuations in U.S. consumer price index, producer price index, electric energy production, and money supply (M2), respectively (Huang et al. 2018).

As China's economy slows, rebalances, and shifts toward less commodity-intensive activities, its demand for commodities is likely to plateau. For example, China's and other EMDEs' rising per capita incomes and slowing growth are expected to slow global consumption growth for metals, which are among the commodities most sensitive to the business cycle, by one-third over the next decade (Baffes et al. 2018; World Bank 2018d). Based on current levels of consumption of commodities and expected growth rates elsewhere, no country or group of countries is expected to come close to replicating China's growth in metals demand, which in turn will provide less support to commodity prices (World Bank 2015a, 2018d).

Conclusion

The United States and China, the world's two largest economies, together account for close to four-tenths of global GDP and more than one-fifth of global trade and world population. Because of the size and international links of these two economies, developments in them are bound to have significant implications for the rest of the world.

BOX 6.2 The global role of the United States and China *(continued)*

FIGURE B6.2.12 Spillovers from China growth shocks

A 1.0-percentage-point increase in China's growth is estimated to boost global growth by 0.2 percentage point after two years.

A. Impact of 1.0-percentage-point increase in BRICS and China growth

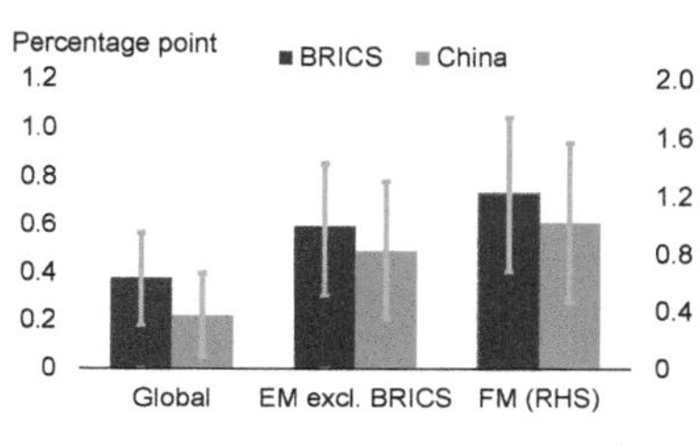

B. Impact of 1.0-percentage-point increase in China growth

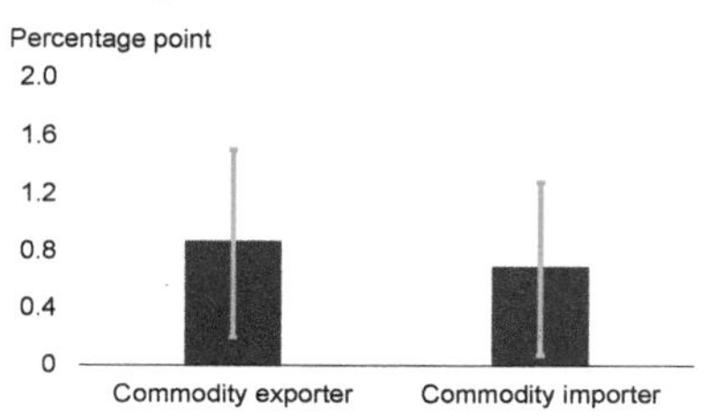

Sources: Haver Analytics; Organisation of Economic Co-operation and Development; World Bank.

A. Cumulated impulse responses at the end of two years due to a 1.0-percentage-point increase on impact in growth in China and in BRICS (Brazil, the Russian Federation, India, China, and South Africa). The shock size is such that China's growth rises by 1.0 percentage point on impact. The shock size for BRICS is calibrated such that its growth rises by exactly the same amount as that of China at the end of two years. Solid bars denote the median and the error bars denote the 16-84 percent confidence bands. EM = emerging market economies.

B. Cumulated impulse responses of trade-weighted commodity prices of commodity exporters, for different horizons, due to a 1.0-percentage-point increase in China's growth. Solid bars denote the median and the error bars denote the 16-84 percent confidence bands. The average quarterly growth rate of commodity prices is about 0.9 percent in the sample.

The United States is the world's largest economy, accounting for almost one-quarter of global output and about one-tenth of total trade flows. It is also the largest international creditor and debtor economy. China, the world's second-largest economy accounts for about 16 percent of global output, one-tenth of global trade, and close to one-fifth of world population. China plays an important role in global commodity markets, currently accounting for about half of global consumption of coal and metals.

Shocks to U.S. growth, changes in U.S. fiscal and monetary policies, or uncertainty in U.S. financial markets or policies all could have sizable global spillovers. The impact is likely to be broad-based and most severe for more financially open economies with stronger trade ties to the United States. A shock to growth in China would also reverberate around EMDEs, with particularly strong impacts on commodity-exporting EMDEs. For now, shocks to China's growth may have somewhat more modest global impacts than shocks to U.S. growth, but policy uncertainty, especially adverse developments, about these two countries' future economic relationship would hit many countries doubly.

FIGURE 6.9 Vulnerabilities in EMDEs

Since 2007, external, corporate sector, and sovereign vulnerabilities have risen in the majority of EMDEs.

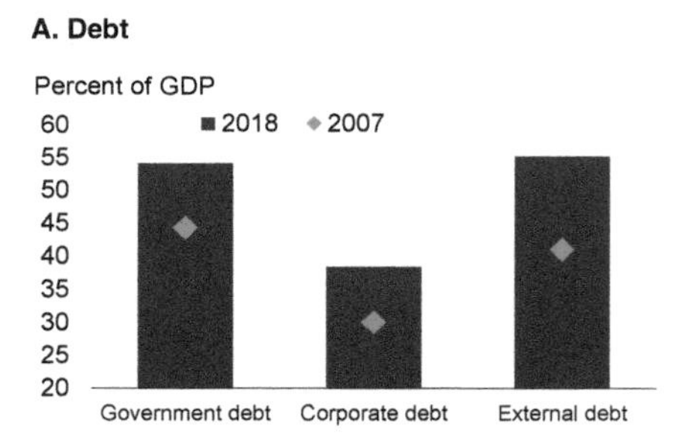

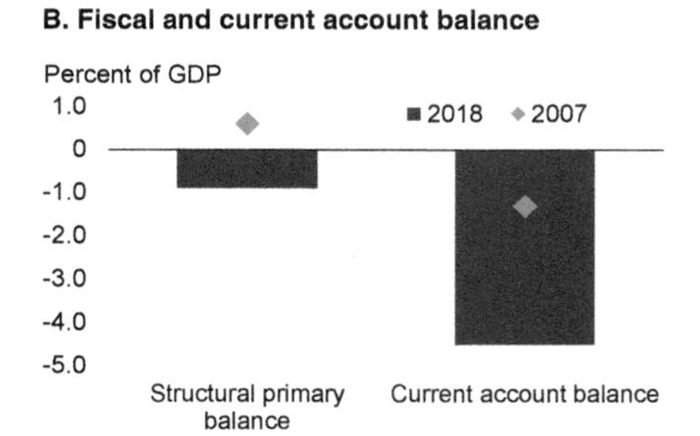

Sources: International Monetary Fund; World Bank.

A. Unweighted averages of gross government debt for 146 emerging market and developing economies (EMDEs), nonfinancial corporate debt for 48 EMDEs, and total external debt for 61 EMDEs.

B. Unweighted averages of the structural primary balance for 149 EMDEs, and current account balances for 143 EMDEs.

oil supply disruptions in MNA can raise global oil prices, depressing global aggregate demand and worsening trade balances in oil-importing economies.

Extreme weather events have been increasing in frequency, severity, and cost (World Bank 2014). Small island economies of the Caribbean and EAP, and economies with large agricultural sectors, including in SSA and SAR, are most at risk (World Bank 2017b). In the median SSA economy, agricultural value added accounted for 21 percent of GDP in 2017—three times larger than in non-SSA EMDEs and 11 times larger than in advanced economies. As natural disasters become more common, their effects on the level and volatility of output in agriculture-dependent economies are likely to increase.

Rising vulnerabilities

Comparison before the global recession. Since 2007, external, corporate sector, and sovereign vulnerabilities have risen in most EMDEs, leaving them less well prepared for the next financial shock (figure 6.9). Vulnerabilities can be defined as conditions that increase the probability of financial or economic crises (or stress) when adverse shocks occur. If risks materialize, their impact on an economy's growth will depend on its vulnerabilities and the ability of policy makers to respond.[12]

Sovereign vulnerabilities. Since 2007, government debt in EMDEs has increased by about 10 percentage points of GDP, on average, to 54 percent of GDP by end-2018,

[12] See Llaudes, Salman, and Chivakul (2010) on the interaction of vulnerabilities in emerging markets and the global financial crisis.

with the most rapid increases seen in commodity exporters (figure 6.10). Debt has risen in three-quarters of EMDEs and by more than 20 percentage points of GDP in one-third of them. Reflecting this rise in sovereign indebtedness, many EMDEs have a lower average sovereign credit rating now than in 2007. Moreover, the average maturity of EMDE sovereign debt has declined from 11.5 years in 2007 to 10.3 years in 2018, with 23 percent of EMDEs in 2018 having an average debt maturity under 6 years.

The rise in EMDE sovereign debt reflects a deterioration in fiscal balances. On average, the primary surplus of 2.4 percent of GDP in 2007 turned into a deficit of 1.3 percent of GDP by 2018. The cyclically adjusted overall fiscal balance has shifted from a surplus of 2.4 percent of GDP to a deficit of 1.5 percent. Nine-tenths of EMDEs now have a cyclically adjusted fiscal deficit, compared to two-thirds in 2007. EMDEs, on average, continued to run cyclically adjusted primary budget deficits in 2018, and have not yet fully unwound fiscal stimulus implemented during the global recession (chapter 5). Commodity-exporting EMDEs experienced the largest deterioration in fiscal balances, on average, and are currently running the largest deficits.

External vulnerabilities. Although external financing helps fund much-needed investment in EMDEs, it can increase EMDEs' vulnerability to global financial market stress. EMDE total external debt has risen by 14 percentage points of GDP since 2007, to 55 percent of GDP on average in 2018. In half of EMDEs, it has risen by 10 percentage points of GDP or more (figure 6.11). This increase has mainly reflected sizable and persistent current account deficits, which averaged 4.5 percent of GDP in 2018, compared with 1.2 percent of GDP in 2007. In 2018, 60 percent of EMDEs had weaker current account balances than in 2007, 76 percent ran current account deficits (compared with 66 percent in 2007), and 44 percent had current account deficits in excess of 5 percent of GDP.

The share of external debt maturing in 12 months or less has remained stable since 2007 at about 12 percent, whereas the share denominated in foreign currency has remained above 90 percent. This buildup of external vulnerabilities has been mitigated somewhat by foreign exchange reserves in most EMDEs. Although still above their 1980s and 1990s averages, international reserves have fallen since 2007 in two-thirds of EMDEs, and in some they have more than halved. In 44 percent of EMDEs, they also appear not to be sufficient to meet their potential balance of payments needs in 2019, according to the reserves assessment metric of the International Monetary Fund (IMF).

A growing share of external liabilities are channeled through domestic bond markets. In some EMDEs, the share of nonresident-held bonds in local currency bond markets has grown to more than 30 percent. The higher participation of nonresidents reduces immediate currency risks, but exposes these countries to the risk of shifts in global risk sentiment (Agur et al. 2018).

Corporate and household debt vulnerabilities. Since 2007, nonfinancial corporate debt has increased on average by 10.3 percentage points of GDP to 48.0 percent in 2018 among EMDEs other than China, often fueled by low global interest rates and

FIGURE 6.10 Sovereign vulnerabilities in EMDEs

Government debt and fiscal deficits had broadbased increases in emerging market and developing economies between 2007 and 2018.

A. Government debt

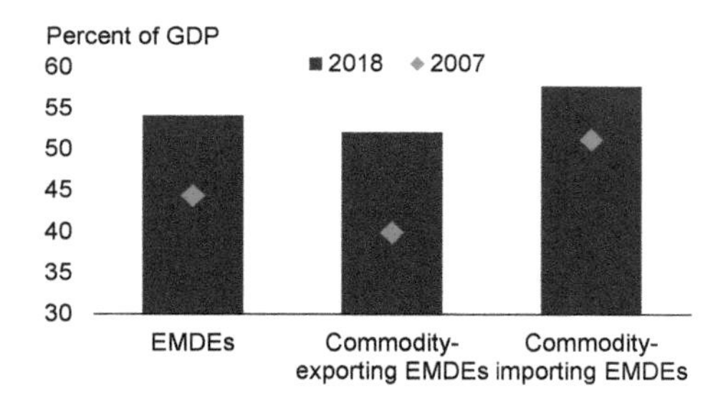

B. Government debt

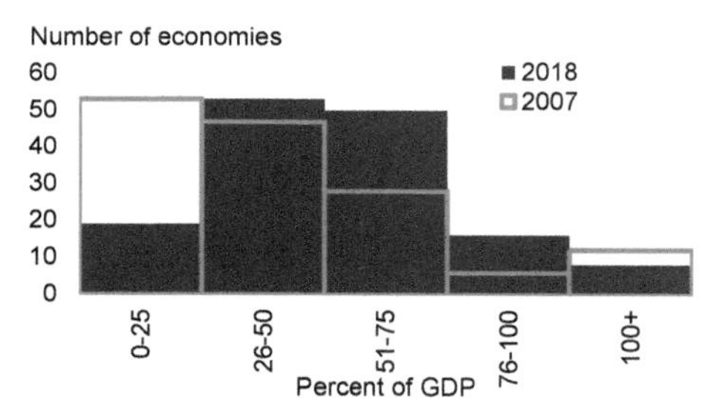

C. Sovereign credit ratings

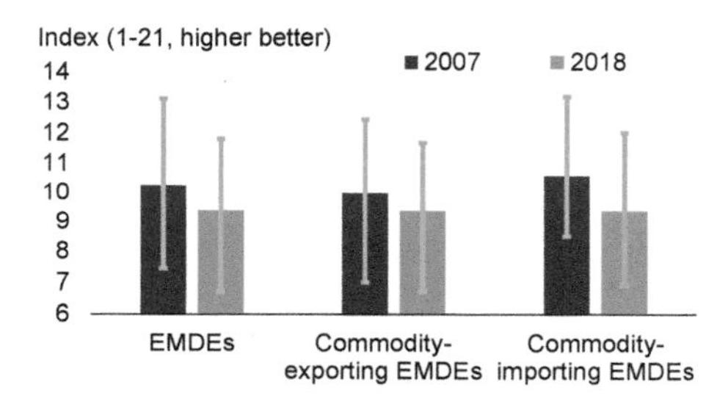

D. Maturity of government debt

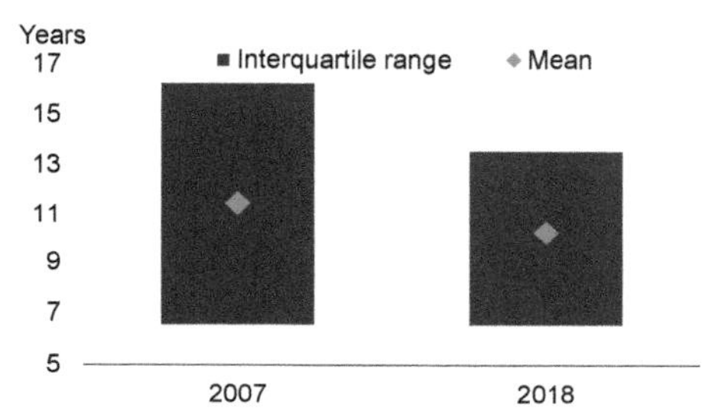

E. Cyclically adjusted primary fiscal balance

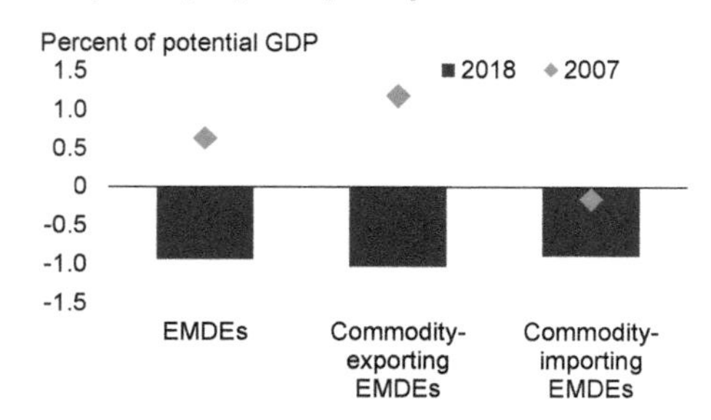

F. Cyclically adjusted primary fiscal balance

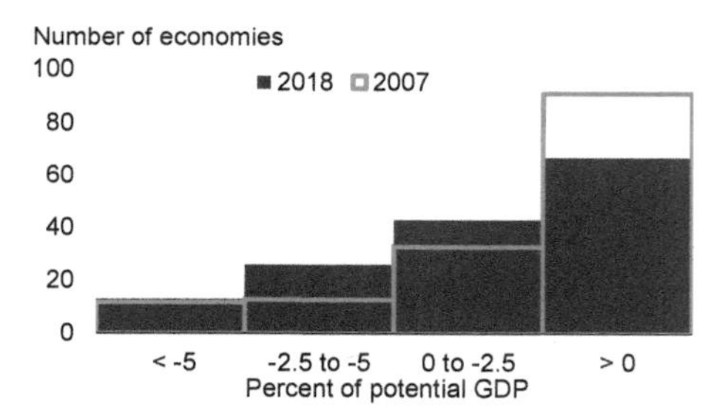

Sources: International Monetary Fund; Kose, Kurlat et al. (2017); World Bank.

Note: EMDEs = emerging market and developing economies.

A. Unweighted average of government debt ratios for 85 EMDE commodity exporters and 60 EMDE commodity importers.

B. Based on data for 146 EMDEs.

C. Unweighted averages of foreign currency sovereign credit ratings for 54 EMDE commodity exporters and 40 EMDE commodity importers. Whiskers denote interquartile ranges.

D. Unweighted averages of the average maturity of government debt based on 38 EMDEs.

E. Unweighted average of cyclically adjusted primary balance-to-potential GDP ratios for 91 EMDE commodity exporters and 64 EMDE commodity importers.

F. Based on data for 149 EMDEs.

FIGURE 6.11 External vulnerabilities in EMDEs

Since 2007, external debt has risen in most EMDEs relative to GDP and current account balances have weakened in commodity exporters. Most EMDEs appear to have adequate foreign reserve coverage to meet balance of payments needs, but significant heterogeneity exists.

A. External debt

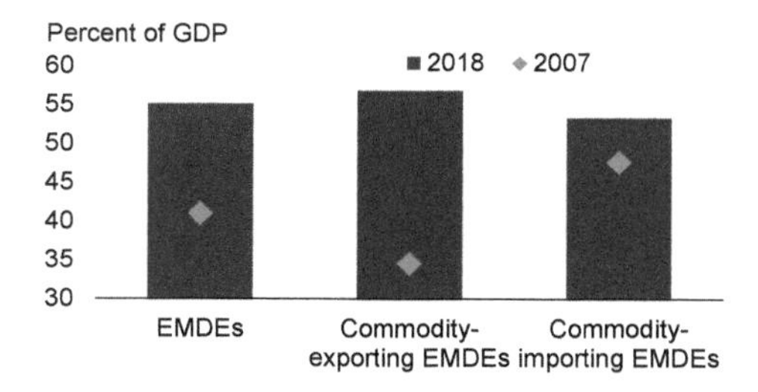

B. External debt

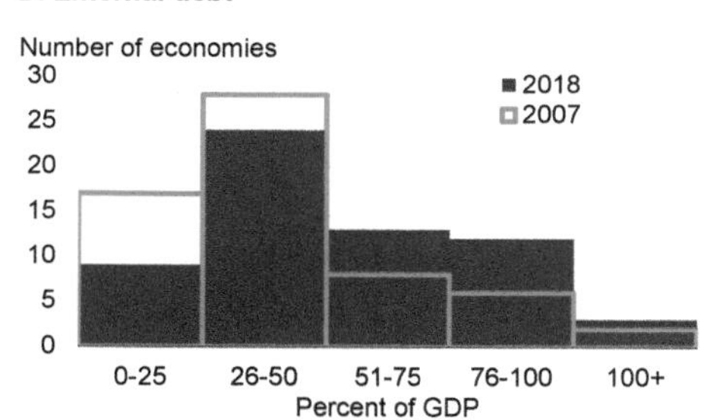

C. Current account balance

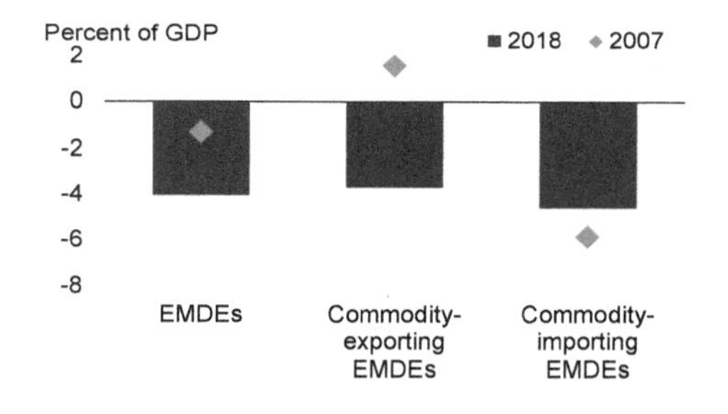

D. Current account balance

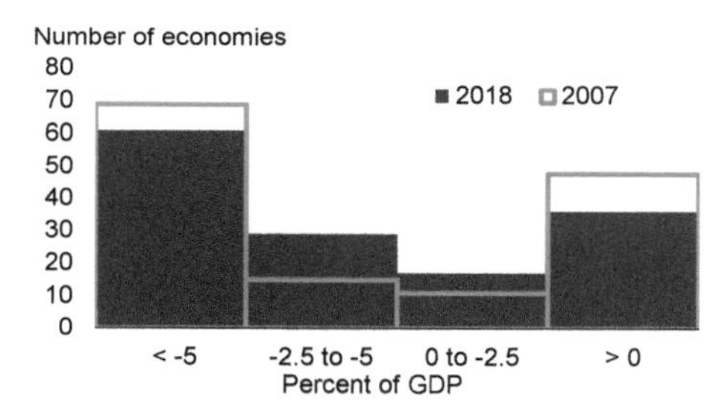

E. Foreign reserves adequacy

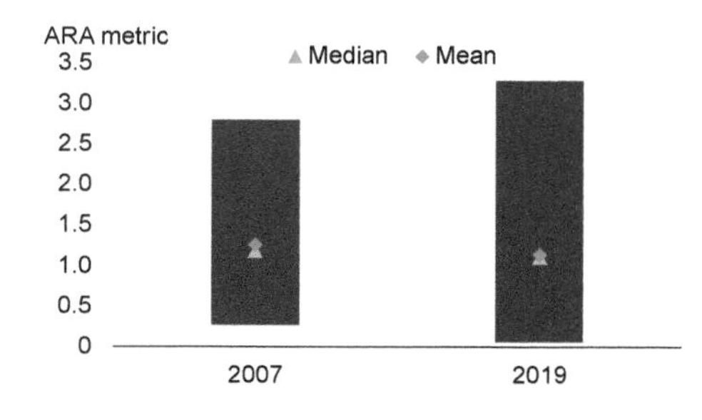

F. Nonresident holdings of local currency debt

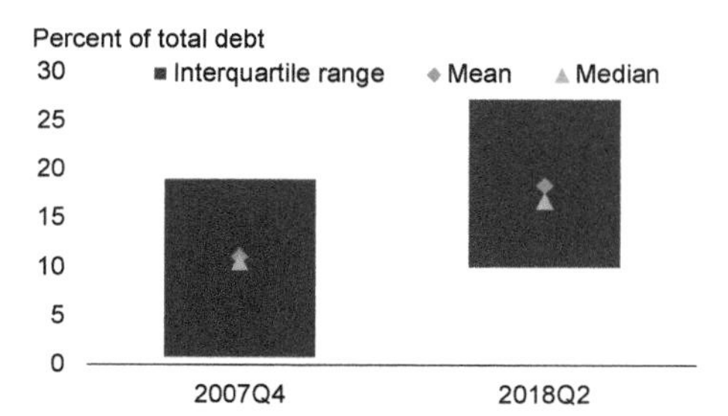

Sources: Ha, Kose, and Ohnsorge (2019); International Monetary Fund; World Bank.

Note: EMDEs = emerging market and developing economies.

A. Unweighted average of total external debt-to-GDP ratios for 31 EMDE commodity exporters and 30 EMDE commodity importers.

B. Based on data for 61 EMDEs.

C. Unweighted average of current account balance-to-GDP ratios for 88 EMDE commodity exporters and 55 EMDE commodity importers.

D. Based on data for 143 EMDEs.

E. Based on data for 48 EMDEs. Dark blue bars show minimum and maximum values. Assessing Reserve Adequacy (ARA) metric is based on IMF (2011), which determines the appropriate reserve cover on a risk-weighted basis covering short-term debt, medium and long-term debt, and equity liabilities. Broad model and export earnings. Risk weights are based on observed outflows during periods of exchange rate pressure. Values above 1 suggest that countries are fully able to meet balance of payments needs using reserves.

F. Based on data for 23 EMDEs.

FIGURE 6.12 Corporate vulnerabilities in EMDEs

Corporate debt has risen most rapidly among commodity-importing EMDEs.

A. Nonfinancial corporate debt

Percent of GDP ■ Latest available ◆ 2007

EMDEs | Commodity-exporting EMDEs | Commodity-importing EMDEs

B. Nonfinancial corporate debt

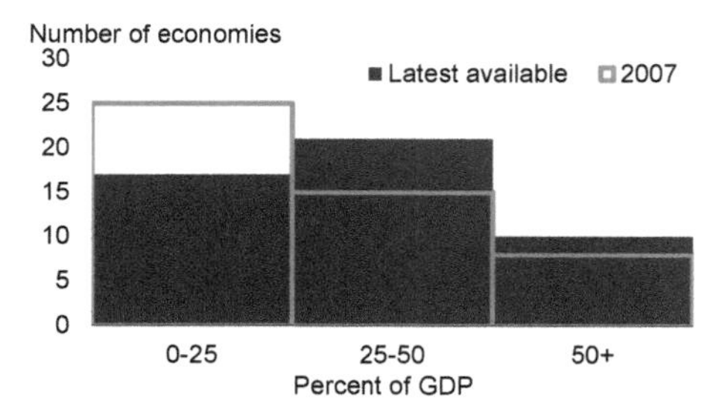

Sources: Bank for International Settlements; International Monetary Fund.

Note: Based on data for 48 emerging market and developing economies (EMDEs). Latest available datapoint is 2019Q1 for Argentina, Brazil, Chile, China, Colombia, Hungary, India, Indonesia, Malaysia, Mexico, Poland, the Russian Federation, Saudi Arabia, South Africa, Thailand, and Turkey; 2016 for Algeria, Malaysia, Peru, and Sri Lanka; and 2017 for the rest. Data from 2008 are used for South Africa and the United Arab Emirates.

A. Unweighted average of nonfinancial corporate debt in 27 EMDE commodity exporters and 21 EMDE commodity importers.

compressed risk premiums (figure 6.12).[13] Corporate debt, as a ratio to GDP, has risen above 2007 levels in eight-tenths of EMDEs and, in one-third of them, by more than 10 percentage points of GDP (Borensztein and Ye 2018; Ohnsorge and Yu 2016).[14] The most rapid increases in nonfinancial corporate debt have occurred in some of the largest EMDEs, particularly China. Outside China, about half of the buildup in EMDE corporate debt since 2010 has been in foreign currency (World Bank 2018c).

Household debt in the average EMDE has also increased by 5 percentage points of GDP since 2007, reaching 25 percent of GDP in 2018. In some EMDEs, household debt has risen by more than 10 percentage points of GDP. The largest increases are in China and Thailand, where household debt swelled by 32 and 24 percentage points of GDP, respectively.

Vulnerabilities in LICs. In LICs also, government debt and current account deficits have grown since 2007. Government debt in the median LIC was 47 percent of GDP in 2018, 10 percentage points higher than in 2007, although significantly lower than before the Multilateral Debt Relief Initiative (MDRI) and Heavily Indebted Poor Countries Initiative (HIPC).[15] The government debt-to-GDP ratio reached a low in 2013 and has since increased by 16 percentage points; it has risen in 90 percent of LICs

---

[13] Based on data for 16 EMDEs that have 2019Q1 data: Argentina, Brazil, Chile, China, Colombia, Hungary, India, Indonesia, Malaysia, Mexico, Poland, the Russian Federation, Saudi Arabia, South Africa, Thailand, and Turkey.

[14] Based on a larger sample of 48 EMDEs with data for 2017 and 2016.

[15] Average LIC debt was 51 percent of GDP in 2018, lower than the 59 percent of GDP in 2007; however, the mean is driven by a minority of LICs that have seen significant declines in debt as part of the Enhanced HIPC initiative of 2009/10.

and, in one-third of them, by more than 20 percentage points. The composition of LIC debt has shifted toward nontraditional sources of funding, including international capital markets and non-Paris Club creditors (World Bank 2019b).[16] Debt has been increasingly financed by nonconcessional and private sources, increasing LICs' vulnerability to financial market disruptions. As a result, interest payments are absorbing an increasing share of government revenues. Separately, the average LIC current account deficit widened to 8.1 percent of GDP in 2018, from 3.1 percent of GDP in 2007.

Vulnerabilities now and during previous crises

EMDEs have periodically witnessed currency, banking, and debt crises (Laeven and Valencia 2018). Reflecting their different triggers and circumstances, these crises were preceded by wide heterogeneity in vulnerabilities. Broadly speaking, however, compared to the average EMDE two years before EMDE crises since the 1980s, today's average EMDE has somewhat higher government and nonfinancial corporate debt and larger fiscal deficits, but smaller current account deficits, lower external debt, and stronger foreign exchange reserve cover (figure 6.13).

- *Higher government and corporate debt.* In the average EMDE, government debt (as of end-2018) is 3 percentage points of GDP higher, and nonfinancial corporate debt is about 7 percentage points of GDP higher, than in the average EMDE two years before it slid into a crisis in the past. Half of EMDEs have government debt levels above the average two years before past crises. Corporate debt levels in about half of EMDEs are above the average two years before past crises. Relative to only sovereign debt crises, however, average government debt in EMDEs today is 18 percentage points of GDP below the average two years preceding past crises.

- *Larger fiscal deficits.* In today's average EMDE, the cyclically adjusted fiscal deficit is 0.5 percentage point of GDP larger than in the average EMDE two years before it slid into a crisis in the past. Over half of EMDEs had a fiscal deficit in 2018 that was larger, in relation to GDP, than the historical average in countries two years away from a crisis.

- *Lower external balances.* In the average EMDE today, the current account deficit, relative to GDP, is 0.7 percentage point smaller than in the average EMDE two years before it slid into crisis. Almost half of EMDEs, however, have current account deficits larger than the average two years before past crises.

- *Lower external debt.* Total external debt is 7 percentage points lower in the average EMDE today compared to the average two years before the crisis; however, 41 percent of EMDEs have external debt levels higher than the average two years prior to crisis.

---

[16] By August 2019, 12 out 28 LICs were regarded as being in debt distress, or at high risk thereof, under the IMF-World Bank debt sustainability framework (two more than at end-2018). A country is considered to be in debt distress if it is experiencing difficulties in servicing its debt, as evidenced, for example, by the existence of arrears or ongoing or impending debt restructuring, or if there are indications that a future debt distress event is probable.

FIGURE 6.13 EMDE vulnerabilities now and during previous crises

Compared to the average EMDE two years ahead of EMDE crises since the 1980s, today's average EMDE has wider fiscal deficits and higher government and corporate debt, but narrower current account balances, lower external debt, and higher foreign exchange reserve cover for short-term external debt.

A. Government debt

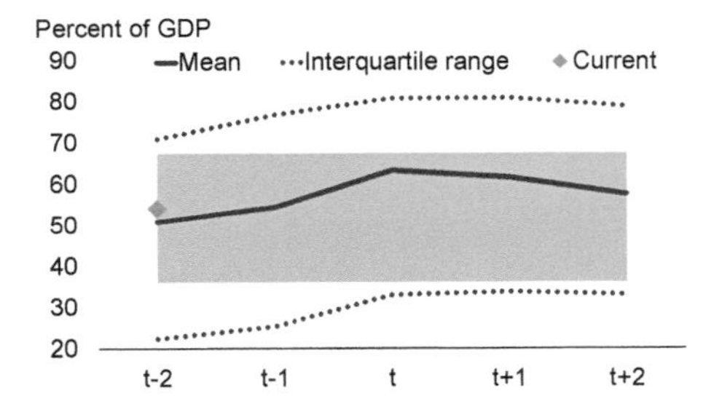

B. Nonfinancial corporate debt

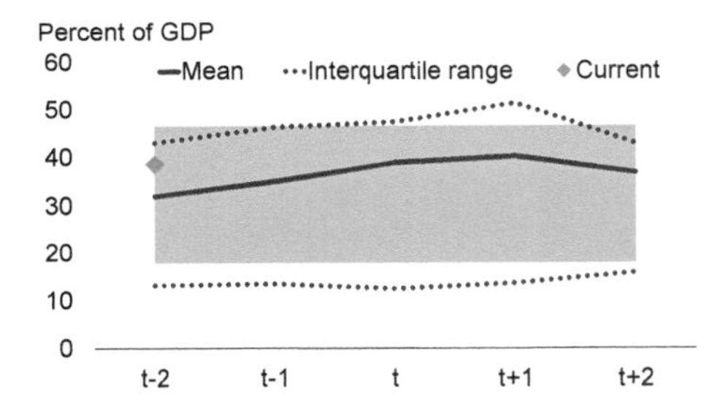

C. Cyclically adjusted fiscal balance

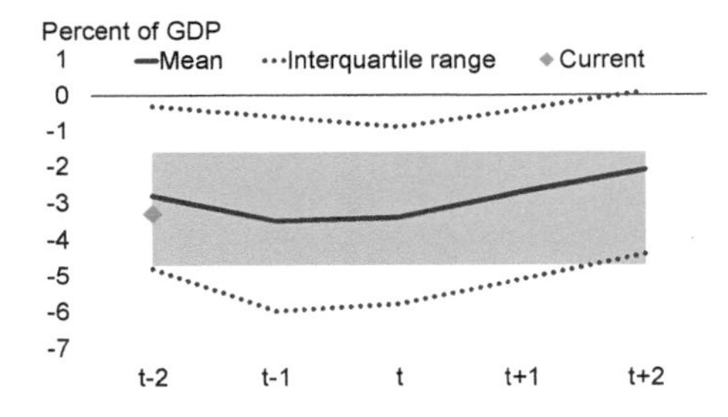

D. Current account balance

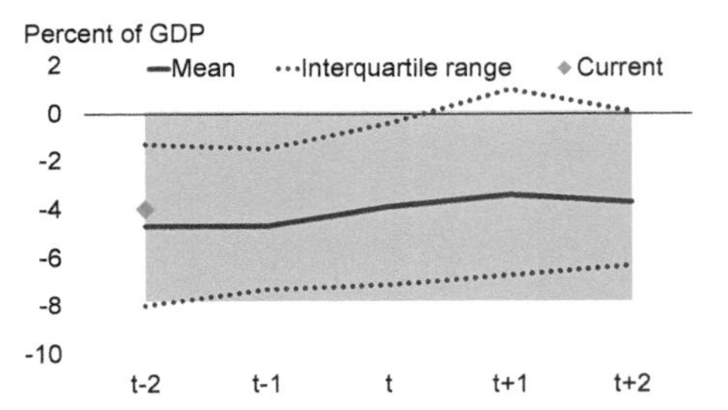

E. External debt

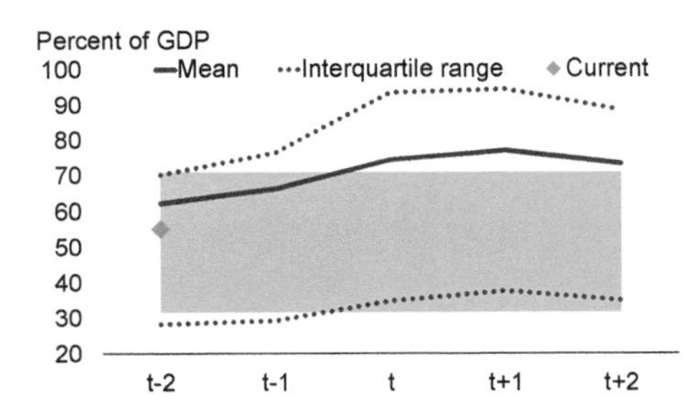

F. Short-term external debt

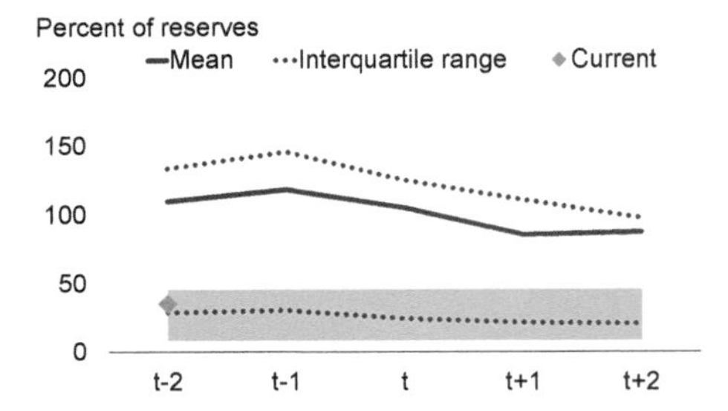

Sources: International Monetary Fund; Laeven and Valencia (2018); World Bank.

Note: Crises are currency, sovereign debt, and banking crises as defined by Laeven and Valencia (2018). Horizontal axis indicates years. "Current" denotes unweighted averages for 2018 for government debt, total external debt, and cyclically adjusted fiscal balance; 2017 for short-term external debt to reserves; 2018Q3 for corporate debt in Argentina, Brazil, Chile, China, Colombia, Hungary, India, Indonesia, Malaysia, Mexico, Poland, the Russian Federation, Saudi Arabia, South Africa, Thailand, and Turkey; 2016 for corporate debt in Algeria, Malaysia, Peru, and Sri Lanka; and 2017 for corporate debt in 29 other EMDEs. Orange shaded area indicates the interquartile range of current observations. t = year of crisis. EMDEs = emerging market and developing economies.

A. Mean and interquartile range based on 94 previous EMDE crisis events.

B. Based on 31 previous EMDE crisis events.

C. Based on 158 previous EMDE crisis events.

D. Based on 295 previous EMDE crisis events.

E. Based on 170 previous EMDE crisis events.

F. Based on 136 previous EMDE crisis events.

- *Higher reserve cover.* In the average EMDE, the ratio of short-term external debt to official international reserves is now only a third of its level in the average EMDE two years before its crisis. More than 80 percent of EMDEs have foreign reserve cover, measured this way, that is larger than levels seen two years before previous crises. Although EMDE reserves have risen since the 1990s, these increases were not evenly distributed across countries. According to the IMF's metric of reserve adequacy, 44 percent of EMDEs appear not to have sufficient reserves to meet their balance of payments needs in 2019.

Many EMDEs have learned the basic lessons from the crises of the 1980s and 1990s and adopted policies that have improved their resilience. These policies include greater exchange rate flexibility, more robust monetary and fiscal policy frameworks, and increased central bank transparency (figure 6.14). Financial sector reforms implemented since the global recession have also increased resilience, particularly the expansion of the Global Financial Safety Net.[17] Resources available in country-specific, regional, and multilateral financial safety nets tripled between 2007 and 2016, including through the creation of regional financing arrangements (RFAs), expanded IMF resources, and international reserve holdings (ECB 2018; IMF 2017a, 2017b). There are also now an estimated 160 bilateral swap lines between central banks around the world (Bahaj and Reis 2018).

The World Bank Group responded to the global recession with unprecedented levels of financing, doubling its commitments (in real terms) during FY09 and FY10, compared to FY07 and FY08 (chapter 8). Lending activity was larger than during any previous crisis, made to more than 100 economies, and larger than any other international financial institution. The World Bank Group has built upon its experience during the global recession in its subsequent work. It has expanded its global economic surveillance capabilities to better identify emerging financial and macroeconomic risks, it has rebuilt its capital, and its lending model has become more flexible and adaptable to the needs of its clients.

Conclusion

EMDE growth has generally disappointed in the past decade, with significant and frequent forecast downgrades, and 2019 is no different. EMDE growth in 2019 has been revised down by 0.7 percentage point between the January 2018 and June 2019 forecasts. Almost 40 percent of EMDEs are projected to experience a slowdown relative to 2018; growth forecasts have also been downgraded for 40 percent of EMDEs.

Growth in EMDEs is expected to bottom out in 2019, but the weak growth of the past few years has taken its toll. As growth has slowed, so has the rate of income convergence with advanced economies. Income gaps with advanced economies will widen in one-

[17] The Global Financial Safety Net consists of four layers: self-insurance against external shocks, on the basis of foreign reserves or fiscal positions at the national level; bilateral currency swap lines among countries; regional financing arrangements; and the global financial backstop provided by the IMF (ECB 2018).

FIGURE 6.14 Policies to improve resilience

Compared to 1999, more EMDEs in recent years have employed flexible exchange rate arrangements, more transparent central banks, and rules-based fiscal and monetary policies.

A. EMDEs with flexible exchange rates

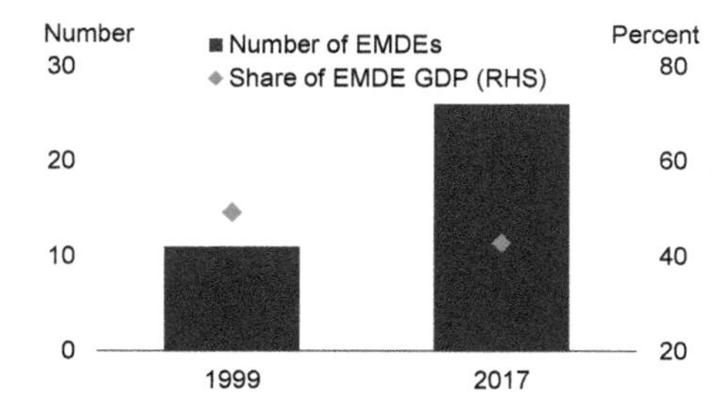

B. EMDEs with inflation targeting

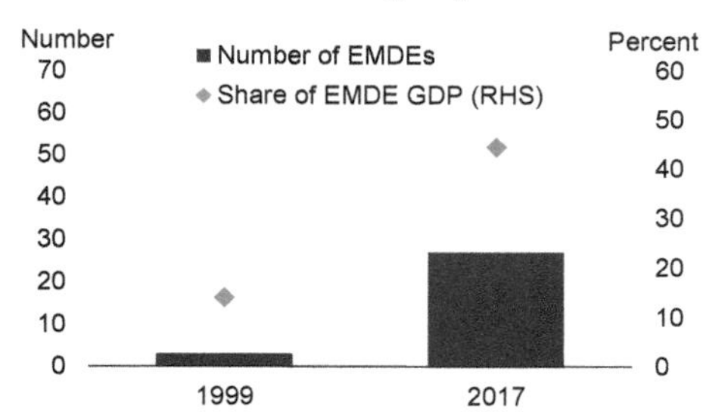

C. Central bank transparency in EMDEs

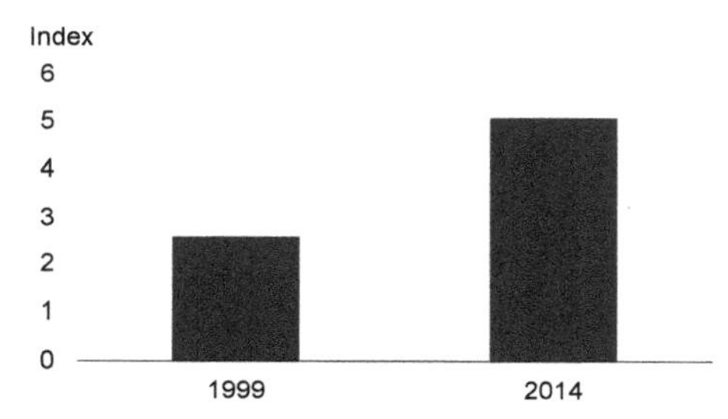

D. EMDEs with fiscal rules

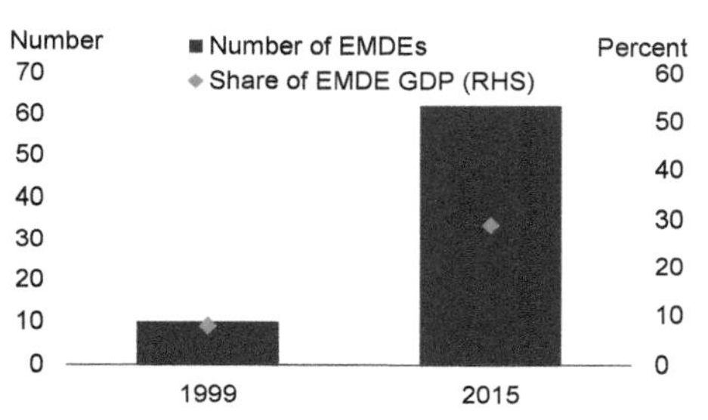

Sources: Dincer and Eichengreen (2014); International Monetary Fund; World Bank.
Note: EMDEs = emerging market and developing economies.
A.B.D. Share of EMDE GDP based on respective year constant 2010 U.S. dollar GDP.
A. An economy is considered to have a flexible exchange rate if it is classified as "floating" or "free floating."
C. Central bank transparency based on the Dincer/Eichengreen Transparency Index. Larger numbers reflect greater transparency. Last observation is 2014.
D. An economy is considered to implement a fiscal rule if it has one or more fiscal rules on expenditure, revenue, budget balance, or debt. Last observation is 2015.

third of EMDEs in 2019, and more in MNA and SSA. With near-zero per capita income growth in SSA—where most of the world's poor will live a decade from now—the goal of reducing global poverty to 3 percent appears out of reach. The prospects for progression of today's LICs, mainly in SSA, to middle-income levels have also dimmed from a decade ago, because of a larger prevalence of countries affected by fragility, conflict, and violence; weaker commodity demand prospects; and higher vulnerability to extreme weather, especially in agriculture-dependent economies (World Bank 2019a).

EMDEs face increased risks from a multitude of sources that could further damage growth. In most cases, these risks relate to a few large economies, where developments could have adverse spillovers to EMDEs. These risks include increased policy uncertainty in advanced economies, as well as rising trade tensions between the United States and some of its major trading partners, most notably China. Where risks originate outside EMDEs, enhanced monitoring and understanding of their likely impact may help prepare a more effective policy response. Where risks originate within EMDE regions, including geopolitical risks and domestic policy uncertainty, EMDEs can take actions to mitigate them or their impacts. If risks materialize, more vulnerable EMDEs are likely to experience more severe downturns. Since the global recession, external, corporate sector and sovereign vulnerabilities have risen in many EMDEs, leaving them less prepared for future shocks.

Over the next few years, EMDEs are expected to experience a modest cyclical upturn. Even after this projected upturn, however, growth is likely to be well below rates enjoyed in the past. Longer-run prospects are weak because of structural factors limiting potential growth. Indeed, the expected slowdown in potential growth is the continuation of a trend. This slowdown reflects sharp deteriorations in capital accumulation and productivity growth amid pronounced weakness in investment, as well as demographic changes. These constraints are unlikely to wane, but structural reforms can dampen their impacts or even counteract them. The next chapter looks at the macroeconomic, financial, and structural policy actions that EMDEs, including LICs, can take to counter the structural factors slowing potential growth, to mitigate their vulnerabilities, and to prepare for future crises.

References

Abbate, A., S. Eickmeier, W. Lemke, and M. Marcellino. 2016. "The Changing International Transmission of Financial Shocks: Evidence from a Classical Time‐Varying FAVAR." *Journal of Money, Credit and Banking* 48 (4): 573-601.

Adrian, T., Crump, R., and E. Moench. 2013. "Pricing the Term Structure with Linear Regressions." *Journal of Financial Economics* 110 (1): 110-38.

Agur, I., M. Chan, M. Goswani, and S. Sharma. 2018. "On International Integration of Emerging Sovereign Bond Markets." IMF Working Paper 18/18, International Monetary Fund, Washington, DC.

Ahmed, S., B. Coulibaly, and A. Zlate. 2017. "International Financial Spillovers to Emerging Market Economies: How Important Are Economic Fundamentals?" *Journal of International Money and Finance* 76 (September): 133-52.

Amiti, M., S. J. Redding, and D. E. Weinstein. 2019. "The Impact of the 2018 Trade War on U.S. Prices and Welfare." Discussion Paper 13564, Centre for Economic Policy Research, London.

Ammer, J., M. De Pooter, C. Erceg, and S. Kamin. 2016. "International Spillovers of Monetary Policy." IFDP Notes, Federal Reserve Board, Washington, DC.

Andolfatto, D., and A. Spewak. 2018. "On the Supply of, and Demand for, U.S. Treasury Debt." Economic Synopses, Federal Reserve Bank of St. Louis.

Arteta, C., M. A. Kose, F. Ohnsorge, and M. Stocker. 2015. "The Coming U.S. Interest Rate Tightening Cycle: Smooth Sailing or Stormy Waters?" Policy Research Note 15/02, World Bank, Washington, DC.

Arteta, C., M. A. Kose, M. Stocker, and T. Taskin. 2016. "Negative Interest Rate Policies: Sources and Implications." Discussion Paper 11433, Centre for Economic Policy Research, London.

Atkinson, T., and S. Morelli. 2010. "Inequality and Banking Crises: A First Look." Paper prepared for Global Labour Forum, Oxford University.

Aziz, I. J., and H. S. Shin. 2015. "Early Warning Indicators for Financial Vulnerabilities." In *Managing Elevated Risk: Global Liquidity, Capital Flows, and Macroprudential Policy—An Asian Perspective*, edited by I. J. Aziz and H. S. Shin. Singapore: Springer.

Baffes, J., A. Kabundi, P. Nagle, and F. Ohnsorge. 2018. "The Role of Major Emerging Markets in Global Commodity Demand." Policy Research Working Paper 8495, World Bank, Washington, DC.

Baffes, J., M. A. Kose, F. Ohnsorge, and M. Stocker. 2015. "The Great Plunge in Oil Prices: Causes, Consequences and Policy Implications." Policy Research Note 1, World Bank, Washington, DC.

Bahaj, S., and R. Reis. 2018. "Central Bank Swap Lines." Staff Working Paper No. 741, Bank of England, London.

Baier, S. L., and J. H. Bergstrand. 2001. "The Growth of World Trade: Tariffs, Transport Costs, and Income Similarity." *Journal of International Economics* 53 (1): 1-27.

Baker, S. R., N. Bloom, and S. J. Davis. 2016. "Measuring Economic Policy Uncertainty." *The Quarterly Journal of Economics* 131 (4): 1593-636.

Bayoumi, T., and A. Swiston. 2009. "Foreign Entanglements: Estimating the source and Size of Spillovers Across Industrial Countries." *IMF Staff Papers* 56: 353-83.

Berg, A., E. Borensztein, G. M. Milesi-Ferretti, and C. Pattillo. 1999. "Anticipating Balance of Payments Crises—The Role of Early Warning Systems," Occasional Paper No. 186, International Monetary Fund, Washington, DC.

Berkmen, S. P., G. Gelos, R. Rennhack, and J. P. Walsh. 2012. "The Global Financial Crisis: Explaining Cross-Country Differences in the Output Impact." *Journal of International Money and Finance* 31 (1): 42-59.

Bloom, N. 2009. "The Impact of Uncertainty Shocks." *Econometrica* 77 (3): 623-85.

Borensztein, E., and L. S. Ye. 2018. "Corporate Debt Overhang and Investment: Firm-Level Evidence." Policy Research Working Paper 8553, World Bank, Washington DC.

Borio, C. and H. Zhu. 2012. "Capital Regulation, Risk-Taking and Monetary Policy: A Missing Link in the Transmission Mechanism?" *Journal of Financial Stability* 8 (4): 236-51.

Bourguignon, F. 2017. *The Globalization of Inequality*. Princeton, NJ: Princeton University Press.

Bowman, D., J. Londono, and H. Sapriza. 2015. "U.S. Unconventional Monetary Policy and Transmission to Emerging Market Economies." *Journal of International Money and Finance* 55 (January): 27-59.

Bruno, V., and H. Shin. 2015a. "Capital Flows and the Risk-Taking Channel of Monetary Policy." *Journal of Monetary Economics* 71 (April): 119-32.

Bruno, V., and H. Shin. 2015b. "Cross-Border Banking and Global Liquidity." *Review of Economic Studies* 82 (2): 535-64.

Cardarelli, R., and M. A. Kose. 2004. "The Economic Impact of U.S. Budget Policies." In *U.S. Fiscal Policies and Priorities for Long-Run Sustainability*, edited by C. Towe and M. Muhleisen. Washington, DC: International Monetary Fund.

Carrière-Swallow, Y., and L. F. Céspedes. 2013. "The Impact of Uncertainty Shocks in Emerging Economies." *Journal of International Economics* 90 (2): 316-25.

Chamon M., and C. Crowe. 2012. "Predictive Indicators of Crises." In *Handbook in Financial Globalization: The Evidence and Impact of Financial Globalization*, edited by G. Caprio. London: Elsevier.

Chen, S., and M. Ravallion. 2010. "Update to the Impact of the Global Crisis on the World's Poorest." World Bank, Washington, DC.

Chitu, L., and D. Quint. 2018. "Emerging Market Vulnerabilities – A Comparison with Previous Crises." ECB Economic Bulletin 8/2018, European Central Bank, Frankfurt.

Chow, J., F. Jaumotte, S. Park, and Y. Zhang. 2015. "Spillovers from Dollar Appreciation." Working Paper 15/02, International Monetary Fund, Washington, DC.

Chui, M. K., I. Fender, and V. Sushko, 2014. "Risks Related to EME Corporate Balance Sheets: The Role of Leverage and Currency Mismatch." *BIS Quarterly Review* (September): 35-47.

Collier, P. 2003. *Breaking the Conflict Trap: Civil War and Development Policy*. Washington, DC: World Bank.

Crump, R., S. Eusepi, and E. Moench. 2018. "The Term Structure of Expectations and Bond Yields." Staff Reports 775, Federal Reserve Bank of New York, NY.

Dahlhaus, T., and A. Lam. 2018. "Assessing Vulnerabilities in Emerging-Market Economies." Discussion Paper 2018-13, Bank of Canada, Ottawa.

Davis, S. J. 2016. "An Index of Global Economic Policy Uncertainty." NBER Working Paper 22740, National Bureau of Economic Research, Cambridge, MA.

De Grauwe, P., and Y. Ji. 2016. "International Correlation of Business Cycles in a Behavioural Macroeconomic Model." Discussion Paper 11257, Center for Economic Policy Research, London.

Development Committee. 2010. "How Resilient Have Developing Countries Been During the Global Crisis?" Joint Ministerial Committee of the Boards of Governors of the World Bank and the International Monetary Fund on the Transfer of Real Resources to Developing Countries, Washington, DC.

Diao, X., M. McMillan, and D. Rodrik. 2019. "The Recent Growth Boom in Developing Economies: A Structural-Change Perspective." *In The Palgrave Handbook of Development Economics*, 281-334. Palgrave Macmillan, Cham.

Dincer, N. N., and B. Eichengreen. 2014. "Central Bank Transparency and Independence: Updates and New Measures." *International Journal of Central Banking* 10 (1): 189-259.

Dollar, D., T. Kleineberg, and A. Kraay. 2013. "Growth Still Is Good for the Poor." Policy Research Working Paper 6568, World Bank, Washington, DC.

Dollar, D., and A. Kraay. 2002. "Growth Is Good for the Poor." *Journal of Economic Growth* 7 (3): 195-225.

Druck, P., N. E. Magud, and R. Mariscal. 2015. "Collateral Damage: Dollar Strength and Emerging Markets' Growth." IMF Working Paper 15/179, International Monetary Fund, Washington, DC.

ECB (European Central Bank). 2018. "Strengthening the Global Financial Safety Net." Occasional Paper Series 207, European Central Bank, Frankfurt am Main.

Ehrmann, M., and M. Fratzscher. 2009. "Global Financial Transmission of Monetary Policy Shocks." *Oxford Bulletin of Economics and Statistics* 71 (6): 739-59.

Ehrmann, M., M. Fratzscher, and R. Rigobon. 2011. "Stocks, Bonds, Money Markets and Exchange Rates: Measuring International Financial Transmission." *Journal of Applied Econometrics* 26 (6): 948-74.

Eickmeier, S. 2007. "Business Cycle Transmission from the US to Germany: A Structural Factor Approach." *European Economic Review* 51 (3): 521-51.

EIA (Energy Information Administration). 2016. "Short-Term Energy Outlook, November 2016." U.S. Energy Information Administration, Washington DC. https://www.eia.gov/outlooks/steo/archives/nov16.pdf.

Fajgelbaum, P. D., P. K. Goldberg, P. J. Kennedy, and A. K. Khandelwal. 2019. "The Return of Protectionism." NBER Working Paper 25638, National Bureau of Economic Research, Cambridge, MA.

Fang, W., S. M. Miller, and C. C. Yeh. 2015. "The Effect of Growth Volatility on Income Inequality." *Economic Modelling* 45 (February): 212-22.

Ferreira, F. H., C. Lakner, M. A. Lugo, and B. Özler. 2014. "Inequality of Opportunity and Economic Growth: A Cross-country Analysis." Policy Research Working Paper 6915, World Bank, Washington, DC.

Feyen, E., N. Fiess, I. Z. Huertas, and L. Lambert. 2017. "Which Emerging Markets and Developing Economies Face Corporate Balance Sheet Vulnerabilities? A Novel Monitoring Framework." Policy Research Working Paper 8198, World Bank, Washington, DC.

Fisher, J., and L. Rachel. 2017. "Assessing Vulnerabilities to Financial Shocks in Some Key Global Economies." *Journal of Risk Management in Financial Institutions* 10 (1): 12-35.

Foster, J. E., and M. Székely. 2008. "Is Economic Growth Good for the Poor? Tracking Low Incomes Using General Means." *International Economic Review* 49 (4): 1143-72.

Frankel, J., and G. Saravelos. 2012. "Can Leading Indicators Assess Country Vulnerability? Evidence from the 2008-09 Global Financial Crisis." *Journal of International Economics* 87 (2): 216-231.

Frazer, G., and J. Van Biesebroeck. 2010. "Trade Growth Under the African Growth and Opportunity Act." *The Review of Economics and Statistics* 92 (1): 128-44.

Freund, C., M. J. Ferrantino, M. Maliszewska, and M. Ruta. 2018. "Impacts on Global Trade and Income of Current Trade Disputes." MTI Practice Notes, Number 2, World Bank, Washington, DC.

FSB (Financial Services Board). 2019. *Global Monitoring Report on Non-Bank Financial Intermediation 2018*. February. Basel: Financial Services Board.

Ghosh, S.R., 2016. "Monitoring Macro-Financial Vulnerability: A Primer." Washington, DC: World Bank.

Glick, R., and S. Leduc. 2013. "The Effects of Unconventional and Conventional U.S. Monetary Policy on the Dollar." Working Paper 2013-11, Federal Reserve Bank of San Francisco, San Francisco, CA.

Goldberg, P. K., and N. Pavcnik. 2004. "Trade, Inequality, and Poverty: What Do We Know? Evidence from Recent Trade Liberalization Episodes in Developing Countries." NBER Working Paper 10593, National Bureau of Economic Research, Cambridge, MA.

Goldberg, P. K., and N. Pavcnik. 2016. "The Effects of Trade Policy." *In Handbook of Commercial Policy, Volume 1A*, edited by K. Bagwell and R. W. Staiger. Amsterdam: Elsevier.

Goldberg, L. S., and C. Tille. 2008. "Vehicle Currency Use in International Trade." *Journal of International Economics* 76 (2): 177-92.

Goodhand, J. 2001. "Violent Conflict, Poverty and Chronic Poverty." CPRC Working Paper 6, Chronic Poverty Research Center, Manchester, U.K.

Grosh, M., M. Bussolo, and S. Freije, eds. 2014. *Understanding the Poverty Impact of the Global Financial Crisis in Latin America and the Caribbean*. Washington, DC: World Bank.

Ha, J., M. A. Kose, and F. Ohnsorge, eds. 2019. *Inflation in Emerging and Developing Economies: Evolution, Drivers, and Policies.* Washington, DC: World Bank.

Habib, B., A. Narayan, S. Olivieri, and C. Sanchez-Paramo. 2010. "The Impact of the Financial Crisis on Poverty and Income Distribution: Insights from Simulations in Selected Countries." *Economic Premise* 7, World Bank, Washington, DC.

Hirata, H., Kose, A. and C. Otrok. 2013. "Regionalization vs. Globalization." IMF Working Paper 13-19, International Monetary Fund, Washington, DC.

Huang, Z., C. Tong, H. Qiu, and Y. Shen. 2018. "The Spillover of Macroeconomic Uncertainty Between the U.S. and China." *Economics Letters* 171 (September): 123-27.

Huidrom, R., M. A. Kose, H. Matsuoka, and F. L. Ohnsorge. 2019. "How Important Are Spillovers from Major Emerging Markets?" *International Finance.* Advance online publication. https://doi.org/10.1111/infi.12350.

IMF (International Monetary Fund). 2007. *World Economic Outlook: Spillovers and Cycles in the World Economy*. Washington, DC: International Monetary Fund.

IMF (International Monetary Fund). 2011. "Assessing Reserve Adequacy." IMF Policy Paper, International Monetary Fund, Washington, DC.

IMF (International Monetary Fund). 2015a. "2015 Spillover Report." July. International Monetary Fund, Washington, DC.

IMF (International Monetary Fund). 2015b. *Spillovers from Dollar Appreciation. Spillover Notes 2.* Washington, DC: International Monetary Fund.

IMF (International Monetary Fund). 2017a. *Adequacy of the Global Financial Safety Net—Considerations for Fund Toolkit Reform.* Washington, DC: International Monetary Fund.

IMF (International Monetary Fund). 2017b. *Collaboration Between Regional Financing Arrangements and the IMF.* Washington, DC: International Monetary Fund.

IMF (International Monetary Fund). 2018. *Global Financial Stability Report. A Decade after the Global Financial Crisis: Are we Safer?* October. Washington, DC: International Monetary Fund.

IMF (International Monetary Fund). 2019. *World Economic Outlook: Growth Slowdown, Precarious Recovery.* April. Washington, DC: International Monetary Fund.

Jansen, W. J., and A. C. Stokman. 2004. "Foreign Direct Investment and International Business Cycle Comovement." ECB Working Paper 401, European Central Bank, Frankfurt.

Jurado, K., S. C. Ludvigson, and S. Ng. 2015. "Measuring Uncertainty." *American Economic Review* 105 (3): 1177-216.

Kolerus, C., M. P. N'Diaye, and C. Saborowski. 2016. "China's Footprint in Global Commodity Markets." *Spillover Notes* 6, International Monetary Fund, Washington, DC.

Kopp, E., and P. Williams. 2018. "A Macroeconomic Approach to the Term Premium." IMF Working Paper 18/140, International Monetary Fund, Washington, DC.

Kose, M. A., S. Kurlat, F. Ohnsorge, and N. Sugawara. 2017. "A Cross-Country Database of Fiscal Space." Policy Research Working Paper 8157, World Bank, Washington, DC.

Kose, M. A., C. Lakatos, F. Ohnsorge, and M. Stocker. 2017. "The Global Role of the U.S. Economy: Linkages, Policies, and Spillovers," Policy Research Working Paper 7962, World Bank, Washington, DC.

Kose, M. A., G. Meredith, and C. Towe. 2005. "How Has NAFTA Affected the Mexican Economy? Review and Evidence." In *Monetary Policy and Macroeconomic Stabilization in Latin America,* edited by R. J. Langhammer and L. V. de Souza. New York: Springer.

Kose, M. A., F. Ohnsorge, and N. Sugawara. Forthcoming. "Global Growth Next Decade: Optimistic Expectations, Disappointing Outcomes." Policy Research Working Paper, World Bank, Washington, DC.

Kose, M. A., E. S. Prasad, and M. E. Terrones. 2004. "Volatility and Comovement in Globalized World Economy: An Exploration." In *Macroeconomic Policies in the World Economy,* edited by H. Siebert. New York: Springer.

Kose, M. A., A. Rebucci, and A. Schipke. 2005. "Macroeconomic Implications of CAFTA-DR." In *Central America: Global Integration and Regional Cooperation,* edited by M. Rodlauer and A. Schipke. IMF Occasional Paper 243, International Monetary Fund, Washington, DC.

Kose, M. A., and M. E. Terrones. 2015. *Collapse and Revival: Understanding Global Recessions and Recoveries.* Washington, DC: International Monetary Fund.

Krugman, P., R. N. Cooper, and T. N. Srinivasan. 1995. "Growing World Trade: Causes and Consequences." *Brookings Papers on Economic Activity* 1: 327-77.

Kutlina-Dimitrova, Z., and C. Lakatos. 2017. "The Global Costs of Protectionism." Policy Research Working Paper 8277, World Bank, Washington, DC.

Laeven, L., and F. Valencia. 2018. "Systemic Banking Crises Revisited." IMF Working Paper 18/206, International Monetary Fund, Washington, DC.

Lane, P. R., and G. M. Milesi-Ferretti. 2007. "The External Wealth of Nations Mark II: Revised and Extended Estimates of Foreign Assets and Liabilities, 1970–2004." *Journal of International Economics* 73 (2): 223-50.

Lee, S. J., K. Posenau, and V. Stebunovs. 2017. "The Anatomy of Financial Vulnerabilities and Crises." FRB International Finance Discussion Paper 1191, Federal Reserve Board, Washington, DC.

Levchenko, A. A., and N. Pandalai-Nayar. 2018. "TFP, News, and 'Sentiments': The International Transmission of Business Cycles." *Journal of the European Economic Association* 18 (1): 302-41.

Llaudes, R., F. Salman, and M. Chivakul. 2010. "The Impact of the Great Recession on Emerging Markets." IMF Working Paper 10/237, International Monetary Fund, Washington, DC.

Mattoo, A., D. Roy, and A. Subramanian. 2003. "The Africa Growth and Opportunity Act and its Rules of Origin: Generosity Undermined?" *The World Economy* 26 (6): 829-51.

McCauley, R. N., P. McGuire, and V. Sushko, 2015. "Dollar Credit to Emerging Market Economies." *BIS Quarterly Review* (December): 27-41.

McMillan, M., D. Rodrik, and C. Sepúlveda. 2016. *Structural Change, Fundamentals, and Growth. Structural Change, Fundamentals, and Growth. A Framework and Case Studies.* Washington, DC: International Food Policy Research Institute Washington.

Narayan, A., and C. Sánchez-Páramo, eds. 2012. *Knowing, When You Do Not Know—Simulating the Poverty and Distributional Impact of An Economic Crisis.* Washington, DC: World Bank.

Neely, C. 2015. "Unconventional Monetary Policy Had Large International Effects." *Journal of Banking and Finance* 52 (March): 101-11.

Ohnsorge, F., and S. Yu. 2016. "Recent Credit Surge in Historical Context." Policy Research Working Paper 7704, World Bank, Washington DC.

Rajan, R. G. 2019. *Is Economic Winter Coming?* Project Syndicate. https://www.project-syndicate.org/commentary/trump-recession-risks-by-raghuram-rajan-2019-11.

Ravallion, M., and S. Chen. 1997. "What Can New Survey Data Tell us about Recent Changes in Distribution and Poverty?" *World Bank Economic Review* 11 (2): 357-82.

Rey, H. 2015. "International Credit Channel and Monetary Policy Autonomy." Paper prepared for the 15th Jacques Polak IMF Annual Research Conference, Washington, DC.

Rojas-Suarez, L. 2015. "Emerging Market Macroeconomic Resilience to External Shocks: Today Versus Pre–Global Crisis." Center for Global Development, Washington, DC.

Romalis, J. 2007. "NAFTA's and CUSFTA's Impact on International Trade." *The Review of Economics and Statistics* 89 (3): 416-35.

Rose, A., and M. Spiegel. 2011. "Cross-Country Causes and Consequences of the Crisis: An Update." *European Economic Review* 55 (3): 309-24.

Sachs, J. D., and A. M. Warner. 1995. "Natural Resource Abundance and Economic Growth." NBER Working Paper 5398, National Bureau of Economic Research, Cambridge, MA.

Santos, M. E., C. Dabus, and F. Delbianco. 2019. "Growth and Poverty Revisited from a Multidimensional Perspective." *Journal of Development Studies* 55 (2): 260-77.

Shen, Y., and T. Abeysinghe. 2016. "International Transmission of Growth Shocks and the World Business Cycle." Working paper 16/02, Singapore Centre for Applied and Policy Economics. http://www.fas.nus.edu.sg/ecs/pub/wp-scape/1602.pdf.

Stiglitz, J. E. 2012. "Macroeconomic Fluctuations, Inequality, and Human Development." *Journal of Human Development and Capabilities* 13 (1): 31-58.

Sun, Y., and W. Samuel. 2009. "ECCU Business Cycles: Impact of the United States." IMF Working Paper 09/71, International Monetary Fund, Washington, DC.

Swiston, A., and M. T. Bayoumi. 2008. "Spillovers across NAFTA." IMF Working Paper 08/3, International Monetary Fund, Washington, DC.

Tingson, E. R., N. Sugawara, V. Sulla, A. Taylor, A. I. Gucoquiva, V. Levin, and K. Subbarao. 2010. *The Crisis Hits Home – Stress-Testing Households in Europe and Central Asia.* Washington, DC: World Bank.

Winters, L. A., N. McCulloch, and A. McKay. 2004. "Trade Liberalization and Poverty: The Evidence So Far." *Journal of Economic Literature* 42 (1): 72-115.

World Bank. 2005. *Toward a Conflict-Sensitive Poverty Reduction Strategy: Lessons from a Retrospective Analysis.* World Bank: Washington, DC.

World Bank. 2006. *World Development Report: Equity and Development.* Washington, DC: World Bank.

World Bank. 2009. *Global Monitoring Report 2009: A Development Emergency.* Washington, DC: World Bank and International Monetary Fund.

World Bank. 2012. *China 2030: Building A Modern, Harmonious, and Creative Society.* Washington, DC: World Bank.

World Bank. 2014. *Turning Down the Heat: Confronting the New Climate Normal.* Washington, DC: World Bank.

World Bank. 2015a. *Commodity Markets Outlook.* July. Washington, DC: World Bank.

World Bank. 2015b. *Global Economic Prospects: Having Space and Using It.* January. Washington, DC: World Bank.

World Bank. 2016a. *Global Economic Prospects: Spillovers and Weak Growth.* January. Washington, DC: World Bank.

World Bank. 2016b. *Commodity Markets Outlook: OPEC in Historical Context.* October. Washington, DC: World Bank.

World Bank. 2016c. *Poverty and Shared Prosperity 2016: Taking on Inequality.* Washington, DC: World Bank.

World Bank. 2017a. *Global Economic Prospects: Weak Investment in Uncertain Times.* January. Washington, DC: World Bank.

World Bank. 2017b. *Climate and Disaster Resilient Transport in Small Island Developing States: A Call for Action.* October. Washington, DC: World Bank.

World Bank. 2017c. *Global Economic Prospects: A Fragile Recovery.* June. Washington, DC: World Bank.

World Bank. 2018a. *Global Economic Prospects: Broad-Based Upturn, but for How Long?* January. Washington, DC: World Bank.

World Bank. 2018b. *Poverty and Shared Prosperity Report 2018: Piecing Together the Poverty Puzzle.* Washington, DC: World Bank.

World Bank. 2018c. *Global Economic Prospects: The Turning of the Tide?* June. Washington, DC: World Bank.

World Bank. 2018d. *Commodity Markets Outlook: The Changing of the Guard—Shifts in Commodity Demand.* June. Washington, DC: World Bank.

World Bank 2019a. *Global Economic Prospects: Heightened Tensions, Subdued Investment.* January. World Bank, Washington, DC.

World Bank. 2019b. *Global Economic Prospects: Darkening Skies.* January. World Bank, Washington, DC.

WTO (World Trade Organization). 2019. *Report on G20 Trade Measures: Mid-October 2018 to Mid-May 2019.* June. Geneva: World Trade Organization.

In the medium term, … the potential for technological catch-up growth and secular convergence remains strong in most emerging countries. The pace of a country's convergence will depend … on the quality of governance and the pace of structural reforms.

Kemal Dervis (2016)

Senior Fellow

Brookings Institution

CHAPTER 7
Policy Challenges

The 2009 global recession demonstrated, once again, the importance of crisis prevention as well as the critical need for preserving policy room so that emerging market and developing economies (EMDEs) can act when hit by shocks. And now, with the global growth outlook weakening and vulnerabilities rising, these lessons underscore the need for comprehensive policies to improve EMDEs' resilience to shocks and to lift long-term growth prospects. On the macroeconomic front, priorities include shoring up fiscal positions, keeping adequate foreign reserves, and strengthening policy frameworks. Financial sector policies to adapt to a changing global financial environment include strengthening home-host supervisor coordination and establishing prudential authorities with the appropriate tools and mandates to mitigate systemic risks. Structural policy priorities include investment in human capital and infrastructure to offset the decline in potential growth that is expected to continue over the next decade. Renewed reform momentum is needed to create the environment that generates private sector-led, productivity-driven growth supported by measures to improve governance and business climates.

Introduction

EMDEs weathered the global recession of 2009 relatively well for three reasons (chapter 3). First, EMDEs were generally not as exposed to the financial sector fragilities that triggered the crisis in advanced economies. Second, many EMDEs had used the 2000s to reduce vulnerabilities and rebuild policy room to respond effectively when the crisis hit. Third, at the onset of the crisis, advanced economies and some large EMDEs provided unprecedented and coordinated monetary and fiscal policy stimulus, which helped shield global economic growth.

Nevertheless, the global recession slowed per capita growth in EMDEs to 0.4 percent in 2009 from an average over much of the preceding decade of close to 5.0 percent. The rebound in 2010-11 was initially strong, but per capita growth never returned to its rates from before the global recession. Commodity exporters faced further headwinds when global commodity prices slid to multiyear lows in 2011-16 and forced commodity-exporting EMDEs to engage in procyclical fiscal tightening. Energy-exporting EMDEs were particularly hard hit by the collapse in oil prices in 2014-16.

Amid slowing growth, most EMDEs were not able to fully unwind the policy stimulus put in place in response to the crisis—fiscal deficits in the average EMDE were about as wide in 2018 as they were in 2010, and external, fiscal, and corporate vulnerabilities have increased since 2007 (chapter 6). Several EMDEs are highly indebted, have elevated levels of debt denominated in foreign currency, or rely on portfolio or bank flows to finance large current account deficits.

Note: This chapter was prepared by Franz Ulrich Ruch.

Since the global recession, structural factors have eroded potential growth. Around 2010, the share of the working-age population in EMDEs stabilized after more than four decades of rapid increases. This demographic shift coincided with a prolonged period of weak investment. As a result, potential growth in EMDEs slowed by 1.2 percentage points after 2003-07, to 4.7 percent in 2013-18.

The years before and during the global recession provided an initial encouragement to adopt business-friendly reforms, when most EMDEs improved their scores in the World Bank's *Doing Business* survey. From DB2008 to DB2010, the number of business-friendly reforms undertaken by EMDEs increased from 170 per year to 243.[1] However, momentum for business climate reforms other than improving financial regulation stalled in DB2010, setbacks in governance appear to have returned EMDE governance indicators to their 1990s levels, and a rethink appears to be taking hold about the appropriate degree of openness to international capital flows.

EMDE growth prospects have dimmed since the global recession because of elevated debt vulnerabilities, slower momentum in structural reforms, diminished policy room to maneuver, and weakening potential growth. Meanwhile, their risks have risen, including those related to trade tensions, weakening commitments to multilateralism, slowing growth among major economies, financial market disruptions, and geopolitical tensions. Shifting demographics, weakening productivity growth, and slowing capital accumulation also raise the possibility of further downgrades to potential growth. Against this backdrop, this chapter addresses the following questions:

- What macroeconomic policies should be implemented to build resilience?
- What financial sector policies should be employed to maintain financial stability?
- How have structural reforms evolved and what policies are needed to boost growth?

Contributions to the literature. A broad literature offers policy recommendations for EMDEs and analysis of the likely effects of possible reforms and other policy actions. This chapter adds to the literature in several ways. First, the chapter assesses both the progress and impact of structural reforms in EMDEs since the global recession. Most studies focus on quantifying the impact these reforms would have on output (Bailiu and Hajzler 2016; Égert 2018) and the evolution of specific aspects of structural reforms (World Bank 2019c).[2] Second, compared to existing studies that focus on individual

---

[1] This refers to reforms of laws, rules, and regulations relating to several activities: starting a business, obtaining construction permits, getting electricity, registering property, access to credit, minority investor protection, paying taxes, trade across borders, enforcing contracts, and resolving insolvencies. The number of reforms is calculated using the business reforms by year and by country, as listed in the World Bank's *Doing Business* publications. "DB" in front of year indicates *Doing Business* publication year.

[2] A large literature offers policy recommendations for EMDEs and analysis of the likely effects of possible reforms and other policy actions. They include reforms to enhance human capital accumulation in such areas as health, education, and gender rights (see, for example, World Bank 2018c, 2018d, 2019a, 2019c, 2020b). They also include policies to improve infrastructure, promote the adoption of new technologies, tackle climate change, and enhance institutional quality and business environments (see, for example, OECD 2018; Rozenberg and Fay 2019; and World Bank 2017b, 2017d, 2019d).

structural reforms, this chapter brings together the policy priorities most relevant at the current juncture, alongside a review of the related literature analyzing the likely impact of their implementation, with a focus on possible complementarities and trade-offs.[3]

Main findings. This chapter reports the following findings. First, it documents the extent to which current macroeconomic policies undermine the resilience of EMDEs to shocks. Over 60 percent of EMDEs have primary fiscal deficits that are too large to stabilize or reduce their debt levels under current economic conditions. The chapter points to several policy implications of this outcome. EMDEs with unsustainable fiscal positions should prioritize raising revenues and improving spending efficiency, while maintaining growth-enhancing expenditure. Measures to enhance tax revenues include broadening the tax base, improving tax collection systems, reducing loopholes, and empowering tax administrators with greater technical skills. To improve spending efficiency and the mix of expenditures, policy makers can enhance the institutions and mechanisms used to determine investment projects and procurement, and to monitor spending, including on government administration and social services. Separately, in several EMDEs, international reserves are currently below levels that would be consistent with reserve adequacy. These EMDEs could focus on rebuilding foreign exchange reserves and restraining foreign currency borrowing.

Second, to improve longer-term resilience, EMDEs need to strengthen fiscal and monetary policy frameworks by adopting transparent and rules-based approaches. Fiscal rules can help countries maintain sustainable finances and accumulate resources when the economy is doing well. Better fiscal frameworks also assist monetary policy by restraining procyclical spending that could contribute to demand pressures. A transparent and independent central bank will be better placed to maintain price stability, thereby helping to create a macroeconomic environment that is conducive to strong growth.

Third, proactive financial sector supervision and regulation can mitigate risks, especially in countries with financial markets that are developing rapidly and becoming more integrated globally. In EMDEs without a prudential authority or prudential powers, creating or empowering these institutions is a priority. In EMDEs with the appropriate institutions, flexible and well-targeted tools are needed to manage balance sheet mismatches, foreign currency risk, and asset price misalignment with fundamentals. In EMDEs facing destabilizing capital flows, capital flow management measures—in

[3] On fiscal policy, recent work looks at the impact of stimulus policies on advanced economies and EMDEs (see Hagedorn, Manovskii, and Mitman 2019; Huidrom et al. 2016, 2019; Huidrom, Kose, and Ohnsorge 2018; Ramey 2019) and at the question of whether fiscal rules can improve policy implementation (Bergman and Hutchinson 2015, 2018; Calderón, Duncan, and Schmidt-Hebbel 2016). On monetary policy, the benefits of low inflation and how a transparent and independent central bank can assist in the anchoring of inflation expectations are studied in Ha, Kose, and Ohnsorge (2019). On financial sector policy, work by the International Monetary Fund (IMF), Financial Stability Board (FSB), and Bank for International Settlements (BIS)—undertaken partly at the request of the Group of Twenty (G20) countries—provides the foundation for a more effective Global Financial Safety Net, contributes to higher standards for macroprudential policy, helps with an overhaul of regulatory and supervisory architecture, and has led to new thinking on the role of capital flow management measures (BIS 2019; Gadanecz and Jayaram 2015; IMF 2011, 2012, 2013a, 2014, 2017, 2018a, 2018b; IMF, FSB, and BIS 2016).

conjunction with sound macroeconomic policies, exchange rate policy, and sufficient levels of financial and institutional development—can reduce the risk of financial instability (IMF 2012). In regions where EMDE-headquartered banks have gained prominence, efforts to strengthen home-host supervisor coordination may pay dividends during the next episode of financial stress.

Fourth, to reverse the trend slowdown in productivity growth, ambitious and comprehensive structural reforms are needed. Although EMDEs made some progress in improving their business climates in the three years before and during the global recession, in many areas momentum was not maintained. Meanwhile, governance in EMDEs has failed to improve since the 1990s and some EMDEs have taken steps to rein in openness to international capital flows. Reform priorities include building institutions that support economic growth and resilience; enhancing productivity and encouraging investment; building human capital; investing in growth-enhancing public infrastructure; helping to address, as well as adapt to, climate change; improving governance; strengthening competition; and reducing regulatory burdens.

This chapter proceeds as follows. First, it examines macroeconomic policies that build resilience. This is timely because EMDEs are more vulnerable today than before the global recession. Next, it explores financial sector policies that address existing and emerging financial stability challenges. Finally, it highlights reforms that address structural impediments to stronger, balanced, and sustainable growth in EMDEs.

Macroeconomic policies to build resilience

As global economic growth slows, EMDE policy makers must strive to make their economies more resilient to shocks. Efforts are needed to strengthen fiscal and monetary policy frameworks and calibrate international reserves, particularly in economies that have experienced rapid increases in debt and have become more exposed to debt-rollover risks, currency volatility, or spikes in interest rates. Countercyclical macroeconomic policies and financial stability can lean against procyclical fluctuations in capital flows. EMDE policy makers must also prepare for spillovers from disorderly market adjustments and policy shocks in advanced economies.

Shoring up fiscal positions. Since 2007, government debt in the average EMDE has increased by 10 percentage points of gross domestic product (GDP), reaching 54 percent of GDP at end-2018 (figure 7.1). The increase was broad-based, with debt rising in three-quarters of EMDEs and all regions experiencing higher average debt. The largest increases in average government debt occurred in Europe and Central Asia (ECA; from a low base), the Middle East and North Africa (MNA), and Latin America and the Caribbean (LAC). Debt rose by more than 20 percentage points of GDP in one-third of EMDEs. The rapid accumulation of debt was due to a significant shift in fiscal policy from 2007: fiscal deficits widened substantially in the postcrisis period and reached a peak in 2016, particularly in commodity-exporting countries that suffered from falling commodity prices. As a result, many EMDEs have deficits well in excess of debt-stabilizing levels, particularly EMDEs in South Asia (SAR), LAC, and Sub-Saharan Africa (SSA), which has also been reflected in credit rating downgrades for many EMDEs.

FIGURE 7.1 Fiscal policy

Government debt and deficits have deteriorated since 2007, damaging debt sustainability and credit quality. Elevated government debt also weakens the effectiveness of fiscal stimulus. More EMDEs have adopted rules for fiscal policy.

A. Government debt

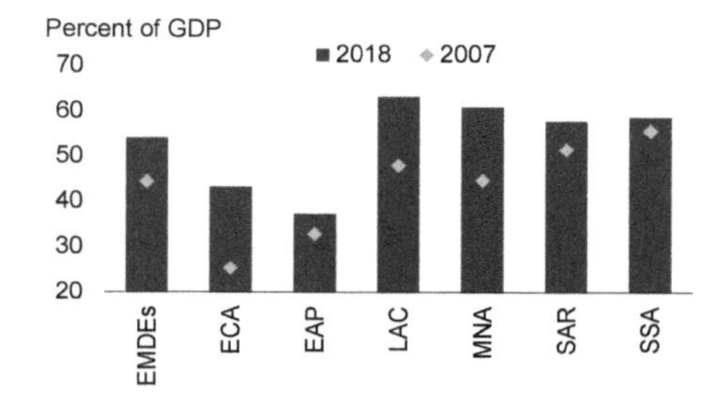

B. Fiscal balance

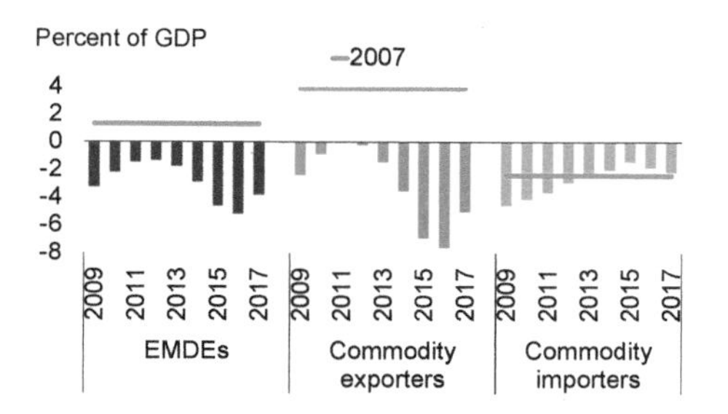

C. Primary fiscal balance sustainability gap

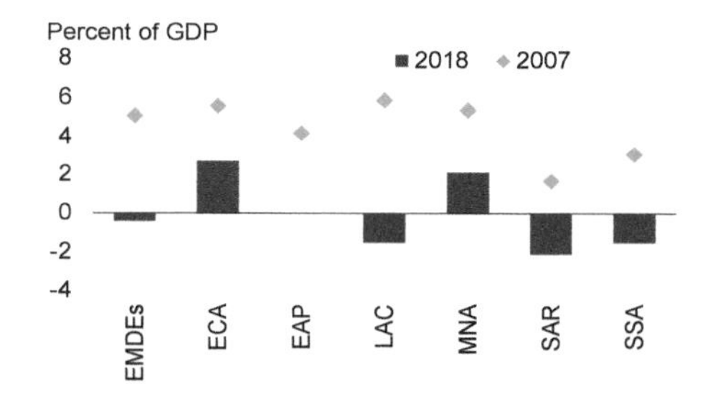

D. Sovereign ratings

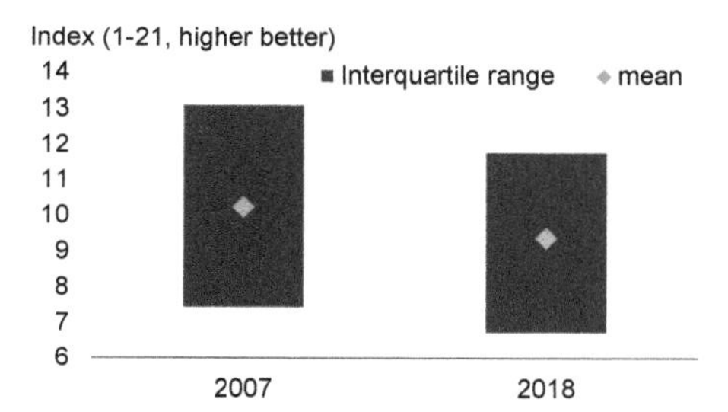

E. Fiscal multiplier, by debt level

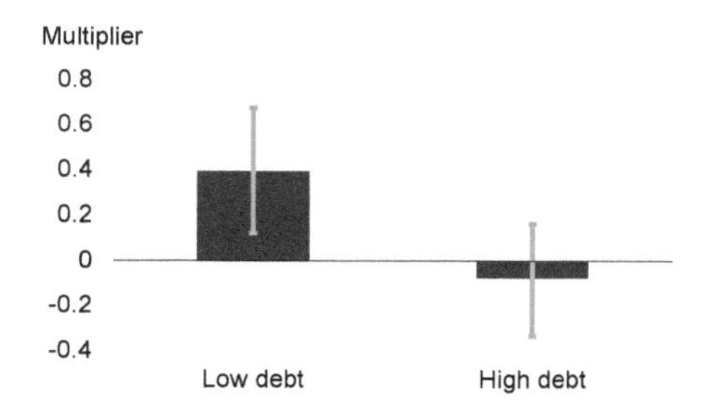

F. Fiscal rules

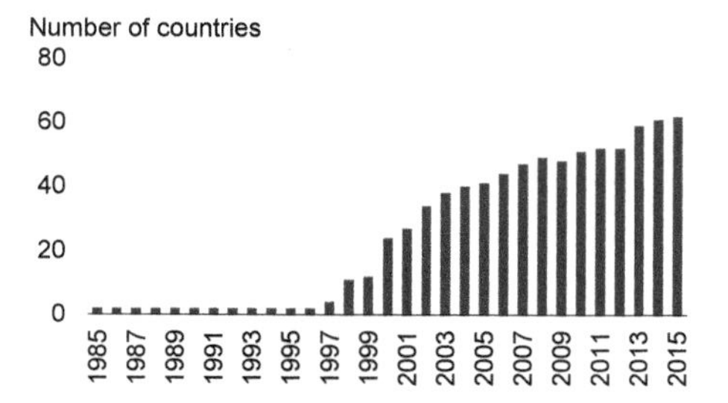

Sources: Huidrom et al. (2019); International Monetary Fund; Kose et al. (2017); World Bank.

Note: EAP = East Asia and Pacific; ECA = Europe and Central Asia; EMDEs = Emerging market and developing economies; LAC = Latin America and the Caribbean; MNA = Middle East and North Africa; SAR = South Asia; SSA = Sub-Saharan Africa.

A.-D. Unweighted averages.

A. Gross government debt.

C. The sustainability gap indicates the difference between the current primary fiscal balance and the debt-stabilizing primary fiscal balance at current growth rates and interest rates. A negative value indicates that government is on a rising trajectory. See Kose et al. (2017) for details.

D. Based on data for 97 EMDEs.

E. Figure shows fiscal multipliers two years from expansionary measures based on estimates from the IPVAR model of Huidrom et al. (2019). An economy is considered to have low debt when government debt is below 40 percent of GDP and high debt when it exceeds 60 percent of GDP. Orange lines represent 16-84 percent confidence bands.

F. An economy is considered to implement a fiscal rule if it has one or more fiscal rules on expenditures, revenues, budget balance, or debt.

Large fiscal deficits and elevated levels of government debt may constrain the ability of policy makers to respond to a downturn. Evidence also suggests that government stimulus tends to be less effective when debt is elevated (Brinca et al. 2016; Hagedorn, Manovskii, and Mitman 2019; Huidrom et al. 2016, 2019; Huidrom, Kose, and Ohnsorge 2018). Policy makers need to take steps to improve fiscal positions and sustainability to ensure that they respond effectively to the next downturn.

For those EMDEs that need to achieve more sustainable fiscal positions, policies should be geared toward minimizing the negative short-term consequences of fiscal consolidation for economic activity, current economic conditions permitting. Doing so requires safeguarding critical poverty-reducing expenditures, implementing growth-enhancing spending, and implementing tax reforms that promote investment and revenue mobilization (Gaspar, Obstfeld, and Sahay 2016; Ramey 2019; World Bank 2019a).

In many EMDEs, weaknesses in revenue collection and mobilization are an important part of the problem. Revenues in EMDEs averaged 29 percent of GDP in 2018, 10 percentage points of GDP below those of advanced economies. They were particularly low in low-income countries (LICs), SSA and SAR. Part of this weakness reflects large informal economies where labor market participants are poor and collecting taxes is difficult, requiring complementary policies that address the challenges of informality but do not undermine its advantages with regard to flexibility and employment. The informal sector accounts for about one-third of GDP in EMDEs and is largest in SSA, LAC, and ECA, whereas informal employment is most common in SSA and SAR (World Bank 2019b). In EMDEs with the most pervasive informal sectors, government revenue is 5-10 percentage points of GDP lower than in those with the least pervasive informal sectors (World Bank 2019b).

In EMDEs with large informal sectors, tax compliance can be improved by simplifying tax codes, using technology to improve tax enforcement, and shifting toward electronic payment methods (see, for example, Awasthi and Engelschalk 2018; Morales and Medina 2017; Rocha, Ulyssea, and Rachter 2018; Ulyssea 2018). Designing taxes that capture informal activity—for example, through value added taxes (VAT)—could improve revenue collection and incentivize formalization, because firms that remain informal will be unable to claim VAT refunds (Loayza 2018). Other methods of encouraging informal firms to register their activities for taxation include improving tax morale through more effective provision of public goods and services, addressing perceptions of fraud and corruption, ensuring that taxes are collected impartially, and having a progressive tax system (Sung, Awasthi, and Lee 2017). Other revenue-focused measures include improving tax collection systems, reducing loopholes, and empowering tax administrators with the technical skills needed to enforce tax compliance and minimize tax avoidance (Akitoby et al. 2018). Revenue collection can also be bolstered through international cooperation aligning international and domestic policies on tax: countering illicit financial flows, tax evasion and avoidance, and profit-shifting to low-tax jurisdictions (United Nations 2019).

On the spending side, policy makers can undertake measures to improve efficiency, shift spending toward growth-enhancing investment from unproductive current spending, and improve governance to contain and eliminate fraud and corruption. To improve spending efficiency, EMDE governments should build credible and transparent medium-term expenditure frameworks that align with the strategic goals of the government (World Bank 2012). Such frameworks can provide clarity on the purpose of expenditures and make government departments accountable for their spending. Further steps could focus on enhancing institutions and mechanisms used to determine the selection, procurement, and monitoring of investment projects and other outlays (IMF 2015a).

Strengthen fiscal frameworks. Policy makers should also focus on strengthening fiscal frameworks, including adopting transparent and rule-based approaches to setting policy and managing debt. Provided there is broad-based public support, fiscal rules can help prevent fiscal slippages and ensure that revenue windfalls are saved during times of strong growth. As extreme weather events become more frequent, frameworks may help prepare for fiscal pressures when disasters occur and help shift public investment toward climate-resilient infrastructure (Pigato 2019). In addition, stronger fiscal frameworks are associated with lower inflation and inflation volatility, so that they can support the central bank in delivering its mandate (Ha, Kose, and Ohnsorge 2019). EMDEs have made important strides in the adoption and comprehensiveness of fiscal rules, catching up to advanced economies in many respects (Schaechter et al. 2012).[4] Fiscal rules appear to be effective in dampening procyclicality of fiscal policy, however, only when a minimum quality of institutions, especially efficiency of government bureaucracy, is achieved (Bergman and Hutchinson 2015, 2018; Calderón, Duncan, and Schmidt-Hebbel 2016).

Any fiscal policy framework should be open and transparent, thereby empowering citizens to hold governments accountable for implementing policy in a sustainable manner to address their needs. Such an approach can be achieved in part by implementing the IMF's Fiscal Transparency Code that was extended to natural resource management by the IMF (2019a). Fiscal policy formulation and implementation can be further improved through independent review processes, including public expenditure reviews, undertaken by a domestic agency or by international organizations.

Government has an important redistributive role to play in society. Tax policy can be used to both redistribute income (through tax credits, tax exemptions, income thresholds, and progressive tax schedules) and change incentives (Joyce and Xu 2019; Piketty, Saez, and Stantcheva 2014). On the spending side, government can improve the targeting of social spending to ensure that constrained fiscal resources benefit vulnerable groups.

[4] Schaechter et al. (2012) create an overall fiscal rule index that captures both the number and characteristics of fiscal rules in operation in advanced economies and EMDEs. They show how EMDEs have made progress in catching up to advanced economies since 2000. That said, about half of LICs implement some form of fiscal rule. Due to weak institutional environments, however, these rules do not seem to improve the countercyclicality of fiscal policy (Bergman and Hutchinson 2018).

Strengthen debt management. As public debt levels rise, governments need to ensure sound debt management. Public debt management is the process used to establish and execute a framework to manage government debt—ideally over a medium-term horizon—which raises an appropriate amount of debt at the lowest possible cost, provides for payment obligations, and is consistent with predefined risk preferences (World Bank and IMF 2009a, 2014). In a recent survey, about 40 percent of low- and middle-income countries did not have debt management strategies in place and 56 percent did not have the legal framework in place to support their development (Cabral 2015).[5] This absence is despite the fact that improvements in debt management helped lower debt ratios in EMDEs during the 2000s (Anderson, Silva, and Velandia-Rubiano 2010; Frankel, Vegh, and Vuletin, 2013).

Recognizing the need for better debt management, the World Bank and the International Monetary Fund (IMF) have developed guidelines, best practices, and frameworks to assist countries in implementing debt management strategies (see World Bank 2007a, 2007b, 2008; World Bank and IMF 2001, 2003, 2009a, 2009b, 2014). Economic crises have often been associated with poorly structured debt portfolios—whether through maturity, currency, or interest rate composition—or large contingent liabilities that were only revealed once they materialized (Jaramillo, Mulas-Granados, and Jalles 2017; Weber 2012; World Bank and IMF 2014). One element of sound debt management is improved debt transparency, which has been associated with lower borrowing costs, increased foreign holdings, and lower government debt (Kemoe and Zhan 2018; Montes, Bastos, and de Oliveira 2019).

Sound debt management is supported by a well-developed and liquid domestic bond market that can reduce the need for foreign lending and ensure stability in government financing (Árvai and Heenan 2008; World Bank and IMF 2001). Investment in infrastructure to lower the cost and increase the efficiency of a local bond market can promote local (currency) bond market development. Similarly, establishing the correct legal and regulatory framework can ensure that such a market operates effectively. A debt management framework has the complementary benefit of also supporting the establishment of a secondary market for government securities.

Among LICs, weaknesses in debt transparency, notably in monitoring and reporting, are widespread, notwithstanding some recent improvements (Essl et al. 2019). This has reflected several factors. First, institutional arrangements are weak. Only 4 of 17 LICs met minimum requirements for debt reporting and evaluation (Essl et al. 2019). About half of LICs implement some form of fiscal rule, but these rules do not seem to improve the countercyclicality of fiscal policy due to weak institutional environments in many LICs (Bergman and Hutchinson 2018). Second, LIC governments and state-owned entities have shifted toward nontraditional creditors. Several LIC sovereigns have accessed international financial markets for the first time since the global recession (Ethiopia, Mozambique, Rwanda, Senegal, Tanzania, Tajikistan) often at terms that

[5] Debt management strategies are only effective, however, if there is an adequate legal framework in place, debt is comprehensively and efficiently recorded, and overall fiscal policy is set in a sustainable and growth-enhancing manner (World Bank and IMF 2009a).

FIGURE 7.2 International reserves

Total global foreign exchange reserve assets grew rapidly following the 1998 Asian crisis but have stagnated since 2012. Significant heterogeneity exists among EMDEs: about 40 percent of them lack adequate reserves to cover balance of payments needs. The reserve positions of 35 percent of EMDEs have deteriorated since 2007.

A. Global foreign reserve assets

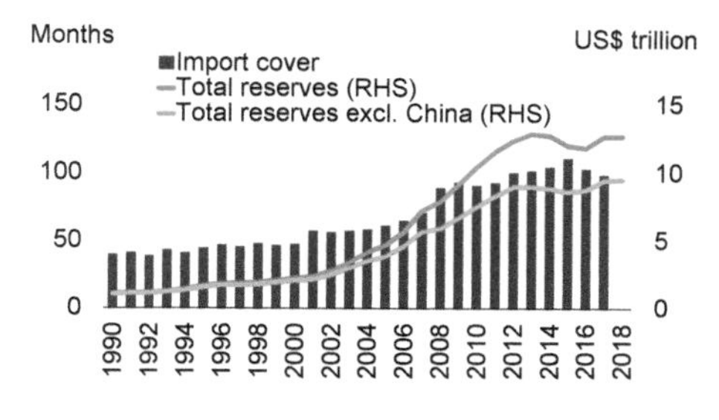

B. Foreign reserves

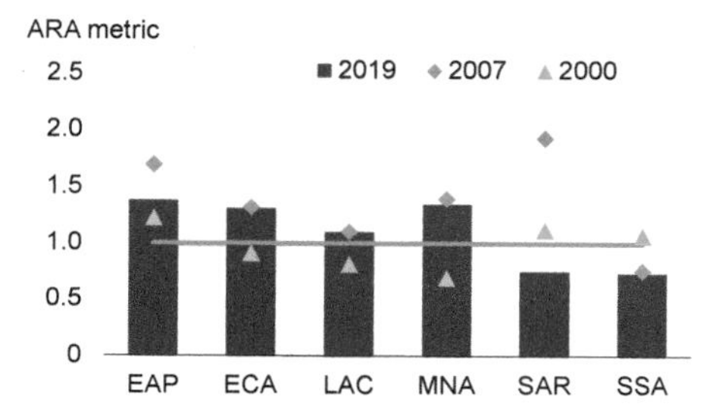

C. Foreign reserve adequacy

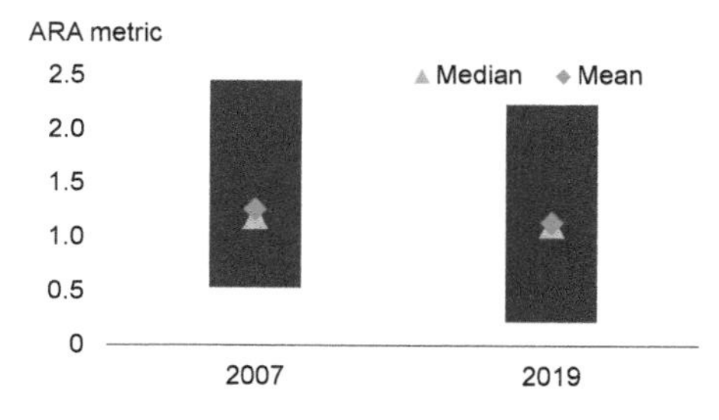

D. Foreign reserve adequacy

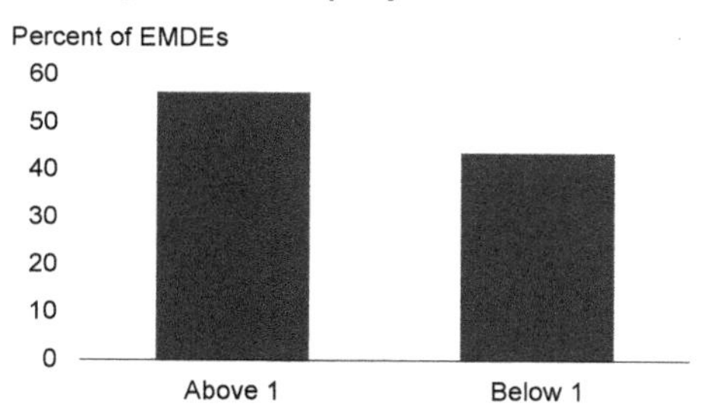

Sources: Haver Analytics; International Monetary Fund.

Note: Assessing Reserve Adequacy (ARA) metric is based on IMF (2011) and determines the appropriate reserve cover on a risk-weighted basis covering short-, medium- and long-term debt, equity liabilities, broad money, and export earnings. Risk weights are based on observed outflows during periods of exchange rate pressure. EAP = East Asia and Pacific; ECA = Europe and Central Asia; EMDEs = emerging market and developing economies; LAC = Latin America and the Caribbean; MNA = Middle East and North Africa; SAR = South Asia; SSA = Sub-Saharan Africa.

B.-D. Based on data for 55 EMDEs.

B. Unweighted averages.

C. Mean is an unweighted average.

D. Data for 2019. A value below 1 suggests that EMDEs do not necessarily have enough reserves to meet their balance of payments requirements as defined by the International Monetary Fund's ARA metric.

expose them to the risk of changing investor sentiment and rising borrowing cost. Non-Paris Club creditors are playing a greater role in lending to LICs. China, for example, accounted for most of the doubling in cross-border claims on SSA economies between 2013 and 2017 (Cerutti, Koch, and Pradhan 2018; Dollar 2016). Debt to non-Paris Club creditors is not always officially reported, and available documentation can be opaque, which can lead to "hidden" debt (Horn, Reinhart, and Trebesch 2019).

Maintain adequate international reserves. Global international reserve assets have grown substantially since the 1998 Asian financial crisis (figure 7.2). In 1998, total global reserves were valued at $1.92 trillion and covered 48 months of imports. By 2018, total reserves were $12.69 trillion and covered nearly 100 months of imports. The rise in reserves, however, has not been distributed evenly among countries. Economies in

East Asia and the Pacific (EAP), ECA, LAC, and MNA have, on average, been able to increase reserves to more adequate levels since 2000. EAP, and especially SAR, however, have seen reserve levels decline since the crisis, and economies in SAR and SSA have not managed to improve reserve levels since 2000. Almost half of EMDEs appear not to have sufficient reserves to meet their balance of payments needs in 2019, according to the IMF's reserves assessment metric.[6]

Adequate foreign exchange reserves can mitigate currency volatility, reducing risks stemming from currency mismatches and volatile capital outflows (IMF 2011, 2015b). Following the taper tantrum of 2013, countries with larger reserve buffers saw less depreciation (BIS 2019). The reserve level that is sufficient to act as insurance against shocks depends on a country's depth and liquidity of domestic financial markets, access to external buffers (such as central bank swap lines of IMF loans), and potential drains on the balance of payments (such as losses of export income, broad money, short-term external debt, and other external liabilities).[7] Commodity-intensive economies often require additional buffers in light of their exposure to sudden changes in their terms of trade and, especially in the case of agricultural producers, to weather-related supply shocks.

Reserve accumulation also comes with potential costs, however, and therefore requires appropriate cost-benefit analysis. In countries where reserves are inadequate, policy makers could establish a medium to long-term plan to build reserves that does not disrupt foreign exchange markets, the sustainability of government budgets, or the economy. Reserve accumulation also requires the sterilization of those reserves—and the availability of monetary policy instruments to implement it—to avoid an inadvertent expansion of the domestic money supply that could cause an undue pickup in inflation. In countries with flexible exchange rate arrangements, policy makers should consider reserve accumulation during periods of currency overvaluation or when the currency is close to fair value, rather than when it is undervalued. Reserve accumulation (or drawdown) can also help LICs that are heavily dependent on foreign aid to mitigate the effects of Dutch disease-type currency overvaluation and aid volatility (Dabla-Norris, Kim, and Shirono 2011; Moldovan, Yang, and Zanna 2019).

Strengthen monetary policy frameworks. With improvements in inflation-targeting frameworks and inflation falling globally, EMDEs have been able to bring average annual inflation down from double-digit rates in the 1990s to an estimated 3.1 percent in 2019 (figure 7.3). In 1999, only 3 EMDEs were inflation targeters and 11 had freely floating exchange rates. By 2018, both numbers were close to 30. EMDEs also significantly improved their central bank transparency over this period, helping to anchor inflation expectations. Despite this progress, some EMDEs still struggle with double-digit inflation. In 2019, almost a third of EMDEs have inflation rates above 5 percent, despite a benign global environment, and 12 percent have double-digit

[6] The Assessing Reserve Adequacy (ARA) metric is based on IMF (2011) and determines appropriate reserve cover on a risk-weighted basis covering short-term debt; medium and long-term debt and equity liabilities; broad money; and export earnings. Risk weights are based on observed outflows during periods of exchange rate pressure.

[7] For models on optimal reserves see IMF (2015b) and Jeanne and Ranciere (2006, 2011).

FIGURE 7.3 Monetary policy

Consumer price inflation in EMDEs declined from double-digit annual rates in the 1990s. More independent and transparent central banks are associated with lower inflation and inflation volatility and less exchange rate pass-through to inflation.

A. Inflation in EMDEs

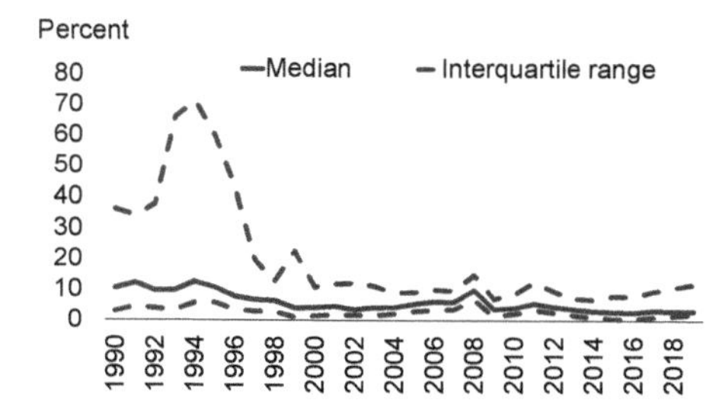

B. EMDEs with inflation targeting

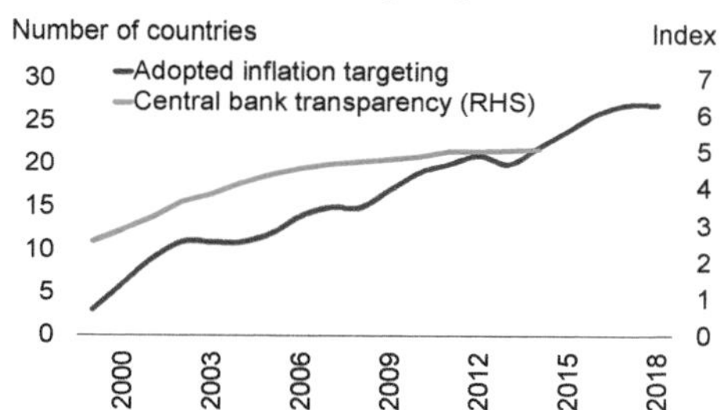

C. Inflation expectations in EMDEs

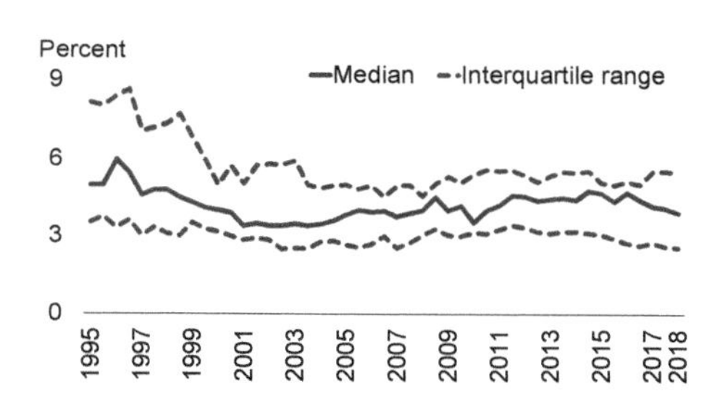

D. Countries with increasing central bank independence and transparency

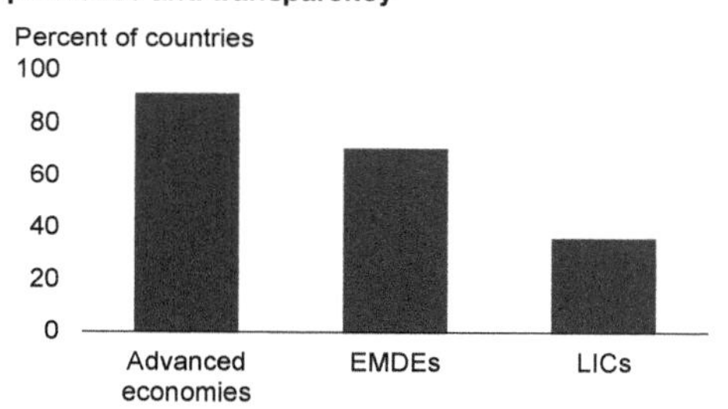

E. Inflation, by central bank independence and transparency

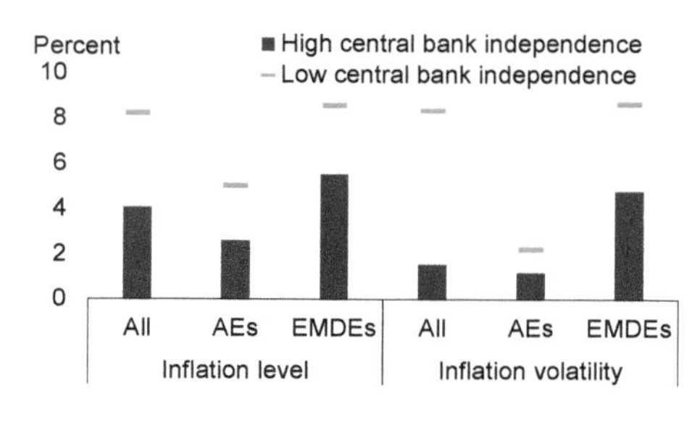

F. Central bank independence and pass-through from exchange rate changes to inflation

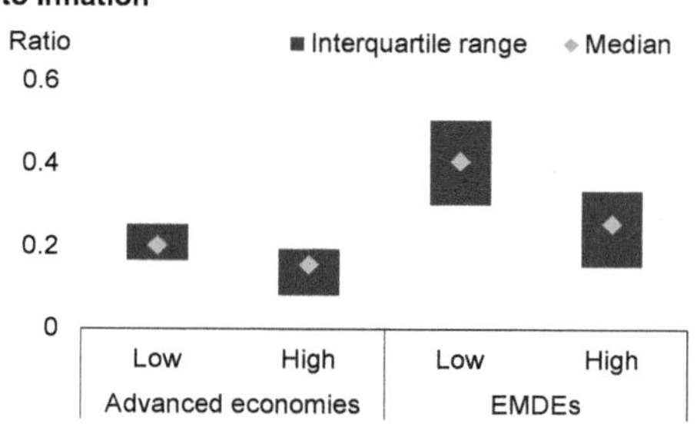

Sources: Dincer and Eichengreen (2014); Ha, Kose, and Ohnsorge (2019); International Monetary Fund; World Bank.

A. Based on data for 155 emerging market and developing economies (EMDEs).

B. Dincer/Eichengreen Transparency Index. The index ranges from 0 (least independent and transparent) to 15 (most independent and transparent).

C. Inflation expectations are long-term (five-year-ahead) expectations of annual inflation, measured at a biannual frequency. Based on a sample of 23 EMDEs during 1995H1-2018H1.

D. Based on data from 1998 to 2014. Figures shows percent of countries with a higher index (by at least 0.1) in 2014 than 1987.

E. Columns indicate median inflation rates and inflation volatility in country-year pairs, with a central bank independence and transparency index in the top quartile of the sample. Bars denote medians for country-year pairs in the bottom quartile. AEs = advanced economies.

F. Pass-through is defined as the ratio between the one-year cumulative impulse response of consumer price inflation and the one-year cumulative impulse response of the exchange rate change estimated from factor-augmented vector autoregression models for 29 advanced economies and 26 EMDEs over 1998-2017. A positive pass-through means that a currency depreciation is associated with higher inflation. Bars show the interquartile range and markers show the cross-country median. The central bank independence index is computed by Dincer and Eichengreen (2014). Low and high central bank independence are defined as below and above the sample average.

inflation. Many have not embraced best practices in their monetary policy frameworks and central bank transparency.

High inflation can be costly to an economy. It is associated with lower growth and financial crises, disproportionately hurts the poor, raises borrowing costs, disincentivizes saving, and erodes household and government balance sheets (Ha, Kose, and Ohnsorge 2019; Mishkin 2008). In turn, a history of stable inflation is generally associated with lower financing costs and better debt tolerance in EMDEs; that is, countries with low inflation may be able to accumulate more debt in a sustainable manner (Reinhart, Rogoff, and Savastano 2003). Embracing a strong, transparent, and independent monetary policy regime can help countries achieve lower and more stable inflation and inflation expectations.

During episodes of financial stress, when EMDE currencies tend to depreciate sharply, strong monetary policy frameworks can be helpful.[8] During these episodes, exchange rate pass-through can spur inflation that constrains EMDE central banks' ability to support activity. But the pass-through tends to be smaller in countries with more credible, transparent, and independent central banks; with inflation-targeting monetary policy regimes; and with better-anchored inflation expectations (Kose et al. 2019).[9] LICs, in particular, can benefit by moving toward coherent and transparent frameworks that reduce interest rate and inflation volatility, promote financial market development, and enhance the transmission of monetary policy to the economy beyond the bank lending channel (Ha et al. 2019).

Financial sector policies for stability and growth

Since the global financial crisis, the global financial architecture has improved, the resilience of major banking systems has strengthened, and new monetary and macroprudential tools have been developed and widely employed. Yet EMDEs face a number of challenges, new and old, related to the financial sector, the architecture of financial regulation and supervision, and macroprudential policy (chapter 5). These challenges include the deterioration of bank balance sheets, the legacy of postrecession credit booms in some countries, the rise in EMDE-headquartered and regional banks, the need for home-host supervisor coordination, the rise in nonbank intermediaries, and the management of volatile capital flows.

The postrecession rebound in EMDE growth, shifts in investor risk appetite, and low borrowing costs have fueled credit to nonfinancial corporations and, in many EMDEs, outright credit booms (Ohnsorge and Yu 2016; chapter 4). Credit extended to the private sector by banks in EMDEs increased by 10.5 percentage points of GDP between 2007 and 2016, with especially rapid increases in EAP and MNA (figure 7.4).

[8] It is, however, no guarantee for success in the context of shifting global financial conditions, and may need to be complemented with macroprudential tools (Cavallino and Sandri 2018; Gopinath 2017; Rey 2015).

[9] Bordo and Siklos (2019) find that EMDEs were able to maintain the levels of central bank transparency and independence they had prior to the crisis, but institutional resilience declined.

FIGURE 7.4 Financial sector developments

EMDEs trail advanced economies in measures of financial deepening and the quality of laws and regulations governing bankruptcy and insolvency. Rapid credit growth and bouts of capital flow reversals since the 2008-09 global financial crisis indicate increased EMDE vulnerabilities. There has also been a shift away from cross-border lending from banks headquartered in advanced economies and toward EMDE-headquartered banks operating regionally.

A. Number of EMDEs in postcrisis credit booms and credit crunches

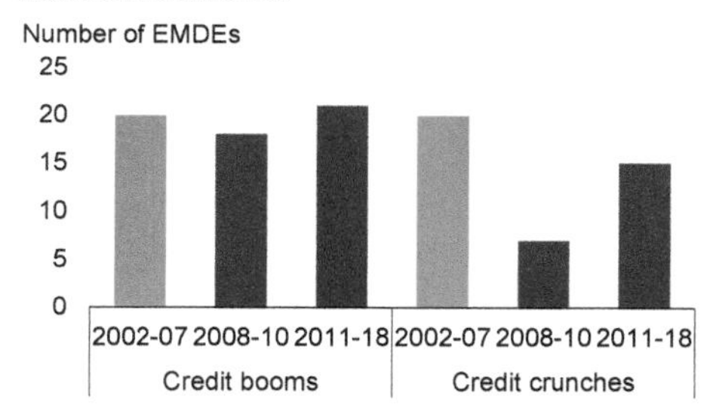

B. EMDEs: Bank credit to private sector

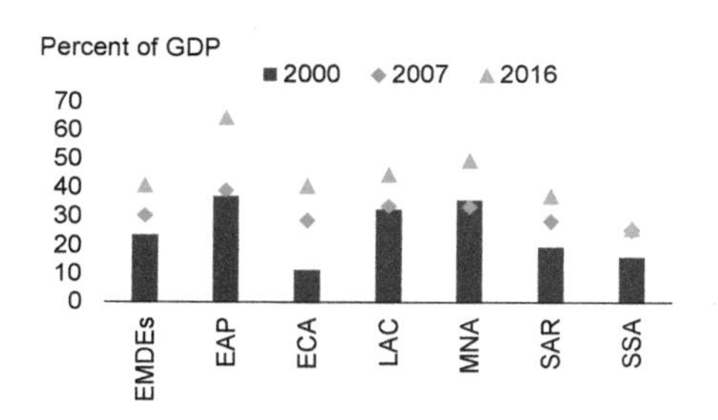

C. Net capital inflows

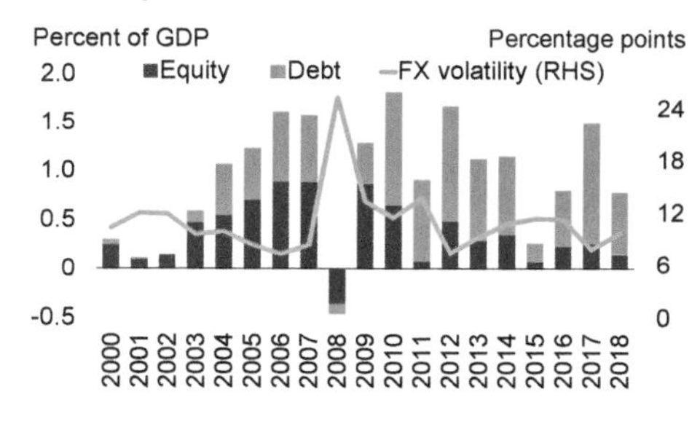

D. Banks' profitability

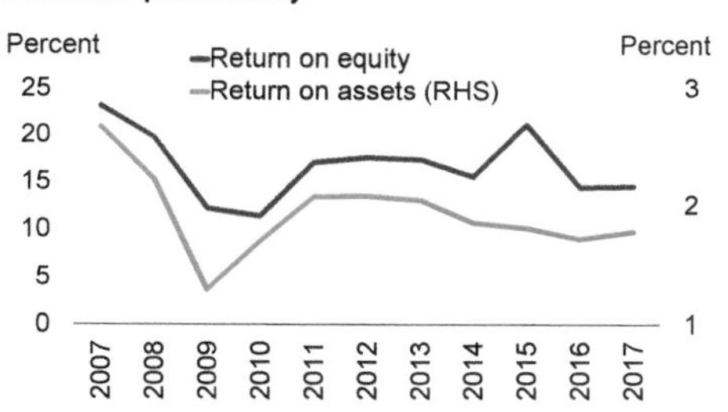

E. Bank assets

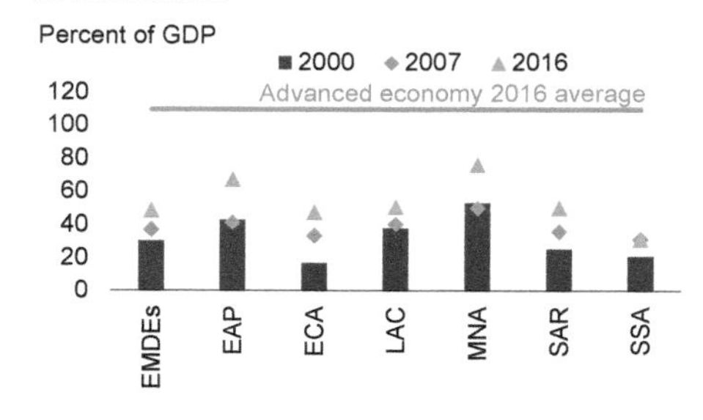

F. EMDE-based banks operating in EMDEs

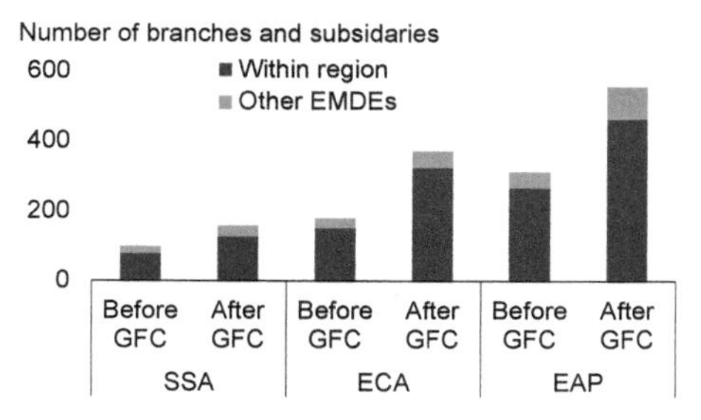

Sources: Institute of International Finance; International Monetary Fund; World Bank.

Note: EAP = East Asia and Pacific; ECA = Europe and Central Asia; EMDEs = emerging market and developing economies; GFC = global financial crisis, 2008/09; LAC = Latin America and the Caribbean; MNA = Middle East and North Africa; SAR = South Asia; SSA = Sub-Saharan Africa.

A. Credit booms (crunches) are episodes when private credit to GDP ratio exceeds (falls below) its long-term trend by 1.65 times one standard deviation of a cyclical component obtained with the Hodrick-Prescott filter. Sample includes about 140 EMDEs with private sector credit data. Weights are based on nominal GDP measured in U.S. dollars at market exchange rates.

B. Unweighted averages. Based on the private credit by deposit money banks and other financial institutions to GDP (%) from the World Bank's Financial Development and Structure Dataset.

C. FX volatility is the J.P. Morgan VXY Global index, a turnover-weighted index of the implied volatility of three-month at-the-money options on 23 U.S. dollar currency pairs.

D. Data from the Financial Soundness Indicators Dataset (International Monetary Fund).

E. Unweighted averages. Based on the deposit money bank assets to GDP (%) from the World Bank's Financial Development and Structure Dataset.

F. Based on annual bank statements. "Before GFC" indicates 2008 or 2009 depending on data availability; "After GFC" indicates 2018 or latest data available.

There has also been a shift toward riskier borrowing by nonfinancial corporations, at least in some EMDEs (see Alfaro et al. 2019; Beltran, Garud, and Rosenblum 2017; Feyen et al. 2017). Although much of the credit growth was domestic, capital inflows (especially, portfolio flows, which can be fickle) also contributed to rising nonfinancial sector debt. On average, portfolio flows accounted for 17 percent of capital flows to EMDEs in 2010-17, up from 8 percent in 2002-07. In some EMDEs, the share of nonresident holdings in local currency bond markets has grown to more than 30 percent (the Czech Republic, Ghana, Indonesia, Mexico, Peru, Poland, South Africa), which exposes these countries to the risk of changing global risk sentiment even if it mitigates currency risk (Agur et al. 2018).

Although these credit booms had largely subsided by 2016, they have left a legacy of elevated private sector debt in a number of EMDEs. This debt, coupled with disappointing economic growth, has contributed to a deterioration in the health of banks' balance sheets. Banks' profitability has declined, with returns on assets and equity recently reaching their lowest levels since 2010. EMDE banks' asset quality has also deteriorated, with the share of nonperforming loans rising in nearly two-thirds of EMDEs between 2007 and 2017, although remaining at still-manageable levels in most EMDEs.

Rapid credit growth in EMDEs partly reflects financial deepening, which is typically associated with long-run economic growth (see Aizenman, Jinjarak, and Park 2015; King and Levine 1993; Levine, Loayza, and Beck 2000). Although bank assets in EMDEs increased by over 10 percentage points of GDP, on average, between 2007 and 2016, they remain only half the advanced economy average (relative to GDP). There is also substantial regional variation: SSA, in particular, has made little progress in financial development, thus measured, since 2000. This disparity in financial development is also reflected in the number of unbanked adults: 63 percent of adults in EMDEs owned an account at a financial institution or mobile money provider in 2017, compared to 94 percent in high-income countries (Demirgüç-Kunt et al. 2018). Although many EMDEs, particularly LICs, have a long way to go to attain adequate access to credit for households and businesses, rapid growth in credit can also lead to financial crises, suggesting that progress is best made gradually and coupled with improvements in financial sector supervision and regulation.

The composition of foreign lenders to EMDEs has changed considerably since the global recession. Changes to the global regulatory framework and financial pressures from the crisis curtailed cross-border lending by international banks. As banks headquartered in the European Union and the United States downsized their EMDE operations, especially in ECA, LAC, and SSA, banks headquartered in these respective regions or in other EMDEs stepped in to fill the void (Cerutti and Zhou 2017, 2018; World Bank 2018a). Chinese banks accounted for two-thirds of EMDE-to-EMDE lending between 2013 and 2017, and for most of the doubling in cross-border claims on SSA economies between 2013 and 2017 (Cerutti, Koch, and Pradhan 2018; Dollar 2016).

EMDE policy makers have a menu of options to strengthen financial sector resilience, spanning the regulatory framework, macroprudential policies, measures to regulate capital flows, and policies to help strengthen corporate balance sheets.

Regulatory and supervisory framework. The design of financial regulation and supervision frameworks and the implementation of oversight policies determine the successful attainment of policy objectives for the financial sector. These objectives include efficient access to, and allocation of, credit in the economy; appropriate risk-taking; adequate competition in the financial sector; financial stability; and the alignment of private incentives with broader public policy objectives. The global financial crisis revealed significant deficiencies in regulation and supervision, and highlighted the importance of getting the basics right through strong, timely, and anticipatory supervisory action and market discipline (Palmer and Cerutti 2009; World Bank 2013). In many EMDEs, especially in LICs, it calls for improved supervisory and regulatory capacity (World Bank 2020b).

A number of policy options can achieve this outcome. First, incentivizing competition by allowing well-capitalized banks, including foreign banks, to enter the market can promote efficiency and risk sharing, and encourage knowledge transfer. Countries with better institutions are more likely to reap the risk-sharing and development benefits of international banking (World Bank 2018a). Second, the regulatory authorities can design reporting systems to promote transparency and reduce counterparty risk (World Bank 2013). Third, regulation can ensure that new technologies (such as mobile banking that reaches formerly unbanked groups) expand financial inclusion to promote development and reduce poverty (World Bank 2014a).

The global financial crisis led to a substantial overhaul of the global regulatory and supervisory environment, designed, in particular, to ensure that banks become better capitalized and less leveraged. The Basel III regulations, approved in late 2010, require banks, especially global systemically important banks (G-SIBs), to increase the level and quality of their capital, limit reliance on short-term wholesale funding, and improve liquidity (BIS 2018).[10] These regulatory reforms have made banks more resilient to financial distress, but they may also have reduced the cross-border activities of global banks and pushed riskier lending outside the banking sector. As of 2019, most Financial Stability Board (FSB) jurisdictions are already compliant with the Basel III rules on capital requirements, on liquidity coverage, and for G-SIBs. Compliance with rules on large exposures, leverage, and net stable funding ratios, however, remains incomplete, and many economies have yet to draft and approve required regulations (BCBS 2019).

The increased regionalization and rise of EMDE-headquartered banks pose regulatory challenges. Although these banks are generally more familiar with the environment for banking in EMDEs and create more competition in the financial sector of the host country, they are also headquartered in less-regulated and institutionally weaker

[10] FSB jurisdictions that agreed to phase in Basel III provisions comprise 24 economies, including 10 EMDEs (Argentina, Brazil, China, India, Indonesia, Mexico, the Russian Federation, Saudi Arabia, South Africa, and Turkey).

countries (World Bank 2018a). As a result, they can accentuate the propagation of shocks between home and host countries. To address such issues, policy makers may benefit from establishing regionally focused regulatory and supervisory frameworks to increase coordination and information sharing. Complementary policy efforts can also assist in mitigating financial sector risks, such as developing financial markets, including capital markets, to improve risk-sharing and lessen reliance on capital flows (Levine 2006).

Macroprudential policies. Macroprudential policies can provide flexible and well-targeted tools for EMDEs to mitigate systemic risk on bank, corporate, and household balance sheets (see IMF 2013a, 2017; IMF, FSB, and BIS 2016; Lim et al. 2011). To implement macroprudential policies effectively, EMDE policy makers need an efficient and well-designed supervision framework and toolkit, an understanding of how macroprudential policies affect the economy, and the capacity to effectively monitor developments in banks and financial markets.

Since 2007, over two-thirds of EMDEs have tightened macroprudential rules—such as standards for bank capital, liquidity buffers, and loan-loss-provisioning—to contain risks from rapid private sector credit growth or house price growth (see Budnik and Kleibl 2018; Kuttner and Shim 2016; Vandenbussche, Vogel, and Detragiache 2015; Zhang and Zoli 2016). Macroprudential regulations have been especially widely used in EAP and ECA (Cerutti, Claessens, and Laeven 2017; figure 7.5). EMDEs have tended to focus on policies aimed at financial institutions, particularly restrictions on foreign currency exposures, reserve requirements on foreign funding, and liquidity-related measures, in efforts to address exposures to volatile capital flows.[11] In 2017, three-quarters of EMDEs applied limits on financial institutions' foreign exchange positions, close to half applied liquidity coverage ratios or liquid asset ratios, and 44 percent and 32 percent implemented capital conservation buffers and limits on leverage ratios, respectively. Such tools can be especially useful for EMDEs that are heavily reliant on foreign capital to fund productive investments.

Tools applying to the household and corporate sectors have been less common: 62 percent and 16 percent of EMDEs have placed some sort of restriction on loans (mainly loan-to-value ratios) to the household and corporate sectors, respectively. Measures targeted at household and corporate foreign currency borrowing have been limited, with less than 16 percent of EMDEs imposing foreign currency borrowing restrictions on households or corporations.

The overall effectiveness of these policies depends on how they interact with macroeconomic and sector-specific policy measures (Bruno, Shim, and Shin 2017; Claessens 2014) and may be weaker in more open economies (Akinci and Olmstead-Rumsey 2018; Cerutti, Claessens, and Laeven 2017), and for larger firms that face fewer borrowing constraints (Ayyagari, Beck, and Martinez Peria 2017). Foreign currency limits in EMDEs have been associated with lower credit growth, especially for corporate

[11] EMDEs often apply macroprudential instruments (e.g., reserve requirements) as a complementary measure to manage credit cycles when open capital accounts make conventional monetary policy less effective (World Bank 2014b).

FIGURE 7.5 Macroprudential policy

More EMDEs are creating macroprudential authorities and implementing tools to curb foreign exchange and credit risk.

A. Macroprudential policy in EMDEs

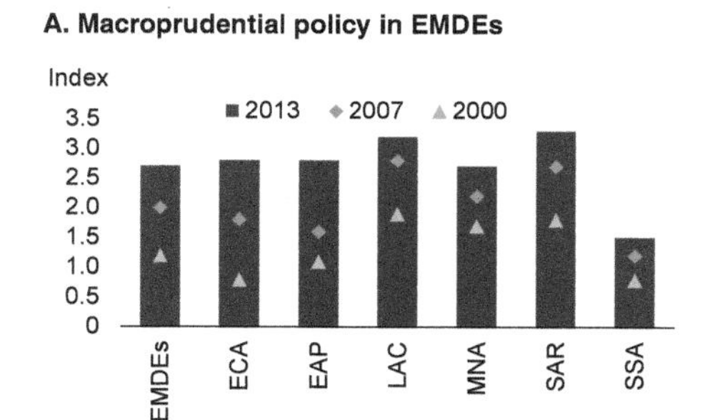

B. Macroprudential tools

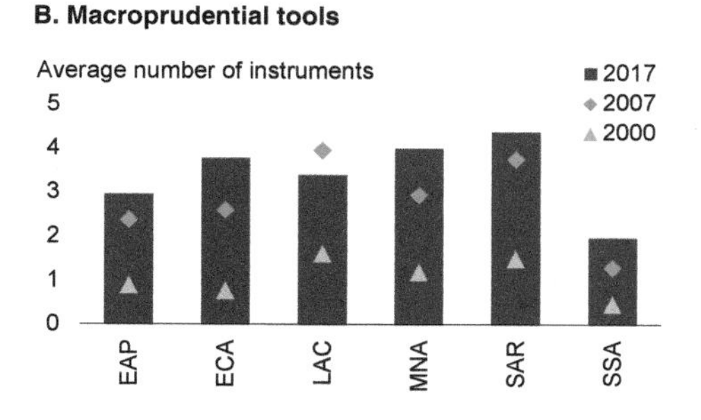

C. Macroprudential tools

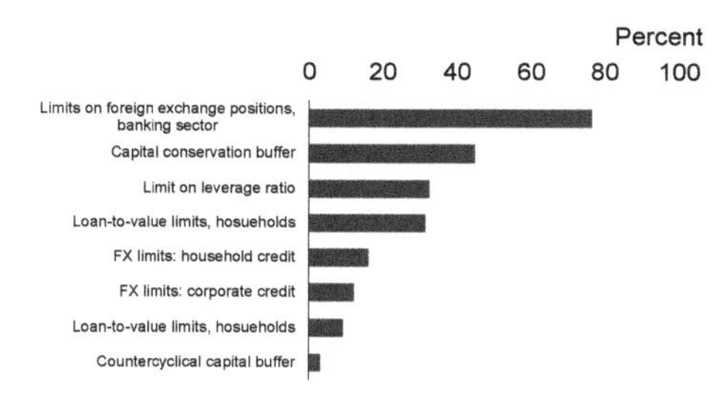

D. Macroprudential institutions in EMDEs

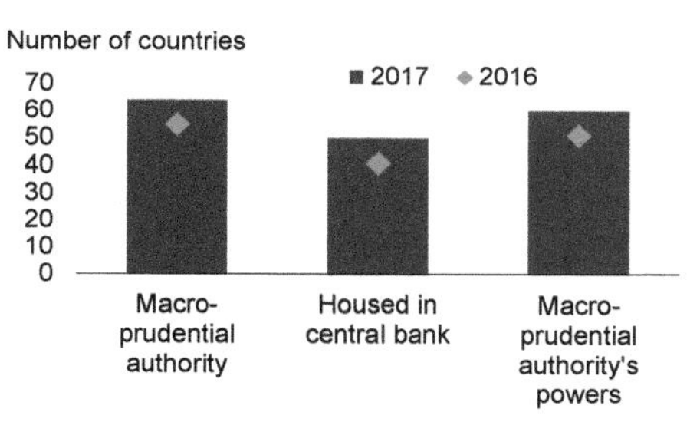

Sources: Cerutti, Claessens, and Laeven (2017); International Monetary Fund (Annual Macroprudential Policy Survey); World Bank.
Note: EAP = East Asia and Pacific; ECA = Europe and Central Asia; EMDEs = emerging market and developing economies; FX = foreign exchange; LAC = Latin America and the Caribbean; MNA = Middle East and North Africa; SAR = South Asia; SSA = Sub-Saharan Africa.

A. Sample includes 123 EMDEs. Unweighted average of the Macroprudential Policy Index of Cerutti, Claessens, and Laeven (2017). The Macroprudential Index measures the tools used by authorities and is based on a simple sum of 12 tools, including the countercyclical capital buffer and loan-to-value ratios.

B. Macroprudential instruments include countercyclical capital buffer, limits on leverage ratios and credit growth, capital conservation buffer, and so on.

C. Based on data for 2017 in 98 EMDEs. Broad-based tools include the countercyclical capital buffer, limits on leverage ratios and credit growth, capital conservation buffer, and so on.

D. Number of EMDEs that have an established macroprudential authority, that is housed in the central bank and has legislative powers to implement macroprudential policy.

credit, but also with a shift toward nonbank or cross-border financing, which is often less regulated or falls outside the mandate of prudential authorities (see Aysan, Fendoglu, and Kilinc 2015; Cerutti, Claessens, and Laeven 2017; IMF, FSB, and BIS 2016). Moreover, there may be trade-offs between macroprudential risk management and rapid financial development (Krishnamurti and Lee 2014).

Having a clear and coherent financial sector oversight framework with an empowered macroprudential authority improves a country's ability to manage systemic risk. By 2017, 64 EMDEs had a designated macroprudential authority and 60 had some form of power to implement macroprudential measures. Better coordination of systemic risk management, crisis preparedness and resolution has been found to help financial stability, particularly in countries with rapid financial deepening (see Brunnermeier et al. 2009; Cecchetti 2008; Claessens et al. 2010; Djikman 2015; Melecky and Podpiera 2010, 2015). Depending on country characteristics, this could be achieved by housing micro- and macroprudential authority "under one roof."[12]

Capital flow management measures (CFMs). Capital inflows to EMDEs come with benefits and costs. They offer EMDEs access to savings in foreign currency that can be used to fund productive investment. They can also, however, contribute to credit and asset price booms, which can disrupt and damage the economy, especially if there is a sudden stop in inflows. CFMs can be used as part of a combination of policies to address issues relating to cross-border capital flows (Ghosh, Ostry, and Qureshi 2017; Heathcote and Perri 2016). These policies can also have unintended consequences and should not be used to avoid addressing other, possibly more fundamental, macroeconomic policy imbalances or to unduly delay necessary exchange rate adjustment (Forbes 2007; Keller 2018; Ostry 2015). In the years following the global recession, EMDEs faced a surge of inflows. More recently, significant capital outflows occurred in the second half of 2015 and in mid-2018.

Generally, EMDEs have relied primarily on macroeconomic policies to manage capital flow reversals. Adjustments to external shocks have been facilitated by exchange rate flexibility—especially in EMDEs where currencies were initially overvalued—foreign exchange market interventions, and monetary and fiscal policy adjustments.

Several EMDEs, however, introduced new CFMs on inflows during 2009-12 as unprecedentedly low interest rates in major advanced economies increased procyclical capital inflows (Forbes et al. 2016; figure 7.6). Most of these measures were either removed (the Russian Federation) or eased (Brazil, Indonesia, Peru) when the inflow surge abated (IMF 2016). In several EMDEs, CFMs were also tightened during stress episodes or when financial stability was threatened by macroeconomic rebalancing, global shocks, significant foreign currency exposures, or financial contagion risks. As these economies implemented macroeconomic adjustment programs, in some cases involving the resolution of failed financial institutions, some CFMs were subsequently eased or removed.

Policies to strengthen corporate balance sheets. Prudential policies, including the monitoring of balance sheets of large, systematically important firms, can help reduce the financial stability risks associated with elevated corporate debt. Structural policies, such as promoting equity market development and strengthening bankruptcy protection rights, can help lift investment and mitigate the medium-term consequences of excessive corporate debt.

[12] An alternative view proposes that a separation of powers between monetary and prudential policies is more appropriate to avoid conflicts between monetary policy objectives and financial stability; reputational risk, because the effectiveness of monetary or financial stability may be undermined by the failures of the other; excessive power in one institution; and moral hazard when the lender of last resort and supervisor are the same (Cecchetti 2008; Gerlach et al. 2009; Masciandaro 2009).

FIGURE 7.6 Capital flow management policies

After easing capital flow restrictions throughout the 1990s and early 2000s, EMDEs reversed course following the global recession to help manage capital flow volatility.

A. Capital inflow restrictions

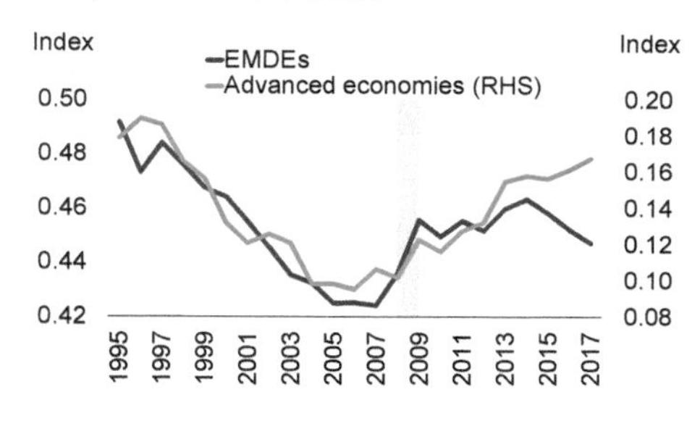

B. Capital outflow restrictions

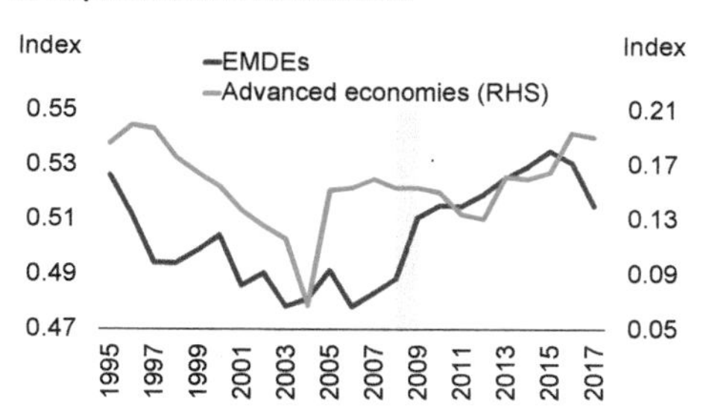

Source: Fernandez et al. (2016).

Note: Based on a database reporting the presence (or absence) of de jure capital controls for 100 countries on an annual basis differentiating between controls on inflows and outflows. This is done for controls on 10 categories of assets, including money market instruments, bonds, equities, collective investment securities, financial credits, commercial credits, derivatives, guarantees, real estate, and direct investment. EMDEs = emerging market and developing economies.

- *Equity financing.* Equity financing helps increase firms' resilience and improves their creditworthiness (World Bank 2015b). A well-developed equity market is also positively associated with growth and capital accumulation (Beck and Levine 2004; Levine and Zervos 1998). There has been some momentum in undertaking equity market reforms in EMDEs, reaching a peak in 2014 (figure 7.7); however, in many EMDEs, such as small economies in SSA and oil importers in MNA, equity market development has been held back by regulatory burdens, weaknesses in corporate governance and shareholder rights, and low domestic savings.

- *Bankruptcy laws.* EMDE bankruptcy protection laws lag international best practices, because creditors often experience long, costly, and weakly enforced debt recovery processes. Strengthening bankruptcy protection can boost investment, facilitate responsible corporate risk-taking, and help to reduce the costs of debt overhangs (World Bank 2014b). Recent reforms in bankruptcy procedures in EMDEs include the introduction of a new bankruptcy law in the Arab Republic of Egypt and in India, the strengthening of secured creditors' rights in India, and the setting up of new restructuring mechanisms in Poland.

Structural policies to boost equitable growth

EMDEs have seen potential growth slow to 4.7 percent in the 2013-18 period, down by 1.2 percentage points compared to 2003-07 (World Bank 2018e; figure 7.8). Part of the slowdown is due to lower productivity growth, attributable to several factors including slower investment growth; diminishing gains from factor reallocation as the pace of urbanization slows; and a stabilization of global value chains. Demographic trends have turned from tailwinds to headwinds as the share of the working-age population stabilized in EMDEs around 2010, following more than four decades of

FIGURE 7.7 Policies to strengthen corporate balance sheets

High corporate debt has triggered calls to further develop equity markets in EMDEs. Strengthening bankruptcy protection rights can help mitigate the systemic consequences of large-scale corporate distress.

A. Equity market governance reforms

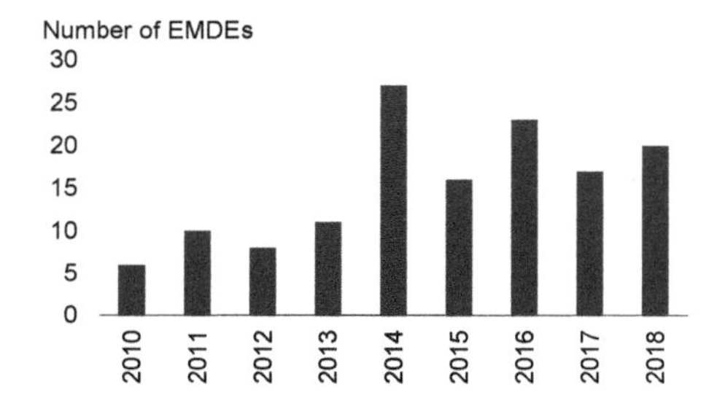

B. Bankruptcy rights protection

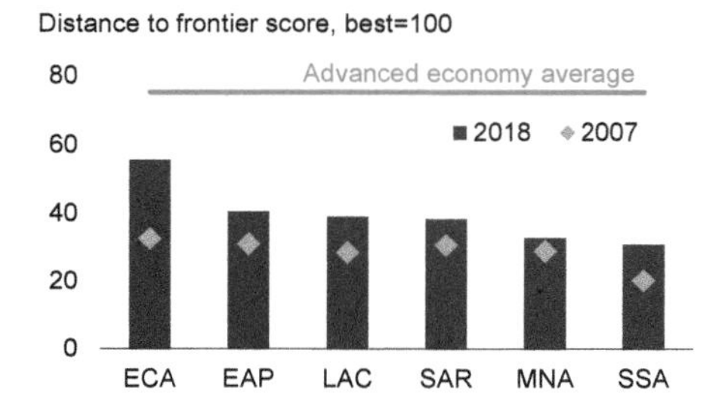

Source: World Bank's *Doing Business*.
Note: EAP = East Asia and Pacific; ECA = Europe and Central Asia; EMDEs = emerging market and developing economies; LAC = Latin America and the Caribbean; MNA = Middle East and North Africa; SAR = South Asia; SSA = Sub-Saharan Africa.
A. Number of EMDEs with an improvement in the score for minority investor rights protection from the previous year.
B. Distance to frontier score for strength of insolvency resolution. A higher index indicates reforms that improve the business climate. EAP, ECA, LAC, MNA, SAR, and SSA include 19, 20, 30, 18, 8, and 46 economies, respectively. Advanced economies include 34 economies. Based on World Bank *Doing Business* report.

steady increases. At this point, all major economies face demographic trends that slow potential growth prospects: economies with rising working-age populations accounted for 19 percent of global GDP in 2013-17, sharply down from 60 percent of global GDP in 2003-07. At current trends, potential growth in EMDEs is expected to continue to slow, to 4.3 percent a year in the next decade, with 60 percent of EMDEs experiencing a slowdown. Demographic trends alone would account for almost one-half of this slowdown and would weigh most heavily on potential growth prospects in EAP and ECA.

Ambitious, credible reform agendas that improve productivity and boost human and physical capital are needed to offset the decline in potential growth over the next decade. Many EMDEs face similar barriers to reaching the efficiency frontier, including poor governance; inflexible labor markets; constraints on human capital arising from poor provision of education, training, and health care; uncompetitive product markets; inadequate contract enforcement; and cumbersome regulations and tax frameworks. Breaking down these barriers is strongly associated with faster growth (Abiad et al. 2012; Berg, Ostry, and Zettelmeyer 2012; World Bank 2018e).

The benefits are greatest when an appropriate mix of policies support each other: the potential benefits of new road and port infrastructure to promote exports, for example, will be achieved only if customs and other border procedures are also streamlined. The timing and sequencing of reforms also matter: product and labor market reforms may be more effective when combined with monetary or fiscal policies that support demand (Bordon, Ebeke, and Shirono 2018; IMF 2019b). Some structural reforms may benefit growth but worsen income inequality, thus involving a trade-off for policy makers that

FIGURE 7.8 Potential growth: Prospects and policies

Potential growth in EMDEs has weakened because of slowdowns in capital accumulation, labor force growth, and productivity growth, and is expected to weaken further. Reforms to raise capital accumulation, labor force participation, and productivity could stem the projected slowdown.

A. Potential output growth

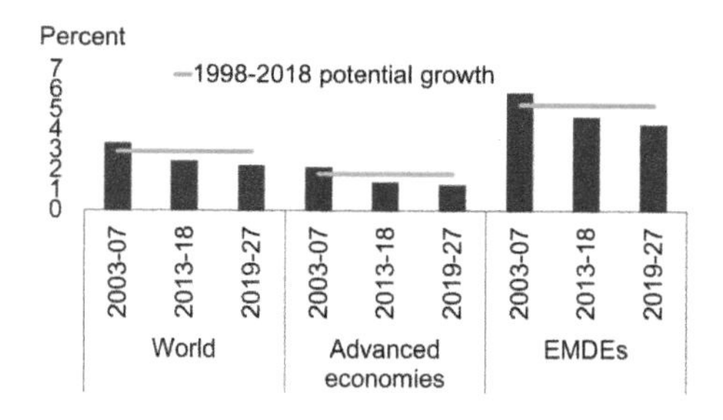

B. Long-term growth forecasts for fixed investment

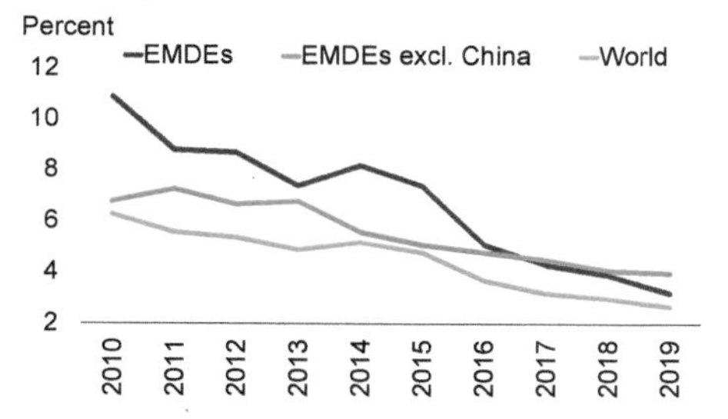

C. Total factor productivity growth in EMDEs

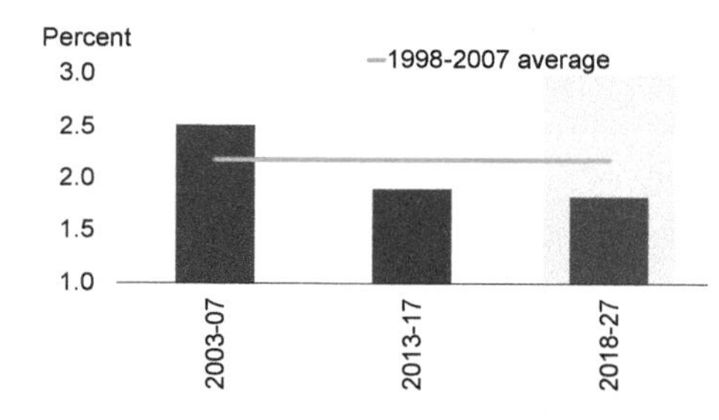

D. Impact of supportive policies on potential output growth in EMDEs

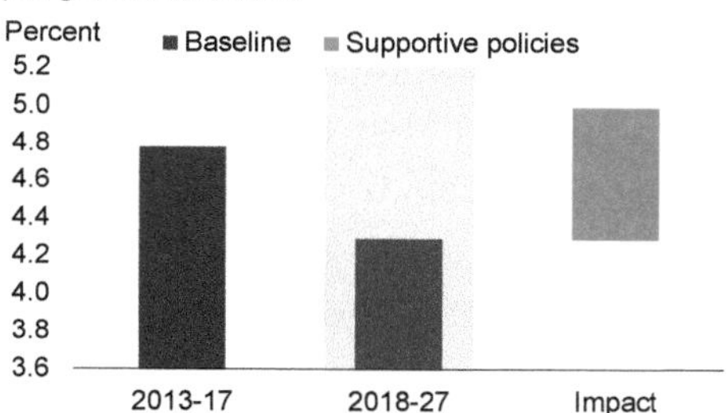

Sources: Consensus Economics; Penn World Table; United Nations Population Prospects; World Bank.

A. Period average of annual GDP-weighted averages. Estimates based on production function approach. World sample includes 50 emerging market and developing economies (EMDEs) and 30 advanced economies.

B. 10-year-ahead forecasts surveyed in indicated year. Aggregate growth rates are calculated using constant 2010 U.S. dollar investment weights. Sample includes 23 advanced economies and 20 EMDEs.

C. Shaded area indicates forecasts. GDP-weighted averages of production function-based potential total factor productivity growth estimates. Sample includes 50 EMDEs.

D. Shaded area indicates forecasts. GDP-weighted averages of production function-based potential growth estimates. Sample includes EMDEs. Supportive policies assume that each country matches over the period 2018-27 its best historical 10-year improvement in educational attainment, schooling, life expectancy, female labor force participation, and investment.

they may need to address by offsetting policies in other areas (Ostry, Berg, and Kothari 2018).

Evolution of structural reforms in EMDEs. Since the global recession, reforms have been implemented to strengthen business climates (which lost momentum since 2010), improve access to finance, strengthen financial supervision, reduce trade costs, and lower energy subsidies (which were mostly sustained). In contrast, governance has deteriorated in EMDEs and they have become less open to international capital flows.[13]

[13] See IMF (2019b) for a complementary discussion of the evolution of structural reforms.

BOX 7.1 Productivity and investment following reforms

Better institutional quality and governance are associated with stronger and more stable growth. Improved business climates empower businesses to invest, enter new markets, expand production, and hire the right staff. In several areas, reform momentum has not been maintained in emerging market and developing economies following the global recession. Yet a renewed reform spurt could help stem the expected decline in potential growth over the next decade.

Introduction

In many emerging market and developing economies (EMDEs), enterprises claim that a wide range of institutional problems form significant obstacles to doing business. Recent World Bank enterprise surveys find that more than 10 percent of EMDEs rank law and order, customs and trade regulation, and tax administration important nonfinancial obstacles to doing business. Weak governance, often manifested in corruption and large informal sectors, was also a common complaint.

By removing obstacles to firms' operations, governance and business climate reforms can raise potential growth through their impact on productivity and investment growth.[a] Against this background, this box addresses the following questions:

- How do weak governance and business climates affect economic growth?
- How has growth of total factor productivity (TFP) and investment evolved during major reform episodes?

How do weak governance and business climates affect growth?

Quality of governance and institutions. Improved quality of governance and institutions clarifies and protects property rights, facilitates contracts between nonrelated parties, and therefore promotes a more efficient allocation of resources (Acemoglu and Johnson 2005). Institutional quality is associated with stronger and more stable long-term growth (Acemoglu and Robinson 2012). In particular, less corruption is typically accompanied by higher growth of output and investment, although such dividends have depended on country circumstances (see de Vaal and Ebben 2011; Hodge et al. 2011; Shleifer and Vishny 1998). Greater political stability encourages stronger growth in output and investment, and lower government spending (Aisen and Veiga 2013). Such elements of the rule of law as the provision of security and the protection of property rights are correlated with higher growth and lower growth volatility (see Acemoglu, Johnson, and Robinson 2001; Haggard and Tiede 2011; World Bank 2017b).

Note: This box was prepared by Sinem Kilic Celik and Franz Ulrich Ruch.

a. Reform payoffs may take some time to materialize, and their growth dividend will depend on the country's stage of development and technology level (Dabla-Norris 2016).

BOX 7.1 Productivity and investment following reforms (continued)

Business climate. The business climate in which firms and entrepreneurs operate directly affects their choices on whether to start a business or enter a new market, who and how many people to hire, and whether to invest in people, capital, or expanded production. Excessively restrictive business climates are not conducive to efficiency for a number of reasons. First, poor business climates encourage anticompetitive practices, curtail innovation, and obstruct an efficient allocation of factors of production (see Aghion and Schankermann 2004; Bourles et al. 2013; Buccirossi et al. 2013). Second, burdensome business regulations amplify the adverse effects of corruption on firms' labor productivity (Amin and Ulku 2019). Third, restrictions on trade are associated with lower firm productivity, especially when accompanied by heavy domestic industrial regulation (Topalova and Khandelwal 2011). Fourth, excessively stringent labor regulations, while sometimes intended to provide social protection, could unintentionally encourage informal employment and constrain firm size (see Bruhn 2011; La Porta and Shleifer 2014; Loayza, Oviedo, and Servén 2005; Loayza and Servén 2010). Finally, weak business environments dampen the crowding-in effects on domestic investment that would otherwise accrue from public and foreign direct investment (Kose et al. 2017). Conversely, reforms that implement major improvements in business environments are associated with increased output growth (Divanbeigi and Ramalho 2015; Kirkpatrick 2014).

How has TFP and investment growth evolved during major reform episodes?

To illustrate the linkages between major governance and business climate reforms and the growth of TFP and investment, an event study and a local projections model are employed.[b] Two sets of events are defined, based on two different datasets of structural indicators. First, major reform spurts and setbacks are defined as those that lift or reduce at least one of four Worldwide Governance Indicators (government effectiveness, control of corruption, rule of law, and regulatory quality) by at least two standard deviations over two years as in Didier et al. (2015). This yields 259 events in 150 EMDEs during 1996-2017. The average of the standard errors at time t and t-2 (the first and last year of the event interval) is used for the standard deviation.

Second, major reform spurts and setbacks are defined as those that lift the score for at least 1 of the 10 World Bank *Doing Business* indicators by at least two standard deviations over two years.[c] This yields 58 events in 149 EMDEs in the period

b. This box analyzes potential TFP growth to assess the long-term effect of structural reforms. Hence, TFP growth refers to potential TFP growth throughout the box.

c. An economy's score is indicated on a scale from 0 to 100, where 0 represents the lowest performance and 100 the frontier, which is constructed from the best performances across all economies and across time.

BOX 7.1 Productivity and investment following reforms *(continued)*

FIGURE B7.1.1 Reform spurts and setbacks

Governance reforms have seen more years of setbacks whereas business climate spurts outnumbered setbacks in all years. Some momentum was gained around the global recession but not maintained in subsequent years.

A. Worldwide Governance Indicators: Number of reform spurts and setbacks

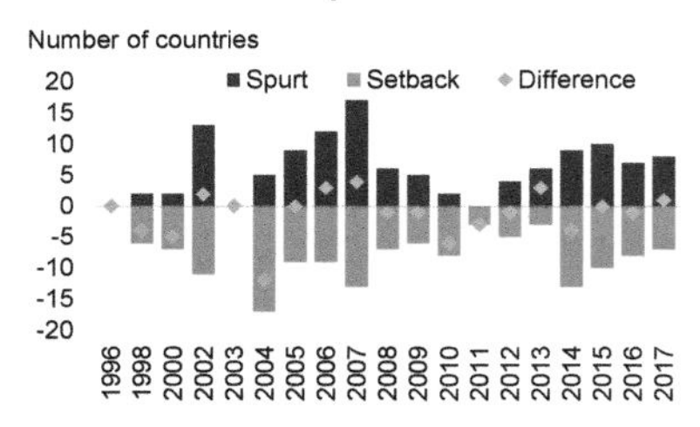

B. *Doing Business* indicators: Number of reform spurts and setbacks

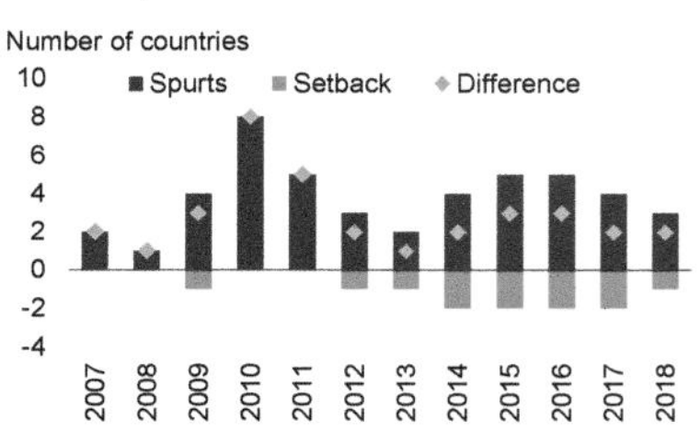

Source: World Bank.
Note: A detailed methodology is available in World Bank (2018e).
A. For Worldwide Governance Indicators, reform events are defined as two standard error changes in one of four Worldwide Governance Indicators for 149 emerging market and developing economies (EMDEs) during 1996-2017.
B. For *Doing Business* indicators, reform events are defined as two standard deviation changes in distance to frontier in 1 of 10 *Doing Business* indicators in 150 EMDEs during the same period during 2004-18.

2004-18. Reform spurts (setbacks) are defined as two-year increases (decreases) by two standard deviations in the score of 1 or more of the 10 indicators: starting a business, dealing with construction permits, getting electricity, registering property, getting credit, protecting minority investors, paying taxes, trading across borders, enforcing contracts, and resolving insolvency. The standard deviation is defined as the cross-country standard deviation in the event year.

Business climate reforms continue to lower trade costs and improve access to finance, but have lost momentum in other areas of business climates since 2010 (figure B7.1.1). In contrast, in governance reforms, there have been more setbacks than reform spurts since the global recession and, in years when many EMDEs have undertaken reforms, many EMDEs have also suffered setbacks.

Around reform episodes, the growth of potential TFP and investment has tended to be higher than during "normal" years. Reform spurts reflected in Worldwide Governance Indicators were, on average, associated with an increase of about 1 percentage point in annual TFP growth globally and somewhat more in EMDEs (figure B7.1.2).[d] Reform setbacks were, on average, associated with annual TFP growth globally and among EMDEs lower by 0.6 percentage point. Investment

---

d. The difference between the simple average of potential TFP (or real investment) growth during all reform spurt (setback) events and the simple average of potential TFP (or real investment) growth during all "normal" years without such events. The averages are calculated both for the full sample and for EMDEs only.

BOX B7.1 Productivity and investment following reforms *(continued)*

FIGURE B7.1.2 Potential TFP and investment growth around reform spurts and setbacks

Reform spurts have, on average, been associated with small increases in TFP growth rates above their "normal-year" averages and statistically significant increases in investment growth two and four years after the reform spurts.

A. Average change in potential TFP growth around Worldwide Governance Indicators reforms

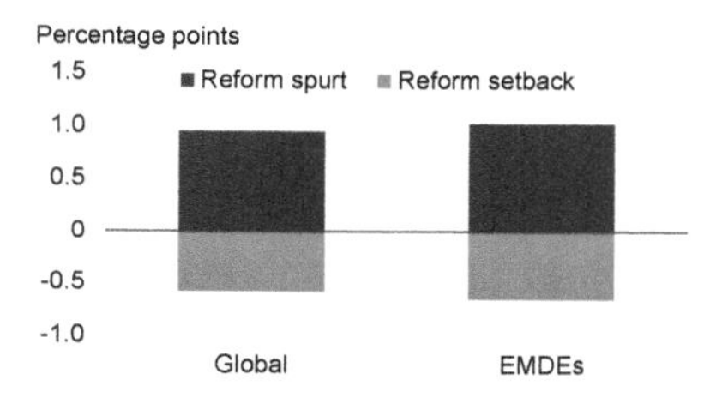

B. Change in potential TFP growth two to four years after reform episodes

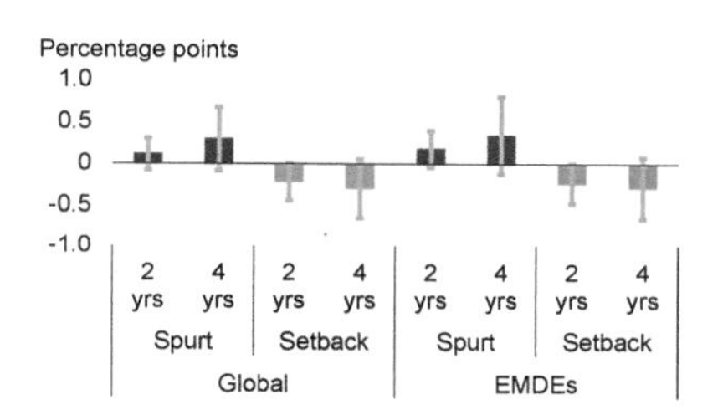

C. Average change in investment growth around *Worldwide Governance Indicators* reforms

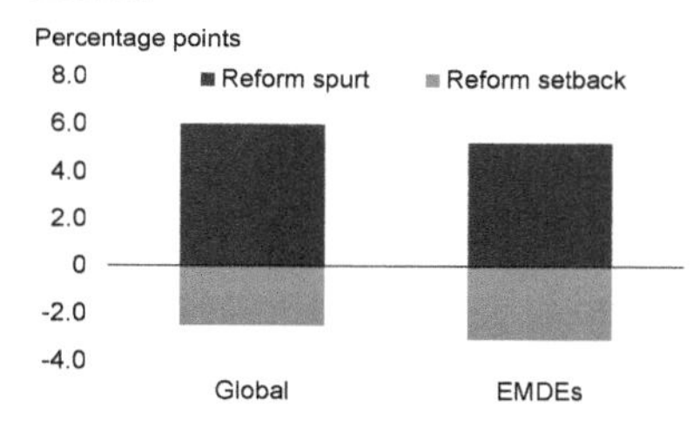

D. Change in investment growth two to four years after reform episodes

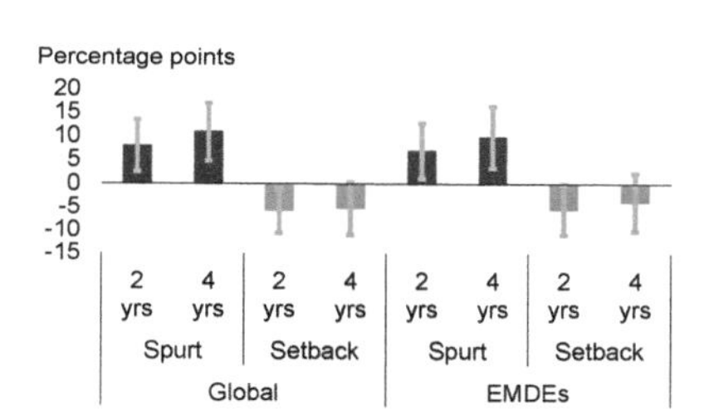

Source: World Bank staff estimates.

Note: Total factor productivity (TFP) growth refers to potential TFP growth, as estimated in World Bank (2018e). EMDEs = emerging market and developing economies.

A.C. Simple averages of potential TFP (A) and investment (C) growth during reform spurts and setbacks (minus simple average potential TFP and investment growth outside such episodes) for all countries ("Global") or for EMDEs only ("EMDEs") using Worldwide Governance Indicators. Based on an event study of statistically significant 305 reform events—defined as two standard error changes in one of four Worldwide Governance Indicators—for 150 EMDEs and 36 advanced economies. Data are from 1996-2017.

C.D. Regression coefficients of potential TFP (C) and investment (F) growth on dummies for structural reform spurts and setbacks—defined as two standard error changes in one of four Worldwide Governance Indicators—from local projections model for lags of two and four years, for a sample of 136 EMDEs and 38 advanced economies during 1996-2017. Vertical bars show 90 percent confidence interval.

growth was 6.0 percentage points a year higher during the average reform spurt and about 2.5 percentage points a year lower during the average reform setback.

For comparison, using industry-level data, Bourles et al. (2013) estimate that the removal of all anticompetitive regulations in upstream industries might have raised TFP growth by 1.7 percentage points per year in the average Organisation for

BOX 7.1 Productivity and investment following reforms *(continued)*

Economic Co-operation and Development country during 1995-2007. Dabla-Norris et al. (2015) estimate that the full elimination of labor and product market distortions would lift TFP in 13 advanced economies by 3.8-19.5 percent. Other studies find that better business climates are associated with 1.0 percentage point higher actual output growth in EMDEs or 0.8 percentage point higher per capita growth in a broader sample of countries (Didier et al. 2015; Divanbeigi and Ramalho 2015).

The local projections model suggests that the effects of governance reform spurts and setbacks build over time (for details, see World Bank 2018e). Typically, it takes four years for growth dividends to materialize after governance reform spurts, but the adverse impact of reform setbacks materializes faster (within about two years) and is less persistent. Potential TFP growth is, on average, about 0.1 percentage point per year above its "normal-year" average (0.8 percent) four years after reform spurts and about 0.2 percentage point per year below two years after setbacks. Investment growth is, on average, about 2.8-3.5 percentage points per year above its "normal-year" average (6.4 percent) two to four years after governance reform spurts and about 2.7 percentage points per year below two years after reform setbacks.

Conclusion

The three years before and during the 2009 global recessions saw a number of reforms to improve business climates that, however, lost momentum after 2010 in some areas. In contrast, governance reforms reversed after the global recession. A renewed boost to both types of reforms could yield sizable dividends for the growth of both productivity and investment.

- *Business environment.* For the private sector to flourish and generate productivity growth, it must operate in an environment conducive to business. This environment includes regulations and arrangements that make it easy to start a business, access electricity and the Internet, register property, and obtain construction permits. It also includes having a tax system that provides appropriate incentives, raises revenue efficiently, and is viewed as fair. In these respects, the general business environment in the average EMDEs has improved since the global recession, with its score improving on average by 13 percentage points since DB2008 (figure 7.9; box 7.1 provides a discussion of statistically significant events).[14] The largest gains in business regulatory environment scores occurred

[14] An economy's score is indicated on a scale from 0 to 100, where 0 represents the lowest performance and 100 the frontier, which is constructed from the best performances across all economies and across time. The number of reforms is calculated using the business reforms by year and by country as listed in the World Bank's *Doing Business* publications.

FIGURE 7.9 Business and financial sector reforms

Business and financial regulatory reforms in EMDEs accelerated in the three years around the financial crisis and paid off with gains in Doing Business indicators. Subsequently momentum in business reforms floundered while financial reforms peaked only recently.

A. Business regulatory environment

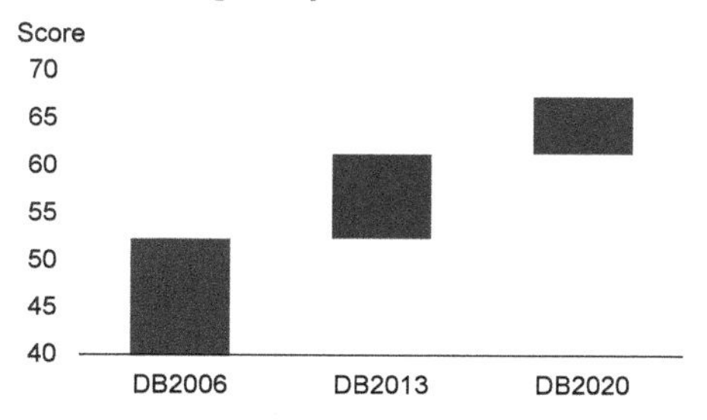

B. Business regulatory reforms

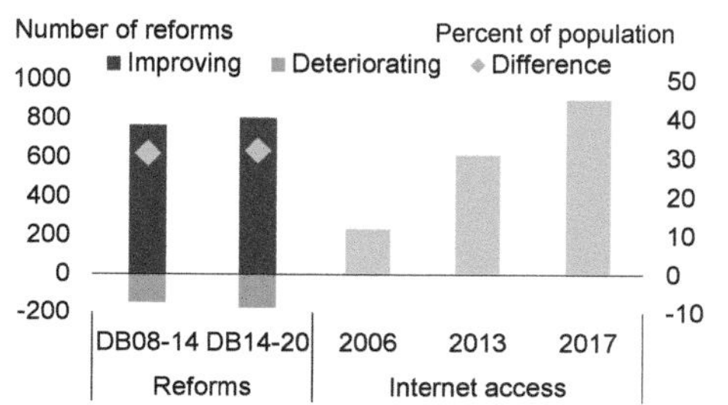

C. Financial regulatory environment

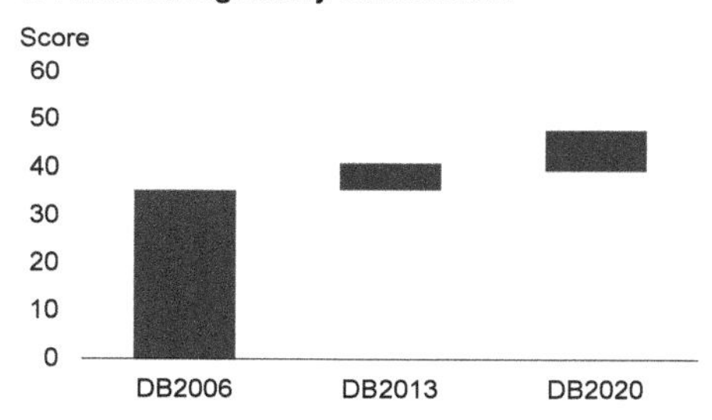

D. Financial regulatory reforms

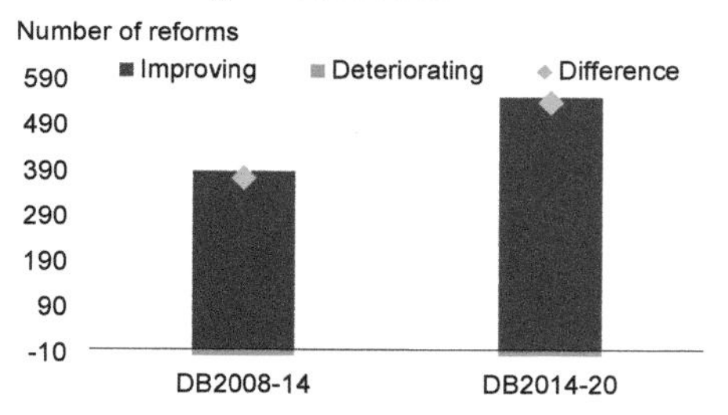

E. Capital account openness

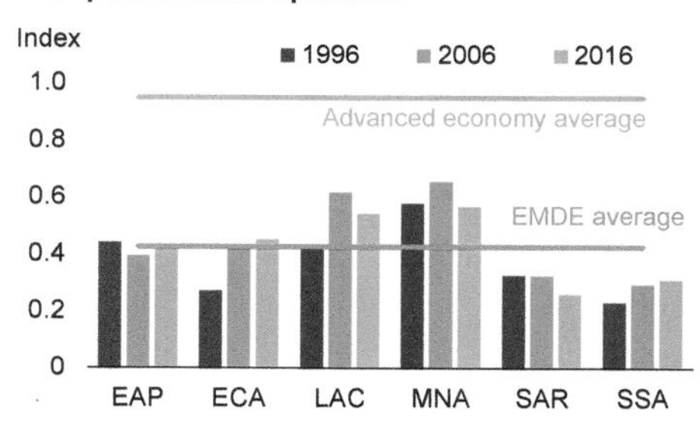

F. Capital account reforms

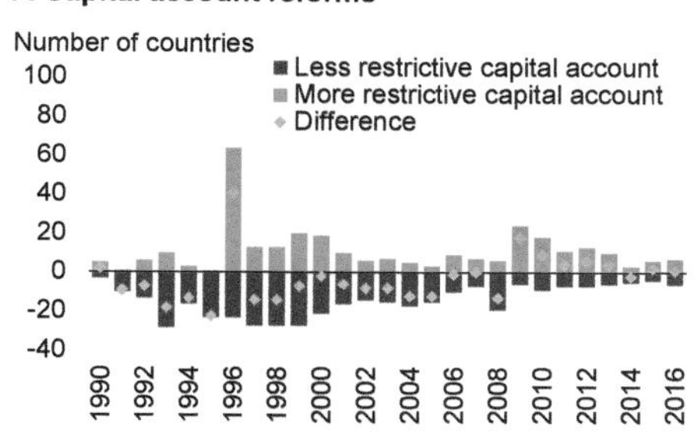

Sources: Chinn and Ito (2006); World Bank.

Note: EAP = East Asia and Pacific; ECA = Europe and Central Asia; EMDEs = emerging market and developing economies; LAC = Latin America and the Caribbean; MNA = Middle East and North Africa; SAR = South Asia; SSA = Sub-Saharan Africa.

A.C. The score is measured on a scale from 0 (weakest) to 100 (best/the frontier). "DB" before the year indicates the related *Doing Business* publication. Average performance of four indicator sets (A: starting a business, dealing with construction permits, registering property, and paying taxes; C: getting credit, protecting minority investors, enforcing contracts, and resolving insolvencies). Indicator sets are spliced backward where methodological changes affected the level.

B.D. The number of reforms is calculated using the business reforms by year and by country as listed in the World Bank's *Doing Business* reports. These are codified from the text list of business reforms as reported by the Doing Business survey.

B. Business regulatory reforms include those business reforms categorized under starting a business, dealing with construction permits, registering property, and paying taxes. Unweighted averages for Internet access.

D. Financial regulatory reforms include those business reforms categorized under getting credit, protecting minority investors, enforcing contracts, and resolving insolvencies.

E. Unweighted regional averages of the Chinn-Ito index (KAOPEN) measuring a country's degree of capital account openness, where 1 represents fully open capital account. Advanced economy and EMDE averages are for 2016.

F. Indicator variable taking on value 1 when a country experiences a year-on-year decrease in the openness index and -1 when a country experiences a year-on-year increase. Based on 145 EMDEs.

during and after the global financial crisis when the number of business-friendly reforms increased from 102 in DB2008 to 147 in DB2010. The share of EMDEs undertaking at least one business-friendly reform measure increased from 57 percent in DB2008 to 73 percent in DB2010; the share of EMDEs undertaking at least three reform measures increased from 15 percent in DB2008 to 25 percent in 2010. Since DB2010, the number of economies undertaking reforms has slowed such that the average improvement between DB2013 and DB2020 was a third smaller than the seven years before DB2013. The number of reforms has not surpassed its DB2010 peak, with reforms slowing significantly to a low in DB2013.

EMDEs have also seen an increase in the use of Internet, with more individuals and businesses using it. The average share of the population using Internet in EMDEs rose from just under 12 percent in 2006 to 45 percent in 2017. This share remains below the 85 percent average in advanced economies.

- *Financial environment.* The global recession placed a spotlight on gaps in financial regulation and supervision. In response, financial sector reform accelerated globally, especially among the major economies, with the adoption of Basel III and improvements in the Global Financial Safety Net (chapter 5). Many EMDEs also accelerated financial environment reforms, but improvements in financial aspects of business including ease of getting credit, protecting minority investors, enforcing contracts, and resolving insolvency indicator sets have been mixed. On average, EMDEs have improved their scores related to the financial regulatory environment (including the ease of getting credit, protecting minority investors, and resolving insolvency) by 10 percentage points between DB2009 and DB2020. Scores have improved by a greater margin in the seven years between DB2013 and DB2020, than the seven prior. EMDEs have done particularly well in improving business access to credit, with the score improving by over 20 percentage points over this same period. Contract enforcement, in contrast, has not materially changed since the global recession. Unlike in business environment reforms, the number of EMDEs undertaking financial reforms has improved more consistently over the postrecession period and the number of reforms reached a peak in DB2019.

- *Openness to international capital flows.* EMDEs have made significant strides toward dismantling capital controls and opening up their capital accounts, starting in earnest in the 1990s. EMDEs on average have fewer open capital accounts than advanced economies do, with LAC and MNA achieving the highest average openness scores among EMDE regions. The pace of capital account liberalization slowed in the 2000s, but with EMDEs on net still shifting toward more openness. After the global financial crisis hit, however, countries on net moved back to more restrictions. In 2009, 17 percent of EMDEs shifted to a more closed capital account. The shift toward less openness has continued in recent years, partly in response to volatile capital flows and shifts in the global debate about its role in macroeconomic management (Didier et al. 2015; IMF 2012; Rey 2015).

- *Governance.* Getting governance right can significantly boost economic growth, and past governance reform spurts in EMDEs have generally been followed by rising productivity and investment growth (box 7.1). Most EMDEs, however, especially those in SSA, still have low scores in regulatory quality and efficiency. Since the global recession, EMDEs experienced fewer governance reform spurts and more setbacks per year than before the recession.[15] The 22 largest EMDEs (EM22) and LICs have not been able to improve governance scores since the 1990s, with scores for regulatory quality, government effectiveness, rule of law, and control of corruption now lower in the average EM22 and LICs than in 1998 (figure 7.10).

- *Trade environment reforms.* Trade remains potentially one of the most important avenues for EMDEs to unlock productivity and efficiency gains. Trade environments remain less supportive in EMDEs than in advanced economies according to measures such as the costs (including time involved) of exporting and importing, the quality of trade- and transport-related infrastructure, and proxy measures (figure 7.11). The average EMDE's overall "trade across borders" score in the *Doing Business* survey improved by 11 percentage points between DB2007 and DB2020.

  Some of this progress has been driven by trade-related reforms, again with increased momentum visible in the three years before and during the global recession. Thus, the number of trade-related reforms in EMDEs increased from 24 to 37 between DB2008 and DB2010. These numbers imply, however, that still only a minority of EMDEs were undertaking reforms that lowered the cost and time required to import and export. Reform momentum slowed after 2010. Since DB2017, however, there seems to have been some renewed vigor in trade reform, with the number of relevant reforms rising to 34 in that year. In contrast to these efforts to lower within-border trade-related costs, Group of Twenty (G20) economies have imposed a growing number of tariffs and nontariff restrictions on trade (WTO 2019).

- *Energy subsidies.* In 2017, governments worldwide spent about $300 billion on fossil fuel subsidies, equivalent to almost six times the funds needed to achieve universal access to electricity and clean cooking (World Bank 2018b). These subsidies disproportionately benefit higher-income households; divert government funds from health, education, and other productive activities; and aggravate carbon emissions and climate change (IMF 2013b; Rentschler and Bazilian 2017a, 2017b; World Bank 2018b). In oil-dependent economies, energy subsidies remain an important barrier to the diversification of exports and production. The significant decline in oil prices in 2014-15 prompted many oil-exporting EMDEs to reform their energy subsidies: between mid-2014 and end-2016, more than half undertook some energy subsidy reform (Stocker et al. 2018).[16] For Gulf Cooperation Council

[15] Reform spurts are improvements in one or more of the Worldwide Governance Indicators that are sufficiently large to exceed the country-specific average by more than 2 standard deviations. Reform setbacks are similarly-sized declines in the indicators.

[16] Economies that undertook reforms include Algeria, Bahrain, Cameroon, Ecuador, Gabon, Ghana, the Islamic Republic of Iran, Iraq, Kazakhstan, Kuwait, Malaysia, Nigeria, Oman, Qatar, Saudi Arabia, Sudan, Trinidad and Tobago, Turkmenistan, the United Arab Emirates, and the Republic of Yemen.

FIGURE 7.10 Governance

The quality of governance is low among EMDEs; it has remained effectively unchanged in the largest 22 EMDEs and deteriorated in low-income countries since the 1990s.

A. Change in governance indicators

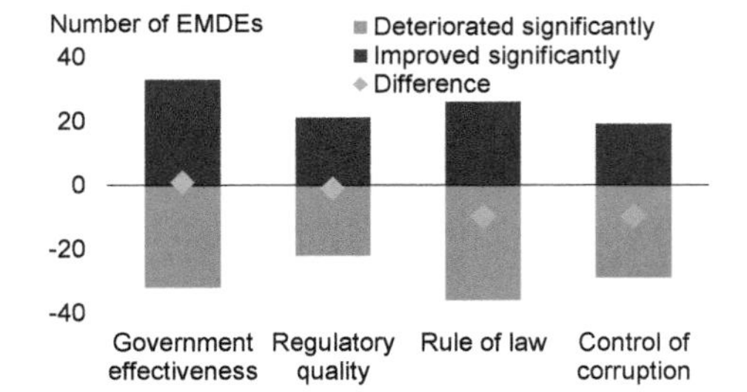

B. Seven largest EMDEs

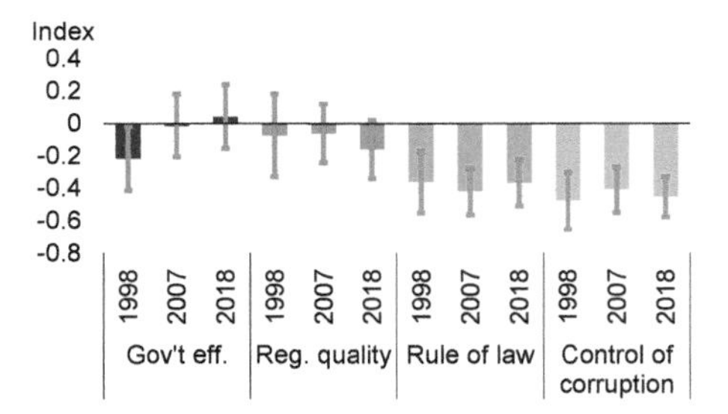

C. Twenty-two largest EMDEs

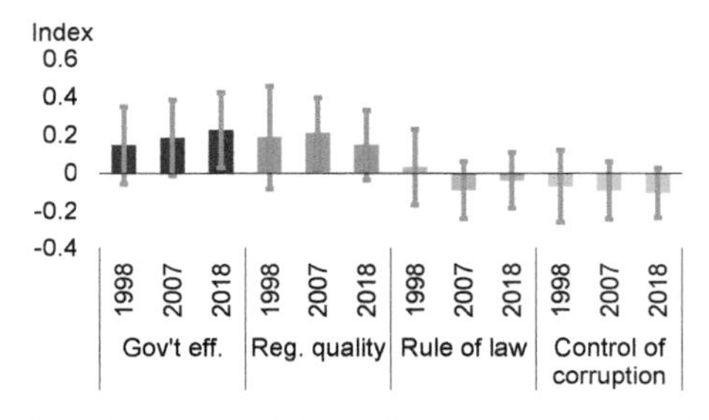

D. Low-income countries

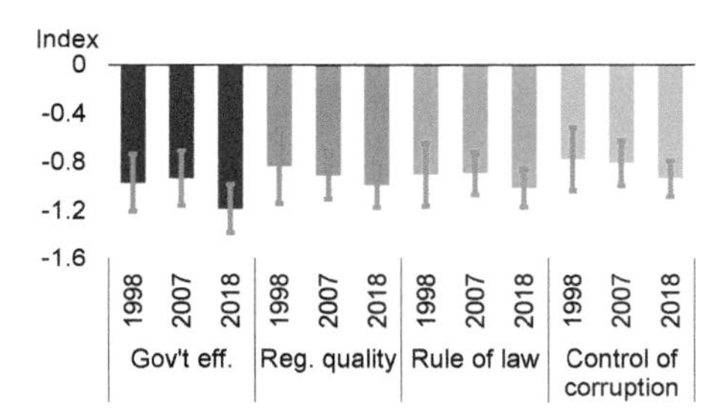

Source: World Bank's Worldwide Governance Indicators (WGI).

Note: Based on indicators from the WGI. WGI defines governance as "the traditions and institutions by which authority in a country is exercised. This includes the process by which governments are selected, monitored and replaced; the capacity of the government to effectively formulate and implement sound policies; and the respect of citizens and the state for the institutions that govern economic and social interactions among them." The four indicators are government effectiveness, regulatory quality, rule of law, and control of corruption. EMDEs = emerging market and developing economies; Gov't eff. = government effectiveness; Reg. quality = regulatory quality.

A. A country significantly improved its rating if it saw a two standard deviation improvement in one of four indicators between 1996 and 2018. The standard errors are the average between two observations.

B.-D. Annual observations are unweighted averages. The seven largest EMDEs are Brazil, China, Mexico, India, Indonesia, the Russian Federation, and Turkey. Low-income countries comprise 26 economies. Error bands are 1 standard deviation.

economies, this represented a substantial change in policy stance (Krane and Hung 2016; World Bank 2017a). As a consequence, the average fiscal cost of energy subsidies among EMDEs declined from about 4.0 percent of GDP in 2014 to 1.9 percent of GDP in 2016. Some of the progress toward reducing energy subsidies was reversed in 2017-18, but subsidies nonetheless remain smaller than before the oil price decline.

Poverty and structural policies. Getting structural reforms right for long-term growth sets the foundation for improving the livelihoods of citizens and fighting extreme poverty. Better governance, more friendly business climates, lower trade barriers, and greater financial inclusion are all associated with lower extreme poverty (figure 7.12; see

FIGURE 7.11 Trade and subsidies reforms

The three years following the financial crisis saw declines in EMDEs' costs of importing and exporting, but the trade environment remains less favorable than in advanced economies. The fiscal costs of energy subsidies and export concentration have fallen.

A. Trade environment

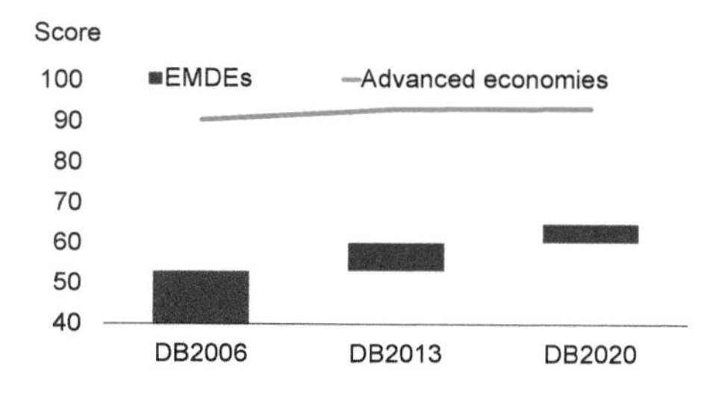

B. Trade reforms

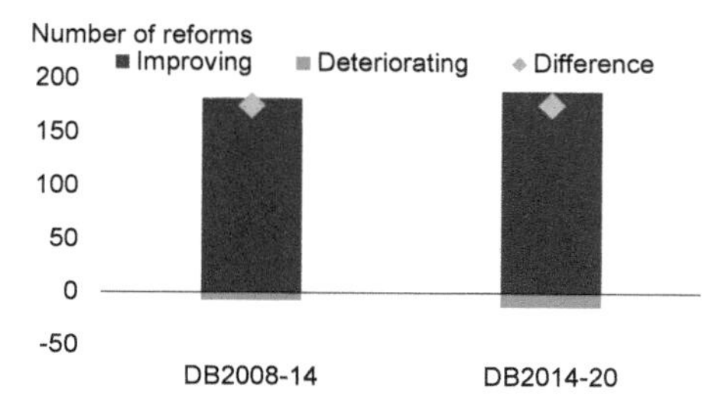

C. Export concentration

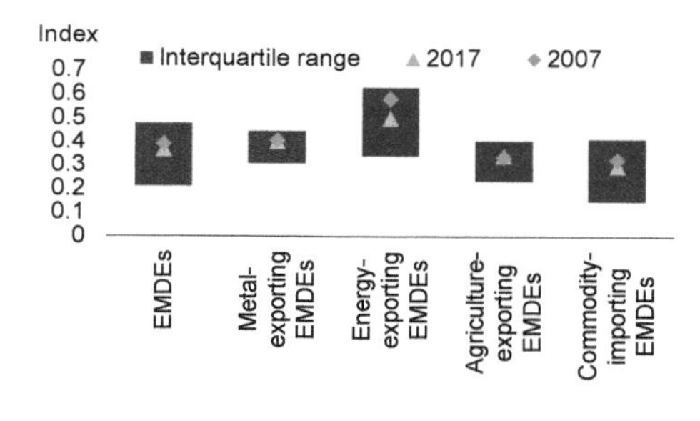

D. Energy subsidies

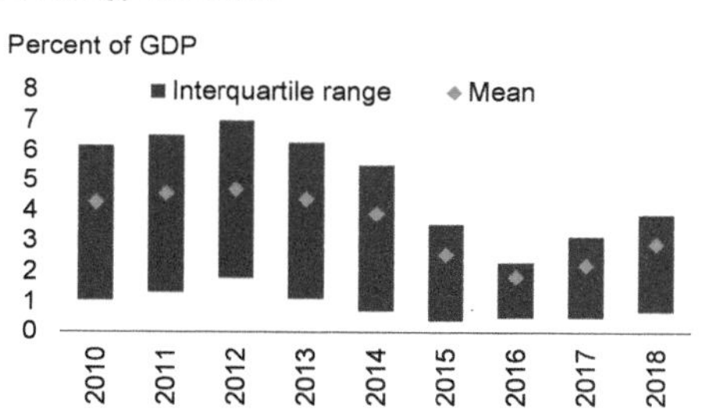

Sources: International Energy Agency; United Nations Conference on Trade and Development; World Bank.

A. Scores are unweighted averages of 39 advanced economies and 148 emerging market and developing economies (EMDEs). The trade across borders indicator set is spliced backward where methodological changes affected the level. An economy's score is indicated on a scale from 0 to 100, where 0 represents the lowest performance and 100 the frontier, which is constructed from the best performances across all economies and across time. "DB" before the year indicates the related *Doing Business* publication.

B. Trade reforms include those business reforms categorized under trading across borders in the *Doing Business* survey. The number of reforms is calculated using the business reforms by year and by country as listed in *Doing Business*. These are codified from the text list of business reforms in the publication.

C. Export concentration measured as the Herfindahl-Hirschmann Index (Product HHI). Observations for 2007 and 2017 are unweighted averages. EMDEs are based on data for 146 economies: 20 metal-exporting economies, 35 energy-exporting economies, 35 agriculture-exporting EMDEs, and 58 commodity-importing economies. Values closer to 1 indicate more concentration.

D. Based on data for 40 EMDEs.

Demenet, Razafindrakoto, and Roubaud 2016; Djankov, Georgieva, and Ramalho 2018; Dollar 2004; Lawless 2013; Paunov 2016; Rashid and Intartaglia 2017; Tebaldi and Mohan 2010).

- *Weak institutions.* Average poverty rates of EMDEs in the quartile with the weakest public institutions are about four times that in the quartile with the strongest public institutions. Nearly 10 times as many of the global poor live in countries with weaker institutions than in countries with the strongest institutions.

FIGURE 7.12 Poverty and structural reforms

Weak governance, lower financial inclusion, unfavorable business climates, and less trade openness are associated with significantly higher poverty rates, highlighting the importance of structural reforms.

A. Poverty rates, by strength of institutions

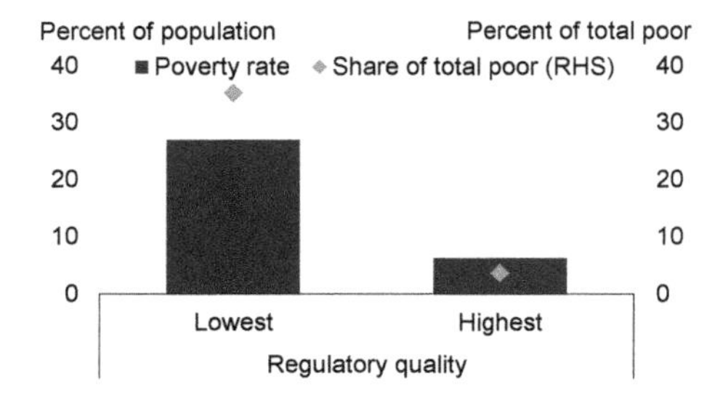

B. Poverty rates, by financial inclusion

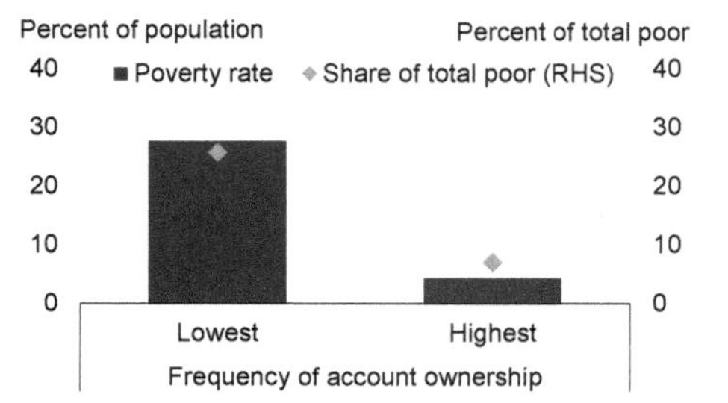

C. Poverty rates, by *Doing Business* ranking

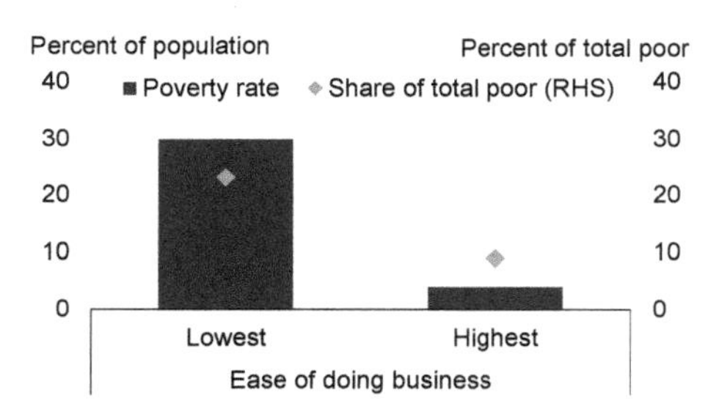

D. Poverty rates, by trade openness

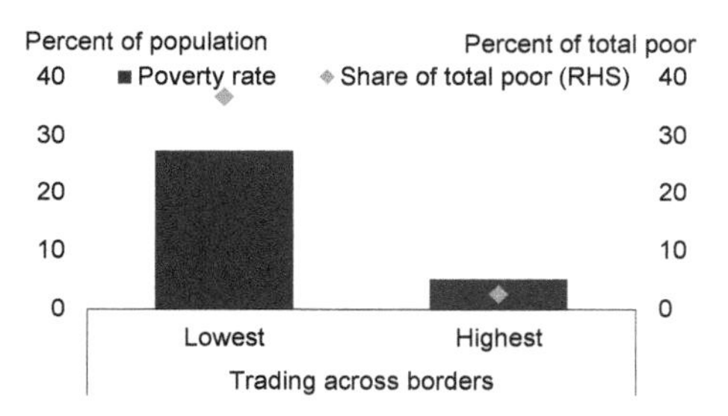

Source: World Bank.

Note: The poverty rate is an unweighted average in each group. Share of population is the cumulative total. Based on poverty data for 2015.

A "Highest" indicates quartile of emerging market and developing economies (EMDEs) with the strongest regulatory quality (based on data for year with latest poverty data). "Lowest" indicates quartile of EMDEs with the weakest regulatory quality. The back data for regulatory quality come from the Worldwide Governance Indicators. Data are for 2017.

B. "Highest" indicates quartile of EMDEs with the highest share of account ownership at a financial institution (greater than 59 percent) in 2017. "Lowest" indicates quartile of EMDEs with the lowest shares (less than 21 percent). India is excluded from the "Best" category.

C. "Highest" indicates quartile of EMDEs with the highest 2019 ease of doing business score (above 67.5). "Lowest" indicates quartile of EMDEs with the lowest 2019 ease of doing dusiness score (below 51.6).

D. "Highest" indicates quartile of EMDEs with the highest 2019 trade across borders score (above 78.1) in the ease of doing business survey. "Lowest" indicates quartile of EMDEs with the lowest 2019 trading across borders score (below 57.1).

- *Barriers to doing business.* EMDEs in the quartile of the *Doing Business* index with the lowest scores experience nearly eight times higher average poverty rates than those in the quartile with the highest scores. More than twice as many of the global poor live in countries with the lowest *Doing Business* rankings than in countries with the highest rankings.
- *Limited access to finance.* The poverty rate in the quartile of EMDEs with the least access to financial institutions is six times that in the quartile with the greatest access.

- *Trade barriers.* The poverty rate in the quartile of EMDEs with the lowest ranking in the trading across borders subcategory of the *Doing Business* index is more than five times that for those in the highest scores: 36 percent of the global poor live in countries with the lowest rankings, compared to only 3 percent in countries with the highest rankings.

Productivity-enhancing reforms. Boosting productivity requires removing barriers to the reallocation of resources toward higher-productivity firms and sectors, and stimulating the creation, innovation, and development of individual firms.

- *Improve business climates.* A more business-friendly environment—with greater access to finance, stronger bankruptcy protection, and simpler tax and regulatory requirements—helps encourage firm creation, entrepreneurship, and productivity-enhancing investment and technology adoption. Policy makers could focus on the following reforms. First, reforms that increase product market flexibility or competition (such as increased openness to international trade and more effective regulation of monopolies and large firms) could raise aggregate productivity growth by encouraging a reallocation of resources away from unsuccessful and sheltered firms to more productive and competitive ones (Bernard, Jensen, and Schott 2006; IMF 2019b; Melitz 2003). Second, labor market reforms that improve the allocation of talent, such as broadening access to occupations and improving access to training and retraining, can generate considerable productivity gains (Hsieh et al. 2013). Third, reforms to level the playing field (for example, state-owned enterprise reforms) could encourage entry of more productive firms and thus raise aggregate productivity (Brandt, van Biesebroek, and Zhang 2012).

- *Enhance governance.* Better institutional quality—such as control of corruption and rent-seeking, fair application of the rule of law, and political stability—is associated with higher productivity and stronger investment growth (box 7.1).

- *Facilitate adoption of new technologies.* Despite the significant gains to productivity and growth through the adoption of new technologies, EMDEs invest far less in research and development than advanced economies do—a so-called innovation paradox (Cirera and Maloney 2017). New technologies, such as industrial automation, advanced robotics, smart factories, the Internet of things, and 3D printing hold the promise of spurring manufacturing productivity, by helping spread innovation; digital technologies may improve government efficiency and the delivery of government services (World Bank 2016a, 2019d). Productivity-enhancing new technologies in the agricultural sector could benefit the two-thirds of the global poor who earn their livelihoods from farming (World Bank 2019e). New technologies are more likely to be adopted successfully if policies are in place to mitigate the costs of adjustment for both workers and firms, and if market failures are addressed (Cirera and Maloney 2017; World Bank 2016a).

- *Increase trade openness.* Openness to international trade increases the competition faced by firms, encourages them to specialize in what they do best, and thus promotes the efficient allocation of resources, helping to raise prosperity and lower poverty (World Bank 2019b, 2020a). In the absence of new multilateral trade agreements, regional trade arrangements could be platforms for further trade integration. Such agreements have become deeper over time, covering areas—some outside the World Trade Organization mandate—such as services, e-trade, competition policy, investment, capital mobility, and property rights (Hofmann, Osnago, and Ruta 2017). EMDEs could focus on policy measures that liberalize services trade and foreign direct investment, areas where barriers remain significant (World Bank 2017c). For example, the 2018 African Continental Free Trade Area could help foster intraregional trade and diversification, generate economies of scale, and encourage higher-value-added production. In LICs, gains from trade can be particularly significant given high trade costs and low trade integration.

- *Diversify economies.* EMDEs that rely heavily on a few export products or on a few trading partners are more vulnerable to shocks, have less diverse sources of growth, and tend to suffer more from volatility in revenue streams (Hausmann, Hwang, and Rodrik 2007; Hesse 2008). Since 2007, EMDEs have made some limited progress in diversifying their exports, with energy exporters achieving the largest improvements (figure 7.11). In the current environment of relatively low commodity prices and predominantly downside risks to global growth, EMDEs should implement reforms to encourage diversification. These reforms include ensuring appropriate trade policies that promote diverse exports, infrastructure investment to enable private sector competition, competition regulation to avoid market concentration, and support for innovation through research and development.[17]

  EMDEs can benefit significantly from further reforms to energy subsidies. Most reforms in this area have been driven by fiscal challenges rather than environmental or socioeconomic objectives (Rentschler and Bazilian 2017a, 2017b). EMDEs should create an energy sector plan with long-term objectives that clearly define the aims and potential benefits of reforms and the cost of subsidies. This plan should follow consultations with stakeholders, and be communicated effectively to the public (IMF 2013b; Rentschler and Bazilian 2017a, 2017b). Such a plan should include phased price increases that are appropriately timed with specific measures to offset the impact on the poor.

Investing in human capital and infrastructure. Increasing investment in infrastructure and human capital can help unlock growth dividends and improve resilience to disruptive technologies and climate change. More effective social safety nets with better coverage can support these investments by helping workers transition to the formal economy or by providing income security in the face of shocks (ILO 2019).

[17] McIntyre et al. (2018) show that export diversification can help to lower output volatility in small countries and that diversification requires structural changes to an economy. Dabla-Norris, Ho, and Kyobe (2016) highlight that reducing trade barriers can help export diversification. Hesse (2008) shows that export diversification can bring stability to export earnings and mitigate risks from terms of trade shocks. Al-Marhubi (2000) shows that export diversification boosts economic growth.

BOX 7.2 Potential growth benefits of reforms

Potential growth has slowed in emerging market and developing economies and is expected to slow further in coming years. These economies can halt and reverse this slowdown and achieve higher potential growth through policy actions that boost investment, improve human capital, raise labor supply, and promote business and governance reforms. Such policy actions offer a critical way to meaningfully raise the standard of living of these economies' citizens.

Introduction

Emerging market and developing economies (EMDEs) have experienced a slowdown in potential growth in the past decade—for more than half of EMDEs, potential growth has slowed below long-term averages—and that growth is expected to slow further in the next decade (World Bank 2018e). If EMDEs are to achieve their development goals and improve the lives of their citizens, they need to boost growth through ambitious and proactive reform agendas.

Using a scenario analysis, this box examines the magnitude of the potential growth dividend from implementing policies that accelerate human and physical capital or labor supply (World Bank 2018e).

To establish the likely effects of these policy choices on potential growth, a counterfactual scenario with higher growth of physical or human capital or labor supply is compared with the baseline scenario.[a] All counterfactual scenarios model a repeat of a country's best 10-year improvement, up to reasonable ceilings. The potential growth dividend in the scenarios therefore depends on each country's track record as well as its room for improvement. The counterfactuals, therefore, most likely provide lower bounds because they disregard nonlinearities in reform effects as well as synergies between different reform measures.

Physical capital

If, over the next decade, each country raised its investment growth by as much as its largest increase over any historical 10-year interval in the period 1981-2017 for which we have data, ratios of global investment to gross domestic product (GDP) would rise by 2.3 percentage points of GDP. Investment-to-GDP ratios would rise somewhat more in EMDEs, by 2.9 percentage points of GDP. It is estimated that such an investment boost would raise global potential output by 2 percent by 2027, reversing the slowdown under the baseline scenario. EMDE potential output would rise even more—by 5 percent cumulatively by 2027 (figure B7.2.1).

Implicit in these scenarios is the premise that the additional investment is used productively. In the context of EMDEs, there is some evidence that absorptive

Note: This box was prepared by Sinem Kilic Celik and Franz Ulrich Ruch.

a. For a detailed description of the methodology, see annex 3.1 in World Bank (2018e).

BOX 7.2 Potential growth benefits of reforms (continued)

FIGURE B7.2.1 Policies to stem declining potential growth

A combination of additional investment, education and health improvements, and labor market reforms could stem and reverse the projected decline in global potential growth over 2018-27.

A. Global potential growth under reform scenarios

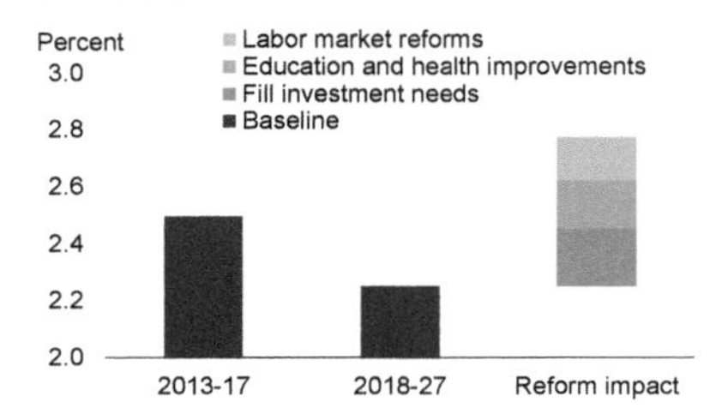

B. EMDE potential growth under reform scenarios

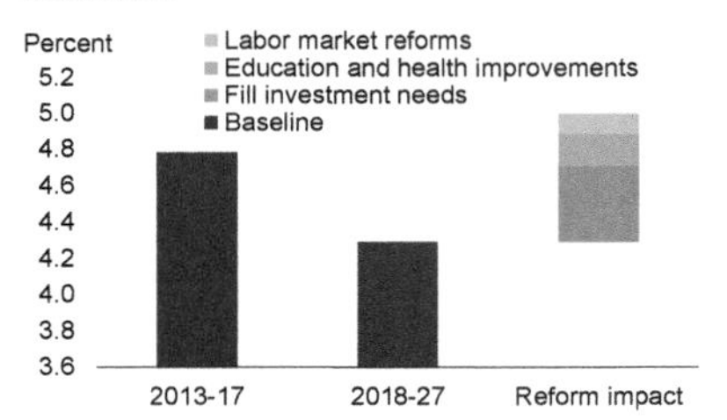

C. EMDE potential growth under reform scenarios, by region

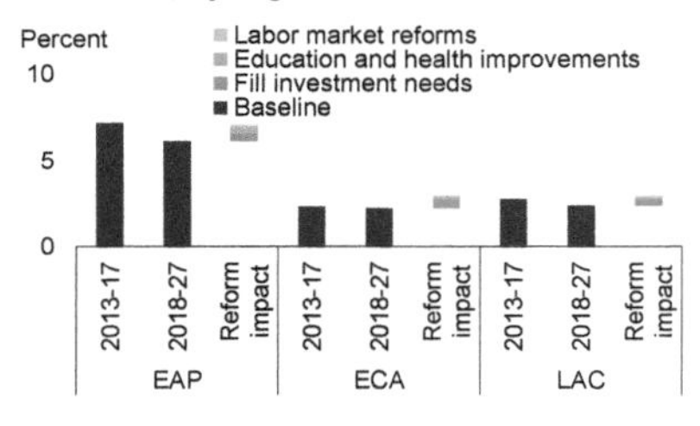

D. EMDE potential growth under reform scenarios, by region

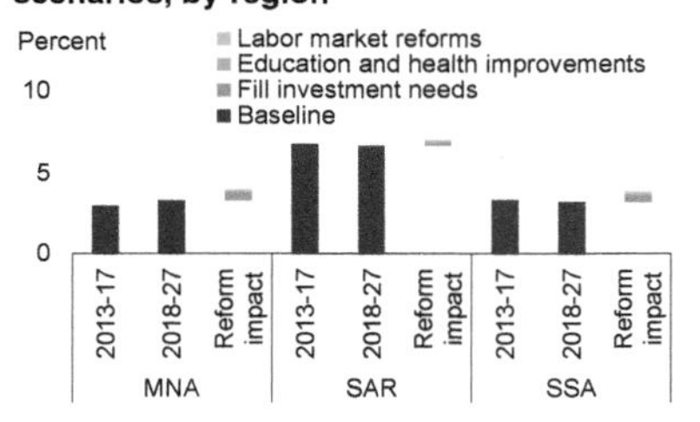

Source: World Bank (2018e).

Note: GDP weighted averages. EAP = East Asia and Pacific; ECA = Europe and Central Asia; EMDE = emerging market and developing economy; LAC = Latin America and the Caribbean; SAR = South Asia; SSA = Sub-Saharan Africa.

A. See annex 3.1 of World Bank (2018e) for more details on the methodology applied.

capacity can limit the success of large scaling-up of public investment, although this adverse effect is small in lower-income and capital-scarce countries (Presbitero 2016). Public investment management is also key to unlocking the growth benefits of investment (IMF 2015a).

Human capital

Education. A better educated workforce is more securely attached to the labor market and more productive (World Bank 2019a, 2019c). In a stylized policy scenario, education-related policy indicators—secondary and tertiary enrollment and completion rates—are assumed to rise over 2018-27 in each EMDE by as

BOX 7.2 Potential growth benefits of reforms *(continued)*

much as their largest historical improvement in any 10-year period during 1981-2017. This improvement would imply that EMDEs, on average, would raise primary school completion rates by 5 percentage points and secondary and tertiary enrollment rates by 7 percentage points, on average, during the next decade. In EMDE regions that have made particularly large strides in improving education outcomes but still have ample room for further improvements, such as South Asia (SAR), secondary school completion rates could rise as much as 16 percentage points over the next decade.

Health policies. At 71 years on average in 2013-17, life expectancy in EMDEs is still below that in advanced economies (82 years). Although regions such as SAR and Sub-Saharan Africa have made large improvements, raising life expectancy by 4-7 years over the past two decades, the average remains about one-eighth below advanced economy levels.

In a stylized scenario of improved health, life expectancy is assumed to rise over 2018-27 in each EMDE by as much as its largest improvement over any historical 10-year period during 1981-2017. This rise would imply an increase in life expectancy in EMDEs of 2.5 years, on average, but as much as 3.8 years in the Middle East and North Africa over the next decade.

Impact on potential growth. These stylized scenarios suggest that improvements in education and health outcomes—via their effect on labor supply and total factor productivity growth—could lift global and EMDE potential growth by 0.2 percentage point a year on average. In some EMDE regions with a strong track record of boosting human capital and ample room for improving education and health outcomes, such as East Asia and Pacific, potential growth could rise by one-and-a-half times as much.

Impact on inequality. Better education and longer life expectancy will not only raise potential output growth but also have implications for income inequality. Whereas economic development may tend to raise income inequality (for example, because of growing urbanization), better education may alleviate some of these pressures.

Labor supply

In 2018, global female labor force participation was two-thirds that of men, and it is even lower in EMDEs, at 48 percent, compared to 75 percent among men. Similarly, in both EMDEs and advanced economies, the average labor force participation rate among workers aged 55 years or older is about one-half that of workers aged 30-45 years, and labor force participation among those aged 19-29 year is only four-fifths that of their peers aged 30-45 years.

In a stylized labor market reform scenario, female labor force participation rates—along cohort-, age-, and country-specific dimensions—surge by 10 percentage

BOX 7.2 Potential growth benefits of reforms *(continued)*

points in each EMDE by 2027 (equivalent to the largest historical 10-year improvement in each EMDE), although they will not reach those of same-aged men. The premise underlying this assumption is that, over the decade, sufficient jobs will be created to absorb this additional labor supply.

Impact on potential growth. In such a stylized labor market reform scenario, global and EMDE potential output growth could rise by 0.2 and 0.1 percentage point a year, respectively, on average, over 2018-27. Again, such a renewed reform push could yield the largest dividends for EMDE regions with a strong track record and sizable remaining gaps between male and female labor force participation rates (such as Latin America and the Caribbean).

Productivity

Institutional reforms could help lift productivity growth. Better institutional quality, such as control of corruption, application of the rule of law, and improved political stability, has accompanied higher and more stable growth (see box 7.1). At the firm-level, more friendly business climates have favored firm productivity and a shift from informal activities to more productive formal activities (see Aghion and Schankermann 2004; Amin and Ulku 2019; Bourles et al. 2013; Buccirossi et al. 2013; Bruhn 2011; Divanbeigi and Ramalho 2015; Kirkpatrick 2014; Kose et al. 2017; La Porta and Shleifer 2014; Loayza, Oviedo, and Servén 2005; Loayza and Servén 2010).

Conclusion

If EMDEs are to achieve their development goals and improve the lives of their citizens, they need to boost economic growth through ambitious and credible reform agendas. These reforms should target increasing productivity-enhancing investment, improving educational outcomes and on-the-job training, encouraging female participation in the workforce, and improving institutional quality and the ease of doing business.

Implementing such reforms could more than offset the decline in global and EMDE potential growth that is expected over the next decade (box 7.2). Instead of potential growth of 4.3 percent a year in 2018-27, such policy reforms could boost annual potential growth to over 5 percent.

- *Strengthen education and training.* An educated workforce is more securely attached to the labor market, more productive, and better able to adjust to disruptive new technologies. For many low- and middle-income EMDEs, improving basic numeracy, literacy, and skills related to information and communications technology remains a key priority (figure 7.13). Although secondary school enrollment rates in the average EMDE are near the levels in advanced economies,

FIGURE 7.13 Human capital and infrastructure

Significant gains are associated with investment in education, health, infrastructure, and mitigation of climate risk.

A. Years of schooling

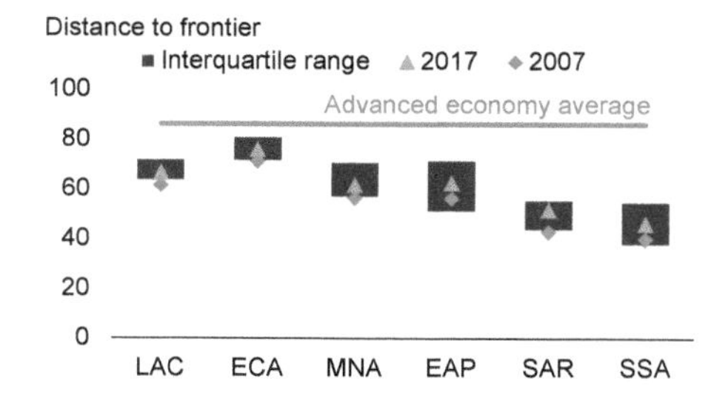

B. Life expectancy

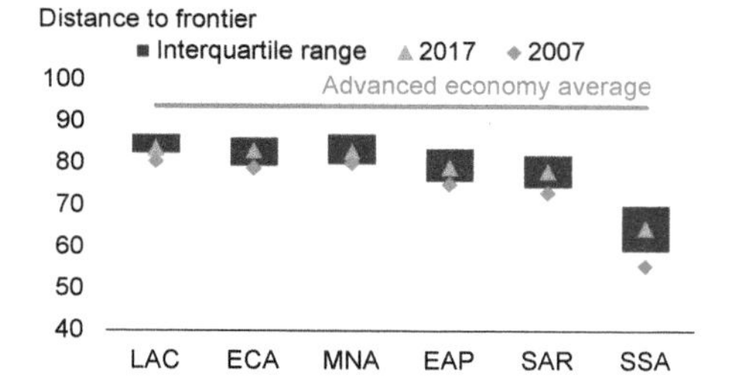

C. Infrastructure gaps

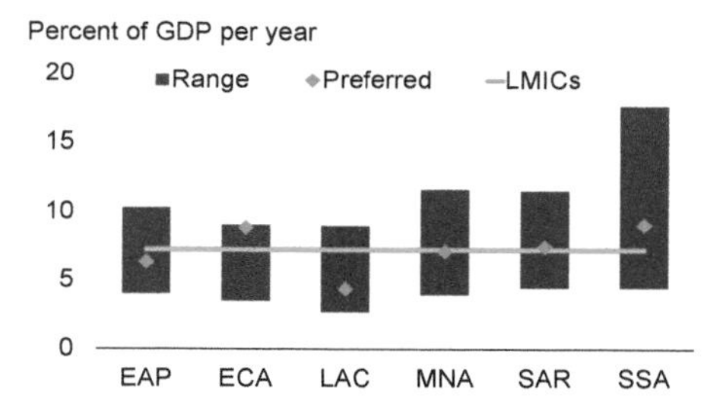

D. Climate risk

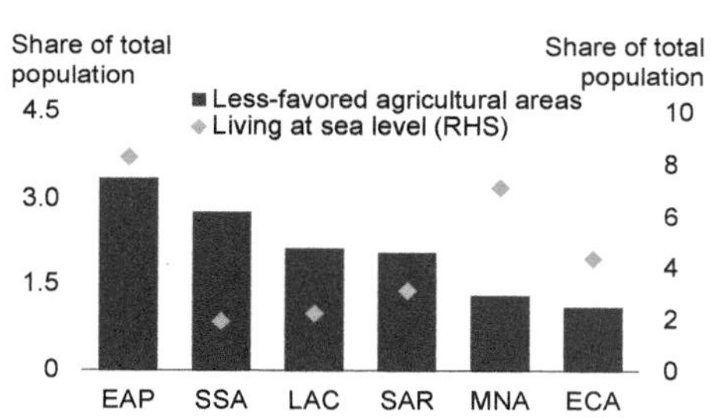

Sources: Barbier and Hochard (2018); Rozenberg and Fay (2019); United Nations Development Program.

Note: EAP = East Asia and Pacific; ECA = Europe and Central Asia; LAC = Latin America and the Caribbean; LMICs = Low- and middle-income countries; MNA = Middle East and North Africa; SAR = South Asia; SSA = Sub-Saharan Africa.

A. Education index from the Human Development Index. 2007 and 2017 are unweighted means in emerging market and developing economies (EMDEs). Interquartile range is for 2017 observations.

B. Life expectancy index from the Human Development Index. 2007 and 2017 are unweighted means in EMDEs. Interquartile range is for 2017 observations.

C. Investment needs based on goals as set out in Rozenberg and Fay (2019), including both new investment and maintenance of existing capital stock. Infrastructure investment includes investment in electricity, transport, water supply and sanitation, flood protection, and irrigation. "Preferred" is defined as the infrastructure "pathway [that] limits stranded assets, has a relatively high per capita consumption due to electric mobility, and invests mostly in renewable energy and storage."

D. Less-favored agricultural areas are agricultural lands constrained by difficult terrain, poor soil quality, limited rainfall, or with limited access to markets. "Sea level" identifies areas where elevation is below 5 meters. Data are from 2010.

tertiary school enrollment rates (40 percent) and secondary and tertiary school completion rates (27 and 10 percent, respectively) were less than two-thirds of advanced-economy averages in 2013-17. As countries increasingly engage in more complex and automated production processes, higher tertiary school enrollment and investment in lifelong learning will be needed to facilitate the training and retraining required for people to meet shifting demands for skills (World Bank 2019c). Improving learning outcomes also requires better measurement and monitoring, more efficient teaching practices, and greater accountability (World Bank 2018c). In LICs, investment in early childhood education can ensure that cognitive and socio-behavioral skills are adequately developed, because addressing deficiencies later in life tends to be much more expensive (World Bank 2019a). To reap the benefits of digital technologies, LICs will require significant investment in human capital.

Reforms to strengthen competition could have synergies with reforms to improve human capital. Firms in EMDEs tend to innovate in marginal process and product improvements rather than engaging in significant technology adoption or new product imitation (Cirera and Maloney 2017). This tendency can partly be attributed to weak managerial capabilities. Better education, especially if combined with more competition, can induce an upgrading of managerial skills that can foster more ambitious innovations.

Finally, better education serves a critical function in reducing inequality both within and between countries. As EMDEs' workforce grows—while that of advanced economies shrinks—and becomes more skilled, the global economy is expected to benefit and global income inequality is expected to fall (World Bank 2018a).

- *Improve health care.* Human capital can be improved by reducing malnutrition and improving health care services. Policy interventions to improve public health, and to ensure and lengthen productive working lives, range widely. Better sanitation and access to clean water would improve public health: 9 percent of the global disease burden may be attributable to unsafe water, inadequate sanitation, and insufficient hygiene (WHO 2008). Improvements in health care provision can be spurred by well-defined and regularly monitored performance indicators (Bradley et al. 2010). Comprehensive provision of health services has been followed by better health outcomes in countries with higher per capita incomes (Maeda et al. 2014). At the local level, programs targeted at local health service providers or groups of patients have generated considerable improvements in health care services and outcomes. For example, in Rwanda, performance-based incentive payments helped significantly improve health indicators for children (Gertler and Vermeersch 2012). In India, enhanced training of primary health care providers led to better identification and treatment of patient ailments (Das et al. 2016).

- *Close infrastructure gaps.* EMDEs have large infrastructure needs that require financing (Rozenberg and Fay 2019). In many EMDEs, access to water and sanitation remains incomplete, power outages are common, access to communication networks is limited, and rail infrastructure is underdeveloped. It is estimated that unfilled global investment needs amount to up to 3 percent of global GDP, and progress towards closing them has been slow during 2014-19, especially in the areas of water, sanitation, and education (UNCTAD 2014, 2019). EMDEs with sound fiscal positions could increase public sector investment, which would both boost short-term demand and help raise potential growth in the long run.

EMDEs that are constrained by fiscal sustainability considerations or high debt could focus on shifting from unproductive expenditures toward productive public investment and improving the management of public investment (World Bank 2017c). Policy and institutional frameworks play a vital role in minimizing the cost of infrastructure needs, including access to electricity, broadband infrastructure, clean water and sanitation, and decarbonization. Reforms that can achieve this include legal and regulatory frameworks that promote renewables, increase public transport utilization, and densify urban areas (Rozenberg and Fay 2019). In many EMDEs, government revenues remain low, indicating that in some cases the best route to increased infrastructure investment may be to increase tax revenues by expanding tax bases or improving the quality of tax administration (World Bank 2015a). To improve infrastructure investment through state-owned enterprises, governments can develop corporate governance frameworks and provide training to boards and government officials (IFC 2018).

The size of investment needs, however, also means that the private sector should be involved through both public-private partnerships and policies that improve the business environment for the private sector to be able to invest and grow. Policy efforts to expand the supply of complementary inputs and capabilities and to raise the returns on investment may foster private investment in infrastructure. These policies would ensure that innovation-related investment rises, especially because these types of investment are low in EMDE firms (Cirera and Maloney 2017). Efficiently designed public guarantees and other forms of credit enhancement can also help unlock additional investment.

- *Encourage labor force participation.* Two broader trends are constraining labor force participation. First, demographic changes have seen the global share of working-age population stabilize since 2010 after more than four decades of rapid increases (World Bank 2016b). Second, in 2018, global female labor force participation was two-thirds that of men, and participation was even lower in EMDEs. Labor supply can be raised by drawing a greater share of the working-age population into the labor force, which can be achieved through policies to "activate" discouraged workers or groups with historically low participation rates, such as women and younger or older workers.

  In both advanced economies and EMDEs, active labor market policies and reforms to social benefits have been followed by higher labor force participation rates (Betcherman, Dar, and Olivas 2004; Card, Kluve, and Weber 2010). Less rigid employment protection regulations and minimum wages have had mixed effects on employment and labor force participation and, at times, unintended side effects such as lower labor force participation of disadvantaged groups (Betcherman 2014).

  In EMDEs, policies aimed at other objectives have sometimes brought important collateral benefits in the form of higher labor force participation. For example, in Nigeria, improved access to finance and training programs increased female labor force participation by encouraging firm startups (Brudevold-Newman et al. 2017). In Uruguay, the extension of the school day was associated with higher adult labor force participation (Alfaro, Evans, and Holland 2015). In ECA, shifting health care systems toward services targeted at the elderly has helped extend productive life times, and providing support services to women with families has helped encourage labor force participation (Bussolo, Koettl, and Sinnott 2015).

- *Increase investment to guard against climate risks.* Poor people are disproportionally affected by climate change because they generally live in riskier areas, depend on income sources such as agriculture that are most vulnerable to extreme weather events, and lack the savings and access to borrowing to help them cope with disasters (World Bank 2017d). Two-thirds of the global poor are estimated to earn their income from farming. In LICs, agriculture remains the largest economic sector. To help mitigate and adapt to climate changes, LICs need to invest in climate-resilient infrastructure, improve irrigation techniques, use fertilizers more effectively, strive to gain access to new markets, and possibly implement land use reform (World Bank 2019e). Building resilient infrastructure can save lives and money. Infrastructure disruptions cost low- and middle-income countries between $391 and $647 billion (about 1.2-2.0 percent of GDP) a year, with natural disasters imposing a significant part of that cost. Building resilient power, water, and sanitation infrastructure would require only about 3 percent of overall investment needs with climate change magnifying the benefits in the long run (Hallegatte, Rentschler, and Rozenberg 2019).

Policy priorities

Fiscal, monetary, and financial policies. In economies with weak demand but with monetary policy room and sound fiscal positions, fiscal or monetary stimulus could help support activity. Where fiscal positions are weak, priorities may include shifting public spending toward more productive and poverty-reducing expenditures and improving revenue frameworks. Some economies in LAC and SSA have experienced rapid debt accumulation and face risks of fiscal unsustainability. Energy-exporting EMDEs, particularly in MNA, face rising vulnerabilities that require policy action. Where central banks lack independence and transparency, policy makers could prioritize implementing rule-based frameworks and building credibility through proper implementation of policy. Where corporate balance sheets face rising vulnerabilities, policy makers can implement macroprudential policies that mitigate risks.

Structural policies. Specific policy priorities will depend on country-specific bottlenecks to growth. The specific policies depend on the extent to which an important market failure has to be rectified and the likelihood of success in governments' efforts to address this failure (Maloney and Nayyar 2018; Rodrik 2008). Several priority areas can be considered.

- Where subsidies remain elevated or undermine investment in other productive activities, governments could establish medium-term plans that unwind these subsidies and replace them with better-targeted tools to protect vulnerable groups.

- Where regulatory or tax burdens constrain growth, priorities may include better public sector effectiveness and governance.

- Where private sector growth is anemic, improved access to finance and better business climates may be among the priorities.

- Where productivity is low and informality is widespread, such as in SSA and LAC, building human capital and enhancing the productivity of workers in the informal sector may be priorities.

- Where the labor force is aging, priorities may include efforts to increase labor force participation, improve health systems, increase lifelong education, and promote financial development to improve the allocation of savings. In countries with large vulnerable populations, better social safety nets may need to be prioritized.

- Where female labor force participation is low, policies aimed at reducing barriers to entry can be prioritized.

- Where climate change threatens human life and infrastructure, particularly in small island states, governments could prioritize climate-resilient infrastructure and fiscal planning.

Conclusion

A decade after the global recession, EMDE policy makers are at a crossroads. EMDE growth has slowed over the past decade, with downside risks becoming more prevalent. At current trends, most EMDEs will face slower potential growth in the next decade than the previous one. Despite some progress in implementing more resilient macroeconomic policy frameworks—including through rules-based policy frameworks, increasing the flexibility of exchange rates, and strengthening prudential policies, including with macroprudential tools—most EMDEs remain some distance from best practices. At the same time, significant policy room that was used in response to the global recession has not yet been restored. There have been efforts to implement business-friendly reforms to improve efficiency and promote investment. But, with governance stalling and reform momentum slowing in several areas, those efforts may not suffice to stem the decline in potential output growth.

To raise per capita incomes, eradicate poverty, and bring about shared prosperity, policy makers need to adopt ambitious and credible reform agendas that focus on all aspects of policy in an integrated way. EMDEs on unsustainable fiscal paths should prioritize actions that can help shore up fiscal positions while protecting growth-enhancing expenditures. Such actions are likely to include cutting unproductive expenditures, improving spending efficiency, and expanding tax revenue bases. EMDEs should also focus on ensuring that other buffers against shocks are adequate. These include foreign exchange reserves, which in many EMDEs today are not sufficient to meet balance of payments needs.

Macroeconomic resilience requires more than addressing the current stance of policy: it also requires transparent and rules-based policy frameworks that help to prevent future policy mistakes and ensure the necessary room to employ countercyclical policy. Fiscal rules can assist countries to maintain sustainable finances and build resources in good times. Transparent and independent central banks are less likely to be diverted from their task of maintaining low inflation by developments that may threaten other policy objectives. Although some EMDEs have made significant progress in establishing such policy frameworks and institutions, many have more to do.

The changing global financial landscape requires increased cross-border regulatory collaboration, adequate prudential responses, and, in some circumstances, the use of capital flow management measures as part of a policy mix to address imbalances. In EMDEs without a prudential authority or prudential powers, policy makers should create and empower such institutions. In EMDEs with the appropriate institutions, financial sector policy makers should use flexible and well-targeted tools to mitigate foreign currency risk and asset price misalignment. In EMDEs where capital flows have created imbalances, policy makers can look to capital flow management measures to help restore macroeconomic balance while allowing appropriate external adjustments, including to exchange rates. In regions where EMDE-headquartered banks have gained prominence, policy makers should ensure that home-host supervisor coordination is adequate to address the risks involved.

With current projections indicating slower long-term productivity growth in most EMDEs, policy makers should undertake ambitious and comprehensive reforms to stimulate private sector-led growth. They should aim to return to and exceed the reform momentum last seen in 2010 and reinvigorate stalling governance. Measures for doing so include building institutions that promote growth and support resilience, reforms to encourage productivity and investment, measures to build human capital and promote investment in growth-enhancing public infrastructure, measures to adapt to climate change, and policies to reduce corruption, strengthen competition, and reduce unnecessary regulatory burdens.

References

Abiad, A., J. Bluedorn, J. Guajardo, and P. Topalova. 2012. "The Rising Resilience of Emerging Market and Developing Economies." IMF Working Paper 12/300, International Monetary Fund, Washington, DC.

Acemoglu, D., and S. Johnson. 2005. "Unbundling Institutions." *Journal of Political Economy* 113 (5): 949-95.

Acemoglu, D., S. Johnson, and J. A. Robinson. 2001. "The Colonial Origins of Comparative Development: An Empirical Investigation." *American Economic Review* 91 (5): 1369-401.

Acemoglu, D. and J.A. Robinson. 2012. *Why Nations Fail: Origins of Power, Poverty and Prosperity*. Crown Publishing Group, Random House.

Aghion, P., and M. Schankerman. 2004. "On the Welfare Effects and Political Economy of Competition- Enhancing Policies." *The Economic Journal* 114 (498): 800-24.

Agur, I., M. Chan, M. Goswani, and S. Sharma. 2018. "On International Integration of Emerging Sovereign Bond Markets." IMF Working Paper 18/18, International Monetary Fund, Washington DC.

Aisen, A., and F. J. Veiga. 2013. "How Does Political Instability Affect Economic Growth?" *European Journal of Political Economy* 29 (March): 151-67.

Aizenman, J., Y. Jinjarak, and D. Park. 2015. "Financial Development and Output Growth in Developing Asia and Latin America: A Comparative Sectoral Analysis." NBER Working Paper 20917, National Bureau of Economic Research, Cambridge, MA.

Akinci, O., and J. Olmstead-Rumsey. 2018. "How Effective are Macroprudential Policies? An Empirical Investigation." *Journal of Financial Intermediation* 33 (January): 33-57.

Akitoby, B., A. Baum, C. Hackney, O. Harrison, K. Primus, and V. Salins. 2018. "Tax Revenue Mobilization Episodes in Emerging Markets and Low-Income Countries: Lessons from a New Dataset." IMF Working Paper 18/234, International Monetary Fund, Washington, DC.

Alfaro, L., G. Asis, A. Chari, and U. Panizza. 2019. "Corporate Debt, Firm Size and Financial Fragility in Emerging Markets." NBER Working Paper 25459, National Bureau of Economic Research, Cambridge, MA.

Alfaro, P., D. K. Evans, and P. Holland. 2015. "Extending the School Day in Latin America and the Caribbean." Policy Research Working Paper 7309, World Bank, Washington, DC.

Al-Marhubi, F. 2000. "Export Diversification and Growth: An Empirical Investigation." *Applied Economics Letters* 7 (9): 559-62.

Amin, M., and H. Ulku. 2019. "Corruption, Regulatory Burden and Firm Productivity." Policy Research Working Paper 8911, World Bank, Washington, DC.

Anderson, P. R. D., A. S. Silva, and A. Velandia-Rubiano. 2010. "Public Debt Management in Emerging Economies: Has This Time Been Different?" Policy Research Working Paper 5399, World Bank, Washington, DC.

Árvai, Z., and G. Heenan. 2008. "A Framework for Developing Secondary Markets for Government Securities." IMF Working Paper 8/174, International Monetary Fund, Washington, DC.

Awasthi, R., and M. Engelschalk. 2018. "Taxation and the Shadow Economy: How the Tax System Can Stimulate and Enforce the Formalization of Business Activities." Policy Research Working Paper 8391, World Bank, Washington, DC.

Aysan, A. F., S. Fendoğlu, and M. Kilinc. 2015. "Macroprudential Policies as Buffer Against Volatile Cross-Border Capital Flows." *The Singapore Economic Review* 60 (1): 1-26.

Ayyagari, M., T. Beck, and M. S. Martinez Peria. 2017. "Credit Growth and Macroprudential Policies: Preliminary Evidence on the Firm Level." Chapter in *BIS Papers 91—Financial Systems and the Real Economy*. Basel: Bank for International Settlements.

Bailliu, J., and C. Hajzler. 2016. "Structural Reforms and Economic Growth in Emerging-Market Economies." *Bank of Canada Review* (Autumn): 47-60.

Barbier, E. B., and J. P. Hochard. 2018. "The Impacts of Climate Change on the Poor in Disadvantaged Regions." *Review of Environmental Economics and Policy* 12 (1): 26-47.

BCBS (Basel Committee on Banking Supervision). 2019. *Sixteenth Progress Report on Adoption of the Basel Regulatory Framework*. Basel: Basel Committee on Banking Supervision.

Beck, T., and R. Levine. 2004. "Stock Markets, Banks, and Growth: Panel Evidence." *Journal of Banking & Finance* 28 (3): 423-42.

Beltran, D., K. Garud, and A. Rosenblum. 2017. "Emerging Market Nonfinancial Corporate Debt: How Concerned Should We Be?" International Finance Discussion Paper Notes, Board of Governors of the Federal Reserve System, Washington, DC.

Berg, A., J. D. Ostry, and J. Zettelmeyer. 2012. "What Makes Growth Sustained?" *Journal of Development Economics* 98 (2): 149-66.

Bergman, U. M., and M. Hutchison. 2015. "Economic Stabilization in the Post-Crisis World: Are Fiscal Rules the Answer?" *Journal of International Money and Finance* 52 (April): 82-101.

Bergman, U. M., and M. Hutchison. 2018. "Fiscal Procyclicality in Developing Economies: The Role of Fiscal Rules, Institutions and Economic Conditions." http://web.econ.ku.dk/okombe /BH_2018.pdf.

Bernard, A. B., J. B. Jensen, and P. K. Schott. 2006. "Trade Costs, Firms and Productivity." *Journal of Monetary Economics* 53 (5): 917-37.

Betcherman, G. 2014. "Labor Market Regulations: What Do We Know about Their Impacts in Developing Countries?" *The World Bank Research Observer* 30 (1): 124-53.

Betcherman, G., A. Dar, and K. Olivas. 2004. "Impacts of Active Labor Market Programs: New Evidence from Evaluations with Particular Attention to Developing and Transition Countries." Social Protection and Labor Policy and Technical Note 29142, World Bank, Washington, DC.

BIS (Bank for International Settlements). 2018. *Global Systemically Important Banks: Revised Assessment Methodology and the Higher Loss Absorbency Requirement.* Basel Committee on Banking Supervision. Basel: Bank for International Settlements.

BIS (Bank for International Settlements). 2019. *Annual Economic Report: Promoting Global Monetary and Financial Stability.* Basel: Bank for International Settlements.

Bordo, M. D. and P.L. Siklos. 2019. "The Transformation and Performance of Emerging Market Economies Across the Great Divide of the Global Financial Crisis." Hoover Institution Economics Working Papers 19111, Stanford.

Bordon, A. R., C. Ebeke, and K. Shirono. 2018. "When do Structural Reforms Work? On the Role of the Business Cycle and Macroeconomic Policies." In *Structural Reforms: Moving the Economy Forward,* edited by J. de Haan and J. Parlevliet. Cham, Switzerland: Springer.

Bourles, R., G. Cette, J. Lopez, J. Mairesse, and G. Nicoletti. 2013. "Do Product Market Regulations in Upstream Sectors Curb Productivity Growth? Panel Data Evidence for OECD Countries." *Review of Economics and Statistics* 95 (5): 1750-68.

Bradley, E. H., S. Pallas, C. Bashyal, P. Berman, and L. Curry. 2010. "Developing Strategies for Improving Health Care Delivery: Guide to Concepts, Determinants, Measurement, and Intervention Design." Health, Nutrition and Population Discussion Paper 59885, World Bank, Washington, DC.

Brandt, L., J. Van Biesebroeck, and Y. Zhang. 2012. "Creative Accounting or Creative Destruction? Firm-Level Productivity Growth in Chinese Manufacturing." *Journal of Development Economics* 97 (2): 339-51.

Brinca, P., H. A. Holter, P. Krusell, and L. Malafry. 2016. "Fiscal Multipliers in the 21st Century." *Journal of Monetary Economics* 77 (C): 53-69.

Brudevold-Newman, A., M. Honorati, P. Jakiela, and O. W. Ozier. 2017. "A Firm of One's Own: Experimental Evidence on Credit Constraints and Occupational Choice." IZA Discussion Paper 10583, IZA Institute for Labor Economics, Bonn, Germany.

Bruhn, M. 2011. "License to Sell: The Effect of Business Registration Reform on Entrepreneurial Activity in Mexico." *The Review of Economics and Statistics* 93 (1): 382-86.

Brunnermeier, M. K, A. Crockett, C. Goodhart, A. Persaud, and H. Shin. 2009. "The Fundamental Principles of Financial Regulation." International Center for Monetary and Banking Studies Centre for Economic Policy Research, Geneva.

Bruno, V., I. Shim, and H. S. Shin. 2017. "Comparative Assessment of Macroprudential Policies." *Journal of Financial Stability* 28 (February): 183-202.

Buccirossi, P., L. Ciari, T. Duso, G. Spagnolo, and C. Vitale. 2013. "Competition Policy and Productivity Growth: An Empirical Assessment." *Review of Economics and Statistics* 95 (4): 1324-36.

Budnik, K. B., and J. Kleibl. 2018. "Macroprudential Regulation in the European Union in 1995-2014: Introducing a New Data Set on Policy Actions of a Macroprudential Nature." ECB Working Paper 2123, European Central Bank, Frankfurt.

Bussolo, M., J. Koettl, and E. Sinnott. 2015. *Golden Aging: Prospects for Healthy, Active, and Prosperous Aging in Europe and Central Asia.* Washington, DC: World Bank.

Cabral, R. 2015. "How Strategically Is Public Debt Being Managed Around the Globe? A Survey on Public Debt Management Strategies." Financial Advisory and Banking Department, World Bank, Washington, DC.

Calderón, C., R. Duncan, and K. Schmidt-Hebbel. 2016. "Do Good Institutions Promote Countercyclical Macroeconomic Policies?" *Oxford Bulletin of Economics and Statistics* 78 (5): 650-70.

Calderón, C., R. Duncan, and K. Schmidt⊠Hebbel. 2014. "Infrastructure, Growth, and Inequality: An Overview." Policy Research Working Paper 7034, World Bank, Washington, DC.

Card, D., J. Kluve, and A. Weber. 2010. "Active Labour Market Policy Evaluations: A Meta⊠ Analysis." *The Economic Journal* 120 (November): F452-77.

Cavallino, P., and D. Sandri., 2018. "The Expansionary Lower Bound: Contractionary Monetary Easing and the Trilemma." IMF Working Paper 18/236, International Monetary Fund, Washington, DC.

Cecchetti, S. G. 2008. "Crisis and Responses: The Federal Reserve and the Financial Crisis of 2007-2008" NBER Working Papers 14134, National Bureau of Economic Research, Cambridge, MA.

Cerutti, E., S. Claessens, and L. Laeven. 2017. "The Use and Effectiveness of Macroprudential Policies: New Evidence." *Journal of Financial Stability* 28 (February): 203-24.

Cerutti, E., C. Koch, and S. Pradhan. 2018. "The Growing Footprint of EME Banks in the International Banking System." *BIS Quarterly Review, December* 2018, Bank for International Settlements, Basel.

Cerutti, M., and H. Zhou. 2017. "The Global Banking Network in the Aftermath of the Crisis: Is There Evidence of De-globalization?" IMF Working Paper 17/232, International Monetary Fund, Washington, DC.

Cerutti, M., and H. Zhou. 2018. "The Global Banking Network: What Is Behind the Increasing Regionalization Trend?" IMF Working Paper 18/46, International Monetary Fund, Washington, DC.

Chinn, M. D., and H. Ito. 2006. "What Matters for Financial Development? Capital Controls, Institutions, and Interactions." *Journal of Development Economics* 81 (1): 163-92.

Cirera, X., and W. F. Maloney. 2017. *The Innovation Paradox: Developing-country Capabilities and the Unrealized Promise of Technological Catch-up*. Washington, DC: World Bank.

Claessens, S. 2014. "An Overview of Macroprudential Policy Tools." IMF Working Paper 14-214. International Monetary Fund, Washington, DC.

Claessens, S., G. Dell'Ariccia, I. Deniz, and L. Laeven. 2010. "Lessons and Policy Implications from the Global Financial Crisis." IMF Working Paper 10/44, International Monetary Fund, Washington, DC.

Dabla-Norris, E., M. S. Guo, M. V. Haksar, M. Kim, M. K. Kochhar, K. Wiseman, and A. Zdzienicka. 2015. *The New Normal: A Sector-Level Perspective on Productivity Trends in Advanced Economies*. Washington, DC: International Monetary Fund.

Dabla-Norris, E., G. Ho, and A. Kyobe. 2016. "Structural Reforms and Productivity Growth in Emerging Market and Developing Economies." IMF Working Paper 16/15, International Monetary Fund, Washington, DC.

Dabla-Norris, E., J. I. Kim, and K. Shirono. 2011. "Optimal Precautionary Reserves for Low-Income Countries: A Cost-Benefit Analysis." IMF Working Paper 11/249, International Monetary Fund, Washington, DC.

Das, J., A. Chowdhury, R. Hussam, and A. V. Banerjee. 2016. "The Impact of Training Informal Health Care Providers in India: A Randomized Controlled Trial." *Science* 354 (6308): 7384.

Demenet, A., M. Razafindrakoto, and F. Roubaud. 2016. "Do Informal Businesses Gain from Registration and How? Panel Data Evidence from Vietnam." *World Development* 84 (August): 326-41.

Demirgüç-Kunt, A., L. Klapper, D. Singer, S. Ansar, and J. Hess. 2018. *The Global Findex Database 2017: Measuring Financial Inclusion and the Fintech Revolution*. Washington, DC: World Bank.

Dervis, K. 2016. *Reflections on Progress: Essays on the Global Political Economy*. Brookings Institution Press.

De Vaal, A., and W. Ebben. 2011. "Institutions and the Relation between Corruption and Economic Growth." *Review of Development Economics* 15 (1): 108-23.

Didier, T., M. A. Kose, F. Ohnsorge, and L. S. Ye. 2015. "Slowdown in Emerging Markets: Rough Patch or Prolonged Weakness?" Policy Research Note 15/04, World Bank, Washington, DC.

Dijkman, M. 2015. "Monitoring Financial Stability in Developing and Emerging Economies: Practical Guidance for Conducting Macroprudential Analysis." Policy Research Working Paper 7248, World Bank, Washington, DC.

Dincer, N. N., and B. Eichengreen. 2014. "Central Bank Transparency and Independence: Updates and New Measures." *International Journal of Central Banking* 10 (1): 189-259.

Divanbeigi, R., and R. Ramalho. 2015. "Business Regulations and Growth." Policy Research Working Paper 7299, World Bank, Washington, DC.

Djankov, S., D. Georgieva, and R. Ramalho. 2018. "Business Regulations and Poverty." *Economics Letters* 165 (April): 82-87.

Dollar, D. 2004. "Globalization, Poverty, and Inequality Since 1980." Policy Research Working Paper 3333, World Bank, Washington, DC.

Dollar, D. 2016. *China's Engagement with Africa: From Natural Resources to Human Resources.* Washington, DC: Brookings Institution.

Égert, B. 2018. "The Quantification of Structural Reforms: Extending the Framework to Emerging Market Economies." CESifo Working Paper 6921, Center for Economic Studies and Ifo Institute, Munich.

Essl, S., S. K. Celik, P. Kirby, and A. Proite. 2019. "Debt in Low-Income Countries: Evolution, Implications, and Remedies." Policy Research Working Paper 8794, World Bank, Washington, DC.

Feyen, E., N. Fiess, I. Z. Huertas, and L. Lambert. 2017. "Which Emerging Markets and Developing Economies face Corporate Balance Sheet Vulnerabilities? A Novel Monitoring Framework." Policy Research Working Paper 8198, World Bank, Washington, DC.

Forbes, K. J. 2007. "The Microeconomic Evidence on Capital Controls: No Free Lunch." In *Capital Controls and Capital Flows in Emerging Economies: Policies, Practices and Consequences,* 171-202. Chicago: University of Chicago Press.

Forbes, K., M. Fratzscher, T. Kostka, and R. Straub. 2016. "Bubble Thy Neighbour: Portfolio Effects and Externalities from Capital Controls." *Journal of International Economics* 99 (March): 85-104.

Frankel, J. A., C. A. Vegh, and G. Vuletin. 2013. "On Graduation from Fiscal Procyclicality." *Journal of Development Economics* 100 (1): 32-47.

Gadanecz, B., and K. Jayaram. 2015. *Macroprudential Policy Frameworks, Instruments and Indicators: A Review.* Basel: Bank for International Settlements.

Gaspar, V., M. Obstfeld, and R. Sahay. 2016. "Macroeconomic Management When Policy Space Is Constrained: A Comprehensive, Consistent, and Coordinated Approach to Economic Policy." IMF Staff Discussion Note 16/09, International Monetary Fund, Washington, DC.

Gerlach, S., A. Giovannini, C. Tille, and J. Viñals. 2009. *Are the Golden Days of Banking Over? The Crisis and the Challenges.* Geneva Reports on the World Economy 10. Geneva: International Center for Monetary and Banking Studies.

Gertler, P., and C. Vermeersch. 2012. "Using Performance Incentives to Improve Health Outcomes." Policy Research Working Paper 6100, World Bank, Washington, DC.

Ghosh, M. A. R., M. J. D. Ostry, and M. S. Qureshi. 2017. "Managing the Tide: How Do Emerging Markets Respond to Capital Flows?" IMF Working Paper 17/69, International Monetary Fund, Washington, DC.

Gopinath, G. 2017. "Rethinking Macroeconomic Policy: International Economy Issues." Paper presented at conference "Rethinking Macroeconomic Policy," Peterson Institute for International Economics, Washington, DC, October 12–13.

Ha, J., A. Ivanova, P. Montiel, and P. Pedroni. 2019. "Inflation in Low-Income Countries." Policy Research Working Paper 8934, World Bank, Washington, DC.

Ha, J., M. A. Kose, and F. Ohnsorge, eds. 2019. *Inflation in Emerging and Developing Economies: Evolution, Drivers, and Policies.* Washington, DC: World Bank.

Hagedorn, M., I. Manovskii, and K. Mitman. 2019. "The Fiscal Multiplier." NBER Working Paper 25571, National Bureau of Economic Research, Cambridge, MA.

Haggard, S., and L. Tiede. 2011. "The Rule of Law and Economic Growth: Where Are We?" *World Development* 39 (5): 673-85.

Hallegatte, S., J. Rentschler, and J. Rozenberg. 2019. *Lifelines: The Resilient Infrastructure Opportunity*. Washington, DC: World Bank.

Hausmann, R., J. Hwang, and D. Rodrik. 2007. "What You Export Matters." *Journal of Economic Growth* 12 (1): 1-25.

Heathcote, J., and F. Perri. 2016. "On the Desirability of Capital Controls." *IMF Economic Review* 64 (1): 75-102.

Hesse, H. 2008. "Export Diversification and Economic Growth." Working Paper 21, Commission on Growth and Development, World Bank, Washington, DC.

Hodge, A., S. Shankar, D. S. Rao, and A. Duhs. 2011. "Exploring the Links Between Corruption and Growth." *Review of Development Economics* 15 (3): 474-90.

Hofmann, C., A. Osnago, and M. Ruta. 2017. *Horizontal Depth: A New Database on the Content of Preferential Trade Agreements*. Washington, DC: World Bank.

Horn, S., C. M. Reinhart, and C. Trebesch. 2019. "China's Overseas Lending." NBER Working Paper 26050, National Bureau of Economic Research, Cambridge, MA.

Hsieh, C. T., E. Hurst, C. I. Jones, and P. J. Klenow. 2013. "The Allocation of Talent and U.S. Economic Growth." NBER Working Paper 18693, National Bureau of Economic Research, Cambridge, MA.

Huidrom, R., M. A. Kose, J. J. Lim, and F. Ohnsorge. 2016. "Do Fiscal Multipliers Depend on Fiscal Positions?" Policy Research Working Paper 7724, World Bank, Washington, DC.

Huidrom, R., M. A. Kose, J. J. Lim, and F. L. Ohnsorge. 2019. "Why Do Fiscal Multipliers Depend on Fiscal Positions?" *Journal of Monetary Economics*. Advance online publication. https://doi.org/10.1016/j.jmoneco.2019.03.004.

Huidrom, R., M. A. Kose, and F. Ohnsorge, 2018. "Challenges of Fiscal Policy in Emerging and Developing Economies." *Emerging Markets Finance and Trade* 54 (9): 1927-45.

IFC (International Finance Corporation). 2018. *Corporate Governance of State-Owned Enterprises*. Washington DC: International Finance Corporation.

ILO (International Labour Organization). 2019. *100 Years of Social Protection: The Road to Universal Social Protection Systems and Floors*. Geneva: International Labour Organization.

IMF (International Monetary Fund). 2011. "Assessing Reserve Adequacy." Policy Paper, International Monetary Fund, Washington, DC.

IMF (International Monetary Fund). 2012. "The Liberalization and Management of Capital Flows—An Institutional View." Policy Paper, International Monetary Fund, Washington, DC.

IMF (International Monetary Fund). 2013a. "Key Aspects of Macroprudential Policy." Policy Paper, International Monetary Fund, Washington, DC.

IMF (International Monetary Fund). 2013b. "Energy Subsidy Reform: Lessons and Implications." Policy Paper, International Monetary Fund, Washington, DC.

IMF (International Monetary Fund). 2014. "Staff Guidance Note on Macroprudential Policy." Policy Paper, International Monetary Fund, Washington, DC.

IMF (International Monetary Fund).2015a. "Making Public Investment More Efficient." Policy Paper, International Monetary Fund, Washington, DC.

IMF (International Monetary Fund). 2015b. "Assessing Reserve Adequacy—Specific Proposals." Policy Paper, International Monetary Fund, Washington, DC.

IMF (International Monetary Fund). 2016. "Capital Flows—Review of Experience With the Institutional View." Policy Paper, International Monetary Fund, Washington, DC.

IMF (International Monetary Fund). 2017. "Increasing the Resilience to Large and Volatile Capital Flows: The Role of Macroprudential Policies." Policy Paper, International Monetary Fund, Washington, DC.

IMF (International Monetary Fund). 2018a. "IMF 2018 Taxonomy of Capital Flow Management Measures." International Monetary Fund, Washington, DC.

IMF (International Monetary Fund). 2018b. "The IMF's Institutional View of Capital Flows in Practice." International Monetary Fund, Washington, DC.

IMF (International Monetary Fund). 2019a. "Fiscal Transparency Initiative: Integration of Natural Resource Management Issues." Policy Paper, International Monetary Fund, Washington, DC.

IMF (International Monetary Fund). 2019b. "Reigniting Growth in Low-Income and Emerging Market Economies: What Role Can Structural Reforms Play?" In *World Economic Outlook: Global Manufacturing Downturn, Rising Trade Barriers*. October. Washington, DC: International Monetary Fund.

IMF, FSB, and BIS (International Monetary Fund, Financial Stability Board, and Bank for International Settlements). 2016. "Elements of Effective Macroprudential Policies: Lessons from International Experience." Joint publication.

Jaramillo, L., C. Mulas-Granados, and J. T. Jalles. 2017. "Debt Spikes, Blind Spots, and Financial Stress." *International Journal of Finance & Economics* 22 (4): 421-37.

Jeanne, O., and R. Ranciere. 2006. "The Optimal Level of International Reserves for Emerging Market Countries: Formulas and Applications." IMF Working Paper 6/229, International Monetary Fund, Washington, DC.

Jeanne, O., and R. Ranciere. 2011. "The Optimal Level of International Reserves for Emerging Market Countries: A New Formula and Some Applications." *The Economic Journal* 121 (555): 905-30.

Joyce, R., and X. Xu. 2019. "Inequalities in the Twenty-first Century: Introducing the IFS Deaton Review." Institute for Fiscal Studies, London.

Keller, L. 2018. "Capital Controls and Risk Misallocation: Evidence from a Natural Experiment." https://rodneywhitecenter.wharton.upenn.edu/wp-content/uploads/2019/12/10-19.Keller.pdf.

Kemoe, L., and Z. Zhan. 2018. "Fiscal Transparency, Borrowing Costs, and Foreign Holdings of Sovereign Debt. IMF Working Paper 18/189, International Monetary Fund, Washington, DC.

King, R. G., and R. Levine. 1993. "Finance and Growth: Schumpeter Might be Right." *The Quarterly Journal of Economics* 108 (3): 717-37.

Kirkpatrick, C. 2014. "Assessing the Impact of Regulatory Reform in Developing Countries." *Public Administration and Development* 34 (3): 162-68.

Kose, M. A., S. Kurlat, F. Ohnsorge, and N. Sugawara. 2017. "A Cross-Country Database of Fiscal Space." Policy Research Working Paper 8157, World Bank, Washington, DC.

Kose, A., H. Matsuoka, U. G. Panizza, and D. L. Vorisek. 2019. "Inflation Expectations: Review and Evidence." Policy Research Working Paper 8785, World Bank, Washington, DC.

Krane, J., and S. Y. Hung. 2016. "Energy Subsidy Reform in the Persian Gulf: The End of the Big Oil Giveaway." Issue Brief, Baker Institute for Public Policy, Rice University, Houston, TX.

Krishnamurti, D., and Y. C. Lee. 2014. *Macroprudential Policy Framework: A Practice Guide.* World Bank, Washington DC.

Kuttner, K. N., and I. Shim. 2016. "Can Non-Interest Rate Policies Stabilize Housing Markets? Evidence from a Panel of 57 Economies." *Journal of Financial Stability* 26 (October): 31-44.

La Porta, R., and A. Shleifer. 2014. "Informality and Development." *Journal of Economic Perspectives* 28 (3): 109-26.

Lawless, M. 2013. "Do Complicated Tax Systems Prevent Foreign Direct Investment?" *Economica* 80 (317): 1–22.

Levine, R. 2006. "Finance and Growth: The Theory, Evidence, and Mechanisms." In *Handbook of Economic Growth,* edited by P. Aghion and S. Durlauf. North Holland: Elsevier.

Levine, R., N. Loayza, and T. Beck. 2000. "Finance and the Sources of Growth." *Journal of Financial Economics* 58 (1-2): 261–300.

Levine, R., and S. Zervos. 1998. "Stock Markets, Banks, and Economic Growth." *American Economic Review* 88 (3): 537-58.

Lim, C., F. Columba, A. Costa, P. Kongsamut, A. Otani, M. Saiyid, T. Wezel, and X. Wu. 2011. "Macroprudential Policy: What Instruments and How to Use Them? Lessons from Country Experiences." IMF Working Paper 11/238, International Monetary Fund, Washington, DC.

Loayza, N. 2018. "Informality: Why Is It So Widespread and How Can It Be Reduced?" Research & Policy Brief 20, World Bank Malaysia Hub, Kuala Lumpur.

Loayza, N., A. M. Oviedo, and L. Servén. 2005. "The Impact of Regulation on Growth and Informality: Cross-Country Evidence." Policy Research Working Paper 3623, World Bank, Washington, DC.

Loayza, N., and L. Servén. 2010. *Business Regulation and Economic Performance.* Washington, DC: World Bank.

Maeda, A., E. Araujo, C. Cashin, J. Harris, N. Ikegami, and M. R. Reich. 2014. *Universal Health Coverage for Inclusive and Sustainable Development: A Synthesis of 11 Country Case Studies.* Washington, DC: World Bank.

Masciandaro, D. 2009. "Politicians and Financial Supervision Unification Outside the Central Bank: Why Do they Do It?" *Journal of Financial Stability* 5 (2): 124-46.

Maloney, W. F., and G. Nayyar. 2018. "Industrial Policy, Information, and Government Capacity." *The World Bank Research Observer* 33 (2): 189-217.

McIntyre, A., M. X. Li, K. Wang, and H. Yun. 2018. "Economic Benefits of Export Diversification in Small States." IMF Working Paper 18/86, International Monetary Fund, Washington, DC.

Melecky, M., and A. M. Podpiera. 2010. "Macroprudential Stress-testing Practices of Central Banks in Central and South Eastern Europe: An Overview and Challenges Ahead." Policy Research Working Paper 5434, World Bank, Washington DC.

Melecky, M., and A. M. Podpiera. 2015. "Placing Bank Supervision in the Central Bank: Implications for Financial Stability Based on Evidence from the Global Crisis." Policy Research Working Paper 730, World Bank, Washington DC.

Melitz, M. J. 2003. "The Impact of Trade on Intra-Industry Reallocations and Aggregate Industry Productivity." *Econometrica* 71 (6): 1695-725.

Mishkin, F. S. 2008. "Does Stabilizing Inflation Contribute to Stabilizing Economic Activity?" NBER Working Paper 13970, National Bureau of Economic Research, Cambridge, MA.

Moldovan, I., S. C. S. Yang, and L. F. Zanna. 2019. "Optimal Fiscal Spending and Reserve Accumulation Policies Under Volatile Aid." IMF Working Paper 19/126, International Monetary Fund, Washington, DC.

Montes, G. C., J. C. A. Bastos, and A. J. de Oliveira. 2019. "Fiscal Transparency, Government Effectiveness and Government Spending Efficiency: Some International Evidence Based on Panel Data Approach." *Economic Modelling* 79 (June): 211-25.

Morales, L., and C. Medina. 2017. "Assessing the Effect of Payroll Taxes on Formal Employment: The Case of the 2012 Tax Reform in Colombia." *Economía* 18 (1): 75-124.

OECD (Organisation for Economic Cooperation and Development). 2018. "OECD on the Crisis: 10 Years, 10 Stories." *OECD Observer,* September 2018. http://oecdobserver.org/news/fullstory.php/aid/6067/OECD_on_the_crisis_and_after:_10_years,_10_stories.html.

Ohnsorge, F., and S. Yu. 2016. "Recent Credit Surge in Historical Context." Policy Research Working Paper 7704, World Bank, Washington, DC.

Ostry J. D. 2015. "Managing Capital Flows — Capital Controls and Foreign Exchange Intervention." In *Taming Capital Flows: Capital Account Management in an Era of Globalization,* edited by J. E. Stiglitz and R. S. Gürkaynak. London: Palgrave Macmillan.

Ostry, J. D., A. Berg, and S. Kothari. 2018. "Growth-Equity Trade-Offs in Structural Reforms." IMF Working Paper 18/5, International Monetary Fund, Washington, DC.

Palmer, J., and C. Cerutti. 2009. "Is There a Need to Rethink the Supervisory Process?" Discussion paper presented at "Reforming Financial Regulation and Supervision: Going Back to Basics," Madrid, June 15.

Paunov, C. 2016. "Corruption's Asymmetric Impacts on Firm Innovation." *Journal of Development Economics* 118 (January): 216-31.

Pigato, M. A. 2019. *Fiscal Policies for Development and Climate Action.* Washington, DC: World Bank.

Piketty, T., E. Saez, and S. Stantcheva. 2014. "Optimal Taxation of Top Labor Incomes: A Tale of Three Elasticities." *American Economic Journal: Economic Policy* 6 (1): 230-71.

Presbitero, A. F. 2016. "Too Much and Too Fast? Public Investment Scaling-Up and Absorptive Capacity." *Journal of Development Economics* 120 (May): 17-31.

Ramey, V. A. 2019. "Ten Years After the Financial Crisis: What Have We Learned From the Renaissance in Fiscal Research?" *Journal of Economic Perspectives* 33 (2): 89-114.

Rashid, A., and M. Intartaglia. 2017. "Financial Development—Does It Lessen Poverty?" *Journal of Economic Studies* 44 (1): 69-86.

Reinhart, C., K. Rogoff, and M. Savastano. 2003. "Debt Intolerance." *Brookings Papers on Economic Activity* 1:1-74.

Rentschler, J., and M. Bazilian. 2017a. "Policy Monitor—Principles for Designing Effective Fossil Fuel Subsidy Reforms." *Review of Environmental Economics and Policy* 11 (1): 138-55.

Rentschler, J., and M. Bazilian. 2017b. "Reforming Fossil Fuel Subsidies: Drivers, Barriers and the State of Progress." *Climate Policy* 17 (7): 891-914.

Rey, H. 2015. "Dilemma Not Trilemma: The Global Financial Cycle and Monetary Policy Independence." NBER Working Paper 21162, National Bureau of Economic Research, Cambridge, MA.

Rocha, R., G. Ulyssea, and R. Rachter. 2018. "Do Lower Taxes Reduce Informality? Evidence from Brazil." *Journal of Development Economics* 134 (September): 28-49.

Rodrik, D., 2008. *One Economics, Many Recipes: Globalization, Institutions, and Economic Growth.* Princeton, NJ: Princeton University Press.

Rozenberg, J., and M. Fay. 2019. *Beyond the Gap: How Countries Can Afford the Infrastructure They Need While Protecting the Planet.* Washington, DC: World Bank.

Schaechter, A., T. Kinda, N. T. Budina, and A. Weber. 2012. "Fiscal Rules in Response to the Crisis-Toward the 'Next-Generation' Rules: A New Dataset." IMF Working Paper12/187, International Monetary Fund, Washington, DC.

Shleifer, A., and R. Vishny. 1998. *The Grabbing Hand: Government Pathologies and Their Cures* Cambridge, MA: Harvard University Press.

Stocker, M., J. Baffes, J., Y. M. Some, D. Vorisek, C. M. Wheeler. 2018. "The 2014-16 Oil Price Collapse in Retrospect: Sources and Implications." Policy Research Working Paper 8419, World Bank, Washington, DC.

Sung, M. J., R. Awasthi, and H. C. Lee. 2017. "Can Tax Incentives for Electronic Payments Reduce the Shadow Economy? Korea's Attempt to Reduce Underreporting in Retail Businesses." Policy Research Working Paper 7936, World Bank, Washington, DC.

Tebaldi, E., and R. Mohan. 2010. "Institutions and Poverty." *Journal of Development Studies* 46 (6): 1047-66.

Topalova, P., and A. Khandelwal. 2011. "Trade Liberalization and Firm Productivity: The Case of India." *Review of Economics and Statistics* 93 (3): 995-1009.

UNCTAD (United Nations Conference on Trade and Development). 2014. *Investment in SGDs: An Action Plan, World Investment Report.* New York: United Nations.

UNCTAD (United Nations Conference on Trade and Development). 2019. *SDG Investment Monitor.* New York: United Nations.

United Nations. 2019. "Follow-Up Note on the Role of Taxation and Domestic Resource Mobilization in Achieving the Sustainable Development Goals." Committee of Experts on International Cooperation in Tax Matters, United Nations, New York.

Ulyssea, G. 2018. "Firms, Informality, and Development: Theory and Evidence from Brazil." *American Economic Review* 108 (8): 2015-47.

Vandenbussche, J., U. Vogel, and E. Detragiache. 2015. "Macroprudential Policies and Housing Prices: A New Database and Empirical Evidence for Central, Eastern, and Southeastern Europe." *Journal of Money, Credit and Banking* 47 (S1): 343-77.

Weber, A. 2012. "Stock-Flow Adjustments and Fiscal Transparency: A Cross-Country Comparison." IMF Working Paper 12/39, International Monetary Fund, Washington, DC.

WHO (World Health Organization). 2008. *Safer Water, Better Health: Costs, Benefits and Sustainability of Interventions to Protect and Promote Health*. Geneva: World Health Organization.

World Bank. 2007a. *Managing Public Debt: From Diagnostics to Reform Implementation*. Washington, DC: World Bank.

World Bank. 2007b. *Developing the Domestic Government Debt Market: From Diagnostics to Reform Implementation*. Washington, DC: World Bank.

World Bank. 2008. "Guide to the Debt Management Performance Assessment Tool (DEMPA)." World Bank, Washington, DC.

World Bank. 2012. *Beyond the Annual Budget: Global Experience with Medium Term Expenditure Frameworks*. Washington, DC: World Bank.

World Bank. 2013. *Global Financial Development Report: Rethinking the Role of the State in Finance*. Washington, DC: World Bank.

World Bank. 2014a. *Global Financial Development Report: Financial Inclusion*. Washington, DC: World Bank.

World Bank. 2014b. *Turning Down the Heat: Confronting the New Climate Normal*. Washington, DC: World Bank.

World Bank. 2015a. *Global Economic Prospects: Having Fiscal Space and Using It*. January. Washington, DC: World Bank.

World Bank. 2015b. *Global Financial Development Report 2015-2016: Long-Term Finance*. Washington, DC: World Bank.

World Bank. 2016a. *World Development Report: Digital Dividends*. Washington, DC: World Bank.

World Bank. 2016b. *Global Monitoring Report 2015/2016: Development Goals in an Era of Demographic Change*. Washington, DC: World Bank

World Bank. 2017a. *Gulf Economic Monitor: Sustaining Fiscal Reforms in the Long-Term*. June. Washington, DC: World Bank.

World Bank 2017b. *World Development Report: Governance and Law*. Washington, DC: World Bank.

World Bank. 2017c. *Global Economic Prospects: Weak Investment in Uncertain Times*. January. Washington, DC: World Bank.

World Bank. 2017d. *Climate and Disaster Resilient Transport in Small Island Developing States: A Call for Action*. October. Washington, DC: World Bank.

World Bank. 2018a. *Global Financial Development Report: Bankers without Borders*. Washington, DC: World Bank.

World Bank. 2018b. *Energy Sector Management Assistance Program Annual Report 2018*. Washington, DC: World Bank.

World Bank. 2018c. *World Development Report: Learning to Realize Education's Promise*. Washington, DC: World Bank.

World Bank. 2018d. *The Human Capital Project*. World Bank, Washington, DC.

World Bank. 2018e. *Global Economic Prospects: Broad-Based Upturn, but for How Long?* January. World Bank, Washington, DC.

World Bank. 2019a. *World Development Report. The Changing Nature of Work*. Washington, DC: World Bank.

World Bank. 2019b. *Global Economic Prospects: Darkening Skies*. January. Washington, DC: World Bank.

World Bank. 2019c. *Doing Business: Training for Reform*. January. Washington, DC: World Bank.

World Bank. 2019d. *Mainstreaming Disruptive Technologies at the World Bank Group*. January. Washington, DC: World Bank.

World Bank. 2019e. *Harvesting Prosperity: Technological Progress and Productivity Growth in Agriculture*. January. Washington, DC: World Bank.

World Bank. 2020a. *World Development Report: Trading for Development in the Age of Global Value Chains*. Washington, DC: World Bank.

World Bank. 2020b. *Global Financial Development Report 2020: Bank Regulation and Supervision a Decade after the Global Recession*. Washington, DC: World Bank.

World Bank and IMF (International Monetary Fund). 2001. *Developing Government Bond Markets: A Handbook*. Washington, DC: World Bank and International Monetary Fund.

World Bank and IMF (International Monetary Fund). 2003. *Guidelines for Public Debt Management*. Washington, DC: International Monetary Fund.

World Bank and IMF (International Monetary Fund). 2009a. "Developing a Medium-Term Debt Management Strategy (MTDS) Guidance Note for Country Authorities." World Bank and International Monetary Fund, Washington, DC.

World Bank and IMF (International Monetary Fund). 2009b. "Managing Public Debt: Formulating Strategies and Strengthening Institutional Capacity." World Bank and International Monetary Fund, Washington, DC.

World Bank and IMF (International Monetary Fund). 2014. "Revised Guidelines for Public Debt Management." IMF Policy Paper, International Monetary Fund, Washington, DC.

WTO (World Trade Organization). 2019. "Report on G20 Trade Measures: Mid-October 2018 to Mid-May 2019." World Trade Organization, Geneva.

Zhang, L., and E. Zoli. 2016. "Leaning Against the Wind: Macroprudential Policy in Asia." *Journal of Asian Economics* 42 (February): 33-52.

PART IV

Implications for the World Bank Group

"Nirvana" is defined as the state of freedom from suffering. For emerging markets, that state is over; but, in some cases, their citizens—still feeling rich from cheap money and high export prices—have no inkling of the suffering that may be upon them. For the sake of political stability, governments would be well advised to inform them.

Andres Velasco (2013)

Dean of the School of Public Policy
London School of Economics and Political Science

CHAPTER 8

The Role of the World Bank Group

The World Bank Group's response to the 2009 global recession was unprecedented in its scale. Annual average financing commitments nearly doubled between fiscal years 2007/08 and 2008/09 and between fiscal years 2009/10 and 2010/11, and reached more than 100 countries, with the largest increases in Latin America and the Caribbean and in Europe and Central Asia. Lending prioritized support for social protection, financial and infrastructure development, and fiscal management. The World Bank Group supplemented traditional instruments such as investment lending and development policy lending with more flexible facilities that supported crisis-impaired activities, including trade finance and infrastructure investment. Since then, the World Bank Group has capitalized on its crisis experience. It has expanded its global economic surveillance capabilities to better identify emerging financial and macroeconomic risks, it has rebuilt its capital, and its operating model has become more flexible and adaptable to the needs of its member countries. The World Bank Group's current policy toolkit contains a comprehensive set of instruments to help countries reduce risk and mitigate the consequences of crises, and to build longer-term structural resilience.

Introduction

The global financial crisis and the subsequent 2009 global recession not only adversely affected global growth and poverty but also demonstrated the limitations and challenges of unilateral responses by national governments (chapter 7). The global recession required rapid and targeted responses by international financial institutions (IFIs)—in particular, it led the World Bank Group to provide unprecedented financing support and advisory services to its member countries.

The previous chapters discussed the broad range of factors that contributed to the global recession and the new vulnerabilities that have been building since then. In emerging market and developing economies (EMDEs), fiscal buffers have eroded, structural changes in financial markets have created new challenges, and reform momentum has weakened after an initial postcrisis burst. Meanwhile, EMDEs face heightened risks from global policy uncertainty, trade tensions, weak growth in advanced economies, and bouts of volatility in global financial markets. This confluence of risks and vulnerabilities raises concerns about the possibility of a global downturn and highlights the continued importance of IFIs in preventing and mitigating economic and financial stress.

Against this backdrop, this chapter examines the following four questions:

- How did the World Bank Group respond during the global recession?

Note: This chapter was prepared by Lei Sandy Ye.

- What was the assessment of the World Bank Group's response?
- How have the World Bank Group's strategy and operating model changed since the global recession?
- What policies can the World Bank Group offer to reduce vulnerabilities and build resilience ahead of future crises?

In addressing these questions, this chapter links the World Bank Group's global recession response to the evolution of its policy toolkit in the subsequent decade. Although an exhaustive analysis of the World Bank Group's role during the global recession is beyond the scope of this chapter, it adds to a set of studies that have examined the World Bank Group's response to the global recession. Most prominently, the World Bank Group's Independent Evaluation Group (IEG) conducted two comprehensive studies that examined the response. The first described the overall response, presented an early evaluation of its effectiveness, and drew initial lessons (IEG 2011a). The second analysis, a year later, examined the effectiveness of the World Bank Group's crisis response in the areas of social protection, financial sector policies, and fiscal management (IEG 2012). These and other studies have documented that the World Bank Group largely retained its lending models and focus areas through the crisis and the subsequent global recession (Guven 2012; Hall 2015; IEG 2012).[1]

The chapter contributes to these works in three ways. First, it analyzes the World Bank Group's crisis response under the lens of the subsequent decade, a longer time span than the existing work. Second, it analyzes how the global recession affected World Bank Group operations. It documents that, while the institution demonstrated a consistent overall policy position that prioritized its traditional areas of expertise, such as social protection, it has also in the last decade made refinements to its strategy and operating model that were motivated by its experience responding to the global recession. Third, the chapter shows that, partly drawing on the lessons from the global recession response, the World Bank Group's current crisis-response strategy in financing and advisory functions combines crisis risk and impact mitigation with longer-term efforts to build structural resilience.

The chapter documents the following findings.

- World Bank Group's financing during the global recession was unprecedented in volume. Financing commitments nearly doubled in real terms (2010 U.S. dollars), from an annual average of $37 billion during fiscal years (FY) 2007/08 and 2008/09 to an annual average of $66 billion during FY2009/10-FY2010/11. This World Bank Group financing was larger than during earlier crises, with commitments

[1] Guven (2012) argues that the thematic distribution of World Bank lending during the crisis was similar to precrisis patterns. Hall (2015) documents that World Bank Group lending aggressively increased its focus on social protection during the crisis, but that its objectives had not changed significantly from the precrisis period. IEG (2012) shows that precrisis lending patterns were an important determinant of lending patterns in the immediate aftermath of the crisis. The IEG is also currently preparing an evaluation of World Bank Group support for policies to address ex ante vulnerabilities between FY2010 and FY2018 (IEG 2019a).

made to more than 100 economies. The World Bank Group's disbursements during the crisis were also larger than those of any other major IFI.

- The forms of World Bank Group financing were diverse across its multiple entities. Lending by the International Bank for Reconstruction and Development (IBRD) nearly tripled, whereas that of the International Development Association (IDA) increased by about 20 percent. The support of the International Finance Corporation (IFC) and Multilateral Investment Guarantee Agency (MIGA) did not surge, but the former provided investments and the latter provided financial guarantees targeted at sectors and regions that were especially hard-hit by the global recession.[2]

- Lending during the global recession increased the most for Latin America and the Caribbean (LAC) and Europe and Central Asia (ECA), the two most crisis-affected regions. About one-fifth of World Bank (comprising the IBRD and IDA) lending was distributed to low-income countries (LICs), equivalent to about 1 percent of their gross domestic product (GDP). Upper-middle-income countries (UMICs) and lower-middle-income countries (LMICs) each received about 40 percent of World Bank crisis commitments, but these represented much smaller shares of recipient GDP than was the case for LICs.

- As in previous global crises, the World Bank Group prioritized its lending in the areas of social protection, infrastructure investment, fiscal management, and financial sector development. Although investment lending served as the primary lending tool during the global recession, the World Bank Group provided development policy lending more heavily than during noncrisis periods because of its faster pace of deployment. It also adopted crisis-specific facilities in targeted areas, such as trade finance and infrastructure investment, where the World Bank Group has long-standing expertise.

- The World Bank Group has built upon its experience during the global recession in its subsequent work. It has improved its monitoring and surveillance of global macroeconomic and financial developments, allowing it to more effectively flag risks in the world economy. It has completed two rounds of global campaigns to improve its capital adequacy, partly to make it better prepared for future crises. It has refined its operating model by introducing new crisis response facilities and implementing a more coordinated Bank-wide strategy in its financing and advisory activities, helping to enhance its ability to respond quickly and flexibly should a future crisis arise. The World Bank Group has an extensive set of both traditional and new support instruments to help members reduce crisis risk and impact and to build longer-term resilience against future crises. These instruments constitute an important strategic capability that better enables it to advance its twin goals of poverty reduction and shared prosperity, including by mitigating the reversals that occur during economic downturns.

[2] Unlike traditional lending, MIGA provides political risk insurance guarantees or credit enhancements to investors and lenders in order to promote cross-border investment.

Response to the global recession

During the global recession, the World Bank Group made an unprecedented volume of loans to EMDEs, nearly doubling its annual financing commitments from the precrisis period and reaching more than 100 member countries.

Magnitude. The World Bank Group financing response to the global recession was notably larger than in previous crises. In real terms, the World Bank Group's annual financing commitments nearly doubled during the global recession, from an average of $37 billion (2010 U.S. dollars) during FY2007/08-FY2008/09 to an average of $66 billion during FY2009/10-FY2010/11, and the World Bank Group registered the highest financing disbursements among all major IFIs (IEG 2011a).[3]

The World Bank Group's crisis financing took diverse forms across the institution's multiple entities. The sharpest increase in lending occurred at the IBRD, where commitments nearly tripled from about an annual average of $14 billion during FY2007/08-FY2008/09 to $39 billion during FY2009/10-FY2010/11 (figure 8.1). Lending by IDA increased less sharply, by about 20 percent, given its less elastic funding envelope. Investments from the IFC and guarantees from MIGA increased less strongly but shifted toward targeted interventions in specific countries or sectors that were particularly affected by the global recession. For example, the IFC significantly shifted its investments toward its Global Trade Finance Program, which provided risk guarantees to mitigate counterparty risk for banks' trade transactions (IEG 2011a). MIGA issued guarantees to provide political risk insurance and facilitate cross-border payments of financial institutions, especially those in the ECA region, one of the hardest-hit regions during the global recession. MIGA also relied heavily on its Global Financial Sector Initiative to issue financial sector guarantees, providing liquidity to subsidiaries of financial institutions in times of stress.

As historical comparisons, during the 1997-98 Asian financial crisis, World Bank (IBRD and IDA) commitments increased from an average of $28 billion a year (2010 U.S. dollars) during FY1996-FY1997 to $38 billion a year during FY1998-FY1999—a substantial increase, but smaller than the doubling of lending in response to the 2009 global recession (figure 8.1). During the 1980s—the decade of the Latin American debt crises—the World Bank's annual increases in lending have not exceeded 12 percent. As lending commitments rose during the global recession, the average size of World Bank projects increased sharply from a FY2003-FY2008 average of about $85 million to nearly $150 million during FY2009-FY2010. There was, in particular, a significant ramp-up in IBRD lending to EMDEs that had experienced sudden stops in capital flows.

Regions and country groups. The regions that suffered the most severe impacts from the global recession were LAC and ECA, and they received the largest shares of the

[3] World Bank Group disbursements, including from previously approved operations, also increased by about 50 percent, from an annual average of $27 billion 2010 U.S. dollars during FY2007-FY2008 to $41 billion during FY2009-FY2010.

FIGURE 8.1 World Bank Group financing during the global recession

During the global recession, the World Bank Group nearly doubled its annual lending commitments. IBRD commitments nearly tripled, whereas other World Bank Group entities provided targeted interventions. The average project size of the World Bank also increased substantially. The increase in IBRD commitments was significantly channeled to economies that experienced sudden stops in capital flows.

A. Financing across World Bank Group entities

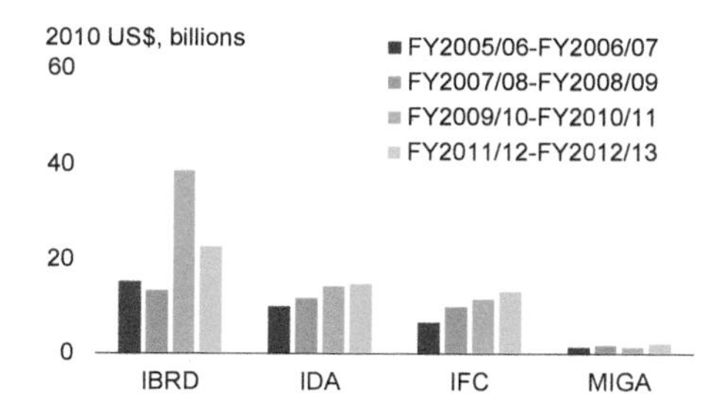

B. World Bank lending commitments

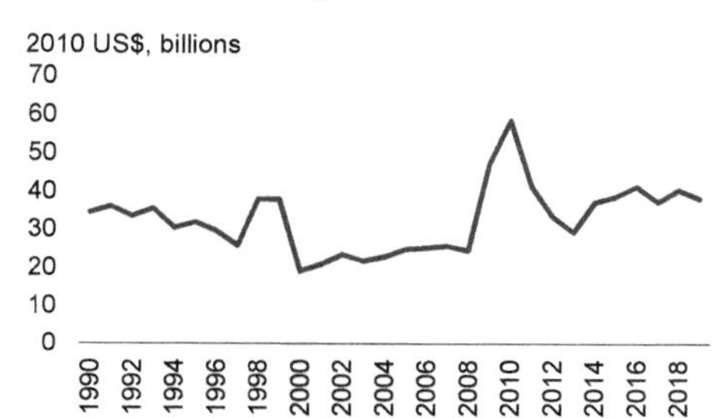

C. World Bank average project size

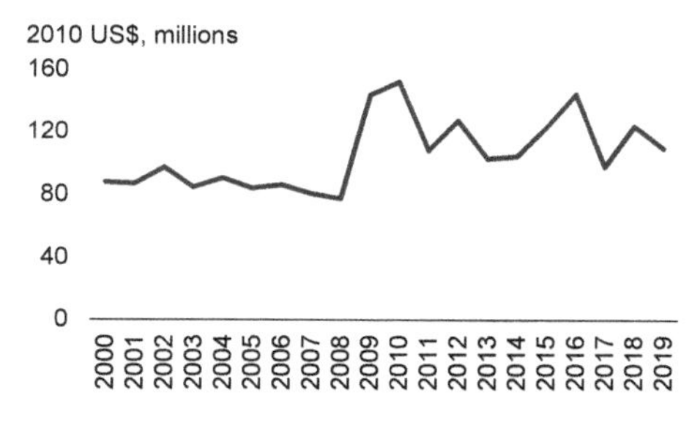

D. IBRD commitments

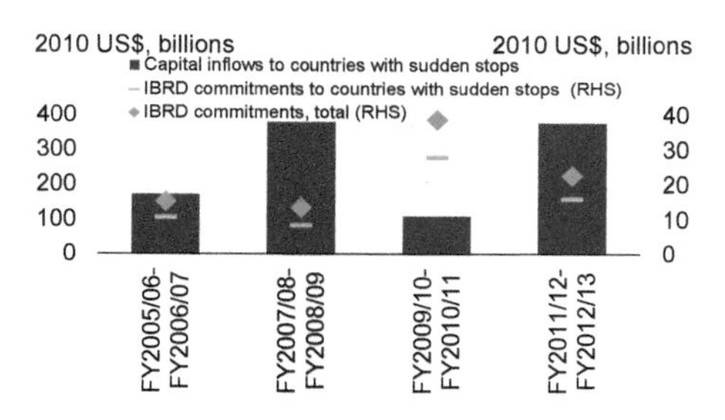

Sources: International Monetary Fund; World Bank.

Note: All years denote fiscal years (FY). IBRD = International Bank for Reconstruction and Development; IDA = International Development Association; IFC = International Finance Corporation; MIGA = Multilateral Investment Guarantee Agency. "World Bank" refers to IBRD and IDA.

A. Annual averages over the periods denoted. Data for IBRD/IDA refer to commitments. Data for IFC refer to investment commitments from own accounts. Data for MIGA refer to guarantee issuances.

B.C. Data refer to IBRD and IDA. Last observation is FY2019.

C. Ratio of total new lending commitment value to number of new projects.

D. Data refer to IBRD. Annual averages. Except for total IBRD commitments, data are based on 20 emerging market and developing economies (EMDEs) where sudden stop episodes (two standard deviations below historical mean of capital inflows) are identified either in 2008 or 2009, as defined in Forbes and Warnock (2012): Argentina, Brazil, Chile, Colombia, Guatemala, Hungary, Indonesia, India, Sri Lanka, Mexico, Malaysia, Panama, Peru, the Philippines, Poland, Romania, the Russian Federation, Thailand, Turkey, and South Africa. Capital inflows include foreign direct investment, portfolio investment, and other investment, and are presented as net inflows.

World Bank's commitments and the largest increases in commitments (figure 8.2).[4] Although lending commitments to the LAC region were the highest in dollar terms, the rise in commitments in relation to recipient GDP was the highest in ECA. In some regions (such as East Asia and Pacific [EAP]), lending occurred in conjunction with

[4] In LAC, growth declined from 6 percent in 2007 to -2 percent in 2009. In ECA, growth declined from 8 percent to -6 percent during the same period. These two regions experienced the most marked slowdowns in growth during the crisis. Similar to lending commitments, World Bank disbursements during FY2009-FY2010 were also the highest in these two regions. The IFC concentrated its investments in LAC, ECA, and Sub-Saharan Africa (SSA), whereas MIGA concentrated its guarantees in ECA.

FIGURE 8.2 Lending commitments during the global recession by region and country group

Both the levels of and increases in World Bank lending during the global recession were greatest in the LAC and ECA regions, reflecting these regions' larger exposure to the effects of the global recession. Lending to LICs constituted about one-fifth of the World Bank's FY2009/10-FY2010/11 commitments and about 1 percent of their combined GDP.

A. Commitments by region

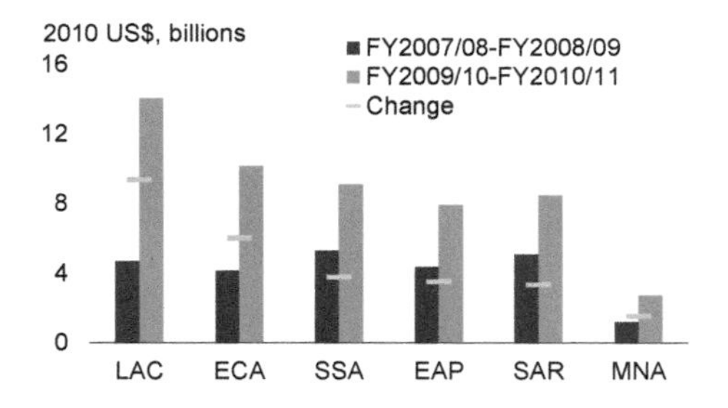

B. Commitments by region

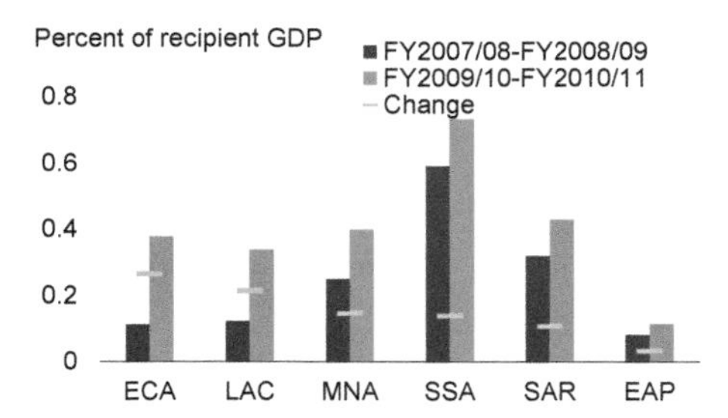

C. Commitments during FY2009/10-FY2010/11

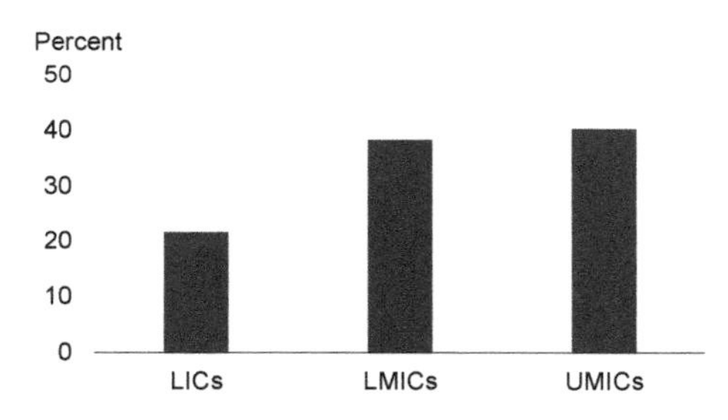

D. Commitments by recipient income level

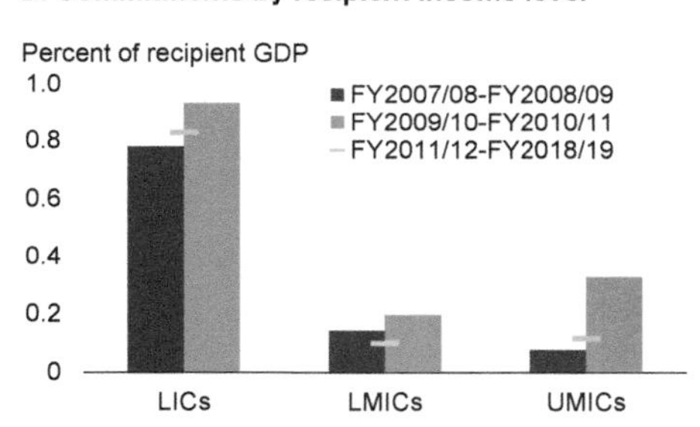

Source: World Bank.

Note: All years denote fiscal years (FY). EAP = East Asia and Pacific; ECA = Europe and Central Asia; LAC = Latin America and the Caribbean; LICs = low-income countries; LMICs = lower-middle-income countries; MNA = Middle East and North Africa; SAR = South Asia; SSA = Sub-Saharan Africa; UMICs = upper-middle-income countries.

A.B.D. Each column shows annual averages over denoted fiscal years for the IBRD and IDA.

C.D. Data refer to IBRD and IDA. Income classification as of FY2009/10. Panel C shows percent of total commitments in each income group.

regional development banks, or in some instances, in the context of International Monetary Fund (IMF) programs.

Lending commitments to LICs during the crisis constituted about one-fifth of World Bank commitments. This was considerably less than the 40 percent of commitments each to LMICs and UMICs, which had stronger financial and trade ties with the advanced economies where the crisis had originated. Relative to the size of their economies, however, lending to LICs was considerably larger (1 percent of GDP) than to middle-income economies (MICs, 0.3 percent of GDP).

Sectors. The World Bank's financial support during the crisis increased most rapidly in the financial (for example, banking), infrastructure (for example, energy and transportation), public (for example, fiscal management), and social protection sectors

FIGURE 8.3 Lending commitments during the global recession by sector and instrument

The largest increases in World Bank lending commitments were in the financial, energy, public, and social protection sectors. Investment lending remained the main form of lending during the global recession. Because development policy lending can be disbursed more quickly, however, its share of lending increased during the global recession, as it did after the Asian financial crisis.

A. Commitments by sector

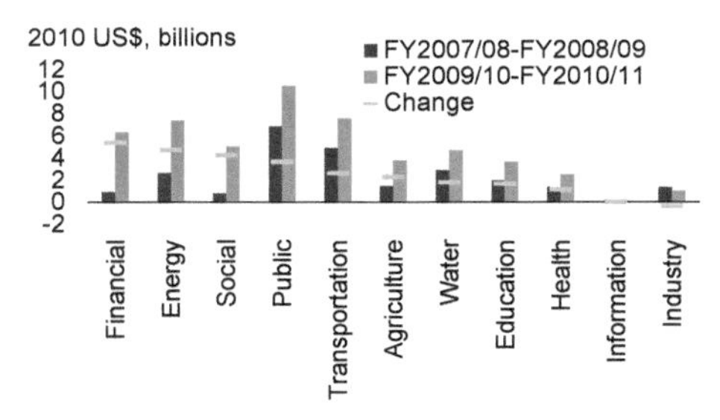

B. Share of commitments by sector

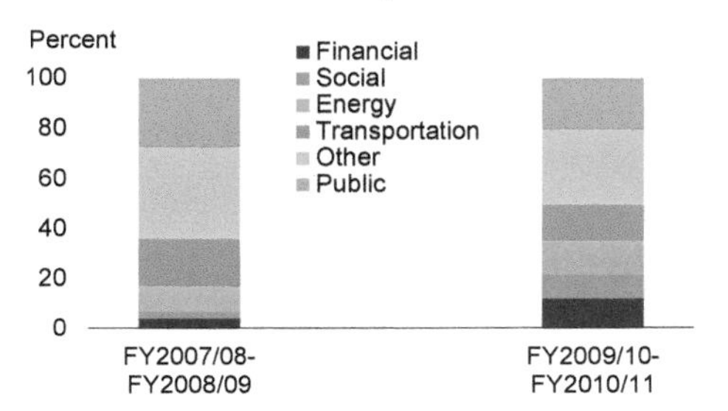

C. Commitments by financing instruments

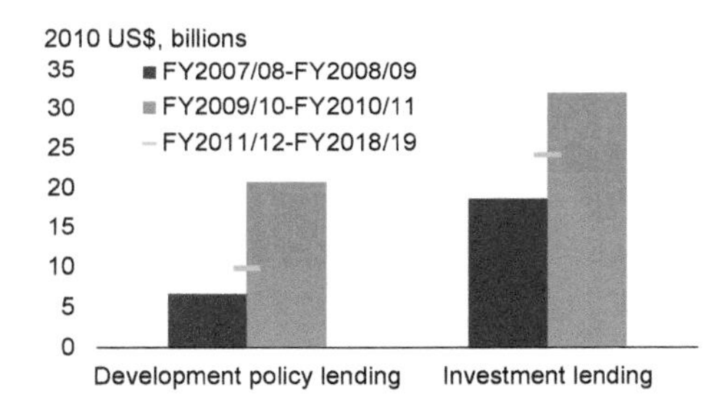

D. Share of development policy lending commitments

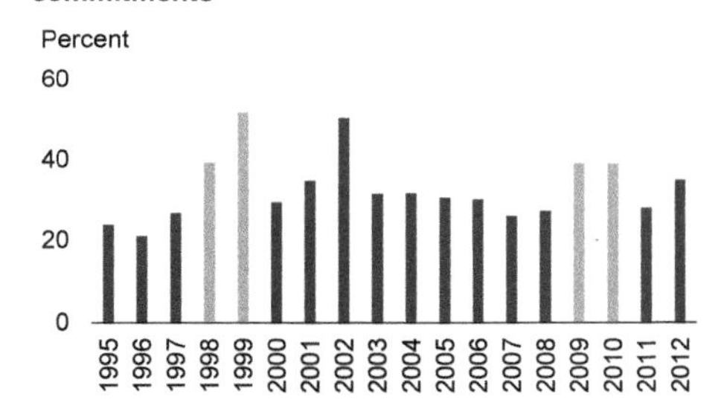

Source: World Bank.

Note: Data refer to the International Bank for Reconstruction and Development and the International Development Association. All years denote fiscal years (FY).

A.B. "Public" denotes reforms in the public sector. Columns in A show annual average commitments.

C.D. Development policy lending provides budget support to governments or their subdivisions for a program of policy and institutional reforms that help sustain growth and poverty reduction, while investment lending finances activities that generate social or physical infrastructure to achieve sustainable growth.

C. Columns show annual average commitments.

D. Denotes annual commitments of development policy lending as a share of total lending. Gray denotes crisis periods' support. Development policy lending was named "adjustment lending" before FY2005.

(figure 8.3). Infrastructure projects accounted for about one-third of the increase in commitments. Social protection lending supported programs like social safety net assistance delivery, for which many economies (especially LICs) lacked effective systems. In terms of identified sectoral shares of crisis lending commitments, public administration took the largest.[5] These operations mostly supported reforms in fiscal policy, expenditure management, and external sector competitiveness in many economies.

[5] Similar to lending commitments, disbursements also prioritized these four sectors.

Financing instruments. During the crisis, the World Bank relied on its traditional instruments of development policy lending (DPL) and investment lending, but more intensively used the former relative to normal times because of its faster-disbursing nature. DPLs provide budget support to governments or subnational bodies for policy and institutional reforms that help sustain growth and poverty reduction, whereas investment lending finances investment in social or physical infrastructure in specific sectors to promote sustainable growth. DPLs may be coupled with a Deferred Drawdown Option (DDO) or packaged as Special Development Policy Loans (SDPLs). DDO provides a contingent credit line that allows disbursement of DPLs to be deferred for up to three years, helping the borrowing country to cope with liquidity constraints during times of economic stress. An SDPL allows countries to participate in international rescue packages during or near crisis times.

For example, DPLs during FY2009/10-FY2010/11 for Mexico supported a strong countercyclical fiscal policy package to reduce crisis vulnerabilities and help build medium-term fiscal sustainability. Similar fiscal policy-related DPLs were provided to other large EMDEs hit significantly by the crisis, such as Brazil. These DPLs often drew on a Public Expenditure Review of the client country's public finances and their sustainability. DDOs were used in economies like Indonesia, for which the World Bank Group provided a contingent credit line of $2 billion in an overall multilateral financing facility of $5.5 billion. This helped Indonesia retain the confidence of global capital markets and allowed it to be one of the first EMDEs to issue bonds internationally during the crisis. The SDPL was used by Latvia to support its social safety net and social sector.[6] In Ukraine, DPLs by the World Bank Group were tailored to address severe stress in the banking sector and involved engagements with private banks. Importantly, they successfully signaled a coordinated response with other international financial institutions to support other areas of economic distress (for example, fiscal policy).

Investment lending projects during the crisis included sector-level loans supporting interventions specific to client countries' special circumstances. These included social protection projects to support vulnerable households or large infrastructure loans to support public investment during the economic downturn. For example, in the World Bank Group's crisis support for Mexico, quick disbursing investment loans in social protection helped the government sustain the financing of two existing large-scale social protection programs (IEG 2018a).

Although investment lending continued to be strong, DPLs increased more rapidly during the global recession, reflecting the instrument's flexibility and high disbursement speed (figure 8.3). Disbursements during FY2009-FY2010 under DPLs were predominantly (91 percent) under new commitments made in the same fiscal years. In contrast, under investment lending, 27 percent of disbursements in FY2009-FY2010 reflected new commitments made in the same fiscal years (IEG 2011a).

[6] Two additional loans, to Latvia and Hungary, were also extended later as SDPLs. This option had been used in other crises, including for Argentina in 1998 and Turkey in 2001.

The IFC and MIGA provided guarantee issuances that improved confidence in financial sectors and their ability to support the real economy. The IFC provided these under its Global Trade Finance Program, helping to ease financing constraints in sectors like the Brazil-Bolivia motor vehicle parts trade, the China-Bangladesh textile trade, and the Russian Federation-Pakistan wheat trade (IEG 2011a). MIGA concentrated its crisis guarantee issuances in the financial sector, especially in ECA, reflecting increased client demand. These guarantees were particularly helpful in recapitalizing many financial institutions in ECA.

Crisis-specific facilities. At the onset of the global financial crisis, a number of new facilities were adopted to accelerate the World Bank Group's response and complement its traditional instruments.

The first, launched at the end of 2008, was IDA's Fast Track Facility. This facility allowed rapid approval of funding for projects related to social safety nets, infrastructure, education, and health.

Starting in early 2009, the IFC established several facilities (in some cases jointly with other IFIs and the private sector) to help member countries cope with the effects of the global recession. The Global Trade Liquidity Program provided risk mitigation and sharing for international banks' trade portfolios. The Microfinance Enhancement Facility targeted loan refinancing to more than 100 microfinance institutions in up to 40 economies. The IFC Capitalization Fund provided capital support to systemically important banks. The Infrastructure Crisis Facility supported privately funded infrastructure projects that faced financial constraints but were otherwise viable. The Debt and Asset Recovery Program provided debt and equity investments to support corporate restructuring.[7]

The World Bank Group also relied more extensively on several facilities that had been established shortly before the global recession. The Global Food Crisis Response Program helped countries deal with food insecurity, an issue that was exacerbated by the global recession. The Rapid Social Response Program helped countries build and deploy protective measures in social protection, including social safety nets and nutrition programming, while the Infrastructure Recovery and Assets Platform targeted lending, diagnostics and partnerships to the energy, communications, water, and transport sectors.

The World Bank Group also provided a wide range of nonfinancing support during the global recession in the form of advisory services and technical assistance. This support includes investment climate assessments to help identify private sector vulnerabilities, workshops on risk management and nonperforming loans resolution, technical assistance and simulation exercises to strengthen authorities' contingency plans, and regional analytical work on pensions to help support DPLs in the ECA region. At the IFC, the Infrastructure Crisis Facility included an advisory component that assisted

[7] This program was later succeeded by the Distressed Asset Recovery Program.

governments in designing public-private partnerships. In some instances (for example, Mongolia), the World Bank Group also proactively led the coordination of international support for client economies (IEG 2012).

Assessment of response

To what extent did the World Bank Group foresee the crisis?

Similar to other major IFIs, the World Bank Group neither predicted the global financial crisis nor immediately perceived its severity as it erupted.[8] Before the onset of the global financial crisis, the World Bank Group's main surveillance publication, the *Global Economic Prospects* report of January that year, pointed to a temporary, moderate slowdown in advanced economies. Although it highlighted several downside risks, such as those associated with the U.S. mortgage market, it expected these disruptions to be temporary and was concerned that monetary authorities might "overstimulate" the economy in the face of uncertainty. The term "crisis" was used only in the context of the U.S. subprime market, and there was no indication of crisis risks of a global nature (World Bank 2008b).[9]

Around April 2008, the World Bank Group's *Global Monitoring Report* on developments in global poverty acknowledged that "the recent financial market turbulence and the resulting global economic slowdown pose difficult challenges for policy makers" (World Bank 2008c). It did not, however, discuss risks of a global financial crisis.

This somewhat sanguine outlook for the global economy before the onset of the global financial crisis was shared in the World Bank Group's regional monitoring publications. For example, the April 2008 edition of the World Bank Group's ECA semiannual regional flagship report, a comprehensive study of the region's long-run productivity prospects, did not flag global economic risks and their potential impact on the region (World Bank 2008d). Similarly, in the World Bank Group's regional update in April 2007 for EAP, although the heightened uncertainty about U.S. growth prospects was acknowledged, a key development highlighted was the tightening of global monetary policies and their impact on East Asia, with no mention of the possibility of a global financial crisis (World Bank 2007).

[8] Qualitatively, this is evident from the views on the global economy expressed in World Bank Group/IMF Development Committee Communiques during 2007-08. In October 2007, the Development Committee stated that "global economic growth remains strong and the direct impact of recent financial market turbulence on developing countries has been limited" (Development Committee 2007). One year later, it acknowledged that markets are "experiencing unprecedented turmoil. Developing countries [...] risk very serious setbacks to their efforts to improve the lives of their populations...." (Development Committee 2008). Similarly, the World Bank Group's financial surveillance publication, the *Global Development Finance* report, acknowledged that the global economy has "entered a period of financial market turmoil" but still expected 3 percent 2019 global economic growth in mid-2018 (World Bank 2008a).

[9] The management response to the IEG study on the World Bank's crisis response pointed to a number of internal briefings in 2008 that highlighted deteriorating global economic conditions and pressure on private capital flows (IEG 2011a).

Other IFIs also failed to flag the risk of a global financial crisis. For example, in the July 2007 *World Economic Outlook* update, IMF staff reported that "the strong global expansion is continuing, and projections for global growth in both 2007 and 2008 have been revised up to 5.2 percent from 4.9 percent [previously]. Risks to this favorable outlook remain modestly tilted to the downside" (IMF 2007). Moreover, in a study of the IMF's response to the global financial crisis, the institution's Independent Evaluation Office concluded that the IMF "prematurely endorsed fiscal consolidation in large advanced economies" in the immediate aftermath of the Lehman collapse, suggesting an insufficient appreciation of the severity of the global financial crisis (IEO 2014).[10]

After the onset of the global recession in 2009, the World Bank Group's analytical and advisory activities at the global, regional, and country levels provided important inputs for World Bank Group DPLs (IEG 2011a).[11] Nonetheless, lending decisions tended to rely on preexisting country engagement dialogues rather than surveillance work (IEG 2011a). Improvements in the World Bank Group's surveillance and analytical work in the postcrisis periods helped strengthen this linkage by incorporating a more harmonized strategy across certain objectives, such as the use of Systematic Country Diagnostics to identify macro-development priorities (discussed in more detail below).

Strengths of and lessons from World Bank Group response

Crisis response policies. During the global recession, the World Bank Group deployed both traditional financing instruments and crisis-specific facilities. Given the speed and flexibility of DPLs, it is not surprising that, as in the Asian crisis (named "adjustment lending" then), the World Bank Group relied heavily on this instrument. Its crisis-specific facilities, although not the main policy tool in the World Bank Group's crisis response, allowed the targeting of specific sectors (for example, finance and trade) where the World Bank Group had well-established expertise.[12]

As in the Asian financial crisis and other episodes, the World Bank Group maintained the focus of its crisis financing on protecting the poor, maintaining infrastructure investment, and sustaining the private sector.[13] This focus was evident in April 2009, when the Development Committee affirmed the critical role of the World Bank Group during the crisis in supporting countercyclical policies, including for social safety nets,

---

[10] The IMF lowered its 2019 global growth forecast from 2.6 percent in April 2008 to 1.1 percent in November 2008, slightly more sanguine than the World Bank Group's forecast of 0.9 percent in November 2008 (IEG 2011a).

[11] Lending to some EMDEs during the global recession was also built on earlier analytical work specific to these economies. For example, the DPL to Jordan during the crisis relied on the Bank's public expenditure review, investment climate assessment, and Financial Sector Assessment Program updates on the country. Similarly, a number of DPLs in ECA (for example, Hungary, Poland, Ukraine) incorporated insights from the region's analytical work on pensions.

[12] The World Bank Group did not adopt as many crisis-specific facilities as the IMF did in its crisis response (IEG 2012); however, the World Bank Group's reliance on traditional instruments helped to keep the cost of borrowing to client countries lower than that at other IFIs (IEG 2011a).

[13] For details, see Development Committee (1998, 2009); Edwards (1994); IEG (2006, 2007, 2009); World Bank (1999, 2009a, 2010a).

sustaining infrastructure and other priority investments, trade finance, and bank recapitalization (Development Committee 2009). This position was reflected in strong lending increases in these sectors during the global recession. The World Bank Group's policies and priorities during the global recession also allowed it to deploy its well-established expertise effectively, including in specialized areas (for example, social protection).

A few studies, most prominently two by the World Bank Group's IEG, documented strengths and weaknesses in the World Bank Group's response (IEG 2011a, 2012). The rest of this subsection draws largely upon the findings of these two studies.

Strengths

- The World Bank Group's response was *deep and broad-based*, supported by its sound financial position on the eve of the crisis. Its disbursements were the largest among all IFIs and reached the vast majority of crisis-affected countries.

- The World Bank Group was able to tap into its *technical expertise* on poverty alleviation in its crisis lending (for example, conditional cash transfers programs; IEG 2011a). It also relied on its well-established country engagements and dialogues, and employed programs tailored toward country-specific needs.

- *Social protection response* was swift, with a sharp increase in lending volume in this area. About half of crisis-related fiscal development policy operations also included provisions to protect social safety nets (IEG 2017b). The World Bank Group also supported medium- and long-term social protection objectives in its lending, capitalizing on the crisis as an opportunity to further reforms in these areas.

- The IFC and IDA were agile in establishing a number of useful *new crisis-specific facilities*. The IFC's Global Trade Liquidity Program along with the expanded Global Trade Finance Program were found to be generally effective in facilitating trade finance, including for LICs (Galat and Ahn 2011; IEG 2011a, 2012). IDA's Fast Track Facility, adopted at the end of 2008, helped reduce the processing time of many eligible operations for LICs (World Bank 2009a).

- The World Bank Group in some instances successfully leveraged its crisis response as opportunities to *build buffers and resilience* for client economies. For example, World Bank Group support for Mexico included a medium-term fiscal sustainability framework and an environmental sustainability framework; in the case of Indonesia, support included a contingency financing facility that improved market confidence. The public expenditure reviews incorporated in some DPLs also included effective diagnostics on the distributional impact of fiscal adjustment.

Despite the successes in many dimensions of the World Bank Group's crisis response, there were also inevitably shortcomings, which have provided lessons for its evolving strategy and operating model (Development Committee 2009).

Shortcomings and lessons

The IEG identified several factors that limited the effectiveness of the World Bank Group's response, which the institution has subsequently worked to address (IEG 2011a, 2012).

- A need was identified for better balance between country-specific engagement and a cross-country, *global strategy* in lending. The World Bank Group's response to the global recession was found to be highly country-specific, often lacking adequate central guidance and monitoring. Moreover, lending was large to some economies that were apparently not severely affected by the global recession, which suggested a need for clearer communication about the bases for World Bank Group's lending decisions under instances of low crisis severity.[14]

- *Financing modalities* lacked the flexibility needed to avoid implementation lags in disbursement. These lags were found in the World Bank Group's global initiatives, such as the IFC Capitalization Fund and Infrastructure Crisis Facility (IEG 2012). In some World Bank Group DPLs, conflicting objectives between reforms and provision of financing contributed to some implementation delays. Financial intermediary loans to provide working capital for the private sector also disbursed slowly at times (IEG 2017b).

- *Crisis-specific policy content* of World Bank Group lending was at times limited. In the context of the World Bank Group's fiscal DPL, some focused on sectors not directly related to the crisis, and they did not always support countercyclical responses. For some infrastructure project support, the realizations of returns were too distant in time to have substantial countercyclical impact, or in other instances, they experienced low disbursements. In some DPLs, more attention could have been devoted to expenditure and revenue strategies to maintain fiscal sustainability and space for possible future countercyclical need (IEG 2017b).

- Although the World Bank Group's response in the *financial sector* was effective in some areas, it was limited in other dimensions. Its financial sector work capacity was low in some instances—at the onset of crisis, Financial Sector Assessment Programs (FSAPs) were available for only about one-third of client economies. The thematic content of the World Bank Group's financial sector operations was found to be similar during the crisis and precrisis periods. During both periods, about 13 percent of lending was allocated to financing of small and medium-sized enterprises and about 14 percent was to banking sector support (IEG 2012). Implementation

[14] The World Bank Group management's response to the IEG findings provides a different view on the low correlation between crisis severity and allocation of Bank financing response. The response posits that financing allocations are based on factors, such as medium-term development sustainability, that are not captured by crisis severity indicators. Ex post correlation between crisis severity and financial allocations also lacks an ex ante counterfactual to assess what would have been the scenario without crisis support (IEG 2011a).

delays in the IFC's trade finance programs, despite their overall success, also limited their full effectiveness.[15]

As the following section discusses, the World Bank Group has in the subsequent decade internalized and capitalized on these lessons in its evolving operating model and strategy.

Changes in strategy and operating model

Partly building on the legacies and lessons of the global recession, the World Bank Group's strategy and operating model have undergone a number of changes. These changes have largely been aimed at improving the World Bank Group's global economic surveillance and monitoring, rebuilding its capital, and refining its operating model, including through the adoption of new crisis-response mechanisms. In addition to adopting a new financial sustainability framework, the World Bank Group's most recent capital increase package in 2018 also set out crisis management as one of the top-five priority areas of leadership in global issues, including an emphasis on crisis management in the cases of fragility, conflict, and violence (FCV) (Development Committee 2018a; World Bank 2018a). These developments are in line with the World Bank Group's "The Forward Look: A Vision for the World Bank Group in 2030" (Forward Look), which explicitly aims to expand the range of innovative financing solutions and analytical capabilities to address crisis risks (Development Committee 2018b). The World Bank Group is also assessing its crisis preparedness along various operational dimensions in response to rapidly changing global economic circumstances and technological progress, as evident in the IEG's comprehensive ongoing evaluation of World Bank Group crisis preparedness in addressing fiscal and financial sector vulnerabilities (IEG 2019a).

Global economic and development surveillance

Since the global recession, the World Bank Group has further enhanced its capacity to monitor the global economy and also sought to link its institutional analytical work more closely to its financing operations. Until mid-2014, the World Bank Group's institutional analysis of global economic and poverty developments was tilted toward conjunctural issues, focusing on recent developments and forecasts in the *Global Economic Prospects* (GEP) series and focused on development progress assessment in the *Global Monitoring Report* series. These analyses have evolved in important ways.

Global economic monitoring. Faced with continuing uncertainties in the global economic outlook after the global recession, in 2014 the flagship *GEP* report expanded its analytical contents to examine in depth global economic issues and their implications

[15] The World Bank Group management's response to the IEG findings points to some differences in views about the financial sector response. Management agreed that, although financial sector skills and capacity were limited in some instances, it was not the case overall (IEG 2011a). The Financial and Private Sector Network also conducted informal work that was valuable during the crisis, and core capabilities were strongly maintained in regions like ECA and in economies like Colombia and Ukraine.

for EMDEs. Global outlook surveillance and discussions are informed by extensive analytical work on risks, vulnerabilities, and structural changes in the global economy.

The January 2015 issue of the *GEP* was the first to take on this expanded effort and analyzed the challenge of limited fiscal space available to EMDEs in the aftermath of the global recession. In subsequent issues, the *GEP* has examined in depth the risks and vulnerabilities most relevant to EMDEs, including the economic growth and financial spillovers from advanced economies to EMDEs and from larger EMDEs to smaller ones (World Bank 2016a). Another issue examined the weakness in investment growth in EMDEs in recent years and its implications for growth prospects (World Bank 2017a). These topics have been complemented by a range of analyses on longer-term challenges facing EMDEs, including assessments of potential output growth, challenges in the informal sector, and growth prospects of LICs (World Bank 2018b, 2019a). The *Commodity Markets Outlook* further complements the analyses in the *GEP* through specialized angles, including analytical work on the oil price collapse of 2014-16 and the role of major EMDEs in global commodity demand (World Bank 2015a, 2015b).

The World Bank Group also pursued additional efforts to monitor macrofinancial risks. This includes an in-depth analysis of risk management in the 2014 *World Development Report* (World Bank 2014). The *Global Financial Development Report* examined special topics on financial development, such as long-term finance (World Bank 2015c). The Equitable Growth, Finance, and Institutions group of the World Bank Group more intensively assessed financial stability risks across the global economy, created new macrofinancial and corporate financial risk indicators to quantitatively benchmark these risks across economies, and established new databases to measure the extent of financial development across the world. With a more targeted focus on the financial sector, these efforts complement the macroeconomic analyses in the semiannual regional updates produced by World Bank Group regions.

The synthesis of analytical and conjunctural work in the *GEP* and other related products is intended to provide, through deeper analysis of policy challenges, a stronger basis for sound policy advice that is both tailored to country-specific needs and globally consistent. It helps flag risks to the global economy and the most pressing vulnerabilities of EMDEs.

Global development monitoring. Three editions of another flagship report of the World Bank Group—the *Global Monitoring Report* (*GMR*) on development and poverty—have examined the impact of the global recession on poverty and related outcomes. The 2009 *GMR* examined the development emergency associated with the crisis; the 2010 *GMR* studied the Millennium Development Goals (MDGs) in the postcrisis era; and the 2011 issue reexamined the challenges of attaining the MDGs in 2015, the target year (World Bank 2009b, 2010b, 2011b). The *GMR* subsequently evolved into the *Poverty and Shared Prosperity* report, dedicated to informing its global audience of the latest and most accurate estimates of global poverty developments (World Bank 2016c).[16] The

[16] These estimates are supported by simulations with microlevel data collection and modeling, including microsimulation models to predict the ex ante poverty and welfare impacts of crises.

comprehensive and overarching analytical guidance in the *GMR* and *Poverty and Shared Prosperity* complement the World Bank's long-standing flagship *World Development Report*, which examines topical issues that affect development outcomes, including those related to learning, gender equality, governance and law, and digital dividends (World Bank 2012, 2016b, 2017b, 2018c).

These surveillance and analytical efforts—some new and some long-established—provide the analytical basis for understanding when countries are at risk of crisis and what remedies match their economic vulnerabilities.

Capital adequacy

During the global recession, the capital adequacy of the World Bank Group declined considerably. The IBRD's equity-to-loans ratio fell from 38 percent at the end of FY2008 to 29 percent at the end of FY2010. This ratio was still above the IBRD's then policy minimum capital adequacy level of 23 percent, showing that the institution still had sufficient capacity to further increase its lending substantially if needed.[17] The decline in capital buffers, however, also led to a recognition that replenishment may be needed should a future global crisis arise, as discussed in communiques before and after the onset of the global financial crisis.[18]

Financially, this recognition led to a capital increase of $86.2 billion in 2010 for the IBRD and $200 million for the IFC, the World Bank Group's first capital increase in more than 20 years. For the IBRD, the increase comprised callable capital of $81.1 billion and paid-in capital of $5.1 billion. Along with this capital increase, preparation for future crises was explicitly set as one of the World Bank Group's five new postcrisis priorities. Similarly, the global recession partly motivated the replenishment of $49.3 billion for IDA (IDA16) in the same year. A new Crisis Response Window to support countries under severe stress was established during this replenishment (World Bank 2011a; discussed in detail in the next section).

In the eight years following the 2010 capital increase, the IBRD continued to expand its commitments to meet growing development challenges: IBRD commitments registered an annual average of $21 billion (2010 U.S. dollars) during FY2011/12-FY2018/19, about 1.5 times the annual average lending level during FY2003/04-FY2008/09. The rise in lending meant that—despite the increase in capital—the equity-to-loan ratio eased somewhat, which partly motivated another capital increase that was approved in

[17] The minimum capital adequacy ratio was later lowered to 20 percent in FY2014. This, along with other internal measures taken in the past several years, such as multiple loan pricing increases, helped the IBRD maintain lending capacity despite prolonged low interest rates serving as a headwind to income generation (World Bank 2018a).

[18] In October 2008, the Development Committee stated that "IBRD has the financial capacity to comfortably double its annual lending to developing countries to meet additional demand from clients" (Development Committee 2008). Half a year later, in April 2009, however, the Development Committee recognized that, "given the possibility of a slow recovery, we considered the potential need to deploy additional resources and asked the World Bank Group to review the financial capacity, including the capital adequacy, of IBRD and IFC, and the adequacy of the concessional resources going to IDA countries, for our further consideration at the 2009 Annual Meetings" (Development Committee 2009).

2018. This capital increase included $13 billion in paid-in capital, $7.5 billion of which was for the IBRD and $5.5 billion of which was for the IFC, and $52.6 billion in callable capital for the IBRD.

The 2018 capital increase was accompanied by a newly formulated priority area for lending—crisis resilience, with the following three dimensions (Development Committee 2018b, 2018c; World Bank 2018a). First, a new IBRD financial sustainability framework was adopted, aiming to balance long-term lending sustainability with crisis needs. In particular, a new metric of long-term financial sustainability, the Sustainable Annual Lending Limit (SALL), was adopted. It indicated a lending level that would be sustainable over a 10-year period, yet permitted the establishment of a crisis buffer that allowed greater lending volume to meet urgent unanticipated needs. Second, for cases of FCV, emphasis was placed on crisis prevention—stemming the escalation of FCV situations and their spillovers—through increased allocation of World Bank Group resources, including support to the private sector to create economic opportunities. Third, the need was recognized to manage potential risks of a regional or global nature, which included recognition of the World Bank Group's role in helping the provision of global public goods, such as mitigation of climate-related risks. These priorities are grounded on the institution's "Forward Look" endorsed by the Development Committee two years earlier (Development Committee 2018b).[19]

Since 2010, IDA has also undergone two further capital replenishments, in 2013 (IDA17) and 2016 (IDA18). The IDA18 replenishment reached an unprecedented level of $75 billion and included additional financial support for crisis management. Under this replenishment, a new $2.5 billion Private Sector Window (PSW), jointly operated by the IFC and MIGA, was introduced to help mobilize private sector capital to deal with LICs' development challenges, including crises related to FCV.

Improvements to the operating model

Since the crisis, the refinements in the World Bank Group's operating model have helped address the limitations associated with its response to the global recession. Refinements include an expanded policy toolkit, tighter Bank-wide alignment of its financing strategy, and new crisis-specific facilities.

During the global recession, some poverty-targeted social safety nets proved to be insufficiently flexible to allow wider coverage or adaptation of benefits to meet needs or to reach newly vulnerable households. In particular, LICs often lacked adequate programs, poverty data, and systems to target and deliver benefits effectively (IEG 2011a). These features constrained the full effectiveness of the World Bank Group's social protection response during the global recession (IEG 2017b). Drawing on this lesson, the World Bank Group has moved from an approach that focused on assistance

[19] In June 2019, the IBRD approved a crisis buffer size that amounted to $10 billion; consequently, the crisis buffer-adjusted sustainable annual lending limit was $28.1 billion for FY2020. For perspective, this limit combined with the crisis buffer amount to about 8 percent of the size of net capital flows contraction to EMDEs during the global recession ($504 billion).

delivery to an approach that focused on building institutions in addressing social vulnerabilities (IEG 2011b, 2019a). This change provides scope for the World Bank Group to play a greater role in helping to design the social safety net systems of client countries, rather than just facilitating the delivery of assistance.

Similarly, the World Bank Group has adopted a more global approach to crisis prevention to complement its country engagement model, part of its Forward Look for 2030 (Development Committee 2018b). In September 2016, the World Bank Group established the Global Crisis Risk Platform (GCRP) to build a Bank-wide approach to the identification and mitigation of crisis risks (World Bank 2018d).[20] This platform seeks to align the World Bank Group's objectives and approach in the areas of crisis expertise, knowledge sharing, and risk monitoring, in addition to promoting further multilateral coordination. It includes initiatives to conduct integrated risk assessments at the Bank level, informing Systematic Country Diagnostics to help client economies identify country-level macrofinancial risks and their corresponding policy responses.

Another global effort the World Bank Group has undertaken is the Maximizing Finance for Development Approach. This approach is based on a "cascade" concept, under which projects prioritize private sector solutions when possible and effective. The approach systematically aims to scale up private sector involvement in addressing development challenges, and it targets reforms in areas where there are market failures and constraints on private sector solutions. The IFC helps implement this approach through its IFC3.0 corporate strategy, which seeks to address major development challenges by creating markets and mobilizing capital to countries where private capital flows are inadequate. This approach is also the basis for the IDA18 IFC-MIGA PSW. The PSW mobilizes private capital and mitigates investment risks to the most underdeveloped markets, including many affected by FCV, through several investment and guarantees facilities. For example, the PSW has already helped mitigate financial risks for private sector-led housing development and agribusiness in South Asia and Sub-Saharan Africa. This approach not only fosters an environment conducive to private investment but could also help mobilize private financing during crises.[21] This facility also exemplifies the World Bank Group's increased emphasis on mobilizing private sector capital to achieve better development outcomes (Development Committee 2015; IEG 2019b).

The World Bank Group has adopted a number of new crisis facilities specific to LICs, drawing on the lessons of the global recession. One of the first innovations adopted in the wake of the global recession by the World Bank Group was the Pilot Crisis Response Window (CRW), approved in December 2009 and intended to help IDA countries cope with severe economic crises and protect core spending on health, education, social safety nets, infrastructure, and agriculture. The CRW was formally established under the

[20] The GCRP was originally named the Global Crisis Response Platform and considers crises across six domains: natural hazard, health, political/security, economic/financial, technological, and societal (World Bank 2018d).

[21] The World Bank Group's response during the global recession involved the private sector in some instances, such as through the IFC's Infrastructure Crisis Facility, where public-private partnerships were managed by the facility. These efforts, however, lacked central coordination at the World Bank Group level (IEG 2011a).

IDA16 replenishment, and now covers economic crises, natural disasters, and public health emergencies.[22] An Immediate Response Mechanism was also adopted in 2011 to allow participating IDA economies to have immediate access to some undisbursed portion of existing investment project balances in the event of crisis. The proposed IDA19 replenishment package seeks to advance the crisis risk management agenda, including allowing the CRW to support earlier responses to crises with slower onsets (that is, disease outbreaks and food insecurity; IDA 2019a). IDA is also looking to introduce commodity hedging intermediation services to member countries before end-IDA18, which will help manage their fiscal exposure to commodity prices. Moreover, IDA19 intends to further address debt vulnerabilities in IDA countries, including strengthening debt sustainability monitoring (IDA 2019b).

The World Bank Group also revived and expanded its use of instruments that were introduced before but not deployed during the global recession. They include Policy-Based Guarantees, a nontraditional form of development policy financing that guarantees principal or interest to international commercial banks, which would in turn provide budget support to national governments on better terms. Policy-Based Guarantees allow for a deeper volume of lending than traditional DPLs and are especially useful during periods of international market turbulence. These instruments helped Western Balkan economies meet financing needs in 2011-14 when they were adversely affected by market conditions associated with the legacies of the global recession (IEG 2016).

The refinements to the operating model since the global recession include deepened engagement with multilateral partners and across World Bank Group entities. The GCRP broadens the World Bank Group's collaboration with multilateral organizations of all types, including development, humanitarian, and private organizations, to ensure stronger service implementation, promote knowledge sharing, and develop an integrated approach to crisis vulnerabilities monitoring. The PSW demonstrates the synergies that collaboration among World Bank Group entities can deliver to promote private investment. In IDA19, a proposed Creditor Outreach Program seeks to strengthen IDA's convening role in sustainable lending practices by promoting information sharing and coordination among borrowers, creditors, and development partners (IDA 2019b).

Support to reduce the risk and impact of crises and to build resilience

The global recession has had a long-lasting and damaging effect on development outcomes (chapter 3). In 2015, about 10 percent of the world's population lived on less than $1.90 a day (World Bank 2018e). LICs and LMICs together account for more than 90 percent of global poverty (figure 8.4). Poor countries face overlapping

[22] CRW resources can be accessed if there is evidence of a severe economic crisis that is caused by an exogenous shock and that affects a significant number of IDA-eligible countries, as follows: (i) the crisis is expected to result in a widespread or regional year-on-year GDP growth decline of 3 percentage points or more; or (ii) a severe price shock did not result in the foregoing GDP growth decline but is broad-based and severe in terms of fiscal impact, or there is consensus a concerted international response is needed; and existing IDA allocations of affected countries are deemed insufficient for crisis response.

FIGURE 8.4 Global and national poverty

LICs and LMICs together account for more than 90 percent of the global poor. Poverty rates are on average about one-third in FCV countries and are above 40 percent in LICs.

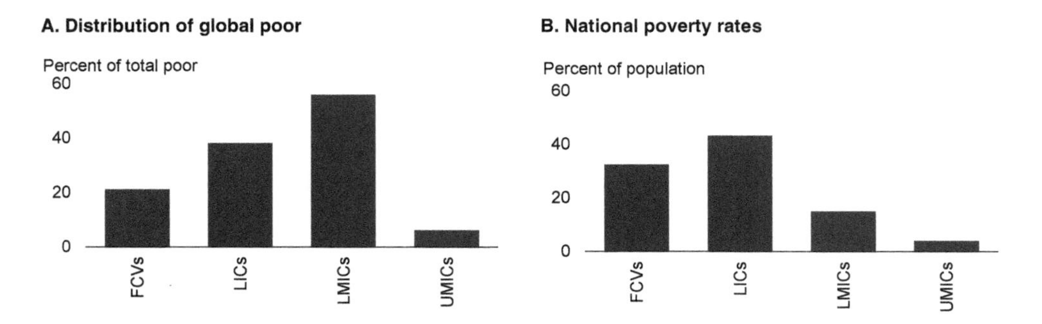

Source: World Bank.

Note: Poverty defined as people living on $1.90 per day or less. FCVs = countries affected by fragility, conflict, and violence; LICs = low-income countries; LMICs = lower-middle-income countries; UMICs = upper-middle-income countries.

A.B. Available data based on 31 FCVs, 27 LICs, 46 LMICs, and 50 UMICs. Based on 2015 poverty estimates. Income classification based on current (2020) fiscal year.

A. Columns denote the percent of total global poor in each respective group denoted.

B. Columns denote the unweighted average poverty rate of each respective group denoted.

constraints on growth of per capita income, including weak institutions, underdeveloped financial systems, and limited integration with global markets. Difficulties in overcoming these constraints are naturally associated with higher poverty rates.

In 2013, the World Bank Group adopted the twin goals of ending poverty and promoting shared prosperity. The World Bank Group's crisis prevention strategy is one of the means to meet the twin goals. This strategy can be viewed as comprising two components: support aimed at reducing crisis risk and impact, and support aimed at building longer-term structural resilience to crises. In the World Bank Group's Forward Look for 2030, building resilience is defined as one of the top priorities. This strategy also incorporates crisis vulnerabilities reduction as part of a vision to lead on the global public goods agenda (Development Committee 2018b). This strategy also balances long -term lending financing sustainability with crisis lending agility, as evident in the most recent IBRD financial sustainability framework (World Bank 2018a).

Support to reduce the risk and impact of crises

The World Bank Group can help its member countries to reduce their vulnerability to crises, and can assist them when crises do materialize, in a number of dimensions.

Countercyclical fiscal adjustment. As the World Bank Group's response to the global recession highlighted, countercyclical support for EMDEs during economic downturns is crucial under environments where national governments' fiscal space is constrained. The World Bank Group can provide this support through its DPLs, which provide direct budget support to national governments and enable them to protect the poor in times of economic stress. This support often takes place as part of broader countercyclical support packages of IFIs and is especially important now given the lack of fiscal buffers in many countries. The SDPL option associated with DPLs can be helpful in accelerating multilateral financing during crises. DPLs can be coupled with World Bank Group technical assistance to support reforms and capacity building that can improve the quality of the fiscal response and signal national governments' policy commitments, thus boosting confidence in financial markets.[23]

Debt management. High debt limits the effectiveness of fiscal policy and increases an economy's vulnerability to financial crises because of risks like higher rollover costs and currency depreciation at times of financial stress (World Bank 2019c). Government debt in EMDEs has risen substantially in the postcrisis period, and private debt has also risen well above historical averages.

Among LICs, debt-related vulnerabilities are a particular concern: since 2013, median government debt of LICs has risen by about 20 percentage points of GDP and has increasingly reflected borrowing from private and other nonconcessional sources (World Bank 2019a). Further, given the high levels of external debt of these economies, most of them would be vulnerable to a sharp weakening in global trade or financial conditions. The need to identify and reduce debt-related vulnerabilities is thus a priority for many LICs. In MICs, elevated private debt may also entail risks to government budgets because, as shown in past crises, private debt can shift to government balance sheets via government support of private institutions under stress.

Effective public debt management is needed to help preserve macroeconomic stability, reduce financial vulnerabilities, and boost investor confidence in sovereign assets (World Bank 2013). Interest and exchange rate volatility requires debt managers to properly assess and mitigate risks, and to maximize financing options. The World Bank Group helps strengthen EMDE debt management through debt performance diagnostic assessments, training, multilateral coordination, and, for LICs, financing through a multilateral trust fund-based Debt Management Facility. The World Bank Group's Debt Management Performance Assessment examines progress in key indicators on government debt management, including those relating to debt strategy formulation, legal frameworks, transparency improvement, and managerial structure. It also shows areas for improvement, especially in auditing and coordination with fiscal policy. Other types of debt management assistance include the provision of tools for medium-term debt management strategies, country visits by staff and expert consultants, regional training events, and support for debt managers' peer learning programs. These efforts are organized as part of a new multipronged approach (joint with the IMF) envisioned in 2018 to address debt vulnerabilities (Development Committee 2018d).

The World Bank Group (jointly with the IMF) has also recently revised the Debt Sustainability Framework for Low-Income Countries to enhance its ability to accurately identify debt risks and incentivize comprehensive debt data coverage. Last, the World Bank Group's Debtor Reporting System publishes detailed information on the terms

---

[23] A recent IEG study of development policy financing in IDA countries finds that having a Public Expenditure Review before DPL and technical assistance during implementation enhance the effectiveness of DPLs (IEG 2018b).

and conditions of public and publicly guaranteed long-term external debt; and participation in the system is a condition of IDA and IBRD borrowing. For MICs, the Government Debt and Risk Management Program provides technical assistance in public debt management, including in areas like capacity expansion of country debt management offices, contingent liabilities risk management training, and capital markets development.

Domestic resource mobilization and revenue management. Government revenue mobilization is essential for the financing of productive government expenditures, including investment in human capital development and infrastructure (Junquera-Varela et al. 2017). Yet economies that are most in need of revenues also often face the largest challenges in tax collection. Domestic resource mobilization is also critical in oil exporting economies, where energy subsidies are high, fiscal buffers are low, and revenues are sensitive to oil price fluctuations. In most LICs, the challenge of resource mobilization has increased with rising debt levels, because interest payments have been absorbing an increasing proportion of government revenues (World Bank 2019a).

The World Bank Group assists EMDEs, and especially LICs, to diversify their domestic revenue bases, including through financial support and assistance in the design of strategies to strengthen domestic resource mobilization, diagnose bottlenecks, and track reform results. DPLs have supported efforts by some countries to reduce fuel subsidies, with implementation guided also by technical assistance for poverty and social impact assessments. Systematic country diagnostic exercises in many oil exporters have identified the policy priorities for revenue diversification of these economies. The World Bank Group is also taking steps to strengthen its analytical capacity related to taxation (IEG 2017a) and to assess the effectiveness of its past implementations of public financial management support (IEG 2018c).

The World Bank Group also provides technical support on public expenditure management to promote equity in fiscal policy (for example, critical protection of programs for the poor in fiscal consolidation programs) and to monitor contingent liabilities. Public Expenditure Reviews can support many development financing operations by identifying detailed spending and investment priorities. These in turn could serve as useful benchmarks for other IFIs' country programs and enhance collaboration with them. For MICs, the IFC provides taxation advisory services in conjunction with client cofinancing, helping to improve business taxation design and efficiency. Both the IBRD and the IFC also promote public investment management, such as through public-private partnerships.

Well-targeted social benefit reforms. Effective social protection helps households cope with job losses and declines in income. With limited precautionary savings, households just above the poverty line are often at high risk of slipping back into poverty during times of economic stress and the poor into further destitution (World Bank 2001, 2019a). The employment of the poor and vulnerable tends to be less secure and informal (World Bank 2019b). The World Bank Group supports universal access to social protection. Building scalable safety net and active labor market programs and effective systems of income support for the unemployed is critical for crisis preparedness.

In many countries the coverage and adequacy of these systems are limited. The World Bank Group strengthens data analysis and research in social protection, supports program design, builds institutional capacity, and provides country-specific financing strategies.

Financial sector reforms. Stable financial systems and intermediation are key to preserving the best risk-benefit trade-off associated with financial deepening and to reducing the amplification of financial crises. The World Bank Group promotes global financial stability by helping governments improve payment systems and enhance banking supervision, as well as by strengthening capital market development and designing sound regulatory frameworks. It helps provide advice on the design and implementation of micro- and macroprudential frameworks, supports the establishment of deposit-insurance systems and financial safety nets, and strengthens crisis management and preparedness.

The FSAP, conducted jointly with the IMF, assesses potential vulnerabilities in the financial sector and promotes financial development. The World Bank Group also contributes to standard-setting bodies and other global engagements, including by serving as a member of the Financial Stability Board and Basel Committee and actively participating in the design of global regulatory reforms. The World Bank Group is also monitoring emerging financial risks, including competitive pressures on traditional banks and financial service providers from financial technology and the growing dependence of financial institutions on information and communication technology outsourcing.[24]

The World Bank Group helps reduce the vulnerabilities of SMEs, which typically lack credit ratings, have fewer financing options, and are less diversified. SMEs' access to external finance is more likely than that of larger firms to depend on specific and close banking relationships, and information asymmetries can be difficult to overcome (Beck and Demirgüç-Kunt 2006). This makes SMEs more vulnerable to bank credit crunches. The World Bank Group supports policies to improve access to finance, including measures to mitigate and overcome information asymmetries, such as the introduction of collateral registries (Love, Martínez Pería, and Singh 2013). The World Bank Group also supports financial inclusion of households to help the poor access critical financial services in times of crisis. Technical assistance in this area also deploys microdata collection at the household level that allows more precise impact evaluation of financial sector policies.

The IFC provides investments and technical assistance designed to directly stimulate private sector investment, such as bond issuances that relieve financing bottlenecks in the underdeveloped capital markets of LICs. It also works with financial institutions to promote investment and advisory support for SMEs and women-owned businesses, to provide technical expertise on risk management, to help reinforce responsible finance

[24] As part of FSAP analyses or stand-alone diagnostics, the World Bank Group also promotes financial stability through technical assistance and capacity building in supporting Anti-Money Laundering/Combating the Financing of Terrorism (AML/CFT) standards.

(for example, introducing environmental standards), and to support trade finance (for example, Global Trade Finance Program to issue risk-mitigating guarantees in markets with limited trade lines). MIGA helps lower the risks and uncertainty associated with private domestic investment and foreign direct investment via its political risk insurance or guarantees. Both entities help to provide a more favorable and resilient environment for private investment, a priority in global financial system reform (G20 2018). Moreover, as the aforementioned IFC-MIGA IDA18 PSW demonstrates, these entities are able to leverage collaborative synergies in joint operations, an identified area for improvement from the global recession experience (IEG 2019a).

Support to build long-term structural resilience

The areas of support discussed in the previous section can reduce the risk and impact of crises for EMDEs. Most of the World Bank Group's other support areas may be viewed as helping to build longer-term structural resilience to crises. These focus areas can be especially relevant for LICs. For these economies, transmission of adverse external developments to the domestic economy is often due less to direct linkages than to an inadequately diversified economic base domestically and a lack of resilience in the economy's institutions and structural policy frameworks.[25]

LICs' growth and development prospects have become more challenging in recent years, partly because today's LICs are further below the middle-income threshold and are more fragile than the LICs in 2001 that have recently graduated to MIC status (World Bank 2019c). Moreover, the reliance on agriculture of today's LICs makes them particularly vulnerable to climate change, including extreme weather events. These challenges call for a broad set of long-term structural policies to build resilience, which the World Bank Group has incorporated into its analytical work, policy advice, and financing efforts across most sectors in the past decade (IEG 2017b).

Institutional and governance reforms. Good governance underpins sustainable growth (World Bank 2017b). Strong institutions help countries prosper and reduce poverty by creating an environment that facilitates private sector growth and job creation and delivers government services efficiently. The World Bank Group helps countries strengthen public policy processes and manage public resources effectively. This includes technical support to strengthen coordination across branches of government, establish e-procurement processes, and create new tools to assess citizen engagement. It also helps enhance trade competitiveness by strengthening trade regulatory and logistics frameworks and by promoting trade integration and connectivity.

Learning-focused education reforms. Effective and inclusive education is key to ensuring equal opportunities, the attainment by individuals of their potential, and the long-term growth of income (World Bank 2018c). The World Bank Group works with

[25] In fact, LICs were somewhat more resilient to the global recession initially than previous global crises because they had relatively better precrisis macroeconomic performance, modest debt burden, high commodity prices, and improved policy frameworks. Nonetheless, their lack of long-term resilience to commodity price collapse and global macroeconomic shocks severely affected growth in LICs after the global recession elapsed (World Bank 2010b).

countries to strengthen their education systems to be inclusive for all children, including in focus areas such as early starts, professional teacher development, teacher-student interaction improvement, and education systems capacity strengthening.

Health care reforms. Access to high quality healthcare reduces the financial risks and social costs associated with ill health and is key to promoting social equity and growth (World Health Organization and World Bank 2017). The World Bank Group provides financing and policy advice to improve health service delivery and quality, including those to eradicate maternal and child mortality, improve child nutrition, and prevent communicable diseases.

Greater female workforce participation and access to services. Women are often the hardest-hit by economic downturns because they are more likely than men to work in precarious employment situations, to receive lower pay, and to have poorer access to health and sanitation services (World Bank 2012, 2015d). The World Bank Group supports programs that increase or sustain women's economic opportunities, including expanded access for women to education and health care through economic downturns and crises, as well as those that finance women-focused labor market programs.

Climate-smart infrastructure investment. Climate change poses ever-growing risks, which vary among EMDE regions. More extensive droughts and extreme heat are causing more harvest failures and desertification. Rapidly spreading forest and grassland fires increasingly threaten built-up areas and resource-based industries. Cyclones of unprecedented power have already caused catastrophic floods in agricultural plains and river deltas, as well as mountain range mudslides.

Because of their location and topography, many LICs and small island developing states are particularly vulnerable to climate-related shocks, especially given that many of these countries depend heavily on agriculture. These vulnerabilities are further exacerbated by limited infrastructure and lack of financial resources. Climate change, including associated natural disasters and extreme weather events, can affect the most vulnerable through lower consumption, poorer health, and lower agricultural yields (World Bank 2016d).

The World Bank Group helps countries address these issues by financing renewable energy projects and climate-smart agricultural investments, as well as by integrating climate-change solutions into lending projects. In 2018, the World Bank Group set out new climate action targets for 2021-25, doubling its five-year investments to about $200 billion to support climate action.[26] It also manages the Global Facility for Disaster Reduction and Recovery, a global partnership that provides financing and technical assistance to strengthen climate change resilience. It supports natural disaster risk insurance, such as the issuance of Pacific Alliance Catastrophe Bond against earthquakes in four LAC economies, helping to transfer risks to financial markets and reduce risks

[26] About 10 percent of the World Bank's financial commitments are now devoted to activities related to disaster risk management, including those that help countries improve fiscal and budgetary resilience to climate and disaster risks (Development Committee 2018e).

borne by investors (Vegh et al. 2018). The IFC helps finance large climate projects involving public-private partnerships and climate-smart agribusiness projects. The World Bank Group also promotes knowledge exchange about climate change resilience among multilateral and national experts through initiatives like the Small Island States Resilience Initiative.

Resilience to fragility, conflict, and violence. FCV economies have limited ability to withstand external shocks. Although they often have limited trade and financial linkages to the rest of the world, the collapse in commodity prices associated with the global recession diminished donor support, constrained access to financial services, and reduced remittances in a number of fragile economies (Allen and Giovannetti 2011). Sustained economic growth is critical for stabilizing FCV economies: the risk of conflict has been estimated to rise by 1 percentage point for each percentage point decline in per capita income growth (World Bank 2000). The global recession highlighted the importance of strengthening state capacity building and resilience against commodity price fluctuations, which formed the main channel of transmission of global economic stress to fragile economies. The World Bank Group supports efforts to address urgent capacity -building needs in fragile economies, including through preventive efforts (for example, risk and resilience assessments), the provision of financing to address forced displacement (for example, Global Concessional Financing Facility), and the promotion of women's inclusion in peace accords (UN and World Bank 2018).[27]

Conclusion

During the global recession, the World Bank Group nearly doubled its annual financing commitments and provided support to a large number of crisis-affected countries. Its extensive and rapid response made use of traditional financing instruments, new crisis-specific facilities, and extensive advisory activities.

Drawing on this experience, the World Bank Group has since enhanced its surveillance of the global economy, rebuilt its capital, and refined its financing and operating model. These efforts have built a more extensive portfolio of support instruments to help member countries in times of economic stress, some directly through the reduction of crisis risk and impact, and others by helping to build longer-term resilience. The World Bank Group has improved its ability to provide countercyclical support, while also retaining the capacity to continue its long-standing focus on strengthening long-term resilience for client economies during normal times.

The global recession highlighted the significant damage that major adverse shocks can do to the achievement of poverty reduction and shared prosperity, and therefore the critical importance of crisis prevention and management for achieving these goals. The current global economic environment is marked by weak growth momentum, and risks to the outlook are heavily tilted to the downside (World Bank 2019c). High levels of

[27] Financial services delivery in fragile economies could be further facilitated by financial technology (World Bank and International Monetary Fund 2018).

public and private indebtedness mean that consumer and business confidence are vulnerable to policy missteps or other shocks—including a further escalation of trade tensions, financial stress, policy uncertainty, or natural disasters. Risks are exacerbated by the lack of fiscal and monetary space and the apparently limited appetite for policy coordination among major economies. Although the World Bank Group's response during the global recession was concentrated on MICs, its current support toolkit can also readily respond to other types of crisis risks that may be more relevant to LICs.

The limited policy room that EMDEs would have in the face of adverse shocks underscores the need for the World Bank Group to proactively engage with member countries to help improve resilience and reduce both the risk and the impact of crises. It also highlights the importance for the World Bank of remaining in a strong position to support its members in the event such risks materialize.

References

Allen, F., and G. Giovannetti. 2011. "The Effects of the Financial Crisis on Sub-Saharan Africa." *Review of Development Finance* 1(1): 1-27.

Basu, K. 2013. "Shared Prosperity and the Mitigation of Poverty: In Practice and in Precept." Policy Research Working Paper 6700, World Bank, Washington, DC.

Beck, T., and A. Demirgüç-Kunt. 2006. "Small and Medium-Size Enterprises: Access to Finance as a Growth Constraint." *Journal of Banking and Finance* 30 (11): 2931-43.

Development Committee. 1998. "Communiqué." Joint Ministerial Committee of the Board of Governors of the Bank and the Fund on the Transfer of Real Resources to Developing Countries, October, World Bank and International Monetary Fund, Washington, DC.

Development Committee. 2007. "Communiqué." Joint Ministerial Committee of the Board of Governors of the Bank and the Fund on the Transfer of Real Resources to Developing Countries, October, World Bank and International Monetary Fund, Washington, DC.

Development Committee. 2008. "Communiqué" Joint Ministerial Committee of the Board of Governors of the Bank and the Fund on the Transfer of Real Resources to Developing Countries, October, World Bank and International Monetary Fund, Washington, DC.

Development Committee. 2009. "G-24 Communiqué." Joint Ministerial Committee of the Board of Governors of the Bank and the Fund on the Transfer of Real Resources to Developing Countries, April, World Bank and International Monetary Fund, Washington, DC.

Development Committee. 2015. "From Billions to Trillions: Transforming Development Finance." Joint Ministerial Committee of the Board of Governors of the Bank and the Fund on the Transfer of Real Resources to Developing Countries, April, World Bank and International Monetary Fund, Washington, DC.

Development Committee. 2018a. Communiqué. Joint Ministerial Committee of the Board of Governors of the Bank and the Fund on the Transfer of Real Resources to Developing Countries, April, World Bank and International Monetary Fund, Washington, DC.

Development Committee. 2018b. "Forward Look—A Vision for the WBG 2030—Implementation Update." Joint Ministerial Committee of the Board of Governors of the Bank and the Fund on the Transfer of Real Resources to Developing Countries, March, World Bank and International Monetary Fund, Washington, DC.

Development Committee. 2018c. "Communiqué." Joint Ministerial Committee of the Board of Governors of the Bank and the Fund on the Transfer of Real Resources to Developing Countries, October, World Bank and International Monetary Fund, Washington, DC.

Development Committee. 2018d. "Debt Vulnerabilities in Emerging and Low-Income Economies." Joint Ministerial Committee of the Board of Governors of the Bank and the Fund on the Transfer of Real Resources to Developing Countries, September, World Bank and International Monetary Fund, Washington, DC.

Development Committee. 2018e. "Progress Report on Mainstreaming Disaster Risk Management in World Bank Group Operations." Joint Ministerial Committee of the Board of Governors of the Bank and the Fund on the Transfer of Real Resources to Developing Countries, April, World Bank and International Monetary Fund, Washington, DC.

Edwards, S. 1994. *The Evolving Role of the World Bank: the Latin American Debt Crisis.* Washington, DC: World Bank.

Forbes, K., and F. Warnock. 2012. "Capital Flow Waves: Surges, Stops, Flight, and Retrenchment." *Journal of International Economics* 88 (2): 235-51.

Galat, B., and H. Ahn. 2011. "The World Bank Group's Response to the Crisis: Expanded Capacity for Unfunded and Funded Support for Trade with Emerging Markets." In *Trade Finance During the Great Trade Collapse*, edited by J.-P. Chauffour and M. Malouche. Washington, DC: World Bank.

G20 (Group of Twenty). 2018. *Making the Global Financial System Work for All.* Report of the G20 Eminent Persons Group on Global Financial Governance, October. https://www.globalfinancialgovernance.org/assets/pdf/G20EPG-Full%20Report.pdf.

Guven, A. B. 2012. "The IMF, the World Bank and the Global Economic Crisis: Exploring Paradigm Continuity." *Development and Change* 43 (4): 869–98.

Hall, A. 2015. "More of the Same: The World Bank's Social Policy Response to Global Economic Crisis." *Global Social Policy* 15 (1): 88–90.

IDA (International Development Association). 2019a. *Towards 2030: Investing in Growth, Resilience, and Opportunity.* Washington, DC: World Bank.

IDA (International Development Association). 2019b. *Addressing Debt Vulnerabilities in IDA Countries: Options for IDA19.* Washington, DC: World Bank.

IEG (Independent Evaluation Group). 2006. *IEG Review of World Bank Assistance to Financial Sector Reform.* Washington, DC: World Bank.

IEG (Independent Evaluation Group). 2007. *Development Results in Middle-Income Countries. An Evaluation of the World Bank's Report.* Washington, DC: World Bank.

IEG (Independent Evaluation Group). 2009. *The World Bank Group's Response to the Global Crisis: Update on an Ongoing IEG Evaluation.* Washington, DC: World Bank.

IEG (Independent Evaluation Group). 2011a. *The World Bank Group's Response to the Global Economic Crisis: Phase 1.* Washington, DC: World Bank.

IEG (Independent Evaluation Group). 2011b. *Social Safety Nets: An Evaluation of World Bank Support, 2000-2010.* Washington, DC: World Bank.

IEG (Independent Evaluation Group). 2012. *The World Bank Group's Response to the Global Economic Crisis: Phase 2.* Washington, DC: World Bank.

IEG (Independent Evaluation Group). 2016. *Findings from Evaluations of Policy-Based Guarantees.* An IEG Learning Product. Washington, DC: World Bank.

IEG (Independent Evaluation Group). 2017a. *Tax Revenue Mobilization: Lessons from World Bank Group Support for Tax Reform.* Washington, DC: World Bank.

IEG (Independent Evaluation Group). 2017b. *Crisis Response and Resilience to Systemic Shocks: Lessons from IEG Evaluations.* Washington, DC: World Bank.

IEG (Independent Evaluation Group). 2018a. "Mexico: Country Program Evaluation. An Evaluation of the World Bank Group's Support to Mexico (2008–17)." World Bank, Washington, DC.

IEG (Independent Evaluation Group). 2018b. "Maximizing the Impact of Development Policy Financing in IDA Countries. A Stocktaking of Success Factors and Risks." An Independent Evaluation Group Meso Evaluation, World Bank, Washington, DC.

IEG (Independent Evaluation Group). 2018c. "Public Finance for Development Evaluation: An IEG Evaluation." Approach Paper, World Bank, Washington, DC.

IEG (Independent Evaluation Group). 2019a. "World Bank Group Support for Crisis Preparedness: Addressing Fiscal and Financial Sector Vulnerabilities. An Independent Evaluation." Approach Paper, World Bank, Washington, DC.

IEG (Independent Evaluation Group). 2019b. "The World Bank Group's Approach to the Mobilization of Private Capital for Development: An IEG Evaluation." Approach Paper, Washington, DC: World Bank.

IEO (Independent Evaluation Office). 2014. *IMF Response to the Financial and Economic Crisis.* International Monetary Fund, Washington, DC.

IMF (International Monetary Fund). 2007. *World Economic Outlook.* April. Washington, DC: International Monetary Fund.

Junquera-Varela, R. F., M. Verhoeven, G. P. Shukla, B. J. Haven, R. Awasthi, and B. Moreno-Dodson. 2017. *Strengthening Domestic Resource Mobilization: Moving from Theory to Practice in Low- and Middle-Income Countries.* Washington, DC: World Bank.

Love, I., M. S. Martínez Pería, and S. Singh. 2013. "Collateral Registries for Movable Assets: Does Their Introduction Spur Firms' Access to Bank Finance?" Policy Research Working Paper 6477, World Bank, Washington, DC.

UN (United Nations) and World Bank. 2018. *Pathways for Peace: Inclusive Approaches to Preventing Violent Conflict.* Washington, DC: World Bank.

Velasco. A. 2013. "Emerging Markets' Nirvana Lost." *Project Syndicate*, September 11, 2013. https://www.project-syndicate.org/commentary/the-absence-of-structural-change-in-latin-america n-economies-by-andres-velasco?barrier=accesspaylog.

Vegh, C., G. Vuletin, D. Riera-Crichton, J. Medina, D. Friedheim, L. Germani Morano, and L. Venturi Grosso. 2018. *From Known Unknowns to Black Swans: How to Manage Risk in Latin*

America and the Caribbean. Latin America and the Caribbean Semiannual Report. Washington, DC: World Bank.

World Bank. 1999. *Annual Report.* Washington, DC: World Bank.

World Bank. 2000. "Economic Causes of Civil War and Their Implications for Policy." World Bank, Washington, DC.

World Bank. 2001. *World Development Report 2000/2001: Attacking Poverty.* World Bank: Washington, DC.

World Bank. 2007. *10 Years After the Crisis: Sustainable Development in East Asia's Urban Fringe.* East Asia and Pacific Economic Update. April. Washington, DC: World Bank.

World Bank. 2008a. *Global Development Finance: The Role of International Banking.* Volume 1. Washington, DC: World Bank.

World Bank. 2008b. *Global Economic Prospects: Technology Diffusion in the Developing World.* Washington, DC: World Bank.

World Bank. 2008c. *Global Monitoring Report: MDGs and the Environment.* Washington, DC: World Bank.

World Bank. 2008d. *Europe and Central Asia Economic Update.* Washington, DC: World Bank.

World Bank. 2009a. *Annual Report.* Washington, DC: World Bank.

World Bank. 2009b. *Global Monitoring Report: A Development Emergency.* Washington, DC: World Bank.

World Bank. 2010a. *Annual Report.* Washington, DC: World Bank.

World Bank. 2010b. *Global Monitoring Report: The MDGs after the Crisis.* Washington, DC: World Bank.

World Bank. 2011a. *Annual Report.* Washington, DC: World Bank.

World Bank. 2011b. *Global Monitoring Report: Improving the Odds of Achieving the MDGs.* Washington, DC: World Bank.

World Bank. 2012. *World Development Report: Gender Equality and Development.* Washington, DC: World Bank.

World Bank. 2013. "Helping Developing Countries Address Public Debt Management Challenges: A World Bank-International Monetary Fund (IMF) Capacity Building Partnership." Debt management performance assessment (DeMPA) background paper, World Bank, Washington, DC.

World Bank. 2014. *World Development Report 2014: Risk and Opportunity – Managing Risk for Development.* World Bank, Washington, DC.

World Bank. 2015a. *Commodity Markets Outlook.* January. Washington, DC: World Bank.

World Bank. 2015b. *Commodity Markets Outlook.* April. Washington, DC: World Bank.

World Bank. 2015c. *Global Financial Development Report 2015-2016: Long-Term Finance.* Washington, DC: World Bank.

World Bank. 2015d. *WBG Gender Strategy (FY16-23): Gender Equality, Poverty Reduction and Inclusive Growth.* World Bank Group, Washington, DC.

World Bank. 2016a. *Global Economic Prospects: Spillovers amid Weak Growth.* January. Washington, DC: World Bank.

World Bank. 2016b. *World Development Report 2016: Digital Dividends.* Washington, DC: World Bank.

World Bank. 2016c. *Poverty and Shared Prosperity: Taking on Inequality.* Washington, DC: World Bank.

World Bank. 2016d. *World Bank Group Climate Change Action Plan 2016-2020.* Washington, DC: World Bank.

World Bank. 2017a. *Global Economic Prospects: Weak Investment in Uncertain Times.* January. Washington, DC: World Bank.

World Bank. 2017b. *World Development Report 2017: Governance and the Law.* Washington, DC: World Bank.

World Bank. 2018a. *Sustainable Financing for Sustainable Development: World Bank Group Capital Package Proposal.* Washington, DC: World Bank.

World Bank. 2018b. *Global Economic Prospects: Broad-Based Upturn, but for How Long?* January. Washington, DC: World Bank.

World Bank. 2018c. *World Development Report 2018: Learning to Realize Education's Promise.* World Bank, Washington, DC.

World Bank. 2018d. *Global Crisis Risk Platform.* Washington, DC: World Bank.

World Bank. 2018e. *Poverty and Shared Prosperity: Piecing Together the Poverty Puzzle.* Washington, DC: World Bank.

World Bank. 2019a. *Global Economic Prospects: Darkening Skies.* January. Washington, DC: World Bank.

World Bank. 2019b. *World Development Report: The Changing Nature of Work.* Washington, DC: World Bank.

World Bank. 2019c. *Global Economic Prospects: Heightened Tensions, Subdued Investment.* June. Washington, DC: World Bank.

World Bank and International Monetary Fund. 2018. "The Bali Fintech Agenda: Chapeau Paper." World Bank and International Monetary Fund, Washington, DC.

World Health Organization and World Bank. 2017. *Tracking Universal Health Coverage: 2017 Global Monitoring Report.* Geneva: World Health Organization.

ECO-AUDIT

Environmental Benefits Statement

The World Bank Group is committed to reducing its environmental footprint. In support of this commitment, we leverage electronic publishing options and print-on-demand technology, which is located in regional hubs worldwide. Together, these initiatives enable print runs to be lowered and shipping distances decreased, resulting in reduced paper consumption, chemical use, greenhouse gas emissions, and waste.

Our books are printed on Forest Stewardship Council (FSC)–certified paper, with a minimum of 10 percent recycled content. The fiber in our book paper is either unbleached or bleached using totally chlorine-free (TCF), processed chlorine–free (PCF), or enhanced elemental chlorine–free (EECF) processes.

More information about the Bank's environmental philosophy can be found at http://www.worldbank.org/corporateresponsibility.